The Quotable Voltaire

Jean Huber, *Voltaire*, circa 1770–1775. Collection of the Château de Versailles. Photograph: ©RMN-Grand Palais (Château de Versailles), Gérard Blot.

The Quotable Voltaire

EDITED BY GARRY APGAR AND
EDWARD M. LANGILLE

Bucknell | UNIVERSITY
UNIVERSITY | PRESS
LEWISBURG, PENNSYLVANIA

Library of Congress Cataloging-in-Publication Data

Names: Voltaire, 1694–1778, author. | Apgar, Garry, editor. |
Langille, Edward M., 1959– editor.
Title: The quotable Voltaire / edited by Garry Apgar and Edward Langille.
Description: Lewisburg, Pennsylvania : Bucknell University Press, [2021] |
Includes bibliographical references and index. |
Each entry in *The Quotable Voltaire* is presented in parallel versions: in English and
the original language, invariably French, but occasionally German, Italian, or Spanish.
Identifiers: LCCN 2020029126 | ISBN 9781684482917 (paperback ; alk. paper) |
ISBN 9781684482924 (hardcover ; alk. paper) | ISBN 9781684482931 (epub) |
ISBN 9781684482948 (mobi) | ISBN 9781684482955 (pdf)
Subjects: LCSH: Voltaire, 1694–1778—Quotations. | Voltaire, 1694–1778—
Translations into English.
Classification: LCC PQ2074 .A64 2021 | DDC 848.509—dc23
LC record available at https://lccn.loc.gov/2020029126

A British Cataloging-in-Publication record for this book is available from the British Library.

www.bucknelluniversitypress.org

Distributed worldwide by Rutgers University Press

Manufactured in the United States of America

To Theodore E. D. Braun, professor emeritus of French and comparative literature, University of Delaware, and Voltaire scholar par excellence; and to George W. Gowen, chairman of the board of the Voltaire Society of America Inc., and its driving force since its inception in 1996

CONTENTS

Figure 1. Jean Huber, *Voltaire and His Apostles*, May 1760. Pencil, ink, and gray wash on paper. Private collection. Voltaire is seated next to his niece, Mme Denis, at their home in Ferney, near Geneva. Facing him is the writer and *philosophe* Jean-François Marmontel, with a black ribbon tied to his wig, and Marmontel's friend, a young man named Gaulard. Voltaire's dramatic gesture is ambiguous: his arm may be raised either to make a point or to bestow a patriarchal blessing on his two admirers.

PREFACE

For almost four hundred years, the King James Bible and Shakespeare formed the twin mother lode of memorable quotations in English. Today, the average American will more likely recall a lyric by Lennon and McCartney or recite a line from *Family Guy* than chapter and verse from the Psalms or a soliloquy by Hamlet.

Purists may lament this seeming triumph of mass culture over time-tested holy or secular writ. But all is not lost. In our increasingly pixelated world of Snapchat and Twitter, revered authors and texts, past and present, still supply instructive words to live by. Countless no-frills, digitally printed dictionaries and internet domains devoted to quotations attest to this happy fact.

Their bill of fare tends to be drawn from standard works such as *Bartlett's Familiar Quotations* or websites such as BrainyQuote.com. Often, in cyberspace especially, the language and attributions are defective. Sometimes they are totally wrong. Most people don't care: for them, it's not the words but the message behind the words that counts.

The popularity of quotations, online and in print, reflects a fundamental thirst for wisdom. Their appeal is all the more powerful if the perceived wisdom is curt, clever, and attached to a celebrated name. Concise, insightful observations, artfully contrived—proverbs, maxims, adages, truisms, quips, and so on—have been around forever. Be they anonymous, or credited to eminent statesmen, poets, or pop stars, quotes help us cope with the mysteries and challenges of life. They are comfort food for the mind, and the soul.

Few men or women have brought as much grist to the quotation mill as Voltaire. "All is for the best in this best of all possible worlds" and "We must cultivate our garden," from *Candide*, are exhibits A and B of his lasting claim on our shared cultural imagination.

"The perfect is the enemy of the good," from Voltaire's *Dictionnaire philosophique*,[1] is a favorite with the ruling class in Washington. In a July 2010

---

1. "The perfect is the enemy of the good" is an English version of a proverb quoted in Italian in "Art Dramatique," an article in Voltaire's *Questions sur l'Encyclopédie, par des Amateurs* (1770), a text later added to editions of the *Dictionnaire philosophique*.

Huffington Post blog, a professor at the University of California, Davis commented on the let's-make-a-deal cynicism he detected in what he called "Obama's-Perfect-Is-the-Enemy-of-Good mantra." One instance of Barack Obama's "favorite platitude," as the blogger put it, occurred during the 2008 presidential campaign. Speaking about an offshore drilling bill pending before Congress, candidate Obama said: "I'm willing to consider it if it's necessary to actually pass a comprehensive plan. I am not interested in making the perfect the enemy of the good—particularly since there is so much good in this compromise that would actually reduce our dependence on foreign oil."[2] Obama's mantra resurfaced in 2013 in connection with legislation to aid victims of Hurricane Sandy. Senator Barbara Mikulski of Maryland, a supporter of the measure, said, "It is not perfect, but it is a very sound bill. Let's not make the perfect the enemy of the good." In March 2017, Speaker of the House Paul Ryan applied Voltaire's remark to the politics of health care reform.[3]

Voltaire is famous not just for aphorisms like this. He may be equally famous for things he never wrote or said, the most notorious being: "I disapprove of what you say, but I will defend to the death your right to say it." Though faithful to Voltaire's core principles, this impassioned call for freedom of speech sprang from the pen of an Englishwoman, Evelyn Beatrice Hall, shortly after the turn of the last century, in her book, *The Friends of Voltaire.*

Writing under the alias "S. G. Tallentyre," Hall meant to convey a succinct summary of Voltaire's reaction to news that an atheistic tract by a fellow *philosophe*, Helvétius (figure 2), had been condemned by the Catholic Church: "'What a fuss about an omelette!' he had exclaimed. . . . How abominably unjust to persecute a man for such an airy trifle as that! 'I disapprove of what you say, but I will defend to the death your right to say it,' was his attitude now."

Hall's qualifying phrase, "his attitude now," was overlooked by virtually everyone who read what she had written.[4]

Her stirring paraphrase, unequivocally assigned to Voltaire, was carved in stone inside the lobby of the Tribune Tower when the *Chicago Tribune*'s new

2. Bob Ostertag, "Gulf Disaster: The Fatal Flaw in Obama's 'Don't Make the Perfect the Enemy of the Good' Politics," *Huffington Post*, July 6, 2010; "Obama's Speech in Lansing, Michigan," *New York Times*, August 4, 2008.

3. John Hayward, "The Cliffhanger, Jan. 29," *Human Events*, January 29, 2013; Rebecca Shabad, "Ryan Says He Doesn't Want to Negotiate with Democrats on Health Care," CBS.com, March 30, 2017. This is what Ryan said on that date on *CBS This Morning*: "If this Republican Congress allows the perfect to become the enemy of the good, I worry we'll push the President to working with Democrats."

4. Hall [S. G. Tallentyre], *The Friends of Voltaire* (1906), 198–199. The controversial tract by Helvétius was *De l'esprit* (1758).

Figure 2. Pierre Sudré, *Portrait of Claude-Adrien Helvétius*, 1825. Lithograph. Copy of an earlier print after a painting from 1755 by Louis-Michel Van Loo. Private collection.

headquarters building was inaugurated in 1925 (figure 3). In June 1934, *Reader's Digest* passed the bogus quote on to its national readership. In 1938, it was further fixed in the public mind by the Hollywood film *Jezebel*, starring Bette Davis, in which a dinner guest declared, "I think it was Voltaire who said, 'I disagree with what you say but I will defend to the death your right to say it.'"

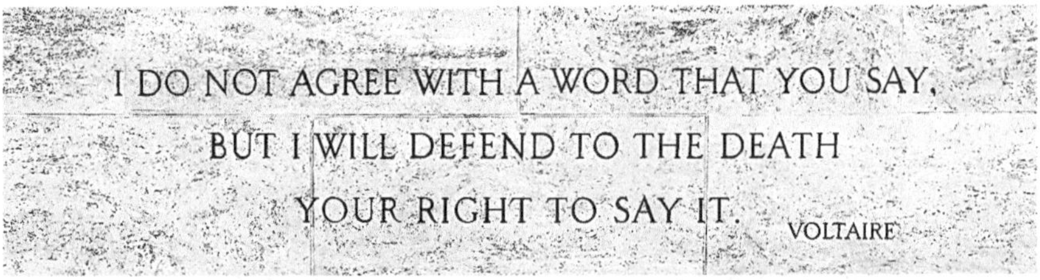

> I DO NOT AGREE WITH A WORD THAT YOU SAY, BUT I WILL DEFEND TO THE DEATH YOUR RIGHT TO SAY IT. VOLTAIRE

Figure 3. The false "I will defend to the death" quote, carved into the wall of the Hall of Inscriptions in the main lobby of the Chicago Tribune building on Michigan Avenue, Chicago. Photograph by John O'Neill.

Lazy, ignorant postwar writers, journalists, and now denizens of the World Wide Web have made the long-debunked quote one of the most commonly misquoted lines in the language.

Voltaire had opinions—not always polite or "politically correct"—on everything from adultery, friendship, and luxury to testicles and Zoroaster. He was, at times, appallingly malicious.

"The fact that Voltaire devoted his life to the noblest of causes," Lytton Strachey said, "must not blind us to another fact," that he could "be a frantic, desperate fighter, to whom all means were excusable; he was a scoundrel, a rogue, he lied, he blasphemed; he was extremely indecent."[5] Both the positive and negative facets of Voltaire's character are in evidence among the more than two thousand quotations in *The Quotable Voltaire.*

In the realm of bons mots, perhaps Voltaire's closest challenger in the eighteenth century was Benjamin Franklin, whose pithy maxims in *Poor Richard's Almanack* remain an integral part of our vernacular.[6] Voltaire could be pithy, too. For Nicholas Cronk, director of the Voltaire Foundation, he was "a master of the one-liner." But his droll one-liners, combined with his many other, more expansive statements—shrewd, cynical, or spiteful—surpass in their totality and depth the range of sayings we associate with Franklin.[7]

In 1925, Emanuel Haldeman-Julius, a Socialist reformer in a small town in Kansas, began selling, at a nickel apiece, copies of a softcover booklet, *The Wit*

---

5. Strachey, "Voltaire," *The Athenæum*, August 1, 1919, 679.

6. See James C. Humes, *The Wit & Wisdom of Benjamin Franklin* (1995). Besides Franklin, two other Anglophone writers in the eighteenth century were masters of the catchy quote: Alexander Pope and Samuel Johnson.

7. Cronk, "Voltaire and the One-liner," *OUPblog*, March 10, 2017.

and Wisdom of Voltaire Famous Skeptic, printed on cheap paper. Haldeman-Julius has been described as "one of the most prolific publishers in U.S. history, putting an estimated 300 million copies of inexpensive 'Little Blue Books' into the hands of working-class and middle-class Americans." In addition to Voltaire, he helped popularize the writings of Will Durant, Bertrand Russell, and Clarence Darrow.[8]

However, *The Wit and Wisdom of Voltaire* is mostly an assortment of windy wooden prose of vague or unspecified origin, not a true collection of quotations. The first bona fide compilation of quotes, *Satirical Dictionary of Voltaire*, was published in 1945 by a professional puppeteer, Paul McPharlin. The lone French dictionary to date, *Sarcasmes*, compiled by a journalist, Pierre Sipriot, came out in 1989.

In 1995, three French academics, Jean Goulemot, André Magnan, and Didier Masseau, assembled a massive compendium, *Inventaire Voltaire*. Scattered throughout its 1,368 articles, contributed by the editors and thirty fellow scholars, are tons of quotable material. In 1994 and in 2013, respectively, a Belgian writer, André Versaille, published two similarly mammoth anthologies of excerpts, drawn à la Haldeman-Julius, from Voltaire's oeuvre: *Dictionnaire de la pensée de Voltaire par lui-même* and *Autodictionnaire Voltaire*. These six antecedents of the present book, the first rigorously curated dictionary of quotations by Voltaire, are listed below, beneath our signature line.

The Quotable Voltaire is unique in terms of its substance, accuracy, and bilingual format. This extends to the inclusion of fourteen quotations misattributed or dubiously ascribed to Voltaire. The second half of the book consists of comments about Voltaire, his life and accomplishments, by Voltaire himself, his contemporaries, and posterity.

In compiling *The Quotable Voltaire*, we relied chiefly on the *Œuvres complètes de Voltaire*, the first critical edition of the whole of Voltaire's works, completed in 2021, in 203 volumes, under the aegis of the Voltaire Foundation at the University of Oxford. All entries in our dictionary are nonetheless fully documented, with specific (usually initial) dates of publication and page numbers for every source we cite, since many early non–*Œuvres complètes* references can be hard to locate. The sole exception to this rule are Voltaire's correspondence and plays. The vast majority of his letters and dramatic works are accessible online or in print in one form or another.[9]

---

8. For the comment on Haldeman-Julius and his Little Blue Books, see Rolf Potts, "The Henry Ford of Literature," *The Believer*, September 2008.

9. The most authoritative collection of Voltaire's letters in print is Theodore Besterman's *The Complete Works of Voltaire. Correspondence and Related Documents. Definitive*

Each entry in *The Quotable Voltaire* is presented in parallel versions: in English and the original language, invariably French, but occasionally German, Italian, or Spanish. Due to their historical, cultural, or literary value, translations for a number of quotes date from the eighteenth or nineteenth century, notably the thirty-six-volume series of Voltaire's works edited by the Scottish poet and novelist Tobias Smollett.

In the back of the book, a timeline of events in Voltaire's life and posthumous critical fortunes precedes a list of books, and one documentary film, for further reading (and viewing) in English. A complete bibliography of texts mentioned within these pages appears at the very end of the volume.

Garry Apgar
Edward M. Langille

Edition (1968–1977), initiated during Besterman's tenure as director of the Institut et Musée Voltaire in Geneva and completed by the Voltaire Foundation at Oxford, now superseded by Electronic Enlightenment (an online research project of the Bodleian Libraries, Oxford; subscription only), which benefits from regular updates and new material. The fifty-one-volume series edited by Besterman contains letters to and by Voltaire. A compact thirteen-volume Pléiade set of the correspondence, culled from Besterman's magnum opus (minus letters to Voltaire), edited by Frédéric Deloffre, has been published by Gallimard. For a relatively complete nineteenth-century edition, available online and thus easily searchable, see Adrien-Jean-Quentin Beuchot, *Œuvres de Voltaire* (1828–1834), vols. 51–70.

PREVIOUSLY PUBLISHED BOOKS
CONTAINING QUOTATIONS AND EXCERPTS
OF WRITINGS BY VOLTAIRE

The Wit and Wisdom of Voltaire Famous Skeptic. Girard, KA: Haldeman-Julius Company (Little Blue Book No. 60), 1925. 64 pp.

Paul McPharlin, ed. *Satirical Dictionary of Voltaire.* New York: Peter Pauper Press, 1945. 110 pp.

Pierre Sipriot, ed. *Sarcasmes.* Monaco: Editions du Rocher, 1989. 216 pp.

André Versaille, ed. *Dictionnaire de la pensée de Voltaire par lui-même.* Brussels: Éditions Complexe, 1994. 1,320 pp.

Jean Goulemot, André Magnan, and Didier Masseau, eds. *Inventaire Voltaire.* Paris: Gallimard, 1995. 1,422 pp.

André Versaille, ed. *Autodictionnaire Voltaire.* Paris: Omnibus, 2013. 624 pp.

The Quotable Voltaire

VOLTAIRE: THE LIFE OF A LEGEND

Garry Apgar

> Voltaire has suffered the greatest misfortune that can befall a writer;
> he has become a legend, which insures that he will not be read
> until someone destroys the legend.
> —W. H. Auden, "A Great Democrat,"
> *The Nation*, March 25, 1939

> A writer is in the end not his books, but his myth.
> —V. S. Naipaul, "Cannery Row Revisited," *Daily
> Telegraph Magazine*, April 3, 1970

The French affectionately refer to English as *la langue de Shakespeare*. They call their own language *la langue de Molière*—and, albeit less frequently, *la langue de Voltaire*. Where Shakespeare is concerned, the play is still the thing. After all, we know so little about who the Immortal Bard really was. That is not the case with François-Marie Arouet, a.k.a. Voltaire, the European Enlightenment personified, and the *exemplum parfait* of the urbane Gallic intellectual. We know a lot about him. Or so we think.

However, some of what we've been told is inaccurate, false, erroneously attributed, or garbled in translation. Part of the problem is that no single author, scholar, or team of scholars, can absorb everything Voltaire did, said, and wrote, not to mention relevant materials generated by his contemporaries and the mass of research that has accumulated since the end of World War II. Nor can any one person fully gauge Voltaire's impact on European and American culture, or hope to collect and assess the multitude of remarks about him made by personalities as diverse as Goethe, Flaubert, and Charles de Gaulle, the science fiction writer Ray Bradbury, and former heavyweight boxing champion Mike Tyson.

No matter. Our mental picture of Voltaire transcends all that. Which is why V. S. Naipaul, in his essay "Cannery Row Revisited," was spot on, and Auden, in his piece "A Great Democrat" in *The Nation*, was dead wrong. Voltaire *is* "his myth." If his legend were laid to eternal rest, chances are he would be less, not more, widely read.

Besides, and contrary to the premise of Auden's contention, the legend of Voltaire is itself extraordinary. Heads of state, political and religious figures aside, before the invention of photomechanical means of reproduction, the image of no other individual circulated as extensively as that of the Patriarch of Ferney. His periodic association with hot-button issues *du jour* likewise set him apart from other giants of world literature such as Dante, Shakespeare, Goethe, or Hemingway.

Voltaire's abiding aura as a physically frail yet dogged crusader for justice, a font of sage witticisms, and the teller of satirical tales like *Candide* is of a piece with his often stormy private life, and the sundry ways he was regarded, by those who knew him, and by succeeding generations. In 1748, in his mid-fifties, he was described in a police file as tall, thin, and resembling a satyr. "Intellectually he is an Eagle," the report continued, "and a very poor subject in matters of the heart, everyone knows his works and his adventures."[1]

The foundational basis of the legend of Voltaire is his prodigious output as a poet, dramatist, historian, prosateur, pamphleteer, and correspondent (the most comprehensive edition of his letters contains over twenty-one thousand items to, from, or about him). Needless to say, most of what Voltaire wrote—including the tragedies and verse that made his reputation early on, circa 1718–1735—have been consigned to the dustbin of our collective memory, even in France. None of his plays, "without any exception," Oscar Wilde asserted, should be read. The poet Richard Aldington called Voltaire's odes "disastrous exercises in rhetoric, completely unreadable."[2]

It would gall the poet of the *Henriade* to be told that of his literary offspring his only canonical text today is *Candide*. On the other hand, writing for Voltaire was primarily a means to an end: Fame. Immediate and lasting fame. By that standard, due in large part to *Candide*, he realized his goal.

Voltaire died in Paris at the age of eighty-four, a rich man, his brow freshly crowned with laurels, two months earlier to be exact, at the Comédie-Française before a packed house, after a performance of the last of his fifty-odd stage plays, *Irène* (figure 4). He remains one of the most renowned men who ever lived, despite the fact that much of that renown was won through

---

1. Annie Angremy et al., *Voltaire* (1979), 49–50 (illus.).

2. Wilde, "To Read or Not to Read," *Pall Mall Gazette*, February 8, 1886, 11; Aldington, *Voltaire* (1925), 148.

Figure 4. C.-É. Gaucher, after J.-M. Moreau the Younger, *Hommages rendus à Voltaire*, 1778–1782. Etching and engraving. Yale University Art Gallery, Department of Prints, Drawings, and Photographs (Everett V. Meeks, B.A. 1901, Fund). At the end of the March 30, 1778, performance of Voltaire's tragedy *Irène* at the Théâtre-Français, members of the cast hold aloft laurel wreaths to honor a bust of Voltaire and the man himself. Voltaire is seated in an upper loge on the left side of the print.

his intermittent antics, histrionic deeds, idiosyncrasies, and the base flattery, polemical commentary, gossip, and effigies he inspired, solicited, or orchestrated.

On one occasion, in the mid-1760s, when the actress Mlle Clairon, Voltaire's invited guest, arrived at Ferney, she theatrically fell to her knees as she came into his presence. The gallant septuagenarian reciprocated her superb gesture: he dropped to the floor and, indicating their mutual posture, said: "Now, Mademoiselle, how do you do?" ("comment vous portez-vous?"). The Genevan artist Jean Huber witnessed and made an etching of this comically endearing scene.[3] On another occasion, it is said, a young houseguest at

3. Voltaire's comment could more literally be translated as "How are you getting along?" For more on this incident, see Lucien Perey and Gaston Maugras, *La Vie intime de Voltaire aux Délices et à Ferney* (1885), 381; for the etching, see Garry Apgar, *L'Art singulier de Jean Huber* (1995), 91 (illus.), 93.

Ferney was roused before dawn and dragged by his host to a nearby hill to watch the sun rise. Overwhelmed by the experience, Voltaire again dropped to the ground, lifted his arms heavenward, and exclaimed: "I believe, I believe in You! God almighty. I believe! As for Monsieur the Son, and Madame his Mother, that's another story."[4] All forms of ancient history, Voltaire once warned, are "des fables convenues," fairy tales, universally agreed upon. So, too, with Voltaire. Any attempt to define his storied genius must entail an element of critical "deconstruction," the good faith correction or destruction, as Auden would have it, of preceding narratives. Nonetheless, no serious assessment of the life, or afterlife, of a fabulous being like Voltaire can discount all previous formulations of his mythic existence. Hence, the subtitle of this essay, "The Life of a Legend."

Voltaire's legend has a way of reaffirming itself at pivotal moments in French history. In 1944, speaking within the sacred precincts of the Sorbonne following the liberation of Paris, the poet Paul Valéry declared: "France is rich in . . . personages of the highest order whose glorious existence is accompanied by a sort of immortal, no doubt, but almost familiar presence."

Montaigne, Pascal, and Jean-Jacques Rousseau were three of the immortals cited by Valéry. Because 1944 was the 250th anniversary year of Voltaire's birth, however, he privileged Voltaire, "whose name," Valéry said, "still arouses among us very sharp and strongly opposed reactions. Voltaire is alive, Voltaire endures: he is infinitely current."[5]

He is still "infinitely current," thanks to his campaign against the three-headed beast he designated *l'infâme*: religious, social, and judicial injustice. "Écrasez l'infâme," Voltaire implored, as he signed off on scores of letters in the 1760s and 1770s, a phrase so universally well-known that as a freshman at Whittier College in California in 1930, Richard Nixon convinced a student group he helped organize to adopt as its credo the words "Écrasons l'Infâme"—"Let us Crush Evil."[6]

Furthermore, Voltaire was lucky. Lucky to have been born at the tail end of the *Grand Siècle*, at the dawn of Modernity, and to have grown up in Paris, the cultural capital of the eighteenth century, in a milieu, the *grande bourgeoisie*, on the fecund cusp of the aristocracy and the middle class. Lucky to have possessed physical and behavioral traits (bright-eyed, lean as a rail, irascible, eccentric) that made for an enduring visual persona, lucky to have

---

4. Quoted by Lord Brougham in his book *Lives of Men of Letters and Science* (1845), 142.
5. Valéry, *Voltaire* (1945), iii.
6. See Conrad Black, *Richard M. Nixon* (2007), 25.

lived long enough to become the dominant nonprincely citizen in Europe, and to make many useful friends, and enemies.

He also was blessed to have been active in an era in which an irreversible drive for religious, political, and personal freedom began to sap the old hier-archical social order. The self-evident truth at the nub of that struggle, that humankind has a natural right to "life, liberty and the pursuit of happiness," was a notion as Voltairian as it was Jeffersonian.[7] And it was fired by a con-current surge in four modes of communication that fit Voltaire to a "T": book publishing, journalism, printmaking, and graphic satire. Finally, he was fortu-nate in that all of this occurred while France, his homeland, ruled the roost in art, literature, and, with England and Scotland, in philosophy, science, and economics.

In his early twenties, François-Marie Arouet had everything going for him. Supremely intelligent, talented, and precocious, with a gift for self-promotion, he benefited from a first-rate education and gilt-edged family connections. A born rebel, he spent eleven months in the Bastille in 1717–1718 for allegedly penning scurrilous verse about the Regent, Philippe d'Orléans. Vain, ambi-tious, and incapable of keeping his tongue, or quill, in check, he would be in and out of hot water until the day he died.

With the premiere in 1718 of his first tragedy, *Œdipe*, he established him-self, at twenty-four, as both the rising star of French letters and its enfant terrible. By adopting the acronym "Voltaire" at this time, he turned his back on another authority figure, Arouet *père*, an ambitious civil law notary who had managed to purchase a position as royal counselor.[8] The decision to adapt, as his debut stage play, Sophocles's *Œdipus the King*, speaks volumes about Voltaire, who insisted repeatedly that his biological father was a noble-man and *homme d'esprit* named Rochebrune.

Acts of rebellion like these helped propel Voltaire to glory. A second, brief stint in the Bastille, for a verbal insult to the chevalier de Rohan, led to volun-tary exile in England. In London, from 1726 to 1728, under the influence of

---

7. The story of Jefferson's esteem for Voltaire, and the little-known parallels between the two men, is told in Garry Apgar, George W. Gowen, and Patrick H. Ryan, *Voltaire & Jefferson: The Sage of Ferney and the Man from Monticello*, a documentary film produced by the Voltaire Society of America (2001).

8. Voltaire never explained how he created his pen name, but "Voltaire" is likely a reordering of the letters in the French equivalent of "Arouet the Younger," in abbreviated form: "Arouet l(e) j(eune)." To make the anagram work, the *u* became a *v*, and the *j* an *i*. In eighteenth-century typography, those characters were interchangeable.

Francis Bacon, John Locke, and Isaac Newton, he raised himself from the status of facile wordsmith to that of philosopher.[9]

When Voltaire returned to France, he seemed to settle down. His liaison with the learned blue blood, the marquise du Châtelet, his *divine* Émilie, begun in Paris in 1733, was no ordinary romance. Their union of the heart and mind, centered on mathematics, science, and writing, presaged the brainy *ménage-à-deux* maintained two centuries later by Jean-Paul Sartre and Simone de Beauvoir.

With the support of another remarkable woman, Mme de Pompadour, Louis XV's arts-friendly *maîtresse en titre*, Voltaire's stock at court rose. In 1745, he was named historiographer to the king and, in 1746, elected to the French Academy.

This blissful interval in Voltaire's career did not last.

He fell from grace, with a careless word to Émilie during a high-stakes card game at Fontainebleau that he believed was rigged. His incautious remark, in English, overheard and understood by players *bien en cour*, obliged the couple to take refuge in the château of Émilie's husband, the marquis du Châtelet, at Cirey, in the eastern province of Champagne.[10] But the marquise was as exploratory in love as she was in math and science. She died in 1749 at Cirey after giving birth to a child fathered by another *ami intime*, the poet Saint-Lambert (the infant also died).[11]

Had Voltaire himself died in 1749, at age fifty-five, a respectable span for his day, he might have won a place as a leading literary light of the period, though he probably would now be viewed, at best, as a curious throwback to the age of Louis XIV. That did not happen. And, out of the crucible of his achievements and misadventures over the remaining three decades of his life, Voltaire became Voltaire.

Mme du Châtelet's death forced him to vacate her husband's house. He was still persona non grata at Versailles and Paris. So, *faute de mieux*, he landed at the court of the Francophile Prussian king, Frederick the Great. His sojourn at Berlin and Potsdam, from 1750 to 1753, dispelled, once and for

---

9. Thomas Jefferson shared Voltaire's admiration for Bacon, Locke, and Newton. In a letter in 1811 to Benjamin Rush, Jefferson said they were "my trinity of the three greatest men the world had ever produced." See Jefferson, *The Papers of Thomas Jefferson, Retirement Series* (2006), 305.

10. According to Sébastien Longchamp, private secretary to Voltaire, his master told Émilie, "en anglais . . . qu'elle jouait avec des fripons" (that she was playing with cheats). See Longchamp, *Anecdotes sur la vie privée de Monsieur de Voltaire* (2009), 56, 161.

11. For an engaging treatment of Voltaire's relationship with Émilie see Nancy Mitford, *Voltaire in Love* (1957).

all, any lingering illusions he had that talent, charm, and good intentions are bound to be rewarded in this world. In a letter to his niece, Mme Denis, he quoted Frederick telling a confidant: "I shall have need of him for another year at most; one squeezes the orange and throws away the peel."[12]

Voltaire's inevitable, and bitter, falling out with Frederick—part soap opera, part surreal psychodrama—once more cast him adrift, with no place to call home. He spent thirteen months with his niece in Colmar, in Alsace. In December 1754 they migrated to French-speaking Switzerland, first to a house near Nyon, in the Pays de Vaud, and from there to Les Délices, a suburban estate in the Republic of Geneva. Ultimately he settled at Ferney, across the border from Geneva, in France, where he found his true home, and niche in history.

From his rustic domain at Ferney, in the company of Mme Denis (figure 5), Voltaire morphed into a kind of philosopher-king. At Ferney, the generous side of his character shone most brightly, as he used his wealth to improve the lot of the peasants who tended his fields and to attract watchmakers and other craftsmen from Geneva to populate the village and grow the local economy. In his *Épître à Horace* he said of this principled benevolence, "I did a little good, it is my greatest work" ("J'ai fait un peu de bien: c'est mon meilleur ouvrage").[13]

In the 1760s, with old age looming large, Voltaire reinvented himself as the Patriarch of Ferney, shifting from the role of *philosophe* to that of *engagé* "public intellectual." Fame was no longer its own reward. He wanted tangible results from his pen. In a letter written in 1765, he told a friend, "A book is justified only if we learn something from it." In a letter to a Calvinist pastor in 1767, he said of Rousseau, "Jean-Jacques writes for the sake of writing," and of himself, "I write in order to act" ("moi j'écris pour agir").[14]

Voltaire's first big step toward doing things with his pen came with his poem inspired by the earthquake that devastated Lisbon in 1755, which contained these lines of verse:

All is well, you say, and all is *necessary*.
What? Would all of Creation be any worse
Without the pit that swallowed up Lisbon?[15]

---

12. Letter from Berlin, September 2, 1751.

13. *Épître à Horace* (1772), 7.

14. Ferney, March 8, 1765, to Étienne-Noël Damilaville; Ferney, April 15, 1767, to the Genevan Pastor Jacob Vernes.

15. *Poèmes sur le désastre de Lisbonne et sur la loi naturelle* (1756), 9.

Figure 5. Marie-Elisabeth de Dompierre de Fontaine, *Portrait of Mme Marie-Louise Denis*, the artist's sister. Pastel copy once owned by Voltaire, circa 1737, of an oil portrait by Carle Van Loo, formerly at the Shelburne Museum in Vermont. Cabinet d'arts graphiques des Musées d'art et d'histoire, Ville de Genève, don Marc Samuel Constant de Rebecque, nº d'inventaire: 1878-0004. Photograph by Bettina Jacot-Descombes.

The lushest fruit born of the "Poème sur le désastre de Lisbonne" (1756) was *Candide*, published in 1759. The action in five of the novel's thirty chapters takes place in the Portuguese capital at the time of the disaster, where, in the name of God, man's inhumanity to man, in the form of expiatory Church-sanctioned auto-da-fés, followed fast on the misery caused by Nature.

Figure 6. Angelika Kauffmann, *Portrait of Dr. John Morgan*. Oil on canvas, 1764. National Portrait Gallery, Smithsonian Institution, Washington, DC.

From his haven at Ferney in the 1760s and 1770s, Voltaire took even more concrete action. Through his exertions on behalf of a Protestant martyr in Toulouse, Jean Calas, the Calas family, and other victims of *l'infâme*, he assumed titular leadership of the loose-knit band of activist brothers known to their supporters as *les Philosophes*, and to their enemies as *les Nouveaux Philosophes*, to distinguish (and diminish) them from classical philosophers such as Plato or Aristotle.

It was at Les Délices and Ferney, that Voltaire's lucky star served up his graphic Boswell, the Genevan artist Jean Huber, who confected scores of portraits and vignettes in various media that by turns exalted and amiably spoofed the venerable activist. Huber created the painting of Voltaire reproduced on the cover of this book and the drawing facing page one of the preface (figure 1).

By the 1760s Voltaire was a superstar, sought out by idolators and sightseers from far and wide: Casanova, Edward Gibbon, James Boswell, and an American, Dr. John Morgan (figure 6), cofounder of the Medical College at the University of Pennsylvania, the first school of its kind in the colonies. These words, addressed to him by Voltaire in English, were recorded by Dr. Morgan in his diary: "The English . . . are I swear by God himself, the first Nation in Europe, & if ever I smell of a Resurrection, or come a second time on Earth, I will pray God to make me be born in England, the land of Liberty. These are four things w'ch I adore that the english boast of so greatly with his fore finger of the right hand counting them up, & naming each distinctly & with an emphasis— *Liberty, Property, Newton & Locke.*"[16] An unprecedented process of secular beatification kicked in as Voltaire entered his twilight years. At an elite gathering in Paris in 1770, hosted by Mme Jacques Necker (Mme de Staël's mother), the sculptor Jean-Baptiste Pigalle was engaged to carve a statue to honor the great man. Pigalle chose to represent him au naturel, in a misguided allusion to the death of the Stoic philosopher Seneca.

The nudity of the seventy-something patriarch, at odds with the male *beau idéal* then still the norm, shocked everyone, and the project was a flop. Pigalle's *Voltaire nu* did, nonetheless, anticipate one of the finest pieces of sculpture of the eighteenth century, the marble effigy of Voltaire from 1781 by Jean-Antoine Houdon (figure 31), who treated his subject with proper dignity: fully clothed, in toga-like attire, in a pose evocative of Michelangelo's seated Moses commissioned by Pope Julius II. Houdon's *Voltaire assis*, a gift from Mme Denis, reigns supreme in the foyer of the Comédie-Française, in its present-day home adjoining the Palais-Royal (Pigalle's statue is on display in the Louvre).

In February 1778 Voltaire returned at last to Paris, where, from a public relations perspective, in an ultimate stroke of good luck, he died, on May 30. For three months prior to his death he experienced one long, tumultuous apotheosis. He was written up in the press, hailed in the street by passersby, lionized at the Théâtre-Français (figure 4), and at the Royal Academy of Sciences, where Benjamin Franklin and he met and embraced.

---

16. Morgan, *The Journal of Dr. John Morgan of Philadelphia* (1907), 220–221.

Figure 7. Pierre-Gabriel Berthault, after Jean-Louis Prieur, *Triomphe de Voltaire, le 11 juillet 1791*, 1802. Engraving. Private collection. The image depicts the procession carrying Voltaire's remains to the Panthéon as it is about to cross the Seine River toward what is now the quai Voltaire, where Voltaire died on May 30, 1778.

Voltaire's passing triggered a second wave of adulation, and soon the first biographies appeared, notably, *Vie de Voltaire* (1786) by the marquis de Condorcet. In 1791, as the kinder, gentler initial phase of the French Revolution held sway, Voltaire was the first of France's *grands hommes* to be entombed in the crypt of the Panthéon. En route to his final resting place, his coffin passed through the streets of Paris in a stately cortege orchestrated by the painter Jacques-Louis David (figure 7). These marks of distinction amounted to a second apotheosis, even if Voltaire's ghost had to share some of the limelight. In the sphere of material culture, for example, he was depicted as one of the kings, along with Molière, La Fontaine, and Rousseau, in packs of playing cards.

In the 1790s, Voltaire's fortunes began a teeter-totter cycle of ups and downs, which in France mirrored political trends, and tended to rise in moments of crisis. A third apotheosis, during the *centenaire* of his birth in 1794, coincided with the bloody excesses of the Terror. In England and America, Voltaire symbolized the Revolution gone awry. In a Federalist cartoon circa 1800, the figure of George Washington, associated with law, order, and religion, was contrasted with a picture of Thomas Jefferson resting on a pile of books, one of them labeled "Voltaire." John Adams, who attended Voltaire and

Franklin's historic meeting in 1778, said of Voltaire, retrospectively, that he "was considered as a vain, profligate wit, and not much esteemed or beloved by anybody, though admired by all who knew his works."[17]

In France, as in America, conservatives scorned him. Radicals simply lost interest. After Napoleon's downfall, fresh-faced Romantics such as Victor Hugo rejected Voltaire as passé—or, like Alfred de Musset, denounced him as an emblem of the soulless spirit of modernity. By and large, Voltaire's French devotees around 1820–1850 were prosperous bourgeois, mocked by Balzac and Flaubert, who stocked their bookshelves with collections of his writings purchased *en bloc*, by the yard.

Voltaire remained in favor with his middle-class base from the July Monarchy into the Second Empire. In 1865, he got a new lease on life in the hearts and minds of leftists and republicans opposed to the self-proclaimed emperor, Napoleon III, when the newspaper *Le Siècle* launched a public subscription to erect a statue to mark the one-hundredth anniversary of Voltaire's death, a date still over a decade off.

That was not the point. The aim was not so much to pay homage to their hero as to inflame popular opinion in opposition to an imperious despot. Hugo, Garibaldi, and Flaubert's mistress, Louise Colet, were conspicuous donors to the cause.

Le Siècle spent the funds it collected on a bronze cast of Houdon's seated Voltaire. In April 1871, a mob toppled a statue of Prince Eugène de Beauharnais, Napoleon's stepson, on the boulevard du Prince-Eugène. The replica of Houdon's masterwork took Eugène's place on the newly renamed boulevard Voltaire. A guillotine was set on fire facing the refurbished monument, to the delight of a mob of spectators (figure 8).

Under the Third Republic, after the Commune was crushed, Voltaire continued to thrive. Statues of him went up in three more public spaces in Paris: on the façade of the Hôtel de Ville, in a square on the Left Bank next to the Institut de France, and in the courtyard of the administrative offices of the ninth arrondissement.[18] The eighth and final volume in the magisterial

17. James A. Leith, professor emeritus, Queens University, Kingston, Ontario, wrote about the outpourings of public adulation Voltaire enjoyed in 1778, 1791, and 1794 in "Les Trois apothéoses de Voltaire," *Annales historiques de la Révolution française*, no. 236 (April–June 1979): 161–209; John Adams's remark appeared in the *Boston Patriot*, May 15, 1811.

18. Three of the four statues were bronze casts. After the fall of France in 1940 they were melted down during the Occupation by the Germans, ostensibly to recover their constituent metals for the production of armaments. *See* Garry Apgar, "'Sage comme une image': Trois siècles d'iconographie voltairienne," *Nouvelles de l'estampe*, July 1994, 20–25.

Figure 8. An engraving, *Les Bois de la guillotine sont brulés aux pieds de la statue de Voltaire, devant la mairie du XIe arrondissement*, published as an illustration in *L'Univers illustré*, April 15, 1871. Private collection. The destruction of the guillotine took place in front of the statue of Voltaire on April 6, 1871. See also fig. 34.

biography by Gustave Desnoiresterres, *Voltaire et la société au XVIIIe siècle*, appeared in 1876.

In his younger days, Victor Hugo disdained the démodé poet and acerbic skeptic. In old age, he cultivated a patriarchal Voltairian persona. And because, much like Voltaire, Hugo had gone into voluntary exile after Louis-Napoléon seized power in 1851, he was seen as the spiritual heir of *l'homme aux Calas*. For these reasons and his rhetorical genius—amid what proved to be Voltaire's fourth and final apotheosis, the centennial jubilee of his death—Hugo served as the keynote speaker on May 30, 1878, before a prestigious assembly at the Théâtre de la Gaîté in Paris.

In his address, Hugo said that Rousseau epitomized "the People," whereas Voltaire embodied "Mankind" as a whole. A generation later, Émile Zola upheld the tradition of the politically committed *homme de lettres* with a combined defense of Captain Dreyfus and attack on anti-Semitism in his open letter, "J'Accuse," published in the Paris daily *L'Aurore*. In "J'Accuse," Zola made no mention of Voltaire, although, in a column in *L'Aurore* in 1866, he praised him as "the most complete personality, and the brightest light of the glorious eighteenth century."[19]

As glittering as these connections to writers of Hugo and Zola's caliber are, arguably the highlight of Voltaire's posthumous association with the arts occurred in February 1916 at the Cabaret Voltaire in Zurich, Switzerland, where the anarchic Dadaist movement came into being. It is fitting that Dada's founders, appalled by the horrors of World War I, should have met at an establishment named after the man who, in chapters 2 and 3 of *Candide*, penned some of the finest antiwar satire in Western literature.

The *bicentenaire* of Voltaire's birth in 1894 had passed barely noticed, and none of the anniversaries to come—1944, 1978, 1994—would match the drama of the events in the 1870s, culminating in Hugo's oration in 1878.

In his remarks *en Sorbonne* in December 1944, Paul Valéry invoked the memory of Voltaire as a symbol of his countrymen's strength of character under the Nazi occupation. In light of the horrors of World War II, Valéry posed this rhetorical question: "Where is the Voltaire, the voice that will rise up today?"[20]

The answer: nowhere. No one voice, anyway.

The French novelist Roger Peyrefitte conceitedly claimed that he shared some of Voltaire's qualities, and before Peyrefitte, Anatole France was likened to Voltaire. In the English-speaking world, Tom Paine, Mark Twain, H. L. Mencken, Gore Vidal, William F. Buckley Jr., Salman Rushdie, Christopher Hitchens, Tom Wolfe, and—nominated, tongue-in-cheek, by Wolfe—Noam Chomsky have all been compared to Voltaire.[21]

In mid-twentieth-century France, Jean-Paul Sartre assumed the role of social and political gadfly once played by the sage of Ferney, and Zola. In 1960, President Charles de Gaulle reportedly was urged to have Sartre arrested for his loud opposition to the government's policy in Algeria. De Gaulle, a keen student of history, replied, "You don't put Voltaire in jail."[22]

---

19. Zola, *Œuvres complètes* (1966–1969), 10:427.

20. Valéry, *Voltaire* (1945), xxxiv.

21. Wolfe, "The Origins of Speech: In the Beginning Was Chomsky," *Harper's*, August 2016, 29. At least four eighteenth-century Britons have been likened to Voltaire: Bolingbroke, Jonathan Swift, Horace Walpole, and Edward Gibbon. See Friedrich Christoph Schlosser, *History of the Eighteenth Century* (1844), 64; Sidney Dark, "The English Voltaire: Jonathan Swift—Satirist," *John O'London's Weekly*, November 29, 1924, 322; Christopher Thacker, *The Wildness Pleases* (1983); and Paul Turnbull, "'Une Marionette Infidèle'" (1997).

22. Jacques Derogy, "Le Défi des 343," *L'Express*, April 12–18, 1971, 15.

Sartre had no real affinity for Voltaire, however. Nor did Sartre's principal successor in the ranks of the French postwar intelligentsia. In 1958, Roland Barthes published an essay in which he maintained that "what separates" Voltaire "from us is that Voltaire was a happy writer"—a writer who gave to "the fight for Reason" a "festive air."[23]

This was an odd but telling point to make. Voltaire *was* a happy writer—the Happy Warrior of Gallic belles-lettres, and the antithesis of his bête noire, Jean-Jacques Rousseau, whose dour, self-absorbed temperament and contrarian, protorevolutionary mentality were more congenial to Barthes and other Marxist-leaning *intellos* in the 1950s and 1960s. An American scholar later condemned what Barthes had said as "an absolute negation of the relevancy of Voltaire to the modern world."[24]

Bernard-Henri Lévy, a *gauchiste* of the rising generation, one of the so-called latter-day *Nouveaux Philosophes* of the 1970s, shared that antipathy. On a visit to Boston in 1979, Lévy was asked whether he preferred Voltaire or Rousseau. His tart response: "I hate Voltaire." Ironically, Lévy's words were uttered not long after the bicentennial commemoration of Voltaire's death.[25]

On the celebratory bill of fare in 1978 were exhibitions in Paris, Bourg-en-Bresse, Sceaux, and Brussels, an international symposium in Paris, and a biographical television miniseries starring Claude Dauphin. Regrettably, the festivities were marred by a pair of tone-deaf decisions by l'État: withdrawal from circulation of the ten-franc note with Voltaire's beaming face on it and removal of the plaster model for Houdon's seated Voltaire from its long-standing site in a ground-floor hallway of the Bibliothèque Nationale.[26]

From the 1970s into the 1990s, while old-school lefties and younger, media-savvy mavericks such as Bernard-Henri Lévy typically despised Voltaire, many conservatives favored him. Two prominent center-right figures who sang Voltaire's praises were the curmudgeonly novelist and essayist, Jean Dutourd, and the aristocratic author and columnist for *Le Figaro*, Jean d'Ormesson, both members of the French Academy. In a deft jab at Roland Barthes, Dutourd said that modern French intellectuals tend to favor Rousseau over Voltaire precisely because Voltaire was so happy ("Le tort de Voltaire est d'avoir été gai"). For d'Ormesson, in volume 2 of his history of French literature,

23. Barthes, "Voltaire, le Dernier des écrivains heureux" (1964), 98.
24. Patrick Henry, "Contre Barthes" (1987), 19.
25. Quoted in the *Canard Enchaîné*, August 8, 1979.
26. Garry Apgar, "Une Célébration bien discrète," *Le Monde*, September 8, 1978, 2.

Jean-Jacques was "a savage and a revolutionary." "Everything is so easy with Voltaire. Nothing is simple with Rousseau."[27]

Comfortably distanced from Gallic cultural politics, the spirit, energy, and ideals of Voltaire often are more highly regarded in Anglo-Saxon precincts than in his native land. In an interview in *Le Monde* in 2015, Roland Barthes's friend, the critic Philippe Sollers, said: "The French don't like Voltaire. . . . The English appreciate him the most."[28]

Notable British enthusiasts were the Liberal statesman, Lord Morley, novelist E. M. Forster, and that all-round man of letters, Lytton Strachey, who owned a painting (figure 9) by Jean Huber, related to the drawing previously mentioned (figure 1), depicting an imaginary dinner party hosted by Voltaire with d'Alembert, Diderot, and Saint-Lambert among his guests. In America, Thomas Jefferson displayed a bust of Voltaire by Houdon at Monticello, and authors as disparate as James Fenimore Cooper, Walt Whitman, Henry Adams, Auden, and Camille Paglia have written about him. Louis Howe, secretary and self-styled "no-man" to President Franklin D. Roosevelt, had business cards printed up that read, "Colonel Louis Rasputin Voltaire Talleyrand Simon Legree Howe."[29]

In retirement after World War II, Winston Churchill discovered *Candide* and pronounced it "extraordinary." In 1952, an enterprising, Polish-born British bibliographer and inveterate *voltairomane*, Theodore Besterman, established the Institut et Musée Voltaire, housed in Voltaire's former abode, Les Délices, in Geneva. From that splendid base of operations, Besterman launched three ambitious projects: the first complete edition of Voltaire's correspondence, a scientific edition of his complete works, and a research series, *Studies on Voltaire and the Eighteenth Century*. This program has been carried on by the Voltaire Foundation at the University of Oxford, where Huber's dinner party picture, acquired in 1983 from one of Strachey's heirs, now hangs.

In the twentieth century, mass culture in the United States latched onto Voltaire. In 1918, America's first "celebrity attorney," Clarence Darrow, devoted a lecture and, in 1929, an essay to Candide's literary father. In 1933, the Oscar-winning English actor, George Arliss, starred in a Hollywood production about Voltaire and the Calas affair. A bust of Voltaire graced the bank offices of Cosmo Topper in the 1937 screwball comedy, *Topper*, starring Cary Grant. (In 1933, Grant's costar in two movies, Mae West, had boasted, "I'm a regular Voltaire when it comes to satire, honey.") In the late 1950s, a

27. Dutourd, *Le Spectre de la rose* (1986), 137; d'Ormesson, *Une Autre histoire de la littérature française* (2000), 71.

28. Sollers, "Il manque, Voltaire, là!," *Le Monde*, April 9, 2015.

29. Alfred B. Rollins Jr., *Roosevelt and Howe* (1962), 436.

Figure 9. Jean Huber, *Voltaire's Last Supper*, 1772–1773. Oil on canvas. The Voltaire Foundation, University of Oxford (once owned by Lytton Strachey). On the far left in this imaginary gathering are Voltaire's resident priest at Ferney, Father Adam, and Friedrich-Melchior Grimm; on the far right, Jean-François Marmontel (in a black tiewig) and Denis Diderot (bare-headed). To Voltaire's immediate right is d'Alembert and to his immediate left the artist himself, Huber.

bust of Voltaire could be seen in the office of television lawyer Perry Mason, and an actor named Voltaire Perkins played the presiding judge in the small-screen series *Divorce Court*.[30]

Leonard Bernstein's musical take on *Candide*, inspired by the specter of McCarthyism, opened on Broadway in 1956 and went on to become a staple

---

30. Other notable namesakes, in addition to Voltaire Perkins, are the winning horse in the 1828 Doncaster Gold Cup race in England and U.S. Army captain Voltaire P. Twombly, who received the Medal of Honor for his heroism in the Civil War. From 2010 to 2016, Voltaire Gazmin was secretary of the Department of Defense of the Philippines. A busy thoroughfare, Voltaire Street, leads to the Voltaire Street Beach in San Diego, and in the fashion world, there is the Paris-based marketer of chic casual attire, Zadig & Voltaire.

in theatrical and operatic repertoires.[31] In 1965, Will and Ariel Durant published a volume in their best-selling *History of Civilization* series, *The Age of Voltaire*. The BBC series *Civilisation*, written and presented by Kenneth Clark, featuring Voltaire in episode 10, "The Smile of Reason," was a big hit on public television stations in the United States in 1969. In 1970, a caricature of the French writer as a sly American-style businessman in a three-piece suit by David Levine (figure 34) accompanied an essay in the *New York Review of Books*.[32]

Candide provided a template of sorts for Preston Sturges's cinematic bildungsroman, *Sullivan's Travels* (1941) and, in 1994, Robert Zemeckis's *Forrest Gump*. In 2005, Penguin brought forth an edition of Voltaire's classic tale, with cover art by the American cartoonist Chris Ware. Voltaire, by then, enjoyed an almost universal reputation in American culture as an impish, freewheeling challenger of the status quo, an image bolstered by his association with Dada. Hence, the poster for the British rock group Cabaret Voltaire, visible in the bedroom of the eponymous main character in *Ferris Bueller's Day Off* (1986), starring Matthew Broderick.

For the tercentenary of Voltaire's birth in 1994, an international congress, "Voltaire et ses combats," was hosted sequentially in two venues, at Oxford and at the Sorbonne. In Paris, an encyclopedic exhibition at the Bibliothèque Nationale showcased nine paintings by Jean Huber of scenes from Voltaire's private life at Ferney, commissioned by Catherine the Great of Russia, and lent by the Hermitage Museum. Of more lasting import was the publication of the final volume of *Voltaire en son temps*, a "remake" of Desnoiresterres's multitome biography, coauthored and presided over by René Pomeau, the dean of twentieth-century *voltairistes*.

On a less lofty cultural plane, plans were made in Geneva and Ferney in 1994 for a revival of Voltaire's tragedy *Le Fanatisme, ou Mahomet le Prophète*. News of the project incensed elements of the Muslim community in the region, for whom the idea of someone playing the part of Muhammad was an abomination. In their view, that the play was written as a veiled attack on the Catholic Church was immaterial. As a result, partly because wealthy Arabs

---

31. Lillian Hellman, who cowrote the book for *Candide*, was blacklisted by the House Committee on Un-American Activities (HUAC); Bernstein was blacklisted by the U.S. State Department.

32. John Weightman, "Cultivating Voltaire," *New York Review of Books*, June 18, 1970, 35–37, was a combined critique of *The Intellectual Development of Voltaire* by the Princeton University scholar Ira O. Wade (1969) and *Voltaire*, an erudite but dry life of the writer by Theodore Besterman (1969).

live and bank in the Canton de Genève, officials there and in neighboring Ferney withdrew support for the production and it was canceled.

This might have been considered a trivial episode when it happened, compared to the violent protests and deaths that ensued when a newspaper in Copenhagen printed a dozen cartoons mocking the Prophet in September 2005. Clearly, core principles of freedom of expression and tolerance—tolerance of non-Western as well as Western values and beliefs—were at stake in the Muhammad cartoons affair and its aftermath.

In hindsight, it is equally clear that the same principles were at stake in 1988, when a fatwa was placed on Salman Rushdie by Ayatollah Khomeini, and in 2004, when an Islamist fanatic brutally murdered the Dutch filmmaker Theo Van Gogh on a sidewalk in Amsterdam.

In Europe or America, whenever religious fanaticism rears its ugly head, Voltaire's name inevitably comes up. Thus, in early February 2006, the Paris newspaper *France-Soir* splashed a photo on its front page of Muslim demonstrators burning the Danish flag, accompanied by the words: "Au secours Voltaire, ils sont devenus fous!" (Help us, Voltaire, they've gone mad!). In March 2006, the *Wall Street Journal* ran a page-one report, "Blame It on Voltaire," about the furor surrounding another attempt to perform *Mahomet*, this time as a public reading, without actors, in a small community next door to Ferney. In this second row over Voltaire's play, braving protests and a riot, the town's mayor stoutly defended the reading as a matter of free speech.

Also in March 2006, in the grand tradition of Sartre, Zola, and Voltaire, twelve writers, journalists, and intellectuals drafted a manifesto in which they declared, "After having overcome fascism, Nazism, and Stalinism, the world now faces a new totalitarian global threat: Islamism." The signatories concluded by saying, "We plead for the universality of freedom of expression, so that a critical spirit may be exercised on all continents, against all abuses and all dogmas. We appeal to democrats and free spirits of all countries that our century should be one of Enlightenment, not of obscurantism."[33] Bernard-Henri Lévy, Salman Rushdie, and Ayaan Hirsi Ali were three of the dozen people who signed the manifesto.

In January 2015 there was the monstrous assault in Paris, Voltaire's birthplace, by Islamic terrorists on the offices of the French satirical weekly *Charlie Hebdo*, which had a history of lampooning (and blaspheming) the Prophet Muhammad. After the attack, flyers were posted around the city (figure 10), bearing a vintage portrait of Voltaire and a caption professing a sense of solidarity shared by millions of Frenchmen: "Je suis Charlie" (I am Charlie). Voltaire's

---

33. Quoted in Irshad Manji, *Liberty and Love* (2011), 145.

Figure 10. Poster of Voltaire plastered on buildings and trees all across Paris after the savage murder of twelve people inside the offices of the satirical weekly *Charlie Hebdo*, January 7, 2015. Photograph by Joel Saget, AFP/Getty Images.

collateral association with the *Charlie Hebdo* tragedy led the American historian Robert Zaretsky, in the title of an article he wrote for the *Chronicle of Higher Education*, to ask, "Where Is France's New Voltaire?"[34]

34. *Chronicle of Higher Education*, June 15, 2015.

As in 1944, the answer is: nowhere. Not in France, at any rate, unless Philippe Sollers was wide of the mark when he said that the French did not really like Voltaire.

If Voltaire were alive today, who knows where he'd hang his hat? In France? In England? The United States? (Probably *not* Switzerland.)

We can, however, assume he'd be media-savvy, quick to condemn every atrocity committed in the name of God—or Allah—and to decry the seemingly endless bloodshed, and Western interventionism, in the Middle East.

With greater assurance, we also can assume he would shun the cheap and obscene shots that are *Charlie Hebdo*'s forte, a brand of satire that, in his interview in *Le Monde*, Sollers argued, perpetuates the utopian, anticlerical tradition of French "anarchists and socialists." Voltaire, Sollers said, was "never caricatural. Irony is not caricatural. Irony does not commit blasphemy."

In an essay in the *New Yorker* in 2005, Adam Gopnik declared, "Voltaire, like God, whom he patronized, is always there."[35]

God's standing in Old Europe is not what it once was, unlike in the United States, where each coin and scrap of currency bears the motto "In God We Trust." In the Land of the Free and the Home of the Brave, the Almighty remains, relatively speaking, "always there."

As does Voltaire.

Indeed, if one had to name one place, France excepted, where Voltaire, or rather the legend of Voltaire, is conspicuously present, it may be in the United States. "There is" (Gopnik once more) "as much of Voltaire in American life as in French life."[36] Not just because of his irrepressible good humor, but because, in more dignified, moral terms, his dedication to fundamental human rights appeals to believers and nonbelievers, Christians and Jews, secularists, libertarians, liberals, and conservatives alike.

That attraction precedes the birth of the Republic. Washington, Jefferson, and Madison, to name but three of the Founders, owned books by Voltaire.[37] Franklin met him in Paris in 1778. John Adams was there on that occasion, and in the audience when Voltaire was applauded at the Comédie-Française.

---

35. Gopnik, "Voltaire's Garden: The Philosopher as a Campaigner for Human Rights," *New Yorker*, March 7, 2005, 74.

36. Gopnik, "Voltaire's Garden," 81.

37. A copy of *Letters, from M. de Voltaire. To Several of His Friends* (1770) at the New York Public Library, translated by Thomas Francklin, bears George Washington's signature and personal bookplate. Washington likely owned other books by Voltaire and, according to historian Kevin Hayes, may have read *Candide*. See Hayes, *George Washington* (2017), 192, 349n7.

In 1791, during Washington's first term as president, Gouverneur Morris witnessed Voltaire's pantheonization, and in 1798, in Paris, prior to his elevation to the U.S. Supreme Court, John Marshall purportedly was on intimate terms with the marquise de Villette, whom Voltaire had taken under his wing as his adoptive daughter. In a letter to a friend in 1802, Alexander Hamilton evoked the wisdom from the last chapter of *Candide*: "A garden, you know, is a very usual refuge of a disappointed politician. Accordingly, I have purchased a few acres about nine miles from town, have built a house, and am cultivating a garden."[38]

In his poem "Le Mondain" (The Worldling), Voltaire called champagne a "brilliant symbol of the French character."[39] He could have been talking about himself. For roughly three hundred years that sparkling specimen of intelligence, waggish humor, mockery, and—yes, on occasion—human warmth, has been esteemed in this country for those very traits, coupled with an intense devotion to truth, justice, intellectual honesty, a generous if imperfect supply of common sense, and reasoned skepticism.

Lewis Galantière, an American journalist and, in the mid-1960s, president of the international writer's organization PEN, said that Voltaire "had the heart of a lion in the skin of a rabbit"[40]—an apt metaphor for the legend that is Voltaire. His scrappy spirit, lodged within the spindly frame of a man eternally at death's door (or so he thought), personifies our never-ending struggle for freedom and tolerance.

Of course, the spirit of Voltaire cannot be compressed into a handful of words. It may best be understood, and savored, by perusing the hundreds of statements he made (or allegedly made), verbally, in his correspondence, and in print, on the 374 subjects (himself included) that comprise the core of this anthology.

Brevity, quoth Polonius in *Hamlet*, is the soul of wit—meaning wit as intelligence, not levity. In a letter in 1763, Voltaire, who once bragged that it was he who first "brought Shakespeare to the attention of the French," applied the wisdom in Polonius's remark to his own stock-and-trade, books: "Henceforth I believe that everything must be put in the form of a dictionary. Life is too short to plow through a lot of big books: woe unto long dissertations! A dictionary instantly delivers exactly what you need. They are especially useful for people already learned, who wish to recall things they

---

38. To Charles C. Pinckney, December 29, 1802, in Hamilton, *The Papers of Alexander Hamilton* (1979), 271.

39. *Le Mondain, ou l'Apologie du Luxe* (1739), 118.

40. Galantière, "Voltaire" (1965), 848.

knew already."[41] *The Quotable Voltaire* may not deliver everything you think you need regarding Voltaire, what he wrote, or where he stood on a given topic. What it does deliver are the wonders and elemental joie de vivre of one of the most powerful minds of all time, in one neat bundle of words that, by turns, are amusing, informative, insightful, astute, and uplifting.

41. Voltaire bragged about having introduced Shakespeare to France in a letter to Horace Walpole, July 15, 1768. His belief in the value of dictionaries was expressed in a letter to the Rev. Élie Bertrand, January 9, 1763.

QUOTATIONS BY VOLTAIRE

Here and in the section of quotes about Voltaire that follows we have, with rare exceptions, respected the integrity of the published source for each entry, including spelling, capitalization, punctuation, use of italics, irregular use of accents, and so on. Quotations of entire paragraphs are indented; excerpts are not. Unless otherwise indicated, all translations are our own.

Abbé

Cet être indéfinissable, qui n'est ny Ecclesiastique ny Seculier; en un mot ce que l'on appelle un Abbé, est une espece inconnuë en Angleterre.

That undefinable being, neither of the Clergy nor the Laity, in a word what we call an Abbé, is a species unknown in England.

"Cinquième Lettre sur la Religion Anglicane," in *Lettres Ecrites de Londres sur les Anglois et autres sujets* (1734), 38; "Sur la religion anglicane," in *Lettres philosophiques* (1964), 1:64. According to the preface, the letters in this volume were written in London between 1728 and 1730. The English translation by the poet John Lockman appeared in print before the French edition. See "Letter V. on the Church of England," in *Letters Concerning the English Nation. By Mr. de Voltaire* (1733), 39.

Où allez-vous, Monsieur l'Abbé? &c. Savez-vous bien qu'Abbé signifie Pere? Si vous le devenez, vous rendez service à l'Etat; vous faites la meilleure œuvre sans doute que puisse faire un homme; il naîtra de vous un être pensant. Il y a dans cette action quelque chose de divin.

Mais si vous n'êtes Monsieur l'Abbé que pour avoir été tonsuré, pour porter un petit colet, & un manteau court, & pour attendre un bénéfice simple, vous ne méritez pas le nom d'Abbé.

Where are you going, Monsieur l'Abbé? &c. Do you know that Abbé means Father? If you become one, you render a service to the State; you perform perhaps the best work that a man can perform; you will give birth to a thinking being. There is in so doing something divine.

But if you are only Monsieur l'Abbé because you have had your head shaved, you wear a small collar and a short cloak, and you expect a handsome income, you do not deserve the name of Abbé.

"Abbé," in *La Raison par Alphabet. Septieme Édition* (1773), 9; Besterman et al., *Œuvres complètes de Voltaire* (2007), 35:286–287. The term *abbé*, or abbot, as Voltaire indicated in this article, was derived from the Hebrew word for father, *ab*.

Abuse of words

Les livres, comme les conversations, nous donnent rarement des idées précises. Rien n'est si commun que de lire et de converser inutilement.

Il faut répéter ici ce que Locke Locke a tant recommandé, définissez les termes.

Books, like conversation, rarely give us any precise ideas: nothing is so common as to read and converse unprofitably.

We must here repeat what *Locke* has so strongly urged—*Define your terms.*

"Abus des mots," in *Questions sur l'Encyclopédie, par des Amateurs* (1770), 1:52–53; Besterman et al., *Œuvres complètes de Voltaire* (2008), 38:67. The translation is from *A Philosophical Dictionary* (1824), 1:36.

Attributed to Voltaire

If you wish to converse with me, define your terms.

Durant, *Philosophy and the Social Problem* (1917), 30. This is probably a compressed version of what Voltaire said in his article "Abus des mots."

Academies

Presque tous les artistes sublimes, ou ont fleuri avant les établissemens des académies, ou ont travaillé dans un goût différent de celui qui régnait dans ces sociétés.

Almost all the great Artists have either flourished before the establishment of Academies, or have employed their pencils in a different taste from that which reigned in such societies.

"Des peintres, sculpteurs, architectes, graveurs, &c.," in *Le Siècle de Louis XIV* (1751), 2:432; Besterman et al., *Œuvres complètes de Voltaire* (2017), 12:210. The translation is from the section "Painters," in *The Age of Louis XIV* (1779), clxxvi–clxxvii.

Les académies sont aux universités ce que l'âge mûr est à l'enfance; ce que l'art de bien parler est à la grammaire; ce que la politesse est aux premières leçons de la civilité. Les académies n'étant point mercenaires, doivent être absolument libres. Telles ont été les académies d'Italie, telle est l'académie Française, & surtout la société royale de Londres.

Academies are to universities, as adulthood is to childhood, oratory to grammar, or politeness to the first lessons in civility. Academies, not being stipendiary, ought to be entirely free: such were the academies of Italy; such is the French Academy; and such, more particularly, is the Royal Society of London.

"Académie," in *Questions sur l'Encyclopédie, par des Amateurs* (1770), 1:57; Besterman et al., *Œuvres complètes de Voltaire* (2007), 38:75. The translation is from *A Philosophical Dictionary* (1824), 1:39.

Adultery

Quand les dames parlent à leurs amies de leurs adultères, elles disent: J'avoue que j'ai du goût pour lui. Elles avouaient autrefois qu'elles sentaient quelque estime; mais depuis qu'une bourgeoise s'accusa à son confesseur d'avoir de l'estime pour un conseiller, & que le confesseur lui dit, Madame, combien de fois vous a-t-il estimée? les dames de qualité n'ont plus estimé personne, & ne vont plus guère à confesse.

When ladies talk of their adulteries to their female friends, they say, "I confess I have some inclination for *him*." They used formerly to confess that they felt some *esteem*; but since the time when a certain citizen's wife accused herself to her confessor of having *esteem* for a counsellor, and the confessor inquired as to the number of proofs of esteem afforded, ladies of quality have *esteemed* no one, and gone but little to confession.

"Adultère," in *Questions sur l'Encyclopédie, par des Amateurs* (1770), 1:78; Besterman et al., *Œuvres complètes de Voltaire* (2007), 38:104. The translation is from *A Philosophical Dictionary* (1824), 1:54–55.

Jean Le Rond d'Alembert (1717–1783)

FRENCH MATHEMATICIAN, *PHILOSOPHE*, MEMBER OF
THE ACADÉMIE FRANÇAISE, LOYAL PROTÉGÉ OF VOLTAIRE,
AND COEDITOR WITH DIDEROT OF THE *ENCYCLOPÉDIE*

Ce d'Alembert, n'est pas welche, c'est un vrai Français.

This d'Alembert is not a *Welche*, he's a true Frenchman.

Letter from Ferney, February 4, 1765, to Pierre-Robert Le Corner de Cideville in Rouen. Voltaire's classmate at the lycée Louis-le-Grand in Paris, Cideville was a magistrate in Normandy and founder of the Academy of Rouen. "Welche" is a derogatory term in German for "Frenchman," often used by Voltaire to mock his compatriots.

Francesco Algarotti (1712–1764)

ITALIAN MATHEMATICIAN AND PHILOSOPHER

S'il n'avait commencé par admirer, il ne se serait pas fait un nom. Admirateur de Newton, il a réussi à mettre les dames en état de parler de la lumière.

If he had not begun by admiring others, he would not have made a name for himself. As an admirer of Newton, he succeeded in making it possible for ladies to talk about light.

To Giacomo Casanova during his visit to Les Délices, Voltaire's home on the outskirts of Geneva, July 1760. Quoted in Casanova, *Histoire de ma vie* (1960), 3:226.

Allies

Vous savez que les alliés sont comme les amis qu'on appelait de mon temps au quadrille, on changeait d'ami à chaque coup.

You know that allies are like what, in my day, we called dancing partners. As we danced a quadrille, we were constantly changing partners.

Letter from Les Délices, circa July 13, 1761, to the duc de Choiseul, chief minister to the king at Versailles.

The Americas—Native Americans

L'Américain farouche est un monstre sauvage
Qui mord en frémissant les fers de l'esclavage.

The wild American is a savage monster
Who quivers as he gnaws on the chains of slavery.

Gusman in *Alzire, ou les Américains* (1736), act 1, scene 1; Besterman et al., *Œuvres complètes de Voltaire* (1989), 14:127. *Alzire* premiered in Paris at the Comédie-Française on January 27, 1736.

Les prétendus Sauvages d'Amérique sont des Souverains qui reçoivent des Ambassadeurs de nos Colonies, que l'avarice & la légéreté ont transplantées auprès de leur Territoire. Ils connaissent l'honneur, dont jamais nos Sauvages d'Europe n'ont entendu parler. Ils ont une Patrie, ils l'aiment, ils la défendent; ils font des Traités; ils se battent avec courage, & parlent souvent avec une énergie héroïque. Y a-t-il une plus belle réponse dans les grands hommes de Plutarque, que celle de ce Chef des Canadiens, à qui une Nation Européenne proposait de lui céder son patrimoine: Nous sommes nés sur cette Terre, nos Peres y sont ensevelis; dirons-nous aux ossements de nos Peres, levez-vous, & venez avec nous dans une Terre étrangere?

The so-called Savages of America are Sovereigns who receive Ambassadors from our colonies that avarice and capriciousness have resettled close to their lands. They have a sense of honor unheard of by our Savages in Europe. They have a homeland, they love and defend it; they make Treaties, fight bravely, and often speak with heroic energy. Is there a finer response in *The Lives of Great Men* of Plutarch than that of the Canadian Chief to whom one European Nation had proposed that he relinquish his patrimony: "We were born on this land, our Fathers are buried here, shall we say to the bones of our Fathers, arise, and come with us into a foreign Land?"

"Des Sauvages," in *La Philosophie de l'Histoire, Par feu l'Abbé Bazin* (1765), 32–33; Besterman et al., *Œuvres complètes de Voltaire* (1969), 59:109.

Se peut-il qu'on demande encore d'où sont venus les hommes qui ont peuplé l'Amérique? On doit assurément faire la même question sur les nations des Terres Australes. Elles sont beaucoup plus éloignées du Port dont partit Christophe Colomb, que ne le sont les Isles Antilles. On a trouvé des hommes & des animaux par-tout où la terre est habitable; qui les y a mis? On l'a déjà dit, c'est celui qui fait croître l'herbe des champs; & on ne devait pas être plus surpris de trouver en Amérique des hommes que des mouches.

Is it possible, even now, to ask where the people that populated the Americas came from? The same question must be asked about the nations of the *Terra Australis*. They are much farther from the port *Christopher Columbus* sailed from than the West Indies. Men and animals have been found in all habitable parts of the world. Who put them there? As we have said before: the same one that made grass grow in the fields. One should be no more surprised to find men in America than flies.

"De l'Amérique," in *La Philosophie de l'Histoire, Par feu l'Abbé Bazin* (1765), 37; Besterman et al., *Œuvres complètes de Voltaire* (1969), 59:115.

Tout change dans les corps & dans les esprits avec le tems; peut-être un jour les Américains viendront enseigner les arts aux peuples de l'Europe.

Everything changes over time, both in body and mind. Perhaps one day the Americans will come to Europe and instruct its peoples in the arts.

"Climat," in *Questions sur l'Encyclopédie, par des Amateurs* (1771), 4:17; Besterman et al., *Œuvres complètes de Voltaire* (2009), 40:132.

Christophe Colombo *devine et découvre un nouveau monde: un marchand, un passager lui donne son nom. Bel exemple des quiproquos de la gloire.*

Christopher Columbus divined and discovered a new world; a merchant lent it his name. Wonderful example of the arbitrary nature of glory.

Pensées, remarques et observations de Voltaire (1802), 21; Besterman et al., *Œuvres complètes de Voltaire* (1968), 82:509. The man who "lent" his name to America was the Florentine merchant, navigator, and explorer Amerigo Vespucci (1454–1512).

Amour-propre

C'est l'amour de nous-mêmes, qui assiste l'amour des autres; c'est par nos besoins mutuels que nous sommes utiles au genre humain; c'est le fondement de tout commerce; c'est l'éternel lien des hommes. Sans lui il n'y auroit pas eu un Art inventé, ni une société de dix personnes formée; c'est cet amour-propre que chaque animal a recû de la nature qui nous avertit de respecter celui des autres. La Loi dirige cet amour propre & la Religion le perfectionne.

Amour-propre helps us love one another; it is through our mutual needs that we are useful to humankind; it is the basis of all commerce; it is the eternal bond among men. Without it not a single art form would have been invented, and no society of more than ten persons ever formed; every creature was endowed by nature with a sense of *amour-propre* in order to remind us to respect the other's *amour-propre*. The Law restrains it and Religion perfects it.

"Vingt-cinquiéme Lettre sur les Pensées de M. Pascal," in *Lettres philosophiques par M. de V.* . . . (1734), 151; Moland, *Œuvres complètes de Voltaire* (1879), 22:36. By *amour-propre* Voltaire did not mean egotism or narcissism but, as he said here, a form of self-regard based on man's interactions with society.

Ce n'est pas l'amour qu'il fallait peindre aveugle, c'est l'amour-propre.

It isn't love we should portray as blind, but *amour-propre*.

Letter from Les Délices, May 11, 1764, to Étienne-Noël Damilaville in Paris. Damilaville, a state functionary and friend of both Voltaire and Diderot, corresponded with Voltaire from the early 1760s until his death in 1778.

L'amour-propre n'est point une scélératesse, c'est un sentiment naturel à tous les hommes; il est beaucoup plus voisin de la vanité que du crime.

Amour-propre is in no way evil, it is a natural sentiment common to all men; it is much closer to vanity than it is to a crime.

"Amour-propre," in *Questions sur l'Encyclopédie, par des Amateurs* (1770), 1:213; Besterman et al., *Œuvres complètes de Voltaire* (2007), 38:256.

Ceux qui ont dit que l'amour de nous-mêmes est la base de tous nos sentimens & de toutes nos actions ont donc eu grande raison. . . . Cet amour-propre est l'instrument de notre conservation; il ressemble à l'instrument de la perpétuité de l'espèce: il est nécessaire, il nous est cher, il nous fait plaisir, & il faut le cacher.

Those who have said that love of self is the basis of all our sentiments and everything we do could not have been more right. . . . *Amour-propre* is the instrument of our preservation; it is like the means of human reproduction; it is necessary, it is dear to us, it gives us pleasure, and we must conceal it.

"Amour-propre," in *Questions sur l'Encyclopédie, par des Amateurs* (1770), 1:214–215; Besterman et al., *Œuvres complètes de Voltaire* (2007), 38:257.

Ancestors

Le premier qui fut Roi, fut un Soldat heureux.
Qui sert bien son païs, n'a pas besoin d'ayeux.

The first man made king, was a successful soldier.
He who serves well his country, needs no ancestors.

Polyphonte, a tyrant in ancient Messene, in *Mérope* (1743), act 1, scene 3; *La Mérope Françoise, avec quelques petites pièces de littérature* (1744), 10; Besterman et al., *Œuvres complètes de Voltaire* (1991), 17:255. *Mérope* premiered at the Comédie-Française on February 20, 1743.

Ancient Greeks

Il n'appartient qu'à l'ignorance & à la présomption, qui en est la suite, de dire qu'il n'y a rien à imiter dans les anciens: il n'y a point de beautés dont on ne trouve chez eux les semences.

Nothing but ignorance, and its natural attendant, presumption, can assert, that the antients have nothing worthy of our imitation: there is scarce one real and essential beauty and perfection, for the foundation of which, at least, we are not indebted to them.

"A Son Altesse Sérénissme Madame la Duchesse du Maine," de facto preface to the first edition of *Oreste, Tragédie, Par M. Arouet de Voltaire* (1750), xix; Besterman et al., *Œuvres complètes de Voltaire* (1992), 31a:410. The translation is from "Letter to Her Most Serene Highness the Dutchess of Maine," in Smollett et al., *The Works of Mr. de Voltaire* (1762), 3:118. *Oreste* premiered in Paris on January 12, 1750.

Je me suis imposé, sur-tout, la loi de ne pas m'écarter de cette simplicité, tant recommandée par les Grecs, & si difficile à saisir; c'étoit-là le vrai caractére de l'invention & du génie; c'étoit l'essence du théâtre.

I have made it a strict rule never to forsake that simplicity so strongly prescribed by the Greeks, and so difficult to achieve, which was the true mark of genius and invention, and which is essential in the theater.

"A Son Altesse Sérénissme Madame la Duchesse du Maine," de facto preface to the first edition of *Oreste, Tragédie, Par M. Arouet de Voltaire* (1750), xix; Besterman et al., *Œuvres complètes de Voltaire* (1992), 31a:410–11.

Que les Athéniens étaient un peuple aimable!
Que leur esprit m'enchante, & que leurs fictions
Me font aimer le vrai sous les traits de la fable!

How very likeble were the people of Athens!
How their intelligence enchants me, and their fictions
Make me love the truth that lies within their fables!

"Les Trois Manières" (1763), in *Contes de Guillaume Vadé* (1764), 50; Besterman et al., *Œuvres complètes de Voltaire* (2014), 57b:123. This poem first appeared in English as "The Three Manners," in Smollett et al., *The Works of Mr. de Voltaire* (1765), vol. 34.

Ancient Rome

Le fruit des guerres civiles à Rome a été l'esclavage, & celui des troubles d'Angleterre la liberté.

The civil wars of *Rome* ended in slavery, and those of the *English* in liberty.

"Huitième Lettre sur le Parlement," in *Lettres Ecrites de Londres sur les Anglois et autres sujets* (1734), 51; "Sur le Parlement," in *Lettres philosophiques* (1964), 1:89. The translation is from "Letter VIII. On the Parliament," in *Letters Concerning the English Nation* (1733), 53.

Angels and demons

Une des premières idées des hommes a toujours été de placer des êtres intermédiaires entre la Divinité & nous; ce sont ces démons, ces génies que l'antiquité inventa; l'homme fit toujours les dieux à son image.

One of mankind's oldest, most enduring ideas has been to place intermediate forms between the Divinity and us. Such were those demons, those genies, that antiquity invented: man has always made gods in his own image.

"Ange," in *Dictionnaire philosophique, portatif* (1764), 23; Besterman et al., *Œuvres complètes de Voltaire* (1994), 35:337.

On ne sçait pas précisément où les Anges se tiennent, si c'est dans l'air, dans le vuide, dans les planètes; Dieu n'a pas voulu que nous en fussions instruits.

We know not where angels abide exactly, whether it be in the air, in a vacuum, or on other worlds. God has not chosen to share that information with us.

"Ange," in *Dictionnaire philosophique, portatif* (1764), 25; Besterman et al., *Œuvres complètes de Voltaire* (1994), 35:342.

Anglicanism

À l'égard des mœurs, le Clergé anglican est plus reglé que celui de France, & en voicy la cause. Tous les Ecclesiastiques sont elevés dans l'Université d'Oxford, ou dans celle de Cambridge, loin de la corruption de la capitale. Ils ne sont apellés aux dignités de l'Eglise que très tard, & dans un âge où les hommes n'ont d'autres passions que l'avarice, lorsque leur ambition manque d'alimens.

With regard to the morals of the *English* Clergy, they are more regular than those of *France*, and for this reason. All the clergy (a very few excepted) are educated in the universities of *Oxford* or *Cambridge*, far from the depravity and corruption of the capital. They are not call'd to dignities till very late, at a time of life when men are sensible of no other passion but avarice, that is, when their ambition craves a supply.

"Cinquième Lettre. Sur la Religion *Anglicane*," in *Lettres Ecrites de Londres sur les Anglois et autres sujets* (1734), 37; "Sur la religion anglicane," in *Lettres philosophiques* (1964), 1:63. The translation is "Letter XIII. On Mr. Locke," in *Letters Concerning the English Nation* (1733), 38–39.

Architecture

Les anciens Romains élevoient des prodiges d'Architecture pour faire combattre des bêtes; & nous n'avons pas sçû depuis un siécle bâtir seulement une Salle passable pour y faire représenter les Chef-d'œuvres de l'Esprit humain.

The ancient Romans raised marvels of Architecture in which beasts might do battle; and yet for more than a century we have not built one passably good Play-house in which to stage the Masterpieces of the human Spirit.

"Copie d'une lettre à un Premier commis," June 20, 1733, in *Oeuvres diverses de Monsieur de Voltaire. Nouvelle édition* (1746), 4:249; Besterman et al., *Œuvres complètes de Voltaire* (1999), 9:322. This was a polemical tract, not a personal letter (a *premier commis* was a government functionary). The translation is based in part on Hall, *Voltaire in His Letters* (1919), 35.

On reproche à la ville de Paris de n'avoir que deux fontaines dans le bon goût; l'ancienne de Jean Gougeon, & la nouvelle de Bouchardon; encor sont-elles toutes deux mal placées. On lui reproche de n'avoir d'autre Théâtre magnifique que celui du Louvre dont on ne fait point d'usage, & de ne s'assembler que dans des salles de spectacles sans goût, sans proportion, sans ornement, & aussi défectueuses dans l'emplacement que dans la construction: tandis que des villes de Provinces donnent à la capitale des exemples qu'elle n'a pas encor suivi.

The city of Paris is faulted for having just two fountains in good taste; the old one of *Jean Gougeon*, and the new one of *Bouchardon*; and even these are poorly situated. It has been faulted because it has no magnificent theater other than that of the Louvre, which is never used, and people must sit in playhouses built without taste, proportion, or ornament, and defective in their location and construction, while provincial cities provide examples to the capital that she has yet to follow.

"Artistes célèbres" ("Des Sculptures, Architectes, Graveurs, &c."), in *Essay sur l'histoire générale, et sur les moeurs et l'esprit des nations* (1757), 7:317; Besterman et al., *Œuvres complètes de Voltaire* (2017), 12:216. The translation is from the section "Of Sculptors, Architects, Engravers, &c.," in *The Age of Louis XIV* (1779), 1:clxxxi. Jean Gougeon was a Renaissance sculptor and architect; the architect Jean-Baptiste Bouchardon died in 1742.

Ariosto (1474–1533)

ITALIAN POET, BEST KNOWN FOR HIS EPIC POEM
ORLANDO FURIOSO

Toute l'Europe sera informée de moi-même de la très humble réparation que je dois au plus grand génie qu'elle ait produit.

All Europe shall be informed by me of the most humble amends which I owe to the greatest genius she has ever produced.

To Casanova at Les Délices in July 1760; from Casanova, *Histoire de ma vie* (1960), 3:229. Earlier in their conversation, Voltaire admitted that in his youth he had misjudged the poet, but now said, "J'adore votre Arioste." The translation is from Casanova, *History of My Life* (1968), 227.

Aristophanes (circa 446–386 B.C.)

GREEK DRAMATIST

Ce poëte comique, qui n'est ni comique ni Poëte, n'aurait pas été admis parmi nous à donner ses farces à la foire St. Laurent; il me paraît beaucoup plus bas & plus méprisable que Plutarque ne le dépeint. Voici ce que le sage Plutarque dit de ce farceur: "Le langage d'Aristophane sent son misérable charlatan; ce sont les pointes les plus basses & les plus dégoûtantes; il n'est pas même plaisant pour le Peuple, & il est insupportable aux gens de jugement & d'honneur; on ne peut souffrir son arrogance, & les gens de bien détestent sa malignité."

This comic poet, who is neither comic nor poetical, would not amongst us have been permitted to exhibit his farces at the fair of St. Lawrence. He appears to me to be much lower and more despicable than Plutarch represents him. Let us see what the wise Plutarch says of this buffoon:—"The language of Aristophanes bespeaks his miserable quackery; it is made up of the lowest and most disgusting puns; he is not even pleasing to the people; and to men of judgment and honor he is insupportable: his arrogance is intolerable; and all good men detest his malignity."

"Athée, Athéisme," in *Dictionnaire philosophique, portatif* (1764), 34; Besterman et al., *Œuvres complètes de Voltaire* (1994), 35:376–377. The translation is from *A Philosophical Dictionary* (1824), 1:318–319.

Aristotle (384–322 B.C.)

GREEK PHILOSOPHER

La logique d'Aristote, *son art de raisonner, est d'autant plus estimable qu'il avait affaire aux Grecs, qui s'exerçaient continuellement à des argumens captieux; & son maître Platon était moins exempt qu'un autre de ce défaut.*

Aristotle's logic, his art of reasoning, is so much the more to be esteemed, as he had to deal with the Greeks, who were continually holding captious arguments; from which fault his master Plato was even less exempt than others.

"Aristote," in *Questions sur l'Encyclopédie, par des Amateurs* (1770), 2:147; Besterman et al., *Œuvres complètes de Voltaire* (2008), 39:1. The translation is from *A Philosophical Dictionary* (1824), 1:257.

Figure 11. Benoît-Louis Prévost, after Charles-Nicolas Cochin the Younger, *École de dessin*, 1763. Etching and engraving. Private collection. From *Recueil de planches sur les sciences, les arts libéraux et les arts méchaniques*, a supplementary companion volume of plates for Diderot and d'Alembert's *Encyclopédie* (1763). The print illustrates the standard academic training program for aspiring artists in France in Voltaire's time. Beginning students copied drawings or prints by their teachers and the old masters. Older students sketched from works of sculpture, and eventually, as they advanced, directly from a live model.

Art—the arts

Dans tous les Arts, il y a un terme par-delà lequel on ne peut plus avancer. On est resserré dans les bornes de son talent: on voit la perfection au-delà de soi, & on fait des efforts impuissans pour y atteindre.

In every art there is a certain point beyond which we can never go: we are confined within the limits of our talents; we see perfection lying beyond us, and are powerless through our efforts to attain it.

Preface to *Hérode et Mariamne* (1725), n.p.; Besterman et al., *Œuvres complètes de Voltaire* (2004), 3:190. The translation is from *The Dramatic Works of Mr. De Voltaire* (1761), 1:115. The text of this tragedy, which premiered at the Comédie-Française on March 6, 1724, and the preface were reprinted in *Oeuvres de Mᵉ de Voltaire. Nouvelle Edition* (1752), 3:317, where a typo in the 1725 text ("void") was, as it is here, corrected to read *voit*.

Je vous avouë, MYLORD, qu'à mon retour d'Angleterre où j'avois passé deux années dans une étude continuelle de votre Langue, je me trouvai embarassé lorsque je voulus composer une Tragédie Françoise. Je m'étois presque accoutumé à penser en Anglois, je sentois que les termes de ma Langue ne venoient plus se présenter à mon imagination avec la même abondance qu'auparavant; ... Je compris bien alors que pour réüssir dans un art, il le faut cultiver toute sa vie.

I confess, My Lord, that upon my return from England, where I spent two years in the continual study of your Language, I found myself at a loss when I started to write a French Tragedy. I had almost grown used to thinking in English, and the idioms of my native Tongue no longer seemed to present themselves as freely to my imagination as they once did. ... I then clearly understood that success in any art requires lifelong practice.

"Discours sur la tragédie à Mylord Bolingbrooke," de facto preface to *Le Brutus de Monsieur de Voltaire* (1731), iv–v; Besterman et al., *Œuvres complètes de Voltaire* (1998), 5:158. *Brutus* premiered at the Comédie-Française on December 11, 1730.

... le secret des arts
Est de corriger la nature.

... the secret of the arts
Is to improve upon nature.

Letter from Paris, March 2, 1731, to Pierre-Robert Le Cornier de Cideville in Rouen.

Vous êtes Anglais, mon cher Ami, & je suis né en France; mais ceux qui aiment les Arts sont tous concitoyens.

You are English, my dear Friend, and I was born in France; but those who love the Arts are all fellow citizens.

"Epitre dédicatoire à Monsieur Fakener Marchand Anglais," in *La Zayre, de M. de Voltaire* (1733); Besterman et al., *Œuvres complètes de Voltaire* (1988), 8:405. The dedicatee was the English silk merchant and diplomat, Everard Fawkener. For a while during his sojourn in London in 1726–1728, Voltaire was a guest at Fawkener's house at Wandsworth, on the south bank of the Thames. *La Zayre*, later retitled *Zaïre*, premiered at the Comédie-Française on August 13, 1732.

C'est toujours sous les plus grands Princes que les Arts ont fleuri; & leur décadence est l'époque de celle d'un Etat.

The Arts have always flourished during the reign of the greatest Monarchs; and their decline mirrors the decline of a State.

"Epitre dédicatoire à Monsieur Fakener Marchand Anglais," in *La Zayre, de M. de Voltaire* (1733); Besterman et al., *Œuvres complètes de Voltaire* (1988), 8:405.

Travaillez plus vos vers:
Le plus bel arbre a besoin de culture.

Work on your verse:
The finest tree needs to be tended to.

Letter from Cirey in eastern France, March 16, 1736, to Voltaire's longtime friend Nicolas-Claude Thieriot in Paris. Voltaire was living at this time with his lover, Mme du Châtelet, on the estate of her absent husband, the marquis du Châtelet, a career army officer. Voltaire's advice to "work on your verse" was contained in nine lines of verse intended, he told Thieriot, to encourage a young poet and admirer, Jules-Claude Grandvoinet de Verrière.

Il faut toujours en suivant la nature
La corriger, c'est le secret des arts.

Always, when using nature as a guide,
Correct her, that is the secret of the arts.

From the same set of rhymed advice intended for Grandvoinet de Verrière quoted in the preceding entry.

Les principes de tous les Arts, qui dépendent de l'imagination, sont tous aisés & simples, tous puisés dans la Nature & dans la Raison.

The principles of all the Arts, those that flow from man's imagination, are all easy and simple, grounded as they all are in Nature and in Reason.

"Préface. D'une Edition d'Oedipe de 1729," in *Oeuvres de M. de Voltaire. Nouvelle Edition. Revue, corrigée & considérablement augmentée* (1738), 2:6; Besterman et al., *Œuvres complètes de Voltaire* (2001), 1:261–262. *Œdipe*, Voltaire's first dramatic work, premiered at the Comédie-Française on November 18, 1718.

C'est le diable au corps qu'il faut avoir pour exceller dans tous les arts!

One must be possessed by the devil in order to excel in any art!

To Mlle Marie-Françoise Dumesnil, who had the starring role in *Mérope*, during the first rehearsal of the play at the Théâtre-Français, in 1742. Quoted in Lekain, *Mémoires de Henri Louis Lekain* (1801), 14. Voltaire's remark must have come anecdotally to Lekain since he was still a boy in 1742. It first appeared in print in l'abbé Duvernet's *La Reconnaissance de Le Kain* (1778), 12.

L'art & le génie consistent à trouver tout dans son sujet, & non pas à chercher hors de son sujet.

Art and genius consist in finding everything it needs within a subject, and not straying off topic.

"A Son Altesse Sérénissme Madame la Duchesse du Maine" (1750), xix; Besterman et al., *Œuvres complètes de Voltaire* (2008), 31a:411.

Quiconque pense, & ce qui est encore plus rare, quiconque a du goût, ne compte que quatre siécles dans l'histoire du monde. ces quatre âges heureux, sont ceux où les arts ont été perfectionnés, & qui servant d'époque à la grandeur de l'esprit humain, sont l'exemple de la posterité.

Whosoever thinks, or, what is still more rare, whosoever has taste, will find but four ages in the history of the world. These four happy ages are those in which the arts were carried to perfection; and which, by serving as the æra of the greatness of the human mind, are examples for posterity.

Introduction to *Le Siècle de Louis XIV* (1751), 1:1; Besterman et al., *Œuvres complètes de Voltaire* (2015), 13a:1. For Voltaire, the four greatest epochs in history were the period in ancient Greece from Pericles to Alexander, Rome under Julius Cæsar and Cæsar Augustus, the Italian Renaissance, and the reign of Louis XIV. The translation is from Smollett et al., *The Works of Mr. de Voltaire* (1761), 6:159.

Le quatrième siécle est celui qu'on nomme le siécle de Louis XIV; & c'est peut-être celui des quatre qui approche le plus de la perfection.

The fourth age is that which is named the Age of Louis XIV. and is, perhaps, the one of the four that approaches nearest to perfection.

Introduction to *Le Siècle de Louis XIV* (1751), 1:4; Besterman et al., *Œuvres complètes de Voltaire* (2015), 13a:3. The translation is from *The Age of Louis XIV* (1779), 1:3.

Il est bien rare qu'un homme puissant, quand il est lui-même artiste, protége sincérement les bons artistes.

Only rarely does a powerful man who is himself an artist give wholehearted support to talented artists.

Le Siècle de Louis XIV (1751), 2:182; Besterman et al., *Œuvres complètes de Voltaire* (2016), 13d:18–19. Cardinal Richelieu, "le protecteur des gens de lettres & non pas du bon goût," was the *homme puissant* Voltaire had in mind. Every great French writer in the age of Louis XIV, Voltaire went on to say, was "known to and protected" by the king himself (188).

A l'égard des arts qui ne dépendent pas uniquement de l'esprit, comme la musique, la peinture, la sculpture, l'architecture; ils avaient fait de faibles progrès en France, avant le tems qu'on nomme le siécle de louis XIV.

As for those arts that do not depend on intellect alone, such as music, painting, sculpture, and architecture, they had made very little progress in France prior to the period that we call *the Age of Louis XIV*.

"Suite des arts," in *Le Siècle de Louis XIV* (1751), 2:193; Besterman et al., *Œuvres complètes de Voltaire* (2016), 13d:31.

Ce n'est pas la philosophie à qui on doit attribuer la décadence des beaux-arts. C'est du temps de Neuton qu'ont fleuri les meilleurs poètes anglais; Corneille était contemporain de Descartes, et Molière était l'éleve de Gassendi. Notre décadence vient peut-être de ce que les orateurs et les poètes du siècle de Louis XIV nous ont dit ce que nous ne savions pas et qu'aujourd'hui les meilleurs écrivains ne pourraient dire que ce qu'on sait.

Philosophy must not be blamed for the decline of the arts. The finest English poets flourished in the time of Newton; Corneille was a contemporary of Descartes, Molière a student of Gassendi. Our decadence may be due perhaps to the fact that orators and poets in the age of Louis XIV told us things we did not know, today the best writers can only tell us what we know.

Letter from Ferney, September 2, 1764, to Michel-Paul-Guy de Chabanon in Paris. Pierre Gassendi was a French mathematician and philosopher.

Les grands plaisirs dans tous les arts ne sont que pour les connaisseurs.

The supreme pleasures in each of the arts are reserved for connoisseurs.

Letter from Ferney, March 7, 1769, to the poet Jean-François de Saint-Lambert in Lunéville in Lorraine. In this letter Voltaire thanked Saint-Lambert for sending a copy of his book of verse, *Les Saisons*, which had arrived the day before.

Ce qui est bien plus Essai sur les mœurs et l'esprit des nations de la postérité, ce qui doit l'emporter sur toutes ces coutumes introduites par le caprice, sur toutes ces lois abolies par le temps, sur les querelles des rois qui passent avec eux, c'est la gloire des arts, qui ne passera jamais. Cette gloire a été, pendant tout le seizième siècle, le partage de la seule Italie. Rien ne rappelle davantage l'idée de l'ancienne Grèce: Car si les arts fleurirent en Grèce au milieu des guerres étrangéres & civiles, ils eurent en Italie le même sort; & presque tout y fut porté à sa perfection; tandis que les armées de Charles-Quint saccagèrent Rome, que Barberousse ravagea les côtes, & que les dissensions des princes & des républiques troublèrent l'intérieur du pays.

What is worthier of the attention of posterity and more important than all the customs born of caprice, all the laws erased by the passage of time, or the long-forgotten disputes of crowned heads, themselves now forgotten, is the glorious reputation of the arts, which is everlasting. This glory, during the sixteenth century, belonged to Italy alone. Nothing more strongly conjures up the idea of ancient Greece: the arts flourished in Italy amidst wars foreign and domestic, as they did in Greece, and nearly all of them had been developed to perfection when Rome was sacked by the troops of Charles V, its coasts laid waste by Barbarossa, and the interior of the country torn apart by dissension among princes and the republics.

"Usages des quinziéme & seiziéme siécles, & de l'état des beaux arts," in Pomeau, *Essai sur les mœurs et l'esprit des nations* (1770), 4:138–139; Besterman et al., *Œuvres complètes de Voltaire* (2012), 25:291.

L'histoire des arts, peut-être la plus utile de toutes, quand elle joint à la connaissance de l'invention & du progrès des arts, la description de leur mécanisme.

The history of the arts may be the most useful branch of history, when it combines a knowledge of artistic invention and progress in the arts with a description of how they work.

"De l'histoire," under the subhead "Définition," in *Questions sur l'Encyclopédie, par des Amateurs* (1771), 7:19; Besterman et al., *Œuvres complètes de Voltaire* (2011), 42a:197.

C'est un crime en fait de beaux-arts de mettre des entraves au génie. Ce n'est pas pour rien qu'on le représente avec des ailes; il doit voler où il veut comme il veut.

Where the fine arts are concerned it is a crime to inhibit genius. It is not for nothing that genius is represented as a winged figure. It must soar wherever and however it wishes.

Letter from Ferney, December 1, 1771, to François Tronchin at Les Délices, in Geneva.

Atheism

L'Athéisme est un monstre très-pernicieux dans ceux qui gouvernent, qu'il l'est aussi dans les gens de cabinet, quoique leur vie soit innocente, parce que de leur cabinet ils peuvent percer jusqu'à ceux qui sont en place; que s'il n'est pas si funeste que le fanatisme, il est presque toujours fatal à la vertu.

Atheism is a most monstrous evil in those who govern, but also in those who counsel them, however decent they be in private, because from their office it may infect their superiors; which, if not as deadly as fanaticism, is nearly always fatal to virtue.

"Athée, Athéisme," in *Dictionnaire philosophique, portatif* (1764), 43; Besterman et al., *Œuvres complètes de Voltaire* (1994), 35:391.

L'athéisme est le vice de quelques gens d'esprit; & la superstition le vice des sots. Mais les fripons! que sont-ils? des fripons.

Atheism is the vice of a few intelligent people; and superstition the lot of fools. But scoundrels! What are they? They are scoundrels.

"Athéisme," in *Questions sur l'Encyclopédie, par des Amateurs* (1770), 2:295; Besterman et al., *Œuvres complètes de Voltaire* (1994), 35:391.

Les athées sont pour la plupart des savans hardis & égarés qui raisonnent mal, & qui ne pouvant comprendre la création, l'origine du mal, & d'autres difficultés, ont recours à l'hypothèse de l'éternité des choses et de la nécessité.

Atheists, by and large, are brash, misguided scholars who, because they cannot think straight or comprehend difficult matters like how life began and the origin of evil, fall back on illusory conjecture about the permanence and inevitability of things.

"Athéisme," in *Dictionnaire philosophique*, in Beaumarchais's edition of the *Œuvres complètes de Voltaire* (1784), 38:119–120; Besterman et al., *Œuvres complètes de Voltaire* (1994), 35:389.

Francis Bacon (1561–1626)

ENGLISH STATESMAN AND PHILOSOPHER

Il a été, comme c'est l'usage parmi les hommes, plus estimé après sa mort que de son vivant. Ses ennemis étoient à la Cour de Londres, ses admirateurs étoient les étrangers.

Lord *Bacon*, as is the Fate of Man, was more esteem'd after his Death than in his Life-time. His Enemies were in the *British* Court, and his Admirers were Foreigners.

"Douzième Lettre. Sur le *Chancelier Bacon*," in *Lettres Ecrites de Londres sur les Anglois et autres sujets* (1734), 82; "Sur le chancelier Bacon," in *Lettres philosophiques* (1964), 1:53. The translation is "Letter XII. On the Lord *Bacon*," in *Letters Concerning the English Nation* (1733), 85.

Pierre Bayle (1647–1706)

PHILOSOPHER

Il faut ajouter à ces nouveautés, celle que produisit Bayle, en donnant une espéce de dictionnaire de raisonnement. C'est le premier ouvrage de ce genre, où l'on puisse apprendre à penser.

Among these literary novelties mention should be made of the works of Bayle, who compiled a kind of dictionary of logic. It was the first work of its kind in which one may learn to think.

"Sciences et arts," in *Le Siècle de Louis XIV* (1751), 2:179; Besterman et al., *Œuvres complètes de Voltaire* (2016), 13d:17. The translation is from an excerpt of *The Age of Louis XIV* in Gay and Cavanaugh, *Historians at Work* (1972), 2:335.

Il a vécu & il est mort en sage.

He lived and died a sage.

"Ecrivains, dont plusieurs ont illustré le siécle," in *Le Siècle de Louis XIV* (1751), 2:350; Besterman et al., *Œuvres complètes de Voltaire* (2017), 12:56. The translation is from *The Age of Louis XIV* (1779), 1:xlii.

C'est par son excellente maniére de raisonner qu'il est sur tout recommandable, non par sa maniére d'écrire trop souvent diffuse, lache, incorrecte & d'une familiarité qui tombe quelquefois dans la bassesse; dialecticien admirable plus que profond philosophe.

It is rather from his excellent method of reasoning that he is chiefly distinguished, than from his manner of writing, which is often diffuse, loose, incorrect, and sometimes censurable for a familiarity of style which frequently sinks into vulgarity; admirable dialectician more than profound philosopher.

"Ecrivains dont plusieurs ont illustré le siécle," in *Le Siecle de Louis XIV* (1753), 368; Besterman et al., *Œuvres complètes de Voltaire* (2017), 12:55. This translation is adapted from *The Age of Louis XIV* (1779), 1:xlii.

Père de l'église des sages.

The father of the sect of sage men.

Letter from Les Délices, May 3, 1756, to Voltaire's friend of long standing, Charles-Augustin de Ferriol, comte d'Argental in Paris.

Bayle, *le plus grand Dialecticien qui ait jamais écrit.*

Bayle, the greatest Dialectician that ever put pen to paper.

"Préface de l'auteur," in *Poëmes sur le désastre de Lisbonne et sur la loi naturelle* (1756), 7; Besterman et al., *Œuvres complètes de Voltaire* (2009), 45a:327.

J'abandonne Platon, je rejette Epicure.
Bayle *en sait plus qu'eux tous; je vais le consulter:*
La balance à la main, Bayle *enseigne à douter.*
Assez sage, assez grand pour être sans systeme,
Il les a tous détruits & se combat lui-même:
Semblable à cet aveugle en butte aux Philistins,
Qui tomba sous les murs abbatus par ses mains.

I forego *Plato*, I reject *Epicurus.*
Bayle knows more than all those; so I shall consult him:
Scales of justice in hand, Bayle teaches us to doubt.
Wise enough, great enough to require no creed,
He destroyed all systems and fought even himself.
Like that blind man in the hands of the Philistines,
Crushed beneath the walls that he himself did bring down.

"Poëme sur le désastre de Lisbonne, ou Examen de cet axiome, Tout est bien," in *Poëmes sur le désastre de Lisbonne et sur la loi naturelle* (1756), 15; Besterman et al., *Œuvres complètes de Voltaire* (2009), 45a:346. The "blind man in the hands of the Philistines" was Samson.

Biography

La curiosité insatiable des lecteurs voudrait voir les ames des grands personnages de l'histoire, sur le papier, comme on voit leur visage sur la toile, mais il n'en va pas de même. L'ame n'est qu'une suite continuelle d'idées & de sentiments qui se succedent & se détruisent; les mouvements qui reviennent le plus souvent forment ce qu'on appelle le caractére, & ce caractére même reçoit mille changements par l'âge, par les maladies, par la fortune. . . . Le caractére de chaque homme est un cahos, & l'écrivain qui veut débrouiller après des siécles de cahos, en fait un autre.

Readers, with their insatiable curiosity, want the souls of great historical figures revealed on the printed page, in the same way that their portraits appear on canvas. But that is not how it works. The soul is a continuous succession of mutually destructive ideas and sentiments; the movements that are repeated most frequently form what we call character, and character is affected in a thousand ways by age, disease, and chance. The character of every man is a chaos, and the writer who seeks to disentangle this chaos, only creates another.

"Réfutation directe" ("contre les Critiques de M. La Beaum"), in *Le Siècle politique de Louis XIV.* (1753), 270; Besterman et al., *Œuvres complètes de Voltaire* (2012), 32c:356–357.

Blenheim Palace

Que c'était une grosse masse de pierre, sans agrément et sans goût.

What a great heap of stone it was, without charm or taste.

In the 1969 companion volume for his BBC television series *Civilisation* (246), Kenneth Clark quoted this line in English. The only known source for this remark (cited in French) is *Diary of a Journey to England in the Years 1761–1762* by Count Friedrich Kielmansegge, translated by Philippa Kielmansegg (1902), 95.

Nicolas Boileau-Despréaux (1636–1711)

POET AND LITERARY CRITIC

Dans la cour du Palais, je nâquis ton voisin,
De ton siécle brillant mes yeux virent la fin.

In the Palace courtyard, your neighbor, I was born,
With my eyes, the end of your brilliant age I saw.

"Epitre à Boileau, ou mon Testament," in *Nouveaux Mélanges philosophiques, historiques, critiques, &c. &c. Huitieme Partie* (1769), 276; Besterman et al., *Œuvres complètes de Voltaire* (2016), 70a:210.

Henry St. John, 1st Viscount Bolingbroke (1678–1751)

ENGLISH FREETHINKER, POLITICAL THEORIST,
AND GOVERNMENT OFFICIAL

Si je dédie à un Anglois un Ouvrage représenté à Paris, ce n'est pas, MYLORD, qu'il n'y ait aussi dans ma Patrie des Juges très-éclairez, & d'excellens Esprits ausquels j'eusse pû rendre cet hommage. Mais vous sçavez que la Tragédie de Brutus est née en Angleterre: Vous vous souvenez, que lorsque j'étois retiré à Wandsworth, chez mon ami M. Faukener, ce digne & vertueux Citoyen, je m'occupai chez lui à écrire en Prose Angloise le premier Acte de cette Piéce, à peu près tel qu'il est aujourd'hui en Vers Français. Je vous en parlais quelquefois, & nous nous éton-nions qu'aucun Anglois n'eût traité ce sujet, qui de tous est peut-être le plus conven-able à votre Théâtre. Vous m'encouragiez à continuer un Ouvrage susceptible de si grands sentimens.

I have here dedicated a French work, represented at Paris, to an English patron; not because there are not in my own country many men of distinguish'd parts and judgment, to whom I might have paid that compliment; but because the tragedy of Brutus is as it were a native of England. Your lordship may remem-ber, that when I retir'd to Wandsworth with my friend, Mr. Fakener, that worthy and virtuous citizen, I employ'd my leisure hours at his house in writ-ing the first act of this play in English prose, pretty nearly the same as it now stands in French verse. I mention'd it to your lordship several times, and we were both equally surpriz'd that no Englishman had ever treated this subject, which seems peculiarly adapted to your theatre. You encouraged me to pur-sue a plan which wou'd admit of such noble sentiments.

"Discours sur la tragédie à Mylord Bolingbrooke," in *Le Brutus de Monsieur de Voltaire, avec un Discours sur la Tragedie* (1731), iii; Besterman et al., *Œuvres complètes de Voltaire* (1998), 5:156. The translation is from *The Dramatic Works of Mr. De Voltaire* (1761), 1:200. Voltaire was mistaken on one point: an Elizabethan tragedy by Nathaniel Lee, *Lucius Junius Brutus, Father of His Country*, was performed in 1681.

Books

Une immense Bibliotheque ressemble à la Ville de Paris, dans laquelle il y a près de huit cent mille hommes: Vous ne vivez pas avec tout ce cahos: vous y choisissez quelque société, & vous en changez. On traite les Livres de même. On prend quelques amis dans la foule. Il y aura sept ou huit mille Controversistes, quinze ou seize mille Romans, que vous ne lirez point, une foule de feuilles Périodiques que vous jetterez au feu après les avoir lûës; l'homme de goût ne lit que le bon: mais l'homme d'Etat permet le bon & le mauvais, les pensées des hommes sont devenues un objet impor-tant du Commerce.

A great library is like the City of Paris, in which there are about eight hun-dred thousand persons: you don't live with the entire mob; you select a cer-tain society, and from time to time change company. One treats books the same way, picking a few friends out of the crowd. There will be seven or eight thousand Controversial books, fifteen or sixteen thousand Novels, which you will never read; a mass of Public prints you will throw into the fire after you've read them. The man of taste will read only what is good; but a Statesman will permit both bad and good. Men's thoughts have become an important article of Commerce.

"Copie d'une lettre à un Premier commis," June 20, 1733, in *Oeuvres diverses de Monsieur de Voltaire. Nouvelle édition* (1746), 4:246–247; Besterman et al., *Œuvres complètes de Voltaire* (1999), 9:320. The translation is based on the text in Hall, *Voltaire in His Letters* (1919), 32–33.

Moi qui trouve toujours tous les livres trop longs, & surtout les miens.

I who have always found all books to be too long, and above all my own.

"Lettre à M. de Cideville, sur Le Temple du Goût" (circa 1733), unpublished in Voltaire's lifetime. In *Poèmes et discours en vers* (1784), 136; Besterman et al., *Œuvres complètes de Voltaire* (1999), 9:206.

Le meilleur effet d'un Livre est de faire penser les hommes.

The best effect of a book is to make men think.

"Réponse de l'auteur à quelques critiques," appended to an anonymous brochure, *Panégyrique de Louis XV* (1749), 39; Besterman et al., *Œuvres complètes de Voltaire* (2004), 30c:301. This translation appeared as the epigraph to Aldridge, *Voltaire and the Century of Light* (1975).

Une première édition n'est jamais qu'un essai.

A first edition is never more than a first draft.

Letter from Potsdam, April 3, 1752, to Robert Le Cornier de Cideville in Rouen.

Il en est des livres comme du feu de nos foyers; on va prendre ce feu chez son voisin, on l'allume chez soi, on le communique à d'autres, & il apartient à tous.

There are books that are like the fire in our hearths; we go fetch it from our neighbors, we kindle it at home, we pass it along to others, and it belongs to everyone.

"De Prior, du Poeme singulier d'Hudibras, & du doyen Swift," in *Mélanges de littérature, d'histoire et de philosophie* (1757), 224; "Sur Mr Pope et quelques autres poetes fameux," in *Lettres philosophiques* (1964), 2:136 (variant).

Un livre n'est excusable qu'autant qu'il apprend quelque chose.

A book is justified only if we learn something from it.

Letter from Ferney, March 8, 1765, to Étienne-Noël Damilaville in Paris.

Si une noble émulation soutenue par le génie, produit les bons livres, l'orgueil et l'envie produisent les critiques, on le sait assez.

Just as worthy imitation bolstered by genius produces good books, pride and envy, we know, produce critics.

Lettre de Gérofle à Cogé (1767), in *Les Choses utiles et agréables* (1769), 2:113; *Réponse catégorique au sieur Cogé*, in Besterman et al., *Œuvres complètes de Voltaire* (1990), 63a:223.

Rien n'est plus aisé à faire qu'un mauvais livre, si ce n'est pas une mauvaise critique. La basse littérature inonde une partie de l'Europe. Le goût se corrompt tous les jours.

Nothing is easier than writing a bad book, nothing, that is, except bad criticism. Bad books are now overrunning parts of Europe. Taste is being corrupted daily.

"Avis au lecteur," in *Théâtre complet de M`r`. de Voltaire* (1768), 4:100; Moland, *Œuvres complètes de Voltaire* (1875), 12:73.

Vous les méprisez, les livres, vous dont la vie est plongée dans les vanités de l'ambition & dans la recherche des plaisirs, ou dans l'oiseveté; mais songez que tout l'univers n'est gouverné que par des livres, excepté les nations sauvages.

You, whose life is devoted entirely to vain ambition and the pursuit of pleasure or sloth, hold books in contempt; but remember that all mankind, except in savage nations, is governed by books.

"Livres," in *Questions sur l'Encyclopédie, par des Amateurs* (1771), 7:338; Besterman et al., *Œuvres complètes de Voltaire* (2012), 42b:58.

Il en est des livres comme des hommes, le très petit nombre joue un grand rôle, le reste est confondu dans la foule.

It is with books as with men, a very small number play a great role, the rest are lost in the crowd.

"Livres," in *Questions sur l'Encyclopédie, par des Amateurs* (1771), 7:338; Besterman et al., *Œuvres complètes de Voltaire* (2012), 42b:58.

Qui mène le genre-humain dans les pays policés? ceux qui savent lire & écrire. Vous ne connaissez ni Hippocrate, ni Boerhaave, ni Sidenham; mais vous mettez votre corps entre les mains de ceux qui les ont lus. Vous abandonnez votre ame à ceux qui sont payés pour lire la Bible, quoiqu'il n'y en ait pas cinquante d'entre eux qui l'ayent lue toute entière avec attention.

By whom, in all civilized lands, is mankind led? By those who can read and write. You are acquainted with neither Hippocrates, nor Boerhaave, nor Sydenham; but you place your body in the hands of those who have read them. You leave your soul entirely to the care of those who are paid to read the Bible, although not fifty of them have read it through carefully.

"Livres," in *Questions sur l'Encyclopédie, par des Amateurs* (1771), 7:339; Besterman et al., *Œuvres complètes de Voltaire* (2012), 42b:59.

Il est des nations chez qui l'on regarde les pensées purement comme un objet de commerce. Les opérations de l'entendement humain n'y sont considérées qu'à deux sous la feuille. Si par hazard le libraire veut un privilège pour sa marchandise, soit qu'il vende Rabelais, *soit qu'il vende les* Pères de l'église, *le magistrate donne le privilège sans répondre de ce que le livre contient.*

There are nations where ideas are considered merely as an article of commerce, the operations of human understanding being valued only at so much per page. If a bookseller happens to desire a privilege for his merchandise, be it *Rabelais* or the *Fathers of the Church*, the magistrate grants the privilege with no thought given to the contents of the book.

"Livres," in *Questions sur l'Encyclopédie, par des Amateurs* (1771), 7:340; Besterman et al., *Œuvres complètes de Voltaire* (2012), 42b:59.

Aujourd'hui on se plaint du trop; mais ce n'est pas aux lecteurs à se plaindre; le remède est aisé, rien ne les force à lire. Ce n'est pas non plus aux auteurs. Ceux qui font la foule ne doivent pas crier qu'on les presse. Malgré la quantité énorme de livres, combien peu de gens lisent! & si on lisait avec fruit, verrait-on les déplorables sottises auxquelles le vulgaire se livre encore tous les jours en proie?

The complaint today is that there are too many. But readers must not complain; the solution is simple: no one forces them to read. The same goes for authors. Those who write the books have no right to condemn the glut. And despite all these books, so few people actually read! If they took care in what they read, would we see such deplorable infatuations as the vulgar still fall prey to each and every day?

"Livres," in *Questions sur l'Encyclopédie, par des Amateurs* (1771), 7:343; Besterman et al., *Œuvres complètes de Voltaire* (2012), 42b:62.

C'est qu'avec des livres on en fait d'autres. C'est avec plusieurs volumes déjà imprimés qu'on fabrique une nouvelle histoire de France ou d'Espagne, sans rien ajouter de nouveau. Tous les dictionnaires sont fait de dictionnaires; presque tous les livres nouveaux de géographie sont des répétitions de livres de géographie.

Books are made from books. A new history of France or Spain is assembled from several volumes already in print, without adding anything new. A new dictionary is made from other dictionaries; almost all geography books are a rehash of earlier geography books.

"Livres," in *Questions sur l'Encyclopédie, par des Amateurs* (1771), 7:343; Besterman et al., *Œuvres complètes de Voltaire* (2012), 42b:63.

La multitude des livres nouveaux, qui ne nous apprennent rien, nous surcharge et nous dégoûte.

The multitude of new books teach us nothing and overwhelm and disgust us.

Letter from Ferney, December 8, 1776, to Denis Diderot in Paris. This sentence comes closest to matching a line often repeated since the 1980s, and almost certainly misattributed to Voltaire: "The multitude of books is making us ignorant." In *A World Treasury of Proverbs from Twenty-Five Languages* (1946, 36), Henry Davidoff attributed this line (unsourced) to Montaigne, but it appeared directly above another quote by Voltaire, hence perhaps the misunderstanding.

Boredom

Fuyons surtout l'ennui, dont la sombre langueur
Est plus insupportable encor que la douleur.
Toi qui détruis l'esprit, en amortit la flamme:
Toi, la honte à la fois et la rouille de l'ame.

Let us, above all, shun boredom, whose grim torpor
Even more than physical pain is hard to bear.
You who would wreck the spirit, and deaden the flame:
You are both the rust of the soul and its shame.

Epitre sur l'amour de l'étude, à Madame la Marquise Du Chastelet, Par un Elève de Voltaire, avec des notes du maitre, first published apparently as a free-standing, eighteen-page text in 1815; Besterman et al., *Œuvres complètes de Voltaire* (2008), 18:41.

Bowels

Heureux les mortels dont les entrailles sont souples, lubrifiées, entourées d'une graisse douce qui rend le jeu des ressorts facile! Malheureux les mortels qui ont des entrailles sèches, dures!

Happy those mortals whose bowels are supple, lubricated, enveloped by soft fatty tissue that eases the act of excretion. Unhappy the mortals whose bowels are parched and hard.

Letter from Ferney, June 18, 1762, to Voltaire's favorite physician, Dr. Théodore Tronchin in Geneva.

Brevity

Peut-être cet ouvrage est-il trop long: toute plaisanterie doit être courte, & même le sérieux devrait bien être court aussi.

Perhaps this work is itself too long: every witticism should be short, and even serious things would do well to be short, too.

"De Prior, du Poeme singulier d'Hudibras, et du doyen Swift," in *Mélanges de littérature, d'histoire et de philosophie* (1757), 115; "Sur Mr Pope et quelques autres poetes fameux," in *Lettres philosophiques* (1964), 2:133 (variant).

Brussels

Pour la triste ville où je suis,	In this sad city in which I dwell,
C'est le séjour de l'ignorance,	Home to torpidity, ignorance,
De la pesanteur, des ennuis,	Boredom, beastly indifference,
De la stupide indifférence;	In this place, they cast their spell;
Un vrai pays d'obédience,	Here, where obedience doth sit,
Privé d'esprit, rempli de foi;	Brimming with faith, devoid of wit;
Mais Emilie est avec moi;	But Emilie is here with me;
Seule, elle vaut toute la France.	Worth all of France, alone, is she.

Second stanza of a two-stanza poem, in a letter from Brussels, April 1, 1740, to Jean-Baptiste-Nicolas Formont in Rouen.

Butchery

Exterminez, grands dieux! De la terre où nous sommes,
Quiconque avec plaisir répand le sang des hommes!

O great Gods! Rid from this world in which we live,
All those who delight in spilling other men's blood!

Zopire, a leader in the holy city of Mecca, to one of Mahomet's slaves, in act 3, scene 8 of *Le Fanatisme, ou Mahomet le Prophete* (1743), 62; Besterman et al., *Œuvres complètes de Voltaire* (2002), 20b:243. This tragedy, first performed in Lille on April 25, 1741, opened in Paris on August 9, 1742.

The Calas affair

Vous avez pu voir, Monsieur, les lettres de la veuve Calas et de son fils. J'ai examiné cette affaire pendant trois mois. Je peux me tromper, mais il me paraît clair comme le jour, que la fureur de la faction, et la singularité de la destinée, ont concouru à faire assassiner juridiquement sur la roue le plus innocent et le plus malheureux des hommes, à disperser sa famille, et à la réduire à la mendicité.

You were able, Monsieur, to see the letters of the widow Calas and her son. I have studied this affair for three months. I may be mistaken, but to me it seems clear as day that rabid factionalism, and the peculiarity of fate, combined to cause the most innocent and unfortunate of men to be lawfully murdered on the rack, to break up his family, and reduce it to beggary.

Letter from Les Délices, July 9, 1762, to Dominique Audibert in Paris. Audibert, a Protestant merchant from Marseille, first made Voltaire aware of the Calas affair. Jean Calas, a merchant in Toulouse, was executed in March 1762 for the alleged murder of his eldest son, who in reality had committed suicide. In 1765, thanks to Voltaire, a royal edict nullified the judgment against Calas.

Jean Calvin (1509–1564)

FRENCH-BORN THEOLOGIAN AND LEADER OF THE
PROTESTANT REFORMATION IN GENEVA

Je passe tout aux hommes, pourvu qu'ils ne soient pas persécuteurs; j'aimerais Calvin, s'il n'avait pas fait brûler Servet; je serais serviteur du concile de Constance, sans les fagots de Jean Hus.

Provided men do not persecute, I can forgive them anything. I would be fond of Calvin if he had not had Servetus burned; I would be the servant of the Council of Constance, had Jan Hus not been burned at the stake.

Letter from Paris, September 14, 1733, to the Calvinist theologian Jacob Vernet in Geneva. Hus was a Czech priest, scholar, and proponent of reform within the Roman Catholic Church a century or more before Martin Luther and Calvin.

Nous avons joué presque toute la piece de Zaïre devant les Tronchin et les syndics: c'est un auditoire à qui nous avions grand envie de plaire. Calvin ne se doutait pas que des catholiques feraient un jour pleurer des huguenots dans le territoire de Genève.

We performed nearly all of *Zaïre* before the Tronchins and the Syndics: it is an audience we wanted very much to please. Calvin was far from imagining that one day Catholics would reduce the Huguenots of Geneva to tears.

Letter from Les Délices, April 2, 1755, to Jean-Robert Tronchin in Lyon. The Syndics were the political leaders in the Republic of Geneva. Presumably, François Tronchin and Dr. Théodore Tronchin were among the members of the Tronchin clan invited to attend the performance of *Zaïre*.

Calvin *passe pour être le fondateur du calvinisme. La vanité d'être chef de secte est la seconde de toutes les vanités de ce monde; car celle des conquérans est, dit-on, la première.*

Calvin is considered the founder of Calvinism. The pride in being the head of a sect is the second of this world's vanities; that of conquest is said to be the first.

"Arianisme," in *Questions sur l'Encyclopédie, par des Amateurs* (1770), 2:130; Besterman et al., *Œuvres complètes de Voltaire* (2007), 38:591. The translation is from *A Philosophical Dictionary* (1824), 1:247.

Canada

La guerre est donc sérieuse. Je voudrais que le tremblement de terre eût englouti cette misérable Acadie au lieu de Lisbonne et de Méquines.

This war is, therefore, serious. I'd prefer that the earthquake had swallowed up the miserable land of Acadia instead of Lisbon and Meknes.

Letter from Monrion, near Lausanne, January 29, 1756, to François Tronchin in Geneva. In this letter, Voltaire linked the earthquake at Lisbon to the start of the Seven Years' War. Meknes was the former imperial capital of Morocco.

On est dans un labyrinthe dont on ne pourra guère sortir que dans des ruisseaux de sang, et sur des corps morts: c'est une chose bien triste d'avoir à soutenir une guerre ruineuse sur mer pour quelques arpents de glace en Acadie, et de voir fondre des armées de cent mille hommes en Allemagne sans avoir un arpent à y prétendre.

We are in a labyrinth from which we cannot escape without crawling over dead bodies and through rivers of blood. It is sad to have to fight a ruinous war for a few acres of ice in Acadia, and to watch as we lose armies of one hundred thousand men in Germany where we have no claim to even a single acre.

Letter from Ferney, February 12, 1758, to Mme Du Deffand in Paris.

Si la philosophie & la justice se mêlaient des querelles des hommes, elles leur feraient voir que les Français & les Anglais se disputaient un pays sur lequel ils n'avaient aucun droit: mais ces premiers principes n'entrent point dans les affaires du Monde.

If Philosophy and Justice had a role in men's quarrels, they would make them see that France and England were fighting over a country over which they had no right: but such basic principles play no part in the affairs of the World.

Essay sur l'histoire générale, et sur les moeurs et l'esprit des nations (1757), 6:196; "De la Guerre entre la France et l'Angleterre en 1756," in *Essay sur l'histoire générale, et sur les moeurs et l'esprit des nations* (1757), 6:80; Moland, *Œuvres complètes de Voltaire* (1878), 15:337.

"Vous savez que ces deux Nations sont en guerre pour quelques arpens de neige vers le Canada, & qu'elles dépensent pour cette belle guerre beaucoup plus que tout le Canada ne vaut."

"You know that these two nations are at war over a few acres of snow out around Canada, and that they are spending on that fine war more than all of Canada is worth."

Candide's companion Martin to Candide in "Candide & Martin vont sur les côtes d'Angleterre, ce qu'ils y voyent," chap. 23 in *Candide, ou L'Optimisme* (1759), 209–210; Besterman et al., *Œuvres complètes de Voltaire* (1980), 48:223. The translation is from *Candide, Zadig, and Other Stories*, translated by Donald M. Frame (2001), with an introduction by John Iverson, former president of the Voltaire Society of America, 78. The two nations fighting over "a few acres of snow" in Canada were France and England, including the thirteen English colonies, during the Seven Years' War.

Cannibalism

Nous avons parlé de l'amour. Il est dur de passer de gens qui se baisent, à gens qui se mangent.

We have spoken of love. It is hard to go from people kissing, to people eating each other.

"Anthropophages," *Mélanges philosophiques, littéraires, historiques, &c.* (1777), 6:210; Besterman et al., *Œuvres complètes de Voltaire* (1994), 35:344. When Voltaire says he had "spoken of love," he was referring to his article "Amour," in *Questions sur l'Encyclopédie, par des Amateurs* (1770), 1:208–213.

Castration

Les sages Romains se gardent bien surtout d'excommunier ces Messieurs qui chantent le dessus dans les Opéra Italiens; car en vérité c'est bien assez d'être châtré dans ce Monde, sans être encor damné dans l'autre.

The wise Romans are particularly careful not to excommunicate those gentlemen who sing treble in the Italian operas; for it is enough, in all conscience, to have been castrated in this world, without being damned in the other.

"Sur la Police des Spectacles," in *Suite des mélanges de littérature, d'histoire et de philosophie* (1757), 238; Besterman et al., *Œuvres complètes de Voltaire* (2006), 28a:79. The translation is from Smollett, "On the Management of publick Shows," in Smollett et al., *The Works of Mr. de Voltaire* (1762), 12:114.

Je suis né à Naples, me dit-il, on y chaponne deux ou trois mille enfans tous les ans, les uns en meurent, les autres acquiérent une voix plus belle que celle des femmes, les autres vont gouverner des Etats.

"'I was born at Naples,' he told me; 'there they caponize two or three thousand boys every year. Some die of it, others acquire a voice more beautiful than a woman's, others go and govern states.'"

The *castrato* to the Old Woman in "Suite des malheurs de la vieille," chap. 12 in *Candide, ou L'Optimisme* (1759), 88; Besterman et al., *Œuvres complètes de Voltaire* (1980), 48:158. In English, *Candide, Zadig, and Other Stories* (2001), 38–39.

Catalonia

La Catalogne est un des pays les plus fertiles de la terre, & des plus heureusement situés. . . . Barcelone est un des plus beaux ports de l'Europe. . . . La Catalogne enfin peut se passer de l'univers entier, & ses voisins ne peuvent pas se passer d'elle.

Catalonia is one of the most fertile lands on earth, and the most fortunately situated. . . . Barcelona is one of the finest ports in Europe. . . . Catalonia can do without the entire universe, but her neighbors cannot do without her.

"Victoire du maréchal de Villars à Dénain," in *Le Siécle de Louis XIV, Auquel on a joint Un Précis du Siécle de Louis XV*, in Cramer and Cramer, eds., *Collection complette des Œuvres de Mr. de Voltaire* (1769), 11:436; Besterman et al., *Œuvres complètes de Voltaire* (2015), 13b:206.

Censorship

S'il y avoit eu une Inquisition Littéraire à Rome, nous n'aurions aujourd'hui ni Horace, ni Juvenal, ni les Oeuvres Philosophiques de Ciceron. Si Milton, Driden, Pope, & Locke n'avoient pas été libres, l'Angleterre n'auroit eu ni de Poëtes, ni de Philosophes; il y a je ne sai quoi de Turc à proscrire l'Imprimerie; & c'est-là pro-scrire, que la trop gêner. Contentés-vous de réprimer sévérement les Libelles diffama-toires; parce que ce sont des crimes: mais tandis qu'on débite hardiment des Recueils de ces infames Calottes, & tant d'autres productions qui méritent l'horreur & le mépris; souffrés aumoins que Bayle entre en France, & que celui qui fait tant d'honneur à sa Patrie n'y soit pas de contrebande.

Had there been a literary censorship in Rome, we should have had today neither Horace, Juvenal, nor the philosophical works of Cicero. If Milton, Dryden, Pope, and Locke had not been free, England would have had neither poets nor philosophers; there is something positively Turkish in proscribing printing; and hampering it is proscription. Be content with severely repressing defamatory libels, for they are crimes: but so long as those infamous calottes are boldly published, and so many other unworthy and despicable productions, at least allow Bayle to circulate in France, and do not put him, who has been so great an honour to his country, among its contraband.

"Copie d'une lettre à un Premier commis," June 20, 1733, in *Oeuvres diverses de Monsieur de Voltaire. Nouvelle édition* (1746), 4:246; Besterman et al., *Œuvres complètes de Voltaire* (1999), 9:319. The translation is from Hall, *Voltaire in His Letters* (1919), 31–32.

Heureusement je n'écris rien que la cour de Vienne et celle de Versailles ne pussent lire avec édification.

Fortunately, I never write anything that the court in Vienna or the court at Versailles would not find edifying.

Letter from Lausanne, January 13, 1758, to Jean-Robert Tronchin in Lyon. Voltaire was making clear to his friend, at the height of the Seven Years' War, that he knew government censors were opening his mail.

Certainty

Toute certitude qui n'est pas démonstration mathématique, n'est qu'une extrême probabilité. Il n'y a pas d'autre certitude historique.

All certainty which does not consist in mathematical demonstration is nothing more than the highest probability; there is no other historical certainty.

"Histoire," in Diderot, d'Alembert, et al., *Encyclopédie, ou Dictionnaire raisonné des Sciences, des Arts et des Métiers* (1765), 8:223; Besterman et al., *Œuvres complètes de Voltaire* (1987), 33:177. The translation is from Redman, *The Portable Voltaire* (1949), 223.

Il n'y a que des charlatans qui soient certains. Nous ne savons rien des premiers principes. Il est bien extravagant de définir Dieu, les anges, les esprits, et de savoir précisément pourquoi Dieu a formé le monde, quand on ne sait pas pourquoi on remue son bras à volonté.
Le doute n'est pas un état bien agréable, mais l'assurance est un état ridicule.

Only charlatans have absolute certainty. We know nothing about first principles. It is outlandish to define God, angels, spirits, and to say precisely why God made the world when we do not even know why we can move our arm at will.
Doubt is not an agreeable state, but total certainty is ridiculous.

Letter from Ferney, November 28, 1770, to Frederick William, Hereditary Prince of Prussia, in Berlin or Potsdam.

Celui qui a entendu dire la chose à douze mille témoins oculaires, n'a que douze mille probabilités égales à une forte probabilité, laquelle n'est pas égale à la certitude.

He who has heard something from twelve thousand eyewitnesses has but twelve thousand probabilities that equal a strong probability, which does not equal certainty.

"Vérité," in *Questions sur l'Encyclopédie, par des Amateurs* (1772), 9:49; Besterman et al., *Œuvres complètes de Voltaire* (2013), 43:445.

Miguel de Cervantes (1547–1616)

SPANISH AUTHOR OF PERHAPS THE FIRST
MODERN NOVEL, *DON QUIXOTE*

Vous savez bien que Michel Cervantes disait que, sans l'inquisition, Don Quichotte aurait été encore plus plaisant.

You know very well that Miguel Cervantes said that without the Inquisition, *Don Quixote* would have been a lot more amusing.

Letter from Ferney, March 25, 1765, to Jean-François Marmontel in Paris.

Champagne

Eglé, Cloris, me versent de leur main
Un Vin d'Aï, dont la mousse pressée,
De la Bouteille avec force élancée,
Comme un éclair fait voler le bouchon;
Il part, on rit; il frappe le plat-fond.
De ce Vin frais l'écume pétillante
De nos Français est l'image brillante.

Aegle, Chloris, serve me by their own hand
Sparkling Wine, whose pressurized froth,
From the Bottle, with great force, shoots forth,
Like lightning, the cork is sent wheeling;
Off it soars, we laugh; it strikes the ceiling.
From this Wine's fizzy foam one may infer,
A brilliant symbol of the French character.

[*Le Mondain, ou l'Apologie du Luxe*], as *L'Homme du Monde, ou Défense du Mondain*, in *Oeuvres de M^r. de Voltaire. Nouvelle Edition* (1739), 118; Besterman et al., *Œuvres complètes de Voltaire* (2003), 16:302. In Greek mythology, the nymph Chloris was associated with spring; Aegle was one of the Naiads. *Le vin d'Aÿ* is a sparkling wine from the Champagne region. In English, the title of this poem is usually given as "The Worldling," but in Smollett et al., *The Works of Mr. de Voltaire* (1764), 32:212–218, it appears as "The Worldly Man."

Character

Ne ressemblons-nous pas presque tous à ce vieux général de quatre-vingt-dix ans, qui ayant rencontré de jeunes officiers qui faisaient un peu de désordre avec des filles, leur dit tout en colère, Messieurs, est-ce là l'exemple que je vous donne?

Are not most of us like the old general of ninety who, coming upon some young officers making merry with loose women, angrily says to them, Gentlemen, is that the example that I set for you?

"Caractère," in *Dictionnaire philosophique portatif par Mr. De Voltaire* (1764), 61; Besterman et al., *Œuvres complètes de Voltaire* (2007), 35:433.

> *Le caractère est formé de nos idées & de nos sentimens: or il est très prouvé qu'on ne se donne ni sentimens ni idées; donc notre caractère ne peut dépendre de nous.*
> *S'il en dépendait, il n'y a personne qui ne fût parfait.*
> *Nous ne pouvons nous donner des goûts, des talens; pourquoi nous donnerions-nous des qualités?*
> *Quand on ne réfléchit pas, on se croit le maître de tout; quand on y réfléchit, on voit qu'on n'est maître de rien.*

Character is shaped by ideas and feelings: it is a proven fact that we create neither our feelings nor our ideas; thus, we have no power over our character.

If we did, we would all be perfect.

We cannot give ourselves tastes or talents; how could we give ourselves other qualities?

When we do not think rationally, we believe we are all-powerful; but when we really think about it, we realize we are masters of nothing.

"Caractère," in *Questions sur l'Encyclopédie, par des Amateurs* (1774), 2:87; Besterman et al., *Œuvres complètes de Voltaire* (2008), 39:501.

Gabrielle-Émilie Le Tonnelier de Breteuil, marquise du Châtelet (1706–1749)

FRENCH MATHEMATICIAN, PHYSICIST, AND COMPANION OF VOLTAIRE

Cette belle âme est une étoffe	This lovely soul is a fabric
Qu'elle brode en mille façons,	That she trims a thousand ways,
Son esprit est très philosophe	Her mind is very logical,
Et son cœur aime les pompons.	And her heart adores bobbles.

"Épître à Émilie," included in a letter from Paris, August 29, 1733, to the libertine uncle of the marquis de Sade, abbé Jacques de Sade, in Avignon.

I would pass some months at Constantinople with you, if I could live without that lady whom I look upon as a great man. She understands Newton, she despises superstition, and in short she makes me happy.

Figure 12. Pierre-Gabriel Langlois, *Gabrielle Emilie de Breteuil, Marquise du Châtelet*, 1780 (detail, without the inscription). Engraved after a portrait painted circa 1740 by Marianne Loir (circa 1715–1769). Private collection.

Letter from Brussels, March 2, 1740, written in English to Sir Everard Fawkener, British ambassador to Constantinople.

Une Etrenne frivole à la docte Uranie,
Peut-on la présenter? oh, très-bien, j'en répons:
Tout lui plait, tout convient à son vaste génie;

Les livres, les bijoux, les compas, les pompons,
Les vers, les diamans, les biribis, l'Optique,
L'Algèbre, les Soupers, le latin, les jupons,
L'Opéra, les procès, le bal & la Physique.

Some frivolous verse for the learned Urania.
May I present it? Oh, alright, I'll run the risk.
Everything delights and suits her vast intellect:
Books, jewelry, compasses, and bobbles,
Poetry, diamonds, playing cards, and optics,
Algebra, supper parties, Latin, ladies' skirts,
Opera, lawsuits, fancy dress balls and Physics.

Untitled seven-line poem, published in Clément, *Les Cinq Années Littéraires* (1754), 13; Besterman et al., *Œuvres complètes de Voltaire* (2008), 28a:424. Urania, Voltaire's nickname here for his lover, Mme du Châtelet, was the daughter of Zeus and the muse of astronomy. The poem was probably written in January 1748. Now commonly referred to as "Étrennes à Uranie," it was published as "Étrennes A Madame la Marquise du Ch**," in *Nouvelle anthologie françoise* (1769), 416.

Philip Dormer Stanhope, Fourth Earl of Chesterfield
(1694–1773)

ENGLISH MAN OF LETTERS, STATESMAN, AND WIT

De tous les Anglais c'est peut-être celui qui a écrit avec le plus de grâces. . . . Il ne se doutait pas que ses lettres seraient imprimées après sa mort et après celle de son bâtard. On les traduit en français en Hollande, ainsi Votre Majesté les verra bientôt. Elle lira le seul Anglais qui ait jamais recommandé l'art de plaire comme le premier devoir de la vie.

Of all Englishmen it is perhaps he who wrote with the most grace. . . . He had no idea that his letters would be published after his death and the death of his bastard son. They are being translated into French in Holland, thus Your Majesty will see them soon. He will read the only Englishman who ever argued for the art of pleasing as the first duty of life.

Letter from Ferney, August 16, 1774, to Frederick the Great in Potsdam.

Children

L'expérience nous apprend que les enfans ne sont qu'imitateurs; que si on ne leur disait rien, ils ne parleraient pas; qu'ils se contenteraient de crier.
Dans presque tous les pays connus on leur dit d'abord baba, papa, mama, maman, ou des mots approchans aisés à prononcer, & ils les répètent.

Experience teaches us that children are merely imitators; if nothing were said to them, they would not speak; they would merely scream.

In almost all known countries, one starts by saying to them *baba*, *papa*, *mama*, *maman*, or some such words, easy to pronounce, and they repeat them.

"Langues," in *Questions sur l'Encyclopédie, par des Amateurs* (1771), 7:300; Besterman et al., *Œuvres complètes de Voltaire* (2012), 42b:2.

China

Il ne faut pas être fanatique du mérite Chinois; la continuation de leur Empire est à la vérité la meilleure qui soit au monde, la seule qui soit toute fondée sur le pouvoir paternel.

One need not be obsessed with the merits of the Chinese; the persistence of their empire is in truth the best in the world, the only one founded on paternal authority.

"De la Chine," in *La Raison par Alphabet. Septieme Édition* (1773), 160; Besterman et al., *Œuvres complètes de Voltaire* (1994), 35:539. *La Raison par alphabet* was the title given by Voltaire to several editions of the *Dictionnaire philosophique portatif* around this time.

Christianity

Je ne suis pas Chrétien, mais c'est pour t'aimer mieux.

I am not a Christian, in order to love you all the more.

"Épître à Uranie," in *Lettre de M. de V*** avec Plusieurs piéces galantes et nouvelles de differens auteurs* (1744), 77; Besterman et al., *Œuvres complètes de Voltaire* (2002), 1b:498. This line of verse is addressed to God ("Dieu que j'implore"). The poem, written in the 1720s and originally titled "Épître à Julie," was reworked over the years and in 1772 was published as "Le Pour et le Contre."

Je conclus que tout homme sensé, tout homme de bien doit avoir la secte Chrétienne en horreur. Le grand nom de Théiste qu'on ne révère pas assez, est le seul nom qu'on doive prendre. Le seul évangile qu'on doive lire, c'est le grand livre de la nature, écrit de la main de Dieu & scellé de son cachet. La seule religion qu'on doive professer est celle d'adorer Dieu & d'être honnête homme. Il est aussi impossible que cette religion pure & éternelle produise du mal, qu'il étoit impossible que le fanatisme Chrétien n'en fit pas.

I conclude, that every sensible man, every honest man, ought to hold Christianity in abhorrence. "The great name of Theist, which we cannot sufficiently revere," is the only name we ought to adopt. The only gospel we should read is the grand book of nature, written in God's own hand, and stamped with his seal. The only religion we ought to profess is "to adore God, and act like honest men." It would be as impossible for this simple and eternal religion to produce evil, as it would be impossible for Christian fanaticism not to produce it.

L'Examen Important de Milord Bolingbroke, Ecrit sur la fin de 1736, in a volume comprised of material not entirely written by Voltaire, *Recueil nécessaire* (1765 [1766]), 287; Besterman et al., *Œuvres complètes de Voltaire* (1987), 62:350. The translation is from *The Important Examination of the Holy Scriptures, Attributed to Lord Bolingbroke, but Written by M. Voltaire, and First Published in 1736* (1819). The phrase, "Le grand nom de théiste qu'on ne révère pas assez," refers to the 3rd Earl of Shaftesbury, who, in *Characteristicks of Men, Manners, Opinions, Times* (1711), said, "that to be a settled Christian, it is necessary to be first of all *a good* THEIST."

Sçache que la religion naturelle est le commencement du Christianisme, & que le vrai Christianisme est la loi naturelle perfectionnée.

You should know that Christianity is rooted in the divinity of nature, and that true Christianity is natural law perfected.

Lettre d'un Quakre, A Jean-George Le Franc de Pompignan (1763), 7–8; Besterman et al., *Œuvres complètes de Voltaire* (2014), 57a:280.

La superstition la plus infâme qui ait jamais abruti les hommes et désolé la terre.

The most infamous superstition that ever rendered men stupid and wreaked havoc upon the earth.

Letter from Ferney, October 11, 1763, presumably to the marquis d'Argence in Paris.

La nôtre est sans contredit la plus ridicule [des religions], *la plus absurde, et la plus sanguinaire qui ait jamais infecté le monde. Votre Majesté rendra un service éternel au genre humain en détruisant cette infâme superstition, je ne dis pas chez la canaille, qui n'est pas digne d'être éclairée, et à laquelle tous les jougs sont propres; je dis chez les honnêtes gens, chez les hommes qui pensent, chez ceux qui veulent penser. . . . Je ne m'afflige de toucher à la mort que par mon profond regret de ne vous pas seconder dans cette noble entreprise, la plus belle et la plus respectable qui puisse signaler l'esprit humain.*

Ours is assuredly the most ridiculous, the most absurd and bloodiest [religion] that has ever infected this world. Your Majesty will do the human race an eternal service by extirpating this infamous superstition, I do not say among the rabble, who are not worthy of being enlightened and who are apt for every yoke; I say among honest people, among men who think, among those who wish to think. . . . My one regret in dying is that I cannot aid you in this noble enterprise, the finest and most respectable that the human mind can point out.

Letter from Ferney, January 5, 1767, to Frederick the Great in Potsdam.

Où est le prince assez instruit pour savoir que depuis dix-sept cents ans la secte chrétienne n'a jamais fait que du mal?

Where is the prince sufficiently educated to know that for seventeen hundred years the Christian sect has done nothing but harm?

Letter from Ferney, April 6, 1767, to Frederick the Great in Potsdam.

Pourquoi dit-on toujours, mon dieu et notre-dame?

Why do we say, "My God," but "Our Lady"?

Notebooks or *cahiers* unpublished in Voltaire's lifetime: Besterman, *Voltaire's Notebooks II* (1968), in *Œuvres complètes de Voltaire* (1968), 82:544; first published in Besterman, *Voltaire's Notebooks* (1952), 2:390.

Circumcision

Les Israëlites, de leur aveu même, prirent beaucoup de coutumes des Egyptiens. . . . Rien n'empêche donc que les Hébreux ayent imité les Egyptiens dans la circoncision, comme faisaient les Arabes leurs voisins.

Il n'est point extraordinaire que Dieu, qui a sanctifié le batême si ancien chez les Afriques, ait sanctifié aussi la circoncision non moins ancien chez les Africains. On a déjà remarqué qu'il est le maître d'attacher ses graces aux signes qu'il daigne choisir.

The Israelites, by their own admission, borrowed many customs from the Egyptians. . . . Nothing would have prevented the Hebrews from imitating the Egyptians in the practice of circumcision, as their neighbors the Arabs did.

It is hardly extraordinary that God, who sanctified the ancient African custom of baptism, sanctified circumcision, which was no less ancient in Africa. We have already noted that He is able to grant his grace to any symbols that he so chooses.

"Circoncision," in *La Raison par Alphabet. Septieme Édition* (1773), 160; Besterman et al., *Œuvres complètes de Voltaire* (1994), 35:607.

Cirey

ESTATE IN CHAMPAGNE OWNED BY THE HUSBAND
OF THE MARQUISE DU CHÂTELET

Asile des beaux-arts, solitude où mon cœur
Est toujours occupé dans une paix profonde,

C'est vous qui donnez le bonheur
Que promettait en vain le monde.

Haven of the arts, private space where my heart,
Profoundly at peace, stays forever busy,
'Tis you who gives me happiness
That the world did vainly promise.

Verse placed by Voltaire on the wall beside one of the doors inside his wing of the château de Cirey, as quoted in a letter from Voltaire, April 24, 1744, to the comte d'Argental and his wife, the comtesse d'Argental, in Paris.

Civilization

Avec quelle lenteur, avec quelle difficulté le Genre-humain se civilise, & la Société se perfectionne!

How slowly, with how much difficulty, is the human race civilized and society perfected!

Essay sur l'histoire générale, et sur les moeurs et l'esprit des nations (1756), 4:231; Besterman et al., *Œuvres complètes de Voltaire* (2015), 26c:180. The translation is from Benrekassa, "Civilisation and Civility" (2001), 1:268.

Plus de la moitié de la terre habitable est encor peuplée d'animaux à deux pieds qui vivent dans un horrible état qui approche de la pure nature, ayant à peine le vivre & le vêtir; jouïssans à peine du don de la parole; s'appercevant à peine qu'ils sont malheureux; vivans & mourans sans presque le savoir.

Over half the habitable parts of the world remain populated by two-legged animals living in a ghastly state of almost unadulterated nature, barely able to feed and clothe themselves, barely capable of speech; only slightly aware of how miserable they are; living and dying almost without taking any notice.

"Homme" (under the subheading "De l'homme dans l'état de pure nature"), in *Questions sur l'Encyclopédie, par des Amateurs* (1771), 7:111; Besterman et al., *Œuvres complètes de Voltaire* (2011), 42a:280.

Climate

Le climat a quelque puissance, le gouvernement cent fois plus; la religion jointe au gouvernement encore davantage.

Climate has some power, government a hundred times more; religion and government combined, even more.

"Climat," in *Questions sur l'Encyclopédie, par des Amateurs* (1771), 4:17; Besterman et al., *Œuvres complètes de Voltaire* (2009), 40:132.

Coffee

Puisque je n'ai point de commissionnaire il faut donc que je vous importune pour avoir quatre livres de café. Si je ne m'occupais que de mes malheurs je demanderais de l'opium. Mais je ne m'occupe que de mon travail et le café me ranime.

Since I have no agent, I must therefore impose on you to obtain four pounds of coffee. If it were just a matter of my personal woes, I would ask for opium. But I'm devoted to my work and coffee gives me renewed energy.

Letter from Colmar, April 9, 1754, to his niece, Mme Denis, in Paris.

Je suis fidelle à mon café, dont j'use depuis soixante et dix ans.

I remain true to my coffee, which I've been drinking for seventy years.

Letter from Ferney, December 8, 1772, to Frederick the Great in Potsdam. This comment suggests that Voltaire began drinking coffee as a preteen. In a text titled "Le Café," published in *Chants et Chansons populaires de la France* (1843), Théophile-Marion Dumersan, quoted in paraphrase a quip to someone who said that coffee was poison: "Oui, répondit Voltaire, mais un poison lent, car voilà cinquante ans que j'en prends, et ne suis pas encore mort." *Bartlett's Book of Anecdotes* (rev. ed., 2000) cites a very similar, undated remark. Having been told to drink less coffee because it was poisonous, he reputedly said, "I think it must be slow, for I have been drinking it for sixty-five years and I am not dead yet." A painting by Jean Huber from around 1775 (Hermitage Museum, St. Petersburg), commissioned by Catherine the Great as part of a series of scenes from Voltaire's daily life at Ferney, represents the writer standing near a fireplace, sipping a small cup of coffee brought to him by a servant. The brew Voltaire consumed (with, it seems, a preference for the mocha variety) likely was not as strong as today's standard *café express*. In another letter to Frederick (November 13, 1772), Voltaire said, "ce matin j'ai pris mon café à la crème."

Coincidence

Les beaux esprits se rencontrent.

Great minds think alike.

Letter from Ferney, June 30, 1760, to Nicolas-Claude Thieriot in Paris.

Comment les Grecs ont ils mis en fables ce que les Hébreux ont mis en histoire? Serait-ce par le don de l'invention? Serait-ce par la facilité de l'imitation? Serait-ce parce que les beaux esprits se rencontrent? Enfin, DIEU l'a permis; cela doit suffire.

How is it that the Greeks put in their fables the same things the Hebrews wrote in their histories? Can it be a gift of invention? Imitation? Is it that great minds think alike? Suffice it to say that God condoned it.

"Bacchus," in *Questions sur l'Encyclopédie, par des Amateurs* (1770), 3:15; Besterman et al., *Œuvres complètes de Voltaire* (2008), 39:277.

Jean-Baptiste Colbert (1619–1683)

MINISTER OF FINANCES UNDER LOUIS XIV

Le grand malheur de Colbert est d'avoir vu ses mesures toujours traversées par les entreprises de Louis XIV. La guerre injuste et ridicule de 1672 obligea le plus grand ministre que nous ayons jamais eu à se conduire d'une manière directement opposée à ses sentiments, et cependant il ne laissa en mourant aucune dette de l'État qui fut exigible. Il créa la marine, il établit toutes les manufactures qui servent à la construction et à l'équipement des vaisseaux; on lui doit l'utile et l'agréable.

The tragedy of Colbert is that his great policies were contravened by Louis XIV and his schemes. The unjust and ridiculous war of 1672 forced the greatest minister this country has ever known to conduct his policy in a manner with which he fundamentally disagreed. When he died, he left the nation free from all outstanding debt. He created the navy, founded naval yards to build and equip ships; we owe him things both elegant and useful.

Letter from Ferney, May 12, 1766, to Étienne-Noël Damilaville in Paris. The phrase "l'utile et l'agréable," variously formulated, recurs frequently in Voltaire's writings and his contemporaries, including Diderot (*Le Rêve de d'Alembert*, 1769) and Frederick the Great, in a letter to Voltaire, November 13, 1777. For Voltaire, it was a societal ideal monarchs and statesmen were duty-bound to try to achieve.

Commerce

ENTREZ dans la Bourse de Londres, cette place plus respectable que bien des Cours, dans laquelle s'assemblent les deputés de toutes les nations pour l'utilité des hommes. Là, le Juif, le Mahometan & le Chrétien, traitent l'un avec l'autre comme s'ils étoient de la même religion, & ne se donnent le nom d'infideles qu'à ceux, qui font banqueroute.

TAKE a view of the *Royal Exchange* in *London*, a place more venerable than many courts of justice, where the representatives of all nations meet for the benefit of mankind. There the Jew, the Mahometan, and the Christian transact as tho' they all profess'd the same religion, and give the name of Infidel to none but bankrupts.

"Sixième Lettre. Sur les Presbyteriens," in *Lettres Ecrites de Londres sur les Anglois et autres sujets* (1734), 42; "Sur les Presbiteriens," in *Lettres philosophiques* (1964), 1:74. The translation is "Letter VI. On the Presbyterians," in *Letters Concerning the English Nation* (1733), 44.

Le Commerce, qui a enrichi les Citoyens en Angleterre, a contribué à les rendre libres, & cette liberté a étendu le commerce à son tour; de là s'est formée la grandeur de l'État. C'est le commerce qui a établi peu-à-peu les forces navales, par qui les Anglois sont les maîtres des mers; ils ont a présent prés de deux cent vaisseaux de guerre.

As Trade enrich'd the Citizens in *England*, so it contributed to their Freedom, and this Freedom on the other Side extended Commerce, whence arose the Grandeur of the State. Trade rais'd by insensible Degrees the naval Power, which gives the *English* a Superiority over the Seas, and they are now Masters of very near two hundred Ships of War.

"Dixième Lettre. Sur le Commerce," in *Lettres Ecrites de Londres sur les Anglois et autres sujets* (1734), 66; "Sur le Commerce," in *Lettres philosophiques* (1964), 1:120. The translation is "Letter X. On Trade," in *Letters Concerning the English Nation* (1733), 69.

Je ne sçais . . . lequel est le plus util à un Etat, ou un Seigneur bien poudré, qui sçait précisement à quelle heure le Roy se leve, à quelle heure il se couche, & qui se donne des airs de grandeur en jouant le rôlle d'esclave dans l'Antichambre d'un Ministre; ou un Negotiant qui enrichit son Pays, donne de son cabinet des ordres à Suratte & au Caire, & contribue au bonheur du monde.

I need not say which is most useful to a Nation; a Lord powder'd in the tip of the Mode, who knows exactly at what a Clock the King rises and goes to bed; and who gives himself Airs of Grandeur and State, at the same Time that he is acting the Slave in the Anti-chamber of a prime Minister; or a Merchant, who enriches his Country, dispatches Orders from his Compting-Office to *Surat* and *Grand Cairo*, and contributes to the Felicity of the World.

"Dixième Lettre. Sur le Commerce," in *Lettres Ecrites de Londres sur les Anglois et autres sujets* (1734), 69; "Sur le Commerce," in *Lettres philosophiques* (1964), 1:122. The translation is "Letter X. On Trade," in *Letters Concerning the English Nation* (1733), 72.

Common sense

On dit quelquefois, le sens commun est fort rare; que signifie cette phrase? Que dans plusieurs hommes raison commencée est arrêtée dans ses progrès par quelques préjugés, que tel homme qui juge très-sainement dans une affaire se trompera toujours grossiérement dans une autre. Cet Arabe qui sera d'ailleurs un bon calculateur, un savant chymiste, un astronome exact, croira cependant que Mahomet a mis la moitié de la lune dans sa manche.

Common sense, it is sometimes said, is quite rare; but what does this expression mean? That in some men a nascent ability to reason is arrested by certain prejudices, that a man who judges wisely in one matter will be grossly mistaken in another. An Arab, who, though good with numbers and a learned chemist and a meticulous astronomer, nevertheless believes that Mohammad put half the moon up his sleeve.

"Sens commun," in *Dictionnaire philosophique portatif: Nouvelle Édition* (1765), 317–319; Besterman et al., *Œuvres complètes de Voltaire* (1994), 36:525. Voltaire's reference to Mohammad putting "half the moon up his sleeve" is connected to the legend that the Prophet had been able to split the moon in two.

Le sens commun nous apprend qu'on ne doit point donner à un mot une acception qui ne lui a jamais été donnée dans aucun livre.

Common sense dictates that we ought to refrain from giving a meaning to words that cannot be found in any book.

"Anthropophages," in *Questions sur l'Encyclopédie, par des Amateurs* (1770), 1:359n; Besterman et al., *Œuvres complètes de Voltaire* (2007), 38:417.

Confucius (551–479 B.C.)

CHINESE SAGE AND PHILOSOPHER

On place souvent le grand Confutsé, *que nous nommons* Confucius, *parmi les anciens Législateurs, parmi les Fondateurs de religions; c'est une grande inadvertance.* Confutsée *est très moderne; il ne vivait que six cent cinquante ans avant-nôtre ere. Jamais il n'institua aucun culte, aucun rite; jamais il ne se dit ni inspiré ni Prophête; il ne fit que rassembler en un corps les anciennes loix de la Morale.*

The great Confutse, whom we call Confucius, is often ranked among the ancient legislators, among the founders of religion; this is a great mistake. Confucius is very modern; he was alive only six hundred and fifty years before the Christian era. He never instituted any doctrine, any rite; he called himself neither inspired nor a prophet; he merely united in one code the ancient laws of morality.

"XLI. De *Confucius*" (Doute no. 41), in *Le Philosophe ignorant* (1766), 114; Besterman et al., *Œuvres complètes de Voltaire* (1987), 62:91. This translation is based in part on a text in *Voltairiana* (1805), selected and translated by Young, under the heading "XXV. Confucius," 48.

Il ne dit point qu'il ne faut pas faire à autrui ce que nous ne voulons pas qu'on fasse à nous-mêmes; ce n'est que défendre le mal: il fait plus, il recommande le bien: Traite autrui comme tu veux qu'on te traite.

He does not say that we must not do unto others what we do not want done to us; that is only forbidding wrongdoing: he does more, he recommends goodness: *Treat others as you want them to treat you.*

"XLI. De *Confucius*" (Doute no. 41), in *Le Philosophe ignorant* (1766), 115; Besterman et al., *Œuvres complètes de Voltaire* (1987), 62:92.

Par quelle fatalité, honteuse peut-être pour les peuples occidentaux, faut-il aller au bout de l'Orient pour trouver un sage simple, sans faste, sans imposture, qui enseignait aux hommes à vivre heureux six cents ans avant notre ère vulgaire, dans un temps où tout le Septentrion ignorait l'usage des lettres, et où les Grecs commençaient à peine à se distinguer par la sagesse?

By what fatality, disgraceful perhaps to the nations of the west, has it happened that we are obliged to travel to the extremity of the east, in order to find a sage of simple manners and character, without arrogance and without imposture, who taught men how to live happily six hundred years before the Christian era, at a period when the whole of the north was ignorant of the use of letters, and when the Greeks had scarcely begun to distinguish themselves by wisdom?

"Philosophe," in *Mélanges philosophiques, littéraires, historiques, &c.* (1777), 6:388; Besterman et al., *Œuvres complètes de Voltaire* (1994), 36:434–435. The translation is from "Philosopher," in *A Philosophical Dictionary* (1824), 5:217.

William Congreve (1670–1729)

ENGLISH PLAYWRIGHT AND POET

Celui de tous les Anglois qui a porté le plus loin la gloire du théatre comique est feu Mr. Congrave. Il n'a fait que peu de pieces, mais toutes sont excellentes dans leur genre. Les regles du théatre y sont rigoureusement observés; elles sont pleines de caracteres nuancés avec une extreme finesse; on n'y essuye pas la moindre mauvaise plaisanterie; vous y voyez par tout le langage des honnêtes gens avec des actions de fripons; ce qui prouve qu'il connoissoit bien son monde, & qu'il vivoit dans ce qu'on appelle la bonne compagnie.

The late Mr. *Congreve* rais'd the Glory of Comedy to a greater Height than any English Writer before or since his Time. He wrote only a few Plays, but they are all excellent in their kind. The Laws of the Drama are strictly observ'd in them; they abound with Characters all which are shadow'd with the utmost Delicacy, and we don't meet with so much as one low, or coarse Jest. The Language is every where that of Men of Honour, but their Actions are those of Knaves; a Proof that he was perfectly well acquainted with human Nature, and frequented with what we call polite Company.

"Dix-neuvième Lettre. Sur la comédie," in *Lettres Ecrites de Londres sur les Anglois et autres sujets* (1734), 175; "Sur la Comédie," in *Lettres philosophiques* (1964), 2:108. The translation is "Letter XIX. On Comedy," in *Letters Concerning the English Nation* (1733), 188.

Controversy

J'ai peur qu'en effet il n'y ait dans ces trois volumes bien des choses qui alarment les fanatiques. Le reste est bien pis. Mais plus la sauce est piquante mieux le poisson se vendra. Ce n'est pas la peine de se gêner pour des gens qui vous gêneront sur tout. Leur impertinence nous rend nôtre liberté toute entière, et c'est un fort bon marché.

I am afraid these three volumes actually contain a number of things that will alarm the fanatics. The rest is even worse. But the spicier the sauce, the more marketable the fish. It is not worth worrying about people who will annoy you about each and every thing. Their impertinence gives us total freedom, and that is a very good deal.

Letter from Ferney, circa October 15, 1770, to Gabriel Cramer, his publisher in Geneva. Voltaire must be referring here to the first three (of a projected nine) volumes of his *Questions sur l'Encyclopédie, par des Amateurs* (1770–1772).

Pierre Corneille (1606–1684)

RACINE AND CORNEILLE WERE THE TWO GREATEST
SEVENTEENTH-CENTURY FRENCH PLAYWRIGHTS

M. Racine n'est si au-dessus des autres qui ont tous dit les mêmes choses que lui, que parce qu'il les a mieux dites. Corneille n'est véritablement Grand, que quand il s'exprime aussi-bien qu'il pense.

Mr. Racine is only superior to all those who have said the same things as himself, because he has said them better: and Corneille is never truly great, but when he expresses himself as well as he thinks.

"Discours sur la tragédie à Mylord Bolingbrooke," in *Le Brutus de Monsieur de Voltaire* (1731), xvii; Besterman et al., *Œuvres complètes de Voltaire* (1998), 5:177. The translation is from *The Dramatic Works of Mr. De Voltaire* (1761), 1:219.

Ce grand & sublime Corneille,	This great and sublime Corneille,
Qui plut bien moins à notre oreille,	Who was less pleasing to the ear,
Qu'à notre esprit, qu'il étonna:	Than to the soul, which he astounded:

Le Temple du goût, in *Oeuvres de M.* de Voltaire. *Nouvelle Édition* (1739), 38; Besterman et al., *Œuvres complètes de Voltaire* (2003), 16:257. These lines of verse were later part of a text, posthumously titled, *Discours de M. de Voltaire en réponse aux invectives et outrages de ses détracteurs.*

C'est Corneille seul, qui commença à faire respecter notre langue des Etrangers, précisément dans le temps que le Cardinal de Richelieu commençoit à faire respecter la Couronne. L'un et l'autre porterent notre gloire dans l'Europe.

It is Corneille alone who began to win respect for our language in foreign lands, at precisely the time Cardinal Richelieu began to win respect for the Crown. Together, they spread our glory throughout Europe.

Discours prononcez dans l'Académie Françoise, Le Lundi 9 Mai MDCCXLVI (1746), 11; Besterman et al., *Œuvres complètes de Voltaire* (2003), 30a:28.

Quoiqu'on ne représente plus que six ou sept piéces de trente-trois qu'il a composées, il sera toujours le pére du théâtre. Il est le premier qui ait élevé le génie de la nation, & cela demande grace pour environ vingt de ses piéces qui sont, à quelques endroits près, ce que nous avons de plus mauvais par le stile, par la froideur de l'intrigue, par les amours déplacées & insipides, et par un entassement de raisonnemens alambiqués, qui sont l'opposé du tragique: mais on ne juge d'un grand homme que par ses chefs-d'œuvre, & non par ses fautes.

Though no more than six or seven of the thirty-three plays he composed are staged, nevertheless he will always be considered the father of theater. He was the first to elevate the genius of the nation, and that should atone for about twenty of his plays that in many places are the worst we have in terms of style, sterility of plot, ill-placed and insipid expressions of love, and a mass of overly refined declamations that are the opposite of true tragedy. But a great man is judged only by his masterpieces, and not by his mistakes.

"Ecrivains, dont plusieurs ont illustré le siécle," in *Le Siècle de Louis XIV* (1751), 2:196; Besterman et al., *Œuvres complètes de Voltaire* (2017), 12:86–87.

Every nation has its Shakespeare—Corneille was our french Shakespeare.

At Ferney, September 16, 1764, speaking in English to Dr. John Morgan, physician from Philadelphia and cofounder of the first medical school in the United States, now affiliated with the University of Pennsylvania. Recorded in Morgan, *The Journal of Dr. John Morgan of Philadelphia* (1907), 227. The pages in Morgan's journal relating to his visit to Ferney were reprinted in de Beer and Rousseau, *Voltaire's British Visitors* (1967), 77.

Country life

C'est la cour qu'on doit fuir, c'est aux champs qu'il faut vivre.

One must shun life at court, it is in the country that one must live.

Épitre à Madame Denis, sur l'agriculture, inscribed "A Ferney, ce 14 Mars 1761," in *Troisieme suite des mélanges de poesie, de littérature, d'histoire et de philosophie* (1765), 194; Besterman et al., *Œuvres complètes de Voltaire* (2013), 51b:299.

Un bon cultivateur est cent fois plus utile
Que ne fut autrefois Hésiode *ou* Virgile.

A good farmer is a hundred times more useful
Than ever were either *Hesiod* or *Virgil*.

Verse from the *Dialogue de Pégase et du vieillard* (1774), 12; Besterman et al., *Œuvres complètes de Voltaire* (2013), 76:530. The "old man" (*le vieillard*), who represents Voltaire, is speaking to the immortal winged Pegasus about the worldly realm of arts and letters from a Parisian perspective.

Courage

Un courage indompté dans le cœur des mortels
Fait ou les grands héros ou les grands criminels.

Untamed courage in the heart of mortal men
Doth either great heroes or great villains make.

Cicero to Cato in *Rome sauvée* (1752), act 5, scene 3; Besterman et al., *Œuvres complètes de Voltaire* (1992), 31a:259.

Criminal justice

Que les supplices des criminels soient utiles. Un homme pendu n'est bon à rien, &
un homme condamné aux ouvrages publics sert encor la patrie, & est une leçon
vivante.

Let the punishment of criminals be useful. A hanged man is good for nothing; and a man condemned to public works still serves his country, and is a living lesson.

"Loix civiles et ecclésiastiques," in *La Raison par Alphabet. Sixiéme édition* (1769), 26; Besterman et al., *Œuvres complètes de Voltaire* (1994), 36:323.

Critics

When critics are silent, it does not so much prove the age to be correct as dull.

Quoted in English by Dr. Charles Burney, who visited Voltaire at Ferney in July 1770. Burney, *The Present State of Music in France and Italy* (1771), 60.

Cuckold

Pline le naturaliste *dit,* coccix ova subdit in nidis alienis; ita plerique alienas uxores faciunt matres. *Le coucou dépose ses œufs dans le nid des autres oiseaux; ainsi force Romains rendent mères les femmes de leurs amis. La comparaison n'est pas trop juste.* Coxis *signifiant un coucou, nous en avons fait cocu. Que de choses on doit aux Romains! mais comme on altère le sens de tous les mots! le cocu, suivant la bonne grammaire, devrait être le galant & c'est le* mari.

Pliny, the naturalist, says: *"Coccyx ova subdit in nidis alienis; ita plerique alienas uxores faciunt matres"*—"the cuckoo deposits its eggs in the nest of other birds; so the Romans not infrequently made mothers of the wives of their friends." The comparison is not over just. *Coccyx* signifying a cuckoo, we have made it *cuckold.* What a number of things do we owe to the Romans! But as the sense of all words is subject to change, the term applied to *cuckold,* which, according to good grammar, should be the gallant, is appropriated to the *husband.*

"Adultère," in *Questions sur l'Encyclopédie* (1771), 1:76–77; Besterman et al., *Œuvres complètes de Voltaire* (2007), 38:102. The translation is from *A Philosophical Dictionary* (1824), 1:54.

Cuisine

Qu'un Cuisinier est un mortel divin!

A Cook is truly a divine mortal!

[*Le Mondain, ou l'Apologie du Luxe*], as *L'Homme du Monde, ou Défense du Mondain,* in *Oeuvres de M*. *de Voltaire. Nouvelle Édition* (1739), 118; Besterman et al., *Œuvres complètes de Voltaire* (2003), 16:302.

Custom—tradition

L'instruction fait tout, & la main de nos Peres
Grave en nos foibles cœurs ces premiers caracteres
Que l'exemple, & le temps nous viennent retracer,
Et que peut-être en nous, Dieu seul peut effacer.

Instruction is all, and the hand of our Fathers
Imprints in our feeble hearts our basic character,
Which example and time, combined, both reinforce,
And which, perhaps, God alone can erase.

Zaïre to Fatime in the opening scene of *Zaïre* (1732). *La Zayre, de M. de Voltaire* (1733), 8; Besterman et al., *Œuvres complètes de Voltaire* (1988), 8:435–436.

L'Empire de la coutume est bien plus vaste que celui de la nature; il s'étend sur les mœurs, sur tous les usages; il répand la variété sur la scène de l'Univers; la Nature y répand l'unité; elle établit partout un petit nombre de principes invariables: ainsi le fonds est partout le même; et la culture produit des fruits divers.

The dominion of custom is much more extensive than that of nature, and influences all manners and all usages. It diffuses variety over the face of the universe. Nature establishes unity, and every where settles a few invariable principles: the soil is still the same, but culture produces various fruits.

"Resumé de toute cette histoire," in *Essay sur l'histoire générale, et sur les moeurs et l'esprit des nations* (1761), 5:347; Besterman et al., *Œuvres complètes de Voltaire* (2015), 26c:331. The translation is from *Modern History Continued* (1761), in Smollett et al., *The Works of Mr. de Voltaire* (1761), 9:152.

Depuis Thalès jusqu'aux Professeurs de nos Universités, & jusqu'aux plus chimériques raisonneurs, & jusqu'à leurs plagiaires, aucun Philosophe n'a influé seulement sur les mœurs de la ruë où ils demeuraient. Pourquoi? Parce que les hommes se conduisent par la coûtume, & non par la Métaphysique.

From Thales down to and including the professors of our universities, the most chimerical reasoners, and their plagiarists, not one philosopher has had the slightest influence on public morals, even in the street where he lived. Why? Because men are led by custom, and not by metaphysics.

"XXIV. *Spinosa*" (*Doute* no. 24), in *Le Philosophe ignorant* (1766), 61–62; Besterman et al., *Œuvres complètes de Voltaire* (1987), 62:64. Thales was a Greek philosopher.

Étienne-Noël Damilaville (1723–1768)

ROYAL FUNCTIONARY IN THE OFFICE OF THE *CONTRÔLEUR GÉNÉRAL DES FINANCES* IN PARIS AND FRIEND AND DEVOTEE OF VOLTAIRE STARTING AROUND 1760

Dieu me devait un homme tel que vous, monsieur. Vous aimez Apollon et Cérès, et je sacrifie à l'un et à l'autre; vous détestez le fanatisme et l'hypocrisie, je les ai abhorrés depuis que j'ai eu l'âge de raison; vous aimez monsieur Thieriot, et il y a quarante ans que je le chéris comme l'homme de Paris qui aime le plus sincèrement la littérature et qui a le goût le plus épuré; vous vous êtes lié avec M. Diderot pour qui j'ai une estime égale à son mérite: la lumière qui éclaire son esprit échauffe son cœur.

God owed me a man like you, sir. You love Apollo and Ceres, and I am a devotee of both; you detest fanaticism and hypocrisy, I have abhorred them since I reached the age of reason; you love Thieriot, and for forty years now I have cherished him as the one man in Paris who most sincerely loves literature and has the most refined taste; you are in contact with M. Diderot whom I hold in esteem equal to his merit: the light which illuminates his mind warms his heart.

Letter from Ferney, November 19, 1760, to Étienne-Noël Damilaville in Paris. Nicolas-Claude Thieriot and Voltaire became friends in 1714 when they both clerked for a Parisian *procureur* named Alain.

Dante Alighieri (1265–1321)

ITALIAN RENAISSANCE POET

Sa réputation s'affermira toujours, parce qu'on ne le lit guères.

His reputation will stand firm forever, because scarcely anyone reads him.

"Lettre sur le Dante," in *Suite des mélanges de littérature, d'histoire et de philosophie* (1757), 4:201; Besterman et al., *Œuvres complètes de Voltaire* (2010), 45b:213.

Death

Va, j'aime mieux mourir que de craindre la mort.

Bah! I'd rather die than fear death.

Julius Cæsar to the Roman senator Dolabella, in act 5, scene 5, of *La Mort de César* (1736), 52; Besterman et al., *Œuvres complètes de Voltaire* (1998), 8:229.

Le coupable la craint, le malheureux l'appelle,
Le brave la défie, & marche au-devant d'elle,
Le sage, qui l'attend, la reçoit sans regrets.

The guilty do fear it, those who suffer seek it,
The fearless defy and rush head on to meet it,
The wise, without regret, await and welcome it.

Zamti, a Mandarin scholar, to his wife in act 1, scene 5, of *L'Orphelin de la Chine* (1755), 11; Besterman et al., *Œuvres complètes de Voltaire* (2009), 45a:138. The play was first staged in Paris at the Comédie-Française on August 20, 1755. The first English edition of the tragedy, *The Orphan of China, A Tragedy* (1759), was dedicated to the English actor David Garrick.

Il est très certain qu'on ne le sent point, ce n'est point un moment douleureux, elle ressemble au sommeil comme deux gouttes d'eau, ce n'est que l'idée qu'on ne se réveillera plus qui fait de la peine, c'est l'appareil de la mort qui est horrible, c'est la barbarie de l'extrême-onction, c'est la cruauté qu'on a de nous avertir que tout est fini pour nous. À quoi bon venir nous annoncer notre sentence? Elle s'exécutera bien sans que le notaire et les prêtres s'en mêlent. Il faut avoir fait ses dispositions de bonne heure, et ensuite n'y plus penser du tout. On dit quelquefois d'un homme, qu'il est mort comme un chien, mais vraiment un chien est très heureux de mourir sans tout cet abominable attirail dont on persecute le dernier moment de notre vie. Si on avait un peu de charité pour nous on nous laisserait mourir sans nous en rien dire.

It is very certain that death is not felt at all; it is not painful for a moment; it is like unto sleep as two drops of water. It is only the idea that we shall never wake again which gives us pain; it is the apparatus of death which is horrible,—the barbarity of extreme unction, the cruelty of notifying us that for us all is over. Of what good is it to us to pronounce our sentence? That sentence will be well executed without the notary and the priests taking any trouble about it. It is necessary for us to make our arrangements in good time, and then never to think of it again. They say sometimes of a man, "He died like a dog." But truly a dog is very happy to die without all that ceremony with which they persecute the last moments of our lives. If they had a little charity for us, they would let us die without saying anything to us about it.

Letter from Les Délices, May 9, 1764, to Mme Du Deffand in Paris. The translation is from James Parton, *Life of Voltaire* (1881), 2:350 (where it is broken into two paragraphs).

Les bêtes ont un grand avantage sur l'espèce humaine; il n'y a point de coup de cloche pour les animaux, quelque esprit qu'ils aient. Ils meurent tous sans qu'ils s'en doutent. Ils n'ont point de théologiens qui leur apprennent les quatre fins des bêtes. On ne gêne point leurs derniers moments par des cérémonies impertinentes et souvent odieuses. Il ne leur en coûte rien pour être enterrés, on ne plaide point pour leurs testaments.

Animals have an advantage over the human species. They do not hear the fatal hour strike, however intelligent they may be. They die having no idea of what has taken place. They have no theologians to instruct them in the Four Last Things for beasts. Their final moments are undisturbed by impertinent, often repellent ceremonies. It costs nothing to bury them, and no one fights over their estate.

Letter from Ferney, August 31, 1769, to Gottlob-Louis, comte de Schomberg, a French army general, and good friend of Friedrich-Melchior Grimm. Traditionally, good Christians were supposed to meditate upon Four Last Things relative to the fate of their souls: Death, Judgment Day, Heaven or Hell.

Les Délices

AN ESTATE AT GENEVA OUTSIDE THE CITY GATES
BUT WITHIN THE REPUBLIC OF GENEVA

J'ai toute ma famille dans un de mes ermitages, nommé les Délices, auprès de Genève. Je suis devenu jardinier, vigneron et laboureur.

I have my entire family housed in one of my retreats, called Les Délices, near Geneva. I have become a gardener, a vintner and plowman.

Letter from Les Délices, July 19, 1758, to Saint-Lambert, in Shuissengin near Mannheim. In the same letter, Voltaire said, "Mes Délices n'ont que 60 arpents, coûtent fort cher et ne me rapportent rien du tout" ("My Délices is just 60 acres in size, costs a fortune and generates no income"). From 1755 until 1760, Voltaire resided episodically on this property that he leased from François Tronchin.

J'achetai, par un marché singulier, & dont il n'y avait point d'exemple dans le Pays, un petit bien d'environ 60 arpens, qu'on me vendit le double de ce qu'il eut coûté auprès de Paris: mais le plaisir n'est jamais trop cher; la maison est jolie & commode; l'aspect en est charmant; il étonne & ne lasse point. C'est d'un côté le lac de Genève, c'est la ville de l'autre; le Rhône en sort à gros bouillons & forme un canal au bas de mon jardin.

I bought, by a very singular kind of contract, of which there was no example in that country, a small estate of about sixty acres, which they sold me for about twice as much as it would have cost me at Paris; but pleasure is never too dear. The house was pretty and commodious, and the prospect charming; it astonishes without tiring: on one side is the Lake of Geneva, and the city on the other. The Rhone runs from the former in vast gushes, forming a canal at the bottom of my garden.

Mémoires pour servir à la vie de Mr. de Voltaire (1784), 78; Besterman et al., *Œuvres complètes de Voltaire* (2010), 45c:401. The translation is from *Memoirs of the Life of Voltaire* (1784), 158–159. The *Mémoires* were begun around 1758.

J'ai encore une plus belle maison & une vue plus étendue à Lausanne; mais une maison près de Génève est beaucoup plus agréable. J'ai dans les deux habitations ce que les Rois ne donnent point, ou plutôt ce qu'ils ôtent, le repos & la liberté; j'ai encore ce qu'ils donnent quelquefois, & je ne le tiens pas d'eux. Je mets en pratique ce que j'ai dit dans le mondain.
    Ah le bon tems que ce siècle de fer!

At Lausanne I have another house, with a more extensive view; but a house near Geneva is much more agreeable. In these two abodes, I enjoy what Kings do not give, or rather what they take away: repose and freedom. I also have what they sometimes give, but had not of them. Here I put into practice what I said in *Le Mondain*:

What good times this be, our Age of Iron!

Mémoires pour servir à la vie de Mr. de Voltaire (1784), 79; Besterman et al., *Œuvres complètes de Voltaire* (2010), 45c:401–402. Voltaire's "house near Geneva" was Les Délices.

Je serai bientot obligé, je crois, de quitter ces Délices que vous m'avez rendues si chères en les célébrant. Il faut que j'habite le printemps, l'été et l'automne, la terre de Ferney que je fais valoir, et dans l'hiver il ne me faut qu'une chambre bien chaude. D'ailleurs, il importe fort peu qu'on soit mangé après sa mort par des vers du pays de Genève, ou par les vers du pays de Gex.

I soon will be obliged, I believe, to leave these Délices that you made so dear to me by your celebration of them. I must spend the spring, summer, and fall on my estate at Ferney, which I am currently improving, and in the winter all I need is one really warm room. Besides, it matters very little once we are gone whether we're food for worms in Geneva or the Pays de Gex.

Letter from Ferney, November 14, 1764, to George Keate in London. The year before Keate had published a poem called "The Alps," in which he made no specific mention of Les Délices. In 1768, however, Keate did pay homage to Ferney, Voltaire's new year-round home, in "Ferney: An Epistle to Monsieur de Voltaire."

Demagoguery

Il y a eu des gens qui ont dit autrefois, vous croyez des choses incompréhensibles, contradictoires, impossibles, parce que nous vous l'avons ordonné; faites donc des choses injustes parce que nous vous l'ordonnons. Ces gens là raisonnoient à merveille. Certainement qui est en droit de vous rendre absurde est en droit de vous rendre injuste. Si vous n'opposez point aux ordres de croire l'impossible l'intelligence que Dieu a mise dans vôtre esprit, vous ne devez point opposer aux ordres de malfaire la justice que Dieu a mise dans votre cœur. Une faculté de votre ame étant une fois tirannisée, toutes les autres facultés doivent l'être également. Et c'est là ce qui a produit tous les crimes religieux dont la terre a été inondée.

Once there were those who said: You believe things that are incomprehensible, inconsistent, impossible because we have commanded you to believe them; therefore, do what is unjust because we command you to do so. Such people showed admirable reasoning. Truly, whoever can make you look absurd can make you act unjustly. If the God-given understanding of your mind does not resist a demand to believe what is impossible, then you will not resist a demand to do wrong to that God-given sense of justice in your heart. Once one faculty of your soul is subject to tyranny, other faculties will follow as well. And from this derives all those crimes of religion that have overrun the world.

"Onzième lettre à l'occasion des miracles, Ecrite par Mr. Théro à Mr. Covelle," in *Collection des lettres sur les miracles* (1765), 136–137; Besterman et al., *Œuvres complètes de Voltaire* (2018), 60d:291. Robert Covelle was a jeweler, "Citoyen de Genève," and a married man who had been condemned by the Consistoire de Genève in March 1764 for adulterous relations with a woman by whom he fathered a child. Norman L. Torrey rendered the core idea in this quote as "any one who has the power to make you believe absurdities has the power to make you commit injustices." See Torrey, *Les Philosophes* (1961), 277.

René Descartes (1596–1650)

MATHEMATICIAN AND PHILOSOPHER

Je ne crois pas qu'on ose à la vérité comparer en rien sa Philosophie avec celle de Newton; la premiere est un essay, la seconde est un chef-d'œuvre. Mais celui qui nous a mis sur la voye de la vérité vaut peut-être celui qui a été depuis au bout de cette carriere.

I do not, in truth, believe one may go so far as to compare his Philosophy in any way with that of Newton: the first is a rough sketch, the second a masterpiece. But he who has set us on the road to truth may be as worthy as he who has since gone the course.

"Quatorzième Lettre. Sur *Des Cartes* et *Newton*," in *Lettres Ecrites de Londres sur les Anglois et autres sujets* (1734), 114–115; "Sur Descartes et Newton," in *Lettres philosophiques* (1964), 2:7.

Le plus grand mathématicien de son tems, mais le philosophe qui connut le moins la nature, si on le compare à ceux qui l'ont suivi.

The greatest mathematician of his time, but the most ignorant in the philosophy of nature, compared to those who appeared in the world since.

"Ecrivains, dont plusieurs ont illustré le siécle," in *Le Siècle de Louis XIV* (1751), 2:370; Besterman et al., *Œuvres complètes de Voltaire* (2017), 12:93.

Abbé Pierre Desfontaines (1685–1745)

FORMER JESUIT, JOURNALIST, TRANSLATOR,
AND PAMPHLETEER

Qu'est devenu l'abbé Desfontaines? Dans quelle loge a-t-on mis ce chien qui mordait ses maîtres? Hélas! je lui donnerais encore du pain, tout enragé qu'il est.

What has become of the Abbé Desfontaines? In what box have they caged that dog who bit the hand of his masters? Alas! rabbid as he is, I would still give him some bread.

Letter from Cirey, circa February 2, 1736, to Claude-François Berger in Paris.

Cet abbé Desfontaines est celui-là même qui, pour se justifier, disait à Mr. le comte d'Argenson: il faut que je vive; *& à qui le Mr. le comte d'Argenson répondit:* je n'en vois pas la nécessité.

This abbé Desfontaines is the very same person who, in order to justify what he'd done, told Monsieur le comte d'Argenson: *I do have to live*; and to whom Monsieur le comte d'Argenson replied: *I don't see the need.*

Commentaire historique sur les Oeuvres de l'auteur de La Henriade. &c. (1776), 12; Moland, *Œuvres complètes de Voltaire* (1883), 1:77. If this conversation took place, it may have occurred in 1724, during d'Argenson's relatively brief tenure as *lieutenant général de police*. D'Argenson might well have shared this anecdote with his friend Voltaire, a former classmate at Louis-le-Grand. The same anecdote had appeared in print eight years earlier, with no names named, in Honoré Lacombe de Prézel, *Dictionnaire des portails historiques, anecdotes, et traits remarquables des hommes illustres* (1758), 1:533.

Desire

On ne peut désirer ce qu'on ne connoit pas.

We cannot desire what we do not know.

Zaïre to Fatime in *Zaïre* (1732), act 1, scene 1. *La Zayre, de M. de Voltaire* (1733), 4; Besterman et al., *Œuvres complètes de Voltaire* (1988), 8:431.

Despair

Quand on a tout perdu, quand on n'a plus d'espoir,
La vie est un opprobre, & la mort un devoir.

When one has lost everything and has no more hope,
'Tis a disgrace to live, and a duty to die.

Mérope, widow of the late king of Messene, to Euriclès, in *Mérope* (1743), act 2, scene 7; *La Mérope Françoise, avec quelques petites pièces de littérature* (1744), 26; Besterman et al., *Œuvres complètes de Voltaire* (1991), 17:283.

Dictionary

Un dictionnaire sans citations est un squelette.

A dictionary without citations is a mere skeleton.

Letter from Les Délices, August 11, 1760, to Charles Pinot Duclos in Paris. In this letter, Voltaire agreed to contribute to a revised dictionary of the French language to be compiled by the French Academy. He faulted the most recent edition (1740) for its lack of quotations illustrating word usage.

Je crois qu'il faudra dorénavant tout mettre en dictionnaire. La vie est trop courte pour lire de suite tant de gros livres: malheur aux longues dissertations! Un dictionnaire vous met sous la main dans le moment, la chose dont vous avez besoin. Ils sont utiles surtout aux personnes déjà instruites, qui cherchent à se rappeler ce qu'ils ont su.

Henceforth I believe that everything must be put in the form of a dictionary. Life is too short to plow through a lot of big books: woe unto long dissertations! A dictionary instantly delivers exactly what you need. They are especially useful for people already learned, who wish to recall things they know already.

Letter from Ferney, January 9, 1763, to the Reverend Élie Bertrand in Berne.

Un dictionnaire doit être un monument de vérité et de goût, et non pas un magasin de fantaisies.

A dictionary must be a monument to truth and good taste, and not a storehouse of whimsy.

Letter from Ferney, October–November 1768, to the Paris-based publisher Charles-Joseph Panckoucke.

Denis Diderot (1713–1784)

FRENCH *PHILOSOPHE*, NOVELIST, ART CRITIC,
PLAYWRIGHT, AND EDITOR IN CHIEF
OF THE *ENCYCLOPÉDIE*

Il a presque désavoué d'Alembert sur l'article Genève. . . . Il faut d'ailleurs que Diderot soit le plus mou et le plus faible des hommes, pour continuer à travailler à l'Encyclopédie sous la potence. . . . d'Alembert se conduit en homme libre, et Diderot en esclave.

He all but denounced d'Alembert over the article on Geneva. . . . Diderot has got to be the weakest, most servile of men to carry on as he does with the *Encyclopédie* under the shadow of the gallows. . . . d'Alembert conducts himself like a free man, Diderot like a slave.

Letter from Monrion (Lausanne), February 25, 1758, to the comte d'Argental in Paris.

Figure 13. Jean-Antoine Houdon, *Denis Diderot*, circa 1771. Terra cotta bust. Yale University Art Gallery (gift of Mrs. Charles Seymour Jr. in memory of her husband). Photograph courtesy of Yale University Art Gallery.

Diderot ne m'a point écrit. C'est un homme dont il est plus aisé d'avoir un livre qu'une lettre.

Diderot has not written to me at all. He's a man whom it is easier to get a book out of than a letter.

Letter from Ferney, circa June 7, 1758, to d'Argental in Paris.

Sans avoir jamais vu M. Diderot, sans trouver Le Père de famille *plaisant, j'ai toujours respecté ses profondes connaissances.*

Without ever having met M. Diderot, or finding his *Père de famille* very pleasurable, I have always respected the depth of his knowledge.

Letter from Les Délices, June 4, 1760, to Charles Palissot in Paris.

Discretion

Il n'y a rien à gagner avec un enthousiaste. Il ne faut pas s'aviser de dire à un homme les défauts de sa maîtresse, ni à un plaideur le faible de sa cause, ni des raisons à un illuminé.

You can get nowhere with a zealot. Never presume to point out the faults of his mistress to a man, the weakness of his case to a claimant, or reason to a mystic.

"De la religion des Quakers," in *Oeuvres de M.* *de Voltaire. Nouvelle Edition* (1752), 2:40; Moland, *Œuvres complètes de Voltaire* (1879), 22:85.

Disputes—quarrels

Sottise des deux parts, est comme on sait la devise de toutes les querelles.

Weakness on both sides is, as we know, the motto of all quarrels.

"Sottise des deux parts" (1728), first published in *Oeuvres de M.* *de Voltaire. Nouvelle Edition* (1750), 167; Besterman et al., *Œuvres complètes de Voltaire* (2004), 3a:219. The translation is from *A Philosophical Dictionary* (1824), 6:346.

Les opinions ont plus causé de maux sur ce petit globe que la peste et les tremblements de terre.

Opinions have caused more evil on this little globe of ours than pestilence and earthquakes.

Letter from Les Délices, January 5, 1759, thought to have been sent to Élie Bertrand in Berne.

Divorce

Le divorce est probablement de la même date à peu-près que le mariage. Je crois pourtant que le mariage est de quelques semaines plus ancien, c'est-à-dire, qu'on se querella avec sa femme au bout de quinze jours, qu'on la battit au bout d'un mois, & qu'on se sépara après six semaines de cohabitation.

Divorce probably dates from about the same time as marriage. However, I do believe that marriage preceded divorce by a few weeks, which is to say that the man quarreled with his wife after two weeks, beat her after a month, and that they separated after six weeks of conjugal living.

"Divorce," in *Questions sur l'Encylopédie* (1770), 3:341; Besterman et al., *Œuvres complètes de Voltaire* (2009), 40:502.

Drama—theater

Monsieur, combien avez-vous de piéces de théatre en France? dit Candide à l'Abbé; lequel répondit, Cinq ou six mille; C'est beaucoup dit Candide; combien y en a-t-il de bonnes? Quinze ou seize, répliqua l'autre.—C'est beaucoup, dit Martin.

"Sir, how many plays do you have in France?" Candide said to the abbé, who replied, "Five or six thousand."
"That's a lot," said Candide. "How many of them are good?"
"Fifteen or sixteen," replied the other.
"That's a lot," said Martin.

"Ce qui arriva en France à Candide & à Martin," chap. 22 in *Candide, ou L'Optimisme, Par Mr. de Voltaire* (1763), 116; Besterman et al., *Œuvres complètes de Voltaire* (1980), 48:211. In English, *Candide, Zadig, and Other Stories* (2001), 70. This passage did not appear in the first edition of *Candide*.

Le théatre instruit mieux que ne fait un gros livre.

The theater is better at instructing than any weighty tome.

In the poem "Les Trois Maniéres" (1763), published in *Contes de Guillaume Vadé* (1764), 24; Besterman et al., *Œuvres complètes de Voltaire* (2014), 57b:123.

Dreams

Les rêves sont les intermèdes de la comédie que joue la Raison humaine. Alors l'Imagination, se trouvant seule, fait la parodie de la pièce que la Raison jouait pendant le jour.

Dreams are breaks in the drama staged by the Mind. Left to itself, Imagination creates a parody of the play staged during waking hours by Reason.

Notebooks or *cahiers* unpublished in Voltaire's lifetime; Besterman, *Voltaire's Notebooks II* (1968), in *Œuvres complètes de Voltaire*, vol. 82 (1968); first published in Besterman, *Voltaire's* (1952), 2:260.

Abbé Jean-Baptiste Du Bos (1670–1742)

FRENCH DIPLOMATIC AGENT UNDER JEAN-BAPTISTE COLBERT,
ART THEORIST AND CRITIC, HISTORIAN, AND MEMBER
OF THE ACADÉMIE FRANÇAISE

Il senno è grande, lo stile cattivo; bisogna legger lo; ma lo rileggerlo sarebbe tedioso. Questa bella prerogativa d'esser spesso riletto è il privilegio dell' ingegno, e quello dell'Ariosto. Io lo releggo ogni giorno mercè alle vostre grazie.

He is very perceptive, his style is poor; he must be read, but to reread him would be dreary. The superb prerogative of being read repeatedly is the privilege of genius, and of Ariosto. I reread him every day, thanks to you.

Letter from Potsdam, circa June 1751, to Francesco Algarotti in Venice.

L'Abbé du Bos, homme d'un très grand sens, qui écrivait son traité sur la poësie & sur la peinture, vers l'an 1714, trouva que, dans toute l'histoire de France il n'y avait de vrai sujet de poëme épique que la destruction de la Ligue par Henri le Grand.

The Abbé *du Bos*, a most sensible man, who wrote his treatise on poetry and painting around the year 1714, believed that in all of French history the only true subject for epic poetry was the destruction of the Ligue by *Henry the Great*.

"Des Beaux Arts," in *Essay sur l'histoire générale, et sur les moeurs et l'esprit des nations* (1757), 6:128; Besterman et al., *Œuvres complètes de Voltaire* (2016), 13d:26.

Duty

Qui fait plus qu'il ne doit, ne sçait point me servir.

He who goes beyond his duty knows it not.

Mahomet to his slave Seid, act 2, scene 3, of *Le Fanatisme, ou Mahomet le Prophete* (1743), 29; Besterman et al., *Œuvres complètes de Voltaire* (2002), 20b:200.

Eh que peut craindre celui qui fait son devoir? Je connais la rage de mes ennemis; je sçais toutes leurs calomnies; mais quand on ne cherche qu'à faire du bien aux hommes, & qu'on n'offense point le Ciel, on ne redoute rien, ni pendant la vie, ni à la mort.

Well, what can he fear who does his duty? I am aware of my enemies' rage, I know all their slanders; but when one seeks only to do right by men, and does not offend heaven, one fears nothing, either in life or in the face of death.

Socrates to Sophronime, act 2, scene 1, of *Socrate, ouvrage dramatique, traduit de l'anglais de feu M. Tompson* (1759), 49; Besterman et al., *Œuvres complètes de Voltaire* (2009), 49b:316. In posthumous editions of the play, the word "Eh" appears as "Eh!" or Hé."

Ecclesiastes

Ce Livre . . . montre le néant des choses humaines; il conseille en même-tems, l'usage raisonnable des biens que Dieu a donné aux hommes. Il ne fait pas de la Sagesse un fantôme hideux & révoltant; c'est un cours de Morale fait pour les gens du monde.

This Book . . . reveals the meaninglessness of human existence; at the same time, it advises the rational use of the good things man has been given by God. It does not make a hideous, revolting illusion of Wisdom; it is a lesson in Morality fit for men of the world.

"Avertissement," in *Précis de l'Ecclésiaste, en vers, par Mr. de Voltaire* (1759), 3; Besterman et al., *Œuvres complètes de Voltaire* (2010), 49a:204.

Egotism

C'est n'être bon à rien, de n'être bon qu'à soi.

To be good only to yourself is to be good for nothing.

Septième discours sur la vraie vertu, in *Discours en vers sur l'homme* (1738), in *Mélanges de Poésies, de littérature, d'histoire et de philosophie* (1757), 50; Besterman et al., *Œuvres complètes de Voltaire* (1991), 17:524.

The eighteenth century

Ah le bon tems que ce Siècle de Fer!

What good times this be, our Age of Iron!

[*Le Mondain, ou l'Apologie du Luxe*], as *L'Homme du Monde, ou Défense du Mondain*, in *Oeuvres de Mᵣ. de Voltaire. Nouvelle Edition* (1739), 114; Besterman et al., *Œuvres complètes de Voltaire* (2003), 16:296. In Smollett et al., *The Works of Mr. de Voltaire* (1764), 32:21, this line was translated as "This iron age brings happy days."

Emotions

On parla des passions: Ah! qu'elles sont funestes! disoit Zadig. Ce sont les vents qui enflent les voiles du vaisseau, repartit l'Hermite: elles le submergent quelquefois; mais sans elles l'homme ne pourroit voguer.

They talked about human passions. Ah! How deadly they are! said Zadig. They are the winds that swell the sails of a vessel, replied the Hermit; sometimes they cause it to capsize; but without them, man could not steer ahead.

"L'Hermite," in *Zadig ou la Destinée. Histoire orientale* (1748), 178; Besterman et al., *Œuvres complètes de Voltaire* (2004), 30b:215.

The *Encyclopédie*

Je suis au service des illustres auteurs de l'Encyclopédie: Je me tiendrai très honoré de pouvoir contribuer, quoique faiblement, au plus grand et au plus beau monument de la nation et de la littérature.

I am at the service of the illustrious authors of the *Encyclopédie*; I consider myself honored to contribute, however inadequately, to the nation's and to literature's finest monument.

Letter from Les Délices, December 9, 1755, to Jean le Rond d'Alembert in Paris.

Ce n'est pas la peine d'écrire pour ne point dire la vérité. Il n'y a déjà dans l'Encyclopédie que trop d'articles de métaphysique pitoyables: si l'on est obligé de leur ressembler, il faut se taire.

There is no point in writing if it isn't to tell the truth. In the *Encyclopédie*, there are already too many sorry articles on metaphysics: if one must follow their example, it is better to say nothing.

Letter from Les Délices, January 7, 1760, to Mme d'Épinay, possibly in Paris.

Jamais vingt volumes in-folio ne feront de révolution; ce sont les petits livres portatifs à trente sous qui sont à craindre. Si l'Évangile avait coûté douze cents sesterces, jamais la religion chrétienne ne se serait établie.

Twenty folio volumes will never cause a revolution; it is pocket-sized books at thirty sous apiece that are to be feared. If the Gospels had cost twelve hundred sesterces, Christianity would never have taken hold.

Letter from Ferney, April 5, 1766, to Jean le Rond d'Alembert in Paris.

*Cet ouvrage immense et immortel semble accuser la briéveté de la vie des hommes. Il a été commencé par messieurs d'*Alembert *et* Diderot, *traversé et persécuté par l'envie et par l'ignorance, ce qui est le destin de toutes les grandes entreprises. Il eût été à souhaiter que quelques mains étrangères n'eussent pas défiguré cet important ouvrage par des déclamations puériles et des lieux communs insipides, qui n'empêchent pas que le reste de l'ouvrage ne soit utile au genre humain.*

This immense and immortal work seems to underscore the brevity of human life. Initiated by Messieurs d'*Alembert* and *Diderot*, it was obstructed and persecuted by envy and ignorance, which is the fate of all great undertakings.

Though we might wish that some few puerile perorations and insipid plati-
tudes by alien hands had not spoilt this important work, what is left will prove
useful to humankind.

Le Siècle de Louis XIV, 270, in Beaumarchais, *Œuvres complètes de Voltaire*, vol. 22 (1785);
Besterman et al., *Œuvres complètes de Voltaire* (2017), 12:217.

Enemies

J'ai toujours fait une prière à Dieu, qui est fort courte. La voici: Mon Dieu, rendez nos ennemis bien ridicules! *Dieu m'a exaucé.*

I have always made one prayer to God, a very short one. Here it is: *Lord, make
our enemies as ridiculous as possible!* And God granted it.

Letter from Ferney, May 16, 1767, to Étienne-Noël Damilaville in Paris.

Rien n'est si ordinaire que d'imiter ses ennemis, & d'employer leurs armes.

Nothing could be more common than to imitate our enemies, and to fight the
way they fight.

"Oracle," in *Questions sur l'Encyclopédie, par des Amateurs* (1774), 4:190; Besterman et al.,
Œuvres complètes de Voltaire (2010), 42b:314.

England

*Je sais que c'est un pays où les arts sont tous honorés et récompensés, où il y a de la
différence entre les conditions, mais point d'autre entre les hommes que celles du
mérite. C'est un pays où on pense librement et noblement sans être retenu par aucune
crainte servile. Si je suivais mon inclination, ce serait là que je me fixerais dans
l'idée seulement d'apprendre à penser.*

I know that this is a country where all the arts are honored and rewarded,
where there is a difference among conditions but no other among men except
merit. This is a country where people think freely and nobly without being
held back by servility. If I followed my inclination, I would settle here with
the idea of simply learning how to think.

Letter from London, August 12, 1726, to Nicolas-Claude Thieriot in Paris.

All that I wish for, is to see you one day in London. . . . You will see a nation
fond of their liberty, learned, witty, despising life and death, a nation of philosophers, not but that there are some fools in England, every country has its
madmen. It may be, French folly is pleasanter, than English madness, but by
god English wisdom and English Honesty is above yours.

Letter written in English from London, October 26, 1726, to Thieriot in Paris.

England is [*the*] meeting [*place*] of all religions, as the Royal exchange is the rendez vous of all foreigners.

Notebooks or *cahiers* unpublished in Voltaire's lifetime: Besterman, *Voltaire's Notebooks I* (1968), in *Œuvres complètes de Voltaire* (1968), 81:51; first published in Besterman, *Voltaire's Notebooks* (1952), 1:31. This entry was written in English in 1726.

Reason is free here and walks her own way, hypochondriacs especially are well come. No manner of living appears strange; we have men who walk six miles a day for their health, feed upon roots, never taste flesh, wear a coat thinner than yr. ladies do in the hottest days.

Letter written in English from London, April 11, 1728, to Rolland Puchot, comte des Alleurs, in Paris.

Un Poëte Anglois, disois-je, est un homme libre qui asservit sa Langue à son génie; le François est un esclave de la rime, obligé de faire quelquefois quatre vers, pour exprimer une pensée qu'un Anglois peut rendre en une seule ligne. L'Anglois dit tout ce qu'il veut, le François ne dit que ce qu'il peut. L'un court dans une carriere vaste, & l'autre marche avec des entraves dans un chemin glissant & étroit.

An English poet, said I, is a freeman, who can subject his language to his genius; whilst the Frenchman is a slave to rhime, oblig'd sometimes to make four verses to express a sentiment, that an Englishman can give you in one [line]. An Englishman says what he will; a Frenchman only what he can. One runs along a large and open field, whilst the other walks in shackles, through a narrow and slippery road.

"Discours sur la tragédie à Mylord Bolingbrooke," in *Le Brutus de Monsieur de Voltaire* (1731), iv–v; Besterman et al., *Œuvres complètes de Voltaire* (1998), 5:159. The translation is from *The Dramatic Works of Mr. De Voltaire* (1761), 1:202.

Il a manqué jusqu'à présent à presque tous les Auteurs Tragiques de votre Nation, cette pureté, cette conduite réguliere, ces bienséances de l'action & du stile, cette élégance, & toutes ces finesses de l'Art, qui ont établi la réputation du Théâtre François depuis le Grand Corneille. Mais vos Piéces les plus irrégulieres ont un grand mérite, c'est celui de l'action.

In nearly all the Tragic Authors of your Nation until now, there has been a want of that purity, that regular conduct, that decorum in action and style, and all those fine strokes of art which have established the reputation of the

French Theatre since the Great Corneille. But even your most irregular Plays do have one great merit, which is their action.

"Discours sur la tragédie à Mylord Bolingbrooke," in *Le Brutus de Monsieur de Voltaire* (1731), vii; Besterman et al., *Œuvres complètes de Voltaire* (1998), 5:163.

C'est icy le pays des Sectes: multae sunt mansiones in domo patris mei*: un Anglais, comme homme libre va au ciel par le chemin qui lui plaît.*

This is the land of Sects: *multae sunt mansiones in domo patris mei.* An Englishman, as a free man, goes to heaven in whatever way pleases him.

"Cinquième Lettre sur la Religion Anglicane," in *Lettres Ecrites de Londres sur les Anglois et autres sujets* (1734), 33; "Sur la Religion anglicane," in *Lettres philosophiques* (1964), 1:61. *Multae sunt mansiones in domo patris mei* is, in Latin, a line from John 14:2: "In my Father's house are many mansions."

S'il n'y avoit en Angleterre qu'une Religion, le Despotisme seroit à craindre; s'il y en avoit deux, elles se couperoient la gorge; mais il y en a trente, & elles vivent en paix & heureuses.

If one religion only were allowed in *England*, the government would very possibly become arbitrary; if there were but two, the people wou'd cut one another's throats; but as there are such a multitude, they all live happy, and in peace.

"Sixième Lettre. Sur les Presbyteriens," in *Lettres Ecrites de Londres sur les Anglois et autres sujets* (1734), 43; "Sur les Presbiteriens," in *Lettres philosophiques* (1964) 1:74. The translation is "Letter VI. On the Presbyterians," in *Letters Concerning the English Nation* (1733), 45.

La nation Angloise est la seule de la terre, qui soit parvenue à regler le pouvoir des Roys en leur resistant, & qui d'effort en efforts ait enfin établi ce gouvernement sage, où le Prince tout puissant pour faire du bien, a les mains liées pour faire le mal, où les Seigneurs sont grands sans insolence, & sans vassaux, & où le peuple partage le gouvernement sans confusion.

The English are the only people on earth who have been able to prescribe limits to the power of Kings by resisting them; and who, by a series of struggles, have at last establish'd that wise Government, where the Prince, is all powerful to do good, and at the same time is restrain'd from committing evil; where the Nobles are great without insolence, tho' there are no Vassals; and where the people share in the government without confusion.

"Huitième Lettre sur le Parlement," in *Lettres Ecrites de Londres sur les Anglois et autres sujets* (1734), 51; "Sur le Parlement," in *Lettres philosophiques* (1964), 1:89. The translation is "Letter VIII. On the Parliament," in *Letters Concerning the English Nation* (1733), 53.

Cette Isle, qui a produit les plus grands Philosophes de la terre, n'est pas aussi fertile pour les beaux arts; & si les Anglais ne s'appliquent sérieusement à suivre les préceptes de leurs excellens citoyens Adisson & Pope, ils n'approcheront pas des autres Peuples en fait de goût & de litterature.

This island, which has produced the finest philosophers in the world, is not equally productive of the fine arts; and if the *English* do not seriously apply themselves to the study of those precepts which were given them by their excellent countrymen, *Addison* and *Pope*, they will never come near to other nations in point of taste and literature.

"À Monsieur le Marquis Scipion Maffei, Auteur de la Mérope Italienne, & de beaucoup d'autres célébres Ouvrages," de facto preface to *La Mérope Françoise, avec quelques petites pièces de littérature* (1744), x; Besterman et al., *Œuvres complètes de Voltaire* (1991), 27:223. This translation is from *The Dramatic Works of Mr. De Voltaire* (1762), 3:253–254.

T'is a great pity that y^r nation is so over-run with such prodigious numbers of scandals and scurrilities. However one ought to look upon 'em as the bad fruits of a very good tree, call'd liberty.

Letter from Paris, March 29, 1749, in English to Sir Everard Fawkener in London. Voltaire mistakenly wrote "lumbers of scandals" when he meant to say "numbers."

I am sorry that England has sunk into romances, the time of Newton, Locke, Pope, Adisson, Steele, Swift, is gone.

Letter from Berlin, March 27, 1752, in English to Sir Everard Fawkener in London.

Dans ce pays-ci il est bon de tuer de tems en tems un Amiral pour encourager les autres.

In this country [England] it is a good thing to kill an admiral from time to time to encourage the others.

Martin to Candide, in reference to the hanging, March 14, 1757, of Admiral Byng by the British government because the French defeated him in battle. "Candide & Martin vont sur les côtes d'Angleterre ce qu'ils y voyent," chap. 23 in *Candide, ou L'Optimisme* (1759), 212; Besterman et al., *Œuvres complètes de Voltaire* (1980), 48:214. In English, *Candide, Zadig, and Other Stories* (2001), 78–79.

J'ai ma charrue, et des livres anglais, car j'aime autant les livres de cette nation que j'aime peu leurs personnes. . . . Il y en a peu qui ressemblent à Bolingbroke; celui-là valait mieux que ses livres, mais pour les autres Anglais leurs livres valent mieux qu'eux.

I have my plow, and some English books, for I like that nation's books more than I like the people who wrote them. . . . Few of them are on a par with Bolingbroke; he was better than his books, whereas other Englishmen pale in comparison to their books.

Letter from Les Délices or the château de Tournay, February 18, 1760, to Mme Du Deffand in Paris.

Les Anglais ont été longtemps plus imbéciles que nous, il est vrai, mais vous voyez comme ils se sont corrigés. Ils n'ont plus de moines ni de couvents, mais ils ont des flottes victorieuses; leur clergé fait de bons livres et des enfants; leurs paysans ont rendu fertiles des terres qui ne l'étaient pas; leur commerce embrasse le monde, et leurs philosophes nous ont appris des vérités dont nous ne nous doutions pas. J'avoue que je suis jaloux, quand je jette les yeux sur l'Angleterre.

The English have long been bigger imbeciles than we are, it is true, but see the progress they have made. They have neither monks nor convents, but victorious fleets; their clergy beget books and children; their commerce encircles the world; and their philosophers have taught us truths we had not an inkling of. I confess to a feeling of envy when I think of England.

Letter from Ferney, November 6, 1762, to Louis-René de Caradeuc de la Chalotais in Rennes.

The English, added he, have some fine Authors, they are I swear by God himself, the first Nation in Europe, and if ever I smell of a Resurrection, or come a second time on Earth, I will pray God to make me be born in England, the land of Liberty. These are four things w'ch I adore that the english boast of so greatly with his fore finger of the right hand counting them up, and naming them distinctly with an emphasis—*Liberty, Property, Newton & Locke.*

At Ferney, September 16. 1764, speaking in English in the presence of Dr. John Morgan; from *The Journal of Dr. John Morgan of Philadelphia: From the City of Rome to the City of London 1764* (1907), 220–221. Reprinted in de Beer and Rousseau, *Voltaire's British Visitors* (1967), 73.

You have the better government. If it gets bad, heave it into the ocean; that's why you have the ocean all about you. You are the slaves of laws. The French are the slaves of men.

Speaking to James Boswell at Ferney, December 27, 1764, from the *Boswell Papers*, 4:130, quoted in Boswell, *James Boswell* (2008), 309.

Tout est soumis à la loi, à commencer par la Royauté & par la Religion.

Everything is subject to the law, starting with the Crown and Religion.

"Troisième entretien. Si l'homme est né méchant & enfant du diable," in *L'A, B, C, ou Dialogues entre A. B. C.* (1769), 2:228; Besterman et al., *Œuvres complètes de Voltaire* (2011), 65:234.

Les Anglais crient property and liberty. C'est le cri de l'amour de soy même.

The English cry out: property and liberty. It is an expression of self-respect.

Le Sottisier de Voltaire (1880), 134. See also Besterman, *Voltaire's Notebooks* (1952), 2:321; Besterman et al., *Œuvres complètes de Voltaire* (1968), 82:462. The so-called *Sottisier* is a compilation of comments by Voltaire copied from his notebooks, purchased by Catherine the Great from Mme Denis after her uncle's death.

Liberty, and property: c'est le cri anglais. Il vaut mieux que St. George & mon droit, St. Denis & mon joie: c'est le cri de la nature.

"Liberty and property" is the great national cry of the English. It is certainly better than "St. George and my right," or "St. Denis and Montjoie"; it is the cry of nature.

"Propriété," in *Questions sur l'Encyclopédie, par des Amateurs* (1771), 8:245; Besterman et al., *Œuvres complètes de Voltaire* (2013), 43:25. The translation is from *A Philosophical Dictionary* (1824), 5:326. "St. George et mon droit" must refer to the British royal motto, "Dieu et mon droit." "Montjoie Saint Denis!" was a French battle cry dating back to the reign of Louis VI.

He compared the British nation to a hogshead of their own strong beer; the top of which is froth, the bottom dregs, the middle excellent.

From a conversation at Ferney, July 1772, quoted in John Moore, *A View of Society and Manners in France, Switzerland, and Germany: With Anecdotes relating to some Eminent Characters* (1779), 270.

Elle est supérieure dans la guerre, dans les loix, dans les arts, dans le commerce.

She is superior in warfare, in law, the arts, and in commerce.

Referring to England in "Éloge historique de la Raison, prononcé dans une académie de province par M. . . . . . ," (1774), in *Nouveaux Mélanges philosophiques, historiques, critiques, &c. &c.* (1775), 198; Besterman et al., *Œuvres complètes de Voltaire* (2013), 76:370.

Quand je vois un Anglois rude & aimant les Procès, je dis, voilà un Normand qui est venu avec Guillaume le Conquérant: quand je vois un homme doux & poli, en voilà un qui est venu avec les Plantagenets; un brutal, voilà un Danois; car votre Nation, est aussi bien que votre Langue, est un galimatias de plusieurs autres.

When I see an Englishman subtle and fond of law-suits, I say: "There is a Norman, who came with William the Conqueror!" When I see a man good-natured and polite, "that is one who came with the Plantagenets;" a brutal character, "that is a Dane;" for your nation, as well as your language, is a medley of many others.

Spoken in English to Martin Sherlock, April 1776; quoted in Sherlock's *Letters from an English Traveller* (1780), 163–164. The translation into French is from Sherlock, *Lettres d'un voyageur anglois* (1779), 148–149.

English (speaking the language)

Pour parler anglois il faut mettre la langue entre les dents, et j'ai perdu mes dents.

To speak English one must place the tongue between the teeth, and I have lost my teeth.

To James Boswell Ferney, December 24, 1764, when Boswell asked if he still spoke English. The reply was "no," followed by this explanation; from the *Boswell Papers*, 4:130, quoted in Boswell, *James Boswell* (2008), 309.

Enlightenment

Il faut que les âmes pensantes se frottent l'une contre l'autre, pour faire jaillir de la lumière.

It is necessary for thoughtful souls to rub against one another in order to produce a spark of light.

Letter from Potsdam, December 4, 1751, to Charles-Emmanuel de Crussol, duc d'Uzès, in Uzès near Nîmes.

Tout ce que je vois jette les semences d'une révolution qui arrivera immanquablement, et dont je n'aurai pas le plaisir d'être témoin. Les Français arrivent tard à tout, mais enfin ils arrivent; la lumière s'est tellement répandue de proche en proche, qu'on éclatera à la première occasion et alors ce sera un beau tapage; les jeunes gens sont bien heureux, ils verront de belles choses.

Everything I observe is sowing the seeds of a revolution that will inevitably come to pass and which I shall not have the pleasure of witnessing. The French always get there late but at last they do arrive. By degrees enlightenment has spread so widely that it will burst forth at the first opportunity, and then there will be a grand commotion. The younger generation are lucky; they will see some great things.

Letter from Les Délices, April 2, 1764, to Bernard-Louis Chauvelin, French ambassador at Turin. The translation is from Bruun, *The Enlightened Despots* (1967), 102.

La lumière s'étend certainement de tous les côtés. Je sais bien qu'on ne détruira pas la hiérarchie établie puisqu'il en faut une au peuple. On n'abolira pas la secte dominante; mais certainement on la rendra moins dominante et moins dangereuse. Le christianisme deviendra plus raisonnable et par consequent moins persécuteur.

Enlightenment is certainly more and more widespread. I know that we will not destroy the established hierarchy because every nation needs one for the people. The dominant sect will not be abolished; but it will certainly be less dominant and less dangerous. Christianity will become more reasonable and therefore less oppressive.

Letter from Ferney, June 26, 1765, to Claude-Adrien Helvétius in Paris.

Enthusiasm

Qu'entendons-nous par enthousiasme? que de nuances dans nos affections! approbation, sensibilité, émotion, trouble, saisissement, passion, emportement, démence, fureur, rage. Voilà tous les états par lesquels peut passer cette pauvre ame humaine.

What do we mean by enthusiasm? How nuanced we are in our feelings! approbation, sensibility, emotion, upset, seizure, passion, transport, dementia, fury, rage. Those are the many states to which the pitiful soul may be subjected.

"Enthousiasme," in *Dictionnaire philosophique, portatif. Nouvelle Édition* (1765), 164; Besterman et al., *Œuvres complètes de Voltaire* (1994), 36:59.

La chose la plus rare est de joindre la raison avec l'enthousiame; la raison consiste à voir toujours les choses comme elles sont. Celui qui dans l'ivresse voit les objets doubles, est alors privé de sa raison; l'enthousiasme est précisément comme le vin. Il peut exciter tant de tumulte dans les vaisseaux sanguins, & de si violentes vibrations dans le nerfs, que la raison en est tout-à-fait détruite. Il peut ne causer que de légeres secousses qui ne fassent que donner au cerveau un peu plus d'activité. C'est ce qui arrive dans les grands mouvements d'éloquence, & sur-tout dans la Poésie sublime. L'enthousiasme raisonnable est le partage des grands Poëtes.

That rarest of things is the union of reason and enthusiasm; reason consists in always being able to see things as they are. He who is drunk and seeing double, is deprived of reason; enthusiasm is just like wine. It can wreak such tumult in the blood vessels, and such violent vibrations in the nerves, that all reason is destroyed. It can also cause shocks so light as to gently stimulate activity in the brain. That is what happens during moments of great eloquence, and above all in the most sublime Poetry. Enthusiasm tempered by reason is a gift bestowed only upon great Poets.

"Enthousiasme," in *Dictionnaire philosophique portatif. Nouvelle Édition* (1765), 165; Besterman et al., *Œuvres complètes de Voltaire* (1994), 36:60.

L'Enthousiasme est une maladie qui se gagne.

Enthusiasm is a communicable disease.

"Troisième lettre sur les Quaquers," in *Lettres philosophiques Par M. de V. . . . .* (1734), 12; "Troisième lettre sur les Quakers," in *Lettres philosophiques* (1964), 1:33.

Chevalière d'Éon (1728–1810)

SOLDIER, DIPLOMAT, SPY, AND TRANSVESTITE

On m'a envoyé un chevalier d'Éon, gravé en Minerve, accompagné d'un prétendu brevet du roi, qui donne douze mille livres de pension à cette amazone, et qui lui ordonne le silence respectueux, comme on l'ordonnait autrefois aux jansénistes. Cela fera un beau problème dans l'Histoire. Quelque académie des inscriptions prouvera que c'est un des monuments les plus authentiques. D'Éon sera une pucelle d'Orléans qui n'aura pas été brûlée. On verra combien nos mœurs sont adoucies.

Someone has sent me an engraving of the Chevalier d'Éon as Minerva, featuring a supposed royal certificate that gives this Amazon a pension of 12,000 livres and orders him to keep a respectful silence in the same terms that were used in the case of the Jansenists. This will make a grand problem for history. What Academy of Inscriptions will prove the case to be authentic? D'Eon will be a *pucelle d'Orléans* who will not have been burned. It will be seen how soft we have become.

Letter from Ferney, circa March 5, 1777, to d'Argental in Paris. The print Voltaire described may have been engraved by Charles-François Le Tellier from a drawing by Johann Michael Baader. The *sieur* d'Eon, who served with distinction in the Seven Years' War, was given the honorific title of chevalier in 1763, and in 1775 that of chevalière. The translation is from Kates, *Monsieur d'Eon Is a Woman* (1995), 34.

Equality

Les mortels sont égaux; ce n'est point la naissance,
C'est la seule vertu qui fait leur différence.

All mortal men are equals; it is not their birth,
It is virtue alone that distinguishes them.

Omar, Mahomet's lieutenant, to Zopire, in act 1, scene 4, of *Le Fanatisme, ou Mahomet le Prophete* (1743), 16; Besterman et al., *Œuvres complètes de Voltaire* (2002), 20b:183. Voltaire also used this line in act 2, scene 1, of his tragedy *Eriphile*, staged for the first time in Paris on March 7, 1732, but the text was not published until 1743.

Que doit un chien à un chien, & un cheval à un cheval? Rien, aucun animal ne dépend de son semblable; mais l'homme ayant reçu le rayon de la divinité qu'on appelle raison, quel en est le fruit? c'est d'être esclave dans presque toute la terre.

What does a dog owe to a dog, and a horse to another horse? Nothing. No animal depends on his kind; but man having received the gleam of divinity called reason, what is the result? To be enslaved almost everywhere on earth.

"Égalité," in *Dictionnaire philosophique, portatif* (1764), 171; Besterman et al., *Œuvres complètes de Voltaire* (1994), 36:42.

Tous les hommes seraient donc nécessairement égaux, s'ils étaient sans besoins. La misère attachée à notre espèce subordonne un homme à un autre homme; ce n'est pas l'inégalité qui est un malheur réel, c'est la dépendance.

All men would then be necessarily equal if they were without needs. It is the poverty connected with our species that subjugates one man to another. Inequality is not the real misfortune, dependency is.

"Égalité," in *Dictionnaire philosophique, portatif* (1764), 172; Besterman et al., *Œuvres complètes de Voltaire* (1994), 36:43.

Le genre humain, tel qu'il est, ne peut subsister à moins qu'il n'y ai une infinité d'hommes utiles qui ne possèdent rien du tout. Car certainement un homme à son aise ne quittera pas sa terre pour venir labourer la votre; & si vous avez besoin d'une paire de souliers, ce ne sera pas un maitre des requêtes qui vous le fera. L'égalité est donc à la fois la chose la plus naturelle, & en même tems la plus chimérique.

The human race, constituted as it is, cannot subsist unless there be an infinite number of useful individuals possessed of no property at all; for most certainly, a man in easy circumstances will not leave his own land to come and cultivate yours; and if you want a pair of shoes you will not get a lawyer to make them for you. Equality, then, is at the same time the most natural and the most chimerical thing possible.

"Égalité," in *Dictionnaire philosophique, portatif* (1764), 173; Besterman et al., *Œuvres complètes de Voltaire* (1994), 36:46. The translation is from *A Philosophical Dictionary* (1824), 3:110.

J'ignore ce qui est arrivé dans l'ordre des temps; mais, dans celui de la nature, il faut convenir que les hommes naissant tous égaux, la violence & l'habilité ont fait les premiers Maîtres, les Loix ont fait les derniers.

I know not how it happened in terms of chronology; but in terms of nature, we must agree that all men are born equal: violence and ability made the first masters, laws the present masters.

"Maître," in *Dictionnaire philosophique portatif, ou Supplément à l'Édition de 1765* (circa 1765), 65; Besterman et al., *Œuvres complètes de Voltaire* (1994), 36:333.

Le système de l'égalité m'a toujours paru l'orgueil d'un fou.

The theory of equality has always seemed to me the vanity of a madman.

Letter from Ferney, July 11, 1770, to the duc de Richelieu in Paris.

Erasmus (1466–1536)

DUTCH HUMANIST

Ces deux hommes sont heureux d'être venus avant ce siècle; il nous faut aujourd'hui quelque chose d'un peu plus fort. Ils sont venus au commencement du repas; nous sommes ivres à présent: nous demandons du vin du Cap, et de l'eau des Barbades.

Those two men are lucky to have lived prior to this century; today we need something a little stronger. They came along at the start of the meal; we, at present, are drunk: we're calling for Cape Port and spiced rum.

Commenting on Erasmus and Hugo de Groot in a letter from Les Délices, May 10, 1757, to Jean Lévesque de Burigny in Paris. Hugo de Groot (or Grotius) was a seventeenth-century jurist and philosopher; *le vin du Cap* was a sweet port wine from South Africa.

The establishment

Il vit qu'il est dangereux d'avoir raison dans des choses où des hommes accrédités ont tort.

He saw how dangerous it is to be right in matters where the establishment is wrong.

Speaking of the French philosopher Bernard Le Bovier de Fontenelle in *Essay sur l'histoire générale, et sur les moeurs et l'esprit des nations* (1756), 7:214, "De la plupart des Ecrivains Français qui ont paru dans le siécle de Louis XIV pour servir à l'Histoire littéraire de ce tems," 228; Besterman et al., *Œuvres complètes de Voltaire* (2017), 12:106.

Europe

Les Germains, disait-il, sont les vieillards de l'Europe; les peuples d'Albion sont les hommes faits; les habitants de la Gaule sont les enfans, & j'aime à jouer avec eux.

"The Germans," he said, "are the old folks of Europe; the peoples of Albion are mature men; the inhabitants of Gaul are the children, and I like to play with children."

Amazan, a shepherd, in *La Princesse de Babylone* (March 1768), from *Œuvres de Monsieur de V**** (1771), 1:300.

Je voudrais que tout homme public, quand il est prêt de faire une grosse sottise, se dit toujours à lui-même: l'Europe te regarde.

I wish every time a public figure were about to commit a major blunder, he would say to himself: Europe is watching you.

Letter from Ferney, August 28, 1765, to Jean le Rond d'Alembert in Paris.

Events

Tout mal arrive avec des ailes, et s'en retourne en boitant. Prendre patience est assez insipide; vivre avec ses amis, et laisser aller le monde comme il va serait chose fort douce. Mais chacun est entraîné comme de la paille dans un tourbillon de vent.

All things evil arrive on wings, and leave with a limp. To be patient is dull; to live among one's friends, and let the world go on as it will, is the answer. But each of us is driven like loose straw in a whirlwind.

Letter written "dans les Vosges," October 14, 1753, to Marie-Ursule von Klinglin, comtesse de Lutzelbourg, in Alsace.

Je crois fermement que tous les hommes ont été, sont et seront menés par les événements.

I firmly believe that men have been, are, and will be driven by events.

Letter from Ferney, circa July 13, 1761, to the duc de Choiseul at Versailles.

Evolution

Combien d'auteurs ont répété qu'on avoit trouvé un ancre de vaisseau sur la cime d'une montagne de Suisse, & un vaisseau entier à cent pieds sous terre? . . . donc la mer a couvert autrefois tout le globe: donc alors le monde n'a été peuplé que de poissons: donc lorsque les eaux se sont retirées & ont laissé le terrain à sec, les poissons se sont changés en hommes! Cela est fort beau; mais j'ai de la peine à croire que je descende d'une morue.

How many authors have told us about a ship's anchor found atop a mountain in Switzerland, and an entire ship a hundred feet beneath the earth? . . . thus, the sea once covered the entire globe: thus, the world was populated entirely by fish: thus, after the waters receded and dry land appeared, the fish changed into men! That is all well and good; but I have a hard time believing I am descended from a codfish.

"Dissertation du Physicien de St. Four" ("Troisième lettre du Révérend Père L'Escarbotier"), in *Les Colimaçons du Reverend Pere L'Escarbotier* (1768), in *Pièces nouvelles de Monsieur de Voltaire* (1769), 107; Besterman et al., *Œuvres complètes de Voltaire* (2017), 65b:144. This letter was a commentary on the concept of "tranformisme" proposed by the natural historian, Benoît de Maillet, and the mathematician and scientist, Pierre-Louis Maupertuis.

C'est une grande question parmi eux s'ils [les Africains] *sont descendus des singes ou si les singes sont venus d'eux. Nos sages ont dit que l'homme est l'image de Dieu: voilà une plaisante image de l'Etre éternel qu'un nez noir épaté, avec peu ou point d'intelligence! Un tems viendra, sans doute, où ces animaux sauront bien cultiver la terre, l'embellir par des maisons & par des jardins, & connaître la route des astres. Il faut du tems pour tout.*

It is a serious question among them [Africans] regarding whether they are descended from monkeys or monkeys came from them. Sage men here say man was created in the image of God: now there is a pretty image of the Divine Maker, with a flat black nose and little or no intelligence. A time will doubtless come when these creatures know how to cultivate the earth, embellish it with houses and gardens, and track the movement of the stars. All things in due time.

Les Lettres d'Amabed (1769), seventh letter (from Amabed), in *Nouveaux Mélanges philosophiques, historiques, critiques, &c. &c.* (1769), 233, and in *Romans, contes philosophiques, &c.* (1771), 477; Besterman et al., *Œuvres complètes de Voltaire* (2016), 70a:389.

Fables

Il est vraisemblable que les fables, dans le goût de celles qu'on attribue à Esope, & qui sont plus anciennes que lui, furent inventées en Asie par les premiers peuples subjugués: des hommes libres n'auraient pas eu besoin de déguiser la vérité: on ne peut guere parler à un tyran qu'en paraboles, encore ce détour même est-il dangereux.

Fables, like those attributed to Æsop, and that also predate him, probably were invented in Asia by the first conquered peoples: free men would not have had to disguise the truth: a tyrant can at best only be spoken to in parables, and even that is dangerous.

"Fable," in *Questions sur L'Encyclopédie, par des Amateurs. Sixieme partie* (1771), 1; Besterman et al., *Œuvres complètes de Voltaire* (2010), 41:132.

Faith

L'intérêt que j'ai à croire une chose, n'est pas une preuve de l'existence de cette chose.

My personal interest in believing in something is no proof that it exists.

Lettres philosophiques Par M. de V. . . . . (1734), 144; "Remarques sur les Pensées de Pascal," in *Lettres philosophiques* (1964), 2:191.

L'histoire du déluge étant la chose la plus miraculeuse dont on ait jamais entendu parler il serait insensé de l'expliquer; ce sont de ces mystères qu'on croit par la foi, & la foi consiste à croire ce que la raison ne croit pas, ce qui est encor un autre miracle.

The story of the flood being the most miraculous thing we have heard of, it would be foolish to try to explain it. It is one of those mysteries of faith, and faith consists in believing what is beyond the power of reason to believe, which is yet another miracle.

"Inondation," in *Dictionnaire philosophique portatif par Mr. De Voltaire* (1764), 225, and *Dictionnaire philosophique, portatif* (1764), 225; Besterman et al., *Œuvres complètes de Voltaire* (1994), 36:232.

Qu'est-ce que la Foi? est-ce de croire ce qui paraît évident? Non; il m'est évident qu'il y a un Etre nécessaire, éternel, suprême, intelligent. Ce n'est pas là de la foi, c'est de la raison. . . . La foi consiste à croire, non ce qui semble vrai, mais ce qui semble faux à notre entendement.

What is Faith? Is it a belief in what is self-evident? No; it is evident to me that there exists a necessary, eternal, supreme and intelligent Being. This is not a matter of faith, but of reason. . . . Faith involves believing not what seems to be true, but what seems false to our understanding.

"Foi," in *Dictionnaire philosophique portatif, ou Supplément à l'Édition de 1765* (circa 1765), 1:34; Besterman et al., *Œuvres complètes de Voltaire* (1994), 36:125.

Croire, c'est très souvent douter.

To believe, is very often to doubt.

"Croire," in *Questions sur l'Encyclopédie, par des Amateurs* (1770), 3:190; Besterman et al., *Œuvres complètes de Voltaire* (2010), 41:319.

Fake news

Il faut toujours en fait de nouvelles attendre le sacrement de la confirmation.

Where news is concerned, always await the sacrament of confirmation.

Letter from Ferney, August 28, 1760, to the comte d'Argental in Paris.

Fame

C'est un poids bien pesant qu'un nom trop tôt fameux.

A heavy load to bear is a name too soon famed.

La Henriade de Mr. de Voltaire (1728), 39, *chant* (canto) 3; Besterman et al., *Œuvres complètes de Voltaire* (1970), 2:416.

La Renommée a toujours deux trompettes:
L'une à sa bouche, apliquée à propos
Va célébrant les exploits des Héros;
L'autre est au cul; puisqu'il faut vous le dire;
C'est celle-là qui sert à nous instruire,
De ce fatras de volumes nouveaux
Vers de Danchet, *prose de* Marivaux.
Productions de plumes mercenaires,
Et du Parnasse insectes éphémères,
Qui l'un par l'autre éclipsés tour-à-tour,
Faits en un mois, périssent en un jour
Ensevelis dans le fond des Collèges;
Rongés des vers, eux et leurs privilèges.

Goddess Fame always carries two trumpets:
One of which, press'd to her lips, and justly so,
Serves to praise the feats of great Heroes;
While a second horn is pressed to her butt,
Placed there that we might know what's what
'Bout all the new works that come and go,
Verse by *Danchet*, prose by *Marivaux*.
Products all of a mercenary quill,
And of ephem'ral lice from Parnassus Hill,
Who eclipse one another, each in turn,
Books writ in mere weeks, in a day spurn'd,
In the bowels of Schools to be interr'd,
Worms' food, they and their royal imprimatur.

La Pucelle d'Orléans (1756), canto 6, 71; Besterman et al., *Œuvres complètes de Voltaire* (1970), 7:370. Best known today as a playwright, Marivaux also wrote several novels. The playwright Antoine Danchet was a member of the Académie.

Fanaticism

N'est-il pas honteux que les fanatiques ayent du zêle & que les sages n'en ayent pas?
Il faut être prudent; mais non pas timide.

Is it not disgraceful that fanatics are so filled with fervor and wise men are not? One ought to be prudent; but not timid.

"Pensées Détachées de M. l'Abbé de Saint-Pierre," a kind of addendum to *Le Dîner du comte de Boulainvilliers* (1728), 63; Besterman et al., *Œuvres complètes de Voltaire* (1990), 63a:408.

Le Fanatique aveugle, & le Chrétien sincere
Ont porté trop souvent le même caractere;
Ils ont même courage, ils ont mêmes desirs.
Le crime a ses Héros, l'Erreur a ses Martirs.
Du vrai zèle & du faux, vains Juges que nous sommes,
Souvent les Scelerats ressemblent aux grands Hommes.

Both blind Fanatics, and Christians sincere
Have too often shared the same character;
They have the same courage, the same desires.
Crime hath its Heroes, error its Martyrs.
Vain Judges are we, of zeal, false or true,
For Villains often act like great Men too.

La Henriade, in *Oeuvres de M. de Voltaire. Nouvelle Edition. Revuë, corrigée, augmentée par l'Auteur* (1732), 1:94–95, canto 5; Besterman et al., *Œuvres complètes de Voltaire* (1970), 2:477.

Quand je délivre le genre humain d'une bête féroce qui le dévore, peut-on me demander ce que je mettrai à la place?

When I deliver the human race from a ferocious monster that devours it, can I be asked what I will put in its place?

During a conversation with Casanova at Les Délices in July 1760; from Casanova, *Histoire de ma vie* (1960), 3:246. Casanova had just said to Voltaire: "You might, it seems to me, spare yourself the trouble of fighting" superstition, "for you will never succeed in destroying it, and even if you did, pray tell me with what you would fill its place."

Quoi que vous fassiez, écrasez l'infâme, et aimez qui vous aime.

Whatever you do, crush *l'infâme,* and love those who love you.

Letter from Ferney, November 28, 1762, to Jean le Rond d'Alembert in Paris. "Écrasez l'infâme," variously understood as an appeal to crush superstition, political and religious abuse, or fanaticism, is strongly identified with Voltaire because he closed numerous letters with those words.

Que répondre à un homme qui vous dit qu'il aime mieux obéir à Dieu qu'aux hommes, & qui en conséquence est sûr de mériter le ciel en vous égorgeant?

How do you respond to a man who says he would rather obey God than men, and is certain he is going to heaven by cutting your throat?

"Fanatisme," in *La Raison par Alphabet. Septieme Édition* (1773), 285; Besterman et al., *Œuvres complètes de Voltaire* (1994), 36:110.

Quelque parti que vous preniez, je vous recommande l'infâme. Il faut la détruire chez les honnêtes gens, et la laisser à la canaille grande et petite, pour laquelle elle est faite.

Whatever action you take, I draw your attention to l'*infâme*. It must be destroyed among respectable people, and left to the rabble large and small, for whom it is intended.

Letter from Ferney, September 25, 1763, to Denis Diderot in Paris.

Bayle devait . . . examiner quel est le plus dangereux, du Fanatisme, ou de l'Athéisme. Le Fanatisme est certainement mille fois plus funeste; car l'Athéisme n'inspire point de passion sanguinaire, mais le Fanatisme en inspire: l'Athéisme ne s'oppose pas aux crimes, mais le Fanatisme les fait commettre.

Bayle should have . . . examined which is the more dangerous, Fanaticism or Atheism. Fanaticism is certainly a thousand times more toxic; Atheism does not inspire savage passion, Fanaticism does: Atheism does not oppose criminal acts, but Fanaticism prompts their commission.

"Athée, Athéisme," in *Dictionnaire philosophique, portatif* (1764), 41; Besterman et al., *Œuvres complètes de Voltaire* (2008), 39:388. Voltaire's remark was prompted by a moral problem raised by Bayle, described by Voltaire as the question of "whether a society of atheists can sustain itself."

Le fanatisme est à la superstition, ce que le transport est à la fièvre, ce que la rage est à la colère.

Fanaticism is to superstition what delirium is to fever, what fury is to anger.

"Fanatisme," in *Dictionnaire philosophique, portatif* (1764), 190; Besterman et al., *Œuvres complètes de Voltaire* (1994), 36:105.

Lorsqu'une fois le Fanatisme a gangrené un cerveau, la maladie est presque incurable.

Once Fanaticism has gangrened a brain, the sickness is almost incurable.

"Fanatisme," in *Dictionnaire philosophique, portatif* (1764), 191; Besterman et al., *Œuvres complètes de Voltaire* (1994), 36:108.

Ne soyons point étonnés de la foule des crimes que l'esprit de parti a fait naitre entre tant de sectes rivales: craignons toujours les excès où conduit le fanatisme. Qu'on laisse ce monstre en liberté, qu'on cesse de couper ses griffes & de briser ses dents, que la raison si souvent persécutée se taise, on verra les mêmes horreurs qu'aux siécles passés; le germe subsiste; si vous ne l'étouffez pas, il couvrira la terre.

Let us not be astonished by the abundance of crimes born of partisan spirit among so many rival sects: let us always be fearful of the excesses that fanaticism leads to. If we let this monster remain on the loose, if we stop clipping its claws and smashing its teeth, if human reason, so often persecuted, does not speak up, we will see the same horrors as in centuries past; the seed still lives; if you do not smother it, it will cover the earth.

Avis au Public sur les Parricides Imputés aux Calas et aux Sirven (1766), 24; Besterman et al., *Œuvres complètes de Voltaire* (2012), 61a:251.

Vous avez quitté, Monsieur, des Welches pour des Welches. Vous trouverez partout des barbares têtus. Le nombre des sages sera toujours petit. Il est vrai qu'il est augmenté, mais ce n'est rien en comparaison des sots, et par malheur on dit que Dieu est toujours pour les gros bataillons. Il faut que les honnêtes gens se tiennent serrés et couverts. Il n'y a pas moyen que leur petite troupe attaque le parti des fanatiques en rase campagne.

You have left, Monsieur, one group of *Welches* for another. You will find headstrong barbarians everywhere. The number of wise individuals will always be few. It is true that more of them exist now, but they are nothing in comparison to the many fools, and unhappily they say that God is always on the side of the big battalions. Right-thinking folk must close ranks and not expose themselves to attack. Their small band of troops can in no way confront the forces of fanaticism in open battle.

Letter from Ferney, February 6, 1770, to François-Louis-Henri Leriche, presumably in eastern France. Leriche had recently been named *receveur des domaines* in Besançon.

Fathers

Pour moi la mort d'un pere est un bienfait des Dieux.

For me, a father's death is a gift from the Gods.

Œdipe to Icare, an elderly citizen of Corinth, in *Œdipe* (1718), act 5, scene 2; *Œdipe, Tragédie. Par Monsieur de Voltaire* (1719), 68.

Ferney

Voltaire purchased this estate across the border from Geneva in 1758, and by 1761 had settled there more or less permanently.

Je n'achète la terre de Ferney que pour y faire un peu de bien.

I am only buying the estate at Ferney in order to do a little good.

Letter from Les Délices, November 18, 1758, to Antoine-Jean Le Bault, one of Voltaire's suppliers of wine, in or near Dijon.

J'ai acquis deux belles terres en France, dans le pays de Gex, qui est un jardin continuel.

I have acquired two beautiful estates in France, in the Pays de Gex, which is one continuous garden.

Letter from Les Délices, December 14, 1758, to Cosimo Alessandro Collini in Paris.

Mon château, l'œuvre de mes mains.

My château, the work of my own hands.

Letter from Ferney, January 14, 1763, to the marquis d'Argence at the château de Dirac, near Angoulême.

Si jamais vous êtes assez bon pour revenir à Ferney. Mon petit château sera entièrement bâti, mes paysans augmentent leurs cabanes à mon exemple, leurs terres et les miennes sont bien cultivées. Tout cet affreux désert s'est changé en paradis terrestre.

If ever you are so good as to return to Ferney. Construction on my little château will be complete; following my example, my laborers are improving their huts. Their lands and mine are beautifully tended. What was once a hostile desert has been transformed into an earthly paradise.

Letter from Ferney, May 12, 1766, to Étienne-Noël Damilaville in Paris.

Tibur, *dont tu nous fais l'agréable peinture,*
Surpassa les Jardins vantées par Epicure.
Je crois Ferney *plus beau.*

Figure 14. François-Marie-Isidore Queverdo, after Jean Signy, *Vue du Chateau de Ferney à Mʳ. de Voltaire, du Côté du Nord.* Etching and engraving, 1769. Private collection. The original drawing (1764), once owned by Voltaire, is in the Cabinet des Estampes, Bibliothèque Nationale de France.

Tivoli, whose pleasing portrait you paint for us,
Did surpass the gardens vaunted by *Epicurus.*
I think *Ferney* more beautiful.

Épitre à Horace (1772), 5; Besterman et al., *Œuvres complètes de Voltaire* (2006), 74b:281. It is thought that Voltaire began writing this fourteen-page verse epistle a year or so earlier.

J'ai de tout dans mes jardins, parterre, petite pièce d'eau, promenades régulières, bois très irréguliers, vallons, prés, vignes, potagers avec des murs de partage couverts d'arbres fruitiers, du peigné et du sauvage.

I've a little of everything in my gardens: neatly planted flowerbeds, small fountain, straight paths, virtually virgin woodland, valleys, fields, vineyards, walled vegetable patches filled with fruit trees, some things nicely manicured, the rest wild and untamed.

Letter from Ferney, August 7, 1772, to William Chambers, presumably in London.

Bernard Le Bovier de Fontenelle (1657–1757)

POET, SCIENTIFIC WRITER, AND PHILOSOPHER

On peut le regarder comme l'esprit le plus universel que le siécle de Louis XIV. *ait produit.*

He may be regarded as the most universal mind produced by the age of *Louis XIV.*

Essay sur l'histoire générale, et sur les moeurs et l'esprit des nations (1757), 7:97, in *Collection complette des Oeuvres de Mr. de Voltaire, Seconde edition* (vol. 17), chap. 214, "De la plupart des Ecrivains Français qui ont paru dans le siécle de Louis XIV pour servir à l'Histoire littéraire de ce tems," 97; Besterman et al., *Œuvres complètes de Voltaire* (2017), 12:105.

Foresight (planning ahead)

Si les hommes étoient assez malheureux pour ne s'occuper que du présent, on ne semeroit point, on ne bâtiroit point, on ne planteroit point, on ne pourvoyeroit à rien, on manqueroit de tout au milieu de cette fausse joüissance. . . . La Nature a établi que chaque homme joüiroit du présent en se nourrissant, en faisant des enfans, en écoutant des sons agréables, en occupant sa faculté de penser & de sentir; & qu'en sortant de ces états, souvent au milieu de ces états même, il penseroit au lendemain, sans quoi il périroit de misere aujourd'hui.

Were mankind so unhappy as to employ their minds only on the time present, no person would sow, build, plant, or make the least provision in any respect, but would be in want of all things in the midst of this false enjoyment. . . . Nature has so settled things, that every man is to enjoy the present by supporting himself with food, by getting children, by listening to agreeable sounds, by employing his faculty, of seeing and feeling; and that at the instant of his quelling these several conditions, and even in the midst of them, he reflects on the morrow, without which he would die for want to-day.

"Sur les Pensées de M. Pascal," in *Lettres philosophiques Par M. de V. . . . .* (1734), 159–160 (*Lettre* XXII); "Remarques sur les Pensées de Pascal," in *Lettres philosophiques* (1964), 2:204–205. This translation is from Smollett, "Remarks on Mr. Pascal's Thoughts," in Smollett et al., *The Works of Mr. de Voltaire* (1763), 26:24–25.

Nicolas Fouquet (1615–1680)

PATRON OF THE ARTS AND *SURINTENDANT DE FINANCES* IN THE EARLY DAYS OF THE REIGN OF LOUIS XIV BEFORE HIS DISGRACE AND EXILE

Il importe fort peu à la postérité qu'un homme nommé Fouquet soit mort en 1680 à Pignerol ou dans une terre de sa femme. L'attention qu'on porte sur ces bagatelles montre seulement combien mémorable est le siècle de Louis XIV, qui met de l'importance et de l'intérêt jusque dans les plus petites choses.

It matters very little whether a man named Fouquet died in 1680 at Pignerol or on his wife's lands. Any attention paid to such bagatelles only proves how memorable the age of Louis XIV was, attaching importance and interest to even the smallest of things.

Letter from Berlin, September 7, 1751, to Charles-Jean-François Hénault, presumably in Paris. Louis XIV had Fouquet arrested in 1661 for embezzlement; he was imprisoned for many years in the fortress at Pignerol, near Turin.

L'un des plus généreux et des plus malheureux hommes qui aient jamais été.

One of the most generous and most unfortunate men that ever was.

Le Siécle de Louis XIV, Auquel on a joint Un Précis du Siécle de Louis XV, in Cramer and Cramer, eds., *Collection complette des Œuvres de Mr. de Voltaire* (1769), 11:148; Besterman et al., *Œuvres complètes de Voltaire* (2017), 12:211. This comment appeared in a passage on the painter Charles Le Brun. Fouquet was Le Brun's first patron.

Jamais dissipateur des finances royales ne fut plus noble & plus généreux que ce Sur-Intendant. Jamais homme en place n'eut plus d'amis personnels, & jamais homme persécuté ne fut mieux servi dans son malheur.

Never was a treasury official more noble and more liberal than this Superintendent of Finances. Never did a government administrator have more personal friends, and never was a persecuted man better served in his misfortunes.

Siécle de Louis XIV, Auquel on a joint Un Précis du siécle de Louis XV (1772), 29; Besterman et al., *Œuvres complètes de Voltaire* (2017), 12:41.

France

In England everybody is publik-spirited, in France everybody is in his own interest only.

Notebooks entry, 1726, in Besterman, *Voltaire's Notebooks I* (1968), in *Œuvres complètes de Voltaire* (1968), 81:54.

We have begun in France to write pretty well, before we have begun to think.

Notebooks entry, 1726, in Besterman, *Voltaire's Notebooks I* (1968), in *Œuvres complètes de Voltaire* (1968), 81:55.

In fact, we are the whipped cream of Europe. There are not twenty Frenchmen who understand Newton.

Letter from Cirey, November 30, 1735, to Pierre-Joseph Thoulier d'Olivet in Paris. A member of the Académie française, abbé d'Olivet was one of Voltaire's teachers at the lycée Louis-le-Grand.

Imaginez toutes les contradictions, toutes les incompatibilités possibles, vous les verrez dans le gouvernement, dans les tribunaux, dans les églises, dans les spectacles de cette drole de nation.

Imagine all possible contradictions and incompatibilities—you will see them in the government, the tribunals, in the churches, the entertainments of this queer nation.

Martin to Candide in "Ce qui arriva en France à Candide & à Martin," chap. 22 in *Candide* (1763), 117; Besterman et al., *Œuvres complètes de Voltaire* (1980), 48:212. In English, *Candide, Zadig, and Other Stories* (2001), 70.

Nous laisserons vous et moi Madame ce monde-ci aussi sot, aussi méchant que nous l'avons trouvé en y arrivant. Mais nous laisserons la France plus gueuse et plus vilipendée.

We will leave this world, you and I, Madame, just as foolish, just as wicked as we found it. But we will leave France the poorer and more maligned.

Letter from Les Délices, March 19, 1760, to Mme de Lutzelbourg in Strasbourg.

J'ai peur que dans ce monde on ne soit réduit à être enclume ou marteau; heureux qui échape à cette alternative!

I am afraid that in this world one must be either the hammer or the anvil; happy the man who is spared the choice!

"Tirannie," in *Dictionnaire philosophique, portatif* (1764), 338; Besterman et al., *Œuvres complètes de Voltaire* (1994), 36:580.

Il faut être en France ou enclume, ou marteau; j'étais né enclume.

In France, one must be either a hammer or an anvil; I was born an anvil.

Mémoires pour servir à la vie de Mr. de Voltaire (1784), 116; Besterman et al., *Œuvres complètes de Voltaire* (2010), 45c:402. James Boswell must have heard Voltaire say much the same thing during his visit to Ferney. In his *Journal* entry for December 27, 1764, he recorded these words by Voltaire: "The French are slaves of men. In France every man must be either the hammer or the anvil."

J'ignore si vous quitterez cette nation de singes et si vous irez chez des ours, mais si vous allez en Oursie passez par chez nous.

I don't know if you will leave this nation of monkeys and go to the homeland of the bear, but if you go to Urssia stop by here.

Letter from Ferney, August 5, 1765, to Jean le Rond d'Alembert in Paris. In 1762, Catherine the Great invited d'Alembert to Russia to tutor her son, but he declined. In light of his troubles with censors in Paris, d'Alembert may have reconsidered the offer. Voltaire's pun combining the words *ours* and *Russie* was oddly prescient. In the twentieth century, the abbreviation in French for the Union of Soviet Socialist Republics was "U.R.S.S."

Je mourrai bientôt, et ce sera en détestant le pays des singes et des tigres, où la folie de ma mère me fit naître il y a bientôt soixante et treize ans.

I shall soon die, and will do so loathing the land of monkeys and tigers in which my mother foolishly gave birth to me, well nigh seventy-three years ago.

Letter from Ferney, circa August 10, 1766, to d'Alembert in Paris.

Allez, mes Welches, Dieu vous bénisse! vous êtes la chiasse du genre humain. Vous ne méritez pas d'avoir eu parmi vous de grands hommes qui ont porté votre langue jusqu'à Moscou. C'est bien la peine d'avoir tant d'académies pour devenir barbares!

Be gone with you, you *Welches*. God bless you! you are the shits of humankind. You deserve not having had amongst you great men who carried your language as far away as Moscow. All our learned academies matter not a jot as we sink into savagery!

Letter from Ferney, September 2, 1767, to the comte d'Argental in Paris.

La France serait un bien joli pays sans les impôts et les pédants.

France would be a wonderful country without taxes and pedants.

Letter from Ferney, February 3, 1769, to Jean-François-René Tabareau in Lyon.

Les Français oublient tout, et trop vite.

The French forget everything, and all too quickly.

Letter from Ferney, January 2, 1770, to the future controller-general of finances, Anne-Robert-Jacques Turgot, in Paris.

J'ai lu l'abbé Galliani; on n'a jamais été si plaisant à propos de famine. Ce drole de Napolitain connaît très bien notre nation. Il vaut encore mieux l'amuser que la nourrir. Il ne fallait aux Romains que panem et circenses. *Nous avons retranché* panem, *il nous suffit* circenses, *c'est-à-dire de l'opéra-comique.*

I've read l'abbé Galliani; no one has ever been as witty on the topic of famine. This peculiar Neapolitan knows our nation well. It is better to amuse her than feed her. All the Romans ever needed was bread and circuses. We've eliminated the bread, all we require is circuses, or, put another way, comic opera.

Letter from Ferney, February 6, 1770, to Mme Suzanne Necker in Paris. The work by Galiani cited by Voltaire is *Le Dialogue sur le Commerce des blés* (1770).

Oui, quant à se promener, à manger tout ce qu'il veut, à se reposer sur son fauteuil, le François est assez libre: mais quant aux impôts—ah, Monsieur, vous êtes heureux, vous pouvez faire tout; nous sommes nés dans l'esclavage, & nous mourons dans l'esclavage; nous ne pouvons pas même mourir comme nous voulons, il faut avoir un Prêtre.

Yes, as to walking, or eating whatever he pleases, or lolling in his elbow-chair, a Frenchman is free enough; but as to taxes—Ah! Sir, you are happy, you may do anything; we are born into slavery, and we die in slavery; we cannot even die as we will, we must have a priest.

In English to Martin Sherlock, April 1776, quoted in Sherlock's *Letters from an English Traveller* (1780), 161–162. The French translation is from Sherlock, *Lettres d'un voyageur anglois* (1779), 146–147.

Les Anglois se vendent, ce qui est une preuve qu'ils valent quelque chose: nous autres François, nous ne nous vendons point; vraisemblablement c'est que nous ne valons rien.

The English sell themselves, which is proof that they are worth something: we French do not sell ourselves; probably because we are worth nothing.

To Martin Sherlock, April 1776, in Sherlock, *Letters from an English Traveller* (1780), 162. The French translation is from Sherlock, *Lettres d'un voyageur anglois* (1779), 147.

Frederick the Great (1712–1786)

KING OF PRUSSIA FROM 1740 UNTIL HIS DEATH

Il faudrait être insensible, pour n'être pas infiniment touché de la lettre dont Votre Altesse Royale a daigné m'honorer: mon amour-propre en a été trop flatté, mais l'amour du genre humain que j'ai eu toujours dans le cœur, et qui, j'ose dire, fait mon caractère, m'a donné un plaisir mille fois plus pur, quand j'ai vu qu'il y a dans le monde un prince qui pense en homme, un prince philosophe qui rendra les hommes heureux.

One would have to be unfeeling not to be profoundly touched by the letter Your Royal Highness deigned to honor me with: my pride was exceedingly flattered, but the love of mankind, which has always filled my heart, and which I will presume to say is my distinguishing characteristic, pleased me a thousand times over when I saw that there was in the world a prince who thinks like a man, a philosopher prince who will make men happy.

Letter from Cirey, circa September 1, 1736, to Frederick, crown prince of Prussia, future Frederick the Great, presumably in Potsdam.

Il dit tout en deux mots, et fait tout en deux mois.

In two words he can say anything, and in two months do anything.

Letter from Brussels, April 9, 1741, to Frederick, crown prince of Prussia.

You must know my Prussian king, when he was but a man, lov'd passionately yr. English gouvernement. But the king has altered the man, and now he relishes despotik power, as much as a Mustapha, a Selim or a Solyman.

Letter written in English from Paris, circa June 1742, to Sir Everard Fawkener in London.

Il me fallait le roi de Prusse pour maître et le peuple anglais pour concitoyen.

I needed the king of Prussia as master and the English people as fellow citizens.

Letter written en route to Brussels from Reims, August 29, 1742, to Frederick, in Aix-la-Chapelle, apparently.

J'aurais besoin de lui encore un an tout au plus; on presse l'orange et on en jette l'écorce.

I shall have need of him for another year at most; one squeezes the orange and throws away the peel.

Letter from Berlin, September 2, 1751, to Mme Denis in Paris. Voltaire was repeating here a malicious comment allegedly made about him by Frederick, shared by the French physician and materialist philosopher La Mettrie, another member of the king's coterie in Berlin.

Voilà le Roi qui m'envoye son linge sale à blanchir: je blanchirai le votre ensuite.

The King has sent me some of his dirty linen to wash; I will wash yours after his.

To General Christian Hermann von Manstein, in Prussia at the court of Frederick the Great. Voltaire was helping Manstein revise a manuscript in proper French when some verse written by the king was delivered for him to work on. The quote appears in Voltaire's third-person, autobiographical narrative, *Commentaire historique sur les Oeuvres de l'auteur de La Henriade* (1776), 60; Moland, *Œuvres complètes de Voltaire* (1883), 1:94.

Les Princes se ruinent aujourd'hui par la guerre; il s'y était enrichi. Ses soins se tournerent alors à embellir la ville de Berlin, à bâtir une des plus belles salles d'Opéra qui soient en Europe, à faire venir des artistes en tout genre, car il voulait aller à la gloire par tous les chemins et au meilleur marché possible.

Princes today ruin themselves by war; but he made himself rich. He then turned his attention to the embellishment of the city of Berlin, building one of the most beautiful opera houses in Europe, summoning artists of all kinds, because he wanted to achieve glory by every means and as cheaply as possible.

Mémoires pour servir à la vie de Mr. de Voltaire (1784), 51–52; Besterman et al., *Œuvres complètes de Voltaire* (2010), 45c:402.

Freedom

Where there is not liberty of conscience, there is seldom liberty of trade, the same tyranny encroaching upon the commerce as upon Relligion.

Notebooks entry, 1726, in Besterman, *Voltaire's Notebooks I* (1968), in *Œuvres complètes de Voltaire* (1968), 81:55.

Croi-moi, la liberté que tout mortel adore,
Que je veux leur ôter, mais que j'admire encore,
Donne à l'homme un courage, inspire une grandeur,
Qu'il n'eût jamais trouvés dans le fond de son cœur.

Believe me: liberty, which all mortals adore,
That I too admire, tho' I wou'd wrest it from them,
Gives courage to a man, and inspires greatness,
That he'd never have found deep within his own heart.

Arons, ambassador to Rome from the Etruscan king Porsenna, to a confidant, Albin, in act 1, scene 3, of *Brutus*, first staged in 1730. The French text is from the first edition of the play *Le Brutus de Monsieur de Voltaire* (1731), 11; Besterman et al., *Œuvres complètes de Voltaire* (1998), 5:196.

L'homme est libre, au moment qu'il veut l'être.

Man is free, at the instant he resolves to be.

Brutus's traitorous son Titus, speaking to his friend Messala, in act 4, scene 4, of *Brutus*. The French text is from the first edition of the play *Le Brutus de Monsieur de Voltaire* (1731), 27; Besterman et al., *Œuvres complètes de Voltaire* (1998), 5:208.

Dieux donnez-nous la mort plutôt que l'esclavage!

O rather give us death, Ye gods! than slav'ry.

Junius Brutus to his fellow Roman consul, Valerius, act 4, scene 6, of *Brutus* (1731), 64; Besterman et al., *Œuvres complètes de Voltaire* (1998), 5:258. The translation is from *The Dramatic Works of Mr. De Voltaire* (1761), 1:295.

Figure 15. Anonymous stipple engraving *en manière de crayon* ("en sanguine") after a drawing by Jean Huber, *La Liberté que tout Mortel adore*. Rosenwald Collection, National Gallery of Art, Washington, DC.

La Liberté dans l'homme, est la santé de l'Ame.

Liberty is the soul's health in a man.

Deuxième Discours, de la Liberté" (possibly written in 1737), in *Discours en vers sur l'homme*, in *Recueil de pieces fugitives en prose et en vers* (1740), 62; Besterman et al., *Œuvres complètes de Voltaire* (1991), 17:476. The translation is from Smollett et al., *Miscellaneous Poems. By Mr. De Voltaire*, "Dissertation the IId. Upon Liberty," in Smollett et al., *The Works of Mr. de Voltaire* (1764), 33:255.

Si l'Homme est créé libre, il doit se gouverner:
Si l'Homme a des tyrans, il les doit détrôner.

If man is created free, he needs to govern himself;
If ruled by tyrants, he must overthrow them.

"Troisième Discours, de l'envie," *Discours en vers sur l'homme*, in *Recueil de pieces fugitives en prose et en vers* (1740), 65; Besterman et al., *Œuvres complètes de Voltaire* (1991), 17:479.

D'ailleurs c'est un ancien usage des sculpteurs, de mettre des esclaves au pied des statuës des rois. il vaudrait mieux y représenter des citoyiens libres & heureux.

Moreover, it is a sculptor's convention to put slaves at the feet of the statues of kings. it would be better to represent free and happy citizens.

"Particularités & anecdotes du régne de Louis XIV," in *Le Siècle de Louis XIV* (1751), 2:104; Besterman et al., *Œuvres complètes de Voltaire* (2016), 13c:101.

> *La liberté consiste à ne dependre que des loix.*
> *Sur ce piéd chaque homme est libre aujourd'hui en Suéde, en Angleterre, en Hollande, en Suisse, à Généve, à Hambourg. . . . On est libre dans quelques villes impériales d'allemagne. Mais il y a encor des provinces & de vastes royaumes chrétiens où la plus grande partie des hommes, est esclave.*

> Liberty consists of depending solely on the rule of law.
> On this basis, every man is free today in Sweden, in England, in Switzerland, in Geneva, in Hamburg. . . . One is free in several imperial cities in Germany. But there are provinces and vast Christian kingdoms in which the majority of men are slaves.

"Pensées sur le gouvernement," in *Oeuvres de M. de Voltaire. Nouvelle Edition* (1752), 6:iv; Besterman et al., *Œuvres complètes de Voltaire* (2006), 32a:321.

Je serais content de la liberté qui inspire les génies Anglais si la passion & l'esprit de parti ne corrompaient pas tout ce que cette précieuse liberté a d'estimable.

I would be glad of the freedom that inspires English geniuses, if passion and factionalism did not corrupt all that is estimable in that precious freedom.

Lord Pococurante to Martin, in the company of Candide, in "Visite chez le seigneur Pococurantè noble vénitien," chap. 25 in *Candide, ou L'Optimisme* (1759), 240; Besterman et al., *Œuvres complètes de Voltaire* (1980), 48:253. In English, *Candide, Zadig, and Other Stories* (2001), 86.

J'entends parler beaucoup de liberté; mais je ne crois pas qu'il y ait en Europe un particulier qui s'en soit fait une comme la mienne. Suivra mon exemple qui voudra ou qui pourra.

I hear much talk about freedom, but I do not think that there has ever been a private individual in Europe who has achieved the kind of freedom I have. May those who have the will or the means follow my example.

Mémoires pour servir à la vie de Mr. de Voltaire (1784), 143; Besterman et al., *Œuvres complètes de Voltaire* (2010), 45c:427.

Le plus modéré, le moins inquiet, & en même tems le plus sensible, est le plus heureux; mais malheureusement le plus sensible est toujours le moins modéré: ce n'est pas notre condition, c'est la trempe de notre ame qui nous rend heureux.

Happiest are those who are the most temperate, the least fretful, and, at the same time, the most sensitive; but unfortunately the most sensitive are always the least temperate: it is not our station in life, it is the natural cast of our soul that makes us happy.

"Heureux," in Diderot, d'Alembert, et al., *Encyclopédie, ou dictionnaire raisonné des sciences, des arts et des métiers* (1765), 8:195. See *Œuvres alphabétiques* in Besterman et al., *Œuvres complètes de Voltaire* (1987), 33:160.

Plus mes Compatriotes chercheront la vérité, plus ils aimeront leur liberté.

The more my Compatriots seek out the truth, the more they will cherish their freedom.

"Onzième lettre à l'occasion des miracles, Ecrite par Mr. Théro à Mr. Covelle," in *Collection des lettres sur les miracles. Écrites a Geneve. Et à Neufchatel. Par Mr. le Proposant Théro, Monsieur Covelle, Monsieur Néedham, Mr. Beaudinet, & Mr. de Montmolin, &c.* (1765), 138; Besterman et al., *Œuvres complètes de Voltaire* (2018), 60d:292.

Etre véritablement libre, c'est pouvoir. Quand je peux faire ce que je veux, voilà ma liberté. . . . Ma liberté consiste à marcher quand je veux marcher & que je n'ai point de goute.

To be truly free, is being able to do things. When I can do what I want, that is freedom. . . . My freedom consists of walking when I want to walk and when I'm not suffering from gout.

"XIII. *Suis-je libre?*" (*Doute* no. 13), in *Le Philosophe ignorant* (1766), 26; Besterman et al., *Œuvres complètes de Voltaire* (1987), 62:45.

Je te dis, mais tout bas, heureux un peuple libre!

I say, but not too loud: how lucky free men be!

Épitre à Horace (1772), 6; Besterman et al., *Œuvres complètes de Voltaire* (2006), 74b:282.

Freedom of the press

Y a-t-il rien de plus tyrannique . . . que d'ôter la liberté de la presse? Et comment un peuple peut-il se dire libre quand il ne lui est pas permis de penser par écrit?

Is there anything more tyrannical . . . than removing the freedom of the press? How can a country say it is free when it is not allowed to write what it thinks?

Letter from Ferney, October 16, 1765, to Étienne-Noël Damilaville in Paris. The translation is from Pearson, *Voltaire Almighty* (2005), 406.

Misattributed to Voltaire

I disapprove of what you say, but I will defend to the death your right to say it.

These words, now widely but mistakenly attributed to Voltaire, were written by Evelyn Beatrice Hall to express Voltaire's attitude with respect to free speech in *The Friends of Voltaire* (1906), 199.

Élie-Catherine Fréron (1719–1776)

ONE OF THE FIRST FRENCH JOURNALISTS AND VOLTAIRE'S IMPLACABLE ENEMY

Vermisseau né du cul de Des Fontaines.

Worm spawned out of Desfontaines's butt.

Le Pauvre Diable (1758), 10; Besterman et al., *Œuvres complètes de Voltaire* (2015), 51:89. Three lines later Voltaire identified the worm as "cet animal se nommait Jean F. . . . ." Fréron edited the cultural journal *L'Année littéraire*. He got his start in journalism working for another of Voltaire's literary enemies, abbé Pierre Desfontaines, who published the periodical *Observations sur les écrits modernes*.

D'où vient que ce nom de Fr. . . .
Est l'emblème du ridicule?

How is it that the name Fréron
Embodies all that is absurd?

"Les Fr. . . . ." ("Les Fréron"), 278 (first two lines in the first stanza), in *Recueil des facéties parisiennes* (1760); Besterman et al., *Œuvres complètes de Voltaire* (2015), 51a:481.

L'autre jour, au fond d'un vallon	The other day, deep in a glen
Un serpent mordit Jean Fréron.	By a snake Jean Fréron was bit.
Devinez ce qu'il arriva?	Can you guess what happened then?
Ce fut le serpent qui creva.	'Twas the snake took the fatal hit.

"Épigramme de M. de Voltaire contre moi," in *L'Année littéraire* (1763), 1:287.

Le ris malin . . . c'est la joie de l'humiliation d'autrui: on poursuit par des éclats moqueurs, . . . c'est huer plutôt que rire. Notre orgueil alors se moque de l'orgueil de celui qui s'en est fait accroire. On hue notre ami Fréron dans l'Ecossaise plus encore qu'on n'en rit: J'aime toujours à parler de l'ami Fréron, cela me fait rire.

Malicious laughter . . . is joy caused by someone else's humilation: one hounds him through outbursts of mockery, . . . it is hooting rather than laughter. Our own pride in that way mocks the pride of someone who's full of himself. In *L'Ecossaise* Fréron is hooted at more than laughed about: I always like to talk about friend Fréron, that makes me laugh.

"Rire," in *Questions sur l'Encyclopédie, par des Amateurs* (1772), 9:238; Besterman et al., *Œuvres complètes de Voltaire* (2013), 43:162. This passage does not appear in earlier versions of what we now call the *Dictionnaire philosophique*.

Friendship

J'ai des adorateurs, & n'ai pas un ami.

I have great admirers, and not a single friend.

Hérode to Mazael in *Hérode et Mariamne* (1725), act 3, scene 5, 53; Besterman et al., *Œuvres complètes de Voltaire* (2004), 3c:256.

Where there is friendship, there is our naturel soil.

Letter from Cirey, believed to date from November 1734, to Nicolas-Claude Thieriot in London.

Dufresny a dit dans une chanson que les rois ne se faisaient la guerre que parce qu'ils ne buvaient jamais ensemble. Il se trompe. François Ier avait soupé avec Charles Quint et vous savez ce qui s'ensuivit. Vous trouverez en remontant plus haut qu'Auguste avait fait cent soupers avec Antoine. Non Madame ce n'est pas le souper qui fait l'amitié.

In a song Dufresny said that kings went to war against each other only because they never drank together. He is wrong. François Ier supped with Charles V and you know what happened there. You will find, further back in time, that Augustus had a hundred suppers with Anthony. No, Madame, it isn't supping together that creates friendship.

Letter from Paris, May–June 1745, to Madame de Pompadour at Versailles. Charles Dufresny was a dramatist, journalist, and chansonnier. Mark Anthony had married Octavian's sister before he and the future emperor Augustus had a bitter falling out.

Il n'y a que les anciens amis de bons.

The only good friendships are the old ones.

Letter from Les Délices, July 28, 1760, to Thieriot in Paris.

Toutes les grandeurs de ce monde ne valent pas un bon ami.

All the splendors of this world are not worth one good friend.

Jeannot et Colin (1764), in *Contes de Monsieur de Voltaire ou de Guillaume Vadé* (1764), 69; Besterman et al., *Œuvres complètes de Voltaire* (2014), 57b:292.

J'ai comme vous des chevaux de trente ans, c'est ce qui fait que je les aime. Il n'y a rien de tel que les vieux amis. Les jeunes pourtant ne sont pas à mépriser les dames.

Like you, I have horses that are thirty years old; which is why I love them. There is nothing like old friends. Young ones, however, are not to be despised, ladies.

Letter from Ferney, August 10, 1768, to Mme Louise-Suzanne Gallatin-Vaudenet at Pré-gny, near Voltaire's property at Tournay. His neighbor's grandson, Albert Gallatin, emi-grated to America where he served in Congress and as secretary of the treasury under President Jefferson. The translation is from Parton, *Life of Voltaire* (1881), 2:442.

On a parlé depuis longtems du temple de l'amitié, & on sait qu'il a été peu fréquenté.

We've long spoken of the temple of friendship, and we know how few people go there.

"Amitié," in *Questions sur l'Encyclopédie, par des Amateurs* (1770), 1:205; Besterman et al., *Œuvres complètes de Voltaire* (2007), 38:247.

L'amitié est le mariage de l'ame; & ce mariage est sujet au divorce.

Friendship is a marriage of the soul; and it is subject to divorce.

"Amitié," in *Questions sur l'Encyclopédie, par des Amateurs* (1770), 1:206; Besterman et al., *Œuvres complètes de Voltaire* (2007), 38:248.

Mon Dieu! délivrez-moi de mes amis: je me charge de mes ennemis.

Lord! deliver me from my friends: I can manage my enemies.

Quoted by Voltaire's "fils adoptif," the marquis de Villette, in a letter, presumably from Ferney, June 4, 1782, to his wife in Paris. Quoted in *Œuvres du Marquis de Villette* (1784), 152. Villette acquired the château at Ferney after Voltaire's death in 1778.

Frivolity

On ne peut guère rester sérieusement avec soi-même. Si la nature ne nous avait faits un peu frivoles, nous serions très-malheureux; c'est parce qu'on est frivole que la plupart des gens ne se pendent pas.

One can scarcely take oneself too seriously. If Nature had not made us a little frivolous, we should be most wretched; it is because we are frivolous that most people do not hang themselves.

Letter from Les Délices, September 12, 1760, to Mme Du Deffand in Paris. In Hall, *The Life of Voltaire* (1903), 1:123. In Durant's *The Story of Philosophy* (1926), the last part of this quote was translated as: "It is because one can be frivolous that the majority do not hang themselves" (230).

Ce qui me persuade le plus de la Providence, disait le profond auteur de Bachabilleboquet, c'est que pour nous consoler de nos innombrables misères, la Nature nous a fait frivoles.

What persuades me still more of the existence of providence, said the profound author of "Bacha Billeboquet," is, that to console us for our innumerable miseries, nature has made us frivolous.

"De la frivolité," in *Nouveaux Mélanges philosophiques, historiques, critiques, &c. &c. &c.* (1765), 3:165; Besterman et al., *Œuvres complètes de Voltaire* (2017), 60a:405. The translation is from *A Philosophical Dictionary* (1824), 3:262. The "profound author" mentioned by Voltaire may be Claude Cherrier, who wrote *L'Homme inconnu, ou les Equivoques de la langue, dedié à Bacha Bilboquet* (1713). Bilboquet seems to have been a fictitious figure, and his last name a play on the French term for the children's game, cup-and-ball.

The future

Le présent accouche du futur.

The present gives birth to the future.

"Chaine, ou Génération des événens," in *Questions sur l'Encyclopédie, par des Amateurs* (1770), 3:291; Besterman et al., *Œuvres complètes de Voltaire* (2009), 40:526.

The Garden of Eden

C'est fort bien fait de cultiver son jardin, mais il est difficile qu'Adam cultivât un jardin de sept à huit cents lieues de long, apparemment qu'on lui donna des aides.

It is a good thing for a man to cultivate his garden, but Adam could hardly cultivate a garden seven to eight hundred leagues long; apparently, he was given helpers.

"Genèse," in *Dictionnaire philosophique portatif, ou Supplément à l'Édition de 1765* (circa 1765), 41; Besterman et al., *Œuvres complètes de Voltaire* (1994), 36:157.

Gardens

Je sçai aussi, dit Candide, qu'il faut cultiver nôtre jardin. Vous avez raison, dit Pangloss; car, quand l'homme fut mis dans le jardin d'Éden, il y fut mis, ut operaretur eum, pour qu'il travaillât, ce qui prouve que l'homme n'est pas né pour le repos. Travaillons sans raisonner, dit Martin; c'est le seul moyen de rendre la vie suportable.

"I also know," said Candide, "that we must cultivate our garden."

"You are right," said Pangloss, "for, when man was put in the Garden of Eden, he was put there *ut operaretur eum*, to work, which proves that man was not born for rest."

"Let us work without reasoning," said Martin, "it is the only way to render life endurable."

Candide, Pangloss, and Martin in the conclusion of *Candide, ou L'Optimisme* (1759), 292; Besterman et al., *Œuvres complètes de Voltaire* (1980), 48:260. In English, *Candide, Zadig, and Other Stories* (2001), 101. The phrase quoted in Latin by Pangloss (in English, "in order that he might work it") was adapted by Voltaire from a passage in Genesis 2:15.

La Religion de Zoroastre *est de l'antiquité la plus haute. C'est là qu'on trouve le nom de jardin pour exprimer la récompense des justes: on y voit le mauvais principe sous le nom de* Sathan *que les Juifs adoptèrent aussi.*

The Religion of *Zoroaster* dates from the remotest antiquity. It is there that one finds the word *garden* used to describe the reward that awaits the righteous; it is there that we meet the notion of evil under the name *Satan*, which the Jews also adopted.

Question no. 39, "De Zoroastre," in *Le Philosophe ignorant* (1766), 70; Besterman et al., *Œuvres complètes de Voltaire* (1987), 62:89.

Geneva

Liberté, liberté! ton Trône est en ces lieux.
Rome depuis Brutus ne t'a jamais revue.

Freedom, Freedom! your Throne is here in this place:
Rome, since Brutus, has ne'er again seen your like.

"Épître de l'Auteur arrivant dans sa Terre près du Lac de Genéve, en Mars 1755," in *Mélanges de Poésies, de littérature, d'histoire et de philosophie* (1757), 4; Besterman et al., *Œuvres complètes de Voltaire* (2009), 45a:259.

Genève n'est plus la Genève de Calvin il s'en faut beaucoup. C'est un pays rempli de vrais philosophes. Le christianisme raisonnable de Loke est la religion de presque tous les ministres, et l'adoration d'un être suprême jointe à la morale est la religion de presque tous les magistrats.

Geneva is no longer the Geneva of Calvin, and far from it. It is a land filled with true philosophers. The rational Christianity of Locke is the religion of almost all the ministers, and the adoration of a supreme being combined with morality is the religion of almost all the magistrates.

Letter from Les Délices, April 12, 1756, to Pierre-Robert Le Cornier de Cideville in Rouen.

Voici ce qu'on dit, car pour moi je ne dis mot. Je ne suis pas de la paroisse.

That is what they are saying; as for me, I say nothing. I am not a member of the parish.

Letter from Ferney, January 22, 1765, to François Tronchin in Geneva, commenting on how Rousseau's writings were being received in the Calvinist citadel.

A gentleman's equipage not coming punctually, who was on a visit to him, he [Voltaire] asked if the coachman was a Genevite; and being answered in the affirmative, he replied, "Oh! there the very servants are kings; no wonder you are so tyrannically used."

"Anecdotes of Mons. de Voltaire in his present situation at Fernex in Burgundy, near Geneva" (1768), 65.

Donnez-vous le plaisir de pulvériser les monstres sans vous commettre. Genève est une pétaudière ridicule, mais du moins de pareilles horreurs n'y arrivent point. On n'y brûlerait pas un jeune homme pour deux chansons faites il y a quatre-vingts ans.

Enjoy yourself destroying the monsters but don't get too involved. Geneva is a den of commotion and confusion, but at least horrors like that do not happen here. A young man would not be put to death for two songs written eighty years ago.

Letter from Ferney, circa August 10, 1766, to Jean le Rond d'Alembert in Paris. The "monsters" were the Jansenists, and the young man put to death in France was the chevalier de La Barre, July 1, 1766.

Quand je secoue ma perruque, je poudre toute la république!

When I shake out my wig, I powder the whole republic!

Figure 16. Benoît-Louis Henriquez, after Nicolas-René Jollain, *Portrait of Jean Le Rond d'Alembert*, 1777. Engraving. Courtesy of the Dibner Library of the History of Science and Technology, Smithsonian Libraries, Washington, DC.

Cited (in French) in Simond, *Switzerland; Or, A Journal of a Tour and Residence in That Country* (1822), 1:563. The translation is from Sedgwick, *Letters from Abroad to Kindred at Home* (1841), 1:247.

Genius

C'est le privilége du vrai génie & surtout du génie qui ouvre une carriére, de faire impunément de grandes fautes.

It is the privilege of true genius, especially in its early stages, to make big mistakes with impunity.

"Sciences et Arts," in *Le Siècle de Louis XIV* (1751), 2:183; Besterman et al., *Œuvres complètes de Voltaire* (2016), 13d:20.

Celui qui invente, quelque gêné qu'il soit, paraît toujours plus à l'aise que celui qui imite. En un mot, on ne traduit point le génie.

He who creates, however awkwardly, always seems more at ease than someone who imitates. In a word, genius is untranslatable.

Letter dated May 2, 1764, in *Aux Auteurs de la Gazette Littéraire*, writing about a French
translation of Hume's *Complete History of England*, in *Œuvres complètes de Voltaire. Mélanges
littéraires* (1821), 2:352.

*Lequel vaut le mieux, de posséder sans maître le génie de son art, ou d'atteindre à la
perfection en imitant & en surpassant ses maîtres?*

Which is better, to be possessed of genius in a given art, having no master, or
to attain perfection imitating and surpassing one's masters?

"Génie," in *Questions sur l'Encyclopédie, par des Amateurs* (1771), 6:255; Besterman et al.,
Œuvres complètes de Voltaire (2011), 42a:59.

*Chacun avouera, pour peu qu'on ait de conscience, que nous respectons les génies qui
ont ébauché les arts, & que les esprits qui les ont perfectionnés sont plus à notre usage.*

Everyone will agree, if they gave it any thought, that we respect the geniuses
who led the way in the arts, and we regard those who perfected them as more
useful.

"Génie," in *Questions sur l'Encyclopédie, par des Amateurs* (1771), 6:256; Besterman et al.,
Œuvres complètes de Voltaire (2011), 42a:60.

German poetry

*Hélas, dit-il tout bas à Martin; j'ai bien peur que cet homme-ci n'ait un souverain
mépris pour nos poëtes Allemands; il n'y aurait pas grand mal à cela, dit Martin. O
quel homme supérieur! disait encore Candide entre ses dents, quel grand génie que ce
Pococurante! rien ne peut lui plaire.*

"Alas!" he whispered to Martin, "I'm very much afraid that this man may
have a sovereign contempt for our German poets."
"There would be no great harm in that," said Martin.
"Oh, what a superior man!" Candide said under his breath. "What a great
genius this Pococurante is! Nothing can please him."

Candide and Martin, "Visite chez le seigneur Pococurantè noble vénitien," chap. 25 in *Candide, ou L'Optimisme* (1759), 242; Besterman et al., *Œuvres complètes de Voltaire* (1980),
48:236. In English, *Candide, Zadig, and Other Stories* (2001), 87.

Germany

*C'est une chose affreuse pour un malade français, qui n'a que des domestiques fran-
çais, de courir la poste en Allemagne. Érasme s'en plaignait il y a deux cents ans.*

It is a frightful thing for an ailing Frenchman, who has only French domestic help, to contend with coach travel in Germany. Erasmus complained about it two hundred years ago.

Letter from Cleves, on the German side of the Rhine River, July 2, 1750, to Frederick the Great in Potsdam.

God

Si dieu nous a faits à son image, nous le luy avons bien rendu, un pape disoit.

If God created us in his own image, we have more than returned the favor, a pope once said.

Entry written circa 1735–1750, in "The Piccini Notebooks," 1:231, in Besterman et al., *Œuvres complètes de Voltaire* (1968), 82:363.

Dieu n'est pas pour les gros bataillons, mais pour ceux qui tirent le mieux.

God does not favor the big battalions, but rather those who are the best shots.

Entry written circa 1735–1750, in vol. 2 of "The Piccini Notebooks," 2:547, in Besterman et al., *Œuvres complètes de Voltaire* (1968), 82:547.

Je respecte mon DIEU, mais j'aime l'Univers:
Quand l'homme ose gémir d'un fléau si terrible,
Il n'est point orgueilleux, hélas! il est sensible.

I respect my God, yet I love this world:
When men dare bemoan so terrible a scourge,
'Tis not out of pride, alas! But plain common sense.

"Poëme sur le désastre de Lisbonne," in *Poëmes sur le désastre de Lisbonne et sur la loi naturelle* (1756), 10; Besterman et al., *Œuvres complètes de Voltaire* (2009), 45a:338.

Dieu nous donna des biens, il veut qu'on en jouisse;
Mais n'oubliez jamais leur cause & leur Auteur;
Et lorsque vous goûtez sa divine faveur,
O mortel! gardez-vous d'oublier sa justice.

God wants us to savor the good things He gave us,
But ne'er forget that which caused them and their Author;
And whenever you taste of His divine favor,
O mortal! be sure to forget not his justice.

Précis de l'Ecclésiaste (1759), 14; Besterman et al., *Œuvres complètes de Voltaire* (2010), 49:219. These lines of verse incorporate a partial paraphrase of Ecclesiastes 5:18, in

French: "Mais, si Dieu a donné à un homme des richesses et des biens, s'il l'a rendu maître d'en manger, d'en prendre sa part, et de se réjouir au milieu de son travail, c'est là un don de Dieu."

DEO EREXIT
VOLTAIRE.
M.DCC.LXI.

ERECTED TO GOD.
VOLTAIRE
M.DCC.LXI.

In a letter, September 14, 1761, to d'Argental in Paris, Voltaire mentioned this inscription "que j'ai mise sur le fronton de mon église, *Deo erexit Voltaire*." The words were engraved on a stone plaque above the entrance to the chapel on his estate at Ferney. The letters in Voltaire's name were bigger than God's.

Je veux que mon procureur, mon tailleur, mes valets, ma femme même, croyent en Dieu; & j'imagine que j'en serai moins volé & moins cocu.

I want my attorney, my tailor, my valets, even my wife, to believe in God; I fancy then that I'll be robbed and cuckolded less often.

"A," in Entretien 16, "Sur des choses curieuses," in *L'A, B, C, Dialogue curieux* (1762), 159.

Des géomètres non philosophes ont rejetté les causes finales, mais les vrais philosophes les admettent; &, comme l'a dit un auteur connu, un catéchisme annonce Dieu aux enfans, & Newton le demontre aux sages.

Some geometricians who are not philosophers have rejected final causes, but true philosophers acknowledge them; and, as one well-known author said, a catechism introduces children to God, whose existence Newton demonstrates to those who are wise.

"Athée, Athéisme," in *Dictionnaire philosophique, portatif* (1764), 43; Besterman et al., *Œuvres complètes de Voltaire* (1994), 35:391. The concept of *causes finales*, a belief in a higher aim or order in nature, is associated with Aristotle.

On ne peut trop répéter que tous les dogmes sont différents, & que la morale est la même chose chez tous les hommes qui font usage de leur raison. La morale vient donc de Dieu comme la lumiere. Nos superstitions ne sont que ténebres.

We cannot repeat too frequently that dogmas differ, and that morality is the same among all men who make use of their reason. Morality proceeds from God, like light; our superstitions are only darkness.

"Morale," in *Dictionnaire philosophique portatif, ou Supplément à l'Édition de 1765* (circa 1765), 2:68–69; Besterman et al., *Œuvres complètes de Voltaire* (1994), 36:398.

Je suis bien sûr au moins que si nous ne voyons pas les choses en Dieu même, nous les voyons par son action toute-puissante.

I am at least certain of this, that if we do not see God Himself in things, we see them through His all-powerful action.

"Idée," in *Dictionnaire philosophique, portatif* (1767), 2:285; Besterman et al., *Œuvres complètes de Voltaire* (1994), 36:202.

Quoi qu'en disent quelques savants de nos jours, on peut être très bon philosophe et croire en Dieu.

No matter what some present-day scholars say, one can be a very good philosopher and believe in God.

Letter from Ferney, August 26, 1768, to the marquis de Villevieille, in Nancy apparently.

Dieu ne doit point pâtir des sottises du prêtre:
Reconnaissons ce Dieu, quoique très mal servi.
De lezards & de rats mon logis est empli,
Mais l'architecte existe, & quiconque le nie
Sous le manteau du sage est atteint de manie.

God must not suffer because of imbecile priests:
Though He be poorly served, let us give Him his due.
The house I live in is rife with lizards and rats,
Yet the builder exists, and he who denies it
Is under a sage's cloak touched with madness.

Épître à l'auteur du nouveau livre des Trois imposteurs (1769), 9; Besterman et al., *Œuvres complètes de Voltaire* (2012), 70a:241. The last page of this fifteen-page pamphlet bears the dateline "Ferney, 31. Mars 1769."

Si Dieu n'existait pas, il faudrait l'inventer.

If God did not exist, it would be necessary to invent Him.

Épître à l'auteur du nouveau livre des Trois imposteurs (1769), 9; Besterman et al., *Œuvres complètes de Voltaire* (2012), 70a:241. This line has been invoked by many famous individuals, including the Jacobin leader Robespierre, who admired Voltaire.

On dit que Dieu est toujours pour les gros bataillons.

They say that God is always on the side of the big battalions.

Letter from Ferney, February 2, 1770, to Francois-Louis-Henri Leriche, presumably in Paris.

Au reste, je pense qu'il est toujours très bon de soutenir la doctrine de l'existence de Dieu rémunérateur et vengeur, la société a besoin de cette opinion. Je ne sais si vous connaissez ce vers,
    Si Dieu n'existait pas, il faudrait l'inventer.

By the way, I believe it is always a very good thing to support the doctrine of the existence of God as rewarder and avenger; society needs this system of belief. I don't know if you are familiar with this line of verse:
    If God did not exist, it would be necessary to invent Him.

Letter from Ferney, November 1, 1770, to the duc de Richelieu, presumably in Paris.

J'ai été très fâché qu'on ait poussé trop loin la philosophie. Ce maudit livre du Système de la nature est un péché contre nature. Je vous sais bon gré de réprouver l'athéisme, et d'aimer ce vers,
    Si Dieu n'existait pas il faudrait l'inventer.
Je suis rarement content de mes vers, mais j'avoue que j'ai une tendresse de père pour celui-là.

That our *philosophie* was taken to such extremes greatly upset me. That accursed book *Le Système de la nature* is a sin against nature. I am grateful for your condemnation of atheism and your affection for this line of verse,
    If God did not exist, it would be necessary to invent Him.
    I am seldom satisfied with my verse, but I confess that I have a father's tender feelings for that one.

Letter from Ferney, November 10, 1770, to the Parisian lawyer, poet, and playwright, Bernard-Joseph Saurin. *Le Système de la nature* (1770) was a controversial new book by Diderot's friend, the German-born baron d'Holbach.

Si Dieu n'existait pas il faudrait l'inventer.
    Mais toute la nature nous crie qu'il existe, qu'il y a une intelligence suprême, un pouvoir immense, un ordre admirable, et tout nous instruit de notre dépendance.
    Dans notre ignorance profonde faisons de notre mieux. Voilà ce que je pense et ce que j'ai toujours pensé parmi toutes les misères et toutes les sottises attachées à soixante et dix-sept ans de vie.

If God did not exist, it would be necessary to invent Him.
    But all nature cries out that He exists, that a supreme intelligence, an immense power, an awesome logic exists, and everything we know tells us that we are but a lesser part of it.

In our profound ignorance, then, let us do our best. That is what I think and what I have always thought amid all the misery and follies that have marked my seventy-seven years of life.

Letter from Ferney, November 28, 1770, to Frederick William, Hereditary Prince of Prussia, presumably in Berlin.

Toutes les sectes des philosophes ont échoué contre l'écueil du mal physique & moral. Il ne reste que d'avouer que DIEU ayant agi pour le mieux n'a pu agir mieux.

All schools of philosophy have run aground on the reef of natural and moral grief. We can only admit that God, having acted for the best, could do no better.

"Puissance, Toute-Puissance," in *Questions sur l'Encyclopédie, par des Amateurs* (1771), 8:260; Besterman et al., *Œuvres complètes de Voltaire* (2013), 43:44.

Je crois, je crois en Toi! Dieu puissant! je crois! Quant à Monsieur le Fils, et à Madame sa Mère, c'est une autre affaire.

I believe, I believe in You! God almighty. I believe! As for Monsieur the Son, and Madame his Mother, that is another story.

Quoted in Lord Brougham's book, *Lives of Men of Letters and Science, Who Flourished in the Time of George III* (1845), 142. Inspired by Rousseau's *Profession de Foi d'un Vicaire Savoyard* (1762), Voltaire made this dramatic statement, according to Brougham, in the presence of a young houseguest he had roused from bed early one spring morning to join him in watching the sun rise. René Pomeau thought this probably occurred in May 1776, and that guest was an army officer, the marquis La Tour Du Pin-Gouvernet. See Pomeau, *On a voulu l'enterrer* (1994), 170–172.

Misattributed to Voltaire

God is a comedian playing to an audience too afraid to laugh.

Geary, *Wit's End* (2018), 110. In *A Book of Burlesques* (1920), 203, H. L. Mencken wrote, "Creator. A comedian whose audience is afraid to laugh."

Good and evil

Le mal a des ailes, et le bien va à pas de tortue.

Evil has wings, but virtue travels at a tortoise pace.

Letter from Cirey, circa April 1, 1737, to Willem Jacobs's Gravesande in Leiden, Dutch Republic.

Pourquoi ne fait-on presque jamais la dixième partie du bien qu'on pourrait faire?

Why do we scarcely ever do one-tenth of the good that we might do?

"Les Pourquoi," probably written circa 1745, from *Mélanges philosophiques, littéraires, histo-riques, &c.* (1771), 4:376; Besterman et al., *Œuvres complètes de Voltaire* (2008), 28b:103.

Aucun Philosophe n'a pu jamais expliquer l'origine du mal Moral.

No philosopher has ever been able to explain the origin of Moral evil.

"Préface de l'auteur," in *Poëmes sur le désastre de Lisbonne et sur la loi naturelle* (1756), 7; Bes-terman et al., *Œuvres complètes de Voltaire* (2009), 45a:327.

Qu'importe, dit le Derviche, qu'il y ait du mal ou du bien? Quand Sa Hautesse envoye un vaisseau en Egypte, s'embarrasse-t-elle si les souris qui sont dans le vais-seau sont à leur aise ou non? Que faut-il donc faire? dit Pangloss. Te taire, dit le Derviche. Je me flatais, dit Pangloss, de raisonner un peu avec vous des effets & des causes, du meilleur des Mondes possibles, de l'origine du mal, de la nature de l'ame & de l'harmonie préétablie. Le Derviche à ces mots leur ferma la porte au nez.

"What does it matter," said the dervish, "whether there is evil or good? When His Highness sends a ship to Egypt, is he bothered by whether the mice in the ship are comfortable or not?"

"Then what should we do?" said Pangloss.

"Hold your tongue," said the dervish.

"I flattered myself," said Pangloss, "that you and I would reason a bit together about effects and causes, the best of all possible worlds, the origin of evil, the nature of the souls, and pre-established harmony." At these words, the dervish shut the door in their faces.

Candide and Pangloss in conversation with "a very famous dervish who was considered the best philosopher in Turkey," in the conclusion of *Candide, ou L'Optimisme* (1759), 287–288; Besterman et al., *Œuvres complètes de Voltaire* (1980), 48:257. In English, *Candide, Zadig, and Other Stories* (2001), 99–100.

DIEU a mis dans tous les cœurs la connaissance du bien avec quelque inclination pour le mal.

God has placed in every breast the knowledge of good, with some inclination to evil.

"Aristote," in *Questions sur l'Encyclopédie, par des Amateurs* (1770), 2:154; Besterman et al., *Œuvres complètes de Voltaire* (2008), 39:8. The translation is from *A Philosophical Dictionary* (1824), 1:262.

Government

La bonté d'un Gouvernement consiste à protéger & à contenir également toutes les Possessions d'un Etat.

The goodness of a Government consists in protecting and containing equally all the Possessions of a State.

La Voix du sage et du Peuple (1750), 3; Besterman et al., *Œuvres complètes de Voltaire* (2006), 32a:239.

Un Ministre est excusable du mal qu'il fait, lorsque le gouvernail de l'état est forcé dans sa main par les tempêtes; mais dans le calme il est coupable de tout le bien qu'il ne fait pas.

A government Minister may be excused for the harm he does when the helm of government has forced his hand during a storm; but when the waters are calm, he is guilty of all the good he does not do.

"Etat de la france, jusqu'à la mort du cardinal mazarin en 1661," in *Le Siècle de Louis XIV* (1751), 1:120–121; Besterman et al., *Œuvres complètes de Voltaire* (2015), 13a:119.

En général, l'art du gouvernement consiste à prendre le plus d'argent qu'on peut à une grande partie des citoyens, pour le donner à une autre partie.

In general, the art of government consists of taking as much money as possible from one large group of citizens to give to another.

"Argent," in *Questions sur l'Encyclopédie, par des Amateurs* (1770), 2:128–129; Besterman et al., *Œuvres complètes de Voltaire* (2007), 38:589.

Il faut que le plaisir de gouverner soit bien grand, puisque tant de gens veulent s'en mêler. Nous avons beaucoup plus de livres sur le gouvernement, qu'il n'y a de princes sur la terre.

The pleasure of governing must certainly be exquisite, if we may judge from the vast numbers who are eager to be concerned in it. We have many more books on government than there are monarchs in the world.

"Gouvernement," in *Questions sur l'Encyclopédie, par des Amateurs* (1771), 6:298; Besterman et al., *Œuvres complètes de Voltaire* (2011), 42a:113–114. The translation is from *A Philosophical Dictionary* (1824), 2:365.

Great men

Tel brille au second rang, qui s'éclipse au premier.

He who shines in the second rank, fades in the first.

La Henriade de Mr. de Voltaire (1728), 2, canto 1; Besterman et al., *Œuvres complètes de Voltaire* (1970), 2:368.

Vous sçavez comment Bacon fut accusé d'un crime qui n'est guere d'un Philosophe, de s'être laissé corrompre par argent. . . . Si vous me demandez ce que j'en pense, je me serviray pour vous répondre d'un mot que j'ai oüi dire à Milord Bolingbroke: On parloit en sa presence de l'avarice dont le Duc de Marlborough avoit été accusé, & on en citoit des traits, sur lesquels on appelloit au temoignage de Milord Boling-broke, qui ayant été d'un parti contraire pouvoit avec bienseance dire ce qui en étoit: C'étoit un si grand homme, répondit-il, que j'ai oublié ses vices.

You know that this great Man was accus'd of a Crime very unbecoming a Philosopher, I mean Bribery and Extortion. . . . In case you should ask what are my Thoughts on this Head, I shall answer you in the Words which I heard the Lord *Bolingroke* use on another Occasion. Several Gentlemen were speaking, in his Company, of the Avarice with which the late Duke of *Marlborough* had been charg'd, the Lord *Bolingroke* was appeal'd to, (who having been in the opposite Party, might perhaps without the Imputation of Indecency, have been allow'd to clear up the Matter): "He was so great a Man, that I have forgot his Vices."

"Douzième Lettre. Sur le *Chancelier Bacon*," in *Lettres Ecrites de Londres sur les Anglois et autres sujets* (1734), 82–83; "Sur le chancelier Bacon," in *Lettres philosophiques* (1964), 1:153–154. The translation is "Letter XII. On the Lord *Bacon*," in *Letters Concerning the English Nation* (1733), 86. Francis Bacon was much admired, along with Newton and John Locke, by both Voltaire and Thomas Jefferson. Bolingbroke's remark about the Duke of Marlborough was first recorded here by Voltaire.

Une écluse du canal qui joint les deux mers, un tableau de Poussin, une belle tragédie, une vérité découverte sont des choses plus précieuses que toutes les annales de cour, que toutes les relations de campagne. Vous savez que chez moi les grands hommes vont les premiers, et les héros les derniers. J'appelle grands hommes tous ceux qui ont excellé dans l'utile ou dans l'agréable.

A lock in a canal connecting two great bodies of water, a painting by Poussin, a beautiful tragedy, a newly discovered truth, are more precious than all the annals of court life, or accounts of military campaigns. You know that for me, great men come first, and heroes last. Great men, I say, are those who have excelled in things that are useful or agreeable.

Letter from Cirey, July 15, 1735, to Nicolas-Claude Thieriot in Paris.

L'amitié d'un grand homme est un bienfait des Dieux;
Je lisois mon devoir & mon sort dans ses yeux.

A great man's friendship is a gift sent by the Gods,
I read my duty and my destiny in his eyes.

Philoctète, Prince d'Eubée, to his friend Dimas, speaking of the recently murdered King Laius of Thebes, in *Œdipe*, act 1, scene 1. The verse is from a revised edition of this 1718 tragedy in *Oeuvres de M*. de Voltaire. Nouvelle Edition* (1748), 4:29; Besterman et al., *Œuvres complètes de Voltaire* (2001), 1a:175.

Il ne s'est fait rien de grand dans le Monde que par le génie & la fermeté d'un seul homme, qui lutte contre les préjugés de la multitude.

Nothing great has been done in this world except by the genius and firmness of a single man, battling the prejudice of the multitude.

"Etat de l'Europe à la fin du quinzième siècle," in *Essay sur l'histoire générale et sur les moeurs et l'esprit des nations* (1756), 2:296.

Le grand homme *est plus difficile à définir que le* grand artiste. *Dans un art, dans une profession, celui qui a passé de loin ses rivaux, ou qui a la réputation de les avoir surpassés, est appellé grand dans son art, & semble n'avoir eu besoin que d'un seul mérite. Mais le grand homme doit réunir des mérites différens. . . . Il est plus aisé de nommer ceux à qui l'on doit refuser l'épithete de* grand homme, *que de trouver ceux à qui on doit l'accorder. Il semble que cette denomination suppose quelques grandes vertus.*

The *great man* is harder to define than the *great artist*. In an art or profession, the man who has far surpassed his rivals, or is reputed to have done so, is called *great* in his art, and seems to require only one type of merit in order to obtain this eminence. But the great man must exhibit other kinds of merit. . . . It is easier to name those who should be refused the distinction of *great man* than it is to identify those to whom it should be granted. The denomination seems to imply at least some great virtues.

"Grand, Grandeur," in Diderot, d'Alembert, et al., *Encyclopédie, ou Dictionnaire raisonné des Sciences, des Arts et des Métiers* (1757), 7:847–848.

Greek (language)

On sçait qu'il est impossible de faire passer dans aucune Langue moderne la valeur des expressions Grecques; elles peignent d'un trait ce qui éxige trop de paroles chez tous les autres Peuples.

We know that no modern Language can imitate the speech of the ancient Greeks; they could communicate in a word or two what other Peoples need many words to say.

"A Son Altesse Sérénissme Madame la Duchesse du Maine," de facto preface to the first edition of *Oreste, Tragédie, Par M. Arouet de Voltaire* (1750), iii; Besterman et al., *Œuvres complètes de Voltaire* (1992), 31a:398.

Grief

Les larmes sont le langage muet de la douleur.

Tears are the silent language of grief.

"Larmes," in *Questions sur l'Encyclopédie, par des Amateurs* (1774), 4:44; Besterman et al., *Œuvres complètes de Voltaire* (2012), 42b:23.

Happiness

La grande affaire et la seule qu'on doive avoir c'est de vivre heureux, et si nous pouvions réussir à le devenir sans établir une caisse de juifrerie ce serait autant de peine d'épargnée.

The great and only question we should concern ourselves with is how to be happy, and if we can succeed in that without paying a Jew's ransom, so much the better.

Letter from Paris, April 1722?, to the marquise de Bernières in Rouen.

Les maux viennent bien vite, et les consolations bien tard.

Misfortunes arrive swiftly, consolations reach us late.

Letter from London, October 16, 1726, to the marquise de Bernières in Rouen or Paris.

Nous cherchons tous le bonheur, mais sans savoir où, comme des ivrognes qui cherchent leur maison, sachant confusément qu'ils en ont une.

We are all looking for happiness, but not knowing where to look, like drunkards trying to find their way home, only dimly aware that they have one.

Entry, circa 1735–1750, in Besterman, *Voltaire's Notebooks* (1952), 1:224; *Le Sottisier de Voltaire* (1880), 64; and Besterman et al., *Œuvres complètes de Voltaire* (1968), 81:355. A variation on this remark is found in the same notebook (134): "Men who look for happiness are like drunkards who cannot find their house but know that they have one" ("Les hommes qui cherchent le bonheur sont comme des ivrognes qui ne peuvent trouver leur maison, mais qui savent qu'ils en ont une").

Le bonheur ressemble à l'île d'Ithaque qui fuyoit toujours devant Ulisse.

Happiness resembles the island of Ithaca, ever eluding Ulysses before his eyes.

Entry, circa 1735–1750, in Besterman, *Voltaire's Notebooks* (1952), 2:231; *Le Sottisier de Voltaire* (1880), 134; and Besterman et al., *Œuvres complètes de Voltaire* (1968), 82:463.

Fais ton bonheur, enfin, par le bonheur d'autrui.

Find your happiness through the happiness of others.

"Deuxième Discours, de la Liberté" (possibly written in 1737), in *Discours en vers sur l'homme*, in *Recueil de pieces fugitives en prose et en vers* (1740), 63; Besterman et al., *Œuvres complètes de Voltaire* (1991), 17:477.

Le Paradis Terrestre est où je suis.

Heaven on Earth is where I am now.

Last line of the poem *Le Mondain*, in *Recueil de pieces fugitives en prose et en vers* (1740), 136; Besterman et al., *Œuvres complètes de Voltaire* (2003), 16:303. By "where I am," Voltaire meant eighteenth-century Europe, and what he later called "our present level of refinement" in places such as Paris, Cirey, or at court.

Un bonheur est un évenement heureux. Le bonheur pris indéfinitivement, signifie une suite de ces évenemens. Le plaisir est un sentiment agréable & passager, le bonheur considéré comme sentiment, est une suite de plaisirs, la prospérité une suite d'heureux évenemens, la félicité une jouïssance intime de sa prospérité.

Good fortune is a happy event. Happiness, understood as something indefinite, signifies a succession of such events. Pleasure is an enjoyable and fleeting feeling while happiness, considered as feeling, is a succession of pleasures, prosperity a succession of happy events, and bliss the lasting delight in one's prosperity.

"Félicité," in Diderot, d'Alembert, et al., *Encyclopédie, ou Dictionnaire raisonné des Sciences, des Arts et des Métiers* (1756), 6:466; Besterman et al., *Œuvres complètes de Voltaire* (1983), 33:75.

Je souris en réfléchissant que le plaisir vient de la douleur. C'est ainsi que la félicité éternelle naîtra des misères de cette vie.

I smile as I consider how pleasure is spawned by pain. So it is that eternal bliss shall be born of suffering in this life.

Socrates, awaiting his death, to his wife and friends in prison, in act 3, scene 3, of *Socrate, ouvrage dramatique, traduit de l'anglais de feu M. Tompson* (1759), 98; Besterman et al., *Œuvres complètes de Voltaire* (2009), 49b:341.

Ayant fait réflexion, depuis quelques années, qu'on ne gagnoit rien à être bon homme, je me suis mis à être un peu gai, parce qu'on ma dit que cela est bon pour la santé.

Having, for some years now, reflected that nothing was to be gained by being virtuous, I have begun to be somewhat merry, for I have been told that it is good for your health.

Open letter, April 17, 1761, addressed to abbé Nicolas Trublet, member of the Académie française. In the 1990 French film *Milou en mai* (Louis Malle, dir.), the second half of this quote, delivered by the actor Michel Piccoli, was refashioned as "J'ai décidé d'être heureux parce que c'est bon pour la santé" ("I've decided to be happy because it is good for my health").

Lorsque Louïs XIV. *lui permit de revenir dans sa patrie sur la fin de ses jours, ce Philosophe dédaigna de regarder cette permission comme une grace; il prouva que la patrie est où l'on vit heureux, & il l'était à Londres.*

When Louis XIV gave him permission to return to his homeland at the end of his life, this Philosopher refused to regard it as an act of grace; he proved that a man's homeland is wherever he lives happily, which he did in London.

Talking about the essayist and critic Charles de Saint-Évremond, in "Sur St. Evremont," in *Additions à l'Essay sur l'Histoire générale* (1763), 341; subsequently added to *Le Siècle de Louis XIV.* See Besterman et al., *Œuvres complètes de Voltaire* (2016), 13c:19. Saint-Évremond is buried in Poets' Corner in Westminster Abbey.

Je me bats les flancs pour trouver la façon d'être le moins malheureux qu'il me soit possible; car pour le mot heureux, il ne me paraît guère fait que pour les romans.

I try my best to find ways to be the least unhappy I can possibly be; the word happy, for me, is a word fit only for novels.

Letter from Les Délices, October 3, 1764, to Mme Du Deffand in Paris.

Pour vivre heureux, mon fils, que faut-il? Savoir vivre.

What do you need, my son, to live a happy life? Know how to live.

La comtesse de Givri to her son, in *Charlot, ou La comtesse de Givri, comédie* (1767), act 1, scene 5; Besterman et al., *Œuvres complètes de Voltaire* (2012), 61b:554.

L'homme doit être content, dit-on; mais de quoi?

Man ought to be content, it is said; but content with what?

Pensées, remarques et observations de Voltaire (1802), 8; Besterman et al., *Œuvres complètes de Voltaire* (1968), 82:503.

Attributed to Voltaire, likely apocryphal

Le bonheur est souvent la seule chose qu'on puisse donner sans l'avoir et c'est en le donnant qu'on l'acquiert.

Happiness is often the only thing we can give that we do not have and it is by giving it that we acquire it.

This quote also has been attributed to Elisabeth of Wied (1843–1916), a.k.a. Carmen Sylva, Queen consort of Romania, in Gilbert de Chambertrand, *Femme, qu'y a-t-il entre moi et toi?* (1976), 54.

Claude-Adrien Helvétius (1715–1771)

FRENCH WRITER AND PHILOSOPHER

J'aimais l'auteur du livre de l'Esprit. Cet homme valait mieux que tous ses ennemis ensemble; mais je n'ai jamais approuvé ni les erreurs de son livre, ni les vérités triviales qu'il débite avec emphase. J'ai pris son parti hautement, quand des hommes absurdes l'ont condamné pour ces vérités mêmes.

I was fond of the author of the book *On the Mind*. He was a man worthier than all his enemies put together; but I never endorsed the errors of his book nor the trivial truths that he so emphatically aired. I have, however, boldly taken his part when absurd men have condemned him for these same truths.

"Homme" (under the subheading "De l'homme dans l'état de pure nature"), in *Questions sur l'Encyclopédie, par des Amateurs* (1774), 3:424; Besterman et al., *Œuvres complètes de Voltaire* (2011), 42a:266. This statement by Voltaire may have inspired the line "I disapprove of what you say, but I will defend to the death your right to say it," in Hall's book *Friends of Voltaire* (1906), still widely misattributed to Voltaire.

Henri IV (1553–1610)

KING OF NAVARRE AND OF FRANCE

Je chante ce Héros, qui régna dans la France,
Et par droit de conquête, & par droit de naissance;

Of this Hero who in France did reign, I sing,
By right of conquest, and by right of birth, a king;

La Henriade (1726), *La Henriade de Mr. de Voltaire* (1726), 1:1, canto 1; Besterman et al., *Œuvres complètes de Voltaire* (1970), 3:365. These are the opening lines of Voltaire's epic narrative poem.

Hermaphrodite

On demande si un animal, un homme par exemple peut avoir à la fois des testicules & des ovaires, ou ces glandes prises pour des ovaires; une verge & un clitoris; un prépuce & un vagin; en un mot si la nature peut faire de véritables hermaphrodites; et si un hermaphrodite peut faire un enfant à une fille & être engrossé par un garçon? Je réponds, à mon ordinaire, que je ne sais rien; & que je ne connais pas la cent milliéme partie des choses que la nature peut opérer. . . . Il est bien hardi de dire: Nous n'avons jamais vu ce phénomène; donc il est impossible qu'il existe.

People wonder if an animal, a man for example, can have both testicles and ovaries, or the glands believed to be ovaries; a penis and a clitoris; a foreskin and a vagina; in a word, if nature can form true hermaphrodites, and whether or not a hermaphrodite can father a child with a woman or be made pregnant by a man? I respond, as is my wont, that I do not know, and that I have not one one-hundred-thousandth of an idea of what nature can do. . . . It is something rather bold to assert: We never saw such a phenomenon; therefore, it cannot possibly exist.

"Testicules. Section seconde," in *Questions sur l'Encyclopédie, par des Amateurs* (1774), 4:440; Besterman et al., *Œuvres complètes de Voltaire* (2013), 43:358.

Historians

Je ne suis qu'un Peintre, qui cherche à représenter d'un pinceau foible, mais vrai, les hommes tels qu'ils ont été. Tout m'est indifferent de Charles XII & de Pierre-le-Grand, excepté le bien que ce dernier a pû faire aux hommes, je n'ai aucun sujet de les flater ni d'en médire; je les traiterai avec le respect qu'on doit aux Têtes couronnées, qui viennent de mourir, & avec le respect qu'on doit à la vérité, qui ne mourra jamais.

I am but a Painter, who seeks to depict with a feeble but true brush, men as they were. I am indifferent to Charles XII and also to Peter the Great, except for the good he was able to do for mankind. I have no cause to flatter them or to speak ill of them; I will treat them with the respect due to all crowned Heads, who have just died, and with the respect due to the truth, which will never die.

"Avis à un journaliste" (1744), 10–11; Besterman et al., *Œuvres complètes de Voltaire* (2003), 20a:486. Better known today as "Conseils à un journaliste," this forty-page essay, described as "l'Ouvrage d'un Ecrivain célébre," was composed in 1737.

Lorsque les historiens sont contemporains, il est difficile au bout de quelque temps de savoir qui est celui qui a pillé l'autre.

When historians are contemporaries of one another, after a while it is hard to know who stole what from whom.

"XIII. Des Croisades," in *Remarques, pour servir de supplément à l'Essay sur l'Histoire générale et sur les mœurs et l'esprit des Nations, depuis Charlemagne jusqu'à nos jours* (1763), 51; Besterman et al., *Œuvres complètes de Voltaire* (2016), 27:53.

Attributed to Voltaire

Historians are gossips who love to tease the dead.

Quoted in Hall, "From Voltaire's Scribbling Books" (1945), 83.

History

J'ai vu un temps où vous n'aimiez guère l'Histoire. Ce n'est après tout qu'un ramas de tracasseries qu'on fait aux morts.

I knew a time when you did not much care for History. It is, after all, nothing but a bag of tricks played on the dead.

Letter from Montriond, near Lausanne, February 9, 1757, possibly to Pierre-Robert Le Cornier de Cideville in Rouen.

Il n'y a que les vérités de l'histoire qui puissent forcer l'esprit à croire et à admirer.

Only historical truths can force us into belief and admiration.

Letter from Ferney, September 18, 1759, to Ivan Shuvalov in St. Petersburg. As a young man, Shuvalov, later a general, supporter of the arts, and minister of education, was taken by the much older Russian empress Elizabeth as her lover.

Toutes les histoires anciennes, comme le disait un de nos beaux esprits, ne sont que des fables convenues; & pour les modernes c'est un cahos qu'on ne peut débrouiller.

All forms of ancient history, as one of our wits once said, are merely mutually agreed upon fables; as for modern history, it is a twisted knot no one can untangle.

Jeannot's tutor to Jeannot's mother, in the short philosophical tale *Jeannot et Colin* (1764), 151; Besterman et al., *Œuvres complètes de Voltaire* (2014), 57b:297–80. The "wit" Voltaire mentioned was Fontenelle, author of the essay "De l'origine des Fables" (1724), in which he said, "il n'y a point d'autres Histoires anciennes que les Fables."

C'est le récit des faits donnés pour vrais; au contraire de la fable, qui est le récit des faits donnés pour faux.

It is a story told with facts presented as true; the opposite of a fable, which is a story told with facts presented as false.

"Histoire," in Diderot, d'Alembert, et al., *Encyclopédie, ou Dictionnaire raisonné des Sciences, des Arts et des Métiers* (1765), 8:220; Besterman et al., *Œuvres complètes de Voltaire* (1987), 33:164.

Autant il est aisé de faire un recueil de gazettes, autant il est difficile aujourd'hui d'écrire l'histoire.

The easier it is to compile a bound volume of printed news, the harder is is to write *history*.

"Histoire," in *Encyclopédie, ou Dictionnaire raisonné des Sciences, des Arts et des Métiers* (1765), 8:225; Besterman et al., *Œuvres complètes de Voltaire* (1987), 33:185.

L'histoire n'est que le tableau des crimes & des malheurs.

History is merely a catalogue of crimes and misfortune.

"L'Ingénu enfermé à la Bastille avec un Janséniste," in *L'Ingénu, Histoire véritable* (1767), 43–44; Besterman et al., *Œuvres complètes de Voltaire* (2006), 63c:260.

J'ai toujours pensé comme vous qu'il faut se défier de toutes les histoires anciennes. Fontenelle, le seul homme du siècle de Louis XIV qui fut à la fois poète, philosophe et savant, disait qu'elles étaient des fables convenues.

Like you, I have always felt that one should be wary of all forms of ancient history. Fontenelle, the only man in the age of Louis XIV to be at once a poet, a philosopher, and a scholar, used to say that they were little more than packs of accepted lies.

Letter from Ferney, July 15, 1768, to Horace Walpole, near London.

L'objet était l'histoire de l'esprit humain, & non pas le détail de faits presque toû-jours défigurés; il ne s'agissait pas de rechercher, par exemple, de quelle famille était le seigneur du Puiset, *ou le seigneur de* Monthléri, *qui firent la guerre à des rois de France; mais de voir par quels degrés on est parvenu de la rusticité barbare de ces tems à la politesse du nôtre.*

It was my aim to write a history of the human spirit, not to compile a long list of almost always distorted facts; I did not, for example, trace the family lines of the lords of *Puiset* or of *Monthléri*, who waged war against the kings of France, but instead sought to discover how, by degrees, from a period of rustic barbarity we reached our present level of refinement.

"Remarques pour servir de supplément à l'Essai sur les moeurs et l'esprit des nations," in Cramer and Cramer, eds., *Collection complette des Œuvres de Mr. de Voltaire* (1769), 10:441. The American historian Will Durant rendered the last part of this quotation as "I want to know what were the steps by which man passed from barbarism to civilization." See Durant and Durant, *The Age of Voltaire* (1965), 484.

Il y a l'histoire des opinions qui n'est guères que le recueil des erreurs humaines.

There is history based on opinion that is little more than a compendium of human error.

"De l'histoire," in *Questions sur l'Encyclopédie, par des Amateurs* (1771), 7:19; Besterman et al., *Œuvres complètes de Voltaire* (2011), 42a:197.

Les premiers fondemens de toute histoire, sont les récits des peres aux enfans, transmis ensuite d'une génération à une autre.

The tales fathers tell their children, handed down from one generation to another, are the foundational basis of any kind of history.

"De l'histoire," in *Questions sur l'Encyclopédie, par des Amateurs* (1771), 7:19; Besterman et al., *Œuvres complètes de Voltaire* (2011), 42a:197–198.

Holland

Il n'y a rien de plus agréable que La Haye quand le soleil daigne s'y montrer. On ne voit ici que des prairies, des canaux et des arbres verts; c'est un paradis terrestre depuis La Haye à Amsterdam. J'ai vu avec respect cette ville qui est le magasin de l'univers. Il y avait plus de mille vaisseaux dans le port. De cinq cent mille hommes qui habitent Amsterdam, il n'y en a pas un d'oisif, pas un pauvre, pas un petit-maître, pas un insolent.

When the sun deigns to show its face, nothing could be more agreeable than The Hague. One sees only fields, canals and verdant trees. From The Hague to Amsterdam it is an earthly paradise. I viewed with respect this latter city, which is the world's warehouse. There were more than a thousand vessels in the port. Of the five hundred thousand men that live in Amsterdam, not one is lazy, poor, puts on airs, or is insolent.

Letter from The Hague, October 7, 1722, possibly to the marquise de Bernières in Rouen.

J'y passe ma vie entre le travail et le plaisir et je vis ainsi à la hollandaise et à la française.

I divide my time here between work and pleasure, living life like both a Dutchman and a Frenchman.

Commenting on his experience at The Hague, in a letter from that city, October 7, 1722, possibly to the marquise de Bernières.

The Holy Roman Empire

Ce Corps qui s'appellait, & qui s'appelle encor, le saint Empire Romain, n'était en aucune maniére, ni saint, ni Romain, ni Empire.

This agglomeration that was called, and still calls itself, the Holy Roman Empire, was neither holy, nor Roman, nor an empire.

"De l'Empereur Charles IV," in *Essai sur les mœurs et l'esprit des nations* (1761), 2:19; Besterman et al, *Œuvres complètes de Voltaire* (2011), 24:41.

Homeland

La patrie est aux lieux où l'ame est enchainee.

Our homeland is that spot to which our heart is bound.

Palmyre (Palmira), a slave, to her master, Zopire, the leader of Mecca and an adversary of Muhammad, in act 1, scene 2, of *Le Fanatisme, ou Mahomet le Prophete* (1743), 9; Besterman et al., *Œuvres complètes de Voltaire* (2002), 20b:174.

Homosexuality

On seroit heureux disoit un vieux bougre si les femmes n'étoient jamais venues en France.

How happy we'd be, one old bugger used to say, if there had never been any women in France.

Besterman, *Voltaire's Notebooks* (1952), 2:253; Besterman et al., *Œuvres complètes de Voltaire* (1968), 82:387.

Comment s'est-il pû faire qu'un vice, destructeur du genre-humain s'il était général, qu'un attentat infame contre la nature, soit pourtant si naturel?

How can it be that a vice, destructive of mankind if it were universal, that an infamous offense against nature, is nonetheless so natural?

"Amour nommé socratique," in *Dictionnaire philosophique, portatif* (1764), 18; Besterman et al., *Œuvres complètes de Voltaire* (2007), 35:328.

Je ne peux souffrir qu'on prétende que les Grecs ont autorisé cette licence. On cite le législateur Solon, parce qu'il a dit en deux mauvais vers:
Tu chériras un beau garçon,

Tant qu'il n'aura barbe au menton.
Mais en bonne foi, Solon était-il législateur quand il fit ces deux vers ridicules? Il
était jeune alors, & quand le débauché fut devenu sage, il ne mit point une telle
infamie parmi les loix de sa république.

I cannot accept the claim that the Greeks authorized such licentiousness.
Solon the Lawgiver's name comes up, because in two lines of bad verse he
said:
You will desire a beautiful boy,
Whilst his chin remains bristle-free.
But, really, was Solon a lawgiver when he wrote those two ridiculous lines?
He was young, and when the rake matured and became wise, no such infamy
had a place among the laws of his republic.

"Amour nommé socratique," in *Dictionnaire philosophique, portatif* (1764), 19; Besterman
et al., *Œuvres complètes de Voltaire* (1994), 35:329–330.

L'amitié chez les Grecs était prescrite par la loi & la religion. La pédérastie était
malheureusement tolérée par les mœurs, il ne faut pas imputer à la loi des abus
indignes.

Affection among Greek males was ordered by law and religion. Pederasty,
unfortunately, was tolerated by custom; one must not blame the law for shameful abuses.

"Amitié," in *Questions sur l'Encyclopédie, par des Amateurs* (1770), 1:207; Besterman et al.,
Œuvres complètes de Voltaire (2007), 38:249.

Ces amusemens ont été assez communs entre les précepteurs & les écoliers. Les
moines chargés d'élever la jeunesse, ont été toujours un peu adonnés à la pédérastie.
C'est la suite nécessaire du célibat auquel ces pauvres gens sont condamnés.
Les seigneurs Turcs & Persans font, à ce qu'on nous dit, élever leurs enfans par
des eunuques; étrange alternative pour un pédagogue d'être ou châtré ou sodomite.

Such tomfoolery has been all too common between tutors and their students. The monks charged with educating the young have always been inclined
toward pederasty. It is the logical consequence of the celibicacy to which those
poor men are condemned.
Turkish and Persian nobility, so we are told, entrust their sons to eunuchs
for their education; what an odd dilemma for a pedagogue, having to choose
between castration and sodomy.

"Amour socratique," in *Questions sur l'Encyclopédie, par des Amateurs* (1774), 1:139; Besterman et al., *Œuvres complètes de Voltaire* (2007), 38:263.

Attributed to Voltaire, almost certainly apocryphal

Faire l'amour avec un garçon une fois, c'est être philosophe; deux fois, c'est être pédéraste.

If you have sex once with a boy, you are a philosopher; twice, you're a pederast.

Roger Peyrefitte ascribed this "maxim" to Voltaire in his novel, *L'Illustre écrivain* (1982), 398. A century earlier, the British Arabist Richard F. Burton cited a "popular anecdote" about Voltaire and an Englishman who found their experience of sex together unsatisfactory. Later, when his English friend said he'd tried it again, Voltaire allegedly replied, "Once: a philosopher; twice: a sodomite!" If true, this incident presumably took place in England between 1726 and 1728. See Burton, *The Book of the Thousand Nights and a Night* (1885), 10:248.

Hope

Il faut, bien loin de se plaindre, remercier l'Auteur de la nature, de ce qu'il nous donne cet instinct qui nous emporte sans cesse vers l'avenir: Le trésor le plus précieux de l'homme est cette esperance *qui nous adoucit nos chagrins, & qui nous peint des plaisirs futurs dans la possession des plaisirs présens. Si les hommes étoient assez malheureux pour ne s'occuper que du présent, on ne semeroit point, on ne bâtiroit point, on ne planteroit point, on ne pourvoyeroit à rien; on manqueroit de tout au milieu de cette fausse joüissance. . . . La nature a établi que chaque homme joüiroit du présent en se nourrissant, en faisant des enfans, en écoutant des sons agréables, en occupant sa faculté de penser & de sentir, & qu'en sortant de ces états, souvent au milieu de ces états même, il penseroit au lendemain, sans quoi il périroit de misere aujourd'hui.*

Far from complaining, we must thank the Author of nature for giving us the instinct that drives us unrelentingly forward to the future: man's most precious treasure is *hope*, which cushions our cares and paints imaginary future pleasures in the form of pleasures we now possess. If men were so ill fated as to think only of the present, we would not build, plant, or provide for anything; all would be lost in the midst of an illusory pleasure. . . . Nature dictates that we should delight in the present, nourishing ourselves, making children, listening to agreeable sounds, exercising our abilities to think and to feel; and that, whenever we set these things aside, often even in the midst of them, we should think also of tomorrow, otherwise we would die a miserable death today.

"Vingt-cinquiéme Lettre sur les Pensées de M. Pascal," in *Lettres philosophiques par M. de V . . . . .* (1734), 159; "Remarques sur les Pensées de Pascal," in *Lettres philosophiques* (1964), 2:204–205.

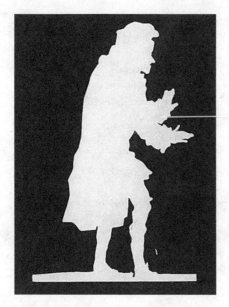

Figure 17. Jean Huber, silhouette of Voltaire cut from a playing card using a pair of scissors (eighteenth-century playing cards were blank on the back). In 1772, during a months-long sojourn in Paris, Huber gave this cutout to Mme Du Deffand. She in turn sent it to Horace Walpole in England. It is now at the Lewis Walpole Library in Farmington, Connecticut, along with three other cutouts by Huber: a profile of a beggar boy, a portrait of the duchess of Grafton and her infant son, and a second standing figure of Voltaire. Photograph courtesy of the Lewis Walpole Library, Yale University.

Jean Huber (1721–1786)

GENEVAN PATRICIAN, CUTOUT ARTIST, PAINTER, CARICATURIST, AND ACQUAINTANCE OF VOLTAIRE

Puisque vous avez vu M. Huber, il fera votre portrait, il vous peindra en pastel, à l'huile, en mezzotinto; il vous dessinera sur une carte avec des ciseaux, le tout en caricature. C'est ainsi qu'il m'a rendu ridicule d'un bout de l'Europe à l'autre.

Now that you have seen M. Huber, he will make your portrait, he will paint you in pastel, in oils, in mezzotint; he will draw your profile on a card with scissors, each one in caricature. That is how he has made me ridiculous from one end of Europe to the other.

Letter from Ferney, August 10, 1772, to Mme Du Deffand in Paris. Huber, his wife, and their children had arrived in Paris from Geneva in May or June 1772. During the year and a half he spent in Paris, Huber worked on a series of paintings depicting scenes in Voltaire's private life commissioned by Catherine the Great. Most of the surviving pictures in the series are now at the Hermitage Museum in St. Petersburg.

David Hume (1711–1776)

SCOTTISH HISTORIAN, PHILOSOPHER, ESSAYIST, AND ECONOMIST

M. Hume, dans son Histoire, ne paroît ni Parlementaire, ni Royaliste, ni Anglican, ni Presbytérien; on ne découvre en lui que l'homme équitable.

M. Hume, in his History, comes across as neither a champion of Parliament nor a Royalist, neither Anglican nor Presbyterian; what we find is simply a fair, unbiased man.

"The Complete History of England, etc.," an anonymous review by Voltaire of Hume's *History of England* (1754–1762) in the *Supplément à la Gazette littéraire de l'Europe*, May 2, 1764, 195; Besterman et al., *Œuvres complètes de Voltaire* (2016), 58:154–155. Voltaire regarded Hume as a new breed—the "nouvel Historien"—a disinterested *philosophe*, "d'aucune Patrie, d'aucune Faction," and he praised Hume's *History* as "la meilleure peut-être qui soit écrite en aucune langue."

Dans le nouvel Historien, on découvre un esprit supérieur à sa matiere, qui parle des foiblesses, des erreurs & des barbaries comme un Médecin parle des maladies épidémiques.

In the modern Historian, one discovers a spirit that rises above his material, who speaks of human weakness, error and barbarity, as a Doctor speaks of an outbreak of infectious diseases.

"The Complete History of England, etc." (1764), 199–200; Besterman et al., *Œuvres complètes de Voltaire* (2016), 58:159.

Humility

L'humilité ne peut pas constituer à se nier à soi-même la supériorité qu'on peut avoir acquise sur un autre. Un bon médecin ne peut se dissimuler qu'il en sait davantage que son malade en délire. Celui qui enseigne l'astronomie doit s'avouer qu'il est plus savant que ses disciples; il ne peut s'empêcher de le croire, mais il ne doit pas s'en faire accroire. L'humilité n'est pas l'abjection; elle est le correctif de l'amour-propre, comme la modestie est le correctif de l'orgueil.

Humility cannot involve denying to yourself the superior skill you may have acquired over someone else. A good doctor cannot disguise the fact that he knows more than his delirious patient. An instructor of astronomy must know that he is more learned than his students; he cannot help but believe it, but must not take excessive pride in it. Humility is not debasement, but serves as a corrective to self-importance, just as modesty has a curative effect on pride.

Cu-Su to Kou, in "Catéchisme chinois" (*sixième entretien*), in *La Raison par Alphabet. Septieme édition* (1773), 126; Besterman et al., *Œuvres complètes de Voltaire* (1994), 35:472.

Humor—laughter

Un bon mot ne prouve rien.

A clever line proves nothing.

L'abbé Couet to the comtesse de Boulainvilliers, in "Second Entretien. Pendant le dîner," in *Le Dîner du comte de Boulainvilliers* (1728), 21; Besterman et al., *Œuvres complètes de Voltaire* (1990), 63a:366.

La plaisanterie expliquée cesse d'être plaisanterie.

Humour explain'd is no longer Humour.

"Vingt-deuzième Lettre. Sur Mr. *Pope* Et quelques autres Poetes Fameux," in *Lettres Ecrites de Londres sur les Anglois et autres sujets* (1734), 196; "Sur Mr Pope et quelques autres poetes fameux," in *Lettres philosophiques* (1964), 2:134–135. The translation is "Letter XXII. On Mr. *Pope*, and Some Other Famous Poets," in *Letters Concerning the English Nation* (1733), 181.

Un malhonnête homme ne fera jamais rire, parce que dans le rire il entre toujours de la gaieté, incompatible avec le mépris et l'indignation.

A bad man will never make us laugh, because laughter always arises from a gayety of disposition, absolutely incompatible with contempt and indignation.

"Préface de l'éditeur," in *L'Enfant prodigue, comédie en vers dissillabes* (1738), 86; Besterman et al., *Œuvres complètes de Voltaire* (2003), 16:96. The translation is from "Preface to the Prodigal," in *The Works of Voltaire* (1901), 19:272.

Mon cher philosophe, somme totale la philosophie de Démocrite est la seule bonne. Le seul parti raisonnable dans un siècle ridicule, c'est de rire de tout.

My dear philosopher, the only philosophy that is any good is that of Democritus. The only reasonable choice we have in this ridiculous century is to laugh at everything.

Letter from Ferney, May 21, 1760, to Jean le Rond d'Alembert in Paris.

Il faut vivre en riant et mourir en riant. Voylà mon avis et la façon dont j'en use.

One must live laughing and die laughing. That is how I feel and the advice that I follow.

Letter from Ferney, May 20, 1764, to the marquis de Thibouville, presumably in Paris.

Ceux qui cherchent des causes métaphysiques au rire, ne sont pas gais: ceux qui savent pourquoi cette espèce de joie qui excite le ris, retire vers les oreilles le muscle zygomatique, l'un des treize muscles de la bouche, sont bien savans.

They who seek metaphysical causes of laughter are not mirthful, while they who are aware that laughter draws the zygomatic muscle backwards towards the ears, are doubtless very learned.

"Rire," in *Questions sur l'Encyclopédie, par des Amateurs* (1772), 9:236; Besterman et al., *Œuvres complètes de Voltaire* (2013), 43:160. The translation is from "Laughter," in *A Philosophical Dictionary* (1824), 4:299.

Toute joie ne fait pas rire, les grands plaisirs sont très sérieux; les plaisirs de l'amour, de l'ambition, de l'avarice, n'ont jamais fait rire personne.

All forms of joy do not make us laugh, the great pleasures are very serious. The pleasures of love, of ambition, of avarice, have never made anyone laugh.

"Rire," in *Questions sur l'Encyclopédie, par des Amateurs* (1772), 9:237; Besterman et al., *Œuvres complètes de Voltaire* (2013), 43:161. The translation is from "Laughter," in *A Philosophical Dictionary* (1824), 4:299.

Ideas

Les idées sont précisément comme la barbe; elle n'est point au menton d'un enfant: les idées viennent avec l'âge.

Ideas are exactly like a beard; a child has none on his chin; ideas come with age.

Entry written circa 1735–1750, in "The Piccini Notebooks," 2:231, in Besterman et al., *Œuvres complètes de Voltaire* (1968), 82:561.

Qu'est-ce qu'une idée?
C'est une image qui se peint dans mon cerveau.
Toutes vos pensées sont donc des images?
Assurément; car les idées les plus abstraites ne sont que les filles de tous les objets que j'ai aperçus. . . . je n'ai d'idées que parce que j'ai des images dans la tête.

What is an idea?
It is an image that has been fixed in my brain.
All your thoughts, then, are images?
Absolutely; for even the most abstract ideas are but the offspring of all the objects that I have perceived. . . . I have ideas only because there are images in my mind.

"Idée," in *Dictionnaire philosophique portatif. Sizieme Edition* (1767), 2:284; Besterman et al., *Œuvres complètes de Voltaire* (1994), 36:201.

Il est bien triste d'avoir tant d'idées, & de ne savoir pas au juste la nature des idées.

It is really sad to have so many ideas, and be unable to fathom their true nature.

"Idée," in *Dictionnaire philosophique portatif. Sizieme Edition* (1767), 2:286; Besterman et al., *Œuvres complètes de Voltaire* (1994), 36:204.

Ignorance

Il y a des sottises convenues qu'on réimprime tous les jours sans conséquence, & qui servent même à l'éducation de la jeunesse.

Some foolish popular notions that appear repeatedly in print day after day are harmless, and actually serve to educate the young.

"Première honnêteté," in *Les Honnêtetés litteraires &c. &c. &c.* (1767), 17; Besterman et al., *Œuvres complètes de Voltaire* (2008), 63b:81.

Indolence

La molesse est douce, & sa suite est cruelle.
Je vois autour de moi cent Rois vaincus par elle.

Indolence is sweet, and its effect is cruel.
All 'round me I see a hundred kings conquered by it.

Orosmane to Zaïre, in *Zaïre* (1732), act 1, scene 2. In *La Zayre, de M. de Voltaire* (1733), 11; Besterman et al., *Œuvres complètes de Voltaire* (1988), 8:439. John Quincy Adams, not yet twenty years old, inscribed a faulty version of the first line of this couplet on the cover of his diary for 1785: "La molesse est douce, mais la suite est cruelle" (translated by young Adams himself, perhaps, as "Ease is delightful, but the consequence is cruel." See Traub, *John Quincy Adams* (2016), 37.

Intellectual freedom

Si les premiers chrétiens n'avaient pas eu la liberté de penser, n'est-il pas vrai qu'il n'y eut point eu de Christianisme?

If the first Christians had not had freedom of thought, is it not true that there would have been no Christianity?

"Liberté de penser," in *Dictionnaire philosophique portatif. Sizieme Edition* (1767), 2:334; Besterman et al., *Œuvres complètes de Voltaire* (1994), 36. From an imaginary dialogue in which an English army officer, Lord Boldmind, puts this question to Count Medroso, another military man, and to an official with the Spanish Inquisition.

Intelligent design

Des êtres intelligens ne peuvent avoir été formés par un être brut, aveugle, insensible: il y a certainement quelque différence entre les idées de Newton & des crottes de mulet. L'intelligence de Newton venait donc d'une autre intelligence.

Intelligent beings cannot have been formed by a crude, blind, insensible being: there is certainly some difference between the ideas of Newton and the dung of a mule. Newton's intelligence, therefore, came from another intelligence.

"Dix-septième entretien. Sur des choses curieuses," in *L'A, B, C, ou Dialogues entre A. B. C.* (1769), 2:327; Besterman et al., *Œuvres complètes de Voltaire* (2011), 65a:337. Sociology professor John Bellamy Foster says, "Nowhere was intelligent design held up to more ridicule in the eighteenth century than in Voltaire's *Candide*." See Foster, Clark, and York, *Critique of Intelligent Design* (2008), 81.

Islam—the Arab world

Il était aisé de s'apercevoir que dans nos siècles de barbarie & d'ignorance, qui suivirent la décadence & le déchirement de l'Empire romain, nous reçumes presque tout des Arabes: astronomie, chimie, medécine, & surtout des remedes plus doux & plus salutaires que ceux qui avaient été connus des grecs et des romains. L'Algèbre est de l'invention de ces Arabes; nôtre aritmétique même nous fut apporté par eux.

It was easy to see that during our centuries of barbarism and ignorance following the decline and destruction of the Roman Empire, we received almost everything from the Arabs: astronomy, chemistry, medicine, especially those medications of a milder and more efficacious nature than those that were known to the Greeks and Romans. Algebra was invented by the Arabs; even our arithmetic was given to us by them.

Preface to *Essai Sur l'Histoire universelle* (1754), 3:11; Moland, *Œuvres complètes de Voltaire* (1879), 24:42–43. The *Essai Sur l'Histoire universelle* was the first published version of Voltaire's *Essai sur les mœurs et l'esprit des nations*.

J'ai dit qu'on réconnut Mahomet *pour un grand homme; rien n'est plus impie, dites-vous. Je vous répondrai que ce n'est pas ma faute, si ce petit homme a changé la face d'une partie du Monde, s'il a gagné des batailles contre des armées dix fois plus nombreuses que les siennes, s'il a fait trembler l'Empire Romain, s'il a donné les prémiers coups à ce colosse que ses Successeurs ont écrasé, & s'il a été Législateur de l'Asie, de l'Afrique, & d'une partie de l'Europe.*

I said that *Muhammad* is recognized as a great man; nothing could be more sinful, say you. I respond to you that it is not my fault that this little man changed the face of part of the World, that he won battles against forces ten times greater than his, that he shook the Roman Empire to its foundation, making an initial assault on that colossus that his Successors were able to crush, that he was the Lawmaker of Asia, Africa, and part of Europe.

"Lettre Civile et Honnête à l'Auteur Malhonnête de la Critique de l'Histoire Universelle (1760), 93–94; Besterman et al., *Œuvres complètes de Voltaire* (2016), 27:364.

Ces mêmes Maures cultivèrent les sciences avec succès, & enseignèrent l'Espagne & l'Italie pendant plus de cinq siécles. Les choses sont bien changées. Le pays de saint Augustin n'est plus qu'un repaire de pirates. L'Angleterre, l'Italie, l'Allemagne, la France qui étaient plongées dans la barbarie, cultivent les arts mieux que les Arabes.

These same Moors cultivated the sciences with success, and taught Spain and Italy for five centuries. Things have greatly changed. The land of Saint Augustine is no longer anything but a den of pirates. England, Italy, Germany, France, once plunged in barbarism, now cultivate the arts better than the Arabs.

"Augustin" (1770), 355; Besterman et al., *Œuvres complètes de Voltaire* (2008), 39:225. The baseline for Voltaire's comparison of Arab and European culture, the era of St. Augustine, was circa 400 A.D.

Il semble que Mahomet *n'ait formé un* peuple *que pour prier, pour pleurer, & pour combattre.*

It seems that Muhammad formed a people solely to pray, to weep, and to wage war.

"De l'alcoran & de la loi musulmane. Examen si la religion musulmane était nouvelle, & si elle a été persécutante," chap. 7 in the *Essai sur les mœurs et l'esprit des nations* (1769), 1:233, in Cramer and Cramer, eds., *Collection complette des Œuvres de Mr. Voltaire*, vol. 8 (1757); Besterman et al., *Œuvres complètes de Voltaire* (2009), 22:158.

Italy

Les Italiens ne sont rien.

The Italians are nothing.

Commenting on the lack of great writers, great men, and so forth, in contemporary Italy, in a letter from Versailles, March 9, 1747, to Frederick the Great in Berlin.

The last centuries are barren in Itali: the inquisition hath damp'd the genious of that warm climate.

Letter written in English from Berlin, March 27, 1752, to Sir Everard Fawkener in London.

Il disoit que les Italiens étoient une Nation de Fripiers: que l'Italie étoit une ancienne Garde-Robe, dans laquelle il y avoit beaucoup de vieux habits d'un goût parfait. C'est encore, à savoir, dit-il, lesquels, des sujets du Grand Turc ou du Pape sont les plus vils.

"The Italians," he said, "were a nation of brokers; that Italy was an old wardrobe, in which there were many old cloaths of exquisite taste. We are still," said he, "to know whether the subjects of the Pope or of the Grand Turk are the most abject."

Voltaire, speaking in English to Martin Sherlock, April 1776, quoted in Sherlock, *Letters from an English Traveller* (1780), 162–163. The French translation is from Sherlock, *Lettres d'un voyageur anglois* (1779), 147–148.

Jansenism

Ce qu'on appelle un Janséniste, est réellement un fou, un mauvais Citoïen, & un rebelle. Il est fou, parce qu'il prend pour des vérités démontrées, des idées particuliéres. S'il se servoit de sa raison, il verroit que les Philosophes n'ont jamais disputé ni pu disputer sur une vérité démontrée. S'il se servoit de sa raison, il verroit qu'une Secte qui mene à des convulsions est une Secte de fous. Il est mauvais Citoïen, parce qu'il trouble l'ordre dans l'Etat. Il est rebelle, parce qu'il desobéit.

He who is called a Jansenist, is really a madman, a bad Citizen, and a rebel. He is a madman because he mistakes certain ideas for demonstrable truths. If he were reasonable, he would see that Philosophers have never disputed or been able to dispute a demonstrable truth. If he were reasonable, he would understand that a Sect that fosters convulsions is a Sect of madmen. He is a bad citizen because he troubles the order of the State: he is a rebel, because he disobeys.

La Voix du sage et du Peuple (1750), 14–15; Besterman et al., *Œuvres complètes de Voltaire* (2006), 32a:243.

Jealousy

La jalousie quand elle est furieuse produit plus de crimes que l'intérêt & l'ambition.

Jealousy, in fury, produces more crimes than self-interest and ambition.

Letter from Potsdam, April 15, 1752, to Johann Heinrich Samuel Formey, member of the Academy of Berlin.

Jesuits

J'ai été élevé pendant sept ans chez des hommes qui se donnent des peines gratuites et infatigables à former l'esprit et les mœurs de la jeunesse.

For seven years I was educated by men who selflessly and tirelessly devoted themselves to forming youthful minds and conduct.

Letter from Versailles or Paris, circa April 1, 1746, to the Jesuit priest Simon de La Tour in Paris. Father La Tour was the headmaster, or principal, of Louis-le-Grand, where Voltaire had received his Jesuit education as a boy.

Jesus

Je demande à présent, si c'est la tolérance, ou l'intolérance qui est de droit divin? Si vous voulez ressembler à JESUS-CHRIST, soyez martirs, & non pas boureaux.

I now desire to know, whether toleration or non toleration appears to be of divine prescription? Let those who would resemble Christ, be martyrs, and not executioners.

"Si l'intolérance a été enseigné par Jésus-Christ," in *Traité sur la Tolérance* (1762), from the 1763 edition, chap. 14, 155; Besterman et al., *Œuvres complètes de Voltaire* (2000), 56c:225. The translation is from *A Treatise Upon Toleration, &c.* in Smollett et al., *The Works of Mr. de Voltaire* (1764), 34:195.

S'il était permis de raisonner conséquemment en fait de Religion, il est clair que nous devrions tous nous faire Juifs, puisque Jesus-Christ, notre Sauveur, est né Juif, a vecu Juif, est mort Juif, & qu'il a dit expressément qu'il accomplissait, qu'il remplissait la Religion Juive.

If it were permitted to reason consistently in matters of Religion, clearly we all should become Jews, because Jesus Christ, Our Savior, was born a Jew, lived a Jew, died a Jew, and explicitly stated that he was carrying out, that he was fulfilling the Jewish Religion.

"Tolérance," in *Dictionnaire philosophique, portatif. Nouvelle Édition* (1765), 333; Besterman et al., *Œuvres complètes de Voltaire* (1994), 36:566.

Jews—Judaism

Vous ne trouverez en eux qu'un Peuple ignorant & barbare, qui joint depuis long-tems la plus sordide avarice à la plus détestable superstition, & à la plus invincible haine pour tous les Peuples qui les tolèrent & qui les enrichissent. Il ne faut pourtant pas les bruler.

You will find in them nothing more than an ignorant and barbarous People, that has long joined the most sordid avarice to the most detestable superstition, and the most stubborn hatred for all Peoples that tolerate and enrich them. *Nonetheless, they should not be burned at the stake.*

"Des Juifs," in *Suite des mélanges de littérature, d'histoire et de philosophie* (1757), 18; Besterman et al., *Œuvres complètes de Voltaire* (2010), 45b:138.

Les lignes dont vous vous plaignez, Monsieur, sont violentes et injustes. Il y a parmi vous des hommes très instruits et très respectables, votre lettre m'en convainc assez. J'aurai soin de faire un carton dans la nouvelle édition. Quand on a un tort il faut le réparer et j'ai tort d'attribuer à toute une nation les vices de plusieurs particuliers.

The lines you object to are violent and unjust. There are among you some very educated and very respectable men; your letter itself convinces me of this. I will be sure to make an insertion in the new edition. When one is in the wrong, amends must be made, and I was wrong to attribute the vices of several individuals to an entire nation.

Letter from Les Délices, July 21, 1762, to Isaac Pinto, a Sephardic financier and moralist, in Paris. In a forty-page tract, *Apologie pour la nation juive* (1762), Pinto had criticized the anti-Semitic "calumnies" in "Des Juifs," a chapter in Voltaire's *Suite des mélanges de littérature, d'histoire et de philosophie* (1756).

Il est étonnant qu'il reste encore des Juifs. . . . Jamais les Juifs n'eurent aucun pays en propre depuis Vespasien, excepté quelques Bourgades dans les Déserts de l'Arabie heureuse, vers la Mer Rouge. Mahomet fut d'abord obligé de les ménager. Mais à la fin il détruisit la petite Domination qu'ils avaient établie au Nord de la Mecque. C'est depuis Mahomet qu'ils ont cessé réellement de composer un corps de Peuple.

It is surprising that there should remain any Jews. . . . The Jews never had any country to themselves since the time of Vespasian, except some hamlets of Arabia Felix towards the Red-Sea. Mahomet was at first obliged to keep terms with them; but he at length destroyed the little dominion which they had established in the north of Mecca. It is from the time of Mahomet that they have actually ceased to exist as a body of people.

"Des Juifs depuis Saül," in *La Philosophie de l'Histoire, Par feu l'Abbé Bazin* (1765), 234–235; Besterman et al., *Œuvres complètes de Voltaire* (1969), 59:234. The translation is from *The Philosophy of History by M. de Voltaire* (1766), 184–185.

En suivant simplement le fil historique de la petite Nation Juive, on voit qu'elle ne pouvait avoir une autre fin. . . . Elle ose étaler une haine irréconciliable contre toutes les Nations; elle se révolte contre tous ses Maîtres; toujours superstitieuse, toujours avide du bien d'autrui, toujours barbare, rampante dans le malheur, & insolente dans la prospérité. Voilà ce que furent les Juifs aux yeux des Grecs & des Romains qui purent lire leurs Livres: mais aux yeux des Chrétiens éclairés par la Foi, ils ont été nos Précurseurs, ils nous ont préparé la voye. Ils ont été les Hérauts de la Providence.

If we simply follow the historical thread of the little Jewish Nation, we see that they could come to no other end. . . . They have the gall to display an irreconcilable hatred against all other Nations; they revolt against all Masters; ever superstitious, ever envious of what others possess; ever barbarous; abject in bad times, and insolent in good times. Such were the Jews in the opinion of the Greeks and Romans, who could read their Books: but in the eyes of Christians, enlightened by the Faith that they persecuted, they prepared the way for us. They have been the Heralds of Providence.

"Des Juifs depuis Saül," in *La Philosophie de l'Histoire, Par feu l'Abbé Bazin* (1765), 235–236; Besterman et al., *Œuvres complètes de Voltaire* (1969), 59:235.

C'est une erreur absurde d'avoir imaginé que les Juifs fussent les seuls qui reconnussent un Dieu unique; c'était la doctrine de presque tout l'Orient; & les Juifs en cela ne furent que des plagiaires comme ils le furent en tout.

It is an absurd mistake to imagine that the Jews were the only people who recognized a single God; that was the doctrine almost everywhere in the East; and the Jews were only plagiarists, in that as in everything they did.

"Job," in *La Raison par Alphabet. Sixiéme édition* (1769), 195, later incorporated into the *Dictionnaire philosophique*; Besterman et al., *Œuvres complètes de Voltaire* (2011), 36:250.

Tous les autres peuples ont commis des crimes, les Juifs sont les seuls qui s'en soient vantés. Ils sont tous nés avec la rage du fanatisme dans le cœur, comme les Germains & les Anglais naissent avec des cheveux blonds. Je ne serais point étonné que cette nation ne fût un jour funeste au genre-humain.

All other races have committed crimes; the Jews are the only ones who have boasted about it. They are all born with fanaticism raging in their hearts, just as the Germans and the English are born with blond hair. I would not in the least be surprised if some day these people did not pose a deadly threat to humankind.

Lettres de Memmius à Cicéron (1771), "Lettre seconde," in *Mélanges philosophiques, littéraires, historiques, &c.* (1771), 4:346; Besterman et al., *Œuvres complètes de Voltaire* (2011), 72:220.

Vous l'avez emporté sur toutes les nations en fables impertinentes, en mauvaise conduite & en barbarie; vous en portez la peine; tel est votre destin.

You have surpassed all nations in impertinent fables, in bad conduct and in barbarism. You deserve to be punished, for this is your destiny.

"Il faut prendre un parti, ou le principe d'action. Diatribe" (1772), under the subhead "Discours d'un théiste," in *Piéces détachées, attribuées à divers hommes célèbres, &c.* (1775), 2:291; Besterman et al., *Œuvres complètes de Voltaire* (1968), 74b:62.

Samuel Johnson (1709–1784)

ENGLISH ESSAYIST, LITERARY CRITIC, BIOGRAPHER, AND LEXICOGRAPHER

A superstitious dog.

Boswell said that Voltaire once applied this term to Dr. Johnson in a conversation at Ferney. When Boswell repeated a disparaging remark by Johnson about the literary ability of Frederick the Great, Voltaire changed his tune, and called him "An honest fellow!" See Boswell, *The Life of Samuel Johnson* (1791), 1:236.

Je ne veux point soupçonner le sieur Jonhson [sic] d'être un mauvais plaisant, & d'aimer trop le vin; mais je trouve un peu extraordinaire qu'il compte la bouffonnerie & l'yvrognerie parmi les beautés du théâtre tragique.

I do not desire to suspect Master Johnson of being a sorry jester, and of being too fond of wine; but I find it somewhat extraordinary that he counts buffoonery and drunkenness among the beauties of the tragic stage.

"Art dramatique, Ouvrages dramatiques, Tragédie, Comédie, Opéra," in *Questions sur l'Encyclopédie, par des Amateurs* (1770), 2:202; Besterman et al., *Œuvres complètes de Voltaire* (2003), 39:52. The translation is from *Voltaire's Philosophical Dictionary* (1924), 110.

Journalism

Vous me demandez comment il faut s'y prendre, pour qu'un Journal plaise à notre Siécle & à la Posterité. Je vous répondrai en deux mots; soyez impartial.

You ask me how you should proceed, in order that a Gazette might find favor in this Century and with Posterity. I will answer you in two words: be impartial.

"Avis à un journaliste," *Mercure de France*, November 1744, 2, and as "Conseils à un journaliste, Sur la Philosophie, l'Histoire, le Théâtre, les Pièces de Poësie, les Mélanges de littérature, les Anecdotes Littéraires, les Langues, & le Stile," in *Collection complete des Œuvres de Monsieur de Voltaire, Nouvelle Édition* (1764), 6:13; Besterman et al., *Œuvres complètes de Voltaire* (2003), 20a:477.

Il faut qu'un bon Journaliste sçache au moins l'Anglois & l'Italien. . . . Ce sont, je crois, les deux langues de l'Europe les plus nécessaires à un François.

A good Journalist must know at least English and Italian. . . . These, I believe, are the two European languages required most by a Frenchman.

"Avis à un journaliste," *Mercure de France*, November 1744, 34, and as "Conseils à un journaliste," in *Collection complete des Œuvres de Monsieur de Voltaire, Nouvelle Édition* (1764), 6:52; Besterman et al., *Œuvres complètes de Voltaire* (2003), 20a:509.

La presse, il le faut avouer, est devenue un des fléaux de la société, & un brigandage intolérable.

The press, we must admit, has become one of the scourges of society, and a form of banditry.

Letter from Potsdam, April 15, 1752, to Johann Heinrich Samuel Formey, member of the Academy of Berlin.

Sallo (Denis) né en 1626. conseiller du parlement de paris. Inventeur des journaux. Bayle perfectionna ce genre, déshonoré ensuite par quelques journaux, que publièrent à l'envie des libraires avides, & que des écrivains obscurs remplirent d'extraits infidéles, d'inepties & de mensonges.

Sallo (Denis), born in 1626. Counsellor of the Parliament of Paris. Inventor of the periodical press, perfected by Bayle, and since dishonored by several gazettes printed by mercenary booksellers, which obscure writers have crammed full of corrupt excerpts, trivial articles and lies.

Le Siecle de Louis XIV. Nouvelle edition revue par l'auteur et considerablement augmentée. Tome second (1753), 467–468; Besterman et al., *Œuvres complètes de Voltaire* (2017), 12:186. In 1665, Denis de Sallo founded the *Journal des sçavans*, still in existence as the *Journal des savants*.

Ce sont des gens bien méprisables, je l'avoüe; mais ils peuvent nuire dans l'occasion, quand ils sont bien dirigés.

I will admit that they are despicable people; but they can do damage from time to time, when properly led.

Anitus, talking about journalists, to three fellow conspirators in his plot against Socrates, in act 3, scene 6, of the second edition of Voltaire's unstaged tragedy, *Socrate*, in *Seconde Suite des mélanges de littérature, d'histoire, et de philosophie* (1761), 165.

Justice—injustice

Ce grand principe: qu'il vaut mieux hazarder de sauver un coupable, que de condamner un innocent.

This great principle: that it is better to risk saving a guilty man, than to condemn one who is innocent.

The philosophy of Zadig as prime minister to the king of Babylon and judge in legal matters. From "Les Jugemens," chap. 6 in *Zadig. Histoire orientale*, in *Oeuvres de Mr. de Voltaire. Nouvelle Edition* (1748), 8:26; Besterman et al., *Œuvres complètes de Voltaire* (2004), 30b:142.

Un jugement trop prompt est souvent sans justice.

A judgement too swiftly rendered is often unjust.

Julius Cæsar to Cato, in act 4, scene 4, of Voltaire's tragedy, *Rome sauvée*, performed for the first time on February 24, 1752; from the 1755 edition, *Rome sauvée, Tragédie. Par M. De Voltaire*, 66; Besterman et al., *Œuvres complètes de Voltaire* (2015), 49b:211.

L'injustice à la fin produit l'indépendance.

In the end, injustice incites independence.

Amenaïde to her father, Argire, a knight in the Norman army at war in Sicily in the year 1005, in *Tancrède*, act 4, scene 6, first staged at the Théâtre de la rue des Fossés in Paris, March 9, 1760. *Tancrède, Tragédie; Par Mr. De Voltaire* (1761), 65; Besterman et al., *Œuvres complètes de Voltaire* (2009), 49b:212.

Je vous réponds, Mesdemoiselles, sur du papier orné de fleurs, parce que je crois que le temps des épines est passé, et qu'on rendra justice à votre respectable mère et à vous.

I reply to you, ladies, on a sheet of paper adorned with flowers because I believe your thorny ordeal is past, and justice will be served to your worthy mother and to you.

Letter from Ferney, January 18, 1763, to Mademoiselles Anne-Rose Calas and Rose Calas in Paris.

La notion de quelque chose de juste me semble si naturelle, si universellement acquise par tous les hommes, qu'elle est indépendante de toute loi, de tout pacte, de toute religion.

Justice seems to me a concept so natural, and so universally accepted by all mankind, as to be independent of all laws, of all agreements, of all religion.

"Utilité réelle. Notion de la justice," in *Le Philosophe ignorant* (1766), 56; Besterman et al., *Œuvres complètes de Voltaire* (1987), 62:78.

Je crois donc que les idées du juste & de l'injuste sont aussi claires, aussi universelles que les idées de santé & de maladie, de vérité & de fausseté, de convenance & d'inconvenance.

I believe that the ideas of just and unjust are as clear-cut, as universal, as the ideas of health and sickness, of truth and falsehood, of propriety and impropriety.

"Utilité réelle. Notion de la justice," in *Le Philosophe ignorant* (1766), 59; Besterman et al., *Œuvres complètes de Voltaire* (1987), 62:80.

Knowledge

Le savoir, en effet, n'est rien sans l'art de vivre.

Without the art of living, knowledge is, indeed, hollow.

Au prince royal de Prusse (1736), in Besterman et al., *Œuvres complètes de Voltaire* (2003), 16:380.

Un Romain était savant quand il savait l'histoire de Rome; un Grec ne savait que sa langue et l'hist. d'Hérodote; nous, religion, langues, mathématiques, histoire de l'univers.

A Roman was well educated when he knew the history of Rome; a Greek had to know only his own language and the history by Herodotus. We know religion, languages, mathematics, world history.

"Appendice: Supplément aux œuvres en prose" ("Traits singuliers du règne de Louis XIV"), in *Œuvres complètes de Voltaire. Commentaires sur Corneille II* (1880), 588. See also *Le Sottisier de Voltaire* (1880), 100; Besterman, *Voltaire's Notebooks* (1952), 2:278; Besterman et al., *Œuvres complètes de Voltaire* (1968), 82:415.

Jean de La Fontaine (1621–1695)

FABULIST

La Fontaine, qui avoit reçû de la Nature l'instinct le plus heureux que jamais homme ait eu.

La Fontaine, who received from Nature, the happiest instinct e'er one man had.

Le Temple du Goust (1733), 53; Besterman et al., *Œuvres complètes de Voltaire* (1999), 9:174.

Maurice-Quentin de La Tour (1704–1788)

FRENCH PASTEL PORTRAITIST

Je vous fais mon compliment, mon cher confrère dans les beaux arts, des grands succès que vous avez à Paris. Je me flatte que vous voulez bien guider le graveur qui fait mon estampe d'après votre pastel.

I compliment you, my dear brother in the arts, for your great success in Paris. I am flattered that you are willing to guide the engraver who is making a print based on your pastel.

Letter from Cirey, October 22, 1738, to de La Tour in Paris, where the artist had been *agréé* as a member of the Académie Royale de Peinture et de Sculpture in May 1737.

Voltaire sat for his portrait in pastel by de La Tour in 1734. The fate of the original is unknown, but Voltaire owned an excellent copy that is still at the château de Ferney. For an engraving after the original, see figure 21.

Malgré tous les efforts des hommes, il n'est aucun langage qui approche de la perfection.

Notwithstanding all the efforts of man, no language comes near to perfection.

"Des Sauvages," in *Nouveaux Mélanges philosophiques, historiques, critiques, &c. &c. &c.* (1765), 1:39; Besterman et al., *Œuvres complètes de Voltaire* (1969), 59:115. The translation is from *The Philosophy of History* (1766), 36.

John Law (1671–1729)

Scottish banker and *contrôleur général des finances* during the regency of the Duke of Orleans who, in 1716, created the Banque Générale and introduced the use of paper currency in France.

Les peuples se précipitèrent d'eux-mêmes dans cette folie, qui enrichit quelques familles, & qui en réduisit tant d'autres à la mendicité.

The people of their own accord ran headlong into this folly, which enriched some families, and reduced many more to beggary.

Speaking of "ce fameux systême de Law," in "Suite du tableau de l'Europe. Régence du duc d'Orléans. Systême de *Law*," chap. 1 in *Précis du siècle de Louis XV*, in *Siècle de Louis XIV. Nouvelle Edition* (1768), 3:264; Moland, *Œuvres complètes de Voltaire* (1878), 15:163. The translation is from *Modern History Continued*, in Smollett et al., *The Works of Mr. de Voltaire* (1761), 8:13.

Un écossais nommé Jean Law, que nous nommons Jean Lass, qui n'avait d'autre métier que d'être grand joueur & grand calculateur, obligé de fuir de la grande Bretagne pour un meurtre, avait dès longtems rédigé le plan d'une compagnie, qui payerait en billets les dettes d'un état, & qui se rembourserait par les profits.

A Scotchman, named John Law, whom we call John Lass, who had no other employment than that of a gamester and calculator, was obliged to fly from Great Britain on account of a murder: he had a long time before [he] digested [drew up] the plan of a company, which was to pay the debts of a state by bank-notes, and reimburse itself with the profits.

"Suite du tableau de l'Europe," chap. 1 in *Précis du siécle de Louis XV*, in *Siécle de Louis XIV. Nouvelle Edition* (1768), 3:264; Moland, *Œuvres complètes de Voltaire* (1878), 15:163. The translation is from *Modern History Continued*, in Smollett et al., *The Works of Mr. de Voltaire* (1761), 8:13.

Law—lawyers

Il le doit, mais sur-tout il doit aimer les Loix:
Il doit en être Esclave, en porter tout le poids;
Qui veut les violer n'aime point sa patrie.

'Tis his duty: but mainly he must love the Laws;
He must be their Slave and endure even their flaws.
He who'd break them does not truly love his country.

Junius Brutus to Messala, a friend of Brutus's son Titus, in act 2, scene 4, of a later, revised version of *Brutus* in *Oeuvres de M. de Voltaire. Nouvelle Edition, Revue, corrigée & considérablement augmentée* (1738), 2:298; Besterman et al., *Œuvres complètes de Voltaire* (1998), 5:217. An *avertissement* in this edition (231) states that the text of the play differs significantly from earlier editions.

Pour moi ce qui m'a dégoûté de la profession d'avocat c'est la profusion de choses inutiles dont on voulut charger ma cervelle. Au fait! est ma devise.

What was repulsive to me about the legal profession is the profusion of useless things they wished to cram into my brain. *To the point! is my motto.*

Letter from Brussels, July 28, 1739, to d'Argenson in Paris. As a young man, Voltaire had briefly trained as a lawyer.

Il n'y a de pays bien policé que celuy dans le quel, la vangeance ce n'est qu'entre les mains des loix.

The only civilized country is the one in which vengeance is in the hands of the law alone.

Besterman, *Voltaire's Notebooks* (1952), 1:111; Besterman et al., *Œuvres complètes de Voltaire* (1968), 81:230. See also *Le Sottisier de Voltaire* (1880), 9.

Un citoyen de Londres me disait un jour, C'est la nécessité qui fait lois, & la force les fait observer. Je lui demandai si la force ne faisait pas aussi quelquefois des loix, & si Guillaume le bâtard & le conquérant ne leur avait pas donné des ordres sans faire de marché avec eux. Oui, dit-il, nous étions des bœufs alors; Guillaume nous mit un joug, & nous fit marcher à coups d'aiguillons; nous avons depuis été changés en hommes, mais les cornes nous sont restées, & nous frappons quiconque veut nous faire labourer pour lui, & non pas pour nous.

A citizen of London once said to me, "Laws are made by necessity, and observed through force." I asked him if force did not also occasionally make laws, and if William, the bastard and conqueror, had not chosen simply to issue his orders without condescending to make any convention or bargain with the English at all. "True," said he, "it was so: we were oxen at that time; William brought us under the yoke, and drove us with a goad; since that period we have been metamorphosed into men; the horns, however, remain with us still, and we use them as weapons against every man who attempts making us work for him and not for ourselves."

"Des Loix," in *Dictionnaire philosophique, portatif* (1764), 251–252; Besterman et al., *Œuvres complètes de Voltaire* (1994), 36:315. The translation is from "Laws," in *A Philosophical Dictionary* (1824), 4:328.

Un Avocat est un homme qui n'ayant pas assez de fortune pour acheter un de ces brillans offices sur lesquels l'Univers a les yeux, étudie pendant trois ans les loix de Théodose & de Justinien pour connaître la coutume de Paris, & qui enfin, étant immatriculé, a le droit de plaider pour de l'argent s'il a la voix forte.

A Lawyer is a man who, being too poor to buy one of those grand offices everyone everywhere has his eye on, studies for three years the laws of *Theodosius and Justinian* in order to learn the ways of Paris, and who, when at last admitted to the bar, has earned the right to plead cases in court for money, if he has a loud voice.

"Des Avocats," in *Nouveaux Mélanges philosophiques, historiques, critiques, &c. &c. &c.* (1765), 3:111–112; Besterman et al., *Œuvres complètes de Voltaire* (2017), 60a:236.

Que toute Loi soit claire, uniforme & précise: l'interpréter, c'est presque toujours la corrompre.

Clear, uniform, and precise be thy Law: in its interpretation it will almost always be corrupted.

"Loix: Fragment d'un Dialogue entre un Bachelier & un Sauvage," in *Les Pensées de Monsieur de Voltaire* (1768), 84; also published, with one slight difference in capitalization, in "Lois civiles et écclésiastiques," in *Dictionnaire philosophique*, 5:481, in Beaumarchais's edition of the *Oeuvres complètes de Voltaire* (1785), vol. 41; Besterman et al., *Œuvres complètes de Voltaire* (1994), 36:323.

Voulez-vous avoir de bonnes loix; brûlez les vôtres & faites-en de nouvelles.

If you want good laws, burn those you have already and make new ones.

"Loix" (1771), 7:353; Besterman et al., *Œuvres complètes de Voltaire* (2012), 42b:74.

*Attributed to Voltaire, almost
certainly apocryphal*

I never was ruined but twice; once when I won a lawsuit, and once when I lost it.

Quoted in English in *The Galaxy of Wit: Or, Laughing Philosopher, Being a Collection of Choice Anecdotes, Many of Which Originated in or about "The Literary Emporium"* (1880), 1:112. Although not attributed to Voltaire, the same witticism was published as a free-standing squib in *The Country Gentleman: A Journal for the Farm, Garden, and Fireside*, August 3, 1865, 88.

Learned men

Décideur impitoyable, pédagogue à phrases, raisonneur fouré, tu cherches les bornes de ton esprit. Elles sont au bout de ton nez.

Heartless critic, wordy pedagogue, cosseted sophist, you pursue the limits of your mind. They are at the tip of your nose.

"Bornes à l'esprit humain," in *Questions sur l'Encyclopédie, par des Amateurs* (1770), 3:153; Besterman et al., *Œuvres complètes de Voltaire* (2008), 39:433.

Ce que les honnêtes gens ont le plus reproche aux savans & ceux qui pretendent l'étre, soit grecs soit barbares c'est d'avoir voulu aller plus loin que la nature. Ils ont creusé des abymes & le terrein est retombe sur eux.

What honest men have most often accused learned men and those who pretend to be learned men of doing, whether they be Greeks or barbarians, is to have wanted to go beyond the bounds of nature. They dug gaping holes, and the earth fell back upon them.

Dialogues d'Évhémère (1777), from the 1779 edition, 115; Besterman et al., *Œuvres complètes de Voltaire* (2009), 80c:267. In this, Voltaire's last published work in his lifetime, the Greek philosopher Euhemerus (Évhémère) makes this statement to his friend Callicrates.

Adrienne Lecouvreur (1692–1730)

FRENCH ACTRESS

*Et dans un champ profane on jette à l'aventure
De ce corps si chéri les restes immortels!*

And in this unhallowed ground they casually throw
The immortal remains of a person once so beloved!

"La Mort de Mlle Lecouvreur" (1730), in *Oeuvres de M. de Voltaire. Nouvelle Édition* (1732), 1:225; Besterman et al., *Œuvres complètes de Voltaire* (1998), 5:558. The greatest actress of her generation was buried in marshland in what is now the Champ de Mars in Paris. Voltaire thought she was poisoned but could not prove it.

On a même reproché aux Anglois d'avoir été trop loin dans les honneurs qu'ils ren-dent au simple merite. On a trouvé à redire qu'ils aïent enterré dans Westminster la celebre Comedienne Mrs. Oldfield à peu près avec les mêmes honneurs rendus à Mr. Newton. Quelques uns ont prétendu qu'ils avoient affecté d'honorer à ce point sa memoire, afin de nous faire sentir davantage la barbare & lâche injustice qu'ils nous reprochent, d'avoir jetté à la voirie le corps de Mademoiselle le Couvreur.

The *English* have even been reproach'd with paying too extravagant Honours to mere Merit, and censured for interring the celebrated Actress Mrs. *Old-field in Westminster-Abbey*, with almost the same Pomp as Sir *Isaac Newton*. Some pretend that the *English* had paid her these great Funeral Honours, purposely to make us more strongly sensible of the Barbarity and Injustice which they object to us, for having buried *Mademoiselle le Couvreur* ignominiously in the Fields.

"Vingt-troisième Lettre. Sur la Consideration Qu'on doit aux Gens de Lettres," in *Lettres Ecrites de Londres sur les Anglois et autres sujets* (1734), 206–207; "Sur la Considération de ce qu'on doit aux gens de lettres," in *Lettres philosophiques* (1964), 2:159. The translation is "Letter XXIII. On the Regard That ought to be shown to Men of Letters," in *Letters Concerning the English Nation* (1733), 227.

Eustache Le Sueur (1617–1655)

FRENCH PAINTER ACTIVE AT THE START OF LOUIS XIV'S REIGN

Il avait porté l'art de la peinture au plus haut point, lorsqu'il mourut à l'âge de 38 ans en 1655.

When he died at the age of 38 in 1655, he had raised the art of painting to the highest degree.

"Artistes célèbres," in "Des peintres, sculpteurs, architectes, graveurs, &c.," in *Le Siècle de Louis XIV* (1751), 2:433; Besterman et al., *Œuvres complètes de Voltaire* (2017), 12:211.

Libraries

Une grande bibliothèque a cela de bon, qu'elle effraye celui qui la regarde. Deux cents mille volumes découragent un homme tenté d'imprimer; mais malheureusement il se dit bientôt à lui-même: on ne lit point la plûpart de ces livres-là; & on pourra me lire.

Il se compare à la goute d'eau qui se plaignait d'être confondue & ignorée dans l'océan: un génie eut pitié d'elle; il la fit avaler par une huitre; elle devint la plus belle perle de l'Orient, et fut le principal ornement du trône du grand-Mogol. Ceux qui ne sont que compilateurs, imitateurs, commentateurs, éplucheurs de phrases, critiques à la petite semaine; enfin ceux dont un génie n'a point eu pitié resteront toûjours goutes d'eau.

One good thing about a large library is that it strikes fear in those who gaze upon it. Two hundred thousand volumes discourage a man tempted to publish something; but unfortunately, he soon says to himself: "People do not read all those books; and they may read mine." He compares himself to the drop of water that complained of being lost in the ocean and ignored: a genie had pity on it; he caused it to be swallowed by an oyster; it became the loveliest pearl in the Orient, and was the chief jewel in the throne of the Great Mogul. Those who are mere compilers, imitators, commentators, splitters of phrases, petty critics, in short those on whom a genie would never take pity, will always remain drops of water.

"Bibliothèque," in *Questions sur l'Encyclopédie, par des Amateurs* (1770), 3:82–83; Besterman et al., *Œuvres complètes de Voltaire* (2007), 39:360.

La bibliothèque publique du roi de France est la plus belle du monde entier, moins encore par le nombre & la rareté des volumes, que par la facilité, & la politesse avec laquelle les bibliothécaires les prêtent à tous les savans. Cette bibliothèque est sans contredit le monument le plus précieux qui soit en France.

The public library of the king of France is the finest anywhere on earth, less on account of the quantity and rarity of its holdings, than the efficiency and kindness with which its librarians lend them to all scholars. This library is unquestionably the most esteemed monument in France.

"Bibliothèque," in *Questions sur l'Encyclopédie, par des Amateurs* (1770), 3:83; Besterman et al., *Œuvres complètes de Voltaire* (2007), 39:361.

Il y a maintenant plus de quatre mille bibliothèques considérables en Europe. Choisissez ce qui vous convient, & tâchez de ne vous pas ennuier.

There are now over four thousand libraries of consequence in Europe. Choose the one that suits you, and try not to be bored.

"Bibliothèque," in *Questions sur l'Encyclopédie, par des Amateurs* (1770), 3:85; Besterman et al., *Œuvres complètes de Voltaire* (2007), 39:364.

La vûë d'une bibliothèque me fait tomber en syncope.

The mere sight of a library makes me feel faint.

Lettre XII, "Sur le Dante, et sur un pauvre homme nommé Martinelli," in *Lettres chinoises, indiennes et tartares adressées A M. Paw par un Bénédictin* (1776), 144; Besterman et al., *Œuvres complètes de Voltaire* (2014), 77b:207.

Lies—lying

Le mensonge n'est un vice que quand il fait du mal; c'est une très grande vertu, quand il fait du bien. Soyez donc plus vertueux que jamais. Il faut mentir comme un diable, non pas timidement, non pas pour un temps mais hardiment et toujours.

A lie is only a vice when it causes harm; it is a great virtue when it does some good. So, be more virtuous than ever. You must lie like the devil, not timidly, not for a brief while, but boldly and constantly.

Letter from Cirey, October 21, 1736, to Nicolas-Claude Thieriot in Paris.

D'un bout du monde à l'autre on ment & l'on mentit;
Nos neveux mentiront comme ont fait nos ancêtres.

From one end of the earth to the other people lie and have lied;
Our nephews will lie, just as our ancestors have done.

Le Dimanche, ou les Filles de Minée (1775), 14; Besterman et al., *Œuvres complètes de Voltaire* (2014), 77a:78.

Life

On entre en guerre en entrant dans le monde.

As soon as we enter this world we are at war.

"Épître sur la calomnie" (1733), dedicated to Mme du Châtelet, from *L'Esprit de Monsieur de Voltaire* (1759), 97; Besterman et al., *Œuvres complètes de Voltaire* (1999), 9:307.

Pourquoi existons-nous? pourquoi y a-t-il quelque chose?

Why do we exist? why is there anything?

"Les Pourquoi" (likely written circa 1745), in *Mélanges philosophiques, littéraires, historiques, &c.* (1771), 4:381; Besterman et al., *Œuvres complètes de Voltaire* (2008), 28b:111. The translation is from "Whys (The)," in *Philosophical Dictionary* (1824), 6:358.

Hélas! grands et petits, et sujets, et monarques,
Distingués un moment par de frivoles marques,
Égaux par la nature, égaux par le malheur,

Tout mortel est chargé de sa propre douleur:
Sa peine lui suffit, et, dans ce grand naufrage,
Rassembler nos débris, voilà notre partage.

Alas! great and small, vassal and monarch alike,
Distinguished a brief while by trifling marks,
Equal by nature, equal by misfortune,
Each mortal must shoulder his own pain and sorrow:
They are his alone, and, as we face this great wreck,
To collect our remains, that is our sad lot.

Idamé to her husband, Zamti, in the tragedy, *L'Orphelin de la Chine* (1755), act 2, scene 4; Besterman et al., *Œuvres complètes de Voltaire* (2009), 45a:148.

Tout meurit par le tems, & s'accroit par l'usage.
Chaque être a son objet, & dans l'instant marqué
Il marche vers le but par le Ciel indiqué.

Every creature ripens with time, and grows through use.
Each has its purpose and at the appointed hour
Moves on toward that goal which Heaven has designed.

"La Loi naturelle; Poëme en Quatre Parties," in *Poëmes sur le désastre de Lisbonne et sur la loi naturelle* (1756), 34; Besterman et al., *Œuvres complètes de Voltaire* (2007), 32b:65.

Un lion mort ne vaut pas
Un moucheron qui respire.

A lifeless lion is worth less
Than a fly that still draws breath.

Précis de l'Ecclésiaste (1759), 10; Besterman et al., *Œuvres complètes de Voltaire* (2010), 49a:212. "Paraphrase" of two lines from Ecclesiastes 9:4, in French, "et même un chien vivant vaut mieux qu'un lion mort" (in English, "for a living dog is better than a dead lion").

Je conçois que la vie est prodigieusement ennuyeuse quand elle est uniforme.

Life as I see it is terribly boring when it is static and unchanging.

Letter from Les Délices or the château de Tournay, February 18, 1760, to Mme Du Deffand in Paris.

Je vous écris rarement, parce que je n'aurais jamais que la même chose à vous mander; et quand je vous aurai bien répété que la vie est un enfant qu'il faut bercer jusqu'à ce qu'il s'endorme, j'aurai dit tout ce que je sais.

I rarely write to you because I should only have the same thing to say; and once I've told you yet again that life is an infant that must be rocked in its cradle until it falls asleep, I shall have told you everything I know.

Letter from Ferney, July 22, 1761, to Mme Du Deffand in Paris.

Je n'ai point peuplé, et j'en demande pardon à Dieu. Mais aussi, la vie est-elle toujours quelque chose de si plaisant qu'il faille se repentir de ne l'avoir pas donné à d'autres?

I have sired no offspring, and for that I beg God's forgiveness. But that said, is life really so pleasurable that one must repent for not having given it to others?

Letter from Ferney, January 2, 1763, to Étienne-Noël Damilaville in Paris.

Adieu, mon cher gros chat, vivons tant que nous pourrons, mais la vie n'est que de l'ennui ou de la crème fouettée.

Adieu, my big beloved pussycat, let us live as best we can, though life is nothing but boredom or whipped cream.

Letter from Les Délices, November 17, 1763, to Mme Antoinette Françoise de Champbonin at Champbonin near Vassy, in Champagne.

La vie est hérissée de ces épines, et je n'y sais d'autre remède que de cultiver son jardin.

Life is bristling with thorns, and I know no other remedy than to cultivate one's garden.

Letter from Ferney, October 21, 1769, to Pierre-Joseph-François Luneau de Boisjermain in Paris.

. . . tout passe & tout meurt; tel est l'arrêt du sort,
L'instant où nous naissons est un pas vers la mort.

. . . all things pass and die; that is the iron law of fate:
The instant we are born is a first step toward death.

"Exhortation à l'agonie d'un curé de C.D.," in *Nouveaux Melanges philosophiques, historiques, critiques, &c. &c. &c. Dixiéme partie* (1770), 382; reprinted as "La Fête de Bellébat. À son Altesse sérénissime Mademoiselle de Clermont" (1725), in Beaumarchais's edition of the *Œuvres complètes de Voltaire* (1784), 12:360; Besterman et al., *Œuvres complètes de Voltaire* (2004), 3a:165. Mlle de Clermont was the sister of the duc de Bourbon.

La fin de la vie est triste, le milieu n'en vaut rien, et le commencement est ridicule.

Life in its final phase is sad, the middle is worthless, and the beginning ridiculous.

Letter from Ferney, April 7, 1770, to Voltaire's nephew by marriage, the marquis de Florian, residing at this time, perhaps, near Abbeville.

Avec toi, l'on apprend à souffrir l'indigence,
A jouir sagement d'une honnête opulence,
A vivre avec soi-même, à servir ses amis,
A se moquer un peu de ses ennemis,
A sortir d'une vie ou triste ou fortunée,
En rendant grâce au Ciel de nous l'avoir donnée.

Like you, one learns how to endure penury,
To sagely delight in honest luxury,
To abide oneself, and to serve one's mates,
To mock just a little those whom one hates,
To exit from life, saddened or joyous,
Thanking Heaven for what it has given to us.

Verse addressed to the Roman poet Horace, one of Voltaire's literary heroes, in *Épitre à Horace* (1772), 12; Besterman et al., *Œuvres complètes de Voltaire* (2010), 74b:288.

Life after death

Je voudrais vous revoir avant d'aller voir Pascal et Rabelais et tutti quanti *dans l'autre monde.*

I'd like to see you again before going to see Pascal and Rabelais *et tutti quanti* in the next world.

Letter from Les Délices, August 23, 1755, to Nicolas-Claude Thieriot in Paris.

Quel homme a jamais su, par sa propre lumiére,
Si lorsque nous tombons dans l'éternelle nuit,
Notre ame avec nos sens se dissout toute entiére,
Si nous vivons encore, ou si tout est détruit?

What man by the light of reason, has ever known,
If, when we tumble into that eternal night,
Our soul with our senses disintegrates entirely,
If we live still on, or whether all is destroyed?

Précis de l'Ecclésiaste, en vers, par Mr. de Voltaire (1759), 10; Besterman et al., *Œuvres complètes de Voltaire* (2010), 49a:213–214.

Ce n'est pas que le néant n'ait du bon, mais je crois qu'il est impossible d'aimer véri-tablement le néant malgré ses bonnes qualités.

It is not that there is nothing good about the state of nothingness, but despite its good qualities I think it impossible to truly love nothingness.

Letter from Les Délices, May 9, 1764, to Mme Du Deffand in Paris.

Literary quarrels

Je suis encore de votre avis sur les guerres littéraires; mais vous m'avouerez que, dans toute guerre, l'agresseur seul a tort devant dieu et devant les hommes.

I am still of your opinion on the subject of literary warfare; however, you must admit that in any war, it is the aggressor alone who is in the wrong, before God and before man.

Letter from Ferney, September 24, 1760, to Charles Palissot de Montenoy in Paris. Palissot was a playwright and author. Though a great admirer of Voltaire, like his friend the journalist Elie-Catherine Fréron, Palissot was a fervent adversary of Diderot and Rousseau.

Les cabales sont affreuses, je le sais; la Littérature en sera toujours troublée, ainsi que tous les autres états de la vie.

Cabals are frightful, this I know; Literature will always be marked by them, along with other aspects of life.

"A Madame la Marquise de Pompadour," prefatory *épitre* to *Tancrède*, first staged at the Théâtre de la rue des Fossés in Paris, March 9, 1760. *Tancrède, Tragédie; Par Mr. De Voltaire* (1761), iv; Besterman et al., *Œuvres complètes de Voltaire* (2009), 49b:128.

Les querelles d'auteurs sont pour le bien de la littérature, comme dans un gouvernement libre les querelles des grands et les clameurs des petits sont nécessaires à la liberté.

Writers' quarrels are good for literature, just as in a free country the quarrels of the great and the clamors of the small are necessary to liberty.

Voltaire, quoted in French in Burney, *The Present State of Music in France and Italy* (1771), 59–60. Dr. Burney visited Voltaire at Ferney in July 1770.

Literature—writing

La profession des lettres, si brillante, et si libre sous Louis XIV, le plus despotique de nos rois, est devenue un métier d'intrigues et de servitude. Il n'y a point de bassesse qu'on ne fasse pour obtenir je ne sais quelles places, ou au sceau, ou dans des académies; et l'esprit de petitesse et de minutie est venu au point que l'on ne peut plus imprimer que des livres insipides. Les bons auteurs du siècle de Louis XIV, n'obtiendraient pas de privilège. Boileau et La Bruyère ne seraient que persécutés. Il faut donc vivre pour soi et pour ses amis, et se bien donner de garde de penser tout haut, ou bien aller penser en Angleterre ou en Hollande.

The literary profession, so brilliant and free under Louis XIV, the most despotic of our kings, has become an occupation marked by intrigue and servility. There are no depths to which one will not stoop to gain a position, or a seal, or to join an academy; and the spirit of pettiness and banality has reached a point where only books of the utmost insipidity make it into print. Good authors from the age of Louis XIV would not be granted permission to publish, Boileau and La Bruyère would now be counted among the persecuted. Thus, we must live for ourselves and for our friends, and take care not to think out loud, or else, go to England or Holland in order to think.

Letter to Jean-Baptiste-Nicolas Formont, June 27, 1734, written, presumably, en route from Autun to Phillipsburg.

Tous les genres sont bons, hors le genre ennuyeux.

All styles are good, except the style that is boring.

"Préface de l'éditeur," in *L'Enfant prodigue, comédie en vers dissillabes* (1738), 86.

Malheur à l'Auteur qui veut toujours instruire;
Le secret d'ennuïer est celui de tout dire.

Authors should not to instruct aspire,
Who speaks too much is ever sure to tire.

"Sixième Discours, De la Nature de l'homme," in *Discours en vers sur l'homme*, in *Recueil de pieces fugitives en prose et en vers* (1740), 93; Besterman et al., *Œuvres complètes de Voltaire* (1991), 17:520. The translation is from Smollett, *Miscellaneous Poems. By Mr. De Voltaire* (1764), "Dissertation the VIth. Upon the Nature of Man," in Smollett et al., *The Works of Mr. de Voltaire* (1764), 33:30. James Parton gave a compressed version of this couplet as "The secret of wearying your reader is to tell him all." See Parton, *Life of Voltaire* (1881), 1:333.

Je ne m'attendais pas à ce nouveau trait de la calomnie, mais qui plume a, guerre a.
Le loyer de nous autres pauvres diables de victimes publiques c'est d'être honnis et persécutés.

I was not expecting this new dose of calumny, but to hold a pen is to be at war. Dishonor and persecution are the price that poor, publicly maligned devils like us must pay.

Letter from the château de La Malgrange, near Nancy, October 4, 1748, to the comtesse d'Argental in Paris. The phrase "Qui plume a, guerre" is a play on the old proverb "Qui terre a, guerre a" ("He who posseses lands, has trouble on his hands").

La vie d'un écrivain sédentaire est dans ses écrits.

The life of a sedentary author is to be found in his writings.

From "Ecrivains, dont plusieurs ont illustré le siécle," in *Le Siècle de Louis XIV* (1751), 2:350–351; Besterman et al., *Œuvres complètes de Voltaire* (2017), 12:55; from the subsection on Pierre Bayle in which Voltaire cites a long biography of Bayle that "ne devait pas contenir six pages" ("ought not have been more than six pages"). The translation is from "Catalogue of the French Writers," in *The Age of Louis XIV* (1779), 1:xlii.

Qui plume a, guerre a. Ce monde est un vaste temple dédié à la discorde.

To hold a pen is to be at war. This world is an immense temple dedicated to disharmony.

Letter from Potsdam, May 22, 1752, to Mme Denis in Paris.

La littérature est un terrain qui produit des poisons comme des plantes salutaires. Il se trouve des misérables qui, parce qu'ils savent lire & écrire, croient se faire un état dans le monde en vendant des scandales à des libraires au lieu de prendre un métier honnête, ne sachant pas que la profession d'un copiste, ou même celle d'un laquais fidèle, est très préférable à la leur.

Literature is a plot of land where plants both poisonous and salubrious grow. There are wretches who, because they can read and write, think they cut a figure in the world by peddling gossip to bookmen rather than take up an honest trade, knowing not that the career of a copyist, even an honest footman, is far preferable to the one they have chosen.

Préface to *Essai Sur l'Histoire universelle* (1754), 3:28; Moland, *Œuvres complètes de Voltaire* (1879), 24:49.

On ne peut corriger son ouvrage qu'après l'avoir oublié.

You can only correct your work properly after you have forgotten it.

Letter from Les Délices, May 4, 1755, to the comte d'Argental in Paris.

Ainsi presque tout est imitation. L'idée des Lettres persanes est prise de celle de l'Espion turc. Le Boiardo a imité le Pulci, l'Arioste a imité le Boiardo. Les esprits les plus originaux empruntent les uns des autres.

Almost everything is imitation. The idea of *The Persian Letters* was taken from *The Turkish Spy*. *Boiardo* imitated *Pulci*, *Ariosto* imitated *Boiardo*. The most original writers borrow from one another.

"De Prior, du Poëme singulier d'Hudibras, & du doyen Swift," in *Mélanges de littérature, d'histoire et de philosophie* (1757), 224; "Sur Mr Pope et quelques autres Poetes fameux," in *Lettres philosophiques* (1964), 2:136 (variant).

Les sots admirent tout dans un Auteur estimé. Je ne lis que pour moi, je n'aime que ce qui est à mon usage.

Fools admire everything in a noted author. I read only for myself; I like only what I can use.

The Venetian nobleman Pococurante, speaking to Candide, in "Visite chez le Seigneur Pococurantè noble vénitien," chap. 25 in *Candide, ou L'Optimisme* (1759), 237; Besterman et al., *Œuvres complètes de Voltaire* (1980), 48:234. In English, *Candide, Zadig, and Other Stories* (2001), 85.

Il faut être court et un peu salé, sans quoi les ministres, les commis et les femmes de chambre font des papillotes du livre.

One should be brief and slightly vulgar, otherwise clergymen, clerks and chambermaids use your book for curling papers.

Letter from Ferney, January 5, 1763, to Pastor Paul Moultou in Geneva.

La vie d'un homme de lettres est un combat perpétuel, et on meurt les armes à la main.

The life of a writer is one of perpetual combat, and he dies holding his weapon in his hand.

Letter from Ferney, November 3, 1766, to the comte and comtesse d'Argental in Paris. Albert Camus recorded a version of this quote in one of his personal notebooks: "On ne réussit dans ce monde qu'à la pointe de l'épée et on meurt les armes à la main." See Camus, *Carnets II: Janvier 1942–mars 1951* (1964), 224.

Il est plus difficile de faire cent beaux vers que d'écrire toute l'histoire de France.

It is harder to produce a hundred lines of beautiful verse than to write the entire history of France.

Letter from Ferney, March 7, 1769, to Saint-Lambert in Lunéville.

L'écriture est la peinture de la voix: plus elle est ressemblante, meilleure elle est.

Writing is a representation of the spoken word: the more perfect the likeness, the better it is.

"Ortographe," in *Questions sur l'Encyclopédie, par des Amateurs* (1771), 8:162; Besterman et al., *Œuvres complètes de Voltaire* (2012), 42b:346.

Je me laisse aller aux idées de l'auteur, c'est lui qui me mène. S'il m'émeut, s'il m'intéresse, si son ensemble et ses détails font sur moi une grande impression, je ne le chicane pas, je ne sens que le plaisir qu'il m'a donné.

I give myself up to the ideas of the author, it is he who leads me. If he moves me, if he interests me, if what he relates both overall and in detail leaves a great impression upon me, I don't complain. I only feel the pleasure he has given me.

Letter from Ferney, April 20, 1775, to Jean-François de La Harpe in Paris.

Misattributed to Voltaire

Si j'avais eu le temps, j'aurais fait plus court.

If I'd had enough time, I'd have made this shorter.

Cited by Alexandre Leupin in *La passion des idoles* (2000), 4, and, in English, by Ian Walker in a letter to the editor in the *Financial Times*, dated November 29, 2012. Diderot expressed this idea in a letter to Mme d'Épinay, September 16, 1761: "Si j'avais eu un peu plus de temps qu'il ne m'en a accordé, j'aurais été meilleur et plus court." Pascal, before Diderot, in a postscript to letter 16 in the *Lettres Provinciales* (1657), wrote: "Je n'ai fait celle-ci plus longue que parce que je n'ai pas eu le loisir de la faire plus courte."

John Locke (1632–1704)

ENGLISH PHILOSOPHER AND PHYSICIAN

Jamais il ne fut peut-être un esprit plus sage, plus méthodique, un logicien plus exact que Locke; cependant il n'était pas grand mathématicien.

Perhaps no Man ever had a more judicious or more methodical Genius, or was a more acute Logician than Mr. Locke, and yet he was not deeply skill'd in the Mathematicks.

"Treisième Lettre. Sur Mr. *Locke*," in *Lettres Ecrites de Londres sur les Anglois et autres sujets* (1734), 91; "Sur Mr. *Loke*," in *Lettres philosophiques* (1964), 1:166. The translation is "Letter XIII. On Mr. *Locke*," in *Letters Concerning the English Nation* (1733), 94.

London

Londres, jadis barbare, est le centre des Arts,
Le magazin du Monde, & l'azile de Mars.

London, once barbarous, is now center of the Arts,
Mart to the World, and sanctuary of Mars.

La Henriade (1726), *La Henriade de Mr. de Voltaire* (1726), 1:15, canto 1; Besterman et al., *Œuvres complètes de Voltaire* (1970), 2:381. Canto 1 is sometimes called the "Éloge de l'Angleterre."

Exemple de l'Europe, ô Londre! heureuse terre,
Ainsi que les Tyrans vous avez sû chasser
Les préjugez honteux qui vous livraient la guerre.
C'est-là qu'on sait tout dire, & tout récompenser,
Nul Art n'est meprisé, tout succès a sa gloire.

Model for Europe, London! blessed land indeed,
As it did with tyrants, had the sense to chase
Shameful biases that civil factions did breed.
There, men speak freely, merit has its rightful place,
No Art is despised, and glory doth crown success.

"La Mort de Mlle Lecouvreur" (1730), in *Oeuvres de M. de Voltaire. Nouvelle Edition* (1732), 1:226; Besterman et al., *Œuvres complètes de Voltaire* (1998), 5:559.

Londres n'est devenue digne d'être habitée que depuis qu'elle fut réduite en cendre. Les rues, depuis cette époque, furent élargies & allignées; Londres fut une ville pour avoir été brulée.

London became worthy of inhabitation only since it was reduced to ashes. The streets, since that time, have been widened and straightened; London became a city only after the Great Fire.

"Loix" (1771), 7:353; Besterman et al., *Œuvres complètes de Voltaire* (2012), 42b:74.

Louis XIV (1712–1786)

KING OF FRANCE

Je ne sais si Louis XIV méritait bien le nom de grand, mais son siècle le méri-
tait, et c'est de ce bel âge des arts et des lettres que je veux parler plus que de sa
personne.

I do not know if Louis XIV deserved to be called great, but the age in which he lived did, and it is that beautiful age of arts and letters that interests me more than his person.

Letter from Paris, April 19, 1735, to the marquis de Caumont in Avignon.

Il y a longtemps que j'ai assemblé quelques matériaux pour faire l'histoire du Siècle de Louis XIV: ce n'est point simplement la vie que j'écris, ce ne sont point les annales de son règne; c'est plutôt l'histoire de l'esprit humain, puisée dans le siècle le plus glorieux à l'esprit humain.

I have, for quite some time now, assembled materials for a history of the Age of Louis XIV: it is not just a life I am writing, not simply a chronicle of his reign; it is instead a history of the human spirit, drawn from the most glorious century produced by the human spirit.

Letter from Cirey, October 30, 1738, to the abbé Jean-Baptiste Du Bos in Paris. In 1739, in Amsterdam, Voltaire would release chapters 1 and 2 of the *Siècle* as *Essai sur l'histoire de Louis XIV*. They were included later that year in *Recueil de pieces fugitives en prose et en vers*, published in Paris, which was condemned by the Parlement and publicly burned on December 4, 1739.

LOUIS XIV se signala par des monumens admirables, par l'amour de tous les arts, par les encouragemens qu'il leur prodiguoit.

LOUIS XIV distinguished himself through superb monuments, his love for each of the arts, and the encouragements he lavished upon them.

Reception speech, May 9, 1746, following Voltaire's election to the Académie française. *Discours prononcez dans l'Académie Françoise, Le Lundi 9 Mai MDCCXLVI* (1746), 20.

Ce n'est pas seulement la vie de Louis XIV qu'on prétend écrire; on se propose un plus grand objet. On veut essaïer de peindre à la posterité, non les actions d'un seul homme; mais l'esprit des hommes dans le siécle le plus éclairé qui fut jamais.

It is not just a life of Louis XIV that we intend to write; we have a grander goal in mind. We want to try to depict for posterity, not the actions of a single man, but the human spirit of the most enlightened century that ever was.

Introduction to *Le siècle de Louis XIV* (1751), 1:1; Besterman et al., *Œuvres complètes de Voltaire* (2015), 13a:1.

Love

L'oreille est le chemin du cœur.

The ear is the road to the heart.

Epitre au prince royal de Prusse (1738), in Besterman et al., *Œuvres complètes de Voltaire* (2007), 18a:316. This epistle, dedicated to the future Frederick the Great, likely first appeared in print in Beaumarchais's edition of the *Oeuvres complètes de Voltaire* (1784), 13:104. The expression "L'oreille est le chemin du cœur" resurfaced in a posthumous edition of *La Pucelle d'Orléans* (1780), 343 (canto XVIII), but it predates Voltaire. See Montfort, *Gasconiana, ou Recueil des bons mots, des pensées les plus plaisantes, et des rencontres les plus vives des Gascons* (1708), 146.

Si ma place est dans votre cœur:
Elle est la première du monde.

If I have a place in your heart
That is the greatest place in the world.

"Stances," in *Œuvres de M. de Voltaire. Nouvelle édition, Considérablement augmentée* (1751), 168; Besterman et al., *Œuvres complètes de Voltaire* (1988), 8:536.

On meurt deux fois, je le vois bien:
Cesser d'aimer & d'être aimable,
C'est une insupportable mort;
Cesser de vivre ce n'est rien.

We die twice o'er, I do believe;
Once we stop loving and being loved,
That is the harshest death by far;
T'is really nothing to cease to live.

"Stances," in *Œuvres de M. de Voltaire. Nouvelle édition, Considérablement augmentée* (1751), 3:168; Besterman et al., *Œuvres complètes de Voltaire* (2015), 20a:564. This couplet dates from 1741, during Voltaire's relationship with Mme du Châtelet.

L'amour; le consolateur du Genre-humain, le conservateur de l'Univers, l'ame de tous les Etres sensibles, le tendre amour.

Love, the consoler of the human race, the preserver of the universe, the soul of all emotional beings, tender love.

Pangloss's polite way of telling Candide how he had contracted syphilis in "Comment Candide rencontra son ancien maître de philosophie le docteur Pangloss, & ce qui en advint," chap. 4 in *Candide, ou L'Optimisme* (1759), 28; Besterman et al., *Œuvres complètes de Voltaire* (1980), 48:130. In English, *Candide, Zadig, and Other Stories* (2001), 23.

Et deux à deux est le bonheur suprême.

And two by two is supreme happiness.

La Pucelle d'Orléans, Poème, divisé en vingt chants (1762), canto 3, 77; Besterman et al., *Œuvres complètes de Voltaire* (1970), 7:331.

Martin Luther (1483–1546)

CATHOLIC PRIEST, THEOLOGIAN, AND LEADING FIGURE
IN THE PROTESTANT REFORMATION

Si on avait dit alors à Luther qu'il détruirait la Religion Romaine dans la moitié de l'Europe, il ne l'aurait pas crû. Il alla plus loin qu'il ne pensait, comme il arrive dans toutes les disputes, & dans presques toutes les affaires.

If one had told Luther back then that he would destroy the Catholic Religion in half of Europe, he would not have believed it: he went further than he thought, and that happens in all disputes and in nearly all human affairs.

"De Luther & de Zuingle," in *Essai sur l'Histoire Universelle depuis Charlemagne* (1757), 57; Besterman et al., *Œuvres complètes de Voltaire* (2012), 25:416.

Luxury

Ceux qui crient contre ce qu'on appelle le luxe ne sont guère que des pauvres de mauvaise humeur.

Those who decry luxury are little more than poor, ill-tempered souls.

Letter from Leyden, Holland, circa January 10, 1737, to Frederick, crown prince of Prussia, future Frederick the Great, in Berlin.

L'Or de la Terre, & les Tresors de l'Onde,
Leurs habitans, & les peuples de l'Air,
Tout sert au luxe, aux plaisirs de ce Monde;
Ah le bon tems que ce Siècle de Fer!
  Le superflu, chose très-nécessaire,
A réuni l'un & l'autre Hémisphére.

The Gold of the Earth, and Ocean's Treasures,
The creatures therein, and those of the Air,
Provide luxury, worldly pleasures.
Ah what good times be this Iron Age of ours!
  Things superfluous, yet de rigueur,
Have united each and every Hemisphere.

[*Le Mondain, ou l'Apologie du Luxe*], as *L'Homme du Monde, ou Défense du Mondain*, in *Oeuvres de M^r. de Voltaire. Nouvelle Edition* (1739), 118; Besterman et al., *Œuvres complètes de Voltaire* (2003), 16:296. The most famous of these lines of verse appears as "Ah le bon tems que ce siècle de fer!" in *Mémoires pour servir à la vie de Mr. de Voltaire* (1784), 115.

Lorsqu'on inventa les ciseaux, qui ne sont certainement pas de l'antiquité la plus haute, que ne dit-on pas contre les premiers qui se rognèrent les ongles, & qui coupèrent une partie des cheveux qui leur tombaient sur le nez? On les traita fans doute de petits-maîtres & de prodigues, qui achetaient chèrement un instrument de la vanité, pour gâter l'ouvrage du créateur.

When scissors, which surely do not go back to the remotest antiquity, were invented, can we doubt that those who first pared their nails and trimmed some of the hair that dropped down to their nose were sorely abused? They were doubtless called fops and spendthrifts, and paid dearly for an instrument of vanity that spoiled the handiwork of the Creator.

"Luxe," in *Dictionnaire philosophique, portatif* (1764), 258; Besterman et al., *Œuvres complètes de Voltaire* (1994), 36:328.

Dans un pays où tout le monde allait les pieds nuds, le premier qui se fit une paire de souliers avait-il du luxe? N'était-ce pas un homme très sensé & très industrieux?

In a nation where everyone was barefoot, was the first man who made himself a pair of shoes indulging in luxury? Wasn't he, rather, a very sensible and very industrious man?

"Luxe," in *Questions sur l'Encyclopédie, par des Amateurs* (1771), 8:22; Besterman et al., *Œuvres complètes de Voltaire* (2012), 42b:122.

Madness—folly

Un fou est un malade dont le cerveau pâtit, comme le gouteux est un malade qui souffre aux piés & aux mains; il pensait par le cerveau, comme il marchait avec les piés, sans rien connaître ni de son pouvoir incompréhensible de marcher, ni de son pouvoir non moins incompréhensible de penser.

A madman has a diseased mind, much as a victim of gout has diseased feet and hands; he thinks with his brain, and walks using his feet, with neither the slightest notion of the unfathomable power that allows him to walk nor the equally unfathomable power that allows him to think.

"Folie," in *La Raison par Alphabet. Septieme Édition* (1773), 296–297; Besterman et al., *Œuvres complètes de Voltaire* (1994), 36:130.

Qu'est-ce que la folie? c'est d'avoir des pensées incohérentes & la conduite de même. Le plus sage des hommes veut-il connaître la folie, qu'il refléchisse sur la marche de ses idées pendant ses rêves. S'il a une digestion laborieuse dans la nuit, mille idées incohérentes l'agitent; il semble que la nature nous punisse d'avoir pris trop d'alimens, ou d'en avoir fait un mauvais choix, en nous donnant des pensées; car on ne pense gueres en dormant que dans une mauvaise digestion. Les rêves inquiets sont réellement une folie passagere.

What is madness? To have erroneous perceptions, and to reason correctly from them? Let the wisest man, if he would understand madness, attend to the succession of his ideas while he dreams. If he is troubled with indigestion during the night, a thousand incoherent ideas torment him; it seems as if nature punished him for having taken too much food, or for having injudiciously selected it, by supplying involuntary conceptions; for we think very little during sleep, except when annoyed by a bad digestion. Unquiet dreams are in reality a transient madness.

"Folie," in *Questions sur l'Encyclopédie, par des Amateurs* (1771), 6:127–128; Besterman et al., *Œuvres complètes de Voltaire* (2010), 41:466. The translation is from Voltaire, "Madness," in *A Philosophical Dictionary* (1824), 2:383.

Man—mankind

Les hommes sont comme les animaux: les gros mangent les petits, et les petits les piquent.

Men are like animals: the little ones get eaten by the big ones, who get stung in return.

Le Sottisier de Voltaire (1880), 100. See also Besterman, *Voltaire's Notebooks* (1952), 2:279; Besterman et al., *Œuvres complètes de Voltaire* (1968), 82:416.

Automates pensans, mûs par des mains divines.

Thinking automatons, by divine hands moved.

"Deuxième Discours, de la Liberté" (possibly written in 1737), in *Discours en vers sur l'homme*, in *Recueil de pieces fugitives en prose et en vers* (1740), 60; Besterman et al., *Œuvres complètes de Voltaire* (1991), 17:473.

On peut juger du caractère des hommes par leurs entreprises.

You can judge the character of men by the projects they undertake.

Le Siècle de Louis XIV (1751), 1:123; Besterman et al., *Œuvres complètes de Voltaire* (2015), 13a:120.

Nous autres sur notre petit tas de boue, nous ne concevons rien au-delà de nos usages.

Here, on our little clump of mud, we can imagine nothing beyond our own ways of doing things.

"Voyage d'un Habitant du monde de l'Etoile Sirius dans le Globe de Saturne," in *Micromégas de Mr. de Voltaire, Avec une Histoire des Croisades* (1752), 5; Besterman et al., *Œuvres complètes de Voltaire* (2017), 20c:65.

Trois choses influent sans cesse sur l'esprit des hommes, le climat, le Gouvernement & la Religion. C'est la seule manière d'expliquer l'énigme de ce Monde.

Three abiding factors affect the mind of man, climate, government and religion. That is the only explanation for the enigmatic ways of this World.

Additions à l'Essay sur l'Histoire générale (1763), 331; Besterman et al., *Œuvres complètes de Voltaire* (2015), 26c:323–324.

On dit à chaque soldat pour l'encourager, Songe que tu ès du régiment de Champagne. On devrait dire à chaque individu, Souviens-toi de ta dignité d'homme.

To stiffen his courage, every soldier is told: Remember that you are in the regiment of Champagne. One should say to each one individually, Remember your dignity as a man.

"Méchant," in *Dictionnaire philosophique, portatif* (1764), 264; Besterman et al., *Œuvres complètes de Voltaire* (1994), 36:346.

En effet, il serait bien singulier que toute la nature, tous les astres obéissent à des loix éternelles, & qu'il y eût un petit animal haut de cinq pieds, qui au mépris de ces loix pût agir comme il lui plairait au seul gré de son caprice. Il agirait au hasard; & on sait que le hazard n'est rien. Nous avons inventé ce mot pour exprimer l'effet connu de toute cause inconnuë.

In fact, it would be highly singular if all nature, every star, should obey eternal laws, and that there should be a little animal five feet tall, who, in contempt of these laws, could do as he pleased, solely according to his caprice. He would be acting randomly; and we know there is no such thing as pure chance. We invented the word chance to describe an identifiable effect resulting from an unknown cause.

"XIII. Suis-je libre" (*Doute* no. 13), in *Le Philosophe ignorant* (1766), 25; Besterman et al., *Œuvres complètes de Voltaire* (1987), 62:44.

Je vous recommande beaucoup de courage et beaucoup de mépris pour le genre humain.

I wish you great courage and a healthy measure of contempt for humankind.

Letter from Ferney, April 8, 1771, to Jean le Rond d'Alembert in Paris.

Les hommes en général ressemblent aux chiens qui hurlent quand ils entendent de loin d'autres chiens hurler.

Men in general are like dogs that howl when they hear other dogs howl in the distance.

"Sommaire des actions de La Bourdonnaye & de Dupleix," *Fragmens sur quelques révolutions dans l'Inde et sur la mort du comte de Lalli* (1773), in *Poësies mêlées, &c.* (1774), 466; Besterman et al., *Œuvres complètes de Voltaire* (2006), 75b:69.

Il faut vingt ans pour mener l'homme de l'état de plante où il est dans le ventre de sa mère, & de l'état de pur animal, qui est le partage de sa première enfance, jusqu'à celui où la maturité de la raison commence à poindre. Il a falu trente siècles pour connaître un peu sa structure. Il faudrait l'éternité pour connaître quelque chose de son ame. Il ne faut qu'un instant pour le tuer.

It takes twenty years to lead man from the vegetative state of his mother's womb, and from the state of pure animal that is the nature of infancy, to a state of maturity where reason begins to take hold. It has taken thirty centuries to understand something of his physical being. It would take all eternity to understand his soul, but only an instant to put him to death.

"Examen d'une pensée de Pascal sur l'homme," under the heading, "Réflexion générale sur l'homme," in *Questions sur l'Encyclopédie, par des Amateurs* (1774), 3:435; Besterman et al., *Œuvres complètes de Voltaire* (2011), 42a:282.

Maternity

Une femme qui nourrit deux enfants, & qui file, rend plus de services à la Patrie que tous les Couvents n'en peuvent jamais rendre.

A woman who nurses two children, and spins at her wheel, serves her country better than all the convents have ever done.

La Voix du sage et du Peuple (1750), 11; Besterman et al., *Œuvres complètes de Voltaire* (2006), 32a:242.

Mathematics

"On étouffe l'esprit des enfans sous un amas de connaissances inutiles; mais de toutes les sciences la plus absurde, à mon avis, & celle qui est la plus capable d'étouffer toute espèce de génie, c'est la géométrie. Cette science ridicule a pour objet des surfaces, des lignes & des points qui n'existent pas dans la nature."

"We smother the spirit of our young under a heap of useless knowledge: but of all the sciences, the most absurd, and that which in my opinion, is most calculated to stifle genius of every kind, is geometry. The objects about which this ridiculous science is conversant are surfaces, lines, and points, that have no existence in nature."

Jeannot's governor, during Jeannot's boyhood in Paris, in *Jeannot et Colin*, first published in *Contes de Guillaume Vadé* (1764), 101–102.

Il y a une imagination *étonnante dans la mathématique pratique; &* Archimede *avoit au moins autant d'imagination qu'*Homere.

There is an astonishing *imagination*, even in the science of mathematics; and *Archimedes* possessed at least as much imagination as *Homer*.

"Imagination," in Diderot, d'Alembert, et al., *Encyclopédie, ou Dictionnaire Raisonné des Sciences, des Arts et des Métiers* (1765), 8:561; Besterman et al., *Œuvres complètes de Voltaire* (1987), 33:209.

May (month of)

Je crois actuellement Votre Majesté à Neisse ou à Glogau, faisant quelques bonnes épigrammes contre les Russes. Je vous supplie, sire, d'en faire aussi contre le mois de mai, qui mérite si peu le nom de printemps, et pendant lequel nous avons froid comme dans l'hiver. Il me paraît que ce mois de mai est l'emblème des réputations mal acquises.

I believe your Majesty is now at Nysa or at Głogów, writing lively epigrams against the Russians. I beseech you, Sire, to also write a few against the month of May, which deserves so little the name of spring, and during which time we are as cold as we are in winter. It seems to me that May is the emblem of ill-deserved reputations.

Letter from Paris, May 15, 1749, to Frederick the Great, by way of Berlin.

Likely misattributed to Voltaire

Voltaire disait que le mois de mai n'était beau que chez les poëtes.

Voltaire was in the habit of saying that "May was fine only in the imaginations of the poets."

Bernardin de Saint-Pierre, *Harmonies de la nature* (1815), 255. The translation is from *Harmonies of Nature* (1815), 1:243.

Medicine—medical doctors

L'espérance de guérir est déjà la moitié de la guérison.

The hope of being cured is already half the cure.

Letter from Paris, December 5, 1723, to Louis-Nicolas Le Tonnelier de Bretueil, Baron de Preuilly, in Paris. Bretueil was the father of Voltaire's future *amie*, the marquise du Châtelet.

Ils ne se vantent pas de guérir toujours, mais ils se vantent de faire tout ce qu'ils peuvent pour soulager les hommes.

They do not claim that in every instance they can cure their patients, but they do claim to do everything they can to provide comfort.

Diatribe du docteur Akakia, Médecin du Pape (1753), 9–10; Besterman et al., *Œuvres complètes de Voltaire* (2012), 32c:134.

Il est vrai que régime vaut mieux que médecine.

It is true that a proper diet is better than medicine.

"Des Médecins," in *Nouveaux Mélanges philosophiques, historiques, critiques, &c. &c. &c.* (1765), 3:107; Besterman et al., *Œuvres complètes de Voltaire* (2017), 60a:223.

Nos jours sont comptés et les erreurs des médecins aussi.

Our days are numbered, and the mistakes of medical doctors, too.

Letter from Ferney, February 28, 1766, to his secretary, Jean-Louis Wagnière near Lausanne, where he may have been visiting a sick or dying family member or friend.

Je ne sais rien de si ridicule qu'un médecin qui ne meurt pas de vieillesse; et je ne conçois guère comment on attend sa santé de gens qui ne savent pas se guérir: cependant il est bon de leur demander conseil, pourvu qu'on ne les croye pas aveuglément.

I know of nothing more laughable than a doctor who does not die of old age; and I can hardly understand how one can depend on someone to care for one's health who cannot cure himself; however, it is good to get their advice, provided you don't follow it blindly.

Letter from Ferney, November 6, 1767, to the comte d'Argental in Paris.

Des hommes qui s'occuperaient de rendre la santé à d'autres hommes par les seuls principes d'humanité & de bienfaisance, seraient fort au-dessus de tous les Grands de la Terre; ils tiendraient de la Divinité. Conserver & réparer est presque aussi beau que faire.

Those who would restore the health of other men, through sheer skill and humanity, are by far the Greatest men on Earth; they are quasi-divine. To save and to mend is nearly as awesome as creation.

"Des Médecins," in *Nouveaux Mélanges philosophiques, historiques, critiques, &c. &c. &c* (1765), 3:108; Besterman et al., *Œuvres complètes de Voltaire* (2017), 60a:224.

La Médecine ayant donc été une profession mercénaire dans le monde, comme l'est en quelques endroits celle de rendre la justice, elle a été sujette à d'étranges abus. Mais est-il rien de plus estimable au monde qu'un Médecin qui ayant dans sa jeunesse étudié la nature, connu les ressorts du corps humain, les maux qui le tourmentent, les remèdes qui peuvent le soulager, exerce son art en s'en défiant, soigne également les pauvres & les riches, ne reçoit d'honoraires qu'à regret, & emploie ces honoraires à secourir l'indigent? Un tel homme n'est-il pas un peu supérieur au Général des Capucins, quelque respectable que soit ce Général?

Medicine, having now become a money-making profession, like the administration of justice in some places, has been subject to strange abuses. But is anything on earth more commendable than a Physician who, from his earliest years studied nature, knows the properties of the human body, the diseases that afflict it, the remedies that may relieve it, exercises his art with caution, treats both the rich and the poor, accepts his fees with regret, and uses them to assist the indigent? Is such a man not just a little better than the General of the Capuchin Order, however respectable the General may be?

"Des Médecins," in *Nouveaux Mélanges philosophiques, historiques, critiques, &c. &c. &c.* (1765), 3:110; Besterman et al., *Œuvres complètes de Voltaire* (2017), 60a:225–226.

Metaphysics

Ce serait le comble de la folie, de prétendre amener tous les hommes à penser d'une manière uniforme sur la Métaphysique. On pourait beaucoup plus aisément subjuguer l'univers entier par les armes, que de subjuguer tous les esprits d'une seule ville.

It would be the height of folly to claim that one could induce all men to think alike based on Metaphysics. One could much more easily subjugate the entire universe by force of arms than conquer the minds of a single city.

"Vertu vaut mieux que science," in *Traité sur la Tolérance* (1763), 184; Besterman et al., *Œuvres complètes de Voltaire* (2000), 56c:245.

Mettons à la fin de presque tous les Chapitres de Métaphysique les deux lettres des Juges Romains quand ils n'entendaient pas une cause: N.L., non liquet; cela n'est pas clair.

Let us add to the conclusion of nearly every Chapter about Metaphysics the two letters used by Roman Jurists when they did not understand a case: N.L. *non liquet*; "it is not clear."

"Tout est bien," in *Dictionnaire philosophique, portatif* (1764), 60; Besterman et al., *Œuvres complètes de Voltaire* (1994), 35:428.

The Middle Ages

Lorsqu'on passe de l'histoire de l'empire romain à celle des peuples qui l'ont déchiré dans l'Occident, on ressemble à un voyageur, qui au sortir d'une ville superbe se trouve dans des déserts couverts de ronces. Vingt jargons barbares succèdent à cette belle langue latine qu'on parlait du fond de l'Illyrie au mont Atlas. Au lieu de ces sages loix qui gouvernaient la moitié de notre hémisphère, on ne trouve plus que des coutumes sauvages. . . . L'entendement humain s'abrutit dans les superstitions les plus lâches & les plus insensées. . . . L'Europe entière croupit dans cet avilissement jusqu'au seiziéme siécle, & n'en sort que part des convulsions terribles.

The history of Western Europe from the Roman Empire down to the time of the peoples who destroyed it, is like a traveler who, leaving a superb city, finds himself in a desert overgrown with thorns. Twenty barbaric dialects succeeded the beautiful Latin tongue that was spoken from the far corners of Illyria to Mount Atlas. Savage customs replaced the wise laws that once governed half of our hemisphere. . . . The human mind was brutalized by the most craven and senseless superstitions. . . . The whole of Europe languished in this debased state until the sixteenth century, and only emerged from it after frightful convulsions.

"Suite de la décadence de l'ancienne Rome," in *Essai sur les mœurs et l'esprit des nations* (1769), 1:260; Besterman et al., *Œuvres complètes de Voltaire* (2009), 22:226–227.

John Milton (1608–1674)

ENGLISH POET

Milton reste la gloire & l'admiration de l'Angleterre; on le compare à Homère, dont les défauts sont aussi grands; & on le met au-dessus du Dante, dont les imaginations sont encor plus bizarres.

Milton remains the glory and the admiration of England; he is compared to *Homer*, whose defects were equally great, and he is raised above *Dante*, whose inventions are even more bizarre.

"Des Beaux-Arts en Europe, du tems to Louis XIV," in *Siécle de Louis XIV. Nouvelle Edition* (1768), 104; Besterman et al., *Œuvres complètes de Voltaire* (2016), 13d:38. The translation is from Bourgeois, *France Under Louis XIV (Le Grand Siècle)* (1897), 336.

Mind your own business

Attributed to Voltaire, very likely apocryphal

Maître André, faites des perruques; faites des perruques, des perruques, des perruques, toujours des perruques et rien que des perruques.

Master André, make wigs; make wigs, wigs, wigs, wigs, always and forever nothing but wigs.

Alleged response by Voltaire, circa 1760, to a wigmaker who sent him a copy of a tragedy he had written, quoted in Pierre Larousse, *Fleurs historiques des dames et des gens du monde* (1862), 228. Voltaire's remark is in the spirit of adages such as "stick to your knitting" or the remark ascribed to the painter Apelles in response to a shoemaker's criticism of his work, "The cobbler should not judge beyond his shoe."

Miracles

Un miracle selon l'énergie du mot est une chose admirable. En ce cas tout est miracle. L'ordre prodigieux de la nature, la rotation de cent millions de globes autour d'un million de soleils, l'activité de la lumière, la vie des animaux, sont des miracles perpétuels.

Selon les idées reçues nous appellons miracle la violation de ces loix divines & éternelles. Qu'il y ait une éclipse de soleil pendant la lune pleine, qu'un mort fasse à pié deux lieues de chemin en portant sa tête entre ses bras, nous appellons cela un miracle.

A miracle, according to the true meaning of the word, is something admirable; and agreeably to this, all is miracle. The stupendous order of nature, the revolution of a hundred million worlds round a million suns, the activity of light, the life of animals, all are grand and perpetual miracles.

According to common acceptation, we call a miracle the violation of these divine and eternal laws. A solar eclipse at the time of the full moon, or a dead man walking two leagues and carrying his head in his arms, we denominate a miracle.

"Miracles," in *Dictionnaire philosophique, portatif* (1764), 1:279–280; Besterman et al., *Œuvres complètes de Voltaire* (1994), 36:374. The translation is from *A Philosophical Dictionary* (1824), 5:45.

Molière (Jean-Baptiste Poquelin) (1622–1673)

ACTOR AND PLAYWRIGHT SPECIALIZING IN COMEDIES

Il y a vingt ans que je n'ai vu Paris. On m'a mandé qu'on n'y jouait plus les pièces de Molière. La raison, à mon avis, c'est que tout le monde les sait par cœur; presque tous les traits en sont devenus proverbes; d'ailleurs il y a des longueurs, les intrigues quelquefois sont faibles, et les dénouements sont rarement ingénieux. Il ne voulait que peindre la nature, et il en a été sans doute le plus grand peintre.

I have not set foot in Paris for twenty years. I have been told that Molière's plays are no longer performed there. The reason, I believe, is that everyone knows them by heart; almost all the good lines in his plays have become proverbs; besides, there are tedious passages, the plots are sometimes weak, and the denouements rarely clever. All he wanted to do was to portray nature, and without a doubt he was its greatest painter.

Letter from Ferney, February 26, 1769, to Aleksander Petrovich Sumarokov in Russia, presumably St. Petersburg.

Monarchy

Est des gouvernements le meilleur ou le pire,
Affreux sous un Tyran, divin sous un bon Roi.

Among forms of government, is the best or worst,
Awful under a Tyrant, divine under a good King.

Messala speaking to Titus about the qualities of monarchy, in act 3, scene 7, of *Brutus* (1730), from the first edition, *Le Brutus de Monsieur de Voltaire* (1731), 324; Besterman et al., *Œuvres complètes de Voltaire* (1998), 5:240.

Ce qui peut arriver de plus heureux aux hommes, c'est que le Prince soit Philosophe.

The best thing that can happen to a nation is to have a philosopher as its King.

La Voix du sage et du Peuple (1750), 13; Besterman et al., *Œuvres complètes de Voltaire* (2006), 32a:243.

Les rois sont avec leurs ministres comme les cocus avec leurs femmes: ils ne savent jamais ce qui se passe.

Kings are to their ministers as cuckolds to their wives: neither one ever knows what is going on.

In Besterman, *Voltaire's Notebooks* (1952), vol. 2; first published in *Le Sottisier de Voltaire* (1880), 508; Besterman et al., *Œuvres complètes de Voltaire* (1968), 82:247.

Michel de Montaigne (1533–1592)

PHILOSOPHER AND ESSAYIST

Le charmant projet que Montagne a eu de se peindre naïvement, comme il a fait! car il peint la nature humaine; & le pauvre projet de Nicole, de Mallebranche, de Pascal, de décrier Montagne!

The lovely project that Montaigne had in painting himself naively as he did! For he painted human nature. And the foolish project of Nicole, Malebranche and Pascal in decrying Montaigne.

Lettres philosophiques Par M. de V. . . . . (1734), 173, number 40 among a list of fifty-seven critical comments in a section titled "Vingt-cinquiéme Lettre Sur les Pensées de M. Pascal"; "Remarques sur les Pensées de Pascal," in *Lettres philosophiques* (1964), 2:216. Pierre Nicole, a Jansenist scholar, died one year after Voltaire was born. Nicole's slightly younger contemporary, Nicolas de Malebranche, was a priest and philosopher. The translation is from Smith, "Montaigne in the World" (2016), 294.

Charles-Louis de Secondat, Baron de Montesquieu (1689–1755)

LAWYER, PHILOSOPHER, MAN OF LETTERS, AND AUTHOR OF THE *LETTRES PERSANES* AND *L'ESPRIT DES LOIS*

L'Esprit des Lois, c'est l'esprit sur les lois, je n'ai pas l'honneur de le comprendre. Mais j'entends bien les Lettres Persanes: bon ouvrage que celui-là.

L'Esprit des Lois is wit applied to the laws; I have not the honor of understanding it. But I quite understand the *Persian Letters*: good book, that one.

Comment at Ferney, summer 1763, recorded by the prince de Ligne in his *Mémoires et mélanges historiques et littéraires, 1827–1829* (1827), 2:159.

MONTESQUIEU fut compté parmi les persecutés: il ne fut qu'un peu molesté pour ses Lettres Persanes, ouvrage . . . au-dessous de son génie.

Montesquieu was counted among the most illustrious men of the eighteenth century, and yet he was not persecuted, he was merely harassed a little on account of his Persian Letters, a work . . . far below his genius.

"Avant-propos," in *Commentaire sur l'Esprit des Loix De Montesquieu Par Mr. de Voltaire* (1778), 3–4. The first part of this quote appeared in French as a footnote in a posthumous volume of the writings of John Adams, in a letter Adams sent to John Taylor in 1814. See *The Works of John Adams, Second President of the United States* (1851), 6:481. The quote was presumably added by Adams's grandson, Charles Francis Adams, who edited the volume.

L'Anglais Hobbes *prétend que l'état naturel de l'homme est un état de guerre, parce que tous les hommes ont un droit égal à tout.*

Montesquieu, plus doux, veut croire que l'homme n'est qu'un animal timide qui cherche la paix.

The Englishman *Hobbes* claims that the natural state of man is a state of war, because all men have an equal claim to everything.

Montesquieu, much gentler, wants to believe that man is an animal that only seeks peace.

"Commentaire sur quelques principales maximes de l'Esprit des lois," in *Commentaire sur l'Esprit des Loix De Montesquieu Par Mr. de Voltaire* (1778), 8; Besterman et al., *Œuvres complètes de Voltaire* (2009), 80b:319.

Likely misattributed to Voltaire

C'est le portefeuille d'un homme, d'esprit, qui a été jette par le fenetre et ramassee [*jeté par la fenêtre et ramassé*] par des sots, said Voltaire.

Comment on *L'Esprit des lois* cited in John Adams, *A Defence of the Constitutions of Government of the United States* (1788), 3:487n. In English: "It is a bundle of papers of a thoughtful man, that has been tossed out the window and collected by fools." Adams's source may, indirectly, have been *Observations sur L'Esprit des Loix* (1751, 49), in which Laurent Angliviel de La Beaumelle remarked, not naming Voltaire or anyone else, "Quelqu'un a appellé Le Livre de l'Esprit des Loix, *le porte-feuille d'un homme d'esprit.*"

Morality

L'adultère & l'amour des garçons seront permis chez beaucoup de nations: mais vous n'en trouverez aucune dans laquelle il soit permis de manquer à sa parole; parce que la société peut bien subsister entre des adultères & des garçons qui s'aiment, mais non pas entre des gens qui se feraient gloire de se tromper les uns les autres.

Adultery and love between boys will be tolerated in many nations; but you will not find one where it is acceptable to break one's word; for society can survive despite adultery and boys loving one another, but not if people take pride in deceiving one another.

"De la vertu & du vice," in *Traité de Métaphysique* (1734–1735); Besterman et al., *Œuvres complètes de Voltaire* (1989), 14:476–477. The French text here is from *Philosophie générale: Métaphysique, morale, et théologie* (1784), 32:70, in Beaumarchais's edition of the *Œuvres complètes de Voltaire*. The *Traité* was unpublished during Voltaire's lifetime.

On ne peut trop répéter que tous les dogmes sont différents, & que la morale est la même chose chez tous les hommes qui font usage de leur raison. La morale vient donc de Dieu comme la lumière. Nos superstitions ne sont que ténebres.

We cannot repeat too frequently that dogmas differ, and that morality is the same among all men who make use of their reason. Morality proceeds from God, like light; our superstitions are only darkness.

"Morale," in *Dictionnaire philosophique portatif, ou Supplément à l'Édition de 1765* (circa 1765), 2:68–69; Besterman et al., *Œuvres complètes de Voltaire* (1994), 36:398.

Moses

Qu'est-ce en effet qu'un vieillard de quatre-vingt ans, pour entreprendre de conduire par lui-même tout un Peuple sur lequel il n'a aucun droit. Son bras ne peut combattre, & sa langue ne peut articuler. Il est peint décrépit & begue. . . . Dieu fait tout, Dieu remédie à tout; il nourrit, il vêtit le Peuple par des miracles. Moïse n'est donc rien par lui-même, and son impuissance montre qu'il ne peut être guidé que par le bras du Tout-Puissant; aussi nous ne considérons en lui que l'homme, & non le Ministre de Dieu.

What can we think of an old man of eighty years of age, who by himself alone undertakes to conduct a whole people over whom he had no authority? His arm cannot fight, nor his tongue articulate. He is described [as] a cripple and a stammerer. . . . God does all things, God remedies all things, he nourishes, he cloaths the people by miracles. Moses, then, is nothing of himself, and his impotence shews, that he can be guided by nothing but the hand of the Almighty: we consider him only as a man, and not the minister of God.

"De Moïse, consideré simplement comme Chef d'une Nation," in *La Philosophie de l'Histoire, Par feu l'Abbé Bazin* (1765), 215–216; Besterman et al., *Œuvres complètes de Voltaire* (1969), 59:223. The translation is from *The Philosophy of History by M. de Voltaire* (1766), 185.

Muhammad (circa 570–632)

THE "HOLY PROPHET" OF ISLAM

Ma vie est un combat.

My life is a battle.

Part of a line Mahomet speaks to his lieutenant, Omar, in act 2, scene 4, of *Le Fanatisme, ou Mahomet le Prophete* (1743), 32; Besterman et al., *Œuvres complètes de Voltaire* (2002), 20b:203.

Music

Un homme qui a l'oreille & la voix juste, peut bien chanter sans les règles de la musique; mais il vaut mieux la savoir.

A man who has a good ear and voice may sing well without musical rules; but it is better to know them.

"Aristote," in *Questions sur l'Encyclopédie, par des Amateurs* (1770), 2:150; Besterman et al., *Œuvres complètes de Voltaire* (2008), 39:4. The translation is from *A Philosophical Dictionary* (1824), 1:259.

Natural law

L'instinct qui nous fait sentir la justice.

The instinct that prompts a sense of justice.

This is the response by A to a question posed by B: "Qu'est-ce que la loi naturelle?" in "Loi naturelle. Dialogue," in *Questions sur l'Encyclopédie, par des Amateurs* (1771), 7:348; Besterman et al., *Œuvres complètes de Voltaire* (2012), 42b:68.

Isaac Newton (1642–1726/1727)

ENGLISH PHYSICIST AND MATHEMATICIAN

Si la vraye Grandeur consiste à avoir reçu du ciel un puissant genie, & à s'en être servi pour s'éclairer soi-meme & les autres, un homme comme M. Newton, tel qu'il s'en trouve à peine en dix siecles, est veritablement le grand homme.

If true Greatness consists in having receiv'd from Heaven a mighty Genius, and in having employ'd it to enlighten our own Minds and that of others; a Man like Sir *Isaac Newton*, whose equal is hardly found in a thousand Years, is a truly great Man.

"Douzième Lettre. Sur *Chancelier Bacon*," in *Lettres Ecrites de Londres sur les Anglois et autres sujets* (1734), 80–81; "Sur le chancelier Bacon," in *Lettres philosophiques* (1964), 1:152. The translation is "Letter XII. On the Lord *Bacon*," in *Letters Concerning the English Nation* (1733), 83–84. Voltaire may have attended Newton's state funeral at Westminster Abbey, March 28, 1727, five years before this text was published.

. . . *Il a vécu 85 ans toujours tranquille, heureux & honoré dans sa patrie.*

Son grand bonheur a été non seulement d'être né dans un pays libre, mais dans un tems où les impertinences scolastiques étant banies, la raison seule étoit cultivée, & le monde ne pouvoit être que son ecolier & non son ennemy.

. . . He liv'd happy, and very much honour'd in his native Country, to the Age of fourscore and five Years.

'Twas his peculiar Felicity, not only to be born in a Country of Liberty, but in an Age when all scholastic Impertinencies were banish'd from the World. Reason alone was cultivated, and Mankind cou'd only be his Pupil, not his Enemy.

Figure 18. Jacob Folkema, after Louis-Fabricius Dubourg, Voltaire in antique garb at his writing table. Engraved allegorical frontispiece to Voltaire's treatise, *Élémens de la philosophie de Neuton* (1738). Courtesy of New York Public Library, Rare Books Division. Mme du Chatelet, held aloft by six chubby cherubs, uses a mirror to reflect the divine genius of Newton onto her lover's desk.

"Treisième Lettre. Sur Mr. *Locke*," in *Lettres Ecrites de Londres sur les Anglois et autres sujets* (1734), III; "Sur Descartes et Newton," in *Lettres philosophiques* (1964), 2:5. The translation is "Letter XIII. On Mr. *Locke*," in *Letters Concerning the English Nation* (1733), 116.

Si vous voulez vous appliquer sérieusement à l'étude de la nature, permettez-moi de vous dire qu'il fait commencer par ne faire aucun système. Il faut se conduire comme les Bayle, les Galilée, les Newton. Examinez, peser, calculer et mesurer, mais ne jamais deviner. M. Newton n'a jamais fait de système: il a vu, et il fait voir; mais il n'a point mis ses imaginations à la place de la vérité: ce que nos yeux et les mathématiques nous démontrent, il faut le tenir pour vrai; dans tout le reste il n'y qu'à dire: J'ignore.

If you want to apply yourself seriously to the study of nature, permit me to say that you must not begin by devising a system. One must proceed as Bayle, Galileo, and Newton did. Examine, weigh, calculate, but never guess. M. Newton never had a system: he saw, and he made us see; but he did not let his imagination supplant the truth: whatever our eyes and mathematics demonstrate must be accepted as true; as for everything else: I cannot know.

Letter from Brussels, April 15, 1741, to Claude-Nicolas Le Cat, a distinguished physician in Rouen.

L'Hôpital (françois marquis de) né en 1662. Le premier qui ait écrit en france sur le calcul *inventé par Newton, qu'il appella* les infiniment petits: *c'était alors un prodige. m. en 1704.*

L'Hôpital (*François*, marquis de) born in 1662. The first in France to have written about the *calculus* invented by Newton, which he called the *infinitely little things*: he was in his time a prodigy: d. in 1704.

"Ecrivains, dont plusieurs ont illustré le siécle," in *Le Siècle de Louis XIV* (1751), 2:384; Besterman et al., *Œuvres complètes de Voltaire* (2017), 12:119.

Novels

Un Roman médiocre est, je le sai bien, parmi les Livres, ce qu'est dans le monde un sot qui veut avoir de l'imagination. On s'en moque, mais on le souffre. Ce Roman fait vivre, & l'Auteur, qui l'a composé & le Libraire qui le débite, & le Fondeur et l'Imprimeur, & le Papetier, & le Relieur, & le Colporteur, & le Marchand de mauvais vin à qui tous ceux-là portent leur argent. L'Ouvrage amuse encore deux ou trois heures quelques femmes, avec lesquelles il faut de la nouveauté en Livres, comme en tout le reste. Ainsi, tout méprisable qu'il est, il a produit deux choses importantes, du profit & du plaisir.

A mediocre Novel is, I well know, to Books what a fool is who wants people to think he is clever. It is mocked but tolerated. Such a Novel provides a living for the Author who wrote it, the Publisher who sells it, the Type-foundry, the Printer, the Paper-maker, the Binder, the man who hawks it in the street, and the Vendor of cheap wine to whom they all take their money. For two or three hours, it will amuse a few women who are drawn to novelty in books, as in everything else. Thus, while it is contemptible, it produced two important things—profit and pleasure.

"Copie d'une lettre à un premier commis," June 20, 1733, in *Oeuvres diverses de Monsieur de Voltaire. Nouvelle édition* (1746), 4:247; Besterman et al., *Œuvres complètes de Voltaire* (1999), 9:320. This translation is based on the text published in Hall, *Voltaire in His Letters* (1919), 33.

Nudity

Pourquoi enferme-t-on un homme, une femme qui marcheraient tout nuds dans les rues, & pourquoi personne n'est-il pas choqué des statues absolument nues, des peintures de Magdelaine & de JESUS qu'on voit dans quelques églises.

Why confine a man, a woman, who walks naked in the street, when no one is shocked by statues that are completely nude, by the paintings of Mary Magdalene and Jesus that one sometimes sees in churches.

"Nudité," in *Questions sur l'Encyclopédie, par des Amateurs* (1772), 9:172; Besterman et al., *Œuvres complètes de Voltaire* (2012), 42b:299.

Old age

Vous avez passé votre jeunesse, vous deviendrez bientôt vieux et infirme; voilà à quoi il faut que vous songiez. Il faut vous préparer une arrière-saison tranquille, heureuse, indépendante. Que deviendrez-vous quand vous serez malade et abandonné? Sera-ce une consolation pour vous de dire: J'ai bu du vin de champagne autrefois en bonne compagnie! Songez qu'une bouteille qui a été fêtée quand elle était pleine d'eau des Barbades est jetée dans un coin dès qu'elle est cassée, et qu'elle reste en morceaux dans la poussière.

Your youth is spent, you will soon become old and infirm; you must remember that. You must prepare yourself for a final stage of life, tranquil, happy, independent. What will become of you when you are sick and all alone? Will it be any consolation to you to say: I once drank champagne with fancy people! Remember that a good bottle that was enjoyed when it was full of Barbados rum is tossed in a corner as soon as it is broken, and it remains there in pieces in the dust.

Letter from Lunéville, June 12, 1735, to Nicolas-Claude Thieriot in Paris.

Un vieillard est un grand arbre qui n'a plus ni fruits ni feuilles, mais qui tient encore à la terre.

An old man is a tall tree that no longer has fruit or leaves, yet still clings to the earth.

Besterman, *Voltaire's Notebooks* (1952), vol. 2; first published in *Le Sottisier de Voltaire* (1880), 60; Besterman et al., *Œuvres complètes de Voltaire* (1968), 82:350.

Je crois qu'il n'y a que les vieux figuiers qui donnent. La vieillesse est encore bonne à quelque chose.

Only old fig trees, I believe, bear fruit. Old age is still good for something.

Letter from Ferney, August 10, 1768, to Mme Louis-Suzanne Gallatin-Vaudenet at Prégny, near Geneva.

Quand on est vieux malade, on se retire bien volontiers du monde. C'est un grand bal où il ne faut pas s'aviser de paraitre lorsqu'on ne peut plus danser.

When you are sick and old, you gladly withdraw from the world. It is a fancy ball one must not think of attending when one can no longer dance.

Letter from Ferney, October 31, 1768, to Jean-François de La Harpe in Paris.

Onanism—masturbation

Un effet très désordonné de l'amour-propre.

A very disordered effect of narcissism.

"Onan et Onanisme," in *Questions sur l'Encyclopédie, par des Amateurs* (1774), 4:186; Besterman et al., *Œuvres complètes de Voltaire* (2012), 42b:304.

On a remarqué que l'espèce des hommes & celle des singes sont les seules qui tombent dans ce défaut contraire au vœu de la nature.

It has been noted that men and apes are the only species afflicted with this flaw contrary to the will of nature.

"Onan et Onanisme," in *Questions sur l'Encyclopédie, par des Amateurs* (1774), 4:187; Besterman et al., *Œuvres complètes de Voltaire* (2012), 42b:307.

Optimism

Tout est bien, dites-vous, & tout est nécessaire.
Quoi? L'Univers entier, sans ce gouffre infernal,
Sans engloutir Lisbonne, eût-il été plus mal?

All is well, you say, and all is *necessary*.
What? Would all of Creation be any worse
Without the pit that swallowed up Lisbon?

"Poëme sur le désastre de Lisbonne," in *Poëmes sur le désastre de Lisbonne et sur la loi naturelle* (1756), 9; Besterman et al., *Œuvres complètes de Voltaire* (2009), 45a:337–338.

Un jour tout sera bien, voilà notre espérance;
Tout est bien aujourdhui, voilà l'illusion.

One day all will be well, *therein lies our every hope*;
All is well right now; *there is the illusion.*

"Poëme sur le désastre de Lisbonne," in *Poëmes sur le désastre de Lisbonne et sur la loi naturelle* (1756), 16; Besterman et al., *Œuvres complètes de Voltaire* (2009), 45a:348.

Il est démontré, disait-il, que les choses ne peuvent être autrement: car tout étant fait pour une fin, tout est nécessairement pour la meilleure fin. . . . *Par conséquent, ceux qui ont avancé que tout est bien, ont dit une sottise: il fallait dire que tout est au mieux.*

"It is demonstrated," he said, "that things cannot be otherwise, for, everything being made for an end, everything is necessarily for the best end. . . . Consequently, those who have asserted that all is well have said a foolish thing; they should have said that all is for the best."

Pangloss to Candide, "Comment Candide fut élevé dans un beau Château, & comment il fut chassé d'icelui," chap. 1 in *Candide, ou L'Optimisme* (1759), 6–7; Besterman et al., *Œuvres complètes de Voltaire* (1980), 48:119. In English, *Candide, Zadig, and Other Stories* (2001), 16.

Qu'est'ce qu'Optimisme? disait Cacambo. Hélas, dit Candide, c'est la rage de soutenir que tout est bien quand on est mal!

"What is optimism?" said Cacambo.
"Alas!" said Candide, "it is the mania of maintaining that all is well when we are miserable!"

"Ce qui leur arriva à Surinam, & comment Candide fit connaissance avec Martin," chap. 19 in *Candide, ou L'Optimisme* (1759), 168–169; Besterman et al., *Œuvres complètes de Voltaire* (1980), 48:196. In English, *Candide, Zadig, and Other Stories* (2001), 61.

Originality

Attributed to Voltaire

Originality is nothing but judicious imitation.

Quoted in "Anecdotes of Voltaire: Collected from the Conversation of several inhabitants of Geneva, and from various learned Characters," *The Edinburgh Magazine, or Literary Miscellany,* June 1786, 410.

The origin of life

Si la matiére quelconque mise en mouvement suffisait pour produire ce que nous voyons sur la terre, il n'y aurait aucune raison pour laquelle de la poussiére bien remuée dans un tonneau ne pourait produire des hommes & des arbres, ni pourquoi un champ semé de bled ne pourrait pas produire des baleines & des écrevisses au lieu de froment.

Were it enough in order to produce the things we see in the world to randomly set in motion any matter whatsoever, there would be absolutely no reason why dust well shaken in a barrel might not produce men and trees, nor any reason why a field sown with grain might not produce whales and crayfish instead of wheat.

Elémens de philosophie de Newton. Divisés en trois parties, part 1, chap. 8, "Des premiers principes de la matiere," in *Mélanges de philosophie avec des figures* (1756), 3:59–60; Besterman et al., *Œuvres complètes de Voltaire* (1992), 15:236.

Painting

Le Poussin sagement peignoit,	Poussin sagely painted,
Le Brun fierement dessinoit,	Le Brun boldly sketched,
Le Sueur entr'eux se plaçoit.	Le Sueur settled in between.

Describing Nicolas Poussin, Charles Le Brun, and Eustache Le Sueur, three leading painters during the reign of Louis XIV, in *Le Temple du Goust* (1733), 31.

Il faut, pour qu'un peintre ait une juste réputation, que ses ouvrages aient un prix chez les étrangers. ce n'est pas assez d'avoir un petit parti, & d'être loué dans de petits livres, il faut être acheté.

For a painter to be held in proper esteem, his work must be prized by foreigners. It is not enough to have a small group of admirers, and to be praised in pamphlets, his work must sell.

"Artistes célèbres," in *Le Siècle de Louis XIV* (1751), 2:431; Besterman et al., *Œuvres complètes de Voltaire* (2017), 12:210.

Il n'en est pas de la PEINTURE comme de la musique. une nation peut avoir un chant qui ne plaise qu'à elle, parce que le génie de sa langue n'en admettra pas d'autres; mais les peintres doivent représenter la nature qui est la même dans tous les païs, et qui est vuë avec les mêmes yeux.

Painting is not at all like music. A nation may have music that is pleasing only to itself, because the genius of its language will accept no other; but painters must represent nature, which is the same in every country, and is seen through the same eyes.

"Artistes célèbres," in *Le Siècle de Louis XIV* (1751), 2:430–431; Besterman et al., *Œuvres complètes de Voltaire* (2017), 12:210.

Quoi! on estimeroit autant un peintre de portrait qu'un Raphaël? Quoi! une tête de Rimbran sera égale au tableau de la transfiguration, ou à celui des noces de Cana?

What! One would rank a portrait painter as highly as Raphael? What! A face by Rembrandt will equal the *Transfiguration*, or the *Wedding at Cana*?

"Parallèle d'Horace, de Boileau et de Pope," in *Contes de Guillaume Vadé* (1764), 253; Besterman et al., *Œuvres complètes de Voltaire* (2014), 52:434. Raphael's thirteen-foot-high *Transfiguration*, commissioned as an altarpiece for the cathedral in Narbonne, is now in the Pinacoteca Vaticana, Rome. Veronese's thirty-three-foot-wide *Wedding of Cana*, is in the Louvre.

To paint well it is necessary to have warm feet. It is hard to paint when your feet are cold.

At Ferney, December 24, 1764, in response to a remark by James Boswell that an academy of painting had been established in Glasgow, "but it did not succeed. Our Scotland is no country for that." Boswell recorded the exchange in his diary. See Pottle, *Boswell on the Grand Tour* (1953), 280.

Paris

Le Paradis terrestre est à Paris.

Paris is heaven on earth.

The final line of *Le Mondain*, in the first published text (1736, 6); Besterman et al., *Œuvres complètes de Voltaire* (2003), 16:303. In the 1739 version of the poem, in the Ledet edition of *Œuvres de M. de Voltaire*, 4:119, inspired by Voltaire's sojourn in Cirey with Mme du Châtelet, the line was changed to "Le Paradis terrestre est où je suis." In Smollett et al., *The Works of Mr. de Voltaire* (1764), vol. 32, the verse is translated as: "Paris to me's a paradise."

Ma chère amie, Paris est un gouffre où se perdent le repos et le recueillement de l'âme, sans qui la vie n'est qu'un tumulte importun.

My dear friend, where the soul is concerned, Paris is a sinkhole of lost repose and reflection, without which life is but a tiresome tumult.

Letter from Les Délices, November 17, 1763, to Mme Antoinette-Françoise de Champbonin at her estate near Vassy in Champagne.

Il est vrai que la vie de Paris me tuerait en huit jours.

It is true that living in Paris would kill me within a week.

Letter from Ferney, July 11, 1770, to the duc de Richelieu in Paris.

Paternal instict

Excepté quelques ames barbares entiérement abruties, ou peut être un philosophe plus abruti encore, les hommes les plus durs aiment par un instinct dominant l'enfant qui n'est pas encor né, le ventre qui le porte, & la mère qui redouble d'amour pour celui dont elle a reçu dans son sein le germe d'un être semblable à elle.

Aside from a few barbarous, utterly brutish souls, or perhaps a philosopher more brutish still, the roughest man, by a prevailing instinct, loves the child that is not yet born, the womb that bears it, and the mother redoubles her love for him from whom she has received in her womb the seed of a being similar to herself.

"Homme" (under the subheading "De l'homme dans l'état de pure nature"), in *Questions sur l'Encyclopédie, par des Amateurs* (1771), 7:102; Besterman et al., *Œuvres complètes de Voltaire* (2011), 42a:273.

The people—the public—rabble

Le peuple n'est pas content quand on ne fait rire que l'esprit. Il faut le faire rire tout haut, et il est difficile de le réduire à aimer mieux des plaisanteries fines, que des équivoques fades, et à préférer Versailles à la rue St-Denis.

For the common people, it is not enough to make the mind laugh. You must make them laugh out loud, and it is hard to get them to prefer subtle pleasantries to insipid puns and Versailles over the rue Saint-Denis.

Letter from Paris, August 20, 1725, to Marguerite-Madeleine du Moutier, marquise de Bernières, in Rouen.

Le public est une bête féroce: il faut l'enchaîner ou la fuir. Je n'ai point de chaînes pour elle; mais j'ai le secret de la retraite. J'ai trouvé la douceur du repos, le vrai bonheur. Irai-je quitter tout cela pour être déchiré par l'abbé Desfontaines, et pour être immolé sur le théâtre des farceurs italiens à la malignité du public et aux rires de la canaille?

The public is a ferocious beast: one must chain it up or flee from it. I have no chains; but I do have a hideaway. I have discovered the sweetness of rest, and real happiness. Would I leave all that only to be torn to shreds by the Abbé Desfontaines, and pilloried on the stage of the Théâtre Italien to satisfy the viciousness of the public and laughter from the rabble?

Letter from Cirey, August 16, 1738, to Jeanne-Françoise Quinault in Paris. Mlle Quinault was an actress and *salonnière*.

La canaille n'est pas faite pour la raison.

The rabble was not made for reason.

Letter from Ferney, February 4, 1757, to Jean le Rond d'Alembert in Paris.

*Vous savez ce que j'entends par le Public. Ce n'est pas l'*Univers, *comme nous autres barbouilleurs de papier l'avons dit quelquefois. Le Public, en fait de livres, est composé de quarante ou cinquante personnes si le livre est sérieux, de quatre ou cinq cent lorsqu'il est plaisant, & d'environ onze ou douze cent s'il s'agit d'une piéce de Théâtre. Il y a toûjours dans Paris plus de cinq cent mille ames qui n'entendons jamais parler de tout cela.*

You know what I mean by the Public. It is not everyone on earth, as we scribblers sometimes say. The Public, for books, is composed of forty or fifty people if the book is serious, four or five hundred when it is amusing, and about eleven or twelve hundred if it is a piece of Theater. There are still more than five hundred thousand souls in Paris who have no interest in any of these things.

Letter presumably from Ferney, September–October 1765, to an unnamed gentleman, probably in Paris, printed in its entirety in the "Préface de l'éditeur," in *Adélaïde du Guesclin, Tragédie,* in *Théatre complet de M.ᵉ de Voltaire* (1768), 3:3. The *éditeur,* likely Gabriel Cramer, said the letter had been sent by Voltaire "à un de ses amis."

Le roi de Prusse mande que sur mille hommes on ne trouve qu'un philosophe; mais il excepte l'Angleterre. À ce compte il n'y aurait guère que deux mille sages en France; mais ces deux mille en dix ans en produisent quarante mille et c'est à peu près tout ce qu'il faut, car il est à propos que le peuple soit guidé, et non pas qu'il soit instruit.

The king of Prussia says that out of a thousand men, you will find just one philosopher, though he makes an exception for England. Thus, there are barely two thousand enlightened souls in France; but these two thousand in ten years will produce forty thousand and that is about all we require, since, and rightly so, the people need to be guided, not educated.

Letter from Ferney, March 19, 1766, to Étienne-Noël Damilaville in Paris.

J'entends par peuple la populace qui n'a que ses bras pour vivre. Je doute que cet ordre de citoyens ait jamais le temps ou la capacité de s'instruire, ils mourraient de faim avant de devenir philosophes, il me paraît essentiel qu'il y ait des gueux igno-rants. . . . Ce n'est pas la manœuvre qu'il faut instruire, c'est le bon bourgeois, c'est l'habitant des villes, cette entreprise est assez forte et assez grande.

I understand by "people" the populace, who have only their arms for suste-nance. I doubt that that class of citizens has the time or the capacity to edu-cate itself, they would starve to death before they would become philosophers; it is, I think, essential for there to be ignorant beggars. . . . It is not the worker that must be educated, it is the solid bourgeois, the city-dweller, and that is already a sufficiently vast and weighty undertaking.

Letter from Ferney, April 1, 1766, to Damilaville in Paris.

Quand la populace se mêle de raisonner, tout est perdu. Je suis de l'avis de ceux qui veulent faire de bons laboureurs des enfants trouvés, au lieu d'en faire des théologiens.

When the masses get mixed up in rational debate, all is lost. I agree with those who would make able ploughmen of foundlings instead of theologians.

Letter from Ferney, April 1, 1766, to Damilaville in Paris.

À l'égard du peuple il sera toujours sot et barbare. . . . Ce sont des bœufs, auxquels il faut un joug, un aiguillon et du foin.

As for the people, they will always be stupid and barbarous. . . . They are like oxen that require a yoke, a goad, and fodder.

Letter from Ferney, February 3, 1769, to Jean-François-René Tabareau in Lyon.

Perfection

Souvent il meglio è l'inimico del bene.

Often the better is the enemy of the good.

Letter from Cirey, June 18, 1744, to the duc de Richelieu in Paris. An equivalent saying in English might be, "Leave well enough alone."

Il meglio è l'inimico del bene.

The better is the enemy of the good.

From "Art dramatique," in *Questions sur l'Encyclopédie, par des Amateurs* (1770), 2:250; Bes-terman et al., *Œuvres complètes de Voltaire* (2008), 39:101. This article was later incorpo-rated into the *Dictionnaire philosophique.*

Dans ses écrits un sage Italien
Dit que le mieux est l'ennemi du bien.

In his writings, a wise Italian
Says that the better is the enemy of the good.

First two lines of an eleven-page fairy tale in verse, *La Bégueule. Conte moral* (1772), 3; Besterman et al., *Œuvres complètes de Voltaire* (2006), 74a:217. The identity of the "wise Italian" is unknown.

Attributed to Voltaire

La perfection marche lentement, il lui faut la main du tems.

Perfection is attained by slow degrees; she requires the hand of time.

Moore, *A Dictionary of Quotations from Various Authors* (1831), 187 (in French and English).

Philippe d'Orléans (1674–1723)

SON OF LOUIS XIV'S YOUNGER BROTHER AND REGENT OF FRANCE FROM 1715 TO 1723

Monseigneur, je remercie votre Altesse Royale de vouloir bien continuer à se charger de ma nourriture; mais je la prie de ne plus se charger de mon logement.

My Lord, I thank your Royal Highness for his continued provision of my board but beg him to no longer concern himself with my lodging.

Condorocet, *Vie de Voltaire, par M. le marquis de Condorcet* (1789), 70:11. In 1717, at age twenty-four, François-Marie Arouet was sent to the Bastille by the regent, Philippe d'Orléans, for having written, among other things, satirical verse implying that Philippe had incestuous relations with his daughter. He remained in prison for eleven months. In 1722, however, the regent granted him an annual pension of two thousand livres. According to Condorcet, this witty line was the poet's way of expressing his gratitude. It was after his stint in the Bastille that Arouet adopted the nom de plume "Voltaire."

Les Philosophes

On crie contre les philosophes. On a raison, car si l'opinion est la reine du monde, les philosophes gouvernent cette reine.

People scream about the *Philosophes*. They are right; because if opinion is queen of the world, the *Philosophes* rule the queen.

Letter from Ferney, July 8, 1765, to Jean le Rond d'Alembert in Paris.

Philosophy—philosophers

Malheur aux philosophes qui ne savent pas se dérider le front! Je regarde l'austérité comme une maladie: j'aime encore mieux mille fois être languissant et sujet à la fièvre, comme je le suis, que de penser tristement. Il me semble que la vertu, l'étude et la gaieté sont trois sœurs, qu'il ne faut point séparer: ces trois divinités sont vos suivantes; je les prends pour mes maîtresses.

Woe unto philosophers who cannot laugh away their wrinkles! I look on solemnity as a disease: I had rather a thousand times more be as I am, feeble and feverish, than surrender to gloomy thoughts. It seems to me that virtue, study and good humor are three sisters who should never be separated: they are your servants those three divinities: I take them as my mistresses.

Letter from Ferney, circa July 30, 1737, to Frederick the Great in Potsdam. The translation is from Hall, *Voltaire in His Letters* (1919), 44–45.

Ce nom de Nouvelle Philosophie ne seroit que le titre d'un Roman nouveau, s'il n'annonçoit que les conjectures d'un Moderne, opposées aux fantaisies des Anciens. . . . Car il y a un nombre innombrable de manieres d'arriver à l'Erreur, il n'y a qu'une seule route vers la Vérité.

This term Nouvelle Philosophie would be but the title of a new Novel, if it merely signaled the conjectures of a Modern, opposed to the fantasies of the Ancients. . . . For there are countless ways of falling into Error, and but one path that leads to the Truth.

Élémens de la philosophie de Neuton, Mis à la portée de tout le monde (1738), 10, in Besterman et al., *Œuvres complètes de Voltaire* (1992), 15:548. Circa 1760, as Voltaire, Rousseau, Diderot, d'Alembert, and their like were making their presence felt, they were sometimes mocked as "les Nouveaux Philosophes."

Sans la philosophie, nous ne serions guères au dessus des animaux qui se creusent des habitations, qui en élèvent, qui s'y préparent leur nourriture, qui prennent soin de leurs petits dans leurs demeures, & qui ont par dessus nous le bonheur de naitre véus.

Without philosophy, we should be little above the animals that dig or erect their habitations, prepare their food in them, take care of their little ones in their dwellings, and, besides, have the good fortune which we have not, of being born ready-clothed.

"Antiquité," in *Questions sur l'Encyclopédie, par des Amateurs* (1770), 1:354; Besterman et al., *Œuvres complètes de Voltaire* (2007), 38:414. The translation is from *A Philosophical Dictionary* (1824), 1:177.

Apprends que tout systeme offense ma raison.

Know this: all systems are offensive in my mind.

The near-parting words of the *vieillard* (Voltaire) to Pegasus, in the *Dialogue de Pégase et du vieillard* (1774), 13; Besterman et al., *Œuvres complètes de Voltaire* (2013), 76:532.

Plagiarism

On dit qu'originairement ce mot vient du latin plaga, *& qu'il signifiait la condamnation au fouet de ceux qui avaient vendu des hommes libres pour des esclaves. Cela n'a rien de commun avec le plagiat des auteurs, lesquels ne vendent point d'hommes, soit esclaves, soit libres. Ils se vendent seulement eux-mêmes quelquefois pour un peu d'argent.*

It is said that this word comes from the Latin *plaga*, and that it signified the condemnation to a public whipping for those who sold freemen as slaves. This has nothing in common with plagiarism among writers, who do not sell men, enslaved or free. They merely sell themselves, sometimes for very little money.

"Plagiat," in *Questions sur l'Encyclopédie, par des Amateurs* (1771), 8:199; Besterman et al., *Œuvres complètes de Voltaire* (2012), 42b:438.

On pourrait appeler plagiaires *tous les compilateurs, tous les feseurs de dictionnaires, qui ne font que répéter à tort & à travers, les opinions, les erreurs, les impostures, les vérités déja imprimés dans les dictionnaires précédens; mais ce sont du moins des plagiaires de bonne foi; ils ne s'arrogent point le mérite de l'invention.*

All makers of dictionaries, all compilers who do nothing but witlessly repeat the opinions, errors, impostures, and truths previously printed in other dictionaries, may be called *plagiarists*; but at least they are honest plagiarists, who lay no claim to being masters of invention.

"Plagiat," in *Questions sur l'Encyclopédie, par des Amateurs* (1771), 8:199; Besterman et al., *Œuvres complètes de Voltaire* (2012), 42b:438.

C'est surtout en poësie qu'on se permet souvent le plagiat, & c'est assurément de tous les larcins le moins dangereux pour la société.

It is chiefly in the field of poetry that plagiarism is most often tolerated; and it is certainly the form of larceny that poses the least danger to society.

"Plagiat," in *Questions sur l'Encyclopédie, par des Amateurs* (1771), 8:201; Besterman et al., *Œuvres complètes de Voltaire* (2012), 42b:442.

Plato (circa 425 B.C.–347 B.C.)

GREEK PHILOSOPHER

. . . Y a-t-il rien dans la littérature de plus dangereux que des rhéteurs sophistes? parmi ces sophistes y en eut-il de plus inintelligibles & de plus indignes d'être enten-dus que le divin Platon?

La seule idée utile qu'on puisse peut-être trouver chez lui, est l'immortalité de l'ame, qui était déja établie chez tous les peuples policés. Mais comment prouve-t-il cette immortalité?

. . . There is nothing in literature more dangerous than rhetorical sophists; and among these sophists none are more unintelligible and unworthy of being understood than the divine Plato.

The only useful idea to be found in him, is that of the immortality of the soul, which was already admitted among cultivated nations; but then how does he prove this immortality?

"Sophiste," in *Questions sur l'Encyclopédie, par des Amateurs* (1771), 8:337–338; Besterman et al., *Œuvres complètes de Voltaire* (2013), 43:287. The translation is from *A Philosophical Dictionary* (1824), 6:141.

Poetry

On demande comment la poësie étant si peu nécessaire au monde, elle occupe un si haut rang parmi les beaux arts? On peut faire la même question sur la musique. La poësie est la musique de l'ame, & surtout des ames grandes & sensibles.

How can poetry, one may ask, being of so little use to the world, occupy such an important place among the arts? The same question may be asked about music. Poetry is the music of the soul, and above all, of great and sensitive souls.

"Des Poëtes," in *Mélanges philosophiques, littéraires, historiques, &c.* (1771), 2:418; Besterman et al., *Œuvres complètes de Voltaire* (2017), 60a:262.

Un mérite de la poësie dont bien des gens ne se doutent pas, c'est qu'elle dit plus que la prose, & en moins de paroles que la prose.

One merit of poetry of which many are unaware, is that it says more, and in fewer words than prose.

"Des Poëtes," in *Mélanges philosophiques, littéraires, historiques, &c.* (1771), 2:419; Besterman et al., *Œuvres complètes de Voltaire* (2017), 60a:262.

*Un jeune homme au sortir du collége délibère s'il se fera avocat, médecin, théolo-
gien, ou poëte; s'il prendra soin de notre fortune, de notre santé, de notre ame, ou
de nos plaisirs.*

A young man, after he leaves school, wonders whether he should become a
lawyer, doctor, theologian, or poet; if he will attend to our property, our health,
our soul, or our pleasure.

"Poètes," in *Dictionnaire philosophique* (M–P), vol. 6 in Beaumarchais's edition
of the *Oeuvres complètes de Voltaire* (1784), 42:331. This line may have appeared in
print for the first time (perhaps exclusively) in Beaumarchais's version of the article
"Poètes."

*La Rime est nécessaire à nos jargons nouveaux,
Enfans demi polis des Normands & des Goths.*

Rhyming is required for these new jargons of ours,
Half-civilized offspring of Normands and Goths.

Épitre à Horace (1772), 13; Besterman et al., *Œuvres complètes de Voltaire* (2006), 74b:281.

Politics

*L'esprit de parti obligé d'avouer les faits en altère les circonstances & les motifs; &
malheureusement c'est ainsi que toutes les histoires contemporaines parviennent fal-
sifiées à la postérité, qui ne peut guère démêler la vérité du mensonge.*

The spirit of faction, forced to accept a set of facts, will alter circumstances
and motives; and unfortunately it is thus that all contemporary histories are
transmitted to posterity, which will be unable to distinguish truth from
lies.

Histoire de l'Empire de Russie, in *Histoire de Charles XII, Roi de Suède*, in Cramer and Cramer, eds., *Collection complette des Œuvres de Mr. de Voltaire* (1768), 2:468; Moland, *Œuvres
complètes de Voltaire* (1877), 4:611.

*La politique a sa source dans la perversité plus que dans la grandeur de l'esprit
humain.*

Politics is rooted more in the perversity than the grandeur of the human
spirit.

"Appendice: Supplément aux œuvres en prose" ("Traits singuliers du règne de Louis XIV"),
in *Œuvres complètes de Voltaire. Commentaires sur Corneille II* (1880), 489; Besterman et al.,
Œuvres complètes de Voltaire (1968), 81:211.

Jeanne-Antoinette Poisson, marquise de Pompadour (1721–1764)

Official mistress, lover and friend of Louis XV, patroness of the arts, supporter of Voltaire and the *Philosophes*.

Sincère et tendre Pompadour,
Car je peux vous donner d'avance
Ce nom qui rime avec l'amour,
Et qui sera bientôt le plus beau nom de France.

Sincere and tender Pompadour,
For I can give you in advance
This name that rhymes with amour,
Soon to be the most beautiful name in France.

First four lines of a twelve-line poem, in a letter from Paris, May–June 1745, to the future Mme de Pompadour at Versailles. In late June, shortly after this poem was composed, the king presented his mistress with an estate and the title of marquise de Pompadour to allow her to appear at court.

Dans le fond de son cœur elle était des nôtres; elle protégeait les lettres autant qu'elle le pouvait: voilà un beau rêve fini.

Deep down she was one of us; she did her best to protect men of letters: there goes a beautiful dream.

Letter from Les Délices, May 8, 1764, to Jean le Rond d'Alembert in Paris, commenting on Pompadour's recent death.

The pope

Le pape est une idole à qui on lie les mains et dont on baise les pieds.

The pope is an idol whose hands are bound and whose feet are kissed.

Notebooks entry, in Besterman, *Voltaire's Notebooks* (1952), 1:101.

La maxime de la France est de le regarder comme une personne sacrée, mais entreprenante, à laquelle il faut baiser les pieds & lier quelquefois les mains.

It is the maxim of France to regard him as a sacred and enterprising person, whose hands must sometimes be tied, though they must kiss his feet.

"Des états Chrêtiens de l'Europe avant Louïs XIV," first chapter in *Essay sur le siècle de Louis XIV. Par Mr. de Voltaire* (1740). Reprinted in *Recueil de nouvelles pièces fugitives en prose et en vers* (1741); Besterman et al., *Œuvres complètes de Voltaire* (2015), 13a:24.

Alexander Pope (1688–1744)

ENGLISH POET

I intend to send you two or three poems of Mr. Pope, the best poet of England, and at present, of all the world.

Letter written in English from London, October 26, 1726, to Nicolas-Claude Thieriot in Paris.

C'est je crois le poëte le plus élégant, le plus correct, & ce qui est encore beaucoup, le plus harmonieux qu'ait eu l'Angleterre. Il a réduit les fifemens aigres de la trompette Angloise aux sons de la flute. On peut le Traduire parce qu'il est extremement clair, & que ses sujets pour la plûpart sont generaux & du ressort de toutes les Nations.

He is in my Opinion the most elegant, the most correct Poet; and at the same Time the most harmonious . . . that England ever gave Birth to. He has mellow'd the harsh Sounds of the English Trumpet to the soft Accents of the Flute. His Compositions may be easily translated, because they are vastly clear and perspicuous; besides, most of his Subjects are general, and relative to all Nations.

"Vingt-Deuzième Lettre. Sur Mr. *Pope* Et quelques Poetes Fameux," in *Lettres Ecrites de Londres sur les Anglois et autres sujets* (1734), 197–198; "Sur Mr Pope et quelques autres poetes fameux," in *Lettres philosophiques* (1964), 2:136. The translation is "Letter XXII. On Mr. *Pope*, and Some Other Famous Poets," in *Letters Concerning the English Nation* (1733), 215–216.

Pope drives a handsome chariot, with a couple of neat trim nags; Dryden a coach, and six stately horses.

Comment to James Boswell at Ferney, presumably December 27, 1764, shared with Samuel Johnson in London, February 1766. See Boswell's *Life of Samuel Johnson* (1791), 1:274.

Nicolas Poussin (1594–1665)

FRENCH NEOCLASSICAL-STYLE PAINTER
AND THE FIRST GREAT MODERN
FRENCH PAINTER

Nicolas *POUSSIN, né aux andelis en normandie en 1594, fut l'éléve de son génie; il se perfectionna à rome. On l'appelle le peintre des gens d'esprit; on pourrait aussi l'appeler le peintre des gens de goût. Il n'a d'autre défaut que celui d'avoir outré le sombre du coloris de l'école romaine. Il était, dans son tems, le plus grand peintre de l'Europe. rappelé de rome à paris, il y céda à l'envie & aux cabales, il se retira. C'est ce qui est arrivé a plus d'un artiste. Le* poussin *retourna à rome, où il vécut pauvre mais content. Sa philosophie le mit au-dessus de la fortune. m. en 1665.*

Nicholas Poussin, born at Les Andelys in Normandy in 1599, was the pupil of his own genius; he perfected himself in Rome. He is called the painter of men of intellect; one might also call him the painter of men of taste. He had no other fault, except having carried too far the dark shadings of the Italian School. He was, in his time, the greatest painter in Europe. Recalled from Rome to Paris, where he fell victim to envy and intrigue, he withdrew: such has happened to more than one artist. *Poussin* returned to Rome, where he lived in poverty, but contented. His philosophy elevated him above his fate: d. in 1665.

Le Siècle de Louis XIV (1751), 2:432; Besterman et al., *Œuvres complètes de Voltaire* (2017), 12:211.

Praise

Ne célébrons jamais que ce que nous aimons.

Let us never celebrate but that which we love.

Épitre à Madame Denis, sur l'agriculture, inscribed "A Ferney, ce 14 Mars 1761," in *Troisieme suite des mélanges de poesie, de littérature, d'histoire et de philosophie* (1765), 195; Besterman et al., *Œuvres complètes de Voltaire* (2013), 51b:300.

Prayer

Prier Dieu, c'est se flatter qu'avec des paroles on changera toute la nature.

To pray to God is to flatter oneself that with words one can alter nature.

Circa 1735, in Besterman, *Voltaire's Notebooks* (1952), 2:260; first published in *Le Sottisier de Voltaire* (1880), 87; Besterman et al., *Œuvres complètes de Voltaire* (1969), 83:396.

L'Eternel a ses desseins de toute éternité. Si la prière est d'accord avec ses volontés immuables, il est très inutile de lui demander ce qu'il a résolu de faire. Si on le prie de faire le contraire de ce qu'il a résolu, c'est le prier d'être faible, léger, inconstant; c'est croire qu'il soit tel; c'est se moquer de lui. Ou vous lui demandez une chose juste; en ce cas il la doit, & elle se fera sans qu'on l'en prie; c'est même se défier de lui que lui faire instance. Ou la chose est injuste; & alors on l'outrage. Vous êtes digne ou indigne de la grace que vous implorez: si digne, il le sait mieux que vous; si indigne, on commet un crime de plus en demandant ce qu'on ne mérite pas.

En un mot, nous ne fesons des prières à DIEU que parce que nous l'avons fait à notre image. Nous le traitons comme un bacha, comme un sultan qu'on peut irriter & appaiser.

The Eternal has had his plans for all eternity. If a prayer accords with His immutable wishes, it is quite useless to ask of Him what He has resolved to do. If you pray to him to do the contrary of what he has resolved, you are praying that He be weak, frivolous, inconstant; to do so is to believe He is thus; you are mocking Him. Either you ask Him a just thing, in which case He must do it, and it will be done without your praying to Him, and so to entreat Him is to distrust Him; or the thing is unjust, and you insult Him. You are worthy or unworthy of the grace you implore: if worthy, He knows it better than you; if unworthy, you commit another crime by requesting what is undeserved.

In a word, we only pray to God because we have made Him in our image. We treat Him like a pasha, like a sultan whom one may provoke or appease.

"Prières," in *Questions sur l'Encyclopédie, par des Amateurs* (1772), 180; Besterman et al., *Œuvres complètes de Voltaire* (2012), 42b:494.

Preaching

ARISTON: *Vous êtes sçavant, & vous avez une éloquence sage; comment comptez-vous prêcher devant des gens de campagne?*

TÉOTIME: *Comme je prêcherais devant les Rois; je parlerais toujours de morale, & jamais de controverse . . . il y a mille choses que mon auditoire n'entendrait pas, ni moi non plus. Je tacherai de faire des gens de bien, & de l'être, mais je ne ferai point des théologiens, & je le ferai le moins que je pourai.*

ARISTON: You are a scholar, and you speak well and wisely; how do you intend to preach to country folk?

TÉOTIME: As I would preach before kings; I would always speak of morality, and never religious controversy . . . there are a thousand things my audience would not understand, nor I. I will try to help people, and myself, to be good, but I will not be making theologians of them, and I will do as little of it as I can.

"Catechisme du Curé," in *Dictionnaire philosophique, portatif* (1764), 124–125; Besterman et al., *Œuvres complètes de Voltaire* (1994), 35:478. This text was reprinted in *Questions sur l'Encyclopédie, par des Amateurs* (1770), as "Le Curé de campagne" ("Dialogue seconde"), 3:205; Besterman et al., *Œuvres complètes de Voltaire* (2009), 40:338–339.

Prejudice

Les Préjugés, ami, sont les Rois du Vulgaire.

Prejudice, my friend, is Monarch of the Rabble.

Mahomet to Omar, his lieutenant, in act 2, scene 4 of *Le Fanatisme, ou Mahomet le Prophete* (1743), 30; Besterman et al., *Œuvres complètes de Voltaire* (2002), 20b:202.

On ne gouverne les hommes que suivant leurs préjugés.

Men are governed only by playing to their prejudices.

Annales de l'Empire depuis Charlemagne. Par l'Auteur du Siècle de Louis XIV. Tome premier. Nouvelle édition (1754), 289; Besterman et al., *Œuvres complètes de Voltaire* (2019), 44b:160.

Que conclure à la fin de tous mes longs propos?
C'est que les préjugés sont la raison des sots.

What then from these, my many words, shall we conclude?
That prejudice is what guides the stupid and the crude.

"La Loi naturelle; Poëme en Quatre Parties" (1756), in *Poëmes sur le désastre de Lisbonne et sur la loi naturelle* (1756), 45; Besterman et al., *Œuvres complètes de Voltaire* (2007), 32b:84.

Gardons nous de heurter ses préjugés au front.

Let us guard against attacking his prejudices head on.

Gourville le jeune to his brother in *Le Dépositaire* (1769), act 4, scene 2, in *Théatre complet de Mr. de Voltaire* (1772), 7:319; Besterman et al., *Œuvres complètes de Voltaire* (2013), 71c:156. This comedy was never staged in Paris.

Pride

Qui s'élève trop, s'avilit;	Degraded he who grows too tall;
De la vanité naît la honte.	For shame is born of vanity.
C'est par l'orgueil qu'on est petit;	It is through pride that we are small;
On est grand quand on le surmonte.	We're great if it surmounted be.

"XXVIII. Stances ou Quatrains, Pour tenir lieu de ceux de Pibrac, qui ont un peu vieilli," in *Épîtres*, vol. 132 of Beaumarchais's edition of the *Oeuvres complètes de Voltaire* (1785), 360; Besterman et al., *Œuvres complètes de Voltaire* (2015), 83:139. The translation is from Harbottle and Dalbiac, *Dictionary of Quotations (French and Italian)* (1901), 196.

L'orgueil des petits consiste à parler toujours de soi. L'orgueil des grands est de n'en jamais parler.

The pride of mediocrities consists of always talking about themselves. The pride of great men is never to do so.

"Du mot *Quisquis* de Ramus, ou La Ramée," in *Questions sur l'Encyclopédie, par des Amateurs* (1775), 6:272; Vercruysse, *Les Éditions encadrées des Œuvres de Voltaire de 1775* (1977), 138, in the series *Studies on Voltaire and the Eighteenth Century.*

Attributed to Voltaire

La vanité rend l'homme content de lui; l'orgueil le rend difficile à contenter.

Vanity renders man content with himself; pride makes him hard to please.

Leysenne, *Le Bréviaire des Éducateurs et des Pères de Famille* (1903), 148.

Priests

Nos Prêtres ne sont pas ce qu'un vain peuple pense,
Notre crédulité fait toute leur science.

Our Priests aren't what a vain people think they may be;
Our credulity is what makes their science work.

Jocasta, the late King Laius's widow, to Œdipus in *Œdipe* (1719), act 4, scene 1; Besterman et al., *Œuvres complètes de Voltaire* (2001), 1a:224.

Prussia

Je me trouve ici en France. On ne parle que notre langue. L'allemand est pour les soldats et pour les chevaux, il n'est nécessaire que pour la route.

Here I feel that I am in France. Our language alone is spoken. German is for soldiers and horses, and required only for travel.

Letter from Potsdam, October 24, 1750, to the marquis de Thibouville in Paris.

Public opinion and customs

On gouverne les hommes par l'opinion régnante, & l'opinion change quand la lumière s'étend.

Men are governed by prevailing opinion, and opinion changes as they become more enlightened.

"Idées de La Mothe le Vayer," in *Recueil nécessaire* (1765 [1766]), 318; Besterman et al., *Œuvres complètes de Voltaire* (2012), 61a:369.

Il est aussi absurde que cruel de punir les violations des usages reçus dans un pays, les délits commis contre l'opinion régnante, & qui n'ont opéré aucun mal physique, du même supplice dont on punit les parricides et les empoisonneurs.

It is as absurd as it is cruel to punish violations of a nation's accepted customs, crimes committed against prevailing opinion, and which have done no physical harm, with the same penalty applied to parricides and poisoners.

Relation de la mort du Chevalier de La Barre (1766 [1767]), 2; Besterman et al., *Œuvres complètes de Voltaire* (2008), 63b:540. The chevalier de La Barre, age nineteen, was tortured and beheaded, his body burned on a pyre along with a copy of Voltaire's *Dictionnaire philosophique portatif* for allegedly having disrespected a Roman Catholic religious procession.

Public service

Ah! qui sert son pays sert souvent un ingrat.

Ah! He who serves his country often serves an ingrate.

Cato to Cicero in act 1, scene 7, of Voltaire's tragedy *Rome sauvée*, performed for the first time on February 24, 1752; from the text published in Berlin in 1752, 14.

Publishers

If our prejudic'd people are fools, booksellers and printers, book jobbers are rogues.

Letter written in English from Berlin, January 24, 1752, to Sir Everard Fawkener in London. A book jobber distributes books.

On m'a volé à Berlin, en Hollande, à Genève, à Paris. On s'empare de mon bien comme si j'étais mort, et on le dénature pour le mieux vendre. Il faudrait traiter tous ces fripons de libraires, comme j'ai fait traiter Grasset qu'on a mis en prison, et qu'on a chassé de la ville, et il est bon qu'on le sache.

I've been robbed in Berlin, Holland, Geneva, and Paris. They grab the fruits of my labors as if I were dead, and mutilate it to make it easier to sell. One should deal with these thieving bookmen the way I dealt with Grasset who was jailed and chased out of town, and these things should be known.

Letter from Les Délices, August 23, 1755, to Cosimo Alessandro Collini in Paris.

Quakers

Guillaume [Penn] hérita de grands biens, parmi lesquels il se trouvoit des dettes de la Couronne. . . . Pen fut obligé d'aller tutoyer Charles Second & ses ministres, plus d'une fois, pour son paiement. Le gouvernement lui donna en 1680, au lieu d'argent la proprieté & la Souveraineté d'une Province d'Amérique, au sud de Maryland. Voilà un Quaker devenu Souverain.

William [*Penn*] inherited great wealth, consisting in part of Crown debts. . . . Penn was obliged, more than once, to go *thee* and *thou* Charles II & his ministers in order to be paid. In 1680, instead of specie, the government granted him the ownership & Sovereignty of a Province of America, south of Maryland. Thus did a Quaker become a Sovereign.

"De l'histoire des Quakers," in *Oeuvres de M^r. de Voltaire. Nouvelle Edition* (1739), 189; "Quatrième lettre sur les Quakers," in *Lettres philosophiques* (1964), 1:47. Charles II gave William Penn the landholdings destined to become the Commonwealth of Pennsylvania in 1681. Voltaire never showed much interest in the future thirteen American colonies. That may explain his imperfect grasp of the geographical location of Pennsylvania.

Je vous dirai sans me répéter que j'aime les quakers. Oui, si la mer ne me faisait pas un mal insupportable, ce serait dans ton sein, ô Pensilvanie! que j'irais finir le reste de ma carrière, s'il y a du reste.

I will tell you, without repeating myself, that I love the Quakers. Yes, if the sea did not make me unbearably ill, it would be in your bosom, O Pennsylvania, that I would go to live out the remainder of my career, if any there is.

"Quaker ou Qouacre, ou Primitif, ou Membre de la primitive Église Chrétienne, ou Pensilvanien, ou Philadelphien," in *Questions sur l'Encyclopédie, par des Amateurs* (1773), 9:201; Besterman et al., *Œuvres complètes de Voltaire* (2013), 43:73.

Questions

Je ne fais aucune de ces questions que pour m'instruire; & j'exige de quiconque voudra m'instruire qu'il parle raisonnablement.

I only ask these questions in order to educate myself; and I demand of whoever wishes to educate me that he speak reasonably.

"Paul," in *La Raison par Alphabet. Sixiéme édition* (1769), 90; Besterman et al., *Œuvres complètes de Voltaire* (1994), 36:422.

Misattributed to Voltaire

Il est encore plus facile de juger de l'esprit d'un homme par ses questions que par ses réponses.

It is much easier to judge a man's mind by his questions rather than by his answers.

Pierre-Marc-Gaston, duc de Lévis, published this adage in his book, *Maximes, préceptes et réflexions sur différens sujets de morale et de politique* (1825), maxim 18, 5. It was wrongly attributed to Voltaire by Halbach and Visser in their article, "The Henkin Sentence," in Manzano, Sain, and Alonso, *The Life and Work of Leon Henkin* (2014), 261. Since the 1970s, a version of this quote has been credited in English to Voltaire as "Judge a man not by his answers, but by his questions."

François Rabelais (circa 1483–1553)

PHYSICIAN, HUMANIST, AND AUTHOR OF
GARGANTUA ET PANTAGRUEL

Ce n'est pas que je mette Rabelais à côté d'Horace, mais si Horace est le premier des faiseurs de bonnes épîtres, Rabelais, quand il est bon, est le premier des bons bouffons. Il ne faut pas qu'il y ait deux hommes de ce métier dans une nation, mais il faut qu'il y en ait un; je me repens d'avoir dit autrefois trop de mal de lui.

It is not that I raise Rabelais to the same level as Horace, but if Horace is first among good versifiers, Rabelais, when he is good, is first among good jesters. A nation does not need two men in that line, but there must be one; I regret that in the past I spoke too disparagingly of him.

Letter from Les Délices, April 12, 1760, to Mme Du Deffand in Paris.

Jean Racine (1639–1699)

VOLTAIRE'S FAVORITE DRAMATIST

Corneille s'était formé tout seul; mais louis XIV, colbert, sophocle & euripide contribuérent tous à former racine.

Corneille developed all on his own; but Louis XIV, Colbert, Sophocles, and Euripides all contributed to Racine's development.

"Sciences et Arts," in *Le Siècle de Louis XIV* (1751), 2:184; Besterman et al., *Œuvres complètes de Voltaire* (2016), 13d:20.

Il n'était pas aussi philosophe que grand poëte.

He was not so much a philosopher as he was a great poet.

Le Siècle de Louis XIV (1751), 2:407; Besterman et al., *Œuvres complètes de Voltaire* (2017), 12:166.

Racine était un homme adroit; il louait beaucoup Euripide, l'imitait un peu (il en a pris tout au plus une douzaine de vers), et il le surpassait infiniment. C'est qu'il a su se plier au goût, au génie de la nation un peu ingrate pour laquelle il travaillait; c'est la seule façon de réussir dans tous les arts.

Racine was a shrewd man; he praised Euripides highly, imitated him a bit (he borrowed no more than a dozen lines), and surpassed him by far. That is because he inclined to the taste, the genius of the ungrateful nation for which he worked, which is the only way to succeed in the arts.

Letter from Ferney, September 2, 1764, to Michel-Paul-Guy de Chabanon in Paris.

Pourquoi sait-on par cœur les vers de Racine? C'est qu'ils sont bons.

Why do we know Racine's verses by heart? Because they are good.

Letter from Ferney, December 18, 1767, to Michel-Paul-Guy de Chabanon in Paris.

Oui, Monsieur, je regarde Racine comme le meilleur de nos poètes tragiques, sans contredit, comme celui qui le seul parle au cœur et à la raison, qui seul a été véritablement sublime sans aucune enflure, et qui a mis dans la diction un charme inconnu jusqu'à lui. Il est le seul encore qui ait traité l'amour tragiquement, car avant lui Corneille n'avait fait bien parler cette passion que dans Le Cid, et Le Cid n'est pas de lui. L'amour est ridicule ou insipide dans presque toutes ses autres pièces.

Yes, Monsieur, I regard Racine as the best of our tragic poets, without question, as the only one who speaks both to the heart and to reason, who alone has been truly sublime without seeming pompous, and whose language was endowed with a charm previously unknown. He is still the only one who has treated love in a tragic manner, because before him Corneille had really only expressed that passion well in *Le Cid* and *Le Cid* is not by him. Love is ridiculous or insipid in nearly all his other plays.

Letter from Ferney, February 26, 1769, to Aleksander Petrovich Sumarokov, presumably in St. Petersburg.

Je suis fâché de ne vous avoir pas instruit plus tôt de ce que j'ai entendu dire souvent il y a plus de quarante ans, à M. le maréchal de Noailles, que Corneille tomberait de jour en jour, et que Racine s'éleverait. Sa prédiction a été accomplie à mesure que le goût s'est formé. C'est que Racine est toujours dans la nature, et que Corneille n'y est presque jamais.

I am sorry not to have informed you sooner of what I often heard from the late Maréchal de Noailles over forty years ago, that day by day Corneille would fall and that Racine would rise. His prediction has been fulfilled as taste over time has improved. That is because Racine is almost always true to nature; Corneille almost never is.

Letter from Ferney, January 22, 1773, to Jean-François de La Harpe in Paris.

Raphael (1483–1520)

ITALIAN RENAISSANCE MASTER

Candide, après le déjeuner, se promenant dans une longue galerie, fut surpris de la beauté des tableaux. Il demanda de quel Maître étaient les deux premiers. Ils sont de Raphaël, dit le Sénateur; je les achetai fort cher par vanité il y a quelques années; on dit que c'est ce qu'il y a de plus beau en Italie; mais ils ne me plaisent point du tout; la couleur en est très rembrunie; les figures ne sont pas assez arrondies, & ne sortent point assez; les draperies ne ressemblent en rien à une étoffe. En un mot, quoi qu'on en dise, je ne trouve point là une imitation vraye de la nature. Je n'aimerai un tableau que quand je croirai voir la nature elle-même: il n'y en a point de cette espéce. J'ai beaucoup de tableaux, mais je ne les regarde plus.

Candide, walking after breakfast in a long gallery, was surprised by the beauty of the pictures. He asked what master painted the first two.

"They are by Raphael," said the senator; "I bought them a few years ago at a very high price out of vanity; they say they are the finest things in Italy, but I do not like them at all: their color has become very dark; the figures are not rounded enough and do not stand out enough; the draperies are not at all like cloth. In a word, no matter what they say, I do not find in them a true imitation of nature. I will like a picture only when I think I am seeing nature itself; and there are none of that kind. I have many pictures, but I no longer look at them."

The Venetian nobleman Pococurante to Candide, in "Visite chez le seigneur Pococurantè noble vénitien," chap. 25 in *Candide, ou L'Optimisme* (1759), 231–232; Besterman et al., *Œuvres complètes de Voltaire* (1980), 48:231. In English, *Candide, Zadig, and Other Stories* (2001), 83–84.

Reason

C'est le triomphe de la raison de bien vivre avec les gens qui n'en ont pas.

It is the triumph of reason to get along well with people who have none.

Socrates to Aglae and Sophronime in act 1, scene 7, of *Socrate, ouvrage dramatique, traduit de l'anglais de feu M. Tompson* (1759), 47; Besterman et al., *Œuvres complètes de Voltaire* (1980), 48:231.

Un proverbe n'est pas une raison; expliquez-vous mieux.

A proverb is not enough; explain yourself better.

"De la liberté," in *Dictionnaire philosophique, portatif* (1764), 244; Besterman et al., *Œuvres complètes de Voltaire* (1994), 36:291.

Religion

L'ABBÉ: *Voilà d'excellent Caffé, Madame; c'est du Moka tout pur.*

LA COMTESSE: *Oui, il vient du pays des Musulmanes; n'est-ce pas grand dommage?*

L'ABBÉ: *Raillerie à part, Madame, il faut une Religion aux hommes.*

THE ABBÉ: That is excellent Coffee, Madame; it is absolutely pure Mocha.

THE COUNTESS: Yes, it comes from the land of the Muslims; isn't that a pity?

THE ABBÉ: Joking aside, Madame, men need a Religion.

"Troisième Entretien. Après dîner," in *Le Dîner du comte de Boulainvilliers* (1728), 45; Besterman et al., *Œuvres complètes de Voltaire* (1990), 63a:390.

LE COMTE: *Quoique j'aye été militaire, je ne veux point faire la guerre aux Prêtres & aux Moines; je ne veux point établir la vérité par le meurtre, comme ils ont établi l'erreur; mais je voudrois au moins que cette vérité éclairât un peu les hommes, qu'ils fussent plus doux & plus heureux, que les peuples cessassent d'être superstitieux, & que les chefs de l'Eglise tremblassent d'être persécuteurs.*

L'ABBÉ: *Il est bien mal-aisé (puisqu'il faut enfin m'expliquer) d'ôter à des insensés des chaînes qu'ils révèrent. Vous vous feriez peut-être lapider par le peuple de Paris, si, dans un temps de pluye, vous empêchiez qu'on ne promenât la prétendue carcasse de Ste. Genevieve par les rues pour avoir du beau temps.*

THE COUNT: Although I was a soldier, I do not wish to wage war against Priests and Monks; I do not wish to establish truth through murder, the way they established errant thought; but I wish at least that truth might enlighten men somewhat, that they were gentler and happier, that people everywhere ceased to be superstitious, and that the leaders of the Church were given fearful pause before becoming persecutors.

THE ABBÉ: It is very difficult (since I must at last give my opinion) to free brutish fools from chains they revere. The people of Paris would stone you if, one rainy day, you impeded the procession of St. Geneviève's supposed cadaver through the streets in order to bring good weather.

"Troisième Entretien. Après dîner," in *Le Dîner du comte de Boulainvilliers* (1728), 47–48; Besterman et al., *Œuvres complètes de Voltaire* (1990), 63a:393. A typo in the French text, "prétendre," has been corrected as "prétendue."

La Coutume, la Loi plia mes premiers ans,
A la religion des heureux Musulmans:
Je le vois trop; les soins qu'on prend de notre enfance,

Forment nos sentimens, nos mœurs, notre créance;
J'eusse été près du Gange esclave des faux Dieux,
Chrétienne dans Paris, Musulmane en ces lieux.

Custom, and Law, did shape my earliest years
To the religion of these contented Muslims.
I see all too well that the pains taken while we're young,
Do form our feelings, our habits, and our beliefs.
By the Ganges I'd have been a slave to false gods,
Christian in Paris, a Muslim where I am here.

Zaïre to her fellow slave Fatime, in the first scene of act 1 in *Zaïre* (1732). In *La Zayre, de M. de Voltaire* (1733), 8; Besterman et al., *Œuvres complètes de Voltaire* (1988), 8:435.

Mes frères, la religion est la voix secrette de Dieu qui parle à tous les hommes; elle doit tous les réunir & non les diviser. Donc toute religion qui n'appartient qu'à un peuple, est fausse.

My brothers, religion is the secret voice of God that speaks to all men; it must unite and not divide them. Therefore, any religion that belongs to just one nation is false.

Le Sermon des Cinquante (1749), 4; Besterman et al., *Œuvres complètes de Voltaire* (2010), 49a:71.

La Religion est instituée pour nous rendre heureux dans cette vie & dans l'autre. Que faut-il pour être heureux dans la vie à venir? Être juste.

Religion was established in order to make us happy in this life and the next. What should we do in order to be happy in the afterlife? Do the right thing.

"Vertu vaut mieux que science," in *Traité sur la Tolérance* (1763), 184; Besterman et al., *Œuvres complètes de Voltaire* (2000), 56c:245.

Oui, il faut une religion; mais il la faut pure, raisonnable, universelle; elle doit être comme le Soleil, qui est pour tous les hommes, & non pas pour quelque petite province privilégiée. Il est absurde, odieux, abominable, d'imaginer que Dieu éclaire tous les yeux, & qu'il plonge presque toutes les âmes dans ses ténèbres. Il n'y a qu'une probité commune à tout l'univers; il n'y a donc qu'une religion. Et quelle est-elle? Vous le savez: c'est d'adorer Dieu & d'être juste.

Yes, we need religion; but it must be pure, reasonable, universal; it must be like the Sun that shines for all, and not for some small privileged part of the world. It is absurd, odious, abominable to imagine that God casts sunlight in everyone's eyes, and that he keeps almost all souls in darkness. There is but one universal morality; thus, there is but one religion. And what is it? You know what it is: it is to worship God and to be virtuous.

"Catéchisme de l'Honnête-homme (1764), 98; Besterman et al., *Œuvres complètes de Voltaire* (2014), 57a:178. The words in this quote were spoken by the *homme de bien* (or *honnête-homme*) to a monk (*caloyer*) in the Greek Orthodox Church.

Toute Secte, comme on sait, est un titre d'erreur; il n'y a point de Sectes de Géometres, d'Algébristes, d'Arithméticiens, parce que toutes les propositions de Géométrie, d'Algebre, d'Arithmétique sont vraies.

Each Sect, as we know, is a fraud; there are no Sects of Geometers, Algebrists, or Arithmeticians, because every proposition in Geometry, Algebra, and Arithmetic is true.

"Tolérance," in *Dictionnaire philosophique, portatif. Nouvelle Édition* (1765), 332; Besterman et al., *Œuvres complètes de Voltaire* (1994), 36:563.

Toute Secte, en quelque genre qui puisse être, est le ralliement du doute & de l'erreur. Scotistes, Thomistes, Réaux, Nominaux, Papistes, Calvinistes, Molinistes, Jansénistes, ne sont que des nom de guerre.

Every Sect, of any kind, represents a rallying of doubt and error. Scotists, Thomists, the order of Réaux-Croix, Nominalists, Papists, Calvinists, Molinists, Jansenists, are merely noms de guerre.

"Secte," in *Dictionnaire philosophique portatif, ou Supplément à l'Édition de 1765* (circa 1765), 80; Besterman et al., *Œuvres complètes de Voltaire* (1994), 36:518.

Il n'y a point de Secte en Géométrie; on ne dit point un Euclidien, un Archimédien.

There are no Sects in Geometry; we don't say a Euclidian, an Archimedian.

"Secte," in *Dictionnaire philosophique portatif, ou Supplément à l'Édition de 1765* (circa 1765), 80; Besterman et al., *Œuvres complètes de Voltaire* (1994), 36:580.

On voit évidemment que toutes les religions ont emprunté tous leurs dogmes et tous leurs rites les unes des autres.

It is clear that all religions copied from one another both their dogma and their rituals.

"De l'Alcoran, & de la loi musulmane. Examen si la religion musulmane était nouvelle, & si elle a été persécutante," chap. 7 in *Essai sur les moeurs et l'esprit des nations*, in Beaumarchais's edition of the *Oeuvres de Voltaire* (1784), 16:333; Besterman et al., *Œuvres complètes de Voltaire* (2007), 22:157.

Republican government

Une République n'est point fondée sur la vertu: elle l'est sur l'ambition de chaque Citoyen, qui contient l'ambition des autres, sur l'orgueil qui réprime l'orgeuil, sur le désir de dominer qui ne souffre pas qu'une autre domine.

A Republic is not founded on virtue: it relies on the ambition of every Citizen, checking the ambition of his fellows, on pride restraining pride, on a desire to dominate wthout being dominated by anyone else.

"Pensées sur l'administration publique" (1764), 17:69; Besterman et al., *Œuvres complètes de Voltaire* (2006), 32a:327.

Il est impossible qu'il y ait sur la terre un état qui ne se soit gouverné d'abord en république; c'est la marche naturelle de la nature humaine. Quelques familles s'assemblent d'abord contre les ours & contre les loups: celle qui a des grains en fournit en échange à celle qui n'a que du bois.

It is inconceivable that any state on earth was not first governed as a republic; it is the natural progression of human nature. At first, a few families join forces against the bears and wolves: the family with some seeds trades them with the one that has firewood.

"Patrie," in *Dictionnaire philosophique, portatif* (1764), 295–296; Besterman et al., *Œuvres complètes de Voltaire* (1994), 36:412.

Resurrection

Le p. Malebranche apporte en preuve de la résurrection des hommes celle des insectes, des vers changés en mouches. Quelle preuve!

Fr. Malebranche provides as proof of the resurrection of man the resurrection of insects, of grubs changed into flies. What kind of proof is that?

Besterman, *Voltaire's Notebooks* (1952), 2:408; Besterman et al., *Œuvres complètes de Voltaire* (1968), 81:179. One work by the seventeenth-century theologian and metaphysician Father Nicolas Malebranche that Voltaire may have had in mind when he made this comment was *De la recherche de la vérité* (1712).

Jean-Baptiste Rousseau (1671–1741)

DRAMATIST, POET, AND ONE OF VOLTAIRE'S
EARLY LITERARY ENEMIES

Savez-vous, notre maître, que je ne crois pas que cette ode arrive jamais à son adresse?

You do know, Master, that I do not think this ode will ever reach its destination?

Comment supposedly made in Paris in late October 1722 to Rousseau in reference to his *Ode à la Postérité*, written at about that time. Voltaire's barbed remark was reported by Théophile Duvernet in *La Vie de Voltaire* (1786, 48), and accepted by Pomeau in *D'Arouet à Voltaire* (1988), 158.

Jean-Jacques Rousseau (1712–1778)

GENEVA-BORN WRITER, PHILOSOPHER, AMATEUR BOTANIST,
AND VOLTAIRE'S MOST FAMOUS BÊTE NOIRE

J'ai reçu, Monsieur, votre nouveau livre contre le genre humain; je vous en remercie; vous plairez aux hommes à qui vous dites leurs vérités, et vous ne les corrigerez pas. Vous peignez avec des couleurs vraies les horreurs de la société humaine dont l'ignorance et la faiblesse se promettent tant de douceurs. On n'a jamais employé tant d'esprit à vouloir nous rendre bêtes.

Il prend envie de marcher à quatre pattes quand on lit votre ouvrage. Cependant comme il y a plus de soixante ans que j'en ai perdu l'habitude, je sens malheureusement qu'il m'est impossible de la reprendre. Et je laisse cette allure naturelle à ceux qui en sont plus dignes que vous et moi.

I have received, Monsieur, your new book against mankind; I thank you for it; you will please those to whom you speak truths that they wish to hear, but you will not correct their ways. You paint in true colors the horrors of human society whose ignorance and weakness promise many consolations. Never has so much thought been expended in an effort to turn us into beasts.

Upon reading your work, one would like to get down on all fours. However, unfortunately, as I lost that habit more than sixty years ago, I don't think it possible for me to resume it. And I leave that natural mode of locomotion to those who are more worthy of it than you and I.

Letter from Les Délices, August 30, 1755, to Rousseau in Paris.

Cet archifou qui aurait pu être quelque chose, s'il s'était laissé conduire par vous, s'avise de faire bande à part, il écrit contre les spectacles, après avoir fait une mauvaise comédie, il écrit contre la France qui le nourrit, il trouve quatre ou cinq douves pourries du tonneau de Diogène; il se met dedans pour aboyer, il abandonne ses amis, il m'écrit, à moi, la plus impertinente lettre que jamais fanatique ait griffonnée.

This stark raving madman, who could have amounted to something had he followed your lead, has decided to go off on his own, he writes against the theater after composing a bad comedy; he writes against France, the land that feeds him, he finds four or five rotten staves from Diogenes's tub and crawls inside to howl, he abandons his friends, he writes to me the most impertinent of letters ever scribbled by a fanatic.

Figure 19. Claude-Antoine Littret, after a pastel drawn by Maurice Quentin de La Tour in 1753, *Vitam Impendere Vero*, 1763. Engraving. Private collection. *Vitam Impendere Vero* ("To devote one's life to truth," from Juvenal) was Rousseau's personal motto.

Letter from Ferney, March 19, 1761, to Jean le Rond d'Alembert in Paris.

L'excès de l'orgeuil et de l'envie a perdu Jean-Jacques, mon illustre philosophe. Ce monstre ose parler d'éducation! lui qui n'a voulu élever aucun de ses fils, et qui les a mis tous aux Enfants-trouvés. . . . Je la [sic] plaindrai s'il est pendu, mais par pure humanité, car je ne le regarde personnellement que comme le chien de Diogène, ou plutôt comme un chien descendu d'un bâtard de ce chien.

An excess of pride and envy has ruined Jean-Jacques, my illustrious philosopher. This monster dares speak of education! He who refused to raise any of his own sons, and placed them all in a foundlings home. . . . I shall be sorry for him if he is hanged, but out of pure humanity, because personally I regard him as no more than Diogenes's dog, or rather as a dog descended from a bastard pup of that dog.

Letter from Ferney, June 17, 1762, to d'Alembert in Paris. In a letter to Théodore Tronchin, March–April 1765, Voltaire called Rousseau "le bâtard du chien de Diogène."

L'infâme Jean-Jacques est le Judas de la confrérie.

That vile Jean-Jacques is the Judas of the brotherhood.

Letter from Ferney, October 16, 1765, to Étienne-Noël Damilaville in Paris.

Jean-Jacques n'écrit que pour écrire, et moi j'écris pour agir.

Jean-Jacques writes for the sake of writing, and I write in order to act.

Letter from Ferney, April 15, 1767, to Pastor Jacob Vernes at Celigny, near Coppet, Pays de Vaud.

Royalty

Rien n'étoit moins assûré alors que l'argent du par le Roi.

Nothing at that time was less secure than money owed by the King.

From commentary about William Penn and Charles II in late seventeenth-century England, in "De l'histoire des Quakers," in *Oeuvres de Mʳ. de Voltaire. Nouvelle Édition* (1739), 180; "Quatrième lettre sur les Quakers," in *Lettres philosophiques* (1964), 1:47.

Satire

L'art d'instruire, quand il est parfait, réussit mieux que l'art de médire, parce que la Satyre meurt avec ceux qui en sont les victimes, & que la raison & la vertu sont éternelles.

The art of instruction, when it succeeds, is better than slander, because once its victims are gone, Satire itself dies, and because reason and virtue are eternal.

Reception speech, May 9, 1746, at the Académie française: *Discours prononcez dans l'Académie Françoise, Le Lundi 9 Mai MDCCXLVI* (1746), 12.

*Peut-être que les Jeunes-Gens qui liront cet essai, apprendront à détester la Sa-
tire; . . . ce genre funeste d'écrire. . . . & les Magistrats qui veillent sur les mœurs,
regarderont peut-être cet Ecrit comme une requête présentée au nom de tous les honnêtes gens pour réprimer un abus intolérable.*

Perhaps Young People who read this essay will learn to detest Satire . . . this
grievous form of writing . . . and the Magistrates who administer our moral
standards will perhaps regard this Text as a petition presented in the name of
all good men to curb this intolerable abuse.

"Mémoire sur la Satire par Mr. Voltaire, De l'Académie Françoise, Gentilhomme ordinaire du Roi & Historiographe de France," in *Le Papillon, ou Lettres parisiennes* (1746), 152;
Besterman et al., *Œuvres complètes de Voltaire* (2003), 20a:163. This *mémoire* was later given
the title "À l'occasion d'un libelle de l'abbé Desfontaines contre l'auteur, 1739."

Qu'une Tragédie est difficile! & qu'une Epitre, une Satyre sont aisées!

How hard it is to write a Tragedy! while an Epistle in verse, a Satire, are so easy!

Pensées philosophiques de M. de Voltaire, ou Tableau encyclopédique des Connaissances humaines
(1766), 2:167; Besterman et al., *Œuvres complètes de Voltaire* (2011), 52:433–34.

Science

*Quand nous ne pouvons nous aider du compas des mathématiques, ni du flambeau
de l'expérience & de la physique, il est certain que nous ne pouvons faire un seul pas.*

When we cannot rely on the compass of mathematics, or the torch of experience and physics, it is certain that we cannot take a single step forward.

"Que toutes les idées viennent par les sens," chap. 3 in *Traité de Métaphysique* (1734–1735),
in Beaumarchais's edition of the *Oeuvres complètes de Voltaire* (1784), 32:36; Besterman et al.,
Œuvres complètes de Voltaire (1989), 14:442.

Sculpture

*C'est principalement dans la sculpture que nous avons excellé, & dans l'art de jettèr
en fonte d'un seul jet des figures équestres colossales.*

It is chiefly in sculpture that we have excelled, and in the art of casting colos-
sal equestrian figures in a single mould.

"Suite des arts," in *Le Siècle de Louis XIV* (1751), 2:197; Besterman et al., *Œuvres complètes
de Voltaire* (2016), 13d:33. Among the great French sculptors in Voltaire's time were Edmé
Bouchardon, Jean-Baptiste Lemoyne, Jean-Baptiste Pigalle, Étienne-Maurice Falconet,
and Jean-Antoine Houdon. The translation is from an excerpt of Voltaire's *Age of Louis
XIV* in Gay and Cavanaugh, *Historians at Work* (1972), 2:344.

La SCULPTURE a été poussée à la perfection sous louis XIV, *& se soûtient dans sa force sous* louis XV.

Sculpture was raised to perfection under Louis XIV, and has sustained itself under *Louis XV.*

"Artistes célèbres," in *Le Siècle de Louis XIV* (1751), 2:435; Besterman et al., *Œuvres complètes de Voltaire* (2017), 12:214.

Sex

Veux-tu avoir une idée de l'amour? Vois les moineaux de ton jardin; vois tes pigeons; contemple le taureau qu'on amène à ta génisse; regarde ce fier cheval que deux de ses valets conduisent à la cavale paisible, qui l'attend & qui détourne sa queue pour le recevoir . . . & songe aux avantages de l'espêce humaine; ils compensent en amour tous ceux que la nature a donnée aux animaux, force, beauté, légéreté, rapidité.

Do you want some idea of love? Behold the sparrows in your garden, and your pigeons; observe the bull led to his heifer, watch the fiery steed led by two footmen to the mare that patiently awaits and turns aside her tail to receive him . . . then consider how in matters of love the advantages of the human species offset all the advantages nature gave to animals: strength, beauty, agility, quickness.

"Amour," in *Dictionnaire philosophique, portatif* (1764), 15; Besterman et al., *Œuvres complètes de Voltaire* (1994), 35:323.

Aucun animal, hors toi, ne connaît les embrassements; tout ton corps est sensible; tes lèvres surtout jouissent d'une volupté que rien ne lasse, & ce plaisir n'appartient qu'à ton espèce; enfin, tu peux dans tous les temps te livrer à l'amour, & les animaux n'ont qu'un temps marqué.

No animal, except you, knows the joy of physical embrace; it affects your entire body; your lips especially experience a delight that never wearies, and is known only to your species; furthermore, you can make love the year round, while animals do so only at certain times.

"Amour," in *Dictionnaire philosophique, portatif* (1764), 16; Besterman et al., *Œuvres complètes de Voltaire* (1994), 35:324.

Le penchant des deux sexes l'un pour l'autre se déclare de bonne heure; mais quoiqu'on ait dit des Africaines & des femmes d'Asie méridionale, ce penchant est généralement beaucoup plus fort dans l'homme que dans la femme; c'est une loi que la nature a établie pour tous les animaux. C'est toujours le mâle qui attaque la femelle.

The affection of the two sexes for one another manifests itself quite early; and despite what has been said about African and South Asian women, in general the inclination is much stronger in the male than in the female; it is a law established by nature for all animals, that the male always attacks the female.

"Amour nommé socratique," in *Dictionnaire philosophique, portatif* (1764), 18; Besterman et al., *Œuvres complètes de Voltaire* (1994), 35:329.

Venez, mesdames, voir le spectacle le plus auguste; vous y verrez la nature dans toute sa majesté.

Come, ladies, to see the most august spectacle, in which you will see nature in all its majesty.

Quoted in the August 1764 issue of the *Correspondance littéraire, philosophique et critique*, a privately circulated newsletter, in which the editor, Friedrich-Melchior Grimm, recalled an incident he witnessed several years earlier at Les Délices. According to Grimm, Voltaire was speaking to a group of ladies from Geneva as he escorted them to observe the mating of an old Danish stallion with six aged mares. See Grimm et al., *Correspondance littéraire, philosophique et critique* (1812), 4:177.

William Shakespeare (1564–1616)

ENGLISH PLAYWRIGHT AND POET

Shakespear . . . avoit un genie plein de force & de fecondité, de naturel & de sublime, sans la moindre etincelle de bon goût, & sans la moindre connoissance des regles. Je vais vous dire une chose hazardée, mais vraie, c'est que le merite de cet Auteur a perdu le Théatre Anglois; il y a de si belles Scenes, des morceaux si grands & si terribles repandûs dans ses farces monstrueuses qu'on appelle Tragedies, que ces pieces ont toujours été jouées avec un grand succés. Le tems qui seul fait la reputation des homme, rend à la fin leurs deffauts respectables. La pluspart des idées bizarres & gigantesques de cet Auteur, ont acquis, au bout de 150 ans, le droit de passer pour sublimes.

Shakespear boasted a strong, fruitful Genius: He was natural and sublime, but had not so much as a single Spark of good Taste, or knew one Rule of the Drama. I will now hazard a random, but, at the same Time, true Reflection, which is, that the great Merit of this Dramatic Poet has been the Ruin of the English Stage. There are such beautiful, such noble, such dreadful Scenes in this Writer's monstrous Farces, to which the name Tragedy is given, that they have always been exhibited with great Success. Time, which only gives Reputation to Writers, at last makes their very Faults venerable. Most of the whimsical, gigantic Images of this Poet, have, thro' Length of Time . . . acquir'd a Right of passing for sublime.

"Dix-Huitième Lettre. Sur la Tragedie," in *Lettres Ecrites de Londres sur les Anglois et autres sujets* (1734), 158–159; "Sur la tragédie," in *Lettres philosophiques* (1964), 2:79. The translation is "Letter XVIII. On Tragedy," in *Letters Concerning the English Nation* (1733), 142–143.

Je suis loin assurément de justifier en tout la Tragédie d'Hamlet; c'est une Piéce grossière & barbare, qui ne seroit pas supportée par la plus vile populace de la France & d'Italie. Hamlet y devient fou au second acte, & sa Maîtresse devient folle au troisiéme; le Prince tue le pere de sa maîtresse feignant de tuer un rat, & l'héroïne se jette dans la riviere. On fait sa fosse sur le Théâtre; des fossoyeurs disent des quolibets dignes d'eux, en tenant dans leurs mains des têtes de morts; le Prince Hamlet répond à leurs grossiéretés abominables par des folies non moins dégoutantes; pendant ce tems-la un des acteurs fait la conquête de la Pologne. Hamlet, sa mere, & son beau-pere boivent ensemble sur le théâtre; on chante à table, on s'y querelle, on se bat, on se tue; on croiroit que cet ouvrage est le fruit de l'imagination d'un Sauvage yvre. Mais parmi ces irrégularités grossiéres, qui rendent encore aujourd'hui le théâtre Anglais si absurde & si barbare, on trouve dans Hamlet, par une bizarrerie encore plus grande, des traits sublimes, dignes des plus grands génies. Il semble que la nature se soit plû à rassembler dans la tête de Shakespear, ce qu'on peut imaginer de plus fort & de plus grand, avec ce que la grossiéreté sans esprit peut avoir de plus bas & de plus détestable.

I do not mean to justify the Tragedy of *Hamlet* in every Particular; it is in Fact a barbarous Piece, abounding with such gross Absurdities, that it would not be tolerated by the Vulgar in *France* and *Italy*. The Hero of the Play runs mad in the second Act, and his Mistress meets with the same Misfortune in the third. The Prince takes *Ophelia*'s Father for a Rat, and kills him, and, in Despair, she throws herself into a River. Her Grave is dug on the Stage, and the Grave-Digger, with a Skull in his Hand, amuses himself with a String of miserable Jests, while the Prince answers them in Language equally disgusting. *Hamlet*, his Mother, and Father-in-Law drink together on the Stage. They divert themselves with Bottle-Songs (*Chansons a boir*), they quarrel, they fight, they kill. One would imagine this Play the Production of a drunken Savage. And yet among these Absurdities, which render the *English* drama absolutely barbarous, there are some Strokes in *Hamlet*, worthy of the most exalted Genius. This has always been [a] Matter of Astonishment to me; it looks as if Nature, in pure Sport, diverted herself with mixing in *Shakespear*'s Head, every thing sublime and great, with all that can be conceived low, mean and detestable.

Dissertation sur la tragédie ancienne et moderne, a son Eminence Monseigneur le Cardinal Querini, noble vénitien, Éveque de Brescia, bibliothécaire du Vatican (1748), "Troisième partie: de Sémiramis," in *La tragédie de Sémiramis, Et quelques autres Piéces de Littérature* (1750), 17–18. The translation, imperfect but well written, is from an open letter to Voltaire by the

Irish barrister and writer, Arthur Murphy (a.k.a. Charles Ranger): "*To Monsieur* Voltaire," in *The Gray's Inn Journal*, no. 12 (December 15, 1753): 68–69. Adam Smith shared Voltaire's dim view of *Hamlet*, calling it "the dream of a drunken savage." See "Anecdotes of the Late Dr. Smith," a letter from Glasgow dated April 9, 1791, and signed "Amicus," in *The Bee, or Literary Weekly Intelligencer*, May 11, 1791, 5.

Vous avez fait accroire à votre nation que je méprise Shakespeare. Je suis le premier qui ait fait connaître Shakespeare aux Français. J'en ai traduit des passages il y a quarante ans, ainsi que de Milton, de Waller, de Rochester, de Dryden et de Pope. Je peux vous assurer qu'avant moi presque personne en France ne connaissait la poésie anglaise, à peine avait-on même entendu parler de Locke. J'ai été persécuté pendant trente ans par une nuée de fanatiques pour avoir dit que Locke est l'Hercule de la métaphysique qui a posé les bornes de l'esprit humain.

Ma destinée a encore voulu que je fusse le premier qui ait expliqué à mes concitoyens les découvertes du grand Newton, que quelques sots parmi nous appellent encore des systèmes. J'ai été votre apôtre et votre martyr. En vérité il n'est pas juste que les Anglais se plaignent de moi.

You have led your countrymen to believe that I disrespect Shakespeare. I was the first who brought Shakespeare to the attention of the French. Forty years ago I translated passages of his plays, along with selected works by Milton, Waller, Rochester, Dryden and Pope as well. I can assure you that before me, nobody in France knew English poetry; hardly anyone had heard of Locke. I have been persecuted for thirty years by a flock of fanatics for having said that Locke is the Hercules of metaphysics who has established the boundaries of the human mind.

Moreover, it was my destiny to be the first to explain to my compatriots the discoveries of the great Newton, which some fools among us still call systems. I have been your apostle and your martyr. In truth, it is not at all fair for the English to criticize me on that point.

Letter from Ferney, July 15, 1768, to Horace Walpole, probably addressed to him at Strawberry Hill, Walpole's country house outside London. In his biography of Voltaire, James Parton said that his writings "contain, perhaps, a hundred allusions to Shakespeare . . . and in almost the last piece he ever wrote, he still speaks of him as an inspired barbarian." See Parton, *Life of Voltaire* (1881), 1:230.

J'avais dit il y a très-longtemps que si Shakespeare était venu dans le siècle d'Adisson, il aurait joint à son génie l'élégance et la pureté qui rendent Adisson recommandable. J'avais dit que son génie était à lui, et que ses fautes étaient de son siècle.

I said a very long time ago that if Shakespeare had come into this world in the age of Addison, his genius would have been combined with the elegance and purity that make Addison so worthy of commendation. I said *that his genius was his own*, and *that his faults were those of his age.*

Letter from Ferney, July 15, 1768, to Horace Walpole, probably at Strawberry Hill.

Slavery

Il n'y a chez les Asiatiques qu'une servitude domestique, & chez les chrétiens qu'une servitude civile. Le paysan Polonais est serf dans la terre, et non esclave dans la maison de son seigneur. Nous n'achetons des esclaves domestiques que chez les nègres. On nous reproche ce commerce: un peuple qui trafique de ses enfans est encor plus condamnable que l'acheteur: ce négoce démontre notre supériorité; celui qui se donne un maître était né pour en avoir.

Among the Asian peoples there is only domestic servitude, and among Christians only civil subjection. A Polish peasant is a serf on the land, but he is not a slave in his master's house. We purchase domestic slaves only in Africa. We are criticized for this trade: a nation that traffics in its own children is more blameworthy than the buyer; this commerce proves our superiority: he who gives himself a master was born to have one.

"De la servitude," in *Essai sur les Mœurs et l'esprit des nations* (1769), 3:430; Besterman et al., *Œuvres complètes de Voltaire* (2015), 26c:332.

Socrates (circa 470 B.C.–399 B.C.)

GREEK PHILOSOPHER

Cet homme dangereux, qui ne prêche que la vertu & la Divinité.

That dangerous man, who preaches only virtue and Divinity.

The high priest Anitus to his mistress, Drixa, in act 1, scene 2, of *Socrate, ouvrage dramatique, traduit de l'anglais de feu M. Tompson* (1759), 16; Besterman et al., *Œuvres complètes de Voltaire* (2009), 49b:303.

Ce vieux nez épaté de Socrate . . . cet insupportable raisonneur, qui corrompt les jeunes gens, & qui les empêche de fréquenter les courtisanes et les saints mystères?

That squash-nosed old Socrates . . . that outrageous rhetorician, who corrupts the youth, and impedes their relations with courtesans and the mysteries of faith?

Drixa in response to Anitus in *Socrate*, in act 1, scene 2, of *Socrate, ouvrage dramatique* (1759), 16; Besterman et al., *Œuvres complètes de Voltaire* (2009), 49b:303.

C'est un hérétique; il nie la pluralité des dieux; il est Déiste; il ne croit qu'un seul Dieu; c'est un Athée.

Il est beau d'être la victime de la Divinité.

Socrate, acte 3.ͤ Scène 3.ͤ

Figure 20. Antoine-Jean Duclos, after Jean-Michel Moreau le Jeune, illustration for the final scene in Voltaire's tragedy *Socrate*. Engraving, 1785. Private collection. The caption reads, "Il est beau d'être la victime de la Divinité." In English, "It is beautiful to be the victim of something Divine."

He's a heretic; he denies the plurality of gods; he's a deist; he believes in just one god; he's an Atheist.

Drixa, speaking as part of a mob demanding Socrates's head, to Anitus, in act 2, scene 9, of *Socrate, ouvrage dramatique* (1759), 69; Besterman et al., *Œuvres complètes de Voltaire* (2009), 49b:327.

The soul

Le divin Platon, maître du divin Aristote, & le divin Socrate, maître du divin Platon, disoient l'ame corporelle & éternelle. Le Demon de Socrate lui avoit apris sans doute ce qui en étoit.

The divine *Plato*, Master of the divine *Aristotle*, and the divine *Socrates* Master of the divine *Plato*, us'd to say that the Soul was corporeal and eternal. No doubt but the Demon of *Socrates* had instructed him in the Nature of it.

"Treisième Lettre. Sur Mr. *Locke*," in *Lettres Ecrites de Londres sur les Anglois et autres sujets* (1734), 93; "Sur M^r. Loke," in *Lettres philosophiques* (1964), 1:167. The translation is "Letter XIII. On Mr. *Locke*," in *Letters Concerning the English Nation* (1733), 96.

La Raison humaine est si peu capable de demontrer par elle même l'immortalité de l'ame que la Religion a été obligée de nous la reveler. Le bien commun de tous les hommes demande qu'on croye l'ame immortelle; la foi nous l'ordonne; il n'en faut davantage: & la chose est decidée. Il n'en est pas de même de sa nature, il importe peu à la Religion de quelle substance soit l'ame, pourvû qu'elle soit vertueuse. C'est un Horloge qu'on nous a donné à gouverner, mais l'ouvrier ne nous a pas dit dequoi le ressort de cet Horloge est composé.

Human Reason is so little able, merely by its own Strength, to demonstrate the Immortality of the Soul, that 'twas absolutely necessary Religion should reveal it to us. 'Tis of Advantage to Society in general, that Mankind should believe the Soul to be immortal; Faith commands us to do this; nothing more is requir'd, and the Matter is clear'd up at once. But 'tis otherwise with respect to Nature; 'tis of little Importance to Religion, which only requires the Soul to be virtuous, what Substance it may be made of. 'Tis a Clock which is given us to regulate, but the Artist has not told us what materials the Spring of this Clock is compos'd.

"Treisième Lettre. Sur Mr. *Locke*," in *Lettres Ecrites de Londres sur les Anglois et autres sujets* (1734), 99; "Sur M^r. Loke," in *Lettres philosophiques* (1964), 1:171. The translation is "Letter XIII. On Mr. *Locke*," in *Letters Concerning the English Nation* (1733), 102–103.

Je suis corps & je pense, je n'en sçais pas davantage.

I am a Body and, I think, that's all I know of the Matter.

"Treisième Lettre. Sur Mr. *Locke*," in *Lettres Ecrites de Londres sur les Anglois et autres sujets* (1734), 99; "Sur M^r. Loke," in *Lettres philosophiques* (1964), 1:172. The translation is "Letter XIII. On Mr. *Locke*," in *Letters Concerning the English Nation* (1733), 103.

Du mouvement de la figure de l'étendue, & de la solidité ne peuvent faire une pensée, donc l'ame ne peur pas être matiere. . . . Je ne connois point du tout la matiere, j'en divine imparfaitement quelques proprietés; or je ne sçai point du tout si ces proprietés peuvent être jointes à la pensée; donc parce que je ne sçai rien du tout, j'assure positivement que la matiere ne sçauroit penser.

Motion, Figure, Extension and Solidity cannot form a Thought, and consequently the Soul cannot be Matter. . . . I am absolutely ignorant what Matter is; I guess, but imperfectly, some Properties of it; now, I absolutely cannot tell whether these Properties may be joyn'd to Thought. As I therefore know nothing, I maintain positively that Matter cannot think.

"Treisième Lettre. Sur Mr. *Locke*," in *Lettres Ecrites de Londres sur les Anglois et autres sujets* (1734), 100; "Sur M^r. Loke," in *Lettres philosophiques* (1964), 1:172. The translation is "Letter XIII. On Mr. *Locke*," in *Letters Concerning the English Nation* (1733), 103–104.

Je puis attribuer à mon corps la faculté de penser & de sentir; donc je ne dois point chercher cette faculté de penser & de sentir dans une autre apelée ame *ou* esprit, *dont je ne puis avoir la moindre idée.*

I can attribute to my Body the ability to think and feel: therefore, I ought not to seek this faculty of thinking and feeling in another faculty called *soul* or *spirit*, of which I cannot have the least idea.

Lettres Philosophiques par M. de V***, letter 26, in *Lettres de M. de V*** avec plusieurs pieces de differens auteurs* (1738), 16; *Lettres philosophiques* (1964), Appendice premier, 1:199. A slightly different version of this passage appeared in La Barre de Beaumarchais, *Amusemens littéraires* (1741), 195.

Je suis Corps & je pense; je n'en sai pas davantage. Si je ne consulte que mes foibles lumiéres, irai-je attribuer à une cause inconnue ce que je puis si aisément attribuer à la seule cause seconde que je connois un peu?

I am a Body and I think; I know no more than that. If I consult my feeble intelligence, will I attribute to an unknown cause that which I can easily attribute to the only secondary cause I know a little about?

"Sur Mr. Locke," in *Réflexions sur les Anglais*, in *Oeuvres de Mr. de Voltaire. Nouvelle Edition* (1739), 239; "Sur M^r. Loke," in *Lettres philosophiques* (1964), 1:172 (with variant). In "Letter XIII. On Mr. *Locke*," in *Letters Concerning the English Nation* (1733), Voltaire also said, in English, "I am a Body and, I think, that's all I know of the Matter."

La matière change & ne périt point; pourquoi l'ame périrait-elle?

Matter changes and does not perish; why should the soul perish?

Socrates to his wife and friends as he awaits his death in act 3, scene 3, of *Socrate, ouvrage dramatique, traduit de l'anglais de feu M. Tompson* (1759), 95. Besterman et al., *Œuvres complètes de Voltaire* (2009), 49b:339.

Ce serait une belle chose de voir son ame. Connais-toi toi-même, *est un excellent précepte; mais il n'appartient qu'à Dieu de le mettre en pratique: quel autre que lui peut connaître son essence?*

It would be a fine thing to see one's soul. *Know thyself* is an excellent precept; but only God can put it into practice: who else but He can know his essence?

"Ame," in *Dictionnaire philosophique, portatif* (1764), 5; Besterman et al., *Œuvres complètes de Voltaire* (1994), 35:304–305. The proverbial words of wisdom, "Know thyself," have been attributed to the ancient Athenian statesman and lawgiver Solon, among others.

Il est vrai qu'on ne sait pas trop bien ce que c'est qu'une âme: on n'en a jamais vu. Tout ce que nous savons c'est que le maître éternel de la nature, nous a donné la faculté de penser et de connaître la vertu. Il n'est pas démontré que cette faculté vive après notre mort, mais le contraire n'est pas démontré davantage. Il se peut que Dieu ait accordé la pensée à une monade qu'il fera subsister après nous. Rien n'est contradictoire dans cette idée.

It is true that we know very little about what a soul is: we have never seen one. All that we know is that the eternal master of nature endowed us with the ability to think and to recognize virtue. It has not been demonstrated how this faculty lives on after we die, but there is no better proof of the inverse. It may be that God shall give the power to reason to a microscopic organism that will survive after we are gone. There is nothing contradictory in this idea.

Letter from Ferney, November 28, 1770, to Frederick William, Hereditary Prince of Prussia, presumably in Berlin.

Spain—the Spanish

Les Espagnols n'ont plus guère de héros, et n'ont pas un écrivain.

The Spanish have few heroes any more, and not a single writer.

Letter from Versailles, March 9, 1747, to Frederick the Great in Berlin.

The spirit of the age

Qui n'a pas l'esprit de son âge,
De son âge a tout le malheur

He that hath not the spirit of the age,
Shall suffer all its misery.

"Stances," in *Œuvres de M. de Voltaire. Nouvelle édition, Considérablement augmentée* (1751), 3:167; Besterman et al., *Œuvres complètes de Voltaire* (2003), 20a:564. This couplet apparently dates from 1741, during Voltaire's relationship with Émilie.

Style

La grace en s'exprimant vaut mieux que ce qu'on dit.

What is said matters less than how well it is expressed.

"Les Trois Manières" (1763), in *Contes de Guillaume Vadé* (1764), 61; Besterman et al., *Œuvres complètes de Voltaire* (2014), 57b:137. In his maiden speech at the Académie française in 1753, Buffon famously said, "le style est l'homme même."

Suffering and torment

Le vautour acharné sur sa timide proie,
De ses membres sanglants se repaît avec joie:
Tout semble bien *pour lui: mais bientôt à son tour*
Une aigle au bec tranchant dévore le vautour.
L'homme d'un plomb mortel atteint cette aigle altiére:
Et l'homme aux champs de Mars couché sur la poussiére,
Sanglant, percé de coups, sur un tas de mourants,
Sert d'aliment affreux aux oiseaux dévorants.
Ainsi du monde entier tous les membres gémissent;
Nés tous pour les tourments, l'un par l'autre ils périssent:
Et vous composerez, dans ce cahos fatal,
Des malheurs de chaque être un bonheur général?

The ferocious vulture with its timid prey,
Upon its bleeding limbs feasts with delight:
All seems *well* for him: but soon enough, in turn,
A sharp-beaked eagle, the vulture doth consume.
The lordly eagle, by a man's deadly shot is felled:
And the man, prostrate on the dusty field of battle,
Bullet-riddled, bleeding, amid the dying,
Serves as frightful provender for ravenous birds.

Thus it is, the world over, that all creatures groan;
Born for torment, they murder one another:
And you would make of this mortal mess,
Of individual misfortune, universal bliss?

"Poëme sur le désastre de Lisbonne," in *Poëmes sur le désastre de Lisbonne et sur la loi naturelle* (1756), 12; Besterman et al., *Œuvres complètes de Voltaire* (2009), 45a:341.

Maximilien de Béthune, duc de Sully (1560–1641)

FRENCH GENERAL AND STATESMAN

Il racheta pour plus de cent cinquante de nos millions de domaines, aujourd'hui aliénés: toutes les places furent réparées, les magasins, les arsenaux remplis, les grands chemins entretenus; c'est la gloire éternelle de Sulli & celle du roi, qui osa choisir un homme de guerre pour rétablir les finances de l'État, & qui travailla avec son ministre.

He bought properties valued at over one hundred fifty million in today's money, since lost: all of the public squares were repaired, the magazines and arsenals stocked, the high roads maintained: to the eternal glory of Sully and of the king, who dared choose a soldier to restore the finances of the state, and who worked with his minister.

Speaking of Henri IV and his first minister, the duc de Sully, in "De Henri IV," in *Essai sur les mœurs et l'esprit des nations* (1769), 3:192; Besterman et al., *Œuvres complètes de Voltaire* (2014), 26b:216.

Superstition

La superstition est à la religion ce que l'Astrologie est à l'Astronomie, la fille très folle d'une mère très sage. Ces deux filles ont longtemps subjugué toute la terre.

Superstition is to religion what Astrology is to Astronomy, the very mad daughter of a very wise mother. These two daughters have long dominated the entire world.

"S'il est utile d'entretenir le peuple dans la Superstition?," chap. 20 in *Traité sur la tolérance* (1763), 179; Besterman et al., *Œuvres complètes de Voltaire* (2000), 56c:242.

Remarquez que les temps les plus superstitieux ont toujours été ceux des plus horribles crimes.

Remember that the most superstitious of times have always been those of the most horrible crimes.

"Superstition," in *Dictionnaire philosophique, portatif* (1764), 336; Besterman et al., *Œuvres complètes de Voltaire* (1994), 35:539.

Il semble que toute superstition ait une chose naturelle pour principe, & que bien des erreurs soient nées d'une vérité dont on abuse.

It seems that every superstition has a basis in some natural occurrence, and that many errors have resulted from an abuse and misconception of the truth.

"Discours préliminaire," in *Essai sur les mœurs et l'esprit des nations* (1769), 1:153; Moland, *Œuvres complètes de Voltaire* (1878), 11:145.

Enfin le superstitieux devient fanatique, & c'est alors que son zèle est capable de tous les crimes au nom du Seigneur.

Finally, the superstitious man becomes a fanatic, and it is then that his zeal is capable of every abuse committed in the name of the Lord.

"IIme homélie. Sur la superstition" (1767), 44; Besterman et al., *Œuvres complètes de Voltaire* (1987), 62:485.

Rejettons donc toute superstition, afin de devenir plus humains; mais en parlant contre le fanatisme, n'irritons point les fanatiques; ce sont des malades en délire, qui veulent battre leurs médecins. Adoucissons leurs maux, ne les aigrissons jamais; & faisons couler goute à goute dans leur ame ce baume divin de la tolérance, qu'ils rejetteraient avec horreur, si on le leur présentait à pleine coupe.

In order to become more human, let us reject all superstition; but in speaking against fanaticism, let us not irritate the fanatics: they are sick and delirious and want to maul their doctors. Let us ease their ills, never embitter them, and drop by drop pour into their souls the divine balm of tolerance, which they would reject with horror if it were administered in a single dose.

"Quatrième homélie," in *Homélies prononcées à Londres en 1765, dans une assemblée particulière*, in *Nouveaux Melanges philosophiques, historiques, critiques, &c. &c. Sixiéme partie* (1768), 358; Besterman et al., *Œuvres complètes de Voltaire* (1987), 62: 485.

Le superstitieux est au fripon ce que l'esclave est au tyran. Il y a plus encore; le superstitieux est gouverné par le fanatique, & le devient.

He who is superstitious is to the knave what the slave is to the tyrant. There is also this: the superstitious man is ruled by fanatics, and becomes one himself.

"Superstition" (section 2), in *La Raison par Alphabet. Sixiéme édition* (1769), 168; Besterman et al., *Œuvres complètes de Voltaire* (1987), 62:485.

En un mot, moins de superstitions moins de fanatisme, & moins de fanatisme, moins de malheurs.

In a word, the less superstition the less fanaticism, and the less fanaticism, the less misery.

"Superstition," in *La Raison par Alphabet. Sixiéme édition* (1769), 171; Besterman et al., *Œuvres complètes de Voltaire* (1994), 36:544.

Jonathan Swift (1667–1745)

ANGLO-IRISH CLERIC, DEAN OF ST. PATRICK'S CATHEDRAL
IN DUBLIN, ESSAYIST, POET, AND SATIRIST

On n'entendra jamais bien en France les livres de l'ingenieux Docteur Swift, qu'on appelle le Rabelais d'Angleterre. . . . Mais on lui fait grand tort, selon mon petit sens, de l'appeller de ce nom.

Dean Swift, who has been call'd the English Rabelais, will never be well understood in France. . . . But in my humble Opinion, the Title of the English Rabelais which is given the Dean is highly derogatory to his Genius.

"Vingt-deuzième Lettre. Sur Mr. *Pope* Et quelques autres Poetes Fameux," in *Lettres Ecrites de Londres sur les Anglois et autres sujets* (1734), 196; "Sur Mr Pope et quelques autres Poetes fameux," in *Lettres philosophiques* (1964), 2:135. The translation is "Letter XXII. On Mr. *Pope*, and Some Other Famous Poets," in *Letters Concerning the English Nation* (1733), 181.

Mr. Swift est Rabelais dans son bon sens, & vivant en bonne compagnie. Il n'a pas à la verité, la gaïté du premier; mais il a toute la finesse, la raison, le choix, le bon goût qui manque à notre Curé de Meudon.

Dean Swift is *Rabelais* in his Senses, and frequenting the politest Company. The former indeed is not so gay as the latter, but then he possesses all the Delicacy, the Justness, the Choice, the good Taste, in which Particulars our giggling rural Vicar *Rabelais* is wanting.

"Vingt-deuzième Lettre. Sur Mr. *Pope* Et quelques autres Poetes Fameux," in *Lettres Ecrites de Londres sur les Anglois et autres sujets* (1734), 197; "Sur Mr Pope et quelques autres Poetes fameux," in *Lettres philosophiques* (1964), 2:135. The translation is "Letter XIII. On Mr. *Locke*," in *Letters Concerning the English Nation* (1733), 182.

Swiss bankers

Likely misattributed to Voltaire

Si vous voyez un banquier suisse sauter d'une fenêtre, sautez derrière lui. Il y a sûrement de l'argent à gagner.

If you see a Swiss banker jump out of a window, jump right after him. There is bound to be money in it.

Quoted as something "Voltaire used to say" by Jean Ziegler, Swiss sociologist and member of the City Council in Geneva, in his book, *Une Suisse au-dessus de tout soupçon* (1976), 76. Two earlier versions of this witticism were not attributed to Voltaire, however. The first of these, cited as something "said in Voltaire's time," was published in 1914 as: "Quand un banquier genevois saute par la fenêtre, il faut sauter après lui. Il y a de l'argent à gagner." Sixty years later, the syndicated columnist Abigail Van Buren credited Herbert R. Mayes, publisher of a London-based newsletter, *The Overseas American*, with this variant on the same line: "The old story about Swiss banks is still valid: if you see a Swiss banker jumping from an office building, follow him out. There's 15 percent to be made on the way down." See Fazy et al., *Genève Suisse* (1914), 249; and Van Buren, "Dear Abby" (1974), 19.

Symbols

Le bœuf Apis était-il adoré à Memphis comme Dieu, comme symbole, ou comme bœuf? Il est à croire que les fanatiques voyaient en lui un Dieu, les sages un simple symbole, & que le sot people adorait le boeuf.

Was the ox Apis idolized in Memphis as a God, a symbol, or as an ox? It may be that the fanatics saw in him a God, the wise men simply a symbol, and the people stupidly worshipped the ox.

"Apis," in *Dictionnaire philosophique, portatif* (1764), 29; Besterman et al., *Œuvres complètes de Voltaire* (1994), 35:358.

Syphilis

O mon cher Candide! vous avez connu Paquette, cette jolie suivante de nôtre auguste Baronne; j'ai goûté dans ses bras les délices du Paradis, qui ont produit ces tourments d'Enfer dont vous me voyez dévoré; elle en était infectée, elle en est peut-être morte. Paquette tenait ce présent d'un Cordelier très savant, qui avait remonté à la source; car il l'avait eue d'une vieille Comtesse, qui l'avait reçuë d'un Capitaine de Cavalerie, qui la devait à une Marquise, qui la tenait d'un Page, qui l'avait reçuë d'un Jésuite, qui, étant novice, l'avait eue en droite ligne d'un des compagnons de Christophe Colomb. Pour moi je ne la donnerai à personne, car je me meurs.

"Oh, my dear Candide! You knew Paquette, that pretty attendant upon our august Baroness; I tasted in her arms the delights of paradise, which produced these torments of hell by which you see me devoured; she was infected and she may have died of it. Paquette had received this present from a very learned Franciscan, who had gone back to the source; for he had got it from an old countess, who had received it from a cavalry captain, who owed it to a marquise, who had it from a page, who had received it from a Jesuit priest, who as a novice got it in a direct line from one of the companions of Christopher Columbus. For my part I shall give it to no one, for I am dying."

Pangloss's reply to Candide, who had asked "about the cause and effect, the sufficient reason" of how he had been infected with syphilis. "Comment Candide rencontra son ancien Maître de Philosophie, le Docteur Pangloss, & ce qui en advint," chap. 4 in *Candide, ou L'Optimisme* (1759), 29–30; Besterman et al., *Œuvres complètes de Voltaire* (1980), 48:130–131. In English, *Candide, Zadig, and Other Stories* (2001), 23.

O Pangloss! s'écria Candide, voilà une étrange généalogie! N'est-ce pas le Diable qui en fut la souche? Point du tout, répliqua ce grand homme; c'était une chose indispensable dans le meilleur des mondes, un ingrédient nécessaire; car si Colomb n'avait pas attrapé, dans une Ile de l'Amérique, cette maladie qui empoisonne la source de la génération, qui souvent même empêche la génération, & qui est évidemment l'opposé du grand but de la nature, nous n'aurions ni le chocolat, ni la cochenille; il faut encore observer que jusqu'aujourd'hui, dans nôtre Continent, cette maladie nous est particuliére, comme la controverse. Les Turcs, les Indiens, les Persans, les Chinois, les Siamois, les Japonois, ne la connaissent pas encore.

Mais il y a une raison suffisante pour qu'ils la connaissent à leur tour dans quelques siécles.

"Oh, Pangloss!" exclaimed Candide, "that is a strange genealogy! Wasn't the devil the root of it?"

"Not at all," replied the great man. "It was an indispensable thing in the best of worlds, a necessary ingredient; for if Columbus had not caught, in an island in America, this disease which poisons the source of generation, which often even prevents generation, and which is obviously opposed to the great purpose of nature, we would not have either chocolate or cochineal. It should also be noted that to this day this malady is peculiar to us in our continent, like religious controversy. The Turks, the Indians, the Persians, the Chinese, the Siamese, the Japanese, are not yet acquainted with it; but there is sufficient reason for their making its acquaintance, within a few centuries."

"Comment Candide rencontra son ancien Maître de Philosophie, le Docteur Pangloss, & ce qui en advint," chap. 4 in *Candide, ou L'Optimisme* (1759), 30–31; Besterman et al., *Œuvres complètes de Voltaire* (1980), 48:131. In English, *Candide, Zadig, and Other Stories* (2001), 23. Cochineal is an insect that yields the chief component in a scarlet dye used to color fabric.

Tacitus (circa 56 A.D.–circa 125 A.D.)

ROMAN ORATOR, LAWYER, AND SENATOR

Je regarde Tacite comme un satirique pétillant d'esprit, connaissant les hommes et les cours, disant des choses fortes en peu de paroles, flétrissant en deux mots un empereur jusqu'à la posterité. Mais je suis curieux; je voudrais connaître les droits du sénat, les forces de l'empire, le nombre des citoyens, la forme du gouvernement, les mœurs, les usages. Je ne trouve rien de tout cela dans Tacite; il m'amuse, et Tite-Live m'instruit.

I regard Tacitus as a satirist sparkling with wit, who knows about men and courts and says harsh things with striking brevity, and in a word or two flays an emperor for all time; but I am curious, I'd like to know about the rights of the senate, the imperial armies, the number of citizens, the form of government, morals, customs. I find none of that in Tacitus; he amuses me, while Livy teaches me.

Letter from Ferney, July 30, 1768, to Mme Du Deffand in Paris.

Taste—connoisseurship

Il est arrivé à notre Téatre ce qu'on voit tous les jours dans une galerie de peinture, où plusieurs tableaux représentent le même sujet. Les Connoisseurs se plaisent à remarquer les diverses manieres; chacun saisit, selon son goût, le caractere de chaque Peintre; c'est une espéce de concours qui sert, à la fois, à perfectionner l'art, & à augmenter les lumieres du Public.

Something is happening in the Theater that goes on every day in a picture gallery, where several paintings depict the same subject. Connoisseurs like to point out differences in technique; they judge a Painter's style according to their own personal taste; it is a kind of game that serves both to perfect art and to educate the Public.

"À Monsieur le Marquis Scipion Maffei, Auteur de la Mérope Italienne, & de beaucoup d'autres célébres Ouvrages," de facto preface to *La Mérope Françoise, avec quelques petites pièces de littérature* (1744), xxi; Besterman et al., *Œuvres complètes de Voltaire* (1991), 17:xviii.

Il ne suffit pas pour le goût, *de voir, de connoître la beauté d'un ouvrage; il faut la sentir, en être touché. Il ne suffit pas de sentir, d'être touché d'une maniere confuse, il faut démêler les différentes nuances; rien ne doit échapper à la promptitude du discernement; & c'est encore une ressemblance de ce goût intellectuel, de ce* goût *des Arts, avec le* goût *sensuel: car si le gourmet sent et reconnoît promptement le mélange de deux liqueurs, l'homme de goût, le connoisseur, verra d'un coup-d'œil prompt le mélange de deux styles; il verra un défaut à côté d'un agrément.*

In order to have *taste*, it is not enough to see or to know what is beautiful in a given work; one must feel it and be touched by it. It is not enough to feel or be touched in some vague way, one must distinguish every nuance; nothing must escape one's immediate discernment; and here again, intellectual *taste* and *taste* in the Arts are rather like sensory taste: just as the gourmet instantly perceives and recognizes a mixture of two liqueurs, so the connoisseur will detect at a glance a mixture of styles; he will spot a flaw next to an embellishment.

"Goût," in Diderot, d'Alembert, et al., *Encyclopédie, ou Dictionnaire raisonné des Sciences, des Arts et des Métiers* (1757), 7:761; Besterman et al., *Œuvres complètes de Voltaire* (1987), 33:128. "Essay on Taste," the first English-language version of this article, was published in Gerard, *An Essay on Taste with Three Dissertations on the same Subject by Mr. De Voltaire* (1759), 214.

Le goût se forme insensiblement dans une nation qui n'en avoit pas, parce qu'on y prend peu-à-peu l'esprit des bons artistes: on s'accoutume à voir des tableaux avec les yeux de Lebrun, du Poussin, de Le Sueur; on entend la déclamation notée des scènes de Quinaut avec l'oreille de Lulli; & les airs, les symphonies, avec celle de Rameau. On lit les livres avec l'esprit des bons auteurs.

Good taste develops gradually in a nation that has hitherto lacked it because, little by little, men are influenced by good artists: they become accustomed to seeing pictures through the eyes of Le Brun, Poussin, Le Sueur; they hear the musical recitation of Quinault's scenes through the ears of Lully; and the melodies of a symphony through the ears of Rameau. They read books with the minds of good authors.

"Goût," in Diderot, d'Alembert, et al., *Encyclopédie, ou Dictionnaire raisonné des Sciences, des Arts et des Métiers* (1757), 7:761; Besterman et al., *Œuvres complètes de Voltaire* (1987), 33:129. The painters Le Brun, Poussin, Le Sueur, the dramatist Philippe Quinault, and the composer Jean-Baptiste Lully were active during the age of Louis XIV. Jean-Philippe Rameau (1683–1764) collaborated with Voltaire on the comedy-ballet *La Princesse de Navarre* and on the opera-ballet *Le Temple de la gloire*, both first performed in 1745.

Si toute une nation s'est réunie dans les premiers tems de la culture des Beaux-Arts, à aimer des auteurs pleins de défauts, et méprisés avec le tems, c'est que ces auteurs avoient des beautés naturelles que tout le monde sentoit, et qu'on n'était pas encore à portée de démêler leurs imperfections.

If an entire nation when the Fine Arts were first developing was united in its admiration of writers whose faults were many, and in due course scorned, it is because those authors possessed many excellent natural qualities that were universally felt, and their imperfections were not yet apparent.

"Goût," in Diderot, d'Alembert, et al., *Encyclopédie, ou Dictionnaire raisonné des Sciences, des Arts et des Métiers* (1757), 7:761; Besterman et al., *Œuvres complètes de Voltaire* (1987), 33:130.

Le goût peut se gâter chez une nation; ce malheur arrive d'ordinaire après les siecles de perfection. Les artistes craignant d'être imitateurs, cherchent des routes écartées;

ils s'éloignent de la belle nature que leurs prédécesseurs ont saisie: il y a du mérite dans leurs efforts; ce mérite couvre leurs défauts, le public amoureux des nouveautés, court après eux; il s'en dégoute bien-tôt, et il en paroit d'autres qui font de nouveaux efforts pour plaire; ils s'éloignent de la nature encore plus que les premiers: le goût se perd, on est entouré de nouveautés qui sont rapidement effacées les unes par les autres; le public ne sait plus où il en est, et il regrette en vain le siecle du bon goût qui ne peut plus revenir.

Taste in a nation can decay. This misfortune usually comes after centuries of perfection. Fearful of being mere imitators, artists seek divergent paths that lead them from the devotion to the beauty of nature their predecessors pursued. There is merit in this, but a merit that masks the weakness in their work. The public, ever fond of novelty, acclaims them, but soon loses interest; artists with a new style try their best to please, but stray even further from nature, and *taste* suffers. Novelty abounds, each one in turn rapidly eclipsed by another; the public no longer knows where things stand, and regrets an age of good *taste* forever lost.

"Goût," in Diderot, d'Alembert, et al., *Encyclopédie, ou Dictionnaire raisonné des Sciences, des Arts et des Métiers* (1757), 7:761; Besterman et al., *Œuvres complètes de Voltaire* (1987), 33:131.

Il est de vastes pays où le goût n'est jamais parvenu; ce sont ceux où la société ne s'est point perfectionnée, où les hommes & les femmes ne se rassemblent point, où certains arts, comme la Sculpture, la Peinture des êtres animés, sont défendus par la religion. Quand il y a peu de société, l'esprit est rétréci, sa pointe s'émousse, il n'y a pas de quoi se former le goût.

There are vast regions on earth where *taste* is unknown, where civil society has not attained perfection, where men and women never mingle, where the representation of the human figure in Sculpture and Painting is forbidden by religious laws. Wherever social intercourse is limited, the mind is narrowed, dulled, and there is no room for *taste* to develop.

"Goût," in Diderot, d'Alembert, et al., *Encyclopédie, ou Dictionnaire raisonné des Sciences, des Arts et des Métiers* (1757), 7:761; Besterman et al., *Œuvres complètes de Voltaire* (1987), 33:132.

Y a-t-il un bon & un mauvais goût? oui sans doute, quoique les hommes diffèrent d'opinions, de mœurs, d'usages.

Le meilleur goût en tout genre est d'imiter la nature avec le plus de fidélité, de force & de grace.

Do good and bad taste exist? Yes, absolutely, even if men differ in opinions, customs, and behavior.

Superior taste in any genre calls for the imitation of nature in as faithful, vigorous, and graceful way possible.

"Goût," in Diderot, d'Alembert, et al., *Encyclopédie, ou Dictionnaire raisonné des Sciences, des Arts et des Métiers* (1757), 7:761; Besterman et al., *Œuvres complètes de Voltaire* (2011), 42a:92.

L'homme de goût a d'autres yeux, d'autres oreilles, ou un autre tact que l'homme grossier; il est choqué des draperies mesquines de Raphaël, *mais il admire la noble correction de son dessein. Il a le plaisir d'appercevoir que les enfans de* Laocoon *n'ont nulle proportion avec la taille de leur père; mais tout le grouppe le fait frisson-ner tandis que d'autres spectateurs sont tranquilles.*

The man of taste has eyes, ears, and judgment different from the uncultivated man; he is appalled by the awful draperies of *Raphael*, but he admires the noble purity of his conception. He notes with some pleasure that the children of *Lao-coon* bear no proportion to the height of their father; and yet the group as a whole makes him tremble, while other spectators are unmoved.

"Goût," in Diderot, d'Alembert, et al., *Encyclopédie, ou Dictionnaire raisonné des Sciences, des Arts et des Métiers* (1757), 7:761; Besterman et al., *Œuvres complètes de Voltaire* (2011), 42a:102–103.

Taxes

Messieurs, il y avait une fois un fermier-général. . . . Ma foi j'ai oublié le reste.

Gentlemen, there was once a tax collector. . . . Oh my, I've forgotten the rest.

Voltaire cracked this joke at Ferney in the presence of d'Alembert and the Genevan artist Jean Huber, in September–October 1770. According to Friedrich-Melchior Grimm, it was proposed that each man tell a humorous tale about a thief. The stories told by Huber and d'Alembert were rated "fort gai," but, Grimm said, Voltaire's one-liner topped them both. See Grimm and Diderot, *Correspondance littéraire, philosophique, et critique* (1813), 2:54.

Testicles

Un Parisien est tout surpris quand on lui dit que les Hottentots font couper à leurs enfans mâles un testicule. Les Hottentots sont peut-être surpris que les Parisiens en gardent deux.

A Parisian is greatly surprised when he is told that the Hottentots cut off one of a male child's testicles. The Hottentots are perhaps surprised that Parisians keep two.

"Circoncision," in *La Raison par Alphabet. Septieme Édition* (1773), 160; Besterman et al., *Œuvres complètes de Voltaire* (1994), 35:613.

Il s'est glissé depuis longtems un préjugé dans l'église latine, qu'il n'est pas permis de dire la messe sans testicules, & qu'il faut au moins les avoir dans sa poche.

For a long time now, a prejudice has crept into the Latin Church, that one is not permitted to say mass without testicles, and that one must at least have them in his pocket.

"Testicules," in *Questions sur l'Encyclopédie, par des Amateurs* (1772), 9:12; Besterman et al., *Œuvres complètes de Voltaire* (2013), 43:356. By "Latin Church," Voltaire meant the Roman Catholic as opposed to the Eastern Orthodox Church.

Mon ami, il faut avoir des couilles pour faire une bonne tragédie; or à quatre-vingt-quatre ans, on n'a plus de couilles.

My friend, one must have balls in order to write a good tragedy; and at eighty-four years of age, one no longer has them.

Comment prompted by a discussion of a tragedy by Mme de Boccage, reported in the December 1777 issue of Grimm and Diderot's *Correspondance littéraire, philosophique et critique* (1812), 4:138 (where the word *couilles* was discreetly replaced by "coui . . ."). In 1817, Lord Byron repeated this line in a letter to John Murray: "When Voltaire was asked why no woman has ever written even a tolerable tragedy, 'Ah (said the Patriarch) the composition of a tragedy requires testicles.'" See Cochran, *Byron at the Theatre* (2009), 63n1.

Thinking—thought

Personne ne me fera jamais croire que je pense toujours, & je ne me sens pas plus disposé à imaginer que quelques semaines après ma conception j'étois une fort sçavante ame, sçachant alors mille choses que j'ai oublié en naissant, & ayant fort inutilement possedé dans l'uterus des connoissances qui m'ont échapé dés que j'ai pu en avoir besoin, & que je n'ai jamais bien pu raprendre depuis.

No one will ever make me believe I have always been capable of thought; and I am no more disposed to think that a few weeks after I was conceived, I was a very learned soul, knowing a thousand things I'd forgotten the moment I was born, and that I possessed in the womb knowledge I lost the instant I needed it; and never have since been able to recover.

"Treisième Lettre. Sur Mr. *Locke*," in *Lettres Ecrites de Londres sur les Anglois* (1734), 96; "Sur M^r. *Loke*," in *Lettres philosophiques* (1964), 1:169.

Puisque nous pensons, nous penserons toujours: la pensée est l'être de l'homme, cet être paraîtra devant un dieu juste, qui récompense la vertu, qui punit le crime, et qui pardonne les faiblesses.

Because we can think, we will always be able to think: thought is the essence of man, this being that will appear before a just God, who rewards virtue, who punishes crime, and forgives weakness.

Socrates, awaiting death, to his wife and friends in act 3, scene 3, of *Socrate, ouvrage dramatique, traduit de l'anglais de feu M. Tompson* (1759), 95; Besterman et al., *Œuvres complètes de Voltaire* (2010), 49b:340.

Nous ne connaissons aucun être à fond; donc il est impossible que nous sachions si un être est incapable ou non de recevoir le sentiment & la pensée. . . . au fond il y a autant de témérité à dire qu'un corps organisé par DIEU même ne peut recevoir la pensée de DIEU même, qu'il serait ridicule de dire que l'esprit ne peut penser.

We cannot fully understand any living creature: therefore, it is impossible for us to know if it is capable or not of feeling and thought. . . . in the end, there is as much temerity in saying that a body organized by God himself cannot receive thought from God as it would be absurd to say that the mind cannot think.

"XXIX. De Locke" (*Doute* no. 29), in *Le Philosophe ignorant* (1766), 78–79; Besterman et al., *Œuvres complètes de Voltaire* (1987), 62:72.

Time—the passage of time

Le tems amollit tout.

Time tempers all things.

Julius Cæsar to Marc-Antoine, in act 1, scene 1, of *La Mort de César* (1736), 10; Besterman et al., *Œuvres complètes de Voltaire* (1998), 8:182.

Il y avoit autrefois un grain de sable qui se lamentoit d'être un atome ignoré dans les déserts. Au bout de quelques années il devint diamant; & il est à présent le plus bel ornement de la couronne du Roi des Indes.

There was once a grain of sand that complained that it was no more than a neglected atom alone in the desert. After a few years, it became a diamond, and it is now the brightest ornament in the crown of the King of the Indies.

"Le Brigand," chap. 13 in *Zadig ou La Destinée* (1748), 119; Besterman et al., *Œuvres complètes de Voltaire* (2004), 30b:181.

La vérité & le bon goût n'ont remis leur sceau que dans la main du tems.

Time alone is entrusted with the seal of approval for truth and good taste.

Letter presumably from Ferney, September–October 1765, to an unnamed gentleman, probably in Paris, printed in its entirety in the "Préface de l'éditeur," in *Adélaïde du Guesclin, Tragédie*, in *Théâtre complet de Mʳ. de Voltaire* (1768), 3:3. The *éditeur*, likely Gabriel Cramer, said the letter had been sent by Voltaire "à un de ses amis."

Tolerance

Qu'est-ce que la Tolérance? c'est l'apanage de l'humanité. Nous sommes tous pêtris de faiblesse & d'erreurs; pardonnons-nous réciproquement nos sottises, c'est la premiere Loi de la nature.

What is Tolerance? It is part of what makes us human. We all have our share of frailty and error; let us pardon one another's follies, that is the first Law of nature.

"Tolerance," in *Dictionnaire philosophique, portatif. Nouvelle Édition* (1765), 326; Besterman et al., *Œuvres complètes de Voltaire* (1994), 36:552.

Nous ne sommes pas faits en France pour arriver les premiers. Les vérités [concernant la religion] nous sont venues d'ailleurs; mais c'est beaucoup de les adopter. Je suis très persuadé que, si on veut s'entendre et se donner un peu de peine, la tolérance sera regardée dans quelques années comme un baume essentiel au genre humain.

We, in France, were not destined to get there first. Truths [about religion] have come to us from abroad; and merely accepting them is a feat by itself. I am utterly convinced that, if we want to get along with one another and will make a little effort, tolerance will be regarded in a few years' time as a curative balm essential for humankind.

Letter from Ferney, June 26, 1765, to Claude-Adrien Helvétius in Paris.

La vraie science amène nécessairement la tolérance.

True learning necessarily breeds tolerance.

Letter from Ferney, July 6, 1766, to Mme d'Épinay, en route to Lyon.

Théodore Tronchin (1709–1781)

RENOWNED GENEVAN PHYSICIAN

Nous avons ici un médecin, M. Tronchin, beau comme Apollon et savant comme Esculape. Il ne fait point la médecine comme les autres. On vient de 50 lieues à la ronde le consulter. Les petits estomacs ont grande confiance en lui.

We have here a doctor, M. Tronchin, handsome as Apollo and as learned as Asclepius. They come from fifty leagues all around to consult him. Sensitive stomachs have great confidence in him.

Letter from Les Délices, September 6, 1755, to his niece, Marie-Élisabeth de Dompierre de Fontaine, in Paris perhaps. Asclepius was a mythical figure with godlike healing abilities.

He is a great physician. He knows the mind.

Adam Smith, speaking with the English poet Samuel Rogers, recalled this remark by Voltaire apparently made to Smith or in Smith's company in Geneva in 1764. See Rae, *Life of Adam Smith* (1895), 59.

Troubles—woes

Le Doge a ses chagrins, les Gondoliers ont les leurs.

"The Doge has his troubles, the gondoliers have theirs."

Martin to Candide, "De Paquette, & de Frère Giroflée," chap. 24 in *Candide, ou L'Optimisme* (1759), 227; Besterman et al., *Œuvres complètes de Voltaire* (1980), 48:229. In English, *Candide, Zadig, and Other Stories* (2001), 83. The Doge in *Candide* was the chief of state of the Republic of Venice.

Abbé Nicolas-Charles-Joseph Trublet (1697–1770)

CANON AT SAINT-MALO, MORALIST, ESSAYIST, AND
MEMBER OF THE ACADÉMIE FRANÇAISE

Il entassait adage sur adage;
Il compilait, compilait, compilait,
On le voyait sans cesse écrire, écrire,
Ce qu'il avait jadis entendu dire.

He stacked adage upon adage;
He compiled, compiled, compiled,
He was seen, always writing and writing,
Down things that he had heard somewhere before.

"Le Pauvre Diable: Ouvrage en Vers aisés, de feu Mr. Vadé," in *Le Pauvre Diable* (1758), 13; Besterman et al., *Œuvres complètes de Voltaire* (2015), 51a:95–96. Trublet first upset Voltaire when he criticized *La Henriade*. But these lines of satirical verse may have been prompted by the abbé's criticism of *De l'esprit*, the controversial tract published in 1758 by Voltaire's protégé, Helvétius.

Truth

Aime la Vérité, mais pardonne à l'Erreur.

Adore Truth, but forgive men their Errors.

"Deuxième Discours, de la Liberté" (possibly written in 1737), in *Discours en vers sur l'homme*, in *Recueil de pieces fugitives en prose et en vers* (1740), 63; Besterman et al., *Œuvres complètes de Voltaire* (1991), 17:477.

Misattributed to Voltaire

On doit des égards aux vivans; on ne doit aux morts que la vérité.

The living deserve our respect; the dead deserve only the truth.

This line first appeared in an editor's note to Voltaire's "Lettres à M. de Genonville" in Beaumarchais's edition of the *Oeuvres complètes de Voltaire* (1785), 1:15. It may have been in part, at least, a kind of proverbial expression. Thirty years earlier, the abbé Trublet commented: "Je suis assez persuadé du principe qu'on ne doit aux morts que la vérité." See "Suite sur M. de Fontenelle, par M. l'Abbé Trublet" (1757), 71.

Tyranny—despotism

Je vous l'ai toujours dit. Si mon père, mon frère ou mon fils étaient premiers ministres dans un état despotique j'en sortirais demain.

I have always said to you. If my father, my brother, or my son were first ministers in the service of a despotic state, I would leave tomorrow.

Letter from Cirey, March 1, 1737, to the comte d'Argental in Paris.

J'ai une observation necessaire à faire ici sur le mot despotique, dont je me suis servi quelquefois. Je ne sai pourquoi ce terme, qui dans son origine n'était que l'expression du pouvoir très-faible & très limité d'un petit vassal de constantinople, signifie aujourd'hui un pouvoir absolu & même tirannique. . . . On ne s'est pas aperçu que le despotisme dans ce sens abominable n'est autre chose que l'abus de la monarchie, de meme que dans les états libres l'anarchie est l'abus de la république.

I have a necessary observation to make here on a word, "despotic," which I have on occasion used. I know not why this term, which originally was used only to describe the weak and very limited power of a minor vassal in Constantinople, now signifies an absolute, even tyrannical power. . . . No one seems to realize that despotism in this detestable sense is nothing but abuse of the monarchy, just as among free men anarchy is the abuse of a republican regime.

"Réfutation directe" ("contre les Critiques de M. La Beaum"), in *Le Siècle politique de Louis XIV.* (1753), 248–249.

On appelle tiran le souverain qui ne connait de loix que son caprice, qui prend le bien de ses sujets, & qui ensuite les enrôle pour aller prendre celui de ses voisins. Il n'y a point de ces tirans-là en Europe.

A monarch who knows no laws but his caprice, who seizes the property of his subjects, then enlists them to seize the property of his neighbors, is called a tyrant. There are no such tyrants in Europe.

"Tirannie," in *Dictionnaire philosophique, portatif* (1764), 337; Besterman et al., *Œuvres complètes de Voltaire* (1994), 36:579.

Une faculté de votre ame étant une fois tirannisée, toutes les autres facultés doivent l'être également. Et c'est là ce qui a produit tous les crimes religieux dont la terre a été inondée.

Once one faculty of your soul is subject to tyranny, all the others will follow. That is how the many crimes that have deluged the world, committed in the name of religion, came about.

"Onzième lettre à l'occasion des miracles, Ecrite par Mr. Théro à Mr. Covelle," in *Collection des lettres sur les miracles* (1765), 136–137; Besterman et al., *Œuvres complètes de Voltaire* (2018), 60d:291.

The universe

L'Univers m'embarrasse & je ne puis songer,
Que cette horloge existe & n'ait pas d'horloger.

The cosmos puzzles me, and I have to wonder,
How this clockwork can exist and have no clockmaker.

Les Cabales, Œuvre pacifique (1772), 9; Besterman et al., *Œuvres complètes de Voltaire* (2006), 74b:179.

Vanity

Malheur à tout mortel, & sur-tout dans nôtre age,
Qui se fait singulier pour être un personnage!
Piron seul eut raison, quand, d'un goût tout nouveau,
Il fit ce vers heureux, digne de son tombeau:
Ci git qui ne fut rien. Quoique l'orgueil en dise,
Humains, foibles humains, voilà votre devise.
Combien de rois, grands-Dieux, jadis si réverés
Dans l'éternel oubli sont en foule enterrés;
La terre a vû passer leur empire & leur trône:
On ne sçait en quel lieu fleurissoit Babylone;
Le tombeau d'Alexandre aujourd'hui renversé
Avec sa ville altière a paru dispersé;

César n'a point d'asyle où sa cendre repose:
Et l'ami Pompignan pense être quelque chose!

Woe to any mortal, and especially these days,
The poseur who seeks to attract attention!
Piron alone was right, when, in a new vein for him,
He penned this happy verse, worthy of his tomb:
Here lies one who was nothing. However great your pride,
Humans, feeble human beings, there is your motto.
How many kings, deities all, once so revered
In the eternal void have by the score been interred;
The world has seen their empire and throne disappear:
We know not where Babylon formerly flourished;
The tomb of Alexander is today destroyed
And with his mighty city scattered to the winds;
Caesar hath no shelter where his ashes now repose;
And friend Pompignan thinks he is really something!

"La Vanité," in *Le Pauvre Diable* (1758), 26; Besterman et al., *Œuvres complètes de Voltaire* (2015), 51a:185–186. These are the last lines in this eighty-two-line poem. The poet Jean-Jacques Lefranc de Pompignan was one of Voltaire's many literary enemies.

Venice

La ville de Venise jouissait d'un avantage plus singulier; c'est que depuis le treizième siecle sa tranquillité intérieure ne fut pas altérée un seul moment; nul trouble, nulle sédition, nul danger dans la ville. Si on allait à Rome & à Florence pour y voir les grands monumens des beaux-arts, les étrangers s'empressaient d'aller goûter dans Venise la liberté & les plaisirs; et on y admirait encore, ainsi qu'à Rome, d'excellens morceaux de peinture. Les arts de l'esprit y étaient cultivés; les spectacles y attiraient les étrangers. Rome était la ville des cérémonies, & Venise la ville des divertissemens.

The city of Venice possessed a still more singular advantage; this was, that since the fourteenth century its internal quiet had not been disturbed for a single moment, the city was wholly exempt from any disorder, sedition, or alarms. Those strangers who went to Rome and Florence to see the noble monuments of the polite arts in those cities, were generally fond of making a visit to Venice, to enjoy the freedom and pleasures which reign there, and where there are several excellent paintings to amuse the curious, as well as at Rome. The liberal arts were cultivated with care, and the magnificent shows attracted strangers. Rome was the city of ceremonies, Venice the city of diversions.

"Suite de l'Italie au dix-septième siècle," in *Essai sur les mœurs et l'esprit des nations* (1769), 3:356; Besterman et al., *Œuvres complètes de Voltaire* (2015), 26c:175. The translation is from Smollett, "Of Venice," in Smollett et al., *The Works of Mr. de Voltaire* (1761), 6:45–46.

Vice

C'est mal connaître les hommes de croire qu'il y ait des sociétés que se soutiennent par les mauvaises mœurs, & qui fassent une loi de l'impudicité. On veut toujours rendre la société respectable à qui veut y entrer. Je ne doute nullement que plusieurs jeunes Templiers ne s'abandonnassent à des excès qui de tout temps ont été le partage de la jeunesse; & ce sont de ces vices passagers qu'il vaut beaucoup mieux ignorer que punir.

It reveals a poor grasp of human nature to think that a society can function that supports immorality and legalizes licentiousness. Every society wants to make itself respectable to those who want to be a part of it. I have no doubt that several young Knights Templars may have given themselves up to those excesses that are common to youth; but they are vices that it is always better to ignore than to punish.

"Du supplice de templiers, et de l'extinction de cet ordre," in *Essay sur l'histoire générale, et sur les moeurs et l'esprit des nations* (1756), 81; Besterman et al., *Œuvres complètes de Voltaire* (2010), 23:542.

Misattributed to Voltaire

Il y a des vices qu'il vaut beaucoup mieux ignorer que punir.

There are vices that it is far better to ignore than punish.

Lacombe, *Voltaire portatif* (1766), 221. This is almost certainly a misquotation of the second half of the last sentence in the preceding entry.

Virginity

C'est une des superstitions de l'esprit humain d'avoir imaginé que la virginité pouvait être une vertu.

It is one of the superstitions of the human mind to have imagined that virginity could be a virtue.

"The Leningrad Notebooks" (circa 1735–1750), first published in Besterman et al., *Œuvres complètes de Voltaire* (1968), 82:455.

Virtue

Les saints ont des plaisirs que je ne connais pas.
Les miracles sont bons; mais soulager son frère,

Mais tirer son ami du sein de la misère,
Mais à ses ennemis pardonner leurs vertus,
C'est un plus grand miracle, & qui ne se fait plus.

Saints have pleasures that are foreign to me.
Miracles are fine; but comforting a brother,
Drawing a friend from the depths of despair,
Forgiving the virtues of our enemies,
These are greater miracles, and something no longer done.

Septième discours sur la vraie vertu, in *Discours en vers sur l'homme* (1738), in *Mélanges de Poésies, de littérature, d'histoire et de philosophie* (1757), 51; Besterman et al., *Œuvres complètes de Voltaire* (1991), 17:526.

O la rage de prétendre que
    Nul n'aura de vertu que nous & nos amis!

O what madness to pretend that
    No one is virtuous but ourselves and our friends!

"Fausseté des vertus humaines," in *Dictionnaire philosophique, portatif. Nouvelle Édition* (1765), 179; Besterman et al., *Œuvres complètes de Voltaire* (1994), 36:114. The exclamatory phrase is Voltaire's clever spin on a line in Molière's comedy, *Les Femmes savantes* (1672): "Nul n'aura de l'esprit, hors nous et nos amis" ("No one will be deemed witty except us and our friends").

Il est vrai que Confucius a dit qu'il avait connu des gens incapables de sciences, mais aucun incapable de vertu; aussi doit-on prêcher la vertu au plus bas peuple.

It is true that Confucius said he had known people incapable of understanding science, but none incapable of virtue; that is why we must preach virtue to the masses.

Letter from Ferney, April 1, 1766, to Étienne-Noël Damilaville in Paris.

Un des malheurs des honnêtes gens, c'est qu'ils sont des lâches.

One of the sad things about decent people is that they are cowards.

Letter from Ferney, circa August 10, 1766, to d'Alembert in Paris.

Qu'est-ce que vertu? bienfaisance envers le prochain.

What is virtue? Compassion for others.

"Vice, Vertu," in *Les Pensées de Monsieur de Voltaire* (1768), 38; Besterman et al., *Œuvres complètes de Voltaire* (1994), 36:581.

La vertu est par-tout la même; c'est qu'elle vient de Dieu, & le reste est des hommes.

Virtue is everywhere the same; because it comes from God, while everything else is of men.

"De la Perse, au tems de Mahomet le prophete, & de l'ancienne religion de Zoroastre," in *Essai sur les mœurs et l'esprit des nations* (1769), 1:212; Besterman et al., *Œuvres complètes de Voltaire* (2009), 22:110. The translation is from Ballou, *Treasury of Thought* (1872), 543.

Vivacity

Je n'ai jamais conçu comment l'on peut être froid; cela me passe. Quiconque n'est pas animé est indigne de vivre. Je le compte au rang des morts.

I've never understood how a man can be indifferent; it is beyond me. A man who isn't spirited is not worthy of living. I count him among the ranks of the dead.

Letter from Ferney or Les Délices, March 11, 1764, to the comte and comtesse d'Argental in Paris.

War

Il est clair que si une nation qui habite entre les Alpes, les Pyrénées & la mer, avait employé à l'amélioration & à l'embellissement du pays la dixième partie de l'argent qu'elle a perdu dans la guerre de 1741, & la moitié des hommes très-inutilement en Allemagne, l'état aurait été plus florissant. Pourquoi ne l'a-t-on pas fait? pourquoi préférer une guerre que l'Europe regardait comme injuste, aux travaux heureux de la paix, qui auraient produit l'agréable & l'utile?

It is clear, that if a nation living between the Alps, the Pyrenees, and the sea, had employed, in ameliorating and embellishing the country, a tenth part of the money it lost in the war of 1741, and one-half of the men killed to no purpose in Germany, the state would have been more flourishing. Why was not this done? Why prefer a war, which Europe considered unjust, to the happy labors of peace, which would have produced the useful and the agreeable?

"Les Pourquoi" (probably written circa 1745), from *Mélanges philosophiques, littéraires, historiques, &c.* (1771), 4:376; Besterman et al., *Œuvres complètes de Voltaire* (2008), 28b:103. The translation is from "Whys (The)," in *A Philosophical Dictionary* (1824), 6:352. By "war of 1741," Voltaire meant the War of the Austrian Succession, which lasted from 1741 to 1748.

Enfin, après d'autres siècles les choses viennent au point où nous les voyons. Ici on représente une tragédie en musique, là on se tue sur la mer dans un autre hémisphère avec mille pièces de bronze; l'opéra et un vaisseau de guerre du premier rang étonnent toujours mon imagination. Je doute qu'on puisse aller plus loin dans aucun des globes dont l'étendue est semée.

So, at long last, things have reached the point we are now at. Here, we stage a tragedy set to music; in another hemisphere, they kill one another on the high seas with a thousand cannon cast in bronze. Grand opera and a ship of the line never cease to boggle my imagination. I doubt they could do better on any other of the many heavenly bodies.

"Homme" (under the subheading "De l'homme dans l'état de pure nature"), in *Questions sur l'Encyclopédie, par des Amateurs* (1771), 7:111; Besterman et al., *Œuvres complètes de Voltaire* (2011), 42a:280.

Je dis au premier coup de canon, en voilà pour sept ans au moins; et j'ai eu le malheur d'être prophète. Cela est un peu plus loin de la paix perpétuelle que Jean-Jacques Rousseau a si généreusement proposée d'après le vertueux visionnaire l'abbé Saint-Pierre. Les hommes seront toujours fous; et ceux qui croient les guérir sont les plus fous de la bande.

I said after the first cannon fire, there we go for at least seven years; and I had the misfortune to be a prophet. That is not quite like the perpetual peace that Jean-Jacques Rousseau so generously proposed, inspired by the abbé Saint-Pierre. Men will always be insane; and those who think they can cure them of their ills are the most insane of the bunch.

Letter from Les Délices, January 30, 1762, to Louise-Dorothée von Meiningen, Duchess of Saxe-Gotha, presumably in Gotha, in the modern-day German state of Thuringia. The abbé de Saint-Pierre was a writer, diplomat, member of the Académie française, and early proponent of world peace.

Philosophes moralistes, brulez tous vos livres. Tant que le caprice de quelques hommes fera loyalement égorger des millions de nos freres, la partie du genre humain consacrée à l'héroïsme sera tout ce qu'il y a de plus affreux dans la nature entière.

Burn your books, ye moralizing Philosophers! Whilst the humour of a few shall make it an act of loyalty to butcher thousands of our fellow creatures, the part of mankind dedicated to heroism will be the most execrable and destructive monsters in all Nature.

"Guerre," in *La Raison Par Alphabet. Septieme Édition* (1773), 1:330–331; Besterman et al., *Œuvres complètes de Voltaire* (1994), 36:194. The translation is from *A Philosophical Dictionary* (1793), 309.

Ce qu'il y a de pis, c'est que la guerre est un fléau inévitable. Si l'on y prend garde, tous les hommes ont adoré le Dieu Mars.

What is worse, war is an inevitable scourge. If we take notice, all men have worshipped Mars.

"Guerre," in *La Raison Par Alphabet. Septieme Édition* (1773), 1:331; Besterman et al., *Œuvres complètes de Voltaire* (1994), 36:194. The translation is from *A Philosophical Dictionary* (1824), 6:345.

Antoine Watteau (1684–1721)

FRENCH ROCOCO PAINTER

Vatau est un Peintre Flamand, qui a travaillé à Paris, où il est mort il y a quelques années. Il a réüssi dans les petites Figures, qu'il a dessinées avec grace et légéreté, & qu'il a très-bien groupées: mais il n'a jamais rien fait de grand & il en étoit incapable.

Watteau is a Flemish Painter, who worked in Paris, where he died a few years ago. He was successful with the little Figures he drew with grace and a lightness of touch, and that he grouped nicely; but he never did anything great; he was incapable of it.

Le Temple du Goust (1733), 9n6; Besterman et al., *Œuvres complètes de Voltaire* (1999), 9:128. Later editions bore the modern spelling of the title of this text, *Le Temple du goût.*

VATEAU a été dans le gracieux à-peu-près ce que téniéres a été dans le grotesque. il a fait des disciples dont les tableaux sont recherchés.

WATTEAU was in the graceful manner something like what Teniers was in the grotesque. He inspired disciples whose pictures are highly prized.

"Artistes célèbres," in *Le Siècle de Louis XIV* (1751), 2:435; Besterman et al., *Œuvres complètes de Voltaire* (2017), 12:213. David Teniers the Younger was a seventeenth-century Flemish artist.

Wealth

Le commerce fait le même effet que le travail des mains; il contribue à la douceur de ma vie. Si j'ai besoin d'ouvrage des Indes, d'une production de la nature, qui ne se trouve qu'à Ceilan ou à Ternate; je suis pauvre par ces besoins. Je deviens riche quand le commerce les satisfait. Ce n'était pas de l'or & de l'argent qui me manquaient; c'était du caffé & de la canelle. Mais ceux qui font six mille lieuës, au risque de leur vie, pour que je prenne du caffé les matins, ne sont que le superflu des hommes laborieux de la nation. La richesse consiste donc dans le grand nombre d'hommes laborieux.

Trade has the same effect as manual labor; it adds to the comfort of my life. If I need some item from the Indies, a product of nature, found only in

Ceylan or the Moluccas, I am the poorer for not having them. I am the richer when trade satisfies those wants. It was not gold and silver that I lacked, it was coffee and cinnamon. But those who travel six thousand leagues, risking their lives, so that I may partake of coffee each morning, are but a small portion of the nation's hard-working men. Wealth consists therefore in the great numbers of men doing productive labor.

"Dialogue III. Entre un Philosophe et un Contrôleur-Général des Finances," in *Oeuvres de M*. *de Voltaire. Nouvelle Édition* (1752), 3:265–266; Besterman et al., *Œuvres complètes de Voltaire* (2006), 32a:85–86.

Wisdom

Le monde est rempli d'automates qui ne méritent pas qu'on leur parle. Le nombre de sages sera toujours extrêmement petit.

The world is full of witless brutes not worth talking to. There will always be precious few truly wise people.

Letter from Ferney, September 16, 1768, to the comte de La Touraille in Paris.

Wit

Malheur à ceux qui cherchent des phrases et de l'esprit, et qui veulent éblouir par des épigrammes quand il faut être solide!

Woe unto those who look for witty words and phrases, and seek to dazzle with clever sayings when they should be serious!

Letter from Ferney, February 28, 1763, to Louis-René de Caradeuc de la Chalotais in Rennes.

Women

Si un opéra d'une femme réussit, j'en serai enchanté. C'est une preuve de mon petit système que les femmes sont capables de tout ce que nous faisons et que la seule différence qui est entre elles et nous, c'est qu'elles sont plus aimables.

If an opera composed by a woman is successful, I shall be delighted. It would prove my theory that women can do anything we can, and the only difference between them and us is that they are nicer.

Letter from Cirey, October 18, 1736, to Claude-François Berger in Paris.

Perdre sa jeunesse, sa beauté, ses passions; c'est-là le vrai malheur. Voilà pourquoi tant de femmes se font dévotes à cinquante ans, & se sauvent d'un ennui par un autre.

To lose one's youth, one's beauty, one's sexual desire; that's a terrible thing. That is why so many women are devout at age fifty, and exchange one bother for another.

"Dialogue II. Entre Madame de Maintenon et Mademoiselle de L'Enclos," in *Oeuvres de Mʳ. de Voltaire. Nouvelle Édition* (1752), 3:260–261; Besterman et al., *Œuvres complètes de Voltaire* (2006), 32a:55. As a boy, Voltaire had been presented to the aged Ninon de Lenclos, one of the great beauties of the age of Louis XIV.

Il faut toujours que la Femme commande.
C'est-là son goût: si j'ai tort, qu'on me pende.

In command the fair sex must always be.
That is what they want: if I'm wrong, then hang me.

Ce qui plaît aux Dames (1764), 13; Besterman et al., *Œuvres complètes de Voltaire* (2014), 57b:52.

Il faut convenir que DIEU n'a créé les femmes que pour apprivoiser les hommes.

One must admit that God created women for the sole purpose of domesticating men.

"La belle St. Yves va à Versailles," in *L'Ingénu, Histoire véritable* (1767), 56; Besterman et al., *Œuvres complètes de Voltaire* (2006), 63c:280.

En général, elle est bien moins forte que l'homme, moins grande, moins capable de longs travaux; son sang est plus aqueux, sa chair moins compacte, ses cheveux plus longs, ses membres plus arrondis, les bras moins musculeux, la bouche plus petite, les fesses plus relevées, les hanches plus écartées, le ventre plus large. Ces caractères distinguent les femmes dans toute la terre, chez toutes les espèces depuis la Lapponie jusqu'à la côté de Guinée, en Amérique comme à la Chine.

In general, she is not as strong as men are, not as tall, less capable of sustained work; her blood is thinner, her flesh less compact, her hair longer, her limbs more rounded, arms less muscular, the mouth smaller, the buttocks more rounded, hips wider, the stomach wider. These characteristics distinguish women the world over, among all races from Lapland to the coast of Guinea, in the Americas as in China.

"Femme," in *Questions sur l'Encyclopédie, par des Amateurs* (1771), 6:29–30; Besterman et al., *Œuvres complètes de Voltaire* (2010), 41:343.

Il n'est pas étonnant qu'en tout pays l'homme se soit rendu le maître de la femme, tout étant fondé sur la force. Il a d'ordinaire beaucoup de supériorité par celle du corps & même de l'esprit.

On a vu des femmes très savantes comme il en fut de guerrières; mais il n'y en a jamais eu d'inventrice.

L'esprit de société & d'agrément est communément leur partage. Il semble générale-ment parlant qu'elles soient faites pour adoucir les mœurs des hommes.

It comes as no surprise that in every land man is master of woman, as a simple matter of force. He is generally far superior physically and mentally.

We have seen very learned women, and warriors as well; but there has never been a female inventor.

A spirit of sociability and charm characterize their role in life. It seems, generally speaking, that they were made to temper the manners of men.

"Femme," in *Questions sur l'Encyclopédie, par des Amateurs* (1771), 6:35; Besterman et al., *Œuvres complètes de Voltaire* (2010), 41:348.

Dans aucune république elles n'eurent jamais la moindre part au gouvernement; elles n'ont jamais régné dans les empires purement électifs; mais elles règnent dans presque tous les royaumes héréditaires de l'Europe, en Espagne, à Naples, en Angleterre, dans plusieurs Etats du Nord, dans plusieurs grands fiefs qu'on nomme féminins.

In no republic have they ever been allowed to take the least part in govern-ment; they have never reigned in purely elective monarchies; yet they reign in almost all the hereditary kingdoms of Europe, in Spain, Naples, England, in several Northern Lands, in several great *feminine* fiefdoms.

"Femme," in *Questions sur l'Encyclopédie, par des Amateurs* (1771), 6:35; Besterman et al., *Œuvres complètes de Voltaire* (2010), 41:349. "Spain," "Italy," "England," are all feminine nouns in French.

Les femmes ressemblent aux girouettes: quand elles se rouillent, elles se fixent.

Women are like weathercocks: once they get rusty, they become set in their ways.

Pensées, remarques et observations de Voltaire (1802), 39; Besterman et al., *Œuvres complètes de Voltaire* (1968), 82:518. Voltaire also used the metaphor of a stuck weathervane to describe himself.

Attributed to Voltaire, probably apocryphal

Ô ciel! voilà bien les femmes! J'en avais ôté Richelieu, Saint-Lambert m'en a expulsé; cela est dans l'ordre, un clou chasse l'autre: ainsi vont les choses de ce monde!

O heaven! That's women for you! I had unseated Richelieu, Saint-Lambert expelled me; that is in the order of things, one nail drives out another: such is the way of the world!

Memoirs of Sébastian Longchamp, in Longchamp and Wagnière, *Mémoires sur Voltaire et sur ses ouvrages* (1826), 2:253–254; Eigeldinger and Trousson, *Anecdotes sur la vie privée de Monsieur de Voltaire* (2009), 226. Longchamp was Voltaire's manservant and occasional copyist from 1746 to 1751. Voltaire supposedly said these words when he learned, after the death of his beloved Émilie, that a portrait of him in miniature, set in a locket ring worn that she wore, had been replaced by a portrait of the poet Saint-Lambert. Mme du Châtelet died in 1749 after giving birth to a child fathered by Saint-Lambert.

A woman can keep one secret—the secret of her age.

Ballou, *Notable Thoughts about Women* (1882), 287.

Words

Craignez en atteignant le grand, de sauter au gigantesque, n'offrez que des images vraies, et servez-vous toujours du mot propre.

Beware, lest in attempting the grand, you overshoot the mark and fall into the grandiose: only employ true similes: and be sure always to use exactly the right word.

Letter from Cirey, February 25, 1739, to Claude-Adrien Helvétius in Paris. The translation is from Hall, *Voltaire in His Letters* (1919), 66. In a letter to Sainte-Beuve (December 23–24, 1862), Flaubert famously spoke of "le mot juste" to express the same idea.

Ils ne se servent de la pensée que pour autoriser leurs injustices, & n'emploient les paroles que pour déguiser leurs pensées.

They use thought only to justify their injustices, and employ words only to conceal their thoughts.

The capon (*chapon*, or young, gelded cockrel), speaking of human beings, "nos éternels ennemis," in the dialogue *Le Chapon et la Poularde* (1763), in *Mélanges philosophiques, littéraires, historiques, &c.* (1771), 337; Besterman et al., *Œuvres complètes de Voltaire* (2017), 60a:444. Variants of this quote have been credited to Talleyrand, but if he used the line he likely borrowed it from Voltaire. It also was misattributed to the Italian Jesuit Gabriel Malagrida by Stendhal as an epigraph for chapter 22 in *The Red and the Black*.

Les paroles sont aux pensées ce que l'or est aux diamants; il est nécessaire pour les enchâsser, mais il en faut peu.

Words are to ideas what gold is to diamonds: some are required to set them off, but a little goes a long way.

From Besterman, *Voltaire's Notebooks* (1952), 2:367; first published, using slightly different wording, in *Le Sottisier de Voltaire* (1880), 60; Besterman et al., *Œuvres complètes de Voltaire* (1969), 82:518.

Work—labor

Plus j'avance dans la carrière de la vie, et plus je trouve le travail nécessaire.

The longer I live, the more I appreciate the need to work.

Letter from Potsdam, August 15, 1751, to Président Charles-Jean-François Hénault in Paris.

Vous devez avoir, dit Candide au Turc, une vaste & magnifique Terre? Je n'ai que vingt arpens, répondit le Turc; je les cultive avec mes enfans; le travail éloigne de nous trois grands maux, l'ennui, le vice, & le besoin.

"You must have a vast and magnificent estate?" said Candide to the Turk.

"I have only twenty acres," replied the Turk; "I cultivate them with my children; work keeps away three great evils: boredom, vice, and need."

Conversation between Candide and a wise old Turk in chapter 30, the conclusion of *Candide, ou L'Optimisme* (1759), 290; Besterman et al., *Œuvres complètes de Voltaire* (1980), 48:258. In English, *Candide, Zadig, and Other Stories* (2001), 100.

L'Ecriture a dit, qui ne travaille pas ne mérite pas de manger. Notre confrère Job . . . dit que l'homme est né pour le travail comme l'oiseau pour voler.

The Bible says, he who does not work does not deserve to eat. Our confrere *Job* . . . says that man was born to work as the bird is to fly.

"Gueux Mendiant," in *Questions sur l'Encyclopédie, par des Amateurs* (1771), 6:345; Besterman et al., *Œuvres complètes de Voltaire* (2011), 42a:168.

The world

J'ai reçu de Buenos Aires le détail de la destruction de Quito. C'est pis que Lisbonne. Notre globe est une mine, et c'est sur cette mine que vous allez vous battre.

I've received details of the destruction of Quito from Buenos Aires. It is worse than Lisbon. This planet of ours is a landmine, and it is on that mine that you'll be fighting.

Letter from Les Délices, April 16, 1756, to the duc de Richelieu, en route to Minorca, where he won a great victory over the English at Port-Mahon, May 20, 1756.

Ce monde, ce théâtre, & d'orgueil & d'erreur,
Est plein d'infortunés qui parlent de bonheur.
Tout se plaint, tout gémit en cherchant le bien-être;
Nul ne voudrait mourir; nul ne voudrait renaître.

This world, this circus, of both pride and wrong,
Teems with unfortunate souls who talk of happiness.
They all complain, and groan, seeking material ease;
No one wants to die; no one wants to return reborn.

"Poëme sur le désastre de Lisbonne," in *Poëmes sur le désastre de Lisbonne et sur la loi naturelle* (1756), 16; Besterman et al., *Œuvres complètes de Voltaire* (2009), 45a:347.

La Terre est un vaste théâtre, où la même tragédie se joue sous des noms différents.

The World is an immense theater, in which the same tragedy is staged under different names.

"Etat de l'Asie au tems des decouvertes des Portugais," in *Essay sur l'histoire générale et sur les moeurs et l'esprit des nations* (1756), 3:247; Besterman et al., *Œuvres complètes de Voltaire* (2013), 26a:314.

Zoroaster (thought to have lived between 1500 and 500 B.C.)

PERSIAN SPIRITUAL LEADER

C'est de lui que les nations tiennent ce grand principe: qu'il vaut mieux hazarder de sauver un coupable que de condamner un innocent.

It is thanks to him that nations hold to this great principle: that it is better to risk sparing a guilty man than to condemn one who is innocent.

Zadig ou La Destinée (1748), 47. Here "him" refers to Zadig, who had been named "chief Judge of all the Tribunals throughout the Empire" by the king of Babylon. The 1756 edition of *Zadig*, however, credits Zoroaster in the preceding paragraph with this "great principle," which Zadig wisely followed. Either way, this statement prefigures a line in Blackstone's *Commentaries on the Laws of England* (1783): "All presumptive evidence of felony should be admitted cautiously; for the law holds, that it is better ten guilty persons escape, than that one innocent suffer."

Si c'est Zoroastre qui le premier annonça aux hommes cette belle maxime: Dans le doute si une action est bonne ou mauvaise, abstiens-toi, Zoroastre était le premier des hommes après Confucius.

If it was Zoroaster who was first to give mankind this splendid maxim: "When in doubt about whether an action is good or bad, do nothing," Zoroaster was the greatest man after Confucius.

"Zoroastre," in *Questions sur l'Encyclopédie, par des Amateurs* (1772), 9:81; Besterman et al., *Œuvres complètes de Voltaire* (2013), 43:516–517.

Figure 21. Louis-Jacques Cathelin, after Maurice Quentin de La Tour, *Post genitis hic carus erit nunc carus amicis*, circa 1773. Etching and engraving. Private collection. The title on the binding of the book in the foreground is "Henriade." The Latin phrase on the ribbon, authored by Mme du Châtelet to honor her lover, translates as "He will be as cherished by posterity as he is today by his friends."

QUOTATIONS ABOUT VOLTAIRE

VOLTAIRE ON VOLTAIRE

J'ai été si malheureux sous le nom d'Arouet que j'en ai pris un autre, surtout pour ne plus être confondu avec le poète Roy.

I was so unhappy with the name Arouet that I chose another, above all in order not to be confused with the poet Roi.

Letter from Paris, circa March 1719, to Jean-Baptiste Rousseau, possibly in Brussels. Pierre-Charles Roy was one of Voltaire's first literary enemies.

Vous trouvez que je m'explique assez clairement; je suis comme les petits ruisseaux; ils sont transparents parce qu'ils sont peu profonds.

You find that I explain myself rather clearly; I am like small streams; they are clear because they are not very deep.

Letter from Cirey, June 20, 1737, to Henri Pitot, possibly in Paris.

Il me fallait le roi de Prusse pour maître et le peuple anglais pour concitoyen.

I needed the king of Prussia as master and the English people as fellow citizens.

Letter written en route to Brussels from Reims, August 29, 1742, to Frederick the Great in Aix-la-Chapelle.

Ma destinée était d'être, je ne sais quel homme public coiffé de trois ou quatre bonnets de laurier, et d'une trentaine de couronnes d'épines.

My destiny was to be some sort of public figure with three or four sheaths of laurel leaves on his head and thirty or so crowns of thorns.

Letter from Potsdam, March 11, 1752, to the comte d'Argental in Paris. This quotation appeared as an epigraph on the title page of Arsène Houssaye, *Le Roi Voltaire* (1858).

A frenchman who thinks like a briton.

Letter from Potsdam, February 1, 1753, to Sir Everard Fawkener in London.

J'ai le malheur d'être un homme de lettres, un ouvrier en paroles et puis c'est tout. Voilà ma vocation dans ce monde.

It has been my unlucky fate to be a man of letters, a wordsmith and that is about it. That is my vocation in this world.

Letter from Colmar, April 16, 1754, to Mme Denis in Paris.

J'ajoute encore un petit mot sur ma triste figure. Je vous jure que je suis aussi laid que mon portrait. Croiez moy. Le peintre n'est pas bon je l'avoue, mais il n'est pas flatteur. Faites en faire mon cher ange une copie pour l'académie. Qu'importe après tout que l'image d'un pauvre diable qui sera bientôt poussière, soit ressemblante ou non. Les portraits sont une chimère, comme tout le reste. L'original vous aimera bien tendrement tant qu'il vivra.

I have one more word to say about my pitiful face. I swear to you that I am as ugly as my portrait. Believe me. The artist is not good, but neither does he flatter me. Have a copy made, *mon cher ange*, for the academy. What difference, after all, does it make whether a portrait of a poor devil who will soon return to dust looks like him. Portraits are illusory fictions, like everything else. The original will love you tenderly for as long as he lives.

Letter from Les Délices, June 16, 1758, to the comte d'Argental in Paris, regarding a copy of the pastel portrait of Voltaire by Maurice-Quentin de La Tour from 1735–1736 (figure 21), destined to join the Académie française collection of portraits of its members.

Je suis flexible comme une anguille, vif comme un lézard, et travaillant toujours comme un écureuil.

I am supple as an eel, quick as a lizard, and, like a squirrel, always busy.

Letter from Tournay, October 22, 1759, to the comte d'Argental in Paris.

Je suis comme les vieilles qui aiment les portraits dans lesquels elles se trouvent embellies.

I am like those old ladies who like portraits of themselves that make them look beautiful.

Letter from Les Délices, April 10, 1760, to the comte d'Albaret in Turin.

Je suis assez semblable aux girouettes, qui ne se fixent que quand elles sont rouillées.

I am rather like a weathercock, which stops moving only when it gets rusty.

Letter from Les Délices, April 10, 1760, to the comte d'Albaret.

J'ai toujours été la mouche du coche, mais je bourdonne de si loin qu'à peine m'entend-on.

I have always been a gadfly, but I buzz about from such a distance that I am barely heard.

Letter from Les Délices, August 11, 1760, to Nicolas-Claude Thieriot in Paris.

J'ai dès l'âge de douze ans . . . connu que mes organes n'étaient pas disposés à aller bien loin dans les mathématiques. J'ai éprouvé que je n'avais nulle disposition pour la musique. Dieu a dit à chaque homme, tu pourras aller jusque-là, et tu n'iras pas plus loin. J'avais quelque ouverture pour apprendre les langues de l'Europe, aucune pour les orientales. Non omnia possumus omnes. Dieu a donné la voix aux ros-signols et l'odorat aux chiens, encore y a-t-il des chiens qui n'en ont pas. Quelle extravagance d'imaginer que chaque homme aurait pu être un Neuton!

By the age of twelve . . . I knew that I could not go far in the study of mathematics. I sensed that I had no talent for music. God said to each man: you may go this far but no farther. I did have some aptitude for European languages, but none for the oriental ones. *Non omnia possumus omnes.* God gave a sweet song to the nightingale and to dogs a keen sense of smell, though admittedly some dogs do not have it. What folly to imagine that anyone can be Newton!

Letter from Ferney, December 22, 1760, to Pierre-Louis d'Aquin de Château-Lyon in Paris. D'Acquin de Château-Lyon was the publisher of *Le Censeur hebdomadaire.* The expression *Non omnia possumus omnes* translates as "We cannot all do everything."

Je suis obligé en conscience de vous dire que je ne suis pas né plus malin que vous; et que dans le fond je suis bon homme. Il est vrai qu'ayant fait réflexion depuis quelques années qu'on ne gagnait rien à être bon homme, je me suis mis à être un peu gai, parce qu'on m'a dit que cela est bon pour la santé.

I must in all conscience tell you that I was not born with more malice in my heart than you; and that at bottom I am a good man. It is true that having, some years ago, taken it into my head that one gained nothing by being virtuous, I took it upon myself to be gay, because I was told it would be good for my health.

Letter from Ferney, April 27, 1761, to abbé Trublet in Paris.

J'ai été pendant quatorze ans l'aubergiste de l'Europe, et je me suis lassé de cette pro-fession. J'ai reçu chez moi trois ou quatre cents Anglais qui sont tous si amoureux de

leur patrie que presque pas un seul ne s'est souvenu de moi après leur départ, excepté
un prêtre écossais nommé Brown, ennemi de M. Hume, qui a écrit contre moi, et
qui m'a reproché d'aller à confesse, ce qui est assurément bien dur.

For fourteen years I was the innkeeper of Europe, and I grew tired of it. I
received three or four hundred Englishmen who were so enamored of their
homeland that nary a one remembered me once they had gone, with the exception of a Scottish clergyman named Brown, an enemy of Hume's, who wrote
lies about me, accusing me of going to confession, which, admittedly, is really
a bit rich.

Letter from Ferney, March 30, 1768, to Mme Du Deffand in Paris. Robert Brown, pastor
of the Scottish Church at Utrecht, apparently called on Voltaire at Les Délices in 1760.

Je me suis lassé d'être l'aubergiste de l'Europe.

I have grown tired of being the innkeeper of Europe.

Letter from Ferney, April 1, 1768, to the duc de Choiseul, chief minister to the king at
Versailles.

J'ai fait plus en mon temps que Luther & Calvin.

I have done more in my time than Luther and Calvin.

Voltaire, *Épître à l'auteur du nouveau livre des Trois imposteurs* (1769); Besterman et al.,
Œuvres complètes de Voltaire (2016), 70a:243.

Mr Pigal doit, dit-on, venir modeler mon visage, on en devinerait à peine la place;
mes yeux sont enfoncés de trois pouces; mes joues sont de vieux parchemin mal collé
sur des os qui ne tiennent à rien. Le peu de dents que j'avais est parti. Ce que je
vous dis là n'est point coqueterie, c'est la pure vérité. On n'a jamais sculpté un pau-
vre homme en cet état. Mr Pigal croirait qu'on s'est moqué de lui, et pour moi j'ai
tant d'amour propre que je n'oserais jamais paraître en sa présence.

Mr Pigalle, they say, must come here to model my features, which are almost
nonexistent; my eyes are sunken by three inches, my cheeks like old parchment loosely glued to bones that are falling apart. The few teeth I had are gone.
What I am saying to you is far from coquetry, it is the absolute truth. No sculpture of a man in such a state has ever been made. Mr Pigalle would think
someone was pulling his leg, and as for me, I have sufficient pride that I would
never appear before him.

Letter from Ferney, May 21, 1770, to Mme Suzanne Necker in Paris. At Ferney, Pigalle
modeled, with great difficulty, a bust of Voltaire in clay. When he returned to Paris, he

carved a marble statue of a seated figure of Voltaire in the nude (a visual reference to the dying Seneca), which pleased no one, least of all Voltaire. The statue is now in the Louvre.

Mes sages voluptés n'ont point de repentirs.
J'ai fait un peu de bien: c'est mon meilleur ouvrage.

My sage pursuit of pleasure has no regrets at all.
I did a little good: it is my greatest work.

Voltaire, *Épitre à Horace* (1772), 7; Besterman et al., *Œuvres complètes de Voltaire* (2010), 74b:282. In a letter in 1758, Voltaire told an acquaintance he had purchased "la terre de Ferney que pour y faire un peu de bien."

Ma destinée était de courir de Roi en Roi, quoique j'aimasse ma liberté avec Idolatrie.

It was my destiny to run from King to King, even though I prized my freedom.

Voltaire, *Mémoires pour servir à la vie de Mr. de Voltaire* (1784), 89; Besterman et al., *Œuvres complètes de Voltaire* (2010), 45c:382.

Je meurs en adorant Dieu, en aimant mes amis, en ne haïssant pas mes ennemis, en détestant la superstition.

I die adoring God, loving my friends, not hating my enemies, and detesting superstition.

Statement recorded in Paris by his secretary, Jean-Louis Wagnière, and signed by Voltaire, February 28, 1778. In Longchamp and Wagnière, *Mémoires sur Voltaire et sur ses ouvrages* (1826), 1:133, and Pomeau, *On a voulu l'enterrer* (1994), 277.

Si Dieu dispose de moi, je meurs dans la sainte religion catholique où je suis né, espérant de la miséricorde divine qu'elle daignera pardonner toutes mes fautes, et que si j'avais jamais scandalisé l'église, j'en demande pardon à Dieu et à elle.

If it pleases God, I die in the Holy Catholic faith into which I was born, hoping that divine mercy will deign forgive me my faults, and if ever I scandalized the Church, I ask God's forgiveness and that of the Church.

Confession signed by Voltaire and witnessed by the abbé Louis-Laurent Gaultier in Paris, March 2, 1778. Longchamp and Wagnière, *Mémoires sur Voltaire et sur ses ouvrages* (1826), 1:453, and Pomeau, *On a voulu l'enterrer* (1994), 278.

Je suis donc un homme mort.

So, I am a dead man.

Voltaire's final words, according to Wagnière, uttered after two priests left his chambers, May 30, 1778. Quoted in Longchamp and Wagnière, *Mémoires sur Voltaire et sur ses ouvrages* (1826), 1:161.

Misattributed to Voltaire

Je m'arrêterais de mourir, s'il me venait un bon mot ou une bonne idée.

I would hold off on dying if a good joke or a good idea came to me.

Jean Dutourd used this line as an epigraph in his novel *Pluche ou l'amour de l'art* (1967), 7. There is no known source for this quote that likely derived from a line in a play by Sacha Guitry, *Le Bien-aimé* (1940), about Louis XV and Mme de Pompadour, in which Voltaire says, "Je m'arrêterais de mourir un instant s'il me venait un bon mot ou une bonne idée." In English, "I'd probably stop dying for a moment if I came up with a *bon mot* or a good idea."

This is no time for making new enemies.

Also said to be Voltaire's last words, cited, with no source given, in English by Susan Ratcliffe in the *Concise Oxford Dictionary of Quotations* (2006), 349. Professor Robert E. Lucas of the University of Chicago quoted this line, also unsourced, in his speech accepting the Nobel Prize in Economic Sciences, December 10, 1995. In recent years, French websites have translated the line as "Ce n'est pas le moment de se faire un ennemi" (or "des ennemis").

CONTEMPORARY OPINION

Abigail Adams (1744–1818)

WIFE OF JOHN ADAMS

I have a thousand fears for my dear Boys as they rise into Life, the most critical period of which is I conceive, at the university; there infidelity abounds, both in example and precepts, there they imbibe the specious arguments of a Voltaire, a Hume and Mandevill. If not from the fountain, they receive them at second hand. These are well calculated to intice a youth, not yet capable of investigating their principals, or answering their arguments. . . . I hope before either of our children are prepaird for colledge you will be able to return and assist by your example and advise, to direct and counsel them; that with undeviating feet they may keep the path of virtue.

Letter from Braintree, Massachusetts, November 11, 1783, to her husband in Paris. In Adams and Adams, *The Book of Abigail and John* (1975), 369. Bernard Mandeville was the author of a controversial book *Fable of the Bees* (1714).

John Adams (1735–1826)

COAUTHOR OF THE DECLARATION OF INDEPENDENCE
AND SECOND PRESIDENT OF THE UNITED STATES

After dinner We went to the Accademy of Sciences, and heard Mr. D'Alembert as Secretary perpetual, pronounce Eulogies on several of their Members lately deceased. Voltaire and Franklin were both present, and there presently arose a general Cry that Monsieur Voltaire and Monsieur Franklin should be introduced to each other. This was done and they bowed and spoke to each other. This was no Satisfaction. There must be something more. Neither of our Philosophers seemed to divine what was wished or expected. They however took each other by the hand. . . . But this was not enough. The Clamour continued, untill the explanation came out "Il faut s'embrasser, a la francoise." The two Aged Actors upon this great Theatre of Philosophy and frivolity then embraced each other by hugging one another in their Arms and kissing each others cheeks, and then the tumult subsided. And the Cry immediately spread through the whole Kingdom and I suppose over all Europe Qu'il etoit charmant. Oh! il etoit enchantant, de voir Solon et Sophocle embrassans. How charming it was! Oh! it was enchanting to see Solon and Sophocles embracing!

Entry, April 29, 1778, in Adams's autobiographical journal, "Travels and Negotiations" (1777–1778), transcribed from the original at the Massachusetts Historical Society. In print see Bailyn, *To Begin the World Anew* (2003), 96.

His reputation was more universal than that of Leibnitz or Newton, Frederick or Voltaire, and his character more loved and esteemed than any or all of them. . . . Voltaire, whose name was more universal than any of those before mentioned, was considered as a vain, profligate wit, and not much esteemed or beloved by anybody, though admired by all who knew his works.

Commenting on how highly esteemed Franklin was in France, in the *Boston Patriot*, May 15, 1811. Quoted in Adams, *The Works of John Adams* (1856), 1:660.

Anonymous or unknown

C'est un homme qui a pour dix millions de gloire et qui en demande deux sous.

He is a man whose glory is valued in the millions and who demands another two cents' worth.

Quoted in Faguet, *Voltaire* (1895), 76.

René-Louis de Voyer de Paulmy, marquis d'Argenson (1694–1757)

VOLTAIRE'S CLASSMATE AT THE *COLLÈGE* LOUIS-LE-GRAND AND MINISTER FOR FOREIGN AFFAIRS, 1744–1747

Ce grand poëte est toujours à cheval sur le Parnasse et sur la rue Quincampoix.

This great poet always has one foot on Mount Parnassus and the other on the rue Quincampoix.

Diary entry, January 12, 1751, in d'Argenson, *Mémoires et journal inédit du marquis d'Argenson* (1858), 9. The rue Quincampoix was the Wall Street of eighteenth-century Paris, and as Roger Pearson says, Voltaire always "had a keen eye for investment opportunities." See Pearson, "Voltaire's Luck" (2016).

James Boswell (1740–1795)

SCOTTISH BIOGRAPHER AND DIARIST

Voltaire's *Candide*, written to refute the system of Optimism, which it has accomplished with great success, is wonderfully similar in its plan and conduct to Johnson's *Rasselas*; insomuch, that I have heard Johnson say, that if they had not been published so closely one after the other that there was not time for imitation, it would have been in vain to deny that the scheme of that which came latest was taken from the other. Though the proposition illustrated by both these works was the same, namely that in our present state there is more evil than good, the intention of the writers was very different. Voltaire, I am afraid, meant only by wanton profaneness to obtain a sportive victory over religion, and to discredit the belief of a superintending Providence: Johnson meant, by shewing the unsatisfactory nature of things temporal, to direct the hopes of man to things eternal.

Boswell, *The Life of Samuel Johnson, L.L.D.* (1791), 1:185, in the section for the year 1759, in which *Candide* and *The History of Rasselas* were published. On May 16, 1778, Johnson told Boswell that he thought *Candide* "had more power in it than any thing that *Voltaire* had written" (*The Life of Samuel Johnson, L.L.D.*, 2:267).

Chevalier Stanislas-Jean de Boufflers (1738–1815)

FRENCH POET AND MEMBER OF THE ACADÉMIE FRANÇAISE

Vous ne pouvez point vous faire d'idée de la dépense & du bien que fait Voltaire. Il est le roi & le père du pays qu'il habite; il fait le bonheur de ce qui l'entoure, & il est aussi bon père de famille que bon poète. Si on le partageait en deux & que je visse d'un côté l'homme que j'ai lu, & de l'autre, celui que j'entends, je ne sais auquel je courrais. Ses imprimeurs auront beau faire, il sera toujours la meilleure édition de ses livres.

You cannot imagine how generous Voltaire is and all the good that he does. He is the king and father of his domain. He makes those around him happy, and is as good a father to them as he is a poet. If he were split in two and I could see on the one hand the man I had read about, and on the other, the man I see and hear today, I cannot say which I would be prefer. Try as his publishers may, he will always be the best edition of his works.

Letter from Ferney, December 12, 1764, to Boufflers's mother, the marquise de Boufflers, in Lunéville. In Boufflers, *Lettres de Monsieur le chevalier de Boufflers pendant* (1771), 21–22.

Giacomo Casanova (1725–1798)

ITALIAN ADVENTURER, WRITER, SPY, AND DIPLOMAT

Voilà, le plus beau moment de ma vie. Je vois, à la fin, mon maître; il y a vingt ans, monsieur, que je suis votre écolier.

This is the happiest moment of my life. At last, I see my master; I have been your pupil, Monsieur, for twenty years.

Addressing Voltaire when they first met, at Les Délices, July 1760. In Casanova, *Histoire de ma vie* (1960), 225.

Ce fut dans ce moment-là que Voltaire m'étonna. Il me récita par cœur les deux grands morceaux du trente-quatrième et du trente-cinquième chant de ce divin poète, où il parle de la conversation qu'Astolphe eut avec l'apôtre St Jean, sans jamais manquer un vers, sans prononcer un seul mot qui ne fût très exact en prosodie; il m'en releva les beautés avec des réflexions de véritable grand homme. On n'aurait pu s'attendre à quelque chose davantage du plus sublime de tous les glossateurs italiens. Je l'ai écouté sans respirer, sans clignoter une seule fois, désirant en vain de le trouver en faute; j'ai dit me tournant à la compagnie que j'étais excédé de surprise, et que j'informerai toute l'Italie de ma juste merveille.

It was then that Voltaire astonished me. He recited by heart the two great passages in the thirty-fourth and thirty-fifth cantos of the divine poet in which he tells of Astolpho's conversation with St. John the Apostle, never skipping a line, never pronouncing a word except in accordance with strict prosody; he pointed out their beauties to me, with reflections which only a truly great man could make. One could have expected nothing more from the greatest of all the Italian commentators. I listened to him without breathing, without once blinking my eyes, hoping in vain to catch him in a mistake; turning to the company, I said that I was overwhelmed with astonishment, and that I would inform all Italy of my wonder and the reason for it.

Conversation at Les Délices, July 1760, in Casanova, *Histoire de ma vie* (1960), 229, and, in English, *History of My Life* (1968), 226–227. The passages Voltaire recited from memory were from Ariosto's *Orlando Furioso*. Duke Astolfo (or Astolpho) was a character in the poem.

Catherine the Great (1729–1796)

PRUSSIAN-BORN EMPRESS OF RUSSIA

Depuis que Voltaire est mort, il me semble qu'il n'y a plus d'honneur attaché à la belle humeur: c'était lui qui était la divinité de la gaité.

Since Voltaire died, it seems to me that honor and good humor have parted ways. He was the divine god of high spirits.

Letter from the imperial palace, Tsarsko-Sélo, outside St. Petersburg, August 11, 1778, to Friedrich Melchior Grimm in Paris, in Moland, *Œuvres complètes de Voltaire* (1883), 1:454.

C'est mon maître; c'est lui ou plutôt ses œuvres qui ont formé mon esprit et ma tête. Je vous l'ai dit plus d'une fois, je pense: je suis son écolière; plus jeune, j'aimais à lui plaire; une action faite, il fallait pour qu'elle me plût qu'elle fût digne de lui être dite, et tout de suite il en était informé. Il y était si bien accoutumé qu'il me grondait lorsque je le laissais manquer de nouvelles et qu'il les apprenait d'autre part.

He is my teacher; he, or rather, his works, shaped my mind, my intellect. I have said to you many times, I think: I am his pupil; when I was younger I loved to please him; my actions satisfied me only when they were worth sharing with Voltaire, and I immediately told him about them. He was so accustomed to this that he scolded me whenever I forgot to tell him the latest news, especially if he heard it from someone else.

Letter from Tsarsko-Sélo, October 1, 1778, to Friedrich Melchior Grimm in Paris, in Moland, *Œuvres complètes de Voltaire: Nouvelle Édition* (1883), 1:454.

Personne avant lui n'écrivit comme lui; à la race future, il servira d'exemple et d'écueil. Il faudrait unir le génie et la philosophie aux connaissances et à l'agrément, en un mot être M. de Voltaire, pour l'égaler.

No one before him wrote as he wrote; for future generations, he will serve as both a model and a hindrance. One would have to combine genius and philosophy with knowledge and charm, in a word, be M. de Voltaire, to equal him.

Letter from St. Petersburg, October 15, 1778, to Mme Denis in Paris; published in the October 1778 *livraison* of Friedrich Melchior Grimm's newsletter *Correspondance littéraire, philosophique et critique* (1812), 4:300.

Attributed to Armand-Louis de Béthune, marquis de Charost (1710–1735)

FRENCH MILITARY OFFICER, MORTALLY WOUNDED DURING THE WAR OF THE POLISH SUCCESSION

M. de V*** . . . est maigre, d'un tempérament sec: il a la bile brûlée, le visage décharné, l'air spirituel & caustique, les yeux étincelans & malins. Tout le feu que vous trouvez dans ses ouvrages, il l'a dans son action; vif jusqu'à l'étourderie: c'est un ardent qui va & vient, qui vous éblouit & qui pétille. . . . Gai par compléxion, sérieux par régime, ouvert sans franchise, politique sans finesse, sociable sans amis, il sait le monde & l'oublie. Le matin Aristippe, & Diogène le soir, il aime la grandeur & méprise les Grands: est aisé avec eux, contraint avec ses égaux. Il commence par la politesse, continuë par la froideur, finit par le dégoût: il aime la Cour & s'y ennuïe; sensible sans attachement, voluptueux sans passion: il ne tient à rien par choix & tient à tout par inconstance. Raisonnant sans principes. Sa raison a ses accès comme la folie des autres; l'esprit droit, le cœur injuste; il pense tout & se moque de tout. Libertin sans tempérament, il sait aussi moraliser sans mœurs; vain à l'excès, mais encore plus intéressé. Il travaille moins pour la réputation que pour l'argent; il en a faim & soif: enfin il se presse de travailler pour se presser de vivre; il étoit fait pour jouir, il veut amasser. Voila l'homme.

M. de V*** . . . is gaunt, brusque by nature: he is fractious, with a thin face, a witty and caustic manner, impish and twinkling eyes. All the fire one finds in his works is present in the way he behaves; lively, almost giddy: his fervor comes and goes, to dazzle & sparkle. . . . Gay by temperament, willfully serious, open without frankness, diplomatic without subtlety, sociable without friends, he sees the world clearly and dismisses it. Aristippus, at dawn, Diogenes by night, he loves grandeur and despises the Great: at ease with them, uneasy with his peers. He is polite at first, then turns cold and in the end grows bored. He loves life at Court and when there is bored; sensitive but without fondness for others, voluptuous without passion: he cares for nothing by choice, and all things by caprice. He reasons without principles. His thinking is as fitful as a madman's; clear-headed, heartless; he has ideas about and mocks everything. Libertine in a passive way, he preaches morality yet is immoral; vain to excess, but self-seeking even more so. He labors less for fame than for money; he hungers and thirsts for it: in sum, he forces himself to work to carry on living; he was made for pleasure but wants to amass a fortune. That is the man.

"Portrait de M. de V***," in *Voltariana ou Eloges amphigouriques de Fr. Marie Arrouet* (1748), 3–4. Aristippus was a pleasure-seeking disciple of Socrates, Diogenes a Cynic who believed in the simple life. According to Louis Nicolardot in *Ménage et finances de Voltaire* (1854, 2–3), this portrait may have circulated privately in Paris as early as 1733. On June 12, 1735, Voltaire wrote Thieriot from Cirey, asking his friend to send him a copy of this four-page "enseigne à bière" (cheap portrait). He wrote again on August 15, claiming "everyone" believed it was written by "the young comte de Charost." Friedrich Melchior Grimm was convinced of Charost's authorship as well. See Grimm, Diderot, et al., *Correspondance littéraire, philosophique, critique, par Grimm, etc.* (1877), 266–267.

Gabrielle-Émilie Le Tonnelier de Breteuil, marquise du Châtelet (1706–1749)

FRENCH MATHEMATICIAN, PHYSICIST, AND COMPANION OF VOLTAIRE

Je l'aime assez, je vous l'avoue, pour sacrifier au bonheur de vivre avec lui sans alarmes, et au plaisir de l'arracher malgré lui à ses imprudences et à sa destinée, tout ce que je pourrais trouver de plaisir et d'agrément à Paris. La seule chose qui m'inquiète et que j'aie à ménager, c'est la présence de M. du Châtelet.

I love him enough, I admit, to sacrifice all the pleasure and delight Paris has to offer for the joy of living, free of all stress, with him and for the pleasure of saving him, despite himself, from his rashness and eventual downfall. The only thing that is cause for concern and which I must manage carefully, is the presence of M. du Châtelet.

Letter from Paris, June 15, 1735, to Voltaire's friend and Émilie's former lover, the duc de Richelieu, on military service along the Rhine. In the same letter, she announced that she and Voltaire were leaving Paris to live on her husband's estate in Cirey. For the French text see Besterman et al., *Œuvres complètes de Voltaire* (1969), 87:146.

Mr. de Voltaire . . . quoy que grand metaphysicien, grand historien, grand philosophe, etc. a donné la preference a la poesie, et l'epithete du plus grand poete français, sera aussi bien son caractere distinctif, que celuy d'homme universel.

Mr. de Voltaire . . . although a great metaphysician, great historian, great philosopher, etc. has chosen to favor poetry. The epithet of France's greatest poet, as well as that of universal man, will be his distinctive characteristic.

From her preface to a translation of Bernard Mandeville's *Fable of the Bees*, circa 1735, unpublished during her lifetime. For the original French see Wade, *Studies on Voltaire* (1947), 132. The translation, with a few minor changes, is from Châtelet's *Selected Philosophical and Scientific Writings* (2009), 44.

Post genitis hic carus erit nunc carus amicis.

He will be as cherished by posterity as he is cherished today by his friends.

Starting in the 1740s, this line in Latin appeared on reproductive prints engraved after La Tour's pastel portrait of Voltaire (figure 21). Voltaire credited Émilie with the phrase in a letter to Nicolas-Louis Bourgeois, January 20, 1746. He enclosed in the letter an earlier print after La Tour's pastel, engraved by Jean-Joseph Balechou.

Philip Dormer Stanhope, Fourth Earl of Chesterfield
(1694–1773)

ENGLISH MAN OF LETTERS, STATESMAN, AND WIT

I have lately read, with great pleasure, his two little Histories of *les Croisades*, and *l'Esprit Humain*; which I recommend to your perusal, if you have not already read them. They are bound up with a most poor performance, called *Micromégas*, which is said to be Voltaire's too; but I cannot believe it, it is so very unworthy of him: it consists only of thoughts stolen from Swift, but miserably mangled and disfigured. But his History of the Croisades shows, in a very short and strong light, the most immoral and wicked scheme, that was ever contrived by knaves, and executed by madmen and fools, against humanity.

Letter from London to his illegitimate son, Philip Stanhope, in Germany, January 1, 1753, in Chesterfield, *Letters Written by the Late Right Honourable Philip Dormer Stanhope* (1774), 6.

I am extremely glad to hear that you are soon to have Voltaire at Mannheim: immediately upon his arrival, pray make him a thousand compliments from me. I admire him exceedingly; and whether as an Epic, Dramatic, or Lyric Poet, or Prose-writer, I think I justly apply to him the *Nil molitur inepté*.

To his son in Germany, March 26, 1754, in Chesterfield, *Letters Written by the Late Right Honourable Philip Dormer Stanhope* (1774), 6. The phrase "nil molitur inepte" ("does not exert himself ineptly") is from *De Arte poetica* by Horace, who happened to be one of Voltaire's favorite Latin poets.

Nicolas de Caritat, marquis de Condorcet (1743–1794)

PHILOSOPHER, MATHEMATICIAN, AND PROTÉGÉ OF VOLTAIRE
WHO DIED MYSTERIOUSLY IN PRISON DURING THE TERROR

Si pour la première fois, la raison commence à répandre sur tous les peuples de l'Europe, un jour égal & pur: par-tout dans l'histoire de ces changements on trouvera le nom de Voltaire; presque par-tout on le verra, ou commencer le combat, ou décider la victoire.

If, now for the first time, reason is starting to advance among the peoples of Europe, some day equal and pure: on every page in the history of those changes, one will find the name of *Voltaire*; and almost always, he will be seen to be either starting the fight or clenching the victory.

Condorcet, *Vie de Voltaire, par M. le marquis de Condorcet* (1789), 70:171.

Jacques-Joseph-Marie Decroix (1746–1826)

LAWYER FROM LILLE, ADMIRER OF THE COMPOSER
RAMEAU, AND EDITOR OF THE MEMOIRS OF
VOLTAIRE'S MANSERVANT, LONGCHAMP

Saint-François de Ferney.

Saint Francis of Ferney.

Quoted in André Magnan, "Poncifs," in Goulemot, Magnan, and Masseau, *Inventaire Voltaire* (1995), 1082.

Denis Diderot (1713–1784)

FRENCH *PHILOSOPHE*, NOVELIST, ART CRITIC, PLAYWRIGHT,
AND EDITOR IN CHIEF OF THE *ENCYCLOPÉDIE*

Cet homme n'est que le second dans tous les genres.

This man is never more than second-rate in all genres.

Diderot, letter from Paris, August 12, 1762, to his mistress, Sophie Volland, also in Paris; from Diderot, *Œuvres complètes de Diderot: Correspondance II* (1876), 100.

Jusqu'à présent, je n'ai connu qu'un homme dont le goût soit resté pur et intact au milieu des barbares. C'est Voltaire; mais quelle conséquence générale à tirer d'un être bizarre qui devient généreux et gai, à l'âge où les autres deviennent avares et tristes.

Till now I've known just one man whose taste remained pure and intact in the midst of barbarians. That is Voltaire; but what general conclusions can be drawn from a bizarre being who turns generous and gay at an age when others become avaricious and glum?

Diderot, *Salon de 1765*, commenting on a painting by Alexandre Roslin. See Diderot, *Salons 1765* (1979), 127.

C'est Voltaire qui ne se connaît ni en architecture, ni en sculpture, ni en peinture, mais qui transmet à la postérité le sentiment de son siècle sur Perrault, Le Sueur et Puget.

Figure 22. Jean-Baptiste Greuze, *Portrait of Denis Diderot*, 1766. Black chalk, stumped, and white chalk on brown paper. The Morgan Library & Museum, 1958.3. Gift of John M. Crawford. Photograph courtesy of Morgan Library & Museum, New York.

It is Voltaire who knows nothing about architecture, sculpture, or painting, and yet he transmits to posterity the views of his time on Perrault, Le Sueur, and Puget.

Letter from Paris, February 1766, to the sculptor Étienne-Maurice Falconet in St. Petersburg, Russia, where he was beginning work on his masterpiece, the equestrian monument to Peter the Great, commissioned by Catherine the Great. See Diderot, *Œuvres complètes de Diderot: Oeuvres diverses II / Correspondance I* (1876), 115.

Je connois telle action que je voudrois avoir faite pour tout ce que je possede. C'est un sublime ouvrage que Mahomet; j'aimerois mieux avoir rehabilité la memoire des Calas.

There are certain things I would give everything I own to have done. *Mahomet* is a sublime work; but I would rather have rehabilitated the memory of the Calas family.

The character "Moi" (the voice of Diderot) to "Lui," the eponymous principal protagonist in *Le Neveu de Rameau* (circa 1762–1773); from Diderot, *Le Neveu de Rameau* (1977), 42. *Le Neveu de Rameau* was first published posthumously in the *Œuvres inédites de Diderot* (1821), 57.

Un poete, c'est de Voltaire; et puis qui encore? de Voltaire; et le troisieme, de Voltaire; et le quatrieme, de Voltaire.

A poet? Well, there's Voltaire; and then who? Voltaire; and in third place? Voltaire. And in fourth? Voltaire.

"Lui," to "Moi," in Diderot, *Le Neveu de Rameau* (1977), 100.

Qui est-ce qui distingue particulièrement Voltaire de tous nos jeunes littérateurs? L'instruction. Voltaire sait beaucoup, et nos jeunes poètes sont ignorants. L'ouvrage de Voltaire est plein de choses; leurs ouvrages sont vides.

What is it that specifically distinguishes Voltaire from all our young writers? Learning. Voltaire knows a great deal and our young poets are ignorant. The work of Voltaire is full of things; their works are empty.

Diderot, *Plan d'une université pour le gouvernement de Russie* (1775), in Diderot, *Œuvres complètes de Diderot* (1875), 3:444. By "poets," Diderot meant dramatic poets as well; Corneille and Racine were mentioned in the same paragraph.

Voltaire écrit contre J. C. quand il se porte bien; est-il malade, il appelle un capucin.

Voltaire denounces Christ when he is feeling well; if he is ill, he calls for a priest.

Undated manuscript note in the Fonds Vandeul, Bibliothèque Nationale de France; from Dieckmann, *Inventaire du fonds Vandeul et inédits de Diderot* (1951), 200.

Quand on voit un historien tel que Voltaire jugeant si platement des arts et des artistes, il importe de peser le jugement de l'historien.

When one sees a historian such as Voltaire judging the arts and artists so dully, one must examine the judgment of the historian.

Undated manuscript note in Dieckmann, *Inventaire du fonds Vandeul et inédits de Diderot* (1951), 231.

Attributed to Marie Anne de Vichy-Chamrond, marquise Du Deffand (1697–1780)

SALONNIÈRE AND PATRON OF THE ARTS

Que voulez-vous de plus? Il a inventé l'histoire.

What more do you want? He invented history.

Supposed reply to someone who said Voltaire lacked invention (had "rien inventé"); from Noël and Carpentier, *Philologie française* (1831), 74.

Abbé Théophile Duvernet (circa 1729–1796)

SCHOOLMASTER, JOURNALIST, AND AUTHOR

Voltaire était tout à-la-fois un sujet d'admiration & d'étonnement; ses écrits, qu'on trouvait partout, semblaient avoir seuls fixé dans toute l'Europe l'universalité de la langue Française. Tous les artistes, sculpteurs, médaillistes, graveurs, peintres, dessinateurs, s'étaient emparés de lui; & c'est sous toutes les formes et toutes les attitudes qu'on variat son portrait; nul homme au monde n'a joui d'un honneur aussi constant & aussi universel.

Voltaire was both a subject of admiration and astonishment; his writings alone, which were everywhere, seemed to establish the universality of the French language all over Europe. He was portrayed by every artist, sculptor, designer of medallions, engraver, painter, and draftsman; and his features were variously drawn in every possible manner and position; no man on earth ever enjoyed an honor as unceasing and universal.

Duvernet, *La Vie de Voltaire, par M**** (1786), 304.

Reverend Timothy Dwight (1752–1817)

CONGREGATIONALIST MINISTER, POET, AND PRESIDENT OF YALE COLLEGE

YOUR Creator endued you with shining talents, and cast your lot in a field of action, where they might be most happily employed: In the progress of a long and industrious life, you devoted them to a single purpose, the elevation of your character above his. For the accomplishment of this purpose . . . you opposed truth, religion, and their authors, with sophistry, contempt, and obloquy; and taught, as far as your example or sentiments extended their influence, that the chief end of man was, to slander his God, and abuse him forever. To whom could such an effort as the following be dedicated, with more propriety than you.

In "To Mons. de Voltaire," Reverend Dwight's dedication to his forty-page verse satire *The Triumph of Infidelity* (1788), iii.

About the year 1728, Voltaire, so celebrated for his wit and brilliancy, and not less distinguished for his hatred of christianity and his abandonment of principle, formed a systematical design to destroy christianity, and to introduce in its stead a general diffusion of irreligion.

Sermon delivered in New Haven, Connecticut, July 4, 1798, from Dwight, *The Duty of Americans, at the Present Crisis* (1798), 10.

André-Hercule de Fleury (1653–1743)

CARDINAL AND FIRST MINISTER UNDER LOUIS XV

Je crois vous connoître parfaitement. Vous êtes un bon et honnête homme . . . mais vous avez été jeune, et peut-être un peu trop longtems. Vous avez été élevé dans la compagnie de tout ce que le monde peu éclairé regardoit comme la meilleure, parce que c'étoient des grands seigneurs. Ils vous ont applaudi et avec raison; mais ils vous l'ont donnée en tout et ils allaient trop loin. Ils vous ont gâté de trop bonne heure, et, à votre âge, cela étoit naturel.

I believe I know exactly who you are. You are a good and decent man . . . but you have been young, and perhaps for a little too long. You were raised in a rather ungodly milieu amidst everything that, because they were great lords, was regarded as the very best. They applauded you and rightly so; and they approved of everything you did, but in that they went too far. They spoiled you much too soon, and, at your age, that was to be expected.

Letter from Fleury at his country home at Issy-les-Moulineaux just outside Paris, November 14, 1740, to Voltaire in Berlin. See Beuchot, *Œuvres de Voltaire avec préfaces, avertissements, notes, etc.* (1832), 54:239; and Besterman, *The Complete Works of Voltaire* (1970), 91:358 (letter D2364).

Benjamin Franklin (1706–1790)

COAUTHOR OF THE DECLARATION OF INDEPENDENCE
AND THE FIRST U.S. MINISTER TO FRANCE

The Occasion of his Writing this *Traité sur la Tolérance*, was what he calls "le *Meurtre* de Jean Calas, *commis* dans Toulouse avec le *glaire* [*glaive*] de la Justice, le 9me Mars, 1762." There is in it an abundance of good Sense and sound

Figure 23. Augustin de Saint-Aubin, after Charles-Nicolas Cochin the Younger, *Benjamin Franklin*, 1777. Etching and engraving. Private collection.

Reasoning mix'd with some of those Pleasantries that mark the Author as strongly as if he had affix'd his Name.

Letter from Philadelphia, September 30, 1764, to Colonel Henry Bouquet at either Fort Loudon, in south-central Pennsylvania, or the colonial outpost at Fort Pitt, future site of

Pittsburgh. See Franklin, *The Papers of Benjamin Franklin* (1967), 367–368. Franklin told Colonel Bouquet that Voltaire's treatise was one "of a Number of new Pamphlets from England and France" that he had "lately receiv'd."

Frederick the Great (1712–1786)

KING OF PRUSSIA FROM 1740 UNTIL HIS DEATH

Les Grands-Hommes Modernes vous auront un jour l'obligation, & à vous unique-ment, en cas que la dispute à qui d'eux ou des Anciens la préférence est due, vienne à renaître, que vous ferez pancher la balance de leur côté.

The Great Men among the Moderns will one day be obliged to you, and to you alone, in the event the debate is reborn over whether they, the Moderns, or the Ancients are superior, for tipping the balance in their favor.

Letter from Berlin, August 8, 1736, to Voltaire at Cirey. In *Oeuvres diverses de Monsieur de Voltaire* (1746), 10–11.

J'ai vu ce Voltaire que j'étois si curieux de connoître. . . . Il a l'éloquence de Cicéron, la douceur de Pline et la sagesse d'Agrippa; il réunit en un mot ce qu'il faut ras-sembler de vertus et de talens de trois des plus grands hommes de l'antiquité. Son esprit travaille sans cesse, chaque goutte d'encre est un trait d'esprit partant de sa plume.

I saw this Voltaire that I was so curious to see. . . . He has the eloquence of Cicero, the tenderness of Pliny, and the wisdom of Agrippa; in a word, he combines all of the virtues and talents that might be borrowed from three of the greatest men in antiquity. His mind never stops, each drop of ink is a dash of wit sprung from his pen.

Letter from Frederick at Wesel in Westphalia, near the Rhine, September 2, 1740, to Charles-Étienne Jordan, presumably in Berlin. Jordan, a Prussian-born Huguenot, and confidante of Frederick, was employed by him as his secretary and librarian. From Frederick II, *Oeuvres posthumes de Frédéric II, Roi de Prusse* (1788), 149.

L'on peut dire, s'il m'est permis de m'exprimer ainsi, que M. de Voltaire valoit seul toute une Académie.

One may say, if I may be permitted to express myself thusly, that Voltaire was by himself the equal of an entire Academy.

Frederick II, *Éloge de Voltaire lu à l'académie royale des Sciences et belles-lettres de Berlin* (1788), 17. This homage to Voltaire was delivered at a special meeting of the Royal Academy in Berlin on November 17, 1778.

Élie-Catherine Fréron (1718–1776)

JOURNALIST, EDITOR, AND CRITIC

Quelques personnes veulent, Mr., ériger une statue à M. de Voltaire. J'en suis enchanté. Il est l'honneur de notre siècle, & la Goute en est le fléau. M. de Voltaire a fait couler des larmes; la Goute fait pousser des soupirs. Les larmes que M. de Voltaire fait répandre sont filles du plaisir, & vous sçavez que l'on dit communément que c'est au plaisir aussi que les douleurs de la Goute doivent leur naissance. Les ouvrages de M. de Voltaire sont entre les mains des grands & des petits; la Goute est de nos jours l'apanage des petits & des grands. On apprend à devenir Philosophe dans les écrits de M. de Voltaire; il n'est certainement personne qui n'apprenne la Philosophie dans un violent accès de Goute. Pourquoi donc ne pas ériger une statue à la Goute comme à M. de Voltaire? Il faudroit la placer à côté de la sienne. Tout est antithèse dans ses écrits; tout seroit antithèse dans les statues.

Some people, Sir, wish to erect a statue to M. *de Voltaire*. I am delighted. He is the most honored figure of our century, and Gout is its scourge. M. *de Voltaire* has caused tears to flow; Gout gives rise to sighs. The tears that M. *de Voltaire* has produced are the tears of pleasure, and you know it is often said that Gout's misery is also the spawn of pleasure. M. *de Voltaire*'s works are in the hands of people both great and small. Now both small and great are blessed with Gout. One learns to become a Philosopher through M. *de Voltaire*'s writings; there is certainly no one who does not learn about philosophy while suffering a violent attack of Gout. Why not erect a statue to Gout as well as to M. *de Voltaire*? It should be placed next to his. Everything he writes is antithetical; everything about these two statues would be antithetical.

"Lettre à l'Auteur de ces Feuilles, en lui envoyant une Chanson sur la Goute," in Fréron, *L'Année littéraire* (1770), 235–236. The statue mentioned here (by Pigalle), now in the Louvre, was commissioned by Mme Necker and a group of subscribers including Catherine the Great.

Marie-Therese Geoffrin (1699–1777)

PARISIAN *SALONNIÈRE*

Quand il a une fois quelque chose dans sa tête, il est hors de lui.

Once he gets an idea in his head, he is beside himself.

Letter from Paris, September 24, 1766, to King Stanislas-Auguste Poniatowski of Poland in Warsaw; from Poniatowski and Geoffrin, *Correspondance inédite du roi Stanislas-Auguste Poniatowski et de Madame Geoffrin* (1875), 243.

Figure 24. Marianne Loir, detail of a presumed portrait of Mme Geoffrin, painted circa 1760. National Museum of Women in the Arts, Washington, DC. Photograph by Lee Stalsworth.

Edward Gibbon (1737–1794)

ENGLISH HISTORIAN

I made a little excursion some days ago to Geneva, not so much for the sake of the town which I had often seen before, as for a representation of Monsieur de Voltaire's. He lives now entirely at Fernay, a little place in France, but only two Leagues from Geneva. He has bought the estate, and built a very pretty tho' small house upon it. After a life passed in courts and Capitals, the Great Voltaire is now a meer country Gentleman, and even (for the honour of the profession) something of a farmer. He says he never enjoyed so much true happiness. He has got rid of most of his infirmities, and tho' very old and lean, enjoys a much better state of health than he did twenty years ago. His playhouse is very neat and well contrived, situated just by his Chappel, which is far inferior to it, tho', he says himself, *que son Christ est du meilleur faiseur, de tout le pays de Gex.*

The play they acted was my favourite Orphan of China. Voltaire himself acted Gengis and Madame Denys Idamé; but I do not know how it happened: either my taste is improved or Voltaire's talents are impaired since I last saw him. He appeared to me now a very ranting unnatural performer. Perhaps indeed as I was come from Paris, I rather judged him by an unfair comparison, than by his own independent value. Perhaps too I was too much struck with the ridiculous figure of Voltaire at seventy acting a Tartar Conqueror with a hollow broken voice, and making love to a very ugly niece of about fifty. The play began at eight in the evening and ended (entertainment and all) about half an hour after eleven. The whole Company was asked to stay and set Down about twelve to a very elegant supper of a hundred Covers. The supper ended about two, the company danced till four, when we broke up, got into our Coaches and came back to Geneva, just as the Gates were opened. Shew me in history or fable, a famous poet of Seventy who has acted in his own plays, and has closed the scene with a supper and ball for a hundred people. I think the last is the more extraordinary of the two.

Gibbon, letter from Lausanne, August 6, 1763, to his mother, Judith Gibbon, in *The Letters of Edward Gibbon* (1956), 1:154–155.

Before I was recalled from Switzerland, I had the satisfaction of seeing the most extraordinary man of the age; a poet, an historian, a philosopher, who has filled thirty quartos, of prose and verse, with his various productions, often excellent, and always entertaining. Need I add the name Voltaire? After forfeiting, by his own misconduct, the friendship of the first of kings, he retired, at the age of sixty, with a plentiful fortune, to a free and beautiful country, and resided two winters (1757 and 1758) in the town or neighborhood of Lausanne. My desire of beholding Voltaire, whom I then rated above his real magnitude, was easily gratified. He received me with civility as an English youth; but I cannot boast of any particular notice or distinction, *Virgilium vidi tantum.*

Gibbon, *The Miscellaneous Works of Edward Gibbon* (1796), 1:72. Gibbon cited a line from Ovid's *Tristia*, "Virgilium vidi tantum" ("So far I have only seen Virgil") to signify that he had not truly gotten to know Voltaire but had merely been in his presence. Voltaire's forfeiture of "the friendship of the first of kings" refers to his spectacular falling out with Frederick the Great.

Johann Wolfgang von Goethe (1749–1832)

GERMAN POET, DRAMATIST, PHILOSOPHER, CRITIC, AND STATESMAN

It has been found that certain monarchs unite all the talents and powers of their race. It was thus with Louis XIV: and it is so with authors. In this sense Voltaire is the greatest of all conceivable Frenchmen.

Quoted in a postscript to a letter by Henry Crabb Robinson, dated May 15, 1808, to Mrs. Thomas Clarkson, published in Samuel Taylor Coleridge, *Notes and Lectures upon Shakespeare and Some of the Old Poets and Dramatists* (1849), 334.

Es gehen mir wunderliche Gedanken durch den Kopf, sagte er, wenn ich bedenke, daß dieses Buch noch jetzt in einer Sprache gilt, in der vor funfzig Jahren Voltaire geherrscht hat. Sie können sich hiebey nicht denken was ich mir denke, und haben keinen Begriff von der Bedeutung, die Voltaire und seine großen Zeitgenossen in meiner Jugend hatten, und wie sie die ganze sittliche Welt beherrschten. Es geht aus meiner Biographie nicht deutlich hervor was diese Männer für einen Einfluß auf meine Jugend gehabt, und was es mich gekostet, mich gegen sie zu wehren und mich auf eigene Füße in ein wahreres Verhältnis zur Natur zu stellen.

I have some singular thoughts in my head, on finding this book translated into a language over which Voltaire had the mastery fifty years since. You cannot understand my thoughts upon this subject, because you can have no idea of the influence which Voltaire and his great contemporaries had over me in my youth, as over the whole civilized world. My biography does not clearly show how powerful was the influence of these men in those years; how difficult it was for me to defend myself against them, to maintain my own ground, and true relation to nature.

Speaking of Voltaire and a French edition of *Faust* he was reading; from Eckermann, *Gespräche mit Goethe in den lezten Jahren seines Lebens* (1836), 1169–1170, entry for January 3, 1830. This translation is from Fuller, *Conversations with Goethe* (1839), 329. Eckermann said that the conversations he published were not exact records but rather reconstructions of his friend's words. Eckermann was himself a poet and an author. Nietzsche hailed *Gespräche mit Goethe* as "the best German book there is." For a recent translation of this passage see Hammer, *Goethe and Rousseau* (2015), 52.

Attributed to Goethe

Voltaire had dissolved all the good old human bonds.

Comment said to date from November 1799, quoted in the section "France and Voltaire," in H. F. Grimm, *Literature* (1886), 89, the English edition of Grimm's book *Fünfzehn Essays* (1874). There seems to be no such quote in the equivalent chapter, "Voltaire und Frankreich," or elsewhere in the German text.

Voltaire will always be regarded as the greatest man in literature of modern times, and, perhaps, even of all times; as the most astonishing creation of the Author of nature, a creation in which he pleased himself to assemble, once, in the frail and perishable body of a man, all the varieties of talent, all the glories of genius, all the powers of thought.

This is part of an extensive quotation reprinted by James Parton in his *Life of Voltaire* (1881, 2:494), from an unnamed edition of Voltaire's complete works. Theodore Besterman published a slightly botched snippet from the same quote in his biography *Voltaire* (1969, 528). He said it came "from Goethe's notes on his edition of Diderot's *Neveu de Rameau*." Arsène Houssaye, a generation before Parton, in his book *Le Roi Voltaire* (1858, 401), offered this French translation of the quote cited here:

Voltaire sera toujours regardé comme le plus grand homme en littérature des temps modernes, et peut-être même de tous les siècles; comme la création la plus étonnante de l'auteur de la nature, création où il s'est plû à rassembler une seule fois, dans la frêle organisation humaine, toutes les variétés du talent, toutes les gloires du génie, toutes les puissances de la pensée.

Après avoir enfanté Voltaire, la nature se reposa.

After giving birth to Voltaire, Nature rested.

Quoted, with no source given, in Houssaye, *Le Roi Voltaire* (1858), i.

Avec Voltaire, c'est un monde qui finit; avec Rousseau, c'est un monde qui commence.

With Voltaire, a world comes to an end; with Rousseau, a new world begins.

Lintilhac, "Le vrai 'système' de Jean-Jacques Rousseau" (1892), 118. According to Lintilhac, Goethe made this prediction "at the start" of the nineteenth century.

Joseph d'Hémery (1722–1806)

FRENCH POLICE OFFICIAL AND ROYAL INSPECTOR
OF THE BOOK TRADE

SIGNALEMENT: Grand, sec et l'air d'un satyre.
    C'est un Aigle pour l'Esprit et un fort mauvais sujet pour les sentimens, tout le monde connoit ses ouvrages et ses aventures. Il est de l'academie francoise. Maď. Denis est sa nièce.

DESCRIPTION: Tall, thin and resembles a satyr.

Intellectually, he is an Eagle, and a very poor subject in matters of the heart, everyone knows his works and his adventures. He is in the Académie française. Mme Denis is his niece.

Comments in the official Paris police file on Voltaire, January 1, 1748. The original is at the Bibliothèque Nationale de France. See Angremy et al., *Voltaire* (1979), 49–50, with a photograph of the document.

Aaron Hill (1685–1750)

ENGLISH AUTHOR, POET, DRAMATIST, AND MANAGER OF THE THEATRE ROYAL, DRURY LANE

I FOUND you born for no one country, by the embracing wideness of your sentiments; for, since you *think* for all mankind, all ages and all languages will claim the merit of your genius.

Letter from Westminster, June 3, 1736, to Voltaire in Paris. In Hill, *The Works of the Late Aaron Hill, Esq* (1753), 1:242. In 1733, Hill adapted Voltaire's tragedy *Zaïre* into English. *Zara*, Hill's play, was staged in London in January 1736. Also in 1736 and 1749, respectively, he staged English-language versions of Voltaire's *Alzire* and *Mérope*.

Jean Huber (1721–1786)

PATRICIAN GENEVAN ARTIST AND NATURALIST

M. de Voltaire (qui par parenthese est le plus inepte des beaux Esprits en fait d'Arts) . . . celui des vrais connoisseurs quand [sic] à la profonde erudition, la finesse et l'étendue des Lumiéres, et le feu du Stile.

M. de Voltaire (who, parenthetically, is the most inept of great Intellects with respect to the Arts) . . . a true connoisseur in terms of his profound erudition, the finesse and range of his Knowledge, and the passion of his Style.

Letter from Geneva, February 10, 1775, to the sculptor Étienne-Maurice Falconet in St. Petersburg, Russia, from a copy in the hand of François Tronchin at the Bibliothèque Publique et Universitaire, Geneva, Tronchin Archives, vol. 180, no. 60. See Besterman, *The Complete Works of Voltaire* (1975), 125:203 (commentary on letter D19192).

David Hume (1711–1776)

SCOTTISH HISTORIAN, PHILOSOPHER, ESSAYIST, AND ECONOMIST

The Fate of poor Voltaire will terrify all men of Genus from trusting themselves with his Prussian Majesty, who, tho' one of the most illustrious

Characters of the Age, is too much a Rival to be a very constant Patron. We have strange Stories with regard to Voltaire. It is pretended, that that sprightly, agreeable, libertine Wit has at last thrown himself into a Convent, has recanted all his Heresies, and is doing voluntary Pennance for his past Transgressions. But this I have a great Difficulty to believe. It is probably the Invention of Bigots, in order to throw a Ridicule on him & other Freethinkers.

Letter from Edinburgh, October 24, 1754, to abbé Jean-Bernard Le Blanc in Paris. In Hume, *The Letters of David Hume* (1932), 207–208.

That Author cannot be depended on with regard to Facts; but his general Views are sometimes sound, & always entertaining.

Letter from Edinburgh, May 1, 1760, to Sir Gilbert Elliot, Lord Minto, presumably at Minto House, Roxburghshire, Scotland. In Hume, *The Letters of David Hume* (1932), 326.

When I arriv'd here, all M Voltaire's Friends told me of the Regard he always express'd for me; and they perswaded me, that some Advances on my part were due to his Age & woud be well taken. I accordingly wrote him a Letter, in which I expressed the Esteem which are undoubtedly due to his Talents; and among other things I said, that, if I were not confind to Paris by public Business, I shou'd have a great Ambition to pay him a Visit at Geneva.

Letter from Paris, January 9, 1764, to Colonel James Edmonstoune in Geneva. In Hume, *The Letters of David Hume* (1932), 423.

Voltaire who never forgives, & never thinks any Enemy below his Notice.

Letter from Paris, April 24, 1764, to Reverend Hugh Blair in Edinburgh. In Hume, *The Letters of David Hume* (1932), 436.

Thomas Jefferson (1746–1826)

COAUTHOR OF THE DECLARATION OF INDEPENDENCE
AND THIRD PRESIDENT OF THE UNITED STATES

Behold me at length on the vaunted scene of Europe! . . . you are perhaps curious to know how this new scene has struck a savage of the mountains of America. Not advantageously I assure you. I find the general fate of humanity here, most deplorable. The truth of Voltaire's observation, offers itself perpetually, that every man here must be either the hammer or the anvil. It is a true picture of that country to which they say we shall pass hereafter, and where we are to see God and his angels in splendor, and crowds of the damned trampled under their feet.

Letter from Paris, September 30, 1785, to Carlo (Charles) Bellini in Williamsburg, Virginia, written one year after Jefferson's arrival as American envoy to France. Bellini was a professor of modern languages at Jefferson's alma mater, the College of William & Mary. See Jefferson, *The Papers of Thomas Jefferson* (1953), 568. While he was in France, Jefferson acquired a bust of Voltaire by Houdon and put it on display in the entrance hall at Monticello. It is not clear which of the two models he purchased, the one with or the one without the wig (figure 25).

Samuel Johnson (1709–1784)

ENGLISH ESSAYIST, LITERARY CRITIC, BIOGRAPHER, AND LEXICOGRAPHER

Why, Sir, it is difficult to settle the proportion of iniquity between them.

To James Boswell when asked if he thought Jean-Jacques Rousseau was "as bad a man as Voltaire." Quoted in the section for the year 1766 in Boswell's *The Life of Samuel Johnson* (1791), 1:278. Johnson had just told Boswell: "Rousseau, Sir, is a very bad man. I would sooner sign a sentence for his transportation, than that of any felon who has gone from the Old Bailey these many years."

He is a man of great intellect and little learning.

The English translation of a comment in Latin to the Paris journalist Élie-Catherine Fréron: "vir est acerrimi ingenii et paucarum literarum." According to Boswell in *The Life of Samuel Johnson* (1:223), the comment was made during Johnson's six-week stay in Paris in 1775, which lasted from late September to early November. In *A Hand-book of English and American Literature* (1883, 230), Esther J. Trimble translated Johnson's caustic description of Voltaire as being one who "possessed sharp intellect, but little learning."

No authours ever had so much fame in their own life-time as Pope and Voltaire.

To the Scottish painter Allan Ramsay at Ramsay's house in London, April 29, 1778, in the company, among others, of Sir Joshua Reynolds, president of the Royal Academy of Arts. Quoted in Boswell, *The Life of Samuel Johnson* (1791), 2:252.

Joseph Joubert (1754–1824)

FRENCH MORALIST, ESSAYIST, AND APHORIST

Voltaire avait l'âme d'un singe et l'esprit d'un ange.

Voltaire had the soul of an ape and the mind of an angel.

From Joubert, *Recueil des Pensées de M. Joubert* (1838), 193.

Il est impossible que Voltaire contente, et impossible qu'il ne plaise pas.

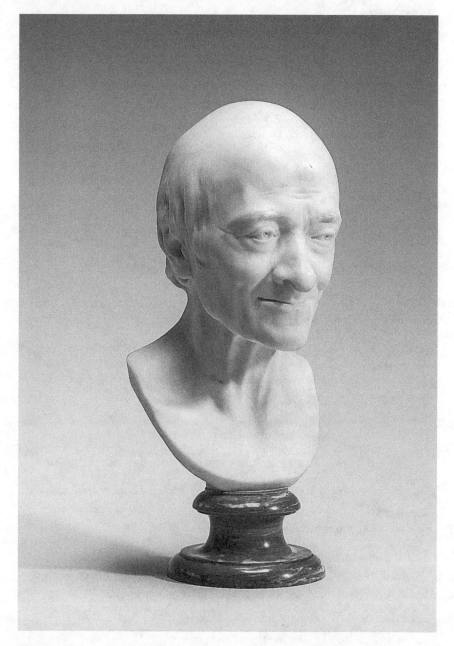

Figure 25. Jean-Antoine Houdon, marble bust of Voltaire, 1778. Chester Dale Collection, National Gallery of Art, Washington, DC. Voltaire's niece, Mme Denis, once owned this bust.

It is not possible to be satisfied with Voltaire, and impossible not to be entertained by him.

From Joubert, *Pensées, essais et maximes* (1842), 181.

Gottfried Ephraim Lessing (1729–1781)

GERMAN PLAYWRIGHT, CRITIC, AND PHILOSOPHER

Doch was hilft es, dem Herrn von Voltaire etwas einzuwenden? Er spricht, und man glaubt.

What good does it do to find fault with Voltaire? He speaks, and people believe him.

Lessing, *Laokoon: Oder über die Grensen der Mahlerey und Poesie* (1766), 384. Quoted in English in Andrews, *Voltaire* (1981), 64.

Attributed to Suzanne-Catherine Gravet de Livry (1694–1778)

ASPIRING ACTRESS AND ONE OF VOLTAIRE'S FIRST LOVERS

Monsieur Arouet était un amant à la neige.

As a lover, Monsieur Arouet was as cold as ice.

Quoted in Orieux, *Voltaire ou la royauté de l'esprit* (1966); paperback edition (1977), 2:103. Voltaire and Mlle de Livry, later marquise de La Tour de Gouvernet, were lovers circa 1716–1718. It was for her that Voltaire had Nicolas de Largillière paint his superb portrait, now at Versailles.

Scipione Maffei (1675–1755)

ITALIAN AUTHOR, PLAYWRIGHT, AND ART CRITIC

Contento ebbi in Inghilterra, quando avendomi Mylord Conte di Burlington, e il Sig. Dottore Mead, l'uno e l'altro talenti rari, . . . condotto alla villa del Sig. Pope, ch'è il Voltaire dell'Inghilterra, come voi siete il Pope della Francia.

I had the pleasure in England, when Mylord the Earl of Burlington and Dr. Mead, both of them rare talents, . . . took me to the villa of Mr. Pope, who is the Voltaire of England as you are the Pope of France.

Open letter to Voltaire, "Al Sig. di Voltaire poeta, insigne, e storico, e filosofo," in the Italian edition of Voltaire's *Mérope* translated by Maffei, *La Merope tragedia Con Annotazioni dell'Autore* (1745), 180. Maffei spent three months in England in 1736.

Elizabeth Montagu (1718–1800)

ENGLISH SOCIAL REFORMER, PATRON OF THE ARTS, CRITIC, AND COFOUNDER OF THE BLUE STOCKINGS SOCIETY

I am not indeed a great admirer of Mr. Voltaire.

Letter from Sandleford, Berkshire, October 23, 1757, to Lord Lyttelton in London. In Montagu, *The Letters of Mrs. Elizabeth Montagu* (1813), 3:66.

The Henriade is a light matter born aloft by the puffing of a little rhyme, and will dance a while in the atmosphere of France: the Iliad is strong and animated, and on immortal wings soars to the very throne of Jove.

Letter, October 23, 1757, to Lord Lyttelton. In Montagu, *The Letters of Mrs. Elizabeth Montagu* (1813), 3:67.

This creature is a downright rebel to his God. Some good may arise from the division of Satan's household; Voltaire directly opposes Lord Bolingbroke, and those who affirm whatever is is right, and that there wants not a future state to make the system just. Lord, what is man! that he shall reject the offer of another world or the enjoyment of this, as pleases his humour and serves his book.

Letter from Sandleford, July 25, 1759, to Mrs. Elizabeth Carter. In Montagu, *The Letters of Mrs. Elizabeth Montagu* (1813), 3:197.

Charles-Louis de Secondat, Baron de Montesquieu (1689–1755)

LAWYER, PHILOSOPHER, MAN OF LETTERS, AND AUTHOR OF THE *LETTRES PERSANES* AND *L'ESPRIT DES LOIS*

Voltaire n'est pas beau, il n'est que joli: il seroit honteux pour l'académie que Voltaire en fût, et il lui sera quelque jour honteux qu'il n'en ait pas été.

Les ouvrages de Voltaire sont comme les visages mal proportionnés qui brillent de jeunesse.

Voltaire n'écrira jamais une bonne histoire. Il est comme les moines, qui n'écrivent pas pour le sujet qu'ils traitent, mais pour la gloire de leur ordre. Voltaire écrit pour son couvent.

Voltaire is not handsome, he is merely pretty: it would be shameful for the Academy if he were a member, and it will some day be a matter of shame that he is not already one.

The works of Voltaire are like poorly proportioned faces that are aglow with youth.

Voltaire will never write a good history. He is like the monks who do not write for the subject at hand but for the glory of their order. Voltaire writes for his convent.

Montesquieu, "Pensées Diverses," under the subhead "Des modernes," in *Œuvres posthumes, pour servir de supplément* (1798), 208.

Attributed to Montesquieu

Il a plus que personne l'esprit que tout le monde a.

He has, more than anyone else, the wit everyone has.

First quoted apparently (with no source given), by Mme de Staël in *De l'Allemagne* (1810), 1:17. As a girl growing up near Geneva, Mme de Staël, née Germaine Necker, had met Voltaire, and she certainly heard a lot about him from family and friends, so these words, attributed properly or not to Montesquieu, must have rung true for her.

Arthur Murphy (1727–1805)

IRISH BARRISTER, JOURNALIST, ACTOR, DRAMATIST, AND CRITIC

I have observed, Sir, that you are apt to reprobate the *English* Stage with some Degree of Acrimony, whenever it comes in your Way, and that you have not hesitated to make free with our immortal *Shakespear*, after a Manner, which, in my Opinion is inconsistent with that relish for manly Sense, which seems to be your Characteristic, and in a Stile, which appears to me destitute of your usual Delicacy.

Murphy, "*To Monsieur* Voltaire" (1753), 68–69. In a later version of this same letter, revised and published in 1756, Murphy famously said, "With us islanders, *Shakespeare* is a kind of established religion in poetry."

Attributed to Alexis Piron (1689–1773)

FRENCH DRAMATIST

S'il n'avait pas écrit, il eût assassiné.

If he'd not been a writer, he'd have been a killer.

Epigram in the August 1770 *livraison* of the manuscript newsletter *Correspondance littéraire*, preceded by the note, "on n'a pu savoir le nom de l'enragé qui l'a composée." In 1818 a Jesuit scholar, François-Xavier de Feller, attributed the poem to Piron. See Grimm, Diderot, et al., *Correspondance littéraire, philosophique et critique* (1812), 263, and de Feller, *Dictionnaire historique, ou Histoire abrégée des hommes qui se sont fait un nom* (1818), 400.

Attributed to Alexander Pope (1688–1744)

ENGLISH POET

The first of the French poets.

Pope described Voltaire this way on February 27, 1727, according to Reverend Joseph Spence in Spence, *Observations, Anecdotes, and Characters* (1966), 222.

Attributed to Père Charles Porée (1665–1741)

FRENCH PRIEST, POET, AUTHOR, AND ONE OF VOLTAIRE'S
TEACHERS AT THE JESUIT *COLLÈGE* LOUIS-LE-GRAND

Il aimait à peser, disait le pere Porée, dans ses petites balances, les grands intérêts de l'Europe.

He loved to weigh in his small set of scales the great interests of Europe.

Quoted in Duvernet, *La Vie de Voltaire* (1786), 24. Père Porée was describing young Arouet, his pupil, at age fifteen or sixteen, circa 1709–1710. See also Pomeau, *D'Arouet à Voltaire* (1988), 45–46.

Jean-Jacques Rousseau (1712–1778)

GENEVA-BORN WRITER, PHILOSOPHER, AMATEUR BOTANIST,
AND VOLTAIRE'S MOST FAMOUS BÊTE NOIRE

Tous mes griefs sont . . . contre votre poëme sur le désastre de Lisbonne, parce que j'en attendois des effets plus dignes de l'humanité qui paroît vous l'avoir inspiré. Vous reprochez à Pope & à Leibniz d'insulter à nos maux en soutenant que tout est bien, & vous amplifiez tellement le tableau de nos miseres que vous en agravez le sentiment. Aulieu des consolations que j'espérois, vous ne faites que m'affliger. On diroit que vous craignez que je ne voye pas assez combien je suis malheureux, & vous croiriez, ce semble, me tranquilliser beaucoup en me prouvant que tout est mal.

All my grievances are . . . against your poem on the Lisbon disaster, because I expected from it something more of the humanity that apparently inspired you to write it. You accuse Pope and Leibnitz of glossing over our misfortunes by maintaining that all is well, and yet the picture you paint of our suffering is so such that you make it even worse: instead of the consolations I had hoped for, you only added to my misery; it is as though you fear that I am not fully aware of how unhappy I am, and you think you are soothing me by proving that everything is bad.

Letter from L'Ermitage at Montmorency, north of Paris, August 18, 1756, to Voltaire at Les Délices, transmitted by Dr. Théodore Tronchin; in Rousseau, *Lettres de J. J. Rousseau* (1765), 3–4. For a modern edition of this long letter see Besterman, *The Complete Works of Voltaire* (1971), 101:280 (letter D6973). Voltaire wrote a polite response to Rousseau's letter on September 12, 1756, but his ultimate response and statement on the Panglossian philosophizing of Pope and Leibniz was *Candide*.

Je ne vous aime point, Monsieur; vous m'avez fait les maux qui pouvaient m'être les plus sensibles, à moi, votre disciple et votre enthousiaste. Vous avez perdu

Genève pour le prix de l'asile que vous y avez reçu; vous avez aliéné de moi mes concitoyens pour le prix des applaudissements que je vous ai prodigués parmi eux; c'est vous qui me rendez le séjour de mon pays insupportable; c'est vous qui me ferez mourir en terre étrangère, privé de toutes les consolations des mourants, et jeté pour tout honneur dans une voirie, tandis que tous les honneurs qu'un homme peut attendre vous accompagneront dans mon pays. Je vous hais, enfin, puisque vous l'avez voulu; mais je vous hais en homme plus digne de vous aimer si vous l'aviez voulu.

I do not like you, Sir; you have inflicted great pain on me, your disciple and ardent admirer. You have brought ruin on Geneva in payment for the asylum accorded you there; you repaid the praises I heaped upon you among my fellow citizens by alienating them from me; you make it impossible for me to live in my native land; because of you, I will die on foreign soil, deprived of the consolations due a dying man, and be thrown, dishonored, into a common grave, while all the honors a man can expect will be granted to you in my native land. In short, I hate you, which is just as you have wished; but I hate you as a man worthy of having loved you, had you but wished it.

Letter from Montmorency, July 17, 1760, to Voltaire at Les Délices.

Frappé de voir ce pauvre homme accablé, pour ainsi dire, de prospérité & de gloire, déclamer toutefois amérement contre les miseres de la vie & trouver toujours que tout étoit mal, je formai l'insensé projet de le faire rentrer en lui-même, & de lui prouver que tout étoit bien. Voltaire, en paroissant toujours croire en Dieu, n'a réellement jamais cru qu'au Diable; puisque son dieu prétendu n'est qu'un être malfaisant, qui, selon lui, ne prend du plaisir qu'à nuire.

Shocked to see this poor man crushed, as it were, by fame and prosperity, and yet railing bitterly against the miseries of life, and declaring everything about it to be bad, I formed the foolish plan of bringing him back to himself, and proving to him that all was well. Voltaire, while always appearing to believe in God, has never really believed in anything but the Devil; since his so-called god is nothing but a malevolent being, who, according to him, derives no pleasure except in malice.

Rousseau, *Les Confessions*, part 2, book 9 (1765), published posthumously in *Seconde Partie des Confessions de J. J. Rousseau* (1790), 355. Rousseau had carried out his "foolish plan" in his famous letter of August 18, 1756, quoted above.

Adam Smith (1723–1790)

SCOTTISH PHILOSOPHER AND ECONOMIC HISTORIAN

Sir, there has been but one Voltaire.

To Samuel Rogers, who, in Rogers's words, happened "to remark of some writer that he was rather superficial, a Voltaire." Quoted in Clayden, *The Early Life of Samuel Rogers* (1887), 110–111, from an entry in Rogers's diary in 1789.

Reason, reason owes him incalculable obligations. The ridicule and sarcasms which he so plentifully bestowed upon fanatics and heretics of all sects have enabled the understanding of men to bear the light of truth, and prepared them for those inquiries to which every intelligent mind ought to aspire. He has done much more for the benefit of mankind than those grave philosophers whose books are read by a few only. The writings of Voltaire are made for all and read by all.

Quoted in Rae, *Life of Adam Smith* (1895, 190), speaking to a French visitor, Barthélemy Faujas de Saint-Fond, as Smith showed him "a fine bust of Voltaire he had in his room."

Reverend Joseph Spence (1699–1768)

ENGLISH SCHOLAR AND COLLECTOR OF ANECDOTES

Voltaire, like the French in general, showed the greatest complaisance outwardly, and the greatest contempt for us inwardly.

Spence, *Observations, Anecdotes, and Characters of Books and Men* (1966), 344. This line does not appear in the first edition of this book, published in London in 1820.

Jonathan Swift (1667–1745)

ANGLO-IRISH CLERIC, DEAN OF ST. PATRICK'S CATHEDRAL
IN DUBLIN, ESSAYIST, POET, AND SATIRIST

The author of the following Discourse, Monsieur *de Voltaire*, is a young *French Gentleman*, and allowed to be the most celebrated Poet of that Kingdom. He hath been some years composing an *Heroick Poem upon Henry the Great*. But being falsely accused for writing a Libel, he was put into the *Bastile*, and confined there in a Dungeon several Months, till the true Author was discovered. He there suffered much in his Health, and having been known to some *English* persons of Quality then at Paris, he was invited over to *England*. His *Heroick Poem* is finished, and now printing in London by Subscription, being encouraged by the Crown and most of the Nobility. He had not been above eleven Months in *England*, when he wrote the following Treatise, intended

Figure 26. Jean-Étienne Liotard, *François Tronchin*, 1757. Pastel on parchment. Cleveland Museum of Art (John L. Severance Fund 1978.54).

as an Assistance to those who shall read his Poem, and may not be sufficiently informed in the History of that Great Prince.

Swift, "A Short Account of the Author," one-page preface to the first Irish edition of Voltaire's *Essay on Epick Poetry* (1728), signed "J.S.D.D.D.S.P.D." ("Jonathan Swift, Doctor of Divinity, Dean of St. Patrick's, Dublin").

François Tronchin (1704–1798)

GENEVAN ART AND LITERARY CONNOISSEUR, FRIEND OF VOLTAIRE, AND COUSIN OF DR. THÉODORE TRONCHIN

Il fait autorité sur la partie de littérature, mais il n'ôte point le bandeau du juge de dessus ses yeux pour rendre ses arrêtés sur les arts.

He passes for an authority in the realm of literature but as a critic is blinkered when making his pronouncements on the fine arts.

Letter from Geneva, February 14, 1775, to Prince Gallitzin, at the court of Catherine the Great in Russia, from a copy in Tronchin's hand at the Bibliothèque Publique et

Universitaire, Geneva, Tronchin Archives, vol. 180, no. 57. Quoted in Tronchin, *Le Conseiller François Tronchin et ses amis* (1895), 289–290, and Besterman, *The Complete Works of Voltaire* (1975), 125:203, in Besterman's commentary on letter D19192.

Voltaire n'avait aucune teinture des arts libéraux. Dessin, peinture, sculpture, architecture, musique, il manquait sur tous ces objets de connaissance et de goût.

Voltaire had not a smattering of the fine arts. Drawing, painting, sculpture, architecture, music, in all these he was wanting in both knowledge and taste.

Manuscript note, circa 1781, Tronchin Archives, Geneva. Quoted in Tronchin, *Le Conseiller François Tronchin et ses amis* (1895), 290, and Diderot, *Correspondance* (1961), 86n7.

Théodore Tronchin (1709–1781)

ONE OF THE LEADING MEDICAL DOCTORS IN EUROPE, WHO PRACTICED IN AMSTERDAM, GENEVA, AND PARIS

Que peut-on attendre d'un homme qui est presque toujours en contradiction avec lui-même, et dont le cœur a toujours été la dupe de l'esprit. Son état moral a été dès sa plus tendre enfance si peu naturel et si altéré que son être actuel fait un tout artificiel qui ne ressemble à rien. De tous les hommes qui coexistent, celui qu'il connaît le moins c'est lui-même. Tous les rapports de lui aux autres hommes et des autres hommes à lui sont dérangés. Il a voulu plus de bonheur qu'il n'en pouvait prétendre, l'excès de ses prétensions l'a conduit insensiblement à cette espèce d'injustice que les lois ne condamnent pas mais que la raison désaprouve. Il n'a pas enlevé le blé de son voisin, il n'a pas pris son bœuf ou sa vache, mais il a fait d'autres rapines pour se donner une réputation et une supériorité que l'homme sage méprise, parce qu'elle est toujours trop chère. Peut-être n'a-t-il pas été assez délicat sur le choix des moyens. Les louanges et les cajoleries de ses admirateurs ont achevé ce que ses prétensions immodérés avaient commencé, et, croyant en être le maître, il est devenu l'esclave de ses admirateurs, son bonheur a dépendu d'eux. Ce fondement trompeur y a laissé des vides immenses, il s'est accoutumé aux louanges; et à quoi ne s'accoutume-t-on pas?

What can one expect from a man who is almost always in contradiction with himself, and whose heart has always been the dupe of his mind. Since his earliest childhood his moral condition has been so unnatural and so impaired that his present being makes up an artificial whole that does not resemble anything. Of all the men who co-exist, the one with whom he is least acquainted is himself. All of his relations with other men and of other men with him are unbalanced. He has wanted more happiness than he could lay claim to, the excessiveness of his claim has led him insensibly to that sort of injustice which the laws do not condemn but of which reason disapproves. He has not carried off his neighbor's grain, he has not taken his ox or his cow, but he has

committed other plundering in order to give himself a reputation and a superiority that the wise man disdains because its cost is always too high. Perhaps
he has not been fastidious enough about the choice of means. The praise and
cajolery of his admirers completed what his immoderate claims had begun and,
while believing he was their master, he has become the slave of his admirers;
his happiness depended on them. This deceptive foundation has left immense
voids in his happiness; he has become accustomed to praises and to what does
one not become accustomed?

Letter from Geneva, September 1, 1756, to Jean-Jacques Rousseau at Montmorency. In
Rousseau, *Correspondance complète de Jean-Jacques Rousseau* (1967), 93. The translation is
from Kelly and Masters, *The Collected Writings of Rousseau* (1995), 557.

*Aujourd'hui que Voltaire est près de sa fin, les bouches s'ouvrent, et je crois aperce-
voir qu'il sera pour le moins regretté. On évalue le mal qu'il a fait à la société, que
des gens qui ne sont pas infiniment sévères équivalent aux guerres, aux pestes et aux
famines qui depuis quelques milliers d'années ont désolé la terre. Ce qui m'a le plus
étonné, c'est que cette évaluation se fait par ce qu'on appelle les gens du monde. J'étais
hier chez M. le duc de Penthièvre, où un élégant entra. Il en parla du même ton.*

Now that Voltaire is almost dead, people are starting to talk, and I get the
impression that, at the very least, he will be missed. They talk about his inim-
ical impact on society that some, far less rigorous than others, compare to the
wars, plagues, and famines that have afflicted the world for thousands of years.
What astonished me most is that these views are held by so-called men of
the world. Yesterday I was at the home of the duc de Penthièvre where an
elegant young man came in speaking in precisely such terms.

Letter from Paris, May 10, 1778, to his cousin François Tronchin at Les Délices. See Besterman, *The Complete Works of Voltaire* (1977), 129:314 (letter D21182).

Abbé Nicolas-Charles-Joseph Trublet (1697–1770)

CANON OF SAINT-MALO IN BRITTANY, AUTHOR,
AND CRITIC OF VOLTAIRE

On a osé dire de la Henriade, *& on l'a dit sans malignité:* Je ne sais pourquoi je
bâille en la lisant.

One has dared say of the *Henriade*, and it was said without malice: *I don't know
why but I yawn as I read it.*

Trublet, *Essais sur divers sujets de Littérature et de Morale* (1760), 232–433. In a letter to
Trublet, April 27, 1761, Voltaire said: "vous aviez imprimé que je vous fesais bâiller, et moi
j'ai laissé imprimer que je me mettais à rire. Il résulte de cela que vous êtes difficile à amuser,

et que je suis mauvais plaisant." In his third *Satire* (1666), the poet and critic Boileau had used the words "Je ne sais pourquoi je bâille en la lisant" to disparage an epic poem by Jean Chapelain.

Ce n'est pas le Poëte qui ennuye *& fait* bâiller *dans la* Henriade, *c'est la poësie, ou plutôt les vers.*

It is not the Poet who *is boring* and makes us *yawn* in the *Henriade*, it is the poetry, or rather the verse.

Trublet, *Essais sur divers sujets de Littérature et de Morale* (1760), 233. On page 234 Trublet said he wished the *Henriade* had been written in prose, adding that no one was more capable of doing so than Voltaire. ("Je voudrois que M. de *Voltaire* eût composé la *Henriade* en prose. Jamais personne ne fut plus capable que lui de la sorte de prose convenable à un pareil ouvrage.")

Attributed to Dr. Edward Young (1683–1765)

ENGLISH LAWYER, POET, AND CLERGYMAN

Thou art so witty, profligate and thin,
Thou seem'st a Milton, with his Death and Sin.

According to the 1766 edition of *The Annual Register*, this epigram was prompted by Voltaire having, in Young's presence, ridiculed Milton and the allegorical figures of death and sin. According to Leigh Hunt, this alleged incident, if true, would have happened at Lord Chesterfield's house while Voltaire was in England in 1726–1728. See "The Life of the Late Celebrated Dr. Edward Young," in *The Annual Register, or a View of the History, Politicks, and Literature, For the Year 1765* (1766), in the section titled "Characters," 35; and Hunt, *The Town* (1848), 174.

Voltaire! Long life's the greatest curse,
   That mortals can receive,
When they imagine the chief end
   Of living is to live;

Young, Quatrain in "Resignation," part 2, in *The Complete Works, Poetry and Prose* (1854), 121. Voltaire is mentioned several times in this long poem.

POSTERITY WEIGHS IN

Henry Adams (1838–1918)

HISTORIAN AND GRANDSON OF JOHN QUINCY ADAMS

He professed in theory equal distrust of English thought, and called it a huge rag-bag of *bric-à-brac*, sometimes precious but never sure. For him, only the

Greek, the Italian or the French standards had claims to respect, and the barbarism of Shakespeare was as flagrant as to Voltaire; but his theory never affected his practice. He knew that his artistic standard was the illusion of his own mind; that English disorder approached nearer to truth, if truth existed, than French measure or Italian line, or German logic.

Henry Adams speaking of himself in the third person in *The Education of Henry Adams* (1907), 368.

Richard Aldington (1892–1962)

ENGLISH WRITER AND POET

Voltaire's poetry . . . in several respects is greatly superior to that of his rivals in the genre; but if the reader has acquired the impression that it is seldom more than half-serious and never profound, that is very nearly correct. Voltaire attempted several kinds of shorter poems, not all with the same success. His *Odes* are disastrous exercises in rhetoric, completely unreadable, and certainly inferior to those of J. B. Rousseau, his master in this very difficult form.

Aldington, *Voltaire* (1925), 148.

A. Owen Aldridge (1915–2005)

PROFESSOR OF FRENCH AND COMPARATIVE LITERATURE AT THE UNIVERSITY OF ILLINOIS

Emilie is said to have had something of the emasculating effect upon Voltaire that Mrs. Clemens is supposed to have had upon Mark Twain in preventing the latter from becoming an American Voltaire.

Aldridge, *Voltaire and the Century of Light* (1975), 141.

Garry Apgar (1945–)

ART HISTORIAN, EDITOR, AND CARTOONIST

He was the classic *artiste engagé*, probably more involved in the passions and tides of his time than any major writer before or since.

Apgar, "Voltaire, Superstar" (1978), 15.

The Grand Old Man of the Enlightenment.

From the script, cowritten and edited by George W. Gowen and Patrick H. Ryan, for the twenty-three-minute documentary *Voltaire & Jefferson*, narrated by Cliff Robertson (2001).

Over the course of his sixty-year career, the sharp-witted French *philosophe* amassed a vaunted and voluminous body of writing. In old age, he was revered as an apostle of tolerance and human freedom, and was the first non-royal to achieve iconic status in his own lifetime.

Apgar, *Mickey Mouse* (2015), 276.

Herbert Aptheker (1925–2003)

AMERICAN MARXIST HISTORIAN, MEMBER OF THE COMMUNIST PARTY, AND POLITICAL ACTIVIST

When the 72-year old Franklin and the 84-year old Voltaire were presented to each other before the Paris Academy of Sciences in 1778, the assembled savants stormed and cheered while Solon and Sophocles embraced and kissed and wept. The tears and cheers reflected the hopes of the Age of Enlightenment that it might yet come into its own. The United States of America was the national embodiment of that international aspiration.

Aptheker, *The American Revolution, 1763–1783* (1960), 206.

Matthew Arnold (1822–1888)

ENGLISH POET AND CRITIC

The chief sources of intellectual influence in Europe, during the last century and a half, have been three chief critics—Voltaire, Lessing, Goethe.

Arnold, "The Bishop and the Philosopher" (1863), 241.

A court of literature can never be very severe with Voltaire: with that inimitable wit and clear sense of his, he cannot write a page in which the fullest head may not find something suggestive: still, because, handling religious ideas, he yet, with all his wit and clear sense, handles them wholly without the power of edification, his frame as a great man is equivocal.

Arnold, "The Bishop and the Philosopher" (1863), 254.

W. H. Auden (1907–1973)

ANGLO-AMERICAN POET

Voltaire was not only one of the greatest Europeans of all time but, though he might be surprised to hear it, one of the greatest fighters for democracy, and one who should be as much a hero to us as Socrates or Jefferson.

Auden, "A Great Democrat" (1939), 352.

Voltaire has suffered the greatest misfortune that can befall a writer; he has become a legend, which insures that he will not be read until someone destroys the legend.

Auden, "A Great Democrat" (1939), 352.

Far off in Paris, where his enemies
Whispered that he was wicked, in an upright chair
A blind woman longed for death and letters. He would write
"Nothing is better than life." But was it? Yes, the fight
Against the false and the unfair,
Was always worth it. So was gardening. Civilise.

Auden, "Voltaire at Ferney," second stanza, in *Collected Poetry of W. H. Auden* (1945), 6. The "blind woman" was the *salonnière* Mme Du Deffand.

A. J. Ayer (1910–1989)

ENGLISH PHILOSOPHER AND PROFESSOR OF PHILOSOPHY AT UNIVERSITY COLLEGE LONDON AND THE UNIVERSITY OF OXFORD

It is clear enough that he was not an atheist. Like other pre-Kantian philosophers, he accepted the argument from design. He saw no fallacy in assuming that it was valid to speak of the world as of a house which pre-supposed an architect. We may allow also that he felt at least an intermittent impulse to worship the God of whose existence he was intellectually convinced. Whether he believed in a personal and benevolent God is more doubtful. The most that can fairly be said, I think, is that he felt that such a God was required to redress the balance of evil in the world over good, and that, with his great sense of justice, he could not bear the thought that it might after all go unredressed. I agree with Mr. Noyes in regarding the lines in the poem on the Lisbon earthquake *Un jour, tout sera bien, voilà notre espérance; Tout est bien aujourd'hui, voilà l'illusion* as truly expressive of Voltaire's attitude. But it must be stressed that this religious optimism was in him no more than a hope.

Ayer, "A Sanctified Voltaire" (1936), 1052, a review of Alfred Noyes's biography *Voltaire* (1936).

Julian Baggini (1968–)

ENGLISH PHILOSOPHER

We must, as Voltaire suggested, defend to the death the rights of people to say what we may strongly disagree with.

Baggini, *The Pig That Wants to Be Eaten* (2006), 98. This is another example of an eminent intellectual or media figure getting Evelyn Beatrice Hall's paraphrase of Voltaire's thinking wrong.

Mikhail Bakunin (1814–1876)

RUSSIAN "SOCIAL ANARCHIST"

Amoureux et jaloux de la liberté humaine, et la considérant comme la condition absolue de tout ce que nous adorons et respectons dans l'humanité, je retourne la phrase de Voltaire, et je dis que: si Dieu existait réellement, il faudrait le faire disparaître.

A jealous lover of human liberty, and deeming it the absolute condition of all that we admire and respect in humanity, I reverse the phrase of Voltaire, and say that, *if God existed, it would be necessary to abolish him.*

Bakunin, *L'Empire Knouto-Germanique et la Révolution sociale* (1908), 48. The original text, written in French in 1871, was first published as *Dieu et l'État* (1882). The translation is from the first American edition, *God and the State* (1883).

Roland Barthes (1915–1980)

FRENCH LITERARY THEORIST AND CRITIC

En somme, ce qui nous sépare peut-être de Voltaire, c'est qu'il fut écrivain heureux. Nul mieux que lui n'a donné au combat de la Raison l'allure d'une fête. Tout était spectacle dans ses batailles: le nom de l'adversaire, toujours ridicule, la doctrine combattue, réduite à une proposition (l'ironie voltairienne est toujours la mise en évidence d'une disproportion); la multiplication des coups, fusant dans toutes les directions, au point d'en paraître un jeu, ce qui dispense de tout respect et de toute pitié; la mobilité même du combattant, ici déguisé sous mille pseudonymes transparents, là faisant de ses voyages européens une sorte de comédie d'esquive, une scapinade perpétuelle.

In short, what may separate us from Voltaire is that he was a happy writer. No one brought a more festive air to the fight for Reason than he. Everything about his battles was spectacular: the name of his adversary, always ridiculous, the doctrine being fought, reduced to a single proposition (Voltairian irony always involves exposing disproportion); the many shots fired in every direction, as if it were a game, doing away with any sense of propriety and pity; the very mobility of the warrior, here hiding behind a thousand obviously fake names, there turning his continental travels into a kind of comic hit-and-run, an unending, impish romp.

Barthes, "Voltaire, le Dernier des écrivains heureux" (1964), 98, first published in *Actualité littéraire*, March 1958. The American scholar Patrick Henry said that Barthes's Marxist perspective in this essay offers "an absolute negation of the relevancy of Voltaire to the modern world" and betrays a "limited view of the most prolific writer of the French Enlightenment." Nicholas Cronk called Barthes's point of view condescending. See Henry, "Contre Barthes," in *Studies on Voltaire and the Eighteenth Century* (1987), 19, and the introduction to Cronk, *The Cambridge Companion to Voltaire* (2009), 4.

Voltaire fut un écrivain heureux, mais ce fut sans doute le dernier.

Voltaire was a happy writer, but he was no doubt the last.

Barthes, "Voltaire, le dernier des écrivains heureux" (1964), 100.

Jacques Barzun (1907–2012)

FRENCH-BORN PROFESSOR OF HISTORY AT CAMBRIDGE UNIVERSITY AND COLUMBIA UNIVERSITY

This fledgling philosopher spoke in a new voice. His prose was rapid, trenchant, sinewy. One might suppose that these adjectives apply as much to Voltaire, but the two styles are worlds apart: Diderot's tone becomes less and less "polite" as he becomes more and more himself.

Barzun referring to Diderot in "Why Diderot?" (1962), 35, reprinted in *A Jacques Barzun Reader* (2002), 207.

It is in the third chapter of this tale that the hero after which it is named takes up the study of nature to console himself for his marital troubles and uses the observation of natural facts to infer facts he has not seen. However implausible and "agrarian" his method, he is the first systematic detective in modern literature, and that priority itself adds to his troubles in the story until his royal vindication.

Talking about Voltaire's character Zadig in Barzun and Taylor, *A Catalogue of Crime* (1971), 417–418.

Needless to say, the spirit of *Candide* is not that of the musical that has been made from it, but neither is Voltaire's advice in *Candide* that of a disillusioned old man. He held the same view of human affairs long before the tale, when he was busy as a writer of histories. The world has forgotten how much he did to inform his age and create in it the sense of history that was to dominate the next century.

Barzun, *From Dawn to Decadence* (2000), 379.

Candide is a tale that takes you all over the world depicting the misfortunes that await an innocent but not stupid young man. The people are appalling and the events entertaining—high comedy.

Barzun, "Why Read Crime Fiction?," in *A Jacques Barzun Reader* (2002), 572.

Charles Baudelaire (1821–1867)

FRENCH CRITIC AND POET

Je m'ennuie en France, surtout parce que tout le monde y ressemble à Voltaire. Emerson a oublié Voltaire dans ses Représentants de l'humanité. *Il aurait pu faire un joli chapitre intitulé:* Voltaire, ou l'anti-poète, *le roi des badauds, le prince des superficiels, l'anti-artiste, le prédicateur des concierges,* ~~la mère-Gig~~ *le père-Gigogne des rédacteurs du Siècle.*

I grow bored in France, chiefly because everybody here resembles Voltaire. Emerson left Voltaire out of his *Representative Men*. He could have written a fine chapter entitled: *Voltaire*, or the *anti-poet*, the king of the boobs, prince of the superficial, the anti-artist, preacher for concierges, ~~the Mothe Go~~ the Father Goose of the journalists at *Le Siècle*.

One of dozens of notes by Baudelaire penned between 1859 and 1866. Titled *Mon cœur mis à nu*, they first appeared in print in Baudelaire's *Œuvres posthumes* (1887). This is note 29, based on the transcription in *Mon cœur mis à nu* (2001). *Le Siècle* was a republican newspaper, opposed to the regime of Napoleon III, and a great admirer of Voltaire.

Dans les oreilles du Comte Chesterfield, Voltaire plaisante sur cette âme immortelle qui a résidé, pendant neuf mois, entre des excréments et des urines. Voltaire, comme tous les paresseux, haïssait le mystère.

In *Lord Chesterfield's Ears*, Voltaire jokes at the expense of that immortal soul which resided, for nine months, amid excrement and urine. Voltaire, like all who are slothful, hates mystery.

Speaking about an unborn child in its mother's womb, in *Baudelaire, His Prose and Poetry* (1919), 233. The French is from note 30, *feuillet* 18 (1859–1866), in Pichois, *Mon cœur mis à nu*. The short tale, *Les Oreilles du comte Chesterfield* (*Lord Chesterfields's Ears*), was first published in 1775.

Simone de Beauvoir (1908–1986)

FRENCH FEMINIST, PHILOSOPHER, AND AUTHOR

Rousseau qui se fait . . . l'interprète de la bourgeoisie voue la femme à son mari et à la maternité. "Toute l'éducation des femmes doit être relative aux hommes. . . . La femme est faite pour céder à l'homme et pour supporter ses injustices," affirme-t-il. Cependant l'idéal démocratique et individualiste du XVIIIème siècle est favorable aux femmes; elles apparaissent à la plupart des philosophes comme des êtres humains égaux à ceux du sexe fort. Voltaire dénonce l'injustice de leur sort. Diderot considère que leur infériorité a été en grande partie faite par la société.

Rousseau is the spokesman of the bourgeoisie and dooms woman to her husband and motherhood. "All the education of women should be relative to men. . . . Woman is made to yield to man and to bear his injustices," he asserts. However, the democratic and individualist ideal of the eighteenth century is favorable to women; for most philosophers they are human beings equal to those of the strong sex. Voltaire denounces the injustice of their lot. Diderot considers their inferiority largely *made* by society.

Beauvoir, *Le Deuxième sexe* (1953), 181. The English-language text is from the unified, one-volume translation of both volumes of *The Second Sex* (2009), 124.

E. C. Bentley (1875–1956)

ENGLISH NOVELIST, AUTHOR OF LIGHT VERSE, AND HUMORIST

It was a weakness of Voltaire's
To forget to say his prayers,
And one which to his shame
He never overcame.

Bentely, *Baseless Biography* (1939), 42.

Isaiah Berlin (1909–1987)

BRITISH SOCIAL AND POLITICAL THEORIST AND PHILOSOPHER, UNIVERSITY OF OXFORD

Voltaire is the central figure of the Enlightenment, because he accepted its basic principles and used all his incomparable wit and energy and literary skill and brilliant malice to propagate these principles and spread havoc in the enemy's camp. Ridicule kills more surely than savage indignation: and Voltaire probably did more for the triumph of civilised values than any writer who ever lived.

Berlin, "The Divorce between the Sciences and the Humanities" (1974), 21, and *The Proper Study of Mankind* (1997), 334. In a radio broadcast in 1952, Berlin called Voltaire and David Hume "really clear elegant thinkers" and Rousseau "the greatest militant lowbrow of history, a kind of guttersnipe of genius." See Berlin, *Freedom and Its Betrayal* (1952), 43, 110.

William Blake (1757–1827)

ENGLISH POET AND ARTIST

Mock on, mock on, Voltaire, Rousseau;
Mock on, mock on, 'tis all in vain!
You throw the sand against the wind,
And the wind blows it back again.
And every sand becomes a gem
Reflected in the beams divine;
Blown back they blind the mocking eye,
But still in Israel's paths they shine.

The Atoms of Democritus
And Newton's Particles of Light
Are sands upon the Red Sea shore,
Where Israel's tents do shine so bright.

Blake, "Mock on, Mock on, Voltaire, Rousseau," from the Rossetti Manuscript, part 2, written circa 1800–1810, as published in *The Selected Poems of William Blake* (1994), 108.

Michael Blankfort (1907–1982)

SCREENWRITER, PLAYWRIGHT, AND CRITIC

Mr. Kaufman has been our foremost Voltaire. (Do I hear the eminent Frenchman turn over in his grave?)

Blankfort, "George S. Kaufman," *The New Masses* (1934), 29. Kaufman won a Pulitzer Prize in 1932 for the Broadway musical *Of Thee I Sing*, cowritten with Morrie Ryskind, and again in 1937, for *You Can't Take It with You*, a play cowritten with Moss Hart.

Harold Bloom (1930–2019)

LITERARY CRITIC, AUTHOR, AND PROFESSOR
OF HUMANITIES AT YALE UNIVERSITY

Disapprovingly, Tolstoy quotes as idolators of Shakespeare a distinguished company that includes Goethe, Shelley, Victor Hugo, and Turgenev. He could have added Hegel, Stendhal, Pushkin, Manzoni, Heine, and scores of others, indeed virtually every major writer capable of reading, with a few unsavory exceptions like Voltaire.

Bloom, *The Western Canon* (1994), 58. Tolstoy rattled off this Who's Who of great names in his 1897 essay *What Is Art?*

Voltaire begins the French tradition of resistance to Shakespeare in the name of neoclassicism and the tragedies of Racine.

Bloom, *The Western Canon* (1994), 73.

Jorge Luis Borges (1899–1986)

ARGENTINE SHORT STORY WRITER,
ESSAYIST, AND POET

No pasa un día sin que usemos la palabra optimismo, que fue acuñada por Voltaire contra Leibniz, que había demostrado (a despecho del Eclesiastés y con el beneplácito de la Iglesia) que vivimos en el mejor de los mundos posibles. Voltaire, muy razonablemente, negó esa exorbitante opinión. (En buena lógica, bastaría una sola pesadilla o un solo cáncer para anularla.) Leibniz pudo haber replicado que un mundo que nos ha regalado a Voltaire tiene algún derecho a que se lo considere el mejor.

Not a day goes by that we don't use the word optimism, coined by Voltaire against Leibniz, who had demonstrated (in spite of the book of Ecclesiastes and with the Church's approval) that we live in the best of all possible worlds. Voltaire, quite reasonably, denied that outlandish opinion. (A single nightmare or cancer would, obviously, suffice to negate it.) Leibniz could have replied that a world that gave us Voltaire has some right to be considered the best.

This is the first paragraph in Borges's preface to a Spanish edition of Voltaire's short stories, *Cuentos* (1986), 9.

Alain Boublil (1941–)

FRANCO-TUNISIAN LYRICIST

and Jean-Marc Natel (1942–)

FRENCH LYRICIST

Je suis tombé par terre, c'est la faute à Voltaire,
Le nez dans le ruisseau, c'est la faute à Rousseau.
Je ne suis pas notaire, c'est la faute à Voltaire
Je suis petit oiseau, c'est la faute à Rousseau!

I've fallen to the ground, it's the fault of Voltaire.
My nose in the gutter, it's the fault of Rousseau.
I am not a notary, it's the fault of Voltaire.
I'm a little bird, it's the fault of Rousseau.

Sung by Gavroche in "C'est la faute à Voltaire," in act 1 of the original French production of *Les Misérables*, which premiered in Paris in September 1980 with music by Claude-Michel Schönberg and words by Boublil and Natel.

Harold Brackman (1946–)

HISTORIAN AND CONSULTANT FOR THE SIMON WIESENTHAL CENTER ON ISSUES OF INTOLERANCE AND TOLERANCE

Voltaire's motto was "Écrasez l'infâme"—by which he meant that all organized religion, not just infamous prejudices, should be eradicated.

Brackman, "The New York Times Whitewashes Voltaire and 'The Dark Enlightenment'" (2019).

Ray Bradbury (1920–2012)

SCIENCE FICTION WRITER

In many ways, a lot of us have shared his dream. Let's hammer together an Idea Factory and summon to it the best thinkers, blueprinters, builders of our century and blow up the concrete to let the green grass through and teach people how to breathe again. Bits and pieces of that dream collided in ancient Rome and Greece and later on in Paris, but only one man finally did it. Damn him if you must, but his Idea Factory, WED, exists and lives amongst us out in Glendale, and from it, blast it as you will, the cornucopia future will be born. Ponce de Leon would have bathed in its founts. Voltaire would have filed it with proper delight in his Philosophical Dictionary.

Talking about Walt Disney, whom Bradbury met and admired, in "Walt Disney, the Man Who Invented a Better Mouse" (1976), U3. Disney's initials were W. E. D. Hence the name WED Enterprises, now Walt Disney Imagineering, a private corporation founded in 1953 by Disney to manage the development and construction of Disneyland.

Sidney D. Braun (1912–1992)

PROFESSOR OF FRENCH AT CITY UNIVERSITY OF NEW YORK

The preëminent literary figure of the eighteenth century, he dominated, as perhaps no single writer did, the intellectual life of his time.

Dictionary of French Literature (1964), s.v. "Voltaire," 483.

Champion of reason, tolerance and progress, Voltaire was the incarnation of the eighteenth-century ideal. Though not a revolutionist, he destroyed many of the existing social abuses of the time. Contributing, through his encyclopediac output, to the philosophic movement, he undermined respect for authority and tradition, and thereby prepared the spirit of the French Revolution.

Dictionary of French Literature (1964), s.v. "Voltaire," 485.

Lionel Brett (1913–2004)

ENGLISH ARCHITECT AND TOWN PLANNER

If Le Corbusier was the Voltaire of the modern movement, Wright was its Rousseau, addressing himself particularly to simple Anglo-Saxon minds which found Le Corbusier (in translated writings and inferior photographs) chilly and highbrow.

Brett, "Wright in New York" (1953), 20.

Arthur Brisbane (1864–1936)

REPORTER, EDITOR, AND COLUMNIST WITH THE *NEW YORK SUN*, THE *NEW YORK WORLD*, AND THE *NEW YORK DAILY MIRROR*

Tex, this is "the best of all possible worlds."

Final words, to his colleague and son-in-law, Tex McCrary, early Christmas morning, 1936. Quoted in "Brisbane Rites to Be Monday" (1936), 11. Like Brisbane, McCrary was an admirer of Voltaire. He once wrote a column for the *New York Daily Mirror* called "Only Human," under the byline "Candide."

Denis W. Brogan (1900–1974)

SCOTTISH-BORN HISTORIAN, AUTHOR, AND PROFESSOR OF POLITICAL SCIENCE AT CAMBRIDGE UNIVERSITY

"Tom Paine," the "filthy little atheist" of Theodore Roosevelt's characteristically vehement denunciation . . . was a man who played a really important part in the making of the United States; who was deeply involved in the French Revolution; and who was long, for English-speaking freethinkers, a lesser Voltaire.

Published anonymously as "The English Voltaire, Tom Paine: Citizen of the World" (1937); reprinted as Brogan, "Tom Paine" (1949), 65.

Van Wyck Brooks (1886–1963)

AMERICAN CRITIC AND CULTURAL HISTORIAN

The great American satirist, the Voltaire, the Swift, the Rabelais of the Gilded Age.

Brooks talking about Mark Twain in *The Ordeal of Mark Twain* (1920), 241. According to Brooks (184), Voltaire, "whom he had read" as a young river pilot, was one of Twain's favorite writers.

Edmund Burke (1729–1797)

BRITISH POLITICAL THINKER, WHIG POLITICIAN, AND STATESMAN

Who ever dreamt of Voltaire and Rousseau as legislators? The first has the merit of writing agreeably; and nobody has ever united blasphemy and obscenity so happily together. The other was not a little deranged in his intellects to my almost certain knowledge. But he saw things in bold and uncommon lights, and he was very eloquent.

Letter to unknown recipient, January 1790, in Burke, *Selected Letters of Edmund Burke* (1984), 268.

Thanks to our sullen resistance to innovation, thanks to the cold sluggishness of our national character, we still bear the stamp of our forefathers. . . . We are not the converts of Rousseau; we are not the disciples of Voltaire; Helvétius has made no progress among us. Atheists are not our preachers; madmen are not our lawgivers. We know that *we* have made no discoveries; and we think that no discoveries are to be made, in morality; nor many in the great principles of government, nor in the ideas of liberty, which were understood long before we were born.

Burke, *Reflections on the Revolution in France* (1790), 127–128.

Aaron Burr (1756–1836)

VICE PRESIDENT UNDER THOMAS JEFFERSON, LATER ACCUSED OF TREASON

Your "nonsense" about Voltaire contains more good sense than all the strictures I have seen upon his works put together.

Letter from Philadelphia, December 15, 1791, to his wife Theodosia Burr in New York. In Charles Felton Pidgin, *Theodosia, The First Gentlewoman of Her Time* (1907), 164. Burr was an avid reader of Voltaire, especially in the 1780s.

Attributed to Burr

If I had read Sterne more, and Voltaire less, I should have known that the world was wide enough for Hamilton and me.

Figure 27. James Gillray, *Voltaire Instructing the Infant Jacobinism*, 1798. Oil painting on paper. Courtesy of New York Public Library, the Miriam and Ira D. Wallach Division of Art, Prints and Photographs.

Quoted in Parton, *The Life and Times of Aaron Burr* (1858), 673. This unsubstantiated quote inspired "The World Was Wide Enough," a song in Lin-Manuel Miranda's musical *Hamilton*, which opened on Broadway on January 20, 2015. In his biography of the man who shot and killed Hamilton, Parton noted that Burr was particularly fond of the novel *Tristram*

Shandy by Laurence Sterne, in which kindly Uncle Toby refuses to kill even a fly, saying: "Why should I hurt thee? This world surely is wide enough to hold both thee and me."

Ian Buruma (1951–)

DUTCH-BORN JOURNALIST, AUTHOR, AND EDITOR

Voltaire was proud of his garden. He thought it was an English garden. . . . He designed it himself. But in fact the style, judging from old prints and from what is still visible today, is too small, too neat, too formal, too fussy—in a word, too French—to be a truly English garden of the eighteenth century.

Buruma, *Voltaire's Coconuts or Anglomania in Europe* (1999), 21.

Voltaire still dominates Ferney today. Wherever you go, you come across the Patriarch, as he is known. There is a Voltaire art gallery, a Voltaire real estate agent, a Voltaire restaurant, a Voltaire stationer's, a Voltaire café, a Voltaire antique shop, a Voltaire school, a Voltaire cinema and a Voltaire fountain in the market square. I had a cup of coffee at the Café le Patriarche, next to a fountain gurgling under Voltaire's bust, and around me I heard French English, German, Italian, Dutch and even Persian. An overweight Iranian was talking loudly into his portable phone, while his wife and children were tackling their baguettes. On their table was a postcard of Voltaire's garden. I could almost hear a sardonic cackle come from the Patriarch's stony lips.

Buruma, *Voltaire's Coconuts or Anglomania in Europe* (1999), 45–46.

Albert Camus (1913–1960)

FRENCH WRITER AND PHILOSOPHER

Voltaire a soupçonné presque tout. Il n'a établi que très peu de choses, mais bien.

Voltaire was suspicious of almost everything. He established only a few things, but he established them well.

Camus, *Carnets II* (1964), 319; first published in Camus, *Carnets: Mai 1935–février 1951* (1962).

Thomas Carlyle (1795–1881)

SCOTTISH PHILOSOPHER, HISTORIAN, AND ESSAYIST

Goethe has been called the German Voltaire; but it is a name which does him wrong, and describes him ill. Except in the corresponding variety of their pursuits and knowledge, in which, perhaps, it does Voltaire wrong, the two cannot be compared. Goethe is all, or the best of all, that Voltaire was; and he was much that Voltaire did not dream of.

Carlyle, *German Romance* (1827), 23.

Voltaire was the *cleverest* of all past and present men; but a great man is something more, and this he surely was not.

Carlyle, *German Romance* (1827), 23.

The unbelieving French believe in their Voltaire. . . . Truly, if Christianity be the highest instance of Hero-worship, then we may find here in Voltaireism one of the lowest! He whose life was that of a kind of Antichrist, does again on this side exhibit a curious contrast. No people ever were so little prone to admire at all as those French of Voltaire. . . . Yet see! The old man of Ferney comes up to Paris; an old, tottering, infirm man of eighty-four years. They feel that he is a kind of Hero; that he has spent his life in unmasking error and injustice, delivering Calases, unmasking hypocrites in high places. . . . They feel withal that, if *persiflage* be the great thing, there never was such a *persifleur*. He is the realised ideal of every one of them; the thing they are all wanting to be; of all Frenchmen the most French. *He* is properly their god,— such god as they are fit for. Accordingly, all persons, from the Queen Antoinette to the Douanier at the Porte St. Denis, do they not worship him? . . . There was nothing highest, beautifulest, noblest in France, that did not feel this man to be higher, beautifuler, nobler.

Carlyle, "The Hero as Divinity," lecture 1 (May 5, 1840), in *On Heroes, Hero-Worship, and the Heroic in History* (1841), 17–18.

François-René, vicomte de Chateaubriand (1768–1848)

FRENCH ROMANTIC WRITER, POLITICIAN, AND DIPLOMAT

Tandis que son imagination vous ravit, il fait luire une fausse raison qui détruit le merveilleux, rapetisse l'âme et borne la vue. Excepté dans quelques-uns de ses chefs-d'œuvre, il n'aperçoit que le côté ridicule des choses et des temps, et montre, sous un jour hideusement gai, l'homme à l'homme.

While his imagination enchants you, he throws around him the glare of a fallacious reason, which destroys the marvellous, contracts the soul, and shortens the sight. Except in some of his master-pieces, he considers only the ludicrous side of things and times, and exhibits man to man in a light hideously diverting.

Chateaubriand, *Le Génie du Christianisme, ou Beautés de la Religion Chrétienne* (1802), 46. The translation, by Frederic Shoberl, is in *The Beauties of Christianity* (1813), 31.

G. K. Chesterton (1874–1936)

ENGLISH WRITER AND CRITIC

If the imaginary traveller knew no alphabet of this earth at all, I think it would still be possible to suppose him seeing a difference between London and Paris, and, upon the whole, the real difference. He would not be able to read the words "Quai Voltaire"; but he would see the sneering statue and the hard, straight roads; without having heard of Voltaire he would understand that the city was Voltairean.

"An Essay on Two Cities," in a collection of essays by Chesterton, *All Things Considered* (1908), 68. The "sneering statue" of Voltaire, erected in 1885 near the quai Voltaire, was destroyed during the German occupation of Paris during World War II.

Voltaire read human nature into Joan of Arc, though it was only the brutal part of human nature.

Chesterton, "The Maid of Orleans," in *All Things Considered* (1908), 268.

Voltaire was a man who believed in cultivating his garden; but it was a very trim and ornamental garden; and science has laid waste that garden more ruthlessly than the Garden of Eden.

Chesterton, "Miracles and Agnosticism" (1923), 2.

When Voltaire told man to cultivate his garden, he did not realise how near the garden was to the Garden of Eden. I do not deny that Voltaire was in a sense the serpent in his own garden. But even he was in some ways a very innocent snake. I mean that he saw the whole problem as much simpler than it has since become—or rather, than it has proved itself to be.

Chesterton, "The Spirit of the Eighteenth Century" (1925), 6.

James L. Christian (1927–2012)

PROFESSOR OF PHILOSOPHY AT SANTA ANA COLLEGE

To laugh is to take a step toward the recovery of our lost humaneness, to rid ourselves of the poison of self-hate and despair. Voltaire, the laughing philosopher, helped France laugh itself back toward sanity.

Christian, *Philosophy* (2009), 156.

Winston Churchill (1874–1965)

ENGLISH POLITICIAN, STATESMAN, HISTORIAN, AND TWICE
PRIME MINISTER OF GREAT BRITAIN

This is an extraordinary book, Charles, have you read it? "The best of all possible worlds" philosophy is attacked with measureless satire. I'm excited about what will come next.

To Sir Charles Watson (Lord Moran), July 27, 1953, from Watson, *Churchill* (1966), 474. Watson prefaced this comment as follows: "When I dined with the P.M. at Chequers he was full of vigour and talk. I found him in bed, though he was already late for dinner, absorbed in *Candide*, in an English translation. He looked up," asked the question about Voltaire's book, then, "with a grin, returning to the famous passage on syphilis," read on "with gurgles in his throat as he savoured Pangloss's explanation to Candide of how he had been reduced to this miserable condition." Putting "down the book reluctantly, he sighed" and said, "I'm burning to get on with it." Watson's reply when asked if he had read *Candide* was, "No, my life has been too full of things to read much."

Sir Kenneth Clark (1903–1983)

BRITISH ART HISTORIAN, AUTHOR, MUSEUM DIRECTOR,
AND PRESENTER OF SEVERAL TELEVISION SERIES
ABOUT ART

The busts of the successful dramatists of eighteenth-century Paris stand in the foyer of the Comédie Française, the national theatre of France, which, strange as it may seem to us today, did a great deal for a hundred years, to promote good sense and humanity. What witty, intelligent faces. And here is the wittiest and most intelligent of them all; in fact, at a certain level, one of the most intelligent men that has ever lived, Voltaire.

Clark, "The Smile of Reason," in *Civilisation* (1969), 245.

The philosophers of the Enlightenment pushed European civilisation some steps up the hill, and in theory, at any rate, this gain was consolidated throughout the nineteenth century. Up to the 1930s people were supposed not to burn witches and other members of minority groups, or extract confessions by torture or pervert the course of justice or go to prison for speaking the truth. Except, of course, during wars. This we owe to the movement known as the Enlightenment, and above all to Voltaire.

Clark, "The Smile of Reason," in *Civilisation* (1969), 245.

Samuel Taylor Coleridge (1772–1834)

ENGLISH POET, LITERARY CRITIC, AND PHILOSOPHER

A petty scribbler.

Comment by Coleridge quoted by Henry Crabb Robinson in a letter to Mrs. Thomas Clarkson, May 15, 1808, published in *Notes and Lectures upon Shakespeare and Some of the Old Poets and Dramatists* (1849), edited by his daughter, Sara Fricker Coleridge, who said that Robinson's letter gave "some account of two Lectures of Mr. Coleridge, delivered in May, 1808."

Of the Heirs of Fame few are more respected by me, though for very different qualities, than Erasmus and Luther: scarcely any one has a larger share of my aversion than Voltaire; and even of the better-hearted Rousseau I was never more than a very lukewarm admirer.

S. T. Coleridge, "Essay V" (1809), 115.

The two *Men* were *essentially* different. Exchange mutually their dates and spheres of action, yet Voltaire, had he been ten-fold a Voltaire, could not have made up an Erasmus; and Erasmus must have emptied himself of half his greatness and all his goodness, to have become a Voltaire.

S. T. Coleridge, "Essay V" (1809), 116–117.

Attributed to Coleridge

A French hairdresser.

This was how Coleridge said Voltaire's smile made him look, according to Richard Holmes in "Voltaire's Grin" (1995), 49.

Alistair Cooke (1908–2004)

BRITISH-BORN BROADCASTER, AUTHOR, AND HOST
OF *MASTERPIECE THEATRE*

From the start Mencken had a reputation among Baltimore newsmen as a boy wonder. . . . But he showed in his early youth very few gleams of the invective style that was to make him within a decade or two the terror of the lawmakers, the churches, the businessmen, and the respectable citzenry, first of Baltimore and then of the whole Republic. . . . Nietzsche and Bernard Shaw were the missing sparks. He discovered them in his mid-twenties, matched himself favorably against their Olympian stature, and decided on his life work: to be the native American Voltaire, the enemy of all puritans, the heretic in the Sunday school, the one-man demolition crew of the genteel tradition, the unregenerate neighborhood brat who stretches a string in the alley to trip the bourgeoisie on its pious homeward journey.

Cooke, "An Introduction to H. L. Mencken" (1955), ix.

James Fenimore Cooper (1789–1851)

AMERICAN NOVELIST

Ferney owes its existence, as a village, to Voltaire. It is neater and better built than common; though it has much of the comfortless, out-of-door look of most French villages. The *château*, as the house is called, is a long, narrow, lantern-like building, a little larger than the "Hall" at Cooperstown, were the latter divided equally lengthwise. It has seven windows in front. The grounds are laid out in the formal French style, and are reasonably extensive. An avenue leads to the building; but there is little taste, and, I think, less comfort, in the general arrangement of the place.

Here, as Voltaire used to say, he "shook his wig and powdered the republic," a feat that was less improbable in his time, when wigs were so large and republics so small, than it would be today. The view is not particularly fine, for the whole of this shore of the lake is low, and the trees are so thick as to shut out the prospect. "Mon lac est le premier," must have alluded to what the lake is, in its finer parts, and not to the particular portion of it which is visible from Ferney.

We entered the house as freely as if it had been an inn. Others were there on the same errand; and, judging from what I saw, I should think the building, at this season of the year more especially, nearly useless as a residence. The rooms are small. In the salon are several copies of the old masters, and a picture that is said to be a conceit of the illustrious philosopher. It is a cumbrous allegory, in which the wit is smothered by the elaboration of the design. In charity, we are to believe that the principal idea was conceived in pleasantry; but the vanity of Voltaire was inordinate. His bedroom is decorated by some vilely executed prints, and his bedstead is worth just one dollar.

Cooper, *Sketches of Switzerland, by an American* (1836), 2:168–170, letter 25. Cooper visited Ferney in September 1828. In the last paragraph of this description of Ferney, Cooper said that the little church on the estate, when he "saw it, had been converted into a receptacle for potatoes."

Victor Cousin (1792–1867)

FRENCH PHILOSOPHER

La métaphysique de Locke, sur les ailes brillantes et légères de l'imagination de Voltaire, traversa le détroit et s'introduisit en France.

Locke's metaphysical philosophy crossed the Channel and arrived in France on the light and brilliant wings of Voltaire's imagination.

Cousin, "Leçons de philosophie, ou Essai sur les facultés de l'âme, par M. Laromiguière . . . Premier extrait," *Journal des Savans*, April 1819, 196.

Nicholas Cronk (circa 1965–)

ENGLISH VOLTAIRE SCHOLAR AND DIRECTOR OF THE
VOLTAIRE FOUNDATION AT THE UNIVERSITY OF OXFORD

The most immediate reason for Voltaire's dominance of his century is simply that he wrote far more than anyone else.

Cronk, introduction to *The Cambridge Companion to Voltaire* (2009), 2.

Voltaire lives on as a master of the one-liner. He presents us with a paradox. Voltaire wrote a huge amount—the definitive edition of his *Complete works* being produced by the Voltaire Foundation in Oxford will soon be finished, in around 200 volumes. And yet he is really famous for his short sentences. He likes being brief, though as a critic once remarked, "Voltaire is interminably brief."

"Voltaire and the One-Liner" (2017). It was René Pomeau who described Voltaire's writing as "interminably brief" in his book *La Religion de Voltaire* (1956), 462 (see the entry by Pomeau later in this chapter).

Robert Darnton (1939–)

PROFESSOR OF HISTORY AT PRINCETON UNIVERSITY AND
DIRECTOR OF THE HARVARD UNIVERSITY LIBRARY

Voltaire—who incessantly cultivated courtiers, tried to become one himself, and at least managed to buy his way into nobility—thought that the Enlightenment should begin with the *grands*; once it had captured society's commanding heights, it could concern itself with the masses—but it should take care to prevent them from learning to read.

Darnton, *The Literary Underground of the Old Regime* (1982), 13.

Rappelons-nous que "l'infâme" est un mal qui dépasse la persécution des huguenots.

Let us remember that "l'infâme" is an evil that involves more than the persecution of Huguenots.

Lacroix, "Nous avons besoin d'un Voltaire dans l'âge de Trump" (2018).

Nous avons besoin d'un Voltaire dans l'âge de Trump.

In the age of Trump, we need a Voltaire.

Lacroix, "Nous avons besoin d'un Voltaire dans l'âge de Trump" (2018).

Clarence Darrow (1857–1938)

DEFENSE ATTORNEY IN THE SCOPES "MONKEY" TRIAL

Had the modern professors of eugenics had power in France in 1694, they probably would not have permitted such a child to have been born. Their scientific knowledge would have shown conclusively that no person of value could have come from the union of his father and mother. In those days, nature had not been instructed by the professors of eugenics and so Voltaire was born.

Darrow, *Voltaire* (1918), 2. This thirty-page booklet contains the text of a lecture delivered at the University of Chicago, February 3, 1918. In the preceding paragraph, Darrow said that Voltaire "was a puny child, whom no one thought would live," hence the reference to eugenics.

There are two things that kill a genius—a fatal disease and contentment. When a man is contented he goes to sleep. Voltaire had no chance to be contented, and so he wrote eternally and unceasingly, more than any other man in the history of the world.

Darrow, *Voltaire* (1918), 11.

Voltaire marks the closing of an epoch. His life and his work stand between the old and the new. When he was old, superstition had not yet died, but had received its mortal wound. Never again can savagery control the minds and thoughts of men. Never again can the prison thumbscrews and the rack be instruments to save men's souls. Among the illustrious heroes who have banished this sort of cruelty from the Western world no other name will stand so high and shine so bright as the illustrious name

VOLTAIRE.

Darrow, *Voltaire* (1918), 30.

He seemed to approach the world with a sneer. But, most people have not the subtlety to judge a sneer. Often it is a protective covering against the pain and anguish suffered by the man who feels the sorrows of the world; what seems to be a sneer is the effort to make himself believe that all of it amounts to nothing, and to loose his consciousness of misery and pain in the contemplation of Nirvana.

Figure 28. *The Best of All Possible Worlds: Voltaire's Romances and Tales* (1929), with an introduction by Clarence Darrow. Dust jacket designed by Art Young, showing Voltaire dropping a splash of light with his pen on a darkened world. Private collection.

Darrow, introduction to *The Best of All Possible Worlds* (1929), xvi.

When haunted by the profoundest tragedies which move the sensitive man, he wore his mocking grin and his cynic's smile, but his tireless brain, his constant energy, even his mocking grin, have done more than was ever accomplished by any other man to rid the world of the cruelty, and intolerance that has blasted the lives and destroyed the hopes of millions of human beings since man came upon the earth.

Darrow, introduction to *The Best of All Possible Worlds* (1929), xvi–xvii.

Eugene V. Debs (1855–1926)

SOCIALIST UNION LEADER AND PRESIDENTIAL CANDIDATE

Voltaire! What a Titan upon the World's vast stage! The American people are densely, pitifully ignorant of him. As a rule they know him only, thanks to their educators (!) and their asinine one hundred percent Americanism, to sneer at him. His towering figure is too tall for them to see above his shoe-tops.

Letter from Terre Haute, Indiana, to Fred D. Warren in Girard, Kansas, January 2, 1912, in Debs, *Letters of Eugene V. Debs* (1990), 442.

Voltairine de Cleyre (1866–1912)

ANARCHIST AND FEMINIST

The pamphlets, periodicals, and books are the crystals wherein *the Zeitgeist* of the 18th century is preserved. Without this acquaintance we cannot realize how the people continually thought. . . . And we shall find by it that the fashion of sneering popularized by Voltaire . . . had so permeated not only French philosophy, but the heads of the common people as well, that religion had become almost a byword, a baseless superstition unaccounted for by, and unnecessary according to, the all-accepted theory of Natural Law.

de Cleyre, "Thomas Paine" (1914), 282. Voltairine's comment about religion may be rooted in her parents' decision to ship her off, at age twelve, to a Catholic convent. Like Voltaire, she never married and was often sickly.

Brenton Dickieson (1975–)

CANADIAN WRITER, ACADEMIC, AND BLOGGER

I don't know that we've had a Voltaire in modern times. Christopher Hitchens may have been close.

Dickieson, "Mark Twain's Letters from Earth" (2016).

The first rule of message-stories is that they should be great stories (unless they are satire, like Voltaire's *Candide*, which is energized by its humour and wit).

Dickieson, "William Morris' Nonsense from Nowhere" (2017).

Wilhelm Dilthey (1833–1911)

GERMAN HISTORIAN AND PROFESSOR OF PHILOSOPHY
AT THE UNIVERSITY OF BERLIN

Voltaire wandte zuerst den neuen Begriff der Kultur auf die Geschichte an. In seinem Zeitalter Ludwigs XIV. *unternahm er, den Zusammenhang darzustellen, in welchem alle Erscheinungen des französischen Lebens während der Regierungszeit dieses Königs verknüpft sind. Ludwig XIV. war ihm die Verkörperung des Machtwillens des französischen Königtums. Sein Kultus dieses Königs beruht auf dem Gedanken, daß die Größe und Festigkeit seines Staates allein die Steigerung des ganzen menschlichen Daseins, die Blüte der Wissenschaften, den Adel und di Formgröße der Kunst und die höfische Verfeinerung der Sitten ermöglicht habe.*

Voltaire was the first to apply the new idea of culture to history. In his *Age of Louis XIV* he undertook to organize all aspects of French life under the king's reign within a coherent framework. For him Louis XIV personified the will to power of the French monarchy. His cult of Louis rested on the idea that only the greatness and solidity of his state had made possible the improvement of man's whole existence: the bloom of science, of the nobility and of the greatness of artistic form and the courtly refinement of manners.

Dilthey, "Das achtzehnte Jahrhundert und die geschichtliche Welt" (1927), 226. The translation is from Gay and Cavanaugh, *Historians at Work* (1975), 4:21, where Dilthey's essay is titled, in English, "The Eighteenth Century and the Historical World."

Michael Dirda (1948–)

PULITZER PRIZE–WINNING *WASHINGTON POST*
BOOK CRITIC

For even the ordinary well-read person, the French Enlightenment is largely restricted to the three big-name philosophes: Diderot, Rousseau, Voltaire.

Dirda, "When the World Spoke French" (2011).

Isaac Disraeli (1766–1848)

ENGLISH SCHOLAR, AUTHOR, AND FATHER OF BENJAMIN DISRAELI

As a univeralist, Voltaire remains unparalleled in ancient or in modern times. . . . The real claims of this great writer to invention and originality are as moderate as his size and variety are astonishing. The wonder of his ninety volumes is, that he singly consists of a number of men of the second order, making up one great man; for unquestionably some could rival Voltaire in any single province, but no one but himself has possessed them all.

Disraeli, *The Literary Character* (1828), 259–260.

Voltaire censures Corneille for making his heroes say continually they are great men. But in drawing the character of an hero he draws his own. All his heroes are only so many Corneilles in different situations.

Disraeli, *Curiosities of Literature* (1835), 113.

Fyodor Dostoyevsky (1821–1881)

RUSSIAN NOVELIST

"Voltaire believed in God, but very little, it seems, and it seems he also loved mankind very little," Alyosha said softly, restrainedly, and quite naturally, as if he were talking to someone of the same age or even older than himself.

Alexei "Alyosha" Karamazov to his younger atheist friend, Kolya Krasotkin, in the original 1880 Russian-language edition of *The Brothers Karamazov*, part 4, book 10, chap. 6. The text in English is from the 1992 edition translated by Pevear and Volokhonsky, 553–554.

Arthur Conan Doyle (1859–1930)

BRITISH PHYSICIAN AND CREATOR OF THE
SHERLOCK HOLMES STORIES

Voltaire was illiterate. Rousseau was a scoundrel. Deists, like Hume, Priestley, or Gibbon, could not be honest men.

Doyle, *Through the Magic Door* (1907), 55.

Sophie Dozoretz (active in Princeton circa 1932–1942)

SECRETARY-TYPIST

"All will be well; that is our hope
All is well; this is our delusion."
—Voltaire

All is and will be well with your typing when you bring it to
Sophie Dozoretz
Room 101 (main Floor) Twenty Nassau.

Classified ad in *The Daily Princetonian*, October 20, 1936, 3.

Alexandre Dumas père (1802–1870)

FRENCH NOVELIST AND PLAYWRIGHT

La première chose que l'on aperçoit avant d'entrer au château, c'est une petite chapelle dont l'inscription est un chef-d'œuvre; elle ne se compose cependant que de trois mots latins:

DEO EREXIT VOLTAIRE.

Elle avait pour but de prouver au monde entier, fort inquiet des démêlés de la créature et du créateur, que Voltaire et Dieu s'étaient enfin réconciliés; le monde apprit cette nouvelle avec satisfaction, mais il soupçonna toujours Voltaire d'avoir fait les premières avances. Nous traversâmes un jardin, nous montâmes un perron elevé de deux ou trois marches, et nous nous trouvâmes dans l'antichambre; c'est là que se recueillent, avant d'entrer dans le sanctuaire, les pélerins qui viennent adorer le dieu de l'irréligion. Le concierge les prévient solennellement d'avance que rien n'a été changé à l'ameublement, et qu'ils vont voir l'appartement tel que l'habitait M. de Voltaire: cette allocution manque rarement de produire son effet. On a vu, à ces simples paroles, pleurer des abonnés du Constitutionnel.

The first thing one notices, just before entering the castle there, is a little chapel on which is an inscription, a work of art in itself, consisting of three words only: DEO EREXIT VOLTAIRE. It had been built with the object of proving to the whole world that the differences between the Creator and his Creation had been healed, and that a reconciliation had been effected between Voltaire and the Almighty. The world at large received the news with satisfaction, but strongly suspected that Voltaire had made the first advances. We passed through a garden, and mounting a flight of three steps, entered an antechamber wherein the pilgrims who come to worship at the shrine of irreligion usually foregather, just in front of the sanctuary proper. A concierge solemnly avers that nothing has been altered in the furnishings of the place, and that the room is just as Voltaire himself used it. This preamble rarely fails in its effect; those simple words have been known to reduce subscribers to *Le Constitutionnel* to tears.

Dumas, "Impressions de voyage" (1833), 178–179. Dumas visited Ferney in September or October 1832. The translation is from Dumas, *Travels in Switzerland* (1958), 11–12.

Will Durant (1885–1981)

HISTORIAN AND PHILOSOPHER

Italy had a Renaissance, and Germany had a Reformation, but France had Voltaire; he was for his country both Renaissance and Reformation, and half the Revolution.

Durant, *The Story of Philosophy* (1926), 220.

Jean Dutourd (1920–2011)

FRENCH AUTHOR AND MEMBER OF THE ACADÉMIE FRANÇAISE

Le tort de Voltaire est d'avoir été gai. Il ne s'est pas méfié de la postérité. Vivant dans un siècle très intelligent, donc porté à rire, il s'est laissé aller pendant quatre-vingt-quatre ans à son esprit facétieux. Il y était encouragé par son public, qui voyait tout ce qu'il y avait de vrai et de profond dans ses écrits et qui était charmé que ceux-ci, en outre, fussent amusants. Ce public était composé de rois, d'impératrices, de seigneurs, de bourgeois éclairés, de gens du peuple qui savaient mieux lire qu'à présent.

Voltaire's mistake was to have been jubilant. He did not concern himself with posterity. Living as he did in a very intelligent age, and thus given to laughter, he let himself go his facetious way for eighty-four years. He was encouraged by his public, who saw everything that was true and profound in his writings and were charmed as well because what he wrote was amusing. His public was composed of kings, empresses, lords, enlightened bourgeois, by ordinary people who were better read than today.

Dutourd, *Le Spectre de la rose* (1986), 137.

Terry Eagleton (1943–)

ENGLISH LITERARY THEORIST, ESSAYIST, AND CRITIC

Voltaire sees the history of civilisation as the story of how it grew bloated on the blood of the poor.

Eagleton, *Culture* (2016), 20.

Julia Edelman (circa 1994–)

COMEDY WRITER AND FILMMAKER

Love is a canvas furnished by Nature and embroidered by imagination.

Voltaire mumbled these famous words while getting very drunk at his first Paint Nite.

From Edelman, "Famous Quotes, Explained," in her spoof self-help book *Love Voltaire Us Apart* (2016).

T. S. Eliot (1888–1965)

AMERICAN-BORN ENGLISH POET, ESSAYIST, AND CRITIC

Only a Christian culture could have produced a Voltaire or a Nietzsche. I do not believe that the culture of Europe could survive the complete disappearance of the Christian Faith.

Broadcast in German on the BBC's German service, March 24, 1946, after Germany's defeat in World War II, published in Eliot, *Die Einheit der Europäischen Kultur* (1946), and in English in "The Unity of European Culture," in *Notes towards the Definition of Culture* (1948), 122.

Ralph Waldo Emerson (1803–1882)

PHILOSOPHER, ESSAYIST, AND LECTURER

Insight is not will, nor is affection will. Perception is cold, and goodness dies in wishes; as Voltaire said, 'tis the misfortune of worthy people that they are cowards; *"un des plus grands malheurs des honnêtes gens c'est qu'ils sont des lâches."* There must be a fusion of these two to generate the energy of will.

Emerson, *The Conduct of Life* (1860), 24–25.

Émile Faguet (1847–1916)

PROFESSOR OF POETRY AT THE SORBONNE AND MEMBER
OF THE ACADÉMIE FRANÇAISE

Il est admirable pour se contredire, pour aller d'un bond jusqu'au bout d'une idée et d'un autre élan jusqu'au bout de l'idée contraire, pour être inconséquent avec une souveraine intrépidité de certitude; pour être athée, déiste, optimiste, pessimiste, audacieux novateur, réactionnaire enragé, toujours avec la même netteté de pensée et de décision d'argument, toujours comme s'il ne pensait jamais autre chose, ce qui fait que chaque livre de lui est une merveille de limpidité, et son œuvre un prodige d'incertitude. Ce grand esprit, c'est un chaos d'idées claires.

He is admirable because of his contradictions, for jumping to the end of one idea, then bounding to the end of the opposite idea, for being flippant with fearless authority; for being an atheist, a deist, optimistic, pessimistic, innovative, bold, rabidly reactionary, always with the same clarity of thought and decisive reasoning, always as if he never thought otherwise, so that each of his books is a marvel of lucidity, and the totality of his work a prodigy of uncertainty. This great mind is a chaos of clear ideas.

Faguet, *Dix-huitième siècle* (1890), 219.

Les exils, forcés ou spontanés, de Voltaire lui furent toujours utiles. D'Angleterre il était revenu philosophe; de Prusse il revint sage.

Voltaire's periods of exile, forced or spontaneous, were always useful. From England he returned a philosopher; from Prussia, a sage.

Faguet, *Voltaire* (1895), 57.

La philosophie de Voltaire se réduit toute entière à une idée négative: éliminer de la pensée de l'homme l'idée d'intervention du surnaturel dans le monde.

Voltaire's philosophy boiled down essentially to one negative idea: to eliminate from man's thinking the idea of supernatural intrusion in the world.

Faguet, *Voltaire* (1895), 82.

Il existe deux esprits voltairiens.

L'un consiste à répéter les plaisanteries de Voltaire et à hériter ses colères contre la religion chrétienne et en général contre toutes les religions. Cet esprit-là manque d'esprit et est extrêmement suranné. . . . Il est inutile, il est ridicule, il n'est pas sans danger moral de s'y laisser aller.

Il existe un autre esprit voltairien; il consiste à être comme Voltaire l'a été, très intelligent, si l'on peut, très sensé, très pratique, à aimer les faits bien observés, à se délier des théories aventureuses, à travailler toutes les questions avec attention, observation, documentation . . . à rêver et à réaliser partiellement un monde de travailleurs honnêtes et de chefs bienfaisants, comme était le petit royaume de Ferney.

Voltaire comes in two forms.

One consists of repeating Voltaire's jokes and maintaining his rage against Christianity and religion in general. That form of wit is foolish and thoroughly obsolete. . . . It is unnecessary, ridiculous, and it runs the moral risk of going too far.

There is another form of Voltairean wit. It involves doing as Voltaire did, being very clever, if possible, being very sensible, very practical, with an affinity for well-observed facts, an aversion to wild theories, and a considered approach to all questions, based on observation and evidence . . . to imagine and in a modest way to fashion a world of honest laborers and benevolent leaders, like the little kingdom at Ferney.

Faguet, *Voltaire* (1895), 236.

Howard Fast (1914–2003)

AUTHOR OF THE NOVEL *SPARTACUS*

Take Voltaire's old epigram—and I call it that with reason—"I do not agree with what he says, but I will defend to the death his right to say it." How often has that been quoted, and what arrant nonsense it is!

Fast, "Free Speech for Fascists?" (1944), 18, Fast's response to a discussion on the subject in the December 7, 1944, issue of the Marxist weekly. Fast was a member of the Communist Party at the time.

Otis Fellows (1908–1993)

PROFESSOR OF HUMANITIES AT COLUMBIA UNIVERSITY
AND SPECIALIST IN DIDEROT STUDIES

A frequent inference in December 1944 was that if Voltaire had been a guide to patriotic Frenchmen during the Occupation, his sagacity and wisdom were equally essential at the time of France's recovery. Whether one likes it or not, it was reiterated, Voltaire represents in the world the liberal concept of French civilization; moreover, he remains one of the great artisans of national unity.

Fellows, *From Voltaire to* La Nouvelle Critique (1970), 16.

Gustave Flaubert (1821–1880)

FRENCH NOVELIST AND SHORT STORY WRITER

J'aime les phrases nettes et qui se tiennent droites, debout tout en courant, ce qui est presque une impossibilité. L'idéal de la prose est arrivé a un degré inouï de difficulté; il faut se dégager de l'archaïsme, du mot commun, avec les idées contemporaines sans leurs mauvais termes, et que ce soit clair comme du Voltaire, touffu comme du Montaigne, nerveux comme du La Bruyère et ruisselant de couleur, toujours.

I like clear-cut sentences that stand up straight and take off running, which is almost an impossibility. The ideal of good prose has reached an unheard-of degree of difficulty: it must be free of archaisms and clichés, express contemporary ideas, but avoid vulgar usage, and it must be as clear as Voltaire, as dense as Montaigne, as brisk as La Bruyère, and—always—brimming with color.

Letter from Flaubert in Croisset, near Rouen, June 13, 1852, to his lover Louise Colet in Paris. In Flaubert, *Correspondance, 1850–1859* (1974), 208.

De roman il en a fait un, lequel est le résumé de toutes ses œuvres, et le meilleur chapitre de Candide *est la visite chez le seigneur* Pococurante, *où Voltaire exprime encore son opinion personnelle sur à peu près tout. Ces quatre pages sont une des merveilles de la prose. Elles étaient la condensation de soixante volumes écrits et d'un demi-siècle d'efforts. Mais j'aurais bien défié Voltaire de faire la description seulement d'un de ces tableaux de Raphaël dont il se moque.*

Among his novels there is one, which sums up all of his works, and the best chapter in *Candide* is the one about the visit to the home of Lord Pococurante, where Voltaire once again expresses his personal opinion about almost everything. Those four pages are a marvel of prose writing. They were the distillation of sixty volumes and half a century of effort. But I would have defied Voltaire to write a description of just one of the paintings by Raphael that he derided.

Letter from Flaubert in Trouville, August 26, 1853, to Louise Colet in Paris. In Flaubert, *Correspondance, 1850–1859* (1974), 399.

Oui, c'est beau Candide! *fort beau!* Quelle justesse! *Y a-t-il moyen d'être plus large, tout en restant aussi net? Peut-être non. Le merveilleux effet de ce livre tient sans doute à la nature des idées qu'il exprime. C'est aussi bien que cela qu'il faut écrire, mais pas comme cela.*

Yes, *Candide* is lovely! Very lovely! *What perfection!* Could anything ever be more broadly, yet clearly written? Perhaps not. The marvelous effect of this book is due no doubt to the nature of the ideas it conveys. It is *as good as that* that one must write, but not *like that.*

Letter from Flaubert in Croisset, September 16, 1853, to Louise Colet in Paris. In Flaubert, *Correspondance, 1850–1859*, 409.

Vous savez bien que je ne partage nullement votre opinion sur la personne de M. de Voltaire. C'est pour moi un saint! Pourquoi s'obstiner à voir un farceur dans un homme qui était un fanatique? . . . j'aime le grand Voltaire autant que je déteste le grand Rousseau.

You well know that I in no way share your opinion of M. de Voltaire the man. For me he is a *Saint!* Why such stubborn insistence in regarding a zealot as a prankster? . . . I love Voltaire the great as much as I detest the great Rousseau.

Letter from Flaubert in Croisset to Mme Roger des Genettes, 1859–1860?, in Flaubert, *Correspondance, 1859–1871* (1975), 23–24.

Son "Écrasons l'infâme" me fait l'effet d'un cri de croisade. Toute son intelligence était une machine de guerre. Et ce qui me le fait chérir, c'est le dégoût que m'inspirent les voltairiens, des gens qui rient sur les grandes choses! Est-ce qu'il riait, lui? Il grinçait!

His "Écrasons l'infâme" affects me like the shout of a crusade. His intellect as a whole was like an engine of war. And what makes me love him especially is the disgust that the Voltairiens inspire in me, the people who laugh at important matters! Did he laugh? He was gnashing his teeth!

Letter from Flaubert in Croisset to Mme Roger des Genettes, 1859–1860?, In Flaubert, *Correspondance, 1859–1871* (1975), 24.

Voltaire ne se doutait pas que le plus immortel de son ouvrage était Candide.

Voltaire had no inkling that *Candide* would be his most immortal work.

Letter from Flaubert in Paris, January 15, 1870, to Léon Pillore. In Flaubert, *Correspondance, 1859–1871* (1975), 544.

Célèbre par son "rictus" épouvantable. Science superficielle.

Famous for his frightful grin. His learning superficial.

Dictionnaire des idées reçues (1910), published posthumously, based on notes compiled by Flaubert in the 1870s, from Flaubert, *Bouvard et Pécuchet: Œuvre posthume* (1910), 6:444.

La fin de Candide: *"Cultivons notre jardin" est la plus grande leçon de morale qui existe.*

The end of *Candide*: "Let us cultivate our garden" is the greatest moral lesson there is.

Letter from Flaubert in Croisset, September 22, 1874, to Edmond de Goncourt in Paris. In Flaubert, *Correspondance, 1871–1877* (1975), 343.

Que dites-vous du centenaire de Voltaire, monté et dirigé par Ménier, chocolatier! L'ironie ne le quitte pas, ce pauvre grand homme; les hommages et les injures persistent comme de son vivant! Après tout je dis une bêtise, car pourquoi un chocolatier serait-il moins digne de le comprendre qu'un autre monsieur?

What do you think of the centenary of Voltaire, orchestrated and run by the chocolatier Ménier! Irony will not leave that poor great man alone; the accolades and insults persist, as if he were still alive! But what a dumb thing to

Figure 29. After Jean Huber, *Esquisse d'aprés nature faite a Fernex en 1769*, circa 1778. Etching and engraving. Private collection.

say, for why should a chocolatier be any less capable of understanding him than another man?

Letter from Flaubert in Paris, March 1, 1878, to Mme Roger de Genettes at Villenauxe-la-Grande, near Nogent-sur-Seine in eastern France. In Flaubert, *Correspondance, 1877–1880* (1975), 37. Voltaire died in Paris on May 30, 1778.

E. M. Forster (1879–1970)

ENGLISH CRITIC, ESSAYIST, AND NOVELIST

Straight ahead of us lay the chateau. . . . Lucky, happy we, to get this last peep at one of the symbols of European civilisation. Civilisation. Humanity. Enjoyment. That was what the agreeable white building said to us, that was what we carried away. It was not a large building and that has been part of the disaster. It was too small to cope with the modern world. A Ferney today would have to be enormous, with rolling staircases and microphones, if it was to function proportionately, and if it was enormous could it be Ferney? Even Voltaire felt that he saw too many people, and that the universe, though fortunately bounded by Russia, was upon too cumbrous a scale. He could just illuminate it, but only just, and he died without knowing that he was the last man who would ever perform such a feat and that Goethe would die asking for more light.

Forster, "Happy Ending" (1940), 442; retitled "Ferney" in Forster's anthology *Two Cheers for Democracy* (1951), 341–342. Forster and a friend took a tram from Geneva to Ferney where they caught a glimpse of Voltaire's estate through the locked front gate in June 1939, shortly before World War II began.

Anatole France (1844–1924)

FRENCH JOURNALIST, POET, AND NOVELIST

Loin d'être infaillible, la postérité a toutes les chances de se tromper. Elle est ignorante et indifférente. Je vois passer en ce moment sur le quai Malaquais la postérité de Corneille et de Voltaire. Elle se promène, égayée par le soleil d'avril. Ella va, la voilette sur le nez ou le cigare aux lèvres, et je vous assure qu'elle se soucie infiniment peu de Voltaire et de Corneille. La faim et l'amour l'ocupent assez.

Far from being infallible, posterity runs a good chance of being mistaken. It is ignorant and indifferent. Just now, on the Quai Malaquais, I am watching the posterity of Corneille and Voltaire. It walks leisurely under a cheerful April sun, a veil over its nose or a cigar on its lips, and I assure you it cares very little about Voltaire and Corneille. Hunger and love keep it busy enough as it is.

France, *La Vie littéraire* (1888), 112–113. The English translation is from Peyre, *Writers and Their Critics* (1944), 263.

Dans ses pirouettes les plus folles, l'incrédule Voltaire ne perd jamais de vue son idéal de raison, de science, de bonté . . . oui, de bonté. Car ce grand satirique ne fut méchant que contre les méchants et les sots.

In his wildest piroutttes, Voltaire the nonbeliever never loses sight of reason, of science, of virtue . . . yes, virtue. For that great satirist was never mean except to mean-spirited people and fools.

France, *Les Matinées de la Villa Saïd* (1921), 83.

Sigmund Freud (1856–1939)

AUSTRIAN PSYCHIATRIST

Das Leben, wie es uns auferlegt ist, ist zu schwer für uns, es bringt uns zuviel Schmerzen, Enttäuschungen, unlösbare Aufgaben. Um es zu ertragen, können wir Linderungsmittel nicht entbehren. . . . Auf die Ablenkungen zielt Voltaire, wenn er seinen Candide in den Rat ausklingen läßt, seinen Garten zu bearbeiten; solch eine Ablenkung ist auch die wissenschaftliche Tätigkeit. Die Ersatzbefriedigungen, wie die Kunst sie bietet, sind gegen die Realität Illusionen, darum nicht minder psychisch wirksam, dank der Rolle, die die Phantasie im Seelenleben behauptet hat.

Life as we find it is too hard for us; it entails too much pain, too many disappointments, impossible tasks. We cannot do without palliative remedies. . . . Voltaire is aiming at a diversion of interest when he brings his *Candide* to a close with the advice that people should cultivate their gardens; scientific work is another deflection of the same kind. The substitute gratifications, such as art offers, are illusions in contrast to reality, but none the less satisfying to the mind on that account, thanks to the place which phantasy has reserved for herself in mental life.

Freud, *Ungbehagen in der Kultur* (1930), 22; translation in *Civilisation and Its Discontents* (1930), 10.

Lewis Galantière (1895–1977)

JOURNALIST, PLAYWRIGHT, TRANSLATOR OF FRENCH LITERATURE, AND PRESIDENT OF PEN

Voltaire said of Louis XIV that he was "not one of the greatest of men but he was one of the greatest of kings." We cannot dispose so neatly of Voltaire himself. He was unquestionably a great man, for the immense influence he came to wield was the product of forces drawn from himself alone: persevering courage, a rapid and imaginative intelligence, an inconceivable capacity for work, and a surprising literary art of persuasion. But he was not one of your Olympians; there was no serenity to him.

Galantière, "Voltaire" (1965), 848.

He published under 150 pseudonyms, was cunning and devious, acted often on impulse or quick-lit anger and was often panicky, for he had the heart of a lion in the skin of a rabbit.

Galantière, "Voltaire" (1965), 848.

Gabriel García Márquez (1927–2014)

COLOMBIAN FICTION WRITER AND JOURNALIST

"Voltaire en latín es casi una herejía."

"Voltaire in Latin is almost a heresy."

Father Cayetano Delauro, a fictional eighteenth-century Colombian priest, commenting on a Latin edition of Voltaire's *Lettres philosophiques* in the personal library of Dr. Abrenuncio, a learned Portuguese Jew. When Abrenuncio says, "His is a perfect prose," Delauro replies, "What a shame it was written by a Frenchman." From García Màrquez, *Del amor y otros demonios* (1994), 155. The translation is from *Of Love and Other Demons* (1995), 113.

Attributed to Charles de Gaulle (1890–1970)

FRENCH ARMY GENERAL, PATRIOT, STATESMAN, AND TWICE PRESIDENT OF FRANCE

On ne met pas Voltaire en prison.

You don't put Voltaire in jail.

Charles de Gaulle's response as president of France to a suggestion in a Council of Ministers meeting in December 1960 that Jean-Paul Sartre be arrested for his loud opposition to the government's policies in Algeria. Quoted in Derogy, "Le Défi des 343" (1971), 15.

Peter Gay (1923–2015)

GERMAN-BORN PROFESSOR OF HISTORY AT YALE UNIVERSITY

He lived too long, wrote too much, expressed opinions too casually, participated in affairs too vividly not to be on opposite sides of various questions at different times. But it does not follow that his political philosophy was a "chaos of clear ideas" as Emile Faguet characterized it in an epigram that has become only too familiar. . . . The variety of his interests and the shifts in his political opinions sprang not from flightiness but from an empiricist's temper, not from detachment but from a deep engagement with reality.

Gay, *Voltaire's Politics* (1959), 9.

Figure 30. Jean Huber, *Differens airs en 30 Têtes de M' de Voltaire calques sur les Tableaux de M' Huber*, circa 1777. Etching. Department of Prints, Drawings, and Photographs. Photograph courtesy of Yale University.

Voltaire was the symbol of his age, and it is the fate of symbols to be exploited rather than to be understood.

Gay, *Voltaire's Politics* (1959), 10.

Far from seeking to make politics a panacea or from dissolving it in ethics, Voltaire sought to humanize it.

Gay, *Voltaire's Politics* (1959), 14.

Voltaire's great trinity—toleration, the rule of law, freedom of opinion—defines the conditions that make it possible for men to realize their purpose on this earth: to live in dignity and in happiness; in a word, it defines Voltaire's platform for social reform.

Gay, *Voltaire's Politics* (1959), 32.

Nothing made Voltaire braver than the fear that he was being a coward.

Gay, *Voltaire's Politics* (1959), 69.

"Ecrasez l'infàme" meant that one must destroy Christianity before one could build a rational society.

Gay, *Voltaire's Politics* (1959), 272.

Voltaire's *Dictionnaire philosophique* is not a dictionary. It is a polemical tract, in turn sober and witty, sensible and outrageous, sincere and disingenuous. It is sometimes angry about the wrong things, sometimes superficial in its explanations, and sometimes almost as cruel as the cruelty it lacerates. But behind the savage humor and partisan analysis stands a passion for humanity and decency, a hatred of fanaticism and stupidity, which Voltaire would not have been embarrassed to acknowledge (and which we should not be too supercilious to recognize) as moral. With its errors and its erudition, its dazzling variety of tactics and brilliant unity of style, the *Dictionnaire philosophique* is Voltaire's most characteristic work—as characteristic as its more famous companion piece, *Candide*.

Gay, *The Party of Humanity* (1964), 7.

He was not a dogmatist but an opportunist; he was never a consistent supporter of any particular form of government. He was a moderate constitutionalist in England, Holland, and Geneva, a vigorous royalist in France, and an advocate of absolutism in Prussia.

Gay, *The Party of Humanity* (1964), 91.

It is true that Voltaire contradicted himself. . . . But his political aims show a complete consistency. The rule of law, freedom of speech, a humane legal code, and a tolerant religious policy—these were desirable everywhere.

Gay, *The Party of Humanity* (1964), 91–92.

Among the men of the Enlightenment François Marie Arouet, self-styled Voltaire, stands first.

Gay, "The Enlightenment," *Horizon*, Spring 1970, 42.

Larry Getlen (circa 1965–)

STAND-UP COMIC, COMEDY WRITER, AND JOURNALIST

Believe it or not, Voltaire was the Jennifer Aniston of the eighteenth century.

Getlen, "Ben Franklin Was the Country's First Fame Whore" (2017).

André Glucksmann (1937–2015)

FRENCH PUBLIC INTELLECTUAL AND "NOUVEAU PHILOSOPHE"

Qui criminalise la liberté d'expression criminalise Voltaire vivant ou mort.

He who criminalizes freedom of expression criminalizes Voltaire, living or dead.

Glucksmann, "L'Europe sera voltairienne ou ne sera pas" (2015).

Voltaire est un contestataire. Plus que de gauche ou de droite, plus que croyant ou athée, il est fondamentalement libre.

Voltaire was a dissenter. Beyond liberalism or conservativism, beyond faith in God or atheism, he was fundamentally free.

Glucksmann, "L'Europe sera voltairienne ou ne sera pas" (2015).

Howard Goldberger (1921–2014)

Some books are good, some books are great. *The Bonfire of the Vanities* is one of the greatest novels of our time. Tom Wolfe is the Voltaire of the twentieth century.

Goldberger, letter to the editor from Wantagh, New York (1998), 8.

Robert Walter Goodman (1914–1969)

CIVIL ENGINEER AND PRESIDENT OF THE
PACIFICA FOUNDATION

We have ample proof in history of the efficacy of satire affecting society. Consider the work of Voltaire, the Karl Marx of the bourgeois revolution, or Aristophanes, who laughed the sophists out of Athens. Certainly Voltaire didn't change the feudal hierarchy of the church (that was left for the people to do), but no intelligent person will argue that the masses under the domination of the church weren't liberated in great measure by his satiric polemics.

Goodman, "The Uses of Satire" (1937), 22. Goodman was a graduate student at Cornell University when he wrote this response to an essay by Robert Forsythe in the August 3, 1937, issue of *The New Masses*.

If we had more *Candides* written today . . . we would make far more rapid progress in our work of enlightenment.

Goodman, "The Uses of Satire" (1937), 22.

Adam Gopnik (1956–)

AMERICAN ESSAYIST, AUTHOR, AND STAFF WRITER
FOR THE *NEW YORKER*

Voltaire, like God, whom he patronized, is always there.

Gopnik, "Voltaire's Garden" (2005), 74.

By the end, he was more like a cross between Andrei Sakharov and Mr. Toad of Toad Hall—a conceited grand bourgeois with a big house who was also one of the first dissidents, embodying a whole alternative set of values, and who came to be treated even by the government almost as an independent state within a state.

Gopnik referring to the final decades of Voltaire's life in "Voltaire's Garden" (2005), 74.

Voltaire was never exactly a "philosopher" in the conventional sense; his philosophy is almost always a moral instinct rendered as a dramatic gesture, rather than consecutive thoughts turned into a logical argument.

Gopnik, "Voltaire's Garden" (2005), 76.

There is . . . as much of Voltaire in American life as in French life. Benjamin Franklin went to him for a blessing, and got it.

Gopnik, "Voltaire's Garden" (2005), 81.

As Tocqueville and Voltaire alike have taught us, the man who cultivates his garden is likelier to be the man who worries about other people's ills than the man who has to scramble for roots or the one who scribbles in his study.

Gopnik, *Angels and Ages* (2009), 91–92. In the same paragraph Gopnik said: "It is not so much the establishment of a garden but the ownership of a gate that moves people from liking a society based on favors to liking one based on rights. Enclosing our garden broadens our circle of compassion."

They were silly, petty, adolescent, impulsive, self-deluding, took absurd revenges for imagined wrongs, and lived lives of privilege and luxury; they were also wise, sublime, adult, saw much farther than their contemporaries, and helped advance the human spirit.

Gopnik commenting on Voltaire and Mme du Châtelet in his introduction to a new edition of Nancy Mitford's book about the couple, *Voltaire in Love* (2012), xiii.

An easily overlooked aspect of Voltaire's thought was the priority it gave, especially in his later life, to practice. Watchmaking, vegetable growing, star charting: the great Enlightenment thinker turned decisively away from abstraction as he aged. The argument of "Candide" is neither that the world gets better nor that it's all for naught; it's that happiness is where you find it, and you find it first by making it yourself. The famous injunction to "cultivate our garden" means just that: make something happen, often with your hands. It remains, as it was meant to, a reproach to all ham-fisted intellects and deskbound brooders. Getting out to make good things happen beats sitting down and thinking big things up.

Gopnik, "Are Liberals on the Wrong Side of History?" (2017), 93.

John Gray (1948–)

ENGLISH POLITICAL PHILOSOPHER AT THE LONDON SCHOOL OF ECONOMICS

Unlike Hume and Kant, he made no contribution to philosophy. Few of his entries in the *Philosophical Dictionary* have to do with philosophical questions. He is significant chiefly as an embodiment of the Enlightenment mentality, which included a rationalist version of racism.

Gray, *Seven Types of Atheism* (2018), 60.

Voltaire's racism was not simply that of his time. Like Hume and Kant, he gave racism intellectual authority by asserting that it was grounded in reason. In a letter he mocked the biblical account of a common ancestry, asking whether Africans descended from monkeys or monkeys from Africans.

Gray, *Seven Types of Atheism* (2018), 61.

More than anyone else, it was Voltaire who embedded Semitic prejudice in Enlightenment thinking. . . . According to Voltaire, anything of value that may have emerged in Jewish life was borrowed from the Greeks or the Romans, the true sources of European civilization.

Gray, *Seven Types of Atheism* (2018), 61–62.

Jean Guéhenno (1890–1978)

FRENCH AUTHOR AND LITERARY CRITIC

"La Faute à Voltaire, la faute à Rousseau." Glorieuses fautes, si elles ont commandé depuis deux cents années beaucoup de ce qui s'est fait pour la liberté et le bonheur des hommes, si elles furent un éclatant refus du monde comme il va, de la tradition hypo-crite, des préjugés intéressés et de la sottise.

"The fault of Voltaire, the fault of Rousseau." Glorious faults, if, for two hun-dred years, they have inspired much of what has been done for human liberty and happiness, if they were a blatant rejection of the world as it is, of run-of-the-mill hypocrisy, bigoted self-interest, and stupidity.

Guéhenno, "Glorieuses fautes" (1978), 1.

Les deux hommes ne s'aimaient guère. Leur mort, à quelques semaines d'intervalle, les a réconciliés, si bien que nous ne pouvons parler de l'un sans parler de l'autre, et l'on s'étonne qu'une France vivante, un Etat vivant, n'ait pas profité d'une coïnci-dence si frappante de ces anniversaires pour se faire une manifestation de sa propre existence.

The two men did not like each other. Their deaths, a few weeks apart, recon-ciled their differences, so much so that we cannot speak of one without speak-ing of the other, and it is astonishing that France, a living State, has failed to profit from such a striking coincidence as these anniversaries to promote its own existence.

Guéhenno commenting on the meager official recognition accorded by France to Vol-taire and Rousseau during the bicentennial year of their deaths in "Glorieuses fautes" (1978), 13.

Evelyn Beatrice Hall (1868–1956)

ENGLISH AUTHOR AND BIOGRAPHER, WHO USED
THE PSEUDONYM S. G. TALLENTYRE

"What a fuss about an omelette!" he had exclaimed. . . . How abominably unjust to persecute a man for such an airy trifle as that! "I disapprove of what you say, but I will defend to the death your right to say it," was his attitude now.

Hall, *The Friends of Voltaire* (1906), 198–199, published under the name S. G. Tallentyre. Hall was trying to express how Voltaire felt when *De l'esprit*, a polemical tract by his fellow *philosophe* Helvétius, got the author in trouble with the church. Her paraphrase of what Voltaire thought ("I disapprove of what you say . . .") is the most widely cited of any misquotation of Voltaire.

Alexander Hamilton (1755–1804)

COAUTHOR OF THE *FEDERALIST PAPERS* AND FIRST
U.S. SECRETARY OF THE TREASURY

A garden, you know, is a very usual refuge of a disappointed politician. Accordingly, I have purchased a few acres about nine miles from town, have built a house, and am cultivating a garden.

Letter to Charles Cotesworth Pinckney, December 29, 1802, in *The Papers of Alexander Hamilton* (1979), 71. Hamilton seems to be invoking the spirit of the wisdom expressed in *Candide*.

Paul Harvey (1918–2009)

RADIO COMMENTATOR AND SYNDICATED NEWSPAPER COLUMNIST

There are hill-country sayings for any occasion: She drove her ducks to a poor market.

Or, as Aunt Betty Ruth says, "The bird never flew so far but what his tail followed him."

Or, "You dance, you have to pay the fiddler."

Voltaire never said it better.

From one of Harvey's syndicated columns, published as "Ozark Folks Dispel Trouble with Homilies," in the *Del Rio News Herald* (Texas), June 20, 1982, 26.

Ben Hecht (1894–1964)

JOURNALIST, SCREENWRITER, AND NOVELIST

The Central Park West Voltaire.

Hecht's epithet for Herman Mankiewicz, his contemporary wit, fellow New Yorker, screenwriter, and good friend. Hecht, *A Child of the Century* (1954), 373.

I have, by the way, never known an intelligent Jew who did not admire Voltaire as one of the great friends of humanity.

Hecht, *A Child of the Century* (1954), 570. Among Voltaire's "intelligent" Jewish admirers were Hecht himself, H. L. Mencken's friend and collaborator, George Jean Nathan, Isaiah Berlin, Leonard Bernstein, Yale historian Peter Gay, and Adam Gopnik.

Arthur Hertzberg (1921–2006)

CONSERVATIVE RABBI AND PROFESSOR OF RELIGION
AT DARTMOUTH COLLEGE

His writings were the great arsenal of anti-Jewish arguments for those enemies of the Jews who wanted to sound contemporary. The "enlightened"
friends of the Jews invariably quoted from Montesquieu and did battle with
Voltaire.

Hertzberg, *The French Enlightenment and the Jews* (1968), 10.

An analysis of everything that Voltaire wrote about Jews throughout his
life establishes the proposition that he is the major link in Western intellectual history between the anti-Semitism of classic paganism and the
modern age.

Hertzberg, *The French Enlightenment and the Jews* (1968), 10.

The defenders of Voltaire have continued to argue that he was not personally
an anti-Semite but only guilty of some rhetorical excesses. That is not how
those who were arguing for and against the emancipation of the Jews, both
in his own time and in the next several generations, read him.

Hertzberg, letter to the editor (1990), 50.

Milton Himmelfarb (1928–2006)

SOCIOGRAPHER

It is not clear how many descendants Voltaire has left. Sade probably has more.

Himmelfarb, "Paganism, Religion and Modernity" (1968), 90.

Christopher Hitchens (1949–2011)

ENGLISH-BORN AUTHOR, JOURNALIST, AND POLEMICIST

Though I dislike to differ with such a great man, Voltaire was simply ludicrous when he said that if god did not exist it would be necessary to invent
him. The human invention of god is the problem to begin with.

Hitchens, *God Is Not Great* (2008), 96. After Hitchens's death, his friend Peter Foges said
this in a letter to the editor of the *New York Times*: "Mr. Hitchens faced death bravely, his
atheism intact. Unlike Voltaire, he never buckled" (Foges, "Hitchens's Atheism, Intact"
[2016], A26).

As a convinced atheist, I ought to agree with Voltaire that Judaism is not just one more religion, but in its way the root of religious evil. . . . Much of the time, I do concur with Voltaire, but not without acknowledging that Judaism is dialectical. . . . Judaism forces its adherents to study and think, it reluctantly teaches them what others think, and it may even teach them how to think.

Hitchens, "Thinking Thrice about the Jewish Question" (2010), 374.

Richard Hofstadter (1916–1970)

PROFESSOR OF AMERICAN HISTORY AT COLUMBIA UNIVERSITY

In the 1790's, when the influence of Deism reached its peak in America, there was a great deal of frightened talk about the incursions of infidelity. These alarms mainly affected the members of the established denominations whose colleges and defecting believers were involved. It is also true that Voltaire and Tom Paine served as whipping boys for preachers during the revivals that broke out after 1795.

Hofstadter, *Anti-Intellectualism in American Life* (1963), 120.

William Dean Howells (1837–1920)

REALIST NOVELIST, LITERARY CRITIC, AND PLAYWRIGHT,
NICKNAMED THE "DEAN OF AMERICAN LETTERS"

Most other readers . . . will share my interest in the devout, the mystical, the knightly treatment of the story of Joan of Arc by Mark Twain. Voltaire tried to make her a laughing-stock and a by-word. He was a very great wit, but he failed to defame her, for the facts were against him. It is our humorist's fortune to have the facts with him, and whatever we think of Joan of Arc, inspired or deluded, we shall feel the wonder of them the more for the light his imagination has thrown upon them.

Howells, *My Mark Twain* (1910), 155–156.

Victor Hugo (1802–1885)

FRENCH DRAMATIST, NOVELIST, AND POET

Voltaire parle à un parti, Molière parle à la société, Shakspeare parle à l'homme.

Voltaire speaks to a party, Molière to society, Shakespeare to mankind.

Hugo, "Butte de cette publication," March 1834, in *Littérature et philosophie mêlées* (1834), lxiii.

Des deux hommes qui ont dominé le dix-huitième siècle, Jean-Jacques a plus fait pour la révolution, Voltaire pour la civilisation.

Of the two men who dominated the eighteenth century, Jean-Jacques did more to promote the revolution, Voltaire, more for civilization.

Hugo, *Choses vues* (1846), 767.

Un livre multiple résumant un siècle, voilà ce que je laisserai derrière moi. Voltaire a résumé dans son oeuvre le dix-huitième siècle, je résumerai le dix-neuvième siècle. Voltaire a sa bible en soixante-quinze volumes, j'aurai la mienne.

A multivolume book summing up an entire century; that is what I shall leave behind. Voltaire summed up in his work the eighteenth century, I shall do the same for the nineteenth. Voltaire has his Bible in seventy-five volumes, I shall have mine.

Draft letter dated December 8, 1859, intended recipient unknown. Quoted in Journet and Robert, *Contribution aux études sur Victor Hugo* (1979), 2:12.

Voltaire, diminué comme poète, a monté comme apôtre. Il a fait plutôt du bien que du beau. Le bien étant inclus dans le beau, ceux qui, comme Dante et Shakespeare, ont fait le beau, dépassent Voltaire; mais au-dessous du poète, la place du philosophe est encore très haute, et Voltaire est le philosophe. Voltaire, c'est du bon sens à jet continu. Excepté en littérature, il est bon juge en tout. Voltaire a été, en dépit de ses insulteurs, presque adoré de son vivant; il est admiré aujourd'hui en pleine connaissance de cause. Le dix-huitième siècle voyait son esprit; nous voyons son âme.

Voltaire, diminished as a poet, rose as an apostle. He produced good deeds instead of works of beauty. The good being included in the beautiful, those who, like Dante and Shakespeare, have produced the beautiful, surpass Voltaire; but below the poet, the place of the philosopher is still very high, and Voltaire is a philosopher. Voltaire is a constant stream of good sense. Aside from literature, he is a good judge of everything. Despite those who abused him, Voltaire was adored in his lifetime; today he is justly admired. The eighteenth century saw his mind; we see his soul.

Hugo, *William Shakespeare* (1864), 470.

On est laid à Nanterre,	They're ugly in Nanterre,
C'est la faute à Voltaire;	Blame it on Voltaire;
On est bête à Palaiseau,	They're dumb in Palaiseau,
C'est la faute à Rousseau.	Blame it on Rousseau.
Je ne suis pas notaire,	I am not a notary,
C'est la faute à Voltaire;	Blame it on Voltaire;

Je suis petit oiseau,	I am a little bird,
C'est la faute à Rousseau.	Blame it on Rousseau.
Joie est mon caractère,	Joy is my character,
C'est la faute à Voltaire;	Blame it on Voltaire;
Misère est mon trousseau,	Misery is my trousseau,
C'est la faute à Rousseau.	Blame it on Rousseau.
Je suis tombé par terre,	I've fallen to the ground,
C'est la faute à Voltaire,	Blame it on Voltaire;
Le nez dans le ruisseau,	My nose in the gutter,
C'est la faute à . . .	Blame it on . . .

Gavroche, the street urchin, was singing this song in Hugo's historical novel *Les Misérables* (1862) when he was shot and killed during a popular protest in Paris in 1832. For the song "La Faute a Voltaire," in the musical version of *Les Misérables*, inspired by this text by Hugo, see the entry "Alain Boublil (1941–) and Jean-Marc Natel (1942–)."

Bonté de l'exil.
   Voltaire est plus Voltaire à Ferney qu'à Paris.

The fortunate outcome of exile:
   Voltaire is more Voltaire at home in Ferney than in Paris.

Hugo, manuscript note in a scrapbook, *Océan prose* (1866–1869), in *Œuvres complètes* (1989), 72.

De certaines destinées ont deux noms. Le premier est comme la préface de l'autre. On est Poquelin avant d'être Molière, Arouet avant d'être Voltaire, et Bonaparte avant d'être Napoléon. Cela tient à ce que ces hommes ont deux aspects, valet de chambre et génie, courtisan et roi, soldat républicain et empereur.

Certain destinies bear two names. The first is as the preface to the other. One is Poquelin before becoming Molière, Arouet before being Voltaire, Bonaparte before Napoléon. That is because these men have two facets: valet and genius, courtier and king, republican soldier and emperor.

Hugo, "Faits et croyances," in *Océan prose* (1866–1869).

On peut dire que, dans ce fécond dix-huitième siècle, Rousseau représente le Peuple; Voltaire, plus vaste encore, représente l'Homme. Ces puissants écrivains ont disparu; mais ils nous ont laissé leur âme, la Révolution.

One may say that in that fruitful eighteenth century, Rousseau represented the People; Voltaire, still more vast, represented Man. Those powerful writers have died, but they left us their soul, the Revolution.

Hugo, "Le Centenaire de Voltaire," speech at the Théâtre de la Gaité in Paris, May 30, 1878, marking the centenary of Voltaire's death, published in the Paris daily cofounded by Hugo, *Le Rappel*, on June 1, 1878.

Voltaire est plus qu'un chef d'État, c'est un chef d'idées.

Voltaire is more than a head of state, he is a leader of ideas.

Final words in Hugo's speech at the Théâtre de la Gaité in Paris, May 30, 1878.

Aldous Huxley (1894–1963)

ENGLISH NOVELIST, ESSAYIST, CRITIC, SCREENWRITER, AND PHILOSOPHER

Mr. Strachey is the eighteenth century grown-up; he is Voltaire at two hundred and thirty.

Aldous Huxley, "The Author of 'Eminent Victorians'" (1922), 41.

Il faut cultiver notre jardin. Yes, but suppose one begins to wonder why?

Aldous Huxley, *On the Margin* (1923), 17.

In the past there was an age of Shakespeare, of Voltaire, of Dickens. Ours is the age, not of any poet or thinker or novelist, but of the Document. Our Representative Man is the travelling newspaper correspondent, who dashes off a best seller between two assignments.

Aldous Huxley, narration in the novel *Time Must Have a Stop* (1944), 295.

T. H. Huxley (1825–1895)

ENGLISH BIOLOGIST AND GRANDFATHER OF ALDOUS HUXLEY

It is said that he lived at Babylon in the time of King Moabdar; but the name Moabdar does not appear in the list of Babylonian sovereigns brought to light by the patience and industry of the decipherers of cuneiform inscriptions in these later years; nor indeed am I aware that there is any other authority for his existence than that of the biographer of Zadig, one Arouet de Voltaire, among whose more conspicuous merits strict historical accuracy is perhaps hardly to be reckoned.

T. H. Huxley, "On the Method of Zadig" (1880), 929. Presumably this jab at Voltaire and *Zadig* was tongue-in-cheek.

Clive James (1939–2019)

AUSTRALIAN-BORN BRITISH WRITER, CRITIC, POET,
AND TELEVISION COMMENTATOR

I have all the correspondence of Voltaire, and enjoy dipping into it: but I will probably never read it through. You need to be very mad about an author to follow him down all his alleys, because you will be spending time on his minutiae that you could be devoting to someone else's main event.

James, *Cultural Amnesia* (2007), 661.

Henri Jeanson (1900–1970)

FRENCH JOURNALIST AND AUTHOR

Voltaire est un mort qu'il faut tuer tous les vingt-cinq ans, car tous les vingt-cinq ans, Voltaire renaît de ses ennemis depuis longtemps oubliés.

Voltaire is a dead man who must be killed every quarter century, because every quarter century Voltaire is reborn out of his long-forgotten enemies.

Jeanson, "Lettres ou pas lettres" (1944), 4.

Walter Kerr (1913–1996)

PULITZER PRIZE–WINNING *NEW YORK HERALD TRIBUNE*
AND *NEW YORK TIMES* THEATER CRITIC, MARRIED
TO AUTHOR JEAN KERR

Three of the most talented people our theater possesses—Lillian Hellman, Leonard Bernstein, Tyrone Guthrie—have joined hands to transform Voltaire's "Candide" into a really spectacular disaster.

Lead paragraph in Kerr's review of the original Broadway production of *Candide* in the *New York Herald Tribune*, December 3, 1956, 10. Kerr called it a "singularly ill-conceived venture." In the *New York Times* almost twenty years later, Kerr called the 1973 revival of *Candide* a "most satisfying resurrection," adding that it "may at last have stumbled into the best of all possible productions." See Kerr, "Is This the Best of All Possible 'Candides'?" (1973), 1.

Russell Kirk (1918–1994)

CONSERVATIVE POLITICAL AND SOCIAL THEORIST

Edmund Burke's conservative argument was a reply to three separate radical schools: the rationalism of the *philosophes*; the romantic sentimentalism of Rousseau and his disciples; and the nascent utilitarianism of Bentham. . . .

Burke was quite aware of the hostility between the rationalism of Voltaire's associates and the romantic idealism of Rousseau's adherents; he assaulted both camps, although generally training his heavy guns on Rousseau.

Kirk, *The Conservative Mind* (1953), 24.

Walter Kirn (1962–)

JOURNALIST, NOVELIST, CRITIC, AND ESSAYIST

Tell it to Voltaire, Mark Twain, and a thousand other pseudonymous & anonymous satirists, critics, etc.

On Kirn's Twitter account, @walterkirn, July 5, 2017, in response to a tweet by opinion writer David Frum: "My view: if you have something to say online, you should sign your name. If you won't sign your name, you shouldn't say it."

Alan Charles Kors (1943–)

PROFESSOR OF HISTORY AT THE UNIVERSITY OF PENNSYLVANIA

That line is the bane of Voltaire scholars around the world.

Kors quoted in Taylor, "Voltaire Wasn't Prepared to Die Defending the Right to Free Speech" (2017). Taylor began this essay by saying, "Surely no phrase has logged more miles in the promotion of ideological liberty than Voltaire's famous statement, 'I disapprove of what you say, but will defend to the death your right to say it.' It is the gold standard for quotations mustered in defence of free speech." Taylor correctly credited Evelyn Beatrice Hall with having "fabricated" the line.

He was no friend of Protestants or Jews, but he was willing to speak out for their rights.

Kors quoted in Taylor, "Voltaire Wasn't Prepared to Die Defending the Right to Free Speech" (2017).

Herbert Kretzmer (1925–)

SOUTH AFRICAN JOURNALIST AND LYRICIST

Master of the house?
Isn't worth me spit!
"Comforter, philosopher"
—and lifelong shit!
Cunning little brain
Regular Voltaire

Thinks he's quite a lover,
But there's not much there
What a cruel trick of nature
Landed me with such a louse
God knows how I've lasted
Living with this bastard in the house!

Sung by Mme Thénardier in "Master of the House," in the British production of *Les Misérables*, which premiered in London on October 5, 1985, with music by Claude-Michel Schönberg, words by Kretzmer. The original French version was first staged in Paris in September 1980, with lyrics by Alain Boublil and Jean-Marc Natel.

Louis Kronenberger (1904–1980)

CRITIC AND EDITOR

For the world at large Voltaire is today merely the author of *Candide*.

Kronenberger, "Candide" (1969), 100.

Voltaire, being both a great ad hoc pamphleteer and one of the supreme comic imps of all time, would not refute Leibnitz with logic; he would smother him in ridicule. Dr. Pangloss was to be made not just a fool, but a byword for foolishness. Optimism was not just to be trounced and stood in a corner; it was to be drawn and quartered and scattered to the winds.

Kronenberger, "Candide" (1969), 102.

Though *Candide* has, right on to the end, its convulsions of laughter, it is more than wild-eyed extravaganza: it manages to refute Leibnitz on realistic as well as surrealist terms; it even manages to neglect a chief theme which has proved so easy a target. Voltaire was not to rest content pulverizing another man's philosophy; he was to promulgate his own opinions and drive home his own point of view. Against optimism he set not just a fantastic pessimism but a reasoned one; against Dr. Pangloss a Martin; and, finally, against a reasoned pessimism a reasoned relativism, a making the best of whatever sort of world ours may be.

Kronenberger, "Candide" (1969), 103.

Gaston Labadie-Lagrave (1842–1919)

FRENCH JOURNALIST

Cet écrivain est célèbre de l'autre côté de l'Atlantique et il commence à être un peu connu en France depuis un récent voyage qu'il a fait à Paris. Il doit sa réputation à de petits romans à thèses dans le goût de Candide, de Zadig et de la Princesse de Baby-lone. C'est un genre un peu démodé chez nous, mais très apprécié aux Etats-Unis.

Ce lointain disciple de Voltaire se distingue par une indisputable fécondité d'imagination, mais il apporte peu de variété dans ses procédés littéraires.

This writer is celebrated on the other side of the Atlantic, and he is begin-ning to be known a little in France since a recent trip he made to Paris. He owes his reputation to little romances in the style of "Candide," "Zadig," and "The Princess of Babylone." It is a style somewhat out of fashion with us, but greatly liked in the United States.

This foreign disciple of Voltaire is distinguished for great fecundity of imag-ination, but there is little variety in his literary work.

Labadie-Lagrave commenting on Mark Twain in "Les appréciations des Américains sur l'œuvre de Paul Bourget" (1895), 19. The translation is from "A Frenchman on Mark Twain and His Criticisms of Bourget" (1895), 11.

Felicia Lamport (1916–1999)

AMERICAN REPORTER, POET, AND SATIRIST

A dictionary without quotations was described by Voltaire as only a skel-eton, but the average or non-scholarly American favors the skeletal in dictionaries.

Lamport, "Dictionaries" (1959), 52.

Gustave Lanson (1857–1934)

FRENCH HISTORIAN AND LITERARY CRITIC

Voltaire est un journaliste de génie: agir sur l'opinion qui agit sur le pouvoir, dans un pays où le pouvoir est faible et l'opinion forte, c'est tout le système du journalisme contemporain; et c'est Voltaire qui l'a créé.

Voltaire is a journalist of genius: to affect public opinion that affects power, in a country where power is weak and opinion strong, is what modern-day jour-nalism is all about; and Voltaire created it.

Lanson, *Histoire de la littérature française* (1896), 750.

Rien n'est plus difficile que de porter un jugement d'ensemble sur Voltaire.

There is nothing more difficult than making an overall assessment of Voltaire.

Lanson, *Histoire de la littérature française* (1896), 756.

En un mot, Voltaire est un grand journaliste. Il représente, à une date où la presse naissait à peine, le génie et la puissance de la presse. Il a tous les défauts du journaliste: information superficielle, affirmations téméraires, plaisanteries ou personnalitiés substituées à la discussion approfondie des idées, partialité passionnée. Mais il a au suprême degré les talents que le journalisme exige: des connaissances universelles, une faculté prodigieuse d'assimilation, un sens juste, rapide, aigu, infiniment plus de sérieux et de solidité qu'on ne dit souvent sous la légèreté du ton, et puis le talent d'exciter la curiosité, d'intéresser l'indifférence, de saisir l'actualité, de tout rendre clair et simple, de tourner toutes les idées du côté qui les fait mieux comprendre et goûter.

In sum, Voltaire was a great *journalist*. He embodied the genius and power of the press at a time when the press was in its infancy. He had all the usual journalistic flaws: a superficial grasp of the facts, a penchant for reckless assertions, joking or making personal jibes rather than engaging in a deep discussion of ideas, and he was passionately partisan. But he had a superb command of the skills journalism requires: a breadth of knowledge, a prodigious ability to assimilate information, judgment that was solid, sharp, and quick. He was often infinitely more serious and grounded than his light touch led one to believe, and he had the ability to arouse curiosity, challenge indifference, seize upon current events, clarify and simplify issues, and cast ideas in a light that made them easier to understand and appreciate.

Lanson, "Voltaire," an unsigned entry in *La Grande Encyclopédie* (1902), 31:1127.

Les Lettres philosophiques *sont la première bombe lancée contre l'ancien régime.*

The *Lettres philosophiques* were the first bomb lobbed at the Ancien Régime.

Lanson, "Voltaire" (1902), 52.

Lewis H. Lapham (1935–)

JOURNALIST, WRITER, AND EDITOR AT *HARPER*'S MAGAZINE

The founders of the American republic devoted themselves to the study of history because they knew that they had nothing else on which to build the future except the blueprint of the past. Well aware of both the continuity and contingency of human affairs, Adams and Madison searched the works of Tacitus and Voltaire and Locke like carpenters rummaging through their assortment of tools, knowing that all the pediments were jury-rigged, all the inscriptions provisional, all the alliances temporary.

Lapham, *Waiting for the Barbarians* (1997), 64.

The marketing directors who make the rules of commercial publishing regard humor of any kind as so specialized a commodity that the chain bookstores make no distinction between the works of Voltaire and those of Garfield the cat; both authors appear under signs marked HUMOR in order that the prospective reader will be advised to approach them with caution. The words might not mean what they say.

Lapham, *Waiting for the Barbarians* (1997), 127.

Harold J. Laski (1893–1950)

ENGLISH POLITICAL THEORIST AND PROFESSOR
OF GOVERNMENT AT THE LONDON SCHOOL OF ECONOMICS

We call the eighteenth century the age of Voltaire because he made its wrongs inescapably known to every man who could read; and he used the whole armory of intelligence to that end. Humor, wit, satire, these were vital weapons in his hands; but he used them, in Mr. Forsyth's phrase, at the point where "it is necessary to stick the stiletto in and twist it around." He made all his enemies angry; that was the proof that he was doing his job as it needed to be done. The times require a Voltaire; but he must do something more than arouse laughter in our enemies.

Laski, "Is Laughter a Weapon?" (1937), 16. Laski was one of five contributors to this symposium in print, inspired by an essay in the August 3, 1937, issue by Robert Forsythe, "Strictly from Anger" containing the phrase "stick the stiletto in and twist it around."

Vladimir I. Lenin (1870–1924)

RUSSIAN COMMUNIST REVOLUTIONARY
AND POLITICAL LEADER

Je ne ferai jamais le pèlerinage de Ferney: je n'aime pas les gens d'esprit.

I will never make the pilgrimage to Ferney: I do not like witty people.

Quoted by André Gide from an unnamed biography of Lenin in "Notes sur Voltaire" (1937), 534. According to Gide, Lenin made this comment in Switzerland (he was in Geneva in 1900).

Bernard-Henri Lévy (1948–)

FRENCH INTELLECTUAL AND AUTHOR

I hate Voltaire.

According to the satirical Parisian weekly *Le Canard Enchaîné*, in the spring of 1979, "dans un appartement chic" in Cambridge, Massachusetts, Lévy was asked whether he preferred

Voltaire or Rousseau. This was his curt reply, delivered in English. See Clémentin, "J'suis pas enceinte, j'suis obèse" (1979), 4.

Simon-Nicolas-Henri Linguet (1736–1794)

JOURNALIST AND LAWYER

Jamais le mot propre ne manque à Racine. *Rarement M. de* Voltaire *le trouve (en* Poesie*). On sent même qu'il n'a pas pris la peine de le chercher.*

The proper word is never wanting in *Racine*. Rarely does M. de *Voltaire* find it (in *Poetry*). One gets the sense that he doesn't even take the trouble to look.

Linguet, *Examen des ouvrages de M. de Voltaire* (1788), 84.

Walter Lippmann (1889–1974)

JOURNALIST AND POLITICAL WRITER

Mr. Mencken . . . sees himself as the companion of a small masterful minority who rule the world and who, because it is so simple to rule the world, have ample leisure for talk. In that circle Mencken is the gayest spirit of the lot, the literary pope, of course, but with a strong flavor of Rabelais and Voltaire about him.

Lippmann, "The Near Machiavelli" (1922), 14.

Dahlia Lithwick (1968–)

CANADIAN-AMERICAN LAWYER AND JOURNALIST

Voltaire once wrote that if God didn't exist, it would be necessary for us to invent him. We did, and we called it the U.S. Supreme Court. But the court, like us, proved to be human in the end.

Lithwick writing about the Supreme Court decision in the Florida recount case that arose from the 2000 presidential election in "Last Count for the Recount" (2000).

James Russell Lowell (1819–1891)

POET, CRITIC, EDITOR OF THE *ATLANTIC MONTHLY*, PROFESSOR OF MODERN LANGUAGES AT HARVARD COLLEGE, AND DIPLOMAT

Freedom of thought owes far more to the jester Voltaire who also had his solid kernel of earnest, than to the sombre Genevese [Jean-Jacques Rousseau], whose earnestness is of the deadly kind.

Lowell, "Rousseau and the Sentimentalists," in *Among My Books* (1870), 353.

Robert Lynd (1879–1949)

ANGLO-IRISH JOURNALIST, ESSAYIST, AND POETRY EDITOR
OF THE *NEWS CHRONICLE* (LONDON)

Thoughtful Christians can no longer accept the old Hell, because it would mean, not the final triumph of righteousness, but the final defeat of God. Many of those who dutifully cling to the dogma of their Church on the point would agree with the French curé who said that he believed in Hell, but he did not think there was anybody in it but Voltaire. And even Voltaire will nowadays seem to most people to be hardly a sufficiently scandalous person to deserve millions of years of anguish.

Lynd, "The Decline and Fall of Hell" (1915), 48–49.

Thomas Babington Macaulay (1800–1859)

BRITISH POET, HISTORIAN, AND WHIG POLITICIAN

The three most eminent masters of the art of ridicule, during the eighteenth century, were, we conceive, Addison, Swift, and Voltaire. Which of the three had the greatest power of moving laughter may be questioned. But each of them, within his own domain, was supreme. Voltaire is the prince of buffoons. His merriment is without disguise or restraint. He gambols; he grins; he shakes his sides; he points the finger; he turns up the nose; he shoots out the tongue. The manner of Swift is the very opposite to this. He moves laughter, but never joins in it. He appears in his works such as he appeared in society. All the company are convulsed with merriment, while the Dean, the author of all the mirth, preserves an invincible gravity, and even sourness of aspect; and gives utterance to the most eccentric and ludicrous fancies, with the air of a man reading the commination-service.

Macaulay, review of Lucy Aikin, *The Life of Joseph Addison* (1843), in "Life and Writings of Addison," *The Edinburgh Review or Critical Journal*, July 1843, 230.

The nature of Voltaire was, indeed, not inhuman; but he venerated nothing. Neither in the masterpieces of art nor in the purest examples of virtue, neither in the Great First Cause nor in the awful enigma of the grave, could he see any thing but subjects for drollery. The more solemn and august the theme, the more monkey-like was his grimacing and chattering. The mirth of Swift is the mirth of Mephistophiles; the mirth of Voltaire is the mirth of Puck.

Macaulay, "Life and Writings of Addison" (1843), 231.

No kind of power is more formidable than the power of making men ridiculous; and that power Addison possessed in boundless measure. How grossly that power was abused by Swift and by Voltaire is well known.

Macaulay, "Life and Writings of Addison" (1843), 231.

Norman Mailer (1923–2007)

NOVELIST, MAN OF LETTERS, AND
PUBLIC INTELLECTUAL

I really do believe that there's a close-knit war between God and the devil that goes on in all our affairs. People hate the thought today, because we live in a technological time where human beings are sick and tired of the heritage of the Middle Ages, a time when we all crawled on our bellies and prayed to God and sobbed and said, Oh, God, please pay attention to me. Oh, God please save me. Oh, Devil, stay away. Well, we've had the Enlightenment since then. We've had Voltaire. We've had several centuries in which to forge our vanity as human beings, and now we are a third force. There's God at one end, the devil at the other, and there we are occupying this huge center. And half of us alive don't believe in God or the devil.

Mailer in an interview in April 2007 in O'Hagan, "Norman Mailer" (2007), reprinted in *The Paris Review Interviews* (2008), 410.

Joseph de Maistre (1753–1821)

LAWYER, AUTHOR, DIPLOMAT FOR THE KINGDOM
OF SAVOY, AND CONSERVATIVE CATHOLIC THINKER

Voyez ce front abject que la pudeur ne colora jamais, ces deux cratères éteints où semblent bouillonner encore la luxure et la haine. Cette bouche.—Je dis mal peut-être, mais ce n'est pas ma faute.—Ce rictus épouvantable, courant d'une oreille a l'autre, et ces deux lèvres pincées par la cruelle malice comme un ressort prêt à se détendre pour lancer le blaspheme ou le sarcasme.—Ne me parlez pas de cet homme, je ne puis en soutenir l'idée.

Look at that wretched forehead, never touched by the blush of modesty, the two extinct craters where lust and hate seem to bubble forth. That mouth.—I express myself poorly, but it is not my fault.—That ghastly *grin*, running from ear to ear, and those two lips, pinched by cruel malice, like a spring ready to uncoil and let loose a blasphemous or sarcastic remark.—Do not speak to me of this man, I cannot abide the thought.

Figure 31. Jean-Antoine Houdon, *Voltaire*, painted plaster and wood statuette, likely made between 1779 and 1793. Ackland Art Museum, Chapel Hill, North Carolina (Ackland Fund, 75.15.1). This a copy of the original maquette from 1778 for the life-sized marble statue commissioned by Mme Denis. The statue, which she presented to the Comédie-Française, was exhibited in the biennial Paris Salon of 1781.

Maistre, *Les Soirées de Saint-Pétersbourg* (1821), 274. De Maistre was describing Voltaire's face on his statue at the Hermitage Palace, now the Hermitage Museum. The statue is a second version, commissioned by Catherine the Great, of Houdon's seated Voltaire at the Comédie-Française.

Joseph Marty (1823–1899)

FRENCH LITERARY SCHOLAR

. . . le siècle de Voltaire.

. . . the century of Voltaire.

This may be the first appearance in print of this familiar phrase. It was used in reference to an obscure poet, playwright, and *académicien*, François Andrieux, whom Marty called "the worthy and last representative of the age of Voltaire." Marty, *Les Principaux monuments funéraires du Père-Lachaise* (1839), under the section heading "Andrieux," 1.

W. Somerset Maugham (1874–1965)

ENGLISH PLAYWRIGHT, NOVELIST, AND SHORT STORY WRITER

It is not an accident that the best prose was written when rococo, with its elegance and moderation, at its birth attained its greatest excellence. . . . It has been said that good prose should resemble the conversation of a well-bred man. Conversation is only possible when men's minds are free from pressing anxieties. Their lives must be reasonably secure and they must have no grave concern about their souls. They must attach importance to the refinements of civilisation. They must value courtesy . . . and they must look upon "enthusiasm" with a critical glance. This is a soil very suitable for prose. It is not to be wondered at that it gave a fitting opportunity for the appearance of the best writer of prose that our modern world has seen, Voltaire. The writers of English . . . have seldom reached the excellence that seems to have come so naturally to him.

Maugham, *The Summing Up* (1938), 77.

Francois Mauriac (1885–1970)

FRENCH WRITER

On n'imagine pas Jean-Jacques ou Voltaire ou Diderot s'interrrompant jamais d'apprendre aux gens ce qu'ils doivent penser de l'homme qui est né bon, de la société qui le corrompt, et des lois, et du progrès des sciences, et de la superstition.

It is difficult to imagine Jean-Jacques, or Voltaire or Diderot ever getting tired of telling men what they should think of Man who is born good, of society which corrupts him, of laws, of the advances of science, of superstition.

Mauriac, *Mémoires intérieurs* (1959), 138. The translation is from the American edition, also titled *Mémoires intérieurs* (1961), 100.

Andre Maurois (1885–1967)

FRENCH WRITER

On a dit que le dix-huitième siècle avait été le siècle de Voltaire, comme le dix-septième celui de Louis XIV. C'est exact.

It has been said that the eighteenth century was the age of Voltaire, just as the seventeenth was the age of Louis XIV. That is exactly right.

Maurois, *Voltaire* (1935), 14–15.

Théiste de nom, humaniste de fait, voilà Voltaire.

A theist in name, a humanist in fact—that is Voltaire.

Maurois, *Voltaire* (1935), 98. The translation is from Maurois, "An Appreciation of Voltaire" (1959), 6.

La rencontre de Franklin et de Voltaire, la démocratie embrassant le déisme, c'est la Révolution qui commence.

The meeting of Franklin and Voltaire, democracy embracing theism, was the dawn of the Revolution.

Maurois, *Voltaire* (1935), 132.

Il était à Ferney comme un lièvre au gîte, mais comme un lièvre belliqueux et qui, dans la jungle politique, tenait parfois les lions en arrêt.

At Ferney he was like a hare in its burrow, but a fierce hare, that in the jungle of politics sometimes held the lions at bay.

Maurois, *Voltaire* (1935), 137.

Jon Meacham (1969–)

AMERICAN JOURNALIST, POPULAR HISTORIAN, AND BIOGRAPHER

Neither conventionally devout nor wholly unbelieving, Jefferson surveyed and staked out an American middle ground between the ferocity of evangelizing Christians on one side and the contempt for religion of secular *philosophes* on the other. The right would like Jefferson to be a soldier of faith, the left an American Voltaire.

Meacham, introduction to *American Gospel* (2006), 4.

H. L. Mencken (1880–1956)

JOURNALIST, EDITOR, AND AUTHOR

Jesus Christ was the inevitable product of his time, just as Shakespeare, Bonaparte and Voltaire were of theirs.

Mencken, *The Philosophy of Friedrich Nietzsche* (1908), 255.

Even today—such is the force of collective opinion—we think of Voltaire and Machiavelli and others of their ilk as criminals rather than truth-tellers.

Mencken, *The Philosophy of Friedrich Nietzsche* (1908), 284.

Vivian Mercier (1919–1989)

IRISH LITERARY CRITIC

The American Voltaire.

Mercier referring to Thorstein Veblen in a review of *The Portable Jonathan Swift* (1948), 362.

Jules Michelet (1798–1874)

FRENCH HISTORIAN

Voltaire est celui qui souffre, celui qui a pris pour lui toutes les douleurs des hommes, qui ressent, poursuit, toute iniquité. Tout ce que le fanatisme et la tyrannie ont jamais fait de mal au monde, c'est à Voltaire qu'ils l'ont fait. Martyr, victime universelle, c'est lui qu'on égorgea à la Saint-Barthélemy, lui qu'on enterra aux ruines du nouveau monde, lui qu'on brûla à Séville, lui que le parlement de Toulouse roua avec Calas. . . . Il pleure, il rit dans les souffrances, rire terrible, auquel s'écroulent les bastilles des tyrans, les temples des Pharisiens.

Voltaire is the one who suffers, who has taken upon him all the agony of mankind, who feels and hunts out every iniquity. All the ills that fanaticism and tyranny have ever inflicted upon the world, have been inflicted upon Voltaire. It was he, the martyr, the universal victim, whom they slaughtered in their Saint Bartholomew, whom they buried in the mines of the new world, whom they burned at Seville, whom the parliament of Toulouse broke on the wheel with Calas.—He weeps, he laughs, in his agony,—a terrible laugh, at which the bastilles of tyrants and the temples of the Pharisees fall to the ground.

Michelet, *Histoire de la Révolution française* (1847), xc–xci. The text in English is from *The History of the French Revolution* (1847), 50–51.

Barbara Mikulski (1936–)

FORMER DEMOCRATIC SENATOR FROM MARYLAND

It is not perfect, but it is a very sound bill. Let's not make the perfect the enemy of the good.

Mikulski quoted in Hayward, "The Cliffhanger, Jan. 29" (2013). Mikulski was talking about a bill before Congress to assist victims of Hurricane Sandy. She was quoting, perhaps unwittingly, Voltaire's oft-repeated line about the better being the enemy of the good.

Nancy Mitford (1904–1973)

ENGLISH BIOGRAPHER

Let it not be thought that Voltaire was indifferent to royal personages. He was one of the great snobs of history.

Mitford, *Madame de Pompadour* (1954), 58.

He thought that an historical study should be composed like a play, with a beginning, a middle and an end, not a mere collection of facts: "If you want to bore the reader, tell him everything."

Mitford, *Voltaire in Love* (1957); in the 2012 edition, 52.

Malcolm Moos (1916–1982)

POLITICAL SCIENTIST AND PRESIDENT OF THE UNIVERSITY OF MINNESOTA

The world has need of its Voltaires in all ages. And no one was around in the twenties who could draw a bead so unerringly on a Dixie demagogue, intolerant lawmaker, preacher, or political jackass. Whatever Mencken may have held dear or central in the way of a political philosophy, no belief had greater priority than that men should work and live unmuzzled.

Moos, introduction to H. L. Mencken, *On Politics* (1956), xx.

Paul Morand (1888–1976)

FRENCH AUTHOR

Aujourd'hui personne n'ignore plus rien: il faudrait appeler cela, l'inculture: le grand soleil fait les déserts. Les primaires savent tout; les secondaires oublient tout; l'homme de demain rentrera dans la définition de Voltaire: "C'est, un imbécile, il a réponse à tout."

Nowadays there is nothing people don't know: we call it a lack of culture: the burning sun creates deserts. Men in charge know everything; those the next level down have forgotten everything; the man of tomorrow will fit Voltaire's definition: "He is an imbecile; he has an answer for everything."

Morand, "Mise au vert" ("Chroniques") (1953), 1073. The line attributed here to Voltaire must be a paraphrase of something he said or wrote.

"C'est un imbécile, il a réponse à tout." Ce mot de Voltaire m'a toujours frappé: une accumulation prodigieuse, un amas de connaissances encyclopédiques . . . se soldant par une soustraction.

"He is an imbecile; he has an answer for everything." I've always been struck by this line by Voltaire: a prodigious accumulation, a mass of encyclopedic knowledge . . . boiled down to its essence.

Morand, private journal entry for October 12, 1969, published posthumously in *Journal inutile 1968–1972* (2001), 279.

Christopher Morley (1890–1957)

JOURNALIST, NOVELIST, AND POET

"Ah, how you need a Voltaire! You have had lots of sentimental Rousseaus, but no Voltaire. But he would have to live as he did near our Geneva, in a bolt-hole prudently close to the frontier. Voltaire at Ferney, like an electric refrigerator secreting his crystalline cubes of clear reason! The electric current of all Europe's thinking was wired through Ferney, and when Voltaire's engine of intellect was at work the lights momentarily dimmed down everywhere dimmed down everywhere else because he was using so many kilowatts. America needs a Voltaire! What cauterizing comedy he could give us!"

The narrator, a Swiss émigré to the United States, to a native New Yorker, in Morley's satirical novel *Swiss Family Manhattan* (1932), 159. Later in the book the narrator defines the role of a philosopher, as he sees it: "a windshield wiper for humanity."

Lord John Morley (1838–1923)

BRITISH JOURNALIST, EDITOR, BIOGRAPHER,
LIBERAL POLITICAN, AND STATESMAN

Voltaire was a stupendous power, not only because his expression was incomparably lucid, or even because his sight was exquisitely clear, but because he saw many new things after which the spirits of others were unconsciously groping and dumbly yearning. . . . Voltaire was ever in the front and centre of the fight. His life was not a mere chapter in a history of literature. He never counted truth a treasure to be discreetly hidden in a napkin. He made it a perpetual war-cry, and emblazoned it on a banner that was many a time rent, but was never out of the field.

Morley, *Voltaire* (1872), 7.

Voltaire left France a poet, he returned to it a sage.

Morely, *Voltaire* (1872), 54; commenting on Voltaire's period of exile in England in 1726–1728.

The rivalry between the schools of Rousseau and Voltaire represents the dead-lock to which social thought had come, a dead-lock of which the catastrophe of the Revolution was both expression and result.

Morley, *Voltaire* (1872), 330.

Frank Luther Mott (1886–1964)

HEAD OF THE JOURNALISM DEPARTMENT AT THE UNIVERSITY OF IOWA AND DEAN OF THE UNIVERSITY OF MISSOURI SCHOOL OF JOURNALISM

and Chester E. Jorgenson (1907–after 1952)

It is the purpose of this essay to show that Franklin, the American Voltaire,—always reasonable if not intuitive, encyclopedic if not sublimely profound, humane if not saintly,—is best explained with reference to the Age of Enlightenment, of which he was the completist colonial representative.

Mott and Jorgenson, introduction to *Benjamin Franklin* (1936), xiii.

Wolfgang Amadeus Mozart (1756–1791)

AUSTRIAN COMPOSER

Nun gebe ich Ihnen eine Nachricht, die Sie vielleicht schon wissen werden, daß näm-lich der gottlose und Erzspitzbub Voltaire sozusagen wie ein Hund, wie ein Vieh krepiert ist—das ist der Lohn!

I must give you a piece of intelligence that you perhaps already know—namely, that the ungodly arch-villain Voltaire has died miserably like a dog—just like a brute. That is his reward!

Letter from Wolfgang Amadeus Mozart to his father, Leopold Mozart, July 3, 1778. Mozart, *Briefe* (1948), 93. The translation is from *The Letters of Wolfgang Amadeus Mozart, 1769–1791* (1865), 218.

Alfred de Musset (1810–1857)

FRENCH ROMANTIC POET

Dors-tu content, Voltaire, et ton hideux sourire
Voltige-t-il encor sur tes os décharnés?

Do you sleep well, Voltaire, and your hideous smile
Does it still flit about o'er your fleshless bones?

Musset, "Rolla," part 4 (1833), 382.

Ogden Nash (1902–1971)

AMERICAN POET SPECIALIZING IN LIGHT VERSE

The Abbé Voltaire, alias Arouet,
Never denounced the seed of the caraway;
Sufficient proof, if proof we need,
That he never bit into a caraway seed.

"The Caraway Seed," in Nash's collection of poems *Good Intentions* (1942), 136.

George Jean Nathan (1882–1958)

DRAMA CRITIC, EDITOR OF *THE SMART SET*,
AND COFOUNDER WITH H. L. MENCKEN OF
THE AMERICAN MERCURY

Frivolity and Criticism—"If Nature had not made us a little frivolous we should be most wretched. It is because one can be frivolous that the majority do not hang themselves." Thus, Voltaire.

I keep the M. Voltaire's dictum pasted conspicuously on my office piano, directly next to the rack of Beethoven's scherzi, to comfort me and assuage my feelings when some nuisance invades my sanctum and deplores my occasional professional levity.

Nathan, *The Intimate Notebooks of George Jean Nathan* (1932), 165. This quotation was attributed to Voltaire by Evelyn Beatrice Hall in her book *The Life of Voltaire* (1903).

Friedrich Nietzsche (1844–1900)

GERMAN PHILOSOPHER

Nicht Voltaire's maassvolle, dem Ordnen, Reinigen und Umbauen zugeneigte Natur, sondern Rousseau's leidenschaftliche Torheiten und Halblügen haben den optimistischen Geist der Revolution wachgerufen, gegen den ich rufe: "Écrasez l'infâme!" Durch ihn ist der Geist der Aufklärung und der fortschreitenden Entwicklung auf lange verscheucht worden: sehen wir zu—ein Jeder bei sich selber—ob es möglich ist, ihn wieder zurückzurufen!

It is not *Voltaire's* temperate nature, inclined to organising, cleansing and restructuring, but rather *Rousseau's* passionate idiocies and half-truths that have called awake the optimistic spirit of revolution, counter to which I shout: *"Ecrasez l'infame!"* Because of him, *the spirit of the Enlightenment and of progressive development* has been scared off for a long time to come: let us see—each one for himself—whether it is not possible to call it back again!

Item 463 in an English edition of short, one-paragraph texts or aphoristic sayings by Nietzsche in *Human, All Too Human* (2008), 91; in the original German, *Menschliches, Allzumenschliches* (1878), 310–311. Earlier in the same book Nietzsche evoked "the banner of enlightenment—a banner bearing the three names: Petrarch, Erasmus, Voltaire" ("die Fahne der Aufklärung—die Fahne mit den drei Namen: Petrarca, Erasmus, Voltaire").

Voltaire ist, im Gegensatz zu allem, was nach ihm schrieb, vor allem ein grandseigneur des Geistes: genau das, was ich auch bin.

Voltaire was, above all, in contrast to every writer who came after him, a *grand seigneur* of the spirit—like me.

Nietzsche, *Ecce Homo* (1908), 76. For a slightly different translation see Rickels, *Looking after Nietzsche* (1990), 129.

Richard M. Nixon (1913–1994)

REPUBLICAN CONGRESSMAN, SENATOR FROM CALIFORNIA, AND THIRTY-SEVENTH PRESIDENT OF THE UNITED STATES

"Écrasons l'Infâme."

During his freshman year at Whittier College in California in 1930, Nixon convinced a student group he helped organize to adopt as its credo this phrase (in English, "Let's Crush Evil"), inspired by Voltaire. Quoted in Black, *Richard M. Nixon* (2007), 25.

Albert Jay Nock (1870–1945)

LIBERTARIAN AUTHOR, CRITIC, THEORIST, CONTRIBUTOR
TO *THE NATION*, AND COEDITOR OF *THE FREEMAN*

Il faut cultiver notre jardin. With these words Voltaire ends his treatise called *Candide*, which in its few pages assays more solid worth, more informed common sense, than the entire bulk of nineteenth-century hedonist literature can show. To my mind, those few concluding words sum up the whole social responsibility of man. The only thing that the psychically-human being can do to improve society is to present society with one improved unit. In a word, ages of experience testify that the only way society can be improved is by the individualist method which Jesus apparently regarded as the only one whereby the Kingdom of Heaven can be established as a going concern; that is, the method of each *one* doing his best to improve *one*.

Nock, *Memoirs of a Superfluous Man* (1943), 307.

William H. Nolte (1928–1999)

LITERARY CRITIC

[H. L. Mencken was no Swift, no Voltaire, but] the nearest thing to these giants that America has ever produced.

Nolte, *H. L. Mencken* (1964), 260.

Michael Novak (1933–2017)

CATHOLIC PHILOSOPHER AND AMBASSADOR TO THE
UNITED NATIONS COMMISSION ON HUMAN RIGHTS

Whoever thought it would come to this? Most secular philosophers today, proudly calling themselves postmodernist, have given up on the Enlightenment and reason in favor of an easygoing moral relativism. In discussing everything from "Paradise Lost" to law to biology, today's "critical thinkers" strip away "patriarchal" objectivity to expose what they think is really real: power and interest. Today, the strongest and most unabashed defender of reason in the world appears to be the Pope. Voltaire, where art thou at this hour?

Novak, "It's Not All Relative" (1998), A27. John Paul II was pope from 1978 to 2005.

Alfred Noyes (1880–1958)

ENGLISH POET, FICTION WRITER, AND PLAYWRIGHT

He was born a poet.

Noyes, *Voltaire* (1936), 6.

Barack H. Obama (1961–)

LAWYER, COMMUNITY ORGANIZER, DEMOCRATIC SENATOR FROM
ILLINOIS, AND FORTY-FOURTH PRESIDENT OF THE UNITED STATES

I'm willing to consider it if it's necessary to actually pass a comprehensive plan.
I am not interested in making the perfect the enemy of the good—particularly
since there is so much good in this compromise that would actually reduce
our dependence on foreign oil.

Quoted in "Obama's Speech in Lansing, Michigan," *New York Times*, August 4, 2008.
Then-Senator Obama was talking about an offshore drilling bill pending in Congress during his first campaign for president, and perhaps unknowingly refrerencing Voltaire's
familiar line about the better being the enemy of the good.

Jean d'Ormesson (1925–2017)

FRENCH AUTHOR, JOURNALIST AND EDITOR WITH *LE FIGARO*,
AND MEMBER OF THE ACADÉMIE FRANÇAISE

*Voltaire vit vieux et il couvre tout son siècle. Son père, homme d'affaires du duc de
Saint-Simon et du duc de Richelieu, avait connu Corneille et Boileau. Lui-même
aurait pu, enfant, croiser les chemins de La Fontaine ou de Racine, il aurait pu,
vieillard, rencontrer Chateaubriand enfant. . . . Parce qu'il est d'une intelligence
merveilleuse et qu'il est partout à la fois, Voltaire est un journaliste de génie. Il tou-
che à tous les genres, et toujours avec succès. Il est dramaturge et historien, philosophe et romancier. Il écrit aussi des vers. Il est tout—sauf poète.*

Voltaire had a long life and embodied the whole of the century he lived in.
His father, who advised the duc de Saint-Simon and the duc de Richelieu in
financial matters, knew Corneille and Boileau. Voltaire, as a boy, could have
met La Fontaine or Racine. In old age, he could have met Chateaubriand when
Chateaubriand was a child. . . . Because he was superbly intelligent and everywhere at once, Voltaire was a journalist of genius. He tried his hand at everything, and always with success. He was a playwright and historian, philosopher and novelist. He also wrote verse. He was everything—but a poet.

Ormesson, *Une Autre histoire de la littérature française* (2000), 55.

Voltaire est le comble de la civilisation et de la culture. Il est l'héritier, indigne, évidemment, de Racine et du classicisme du Grand Siècle. Il appartient tout entier à une société dont il combat les excès et les injustices—mais seulement les excès et les injustices. Il aime le luxe, l'argent, la vie facile, le plaisir. C'est un jouisseur et un intellectuel.

Voltaire is the epitome of civilization and culture. He was the heir, unworthy, of course, of Racine and the classicism of the great seventeenth century. He fit in perfectly in a society whose excesses and injustices he opposed—but only its excesses and injustices. He loved luxury, money, the creature comforts, pleasure. He was a sensualist and an intellectual.

Ormesson, *Une Autre histoire de la littérature française* (2000), 71.

Sentimental et passionné, Jean-Jacques aime la nature par-dessus tout et il n'est à l'aise ni dans la société ni avec lui-même. . . . Tout est si facile avec Voltaire. Rien n'est simple avec Rousseau.

Sentimental and passionate, Jean-Jacques loved nature more than anything else and he was uncomfortable in society and with himself. . . . Everything is so easy with Voltaire. Nothing is simple with Rousseau.

Ormesson, *Une Autre histoire de la littérature française* (2000), 71.

George Orwell (1903–1950)

ENGLISH JOURNALIST, ESSAYIST, CRITIC, AND NOVELIST

Mark Twain has sometimes been compared with his contemporary, Anatole France. This comparison is not so pointless as it may sound. Both men were the spiritual children of Voltaire, both had an ironical, sceptical view of life, and a native pessimism overlaid by gaiety; both knew that the existing social order is a swindle and its cherished beliefs mostly delusions.

Orwell, "Mark Twain—The Licensed Jester" (1943), 14. George Bernard Shaw also compared Twain to Voltaire. Oddly enough, although Twain seems to have admired Voltaire, and jotted down quotes from his writings in his notebooks, there is no record of him ever actually commenting on Voltaire.

Twain mildly satirized his contemporaries in *The Gilded Age*, but he also gave himself up to the prevailing fever, and made and lost vast sums of money. He even for a period of years deserted writing for business; and he squandered his time on buffooneries, not merely lecture tours and public banquets, but, for instance, the writing of a book like *A Connecticut Yankee in King Arthur's Court*, which is a deliberate flattery of all that is worst and most vulgar in American life. The man who might have been a kind of rustic Voltaire became the world's leading after-dinner speaker, charming alike for his anecdotes and his power to make businessmen feel themselves public benefactors.

Orwell, "Mark Twain—The Licensed Jester" (1943), 15.

Camille Paglia (1947–)

CULTURE AND SOCIAL CRITIC AND PROFESSOR OF
HUMANITIES AND MEDIA STUDIES AT THE UNIVERSITY
OF THE ARTS, PHILADELPHIA

Candide is about a simple and naive person who does not fully understand the complex world. Chauncey Gardiner, in *Being There*, was another. So the movies are symptomatic of the quest for truth, a turn away from false complexity.

Quoted in Sheff, "Playboy Interview: Camille Paglia" (1995), 57.

Theodore Parker (1810–1860)

UNITARIAN MINISTER AND ABOLITIONIST

The Roman Church forbade science, burnt Jordano Bruno, and reduced Galileo to silence and his knees. So much the worse for the Church. The French philosophy of the last century, its Encyclopædia of scoffs at religion, were the unavoidable counterpart. Voltaire and Diderot took vengeance for the injustice done to their philosophic forerunners. The fagots of the Middle Ages got repaid by the fiery press of the last generation.

Parker, *Ten Sermons of Religion* (1853), 145–146. The Dominican friar, mathematician, and philosopher, Giordano Bruno, was convicted of heresy and burned at the stake by the Roman Inquisition in 1600.

Walter Pater (1839–1894)

ENGLISH ESSAYIST AND ART CRITIC

Voltaire belongs to that flimsier, more artificial classical tradition, which Winckelmann was one day to supplant.

Pater, "Winckelmann" (1867), 82.

Roger Pearson (1949–)

PROFESSOR OF FRENCH AT THE UNIVERSITY OF OXFORD

The one work which influenced his thinking perhaps more than any other: *Locke's Essay on Human Understanding.*

Pearson, introduction to *Candide and Other Stories* (1990), viii–ix.

Voltaire's *contes* demonstrate that *systems* are an unwarranted and unsustainable imposition of false order on the facts of life.

Pearson, introduction to *Candide and Other Stories* (1990), xlii.

Voltaire's stories mix education and entertainment to the point where they are indistinguishable.

Pearson, introduction to *Candide and Other Stories* (1990), xliii.

And *Candide* . . . Mirthful and wise, the best of all possible stories, an allegory of life and living that does the work of a hundred bibles and a thousand moral tracts. And does not tell us what to do. For that above all was the objective of Voltaire Almighty: to confer freedom on his reader, the freedom to think and to feel and to speak as *we* consider fit. By the light of human reason.

Pearson, *Voltaire Almighty* (2005), 408.

Voltaire valued freedom above all else.

Pearson, *Voltaire Almighty* (2005), 408.

Anthony Peregrine (circa 1955–)

ENGLISH JOURNALIST AND TRAVEL WRITER FOR *THE TELEGRAPH*

A glass of Calvados contains seven apples, which is two more than you need. Obviously, the more you drink the longer the doctor stays away. Cognac is among the warmest, deepest drinks on Earth, while Armagnac is what keeps Gascons going. Thus will you finish the meal like a French person—happy but conscious and sufficiently inspired to discourse about Voltaire until midnight. When presents are exchanged.

Peregrine talking about the intake of alcohol at a typical Christmas Eve dinner in France, in "Nine Things That Might Surprise You about Christmas in France" (2019).

Eli Perry (active circa 1905–1930)

SPECIAL DEPUTY COLLECTOR AT THE PORT OF BOSTON

The question arose some time ago in connection with "Candide" as to whether or not the text was obscene, and a volume of the book was referred to the department at Washington. After the complete text of the specimen volume submitted to the department had been read it was found that numerous passages of said book were either obscene or indecent within the meaning of the terms contained in section 305 of the tariff act and sections 211 and 245 of the United States criminal code.

Letter to Boston bookseller W. B. Dumas, whose shipment of thirteen copies of *Candide*, presumably imported from France, were seized by customs authorities. Quoted in "Voltaire's 'Candide' Is Adjudged Obscene by Treasury of U.S." (1929), 2.

Henri Peyre (1901–1988)

PROFESSOR OF FRENCH AT YALE UNIVERSITY

Limiting ourselves to the nimblest and most acute intellect of the period, that of Voltaire, we are surprised at the number of erratic judgments he expressed of his contemporaries, while he proved, whenever prejudice or partisanship did not obscure his vision, a splendid critic of past literature.

Peyre, *Writers and Their Critics* (1944), 88. The seven chapters in this book were based on a series of lectures Peyre gave at Cornell University in the spring of 1943.

Roger Peyrefitte (1907–2000)

FRENCH NOVELIST

Le début de Candide *est demeuré pour moi la lecture la plus réinvigorante: je me le récite souvent, telle une prière à la langue française et à l'esprit français. Il n'y en aura jamais de plus parfaite.*

The beginning of *Candide* has remained for me the most exhilarating reading: I recite it often to myself, like a prayer to the French language and the French spirit. There will never be anything more perfect.

Peyrefitte, preface to *Romans de Voltaire* (1961), 5–6.

Jean-Charles Pichon (1920–2006)

FRENCH POET, PLAYWRIGHT, PHILOSOPHER, AND MATHEMATICIAN

Anatole France a été un Voltaire repenti.

Anatole France was a repentent Voltaire.

Pichon quoted in Tendron, *Anatole France inconnu* (1995), 16.

Figure 32. Jean Dambrun, after Jean-Michel Moreau le Jeune, illustration for the first chapter of *Candide*. Engraving, 1785. Private collection.

Edwy Plenel (1952–)

FRENCH JOURNALIST AND EDITOR WITH *LE MONDE*, AUTHOR,
AND PUBLISHER OF THE ONLINE NEWS SITE MEDIAPART

The father of investigative journalism.

This expression, applied to Voltaire apparently in 1994, before Plenel was promoted to editor at *Le Monde*, was cited in Richard Holmes, "Voltaire's Grin" (1995), 49.

René Pomeau (1917–2000)

PROFESSOR OF FRENCH AT THE SORBONNE AND DEAN
OF TWENTIETH-CENTURY VOLTAIRE SCHOLARS

La religion de Voltaire fut la rencontre d'un caractère et d'un siècle. Il n'est pas possible de mettre ce déisme ou théisme sur le compte de la frivolité. Il ne fut pas une doctrine de colportage empruntée à Chaulieu et aux Anglais, et répandue par espièglerie, pour faire la nique aux prêtres.

Voltaire's religion reflects the intersection of an individual character and an age. It is impossible to impute his deism or theism to frivolity. It was not a huckster's doctrine, borrowed from Chaulieu and the English, and propagated out of mischievousness to defy the priesthood.

Pomeau, *La Religion de Voltaire* (1956), 455. This book was based on Pomeau's Sorbonne dissertation. For the translation in English see Pomeau, "Voltaire's Religion" (1968), 140.

Voltaire, vieil ami, s'il est permis de s'adresser à toi, après avoir écrit sur toi tant de pages, ce doit être d'abord pour s'excuser: comment être court sur toi qui fus si interminablement bref? Qu'avais-tu tant à dire?

Voltaire, old friend, if we may address you after writing so many pages about you, we must begin by apologizing: how can one be laconic in speaking of you who were so interminably brief? What was it that you had to say at such great length?

Pomeau, *La Religion de Voltaire* (1956), 462. In English, Pomeau "Voltaire's Religion" (1968), 148.

Comment expliquer le bonheur d'une telle œuvre? De quelle tension portée à un niveau supérieur sont nés ces phrases, ces chapitres, cette fable? L'intimité créatrice de l'écrivain interpose devant le biographe une frontière qu'il ne saurait franchir. C'est le cas de répéter ici le mauvais latin que Voltaire appliquait à un mystère d'une autre sorte: procedes huc, et non ibis amplius.

How to explain such a masterwork? To what peak of creative intensity do we owe each sentence, each chapter, the tale as a whole? An author's unique individual talent limits what a biographer can do. One can only repeat the line in imperfect Latin used by Voltaire himself to describe a mystery of another order: *procedes huc, et non ibis amplius.* You will go this far and no farther.

Pomeau commenting on *Candide* in *De la Cour au jardin, 1750–1759* (1991), 374. *De la Cour au jardin* was the third volume in Pomeau's five-volume biography *Voltaire en son temps.*

Laurence M. Porter (1936–)

FORMER CHAIR OF THE DEPARTMENT
OF ROMANCE LANGUAGES AND CLASSICS AT
MICHIGAN STATE UNIVERSITY

Among the many eighteenth-century authors of the Enlightenment, Voltaire was probably the one who most influenced Flaubert.

Porter, *A Gustave Flaubert Encyclopedia* (2001), 343.

John Cowper Powys (1872–1963)

BRITISH PHILOSOPHER AND MAN OF LETTERS

Except for "Candide" and a few excerpts from the "Philosophical Dictionary," I must confess I have no wish to turn over another page of Voltaire.

Powys, "Voltaire," in *Suspended Judgments* (1916), 64. Powys also said that *Candide* "is not only a clever book, a witty book, a wise book. It is a book preposterously and outrageously funny."

Voltaire!—He was well advised to choose that name for himself; a name which sounds even now like the call of a trumpet. And a call it is; a call to the clear intelligences and the unclouded brains; a call to the generous hearts and the unperverted instincts; a call to sanity and sweetness and clarity and noble commonsense; to all that is free and brave and gay and friendly, to rally to the standard of true civilisation against the forces of stupidity, brutality and obscurantism!

Powys, "Voltaire," in *Suspended Judgments* (1916), 65–66.

Theodosia Bartow Prevost (1746–1794)

ARDENT SUPPORTER OF THE AMERICAN REVOLUTION,
WHOSE SECOND HUSBAND WAS AARON BURR

The English, from national jealousy and envy to the French, detract him; but, without being his disciple, we may do justice to his merit, and admire him as a judicious and ingenious author.

Prevost's letter to her lover and future spouse, Aaron Burr. Quoted in Parton, *The Life and Times of Aaron Burr* (1858), 132.

Sir Ralph Richardson (1902–1983)

ENGLISH ACTOR

What a man. When Voltaire was on his deathbed a clever priest came asking him to renounce the devil and all his works. Voltaire told him, "I don't think at this time of life I should start making enemies."

Richardson quoted in Campbell, "A Lunch as Good as a Matinee," *The Gleaner* (Kingston, Jamaica), September 21, 1974, 8. The quote cited by Richardson is apocryphal.

Claude Roy (1915–1997)

FRENCH POET, JOURNALIST, AND AUTHOR

C'est un grand crime que d'avoir de l'esprit, on risque de s'en servir.

It is a great crime to be quick-witted, there's always a chance you'll use it.

Roy, "Un Fauteuil nommé Voltaire" (1958). Comment prompted by a young man who had once recited to Roy what Lenin said about Voltaire: "I will never make the pilgrimage to Ferney: I do not like witty people."

Salman Rushdie (1947–)

ANGLO-INDIAN NOVELIST AND PUBLIC INTELLECTUAL

Voltaire's great fable ends with the suggestion that in appalling times we would be well advised to keep our minds off high ideas and our noses out of great affairs, and simply cultivate our gardens.

Rushdie commenting on *Candide* in "How Politics Took a Leaf from Voltaire's Garden" (2002).

Voltaire was not the sort to recommend apathy as a general cure for life's ills, however; and yet, such is our penchant for sloppy reading and sloppier thinking, the conclusion of his most celebrated work of fiction has come to mean exactly that, has come to be read as an endorsement of apathy, passivity, withdrawal.

Rushdie, "How Politics Took a Leaf from Voltaire's Garden" (2002).

Bertrand Russell (1872–1970)

ENGLISH PHILOSOPHER

There's a Bible on that shelf there. But I keep it next to Voltaire—poison and antidote.

From an interview with Russell, conducted January 6, 1958, in K. Harris, "Kenneth Harris Talks to Bertrand Russell" (1970), 7.

Paul Ryan (1970–)

FORMER REPUBLICAN CONGRESSMAN FROM WISCONSIN
AND SPEAKER OF THE HOUSE

If this Republican Congress allows the perfect to become the enemy of the good, I worry we'll push the President to working with Democrats.

Ryan quoted in Shabad, "Ryan Says He Doesn't Want to Negotiate with Democrats on Health Care" (2017). Ryan was quoting, perhaps unwittingly, Voltaire's oft-repeated line about the better being the enemy of the good.

George Sand [a.k.a. Amantine-Lucile-Aurore Dupin] (1804–1876)

FRENCH NOVELIST AND MEMOIRIST, REMEMBERED
IN PART FOR HER AFFAIRS WITH FRÉDÉRIC CHOPIN
AND ALFRED DE MUSSET

Le progrès est un rêve. Sans cet espoir, personne n'est bon à rien. . . . ces grands esprits auxquels le besoin de ton âme se rattache, Shakespeare, Molière, Voltaire, etc., n'ont que faire d'exister et de se manifester.

Progress is a dream. Without that hope, no one is good for anything. . . . those great minds to which your needy soul is attached, Shakespeare, Molière, Voltaire, etc., need merely exist and do as they please.

Letter from Sand, September 16, 1871, from Nohant in central France, to Gustave Flaubert, at Croisset, near Rouen. Sand, "Lettres de George Sand à Gustave Flaubert" (1883), 61.

Antonin Scalia (1936–2016)

ASSISTANT ATTORNEY GENERAL IN THE FORD ADMINISTRATION
AND ASSOCIATE JUSTICE OF THE U.S. SUPREME COURT

Believe, if you wish, that religion is, as Marx said, the opiate of the masses—so long as you acknowledge it to be our tradition that it is better for the republic that the masses be thus opiated. Or believe, with Voltaire, *si Dieu n'existait, il faudrait l'inventer*—if God did not exist, we would have to invent Him.

Scalia's speech at the Union League Club of Chicago, February 14, 2014, in *Scalia Speaks* (2017), 71.

Friedrich Schlegel (1772–1829)

GERMAN POET AND CRITIC

Könnte unser Dichter auch wohl ein deutscher Voltaire genannt werden.

Our poet could also probably be called a German Voltaire.

Schlegel speaking about Goethe in *Geschichte der alten und neuen Litteratur* (1815), 317.

Friedrich Christoph Schlosser (1776–1861)

PROFESSOR OF HISTORY AT THE UNIVERSITY OF HEIDELBERG

Bolingbroke war der englische Voltaire.

Bolingbroke was the English Voltaire.

Schlosser, *Geschichte des achtzehnten Jahrhunderts und des neunzehnten bis zum Sturz des französischen Kaiserreichs* (1842), 3:581. In English, *History of the Eighteenth Century and of the Nineteenth till the Overthrow of the French Empire* (1844), 2:64.

George Scialabba (1948–)

LITERARY CRITIC

Voltaire and Rousseau have corrupted better men than me.

Scialabba talking about why, as a Harvard undergraduate, he renounced his membership in the ultra-Catholic organization, Opus Dei. Quoted in Haslett, "The Private Intellectual" (2015).

James C. Scott (1936–)

PROFESSOR OF POLITICAL SCIENCE AND ANTHROPOLOGY
AT YALE UNIVERSITY

One could say that Catherine the Great, being Prussian born and an avid correspondent with several of the Encyclopedists, including Voltaire, came by her mania for rational order honestly.

Scott, *Seeing Like a State* (1998), 397n4.

Sir Walter Scott (1771–1832)

ENGLISH NOVELIST

Goethe is different, and a wonderful fellow, the Ariosto at once, and almost the Voltaire of Germany.

Entry in Scott's diary, February 20, 1827. Quoted in Lockhart, *Memoirs of the Life of Sir Walter Scott, Bart.* (1838), 30.

Gilbert Seldes (1893–1970)

CULTURE CRITIC, DIRECTOR OF TELEVISION FOR CBS
NEWS, AND FOUNDING DEAN OF THE ANNENBERG SCHOOL FOR
COMMUNICATION AT THE UNIVERSITY OF PENNSYLVANIA

There is something hopeless about opera as we know it in the United States. . . . For it is pretentious and it appeals not to our sensibilities but to our snobbery. It neither excites nor exalts; it does not amuse. Over it and under it and through it runs the element of fake; it is a substitute for symphonic music and an easy expiatory offering for ragtime. *Ecrasez l'infâme!*

Seldes, *The 7 Lively Arts* (1924), 312–314.

If I were a Hollywood producer with a huge investment in sets and costumes and, above all, overpublicized stars, I think I would protect myself today by hiring a few gangsters to wreck the studios of Mr. Walt Disney. When the heads of the great studies are congratulating Mr. Disney on his first full-length picture, I think they are like the aristocrats of France who invited Voltaire, Diderot, and Rousseau into their salons and who thought that revolutionary ideas were quaint and charming without knowing that these men had laid a mine under their palaces. For it seems to me that Mr. Disney has dug deep under the foundations of the Hollywood feature-picture industry and successfully placed his dynamite, so that now it requires only the striking of a match to blow the whole thing up.

Seldes, review of *Snow White and the Seven Dwarfs* in "Motion Pictures" (1938), 65.

Ben Shapiro (1984–)

CONSERVATIVE POLITICAL COMMENTATOR, EDITOR IN
CHIEF OF *THE DAILY WIRE*, AND AUTHOR

Like an eighteenth-century Bill Maher, Voltaire delighted in ridiculing the most facially ridiculous statements of the Bible and declaring the Bible's morality abhorrent on its face.

Shapiro, *The Right Side of History* (2019), 106.

So where did Voltaire find purpose and morality? Like Francis Bacon, one of his intellectual heroes, he found it in the betterment of the human condition materially. And this led him toward a hedonistic, materialist morality as well. For those capable of exercising reason properly, the maximization of pleasure and minimization of pain were the paramount goals of life.

Shapiro, *The Right Side of History* (2019), 107.

Voltaire's morality tends toward the more fully libertarian, then—freedom from control, liberty in behavior. But such a system, absent the virtue of a citizenry, quickly collapses. Voltaire knew that, which is why he wished that those of lesser rational capacity worship an omnipotent, omniscient God— God was necessary for others, but not for Voltaire.

Shapiro, *The Right Side of History* (2019), 108.

William Sharp (1855–1905)

SCOTTISH AUTHOR, EDITOR, POET, AND LITERARY BIOGRAPHER

Twickenham . . . was the Ferney of the eighteenth-century literary world. . . . Pope was the English Voltaire.

Sharp, "Literary Geography" (1904), 385.

Roger Shattuck (1912–2005)

SCHOLAR, ESSAYIST, AND AUTHOR, SPECIALIZING IN FRENCH LITERATURE

No one has mocked the abuses of reason more effectively than Swift and Voltaire, who represent the Age of Reason.

Shattuck, *Forbidden Knowledge* (1996), 45.

George Bernard Shaw (1856–1950)

ANGLO-IRISH PLAYWRIGHT, CRITIC, AND ESSAYIST

I am persuaded that the future historian of America will find your works as indispensable to him as a French historian finds the political tracts of Voltaire.

Shaw, letter from London, July 3, 1907, to Mark Twain, then visiting in England. In late June, Twain had received an honorary degree from the University of Oxford. Quoted in Kaplan, *Mr. Clemens and Mark Twain* (2003), 381.

Voltaire . . . burlesqued Homer in a mock epic called La Pucelle. It is the fashion to dismiss this with virtuous indignation as an obscene libel; and I certainly cannot defend it against the charge of extravagant indecorum. But its purpose was not to depict Joan, but to kill with ridicule everything that Voltaire righteously hated in the institutions and fashions of his own day. He made Joan ridiculous, but not contemptible nor (comparatively) unchaste; and as he also made Homer and St Peter and St Denis and the brave Dunois ridiculous, and the other heroines of the poem very unchaste indeed, he may be said to have let Joan off very easily. . . . Certainly Voltaire should not have asserted that Joan's father was a priest; but when he was out to *écraser l'infâme* (the French Church) he stuck at nothing.

Shaw, "Preface to Saint Joan," in *Saint Joan: A Chronicle Play in Six Scenes and an Epilogue* (1924), xxxvii–xxxviii.

Bishop Fulton J. Sheen (1895–1979)

ROMAN CATHOLIC BISHOP OF ROCHESTER, NEW YORK, AND TELEVANGELIST

Voltaire boasted that if he could find but ten wicked words a day he could crush the "infamy" of Christianity. He found the ten words daily, and even a daily dozen, but he never found an argument, and so the words went the way of all words and the thing, Christianity, survived.

Sheen, *Old Errors and New Labels* (1931), 96. *Time* magazine once called Bishop Sheen "the first televangelist."

Sydney Smith (1771–1845)

ANGLICAN CLERGYMAN, WIT, AND ESSAYIST

It is a very easy thing to talk about the shallow impostures, and the silly ignorant sophisms of Voltaire, Rousseau, Condorcet, D'Alembert, and Volney, and to say that Hume is not worth answering. This affectation will not do. While these pernicious writers have power to allure from the Church great numbers of proselytes, it is better to study them diligently, and to reply to them satisfactorily, than to veil insolence, want of power, or want of industry, by a pretended contempt; which may leave infidels and wavering Christians to suppose that such writers are abused, because they are feared; and not answered, because they are unanswerable.

Smith's review of *Discourses on Various Subjects* by Dr. Thomas Rennel (1802), 88.

Philippa Snow (1988–)

ENGLISH WRITER AND SELF-STYLED "LINDSAY LOHAN SCHOLAR"

If Paris Hilton did not exist, to paraphrase the philosopher Voltaire, it would be necessary for us to invent her.

Snow, "Paris Hilton Is the Greatest Performance Artist of Our Time" (2019).

Philippe Sollers (1937–)

FRENCH NOVELIST

Les Français n'aiment pas Voltaire, vous savez. . . . Ce sont les Anglais qui l'apprécient le plus.

The French don't like Voltaire, you know. . . . The English appreciate him the most.

Sollers, "Il manque, Voltaire, là!" (2015).

Jean Starobinski (1920–2019)

SWISS PHYSICIAN AND SCHOLAR, SPECIALIZING
IN FRENCH LITERATURE

L'ironie, dans Candide, *a fonction d'arme offensive; elle est orientée vers le dehors, elle mène le combat de la raison contre tout ce qui usurpe l'autorité que la pensée rationnelle devrait seule posséder.*

In *Candide*, irony functions as an offensive weapon; aimed outward, it wages war in the name of reason against anything that usurps the authority which rational thought alone should possess.

Starobinski, "Le fusil à deux coups de Voltaire" (1966). Reprinted in Starobinski, *Le Remède dans le mal* (1989), 129.

Qui peut douter que pendant quelques dizaines d'années le centre nerveux de l'Europe des Lumières n'ait logé dans le corps malingre et indomptable de Voltaire?

Who can doubt that for several decades the nerve center of the European Enlightenment had lodged within the sickly, indomitable body of Voltaire?

Starobinksi, "Est-il tolérant? Est-il odieux?" (1994), 1.

Stendhal [a.k.a. Henri Beyle] (1783–1842)

FRENCH NOVELIST

J'ai été exclusivement élevé par mon excellent grand-père, M. Henri Gagnon. Cet homme rare avait fait un pèlerinage à Ferney pour voir Voltaire et avait été reçu avec distinction. Il avait un petit buste de Voltaire, gros comme le poing, monté sur un pied de bois d'ébène de six pouces de haut. (C'était un singulier goût, mais les beaux-arts n'étaient le fort ni de Voltaire, ni de mon excellent grand-père.)

I was raised exclusively by my excellent grandfather, M. Henri Gagnon. This man of rare qualities had made a pilgrimage to Ferney to visit Voltaire, and was received by him with distinction. He had a small bust of Voltaire, the size of your fist, mounted on an ebony base six inches high. (This was unusual as a matter of taste, but the fine arts were not Voltaire's strong suit, nor that of my excellent grandfather.)

Stendhal, *Vie de Henri Brulard*, unfinished autobiography, unpublished during Stendhal's lifetime; from the 1913 edition, 1:34. There is no reference to Stendhal's maternal grandfather in the literature on Voltaire. Henri Gagnon (1762–1813) practiced medicine in Grenoble, roughly ninety miles from Ferney.

Moi, qui abhorrais la puérilité *de Voltaire dans l'histoire et sa* basse envie *contre Corneille.*

I abhorred Voltaire's *puerility* in history, and his *base envy* of Corneille.

Stendhal, *Vie de Henri Brulard* (1913), 2:26.

James Fitzjames Stephen (1829–1894)

ENGLISH JURIST AND WRITER

If Dante had been personally happy, or Shakespeare personally wretched, if Byron had married Miss Chaworth, if Voltaire had met with no personal ill-usage, their literary influence would have been very different. The result is that we can assign no limits at all to the importance to each other of men's acts and thoughts.

Stephen, *Liberty, Fraternity, Equality* (1873), 138.

Jessi Jezewska Stevens (1990–)

WRITER

If there is precedent for the narrative utility of the acquiescent disposition, then its first and most famous exponent must be Voltaire's optimist,

Candide. . . . At first characterization, Candide is a little stupid, and that is exactly his charm. Too gullible for cynicism, too simple for ambition, he instigates almost none of the obstacles on his ill-fated, picaresque path. He is, in a sense, the anti-Virgil of the absurd.

Stevens, "The Hidden Power of the Passive Protagonist" (2020).

Rather than rejecting the vengeful illogic of a world uniquely designed to screw him over, Candide exists in the moment. He is good-natured, genial, fundamentally optimistic and only ever accidentally wise—the kind of person who throws others' intelligence and cynicism into relief. Here lie the Berty Woosters of the world, through whom we meet a Jeeves.

Stevens, "The Hidden Power of the Passive Protagonist" (2020). The English fiction writer P. G. Wodehouse created the amiable, rather naive Bertie Wooster and his resourceful valet Jeeves.

Robert Stone (1937–2015)

NOVELIST

"You know, Tecan is a special situation—it's still the fifties there. Our ambassador is a Birchite moron. The cops lock you up for reading Voltaire."

The narrator, anthropologist Frank Holliwell, to his friend Marty, talking about Tecan, a fictional Central American country, in Stone's novel *A Flag for Sunrise* (1981), 24. The term "Birchite" refers to the far-right John Birch Society, founded in the United States in 1958.

Rex Stout (1886–1975)

FICTION WRITER AND CREATOR OF THE NERO WOLFE DETECTIVE STORIES

At the dinner table, and with coffee in the office afterwards, Wolfe resumed on the subject he had started at lunch—Voltaire. The big question was, could a man be called great on account of the way he used words, even though he was a toad, a trimmer, a forger, and an intellectual fop. That had been dealt with at lunch, and Voltaire had come out fairly well except on the toady count. How could you call a man great who sought the company and the favors of dukes and duchesses, of Richelieu, of Frederick of Prussia? But it was at dinner and in the office that Voltaire really got it. What finally ruled him out was something that hadn't been mentioned at lunch at all: he had no palate and not much appetite. He was indifferent to food; he might even eat only once a day; and he drank next to nothing. All his life he was extremely skinny, and in his later years he was merely a skeleton. To call him a great man was absurd; strictly speaking, he wasn't a man at all, since he had no palate and a dried-up stomach. He was a remarkable word-assembly plant, but he wasn't a man, let alone a great one.

Archie Goodwin, private detective Nero Wolfe's assistant and the narrator of Stout's Wolfe mystery novel *Gambit* (1962), 87.

John St. Loe Strachey (1860–1927)

ENGLISH JOURNALIST AND EDITOR OF *THE SPECTATOR*

If in the Elysian Fields they are moved at all by mortal things, we may be sure . . . that Voltaire, if he writes as well as watches, is full of sympathetic reflections on the English, for he loved our nation; and if he did not build us a synagogue, he at any rate raised to us an eternal monument in his letters on England—*Anglis erexit Voltaire.*

"Voltaire on the Fleet," *The Spectator*, June 10, 1916, 713. The Latin phrase *Anglis erexit Voltaire* (Erected to England by Voltaire) is a clever play by Strachey on the inscription placed by Voltaire over the entrance to the chapel on his estate at Ferney, *Deo erexit Voltaire.* John Strachey and Lytton Strachey, a regular contributor to *The Spectator*, were cousins.

Lytton Strachey (1880–1932)

SCHOLAR, ESSAYIST, AND AUTHOR, SPECIALIZING
IN FRENCH LITERATURE

The visit of Voltaire to England marks a turning-point in the history of civilisation. . . . It was he who planted the small seed of friendship which, in spite of a thousand hostile influences, in spite of the long wars of the eighteenth century, in spite of Napoleon, in spite of all the powers of hereditary enmity and instinctive distrust, was to grow and flourish so mightily. Doubtless the seed fell on good ground; doubtless if Voltaire had never left his native country some chance wind would have carried it over the narrow seas, and, in the main, history would have been unaltered. Yet it is worth remembering that actually his was the hand which did the work.

Strachey, "Voltaire and England" (1914), 392.

Between the collapse of the Roman Empire and the Industrial Revolution, three men were the intellectual masters of Europe—Bernard of Clairvaux, Erasmus, and Voltaire. In Bernard the piety and the superstition of the Middle

Ages attained their supreme embodiment; in Erasmus the learning and the humanity of the Renaissance. But Erasmus was a tragic figure. The great revolution in the human mind, of which he had been the presiding genius, ended in failure; he lived to see the tide of barbarism rising once more over the world; and it was to Voltaire to carry off the final victory.

Strachey, "Voltaire," published in both the English weekly *The Athenæum* (1919), 677, and the American weekly *The New Republic* (1919), 14. The American text contains minor defects not found in the *Athenæum* version, notably its misidentification of the author of a recent book on Voltaire, S. G. Tallentyre (Evelyn Beatrice Hall), as "Mr." Tallentyre.

The fact that Voltaire devoted his life to the noblest of causes must not blind us to another fact—that he was personally a very ugly customer. He was a frantic, desperate fighter, to whom all means were excusable; he was a scoundrel, a rogue, he lied, he blasphemed; he was extremely indecent. He was, too, quite devoid of dignity, adopting, whenever he saw fit, the wildest expedients and the most extravagant postures; there was in fact a strong element of farce in this character which he had the wit to exploit for his own ends. At the same time he was inordinately vain, and mercilessly revengeful, he was as mischievous as a monkey, and as cruel as a cat. At times one fancies him a puppet on wires, a creature raving in a mechanical frenzy—and then one remembers that lucid piercing intellect, that overwhelming passion for reason and intellect.

Strachey, "Voltaire," *The Athenæum* (1919), 679, and *The New Republic* (1919), 15.

Don Surber (1953–)

RETIRED JOURNALIST, *CHARLESTON* (WEST VIRGINIA)
DAILY MAIL, AND BLOGGER

TV is run by pretty faces. The Internet by people in pajamas. Newspapers have to stand up for the rights [of journalists]. We're the heirs of Voltaire.

Surber, "Bill Keller Wasn't Defending Robert Novak" (2006).

Attributed to Charles-Maurice de Talleyrand-Périgord (1754–1838)

FRENCH POLITICIAN AND STATESMAN IN
THE NAPOLEONIC ERA

Je connais quelqu'un qui a plus d'esprit que Napoléon, que Voltaire, que tous les ministres présents et futurs: c'est l'opinion.

I know someone who is cleverer than Napoleon, Voltaire, and any government minister present or future: public opinion.

Comment reputedly made in the French Chamber of Peers in 1821. Quoted in Campan, *Journal anecdotique de Mme Campan* (1824), 50.

Philip M. Taylor (1954–2010)

ENGLISH HISTORIAN AND PROFESSOR OF COMMUNICATIONS
AT THE UNIVERSITY OF LEEDS

To the French, Franklin *was* the American Revolution, and the ageing philosopher-scientist appeared as an American Voltaire.

Taylor, *Munitions of the Mind* (2003), 140.

Margaret Thatcher (1925–2013)

CONSERVATIVE MEMBER OF PARLIAMENT AND
PRIME MINISTER OF GREAT BRITAIN

"Europe" in anything other than the geographical sense is a wholly artificial construct. It makes no sense at all to lump together Beethoven and Debussy, Voltaire and Burke, Vermeer and Picasso, Notre Dame and St Paul's, boiled beef and bouillabaisse, and portray them as elements of a "European" musical, philosophical, artistic, architectural or gastronomic reality. If Europe charms us, as it has so often charmed me, it is precisely because of its contrasts and contradictions, not its coherence and continuity.

Thatcher, *Statecraft* (2003), 328.

With all due respect to the drafters of the American Declaration of Independence, all men (and women) are not created equal, at least in regard to their characters, abilities and aptitudes. And if they were, their family and cultural backgrounds—not to mention the effect of mere chance—would soon change that. On one thing, nature and nurture agree: we are all different. If this is unjust, then life is unjust. But, though one hears this expression—usually in the form of the complaint that "life is unfair"—it really means nothing. In the same vein, someone once said to Voltaire, "Life is hard." To which he replied: "Compared with what?"

Thatcher, *Statecraft* (2003), 431. Voltaire almost certainly never said the words attributed to him here. This quote first appeared in print, unsourced, in the introduction to *The State of Humanity* (1995, 6), edited by Julian L. Simon, a conservative American economics and business administration professor.

Mark Thompson (1957–)

ENGLISH MEDIA EXECUTIVE, FORMER DIRECTOR-GENERAL
OF THE BBC, AND FORMER PRESIDENT AND CEO OF
THE *NEW YORK TIMES* COMPANY

We can think of freedom of expression as an absolute right and defend it stalwartly as such, offering like Voltaire to lay down our lives to defend the right of people to say and do things we ourselves regard as hateful and false. Or we can think of it as something relative, a right that needs to be balanced with other duties and obligations if our societies are to remain tranquil. To propose . . . that we can magically do both . . . is an uncomfortable middle position that is ultimately unlikely to satisfy anyone. Indeed, a secure and settled answer to the dilemma . . . remains an unanswered dissonance at the core of the modern liberal project.

Thompson, *Enough Said* (2016), 255. This is one more glaring example of the persistent misuse of Evelyn Beatrice Hall's paraphrase of Voltaire's views on free speech, and Thompson got it doubly wrong. Hall said that Voltaire would "defend to the death your right" to say something he disagreed with; he did not defend the right to "do" whatever you please. On the contrary, Voltaire's campaign against *l'infâme* was a direct assault on such concrete abuses.

James Thurber (1894–1961)

HUMORIST, AUTHOR, PLAYWRIGHT, AND CARTOONIST

"Goethe," he would say, "was a wax figure stuffed with hay. When you say Proust was sick, you have said everything. Shakespeare was a dolt. If there had been no Voltaire, it would not have been necessary to create one."

Thurber, "Something to Say," a fictional satire about an arrogant writer named Elliot Vereker (1932), 17.

Norman L. Torrey (1894–1980)

PROFESSOR OF FRENCH AT COLUMBIA UNIVERSITY

Only by a frank acceptance of man's fate, with all its limitations, can life be made endurable. Man should therefore work without theorizing, because "work keeps at bay three great evils: boredom, vice and need." Voltaire's answer is that we should cultivate our gardens. By implication, however, there is no law against uprooting noxious weeds.

Torrey, introduction to *Candide or Optimism* (1946), x.

Frank M. Turner (1944–2010)

PROFESSOR OF HISTORY AT YALE UNIVERSITY

Voltaire brought the force of critical reason and biting satire to bear against many of the institutions of the day. . . . Yet it is Rousseau who remains the most problematical and haunting intellectual of the eighteenth century.

From one of fifteen undergraduate lectures Turner delivered annually at Yale, collected and published as *European Intellectual History from Rousseau to Nietzsche* (2014), 1. Turner regarded Jean-Jacques as more consequential than Voltaire—also Newton, Hume, Montesquieu, and Adam Smith—because Rousseau stood as "the fountainhead of modern European thought."

Mark Twain (1835–1910)

NOVELIST AND HUMORIST

True friends of mankind and haters of intolerance have their rheumatism or colic on August 24th, the day of the Massacre of St. Bartholomew. Voltaire always timed his boils so and got a rash or the itch on May 14th for good measure.

Twain quoted in Fisher, *Abroad with Mark Twain and Eugene Field* (1922), 153. Twain made this comment in London in the Dr. Johnson Room of the Cheshire and Cheese in the Strand. It was on May 14, 1610, Twain explained to his tablemates, that Henri IV was assassinated "by a damn monk."

Mike Tyson (1966–)

FORMER WORLD HEAVYWEIGHT BOXING CHAMPION

I loved *Candide*. . . . And Voltaire himself, he was something, man. He wasn't afraid. They kept putting him in jail, and he kept writing the truth.

Interview during Tyson's imprisonment in Indiana on a rape conviction, in which he spoke about books he'd been reading. Tyson quoted in Hamill, *Piecework* (1996), 330.

John Updike (1932–2009)

NOVELIST, SHORT STORY WRITER, AND LITERARY
AND ART CRITIC

3. Voltaire, *Candide*, 1759. A slim book written in three days, and published anonymously, *Candide* distills the sparkling spirit of Voltaire and the Enlightenment. Like *Don Quixote*, it dramatizes the clash between ideas and reality—the ideas are those of the philosopher Leibniz, which explained away evil,

and reality is represented by the Lisbon earthquake and other sufferings endured by the titular hero and his cheerful tutor, Dr. Pangloss.

From Updike, "The Ten Greatest Works of Literature, 1001–2000" (1999), 847. Updike was mistaken, or exaggerating for effect, when he said that *Candide* was "written in three days."

Paul Valéry (1871–1945)

FRENCH WRITER, POET, AND PHILOSOPHER

La France est riche en . . . personnages de première grandeur, dont l'entité glorieuse s'accompagne d'une sorte de présence, immortelle, sans doute, mais presque familière. . . . Même pour ceux qui ne les ont qu'à peine lus, Montaigne signifie quelqu'un, Pascal signifie quelqu'un, Voltaire aussi. Ce sont des individus significatifs.

France is rich in . . . supremely great figures whose glorious existence is accompanied by a sort of immortal, no doubt, but almost familiar presence. . . . Even for those who have scarcely read them, Montaigne is somebody, Pascal is somebody, Voltaire, too. They are significant individuals.

Valéry, *Voltaire* (1945), iii.

Il avait, je le crains, presque tous les défauts que l'on se plaît à nous donner; et s'il n'eut pas toutes nos qualités, il en possédait quelques-unes à leur plus haute puissance. Il nous faut avouer ou proclamer—selon les goûts—qu'il est spécifiquement français, inconcevable sous d'autres cieux, je dirai même sous un autre ciel que celui de Paris. Il en résulte que son nom excite encore chez nous, après 250 ans, des réactions très sensibles et fortement opposées. . . . Voltaire vit, Voltaire dure: il est indéfiniment actuel.

He had, I fear, almost all of the faults that we are known for: and if he did not have all our virtues, he possessed some of them at their most intense and highest level. We must confess, or proclaim—either way—that he is quite specifically French and unimaginable under any other skies, I would even say under any other sky than Paris. The result is that in France, after 250 years, his name still provokes very sharp and strongly opposed reactions. . . . Voltaire is alive, Voltaire endures: he is infinitely current.

Valéry, *Voltaire* (1945), iv.

Où est le Voltaire, la voix qui s'élèvera aujourd'hui?

Where is the Voltaire, the voice that will rise up today?

Valéry, *Voltaire* (1945), xxxiv.

Le défenseur de Calas consolé de n'avoir pu défendre Bailly, André Chénier et Camille Desmoulins.

Figure 33. Honoré Daumier, lithograph, *Le Charivari*, April 16, 1871. Private collection. The caption reads, "Le défensur de Calas consolé de n'avoir pu défendre Bailly, André Chénier et Camille Desmoulins." In English, "The defender of Calas consoled for not having been able to defend Bailly, André Chénier, and Camille Desmoulins." Chénier, Desmoulins, and Jean-Sylvain Bailly, the first mayor of Paris, were moderate revolutionaries executed during the Reign of Terror. Daumier's cartoon depicts the statue of Voltaire then located in front of the town hall of Paris's eleventh arrondissement, rising to applaud the ceremonial burning of a guillotine during the Commune. See also figure 8.

André Versaille [a.k.a. André Asaël] (1949–)

BELGIAN AUTHOR AND PUBLISHER

Voltaire! Depuis quelques décennies, toute occasion est bonne pour héler le patriarche de Ferney. Combien de "Voltaire, reviens! Ils sont devenus fous!" n'a-t-on pas entendu ces dernières années! Mais est-ce le philosophe que l'on appelle à l'aide, ou ne s'agit-il que de l'agitation d'un symbole, d'un principe quasi abstrait de la liberté d'expression? Il est si souvent brandi en ignorance de cause.

Voltaire! For the past few decades, every opportunity has been seized upon to hail the Patriarch of Ferney. How many times have we heard: "Voltaire, come back! They've gone mad!" in recent years! But is it Voltaire the *"philosophe"* who is appealed to for help, or rather the almost abstract principle of freedom of expression? Voltaire's name is often invoked without people really knowing what he stood for.

Versaille, "De l'héritage de Voltaire et de ce que nous n'en avons pas fait" (2017).

Et s'il revenait? Lui qui, tout en détestant les monothéismes, considérait l'islam avec cent fois moins d'hostilité que le judaïsme et le christianisme, quelle consternation serait la sienne devant cette explosion de fanatisme venue du monde musulman, un monde qui, au XVIIIᵉ siècle, était regardé non seulement sans hostilité, mais avec un très grand intérêt?

And what if he came back? He who, while he had nothing but scorn for monotheism, nevertheless considered Islam with more indulgence than he ever did either Judaism or Christianity. How dismayed he would be to witness this explosion of fanaticism from the Muslim world, a world that, in the eighteenth century, was regarded not only without hostility, but with great interest?

Versaille, "De l'héritage de Voltaire et de ce que nous n'en avons pas fait" (2017).

Gore Vidal (1925–2012)

NOVELIST, PLAYWRIGHT, AND ESSAYIST

"Yes, sir. He has foresworn the demon rum; and preaches against it."

"That is to the good. I've often thought that if he had not so . . . handicapped himself in life, he might have been the American Voltaire."

"Do we really need one of those, sir?" Hay feigned a bumpkin's innocence.

"Now, John, you must never ask a politician such a question before an election."

From a conversation between President Lincoln and his private secretary, John Hay, in Vidal's *Lincoln: A Novel* (1984), 380. They were talking about William Herndon, Lincoln's former law partner in Springfield, Illinois.

Mario Praz once pointed out that Voltaire had influenced my work, and he was right.

Parini, "An Interview with Gore Vidal" (conducted in 1990), in Parini, *Gore Vidal* (1992), 281. In "Washington's Poisonous Games" (2000) Bruce Allen called Vidal "a Voltaire for our time." An online memorial piece signed ArkDem14 in the *Daily Kos*, August 2, 2012, was titled "Gore Vidal: An American Voltaire."

Peter Viereck (1916–2006)

POET, PROFESSOR OF HISTORY AT MOUNT HOLYOKE COLLEGE, AND AUTHOR

In contrast with what he deemed the rootless skepticism of a Voltaire and the social chaos of a Rousseau, Burke defended the Church of England for its political as well as religious function: "To keep moral, civil, and political bonds together binding human understanding."

Viereck, *Conservative Thinkers* (1956), 31. The phrase attributed to Edmund Burke is an apparently garbled quotation of a passage in Burke's *Reflections on the Revolution in France* (1790), 137.

Alexandre Vinet (1797–1847)

SWISS CALVINIST PASTOR, PHILOSOPHER, JOURNALIST, AND CRITIC

Voltaire ne s'est jamais connu, ni a cherché à se connaître.

Voltaire never analyzed himself, nor did he ever try to.

Vinet, *Histoire de la Littérature française au dix-huitième siècle* (1853), 2.

Kurt Vonnegut Jr. (1922–2007)

NOVELIST AND SATIRIST

The function of an artist is to respond to his time. Voltaire, Swift, and Mark Twain did it.

Vonnegut quoted in Noble, "'Unstuck in Time' . . . a Real Kurt Vonnegut" (1972), reprinted in Allen, *Conversations with Kurt Vonnegut* (1988), 64. In a sermon at St. Clement's Church in New York City on Palm Sunday, 1980, Vonnegut said that his German-born paternal great-grandfather "spoke French fluently" and "greatly admired Voltaire." The text of the sermon was published as "Hypocrites You Always Have with You" (1980), 469.

Ira O. Wade (1896–1983)

PROFESSOR OF FRENCH AT PRINCETON UNIVERSITY

We are beginning at last to realize that Voltaire stands in the dead center of modern times—at the turning-point beween a classical humanism and a romantic existentialism. He—and his time—must accept the responsibilty for upsetting the balance of classical humanism, for cheapening or at any rate modifying taste, and for confusing or revising the issues of life. But he—and his time—should be credited with seeing and expressing unambiguously the need for a new synthesis, for a broader grasp of principles, for a clearer insight into meaning. That explains why he seems to end the line Montaigne-Descartes-Pascal and begin the line Stendhal-Balzac-Flaubert, a turning-point between the aesthetic search for truth and the realistic search for beauty, a sort of impossible focus where the good is part truth, part beauty.

Wade, "Towards a New Voltaire," in *The Search for a New Voltaire* (1958), 110.

Voltaire seems to have been constantly on the move: from one place to another . . . from one kind of work to another . . . from one preoccupation to another . . . and even from one idea to another—from Newtonian attraction to free will, to good and evil, to kinetic energy, to equality.

Wade, introduction to *The Intellectual Development of Voltaire* (1969), xi.

Voltaire in his English experience learned two things: the necessity for harmony in the elements of a civilization in order to guarantee its vitality, and the present superiority of science and philosophy over arts and letters. . . . He was therefore forced to reeducate himself, to supplant the "poetry and nonsense" he had learned at Louis-le-Grand by more substantial subjects like metaphysics, physics, history, biblical criticism, and philosophy . . . and in responding to it Voltaire was compelled literally to reconsider the elements of a civilization (seen in the context of history) and the categories of life (viewed in the light of the relationship between thought and art).

Wade, *The Intellectual Development of Voltaire* (1969), xxi. In the next paragraph Wade went on to say that "the making of this world" was "the core" of his book. "It is our contention that Voltaire, more than anyone else, effected it, but the really important point is that he did not bring it about single-handed. There was always a close coordination between his response to the conditions of his time and that of his contemporaries."

John Weightman (1915–2004)

ENGLISH CRITIC, PROFESSOR OF FRENCH LITERATURE AT
THE UNIVERSITY OF LONDON, AND BROADCASTER WITH
THE BBC DURING WORLD WAR II

Voltaire was undoubtedly a very great man, and being the outstanding representative of the most widely respected national culture of his time, he dominated

Figure 34. David Levine, pen-and-ink caricature of Voltaire. Illustration for John Weightman's review of two works about Voltaire in the *New York Review of Books*, June 18, 1970. © Matthew and Eve Levine.

the atmosphere of eighteenth-century Europe in a way that is almost unimaginable today. The postwar apotheosis of Winston Churchill, statesman, writer, soldier, aviator, bricklayer, and painter, with a long career of fame and notoriety behind him, can perhaps give some idea of the remarkable prestige of the extraordinary Frenchman. Voltaire was probably the first private individual—that is, someone not a hereditary ruler, politician, or religious leader—ever to become such a social force. His celebrity increased as he grew older until, on his return to Paris in his eighty-fourth year after a long exile, he was given a hysterical welcome such as had never been accorded to anyone before, and has possibly only been equaled since by General de Gaulle's triumphant reentry after the Liberation.

Weightman, "Cultivating Voltaire" (1970), 35, in a dual review of Theodore Besterman's biography *Voltaire* (1969) and *The Intellectual Development of Voltaire* (1969) by Ira O. Wade.

The paradox of this tremendous career . . . is that nothing remains immediately alive for the average reader except the one little book, *Candide*.

Weightman, "Cultivating Voltaire" (1970), 35.

Barrett Wendell (1855–1921)

PROFESSOR OF ENGLISH AT HARVARD UNIVERSITY

If there be any one European figure whose position in world literature is analogous to that of Holmes in the literature of New England, it is Voltaire. The differences between Voltaire and Holmes, to be sure, are so much more marked than the analogies that any analogy may at first seem fantastic. For all his eminence, Voltaire was not born a gentleman and never had quite the traits of one; in our little New England there was never a better gentleman than Holmes. Voltaire was a man of licentious life and pitiless temper, incensed and distracted by all the old-world corruptions which he spent his wits in stabbing to death; Holmes's life had all the simple provincial decency and kindliness of his country. Voltaire's wit was the keenest and most sustained of Europe; the wit of Holmes, after all, was only the most delightful which has amused nineteenth-century Boston. For all these differences, there is a true analogy between them: both alike, with superficial frivolity, bravely devoted themselves to lifelong war against what they believed to be delusions which terribly impeded the progress of human nature towards a better future. . . . Voltaire's wit, then, teems with blasphemy and licentiousness; that of Holmes is pure of either. This does not mean that one man was essentially better or worse than the other; it means rather that the worlds in which they lived and the superstitions which they combated were different.

Wendell, "Oliver Wendell Holmes," in *A Literary History of America* (1900), 423.

Mae West (1893–1980)

MOTION PICTURE ACTRESS AND COMEDIENNE

The women don't razz me because I don' make 'em jealous. The only censorship directed at me comes from men because intelligent men resent my satire. In one way I'm a regular Voltaire when it comes to satire, honey, because I show that bigshot guys with a lot of dough and tailcoats and culture will fall like shooting gallery ducks for a lady lion tamer or any Madame Honky Tonk that gets a range on them. Once in a while that burns up an intelligent man because it makes him feel inferior.

"Mae West: Philosophy" (1934). In *I'm No Angel*, co-starring Cary Grant (released in October 1933), West's character performs in a lion taming act.

Edmund White (1940–)

NOVELIST, MEMOIRIST, AND ESSAYIST

Just as Voltaire attributed everything good to a China he had never seen, so La Fayette idealised an America he had forgotten.

White, *Fanny* (2003), 40.

Walt Whitman (1819–1892)

POET, ESSAYIST, AND JOURNALIST

They say the French Voltaire in his time designated the grand opera and a ship of war the most signal illustrations of the growth of humanity's and art's advance beyond primitive barbarism.

Whitman, *Specimen Days & Collect* (1887), 140.

Oscar Wilde (1854–1900)

ANGLO-IRISH PLAYWRIGHT, ESSAYIST, NOVELIST, POET, AND WIT

Books not to read at all, such as Thomson's *Seasons*, Rogers's *Italy*, Paley's *Evidences*, all the Fathers except St. Augustine, all John Stuart Mill except the essay on *Liberty*, all Voltaire's plays without any exception, Butler's *Analogy*, Grant's *Aristotle*, Hume's *England*, Lewes's *History of Philosophy*, all argumentative books and all books that try to prove anything.

"To Read or Not to Read" (unsigned) (1886), 11. Wilde began this brief article by dividing literature into three groups: "Books to read, such as Cicero's *Letters*," books to "re-read, such as Plato and Keats," and a third class, those that should not be read at all, by far the most "eminently needed" category in his day. Wilde stayed for a while at the Hôtel Voltaire on the quai Voltaire in Paris in 1883, but he rarely commented in print on Voltaire.

Bernard Williams (1929–2003)

ENGLISH PHILOSOPHER AND KNIGHTBRIDGE
PROFESSOR OF PHILOSOPHY AT CAMBRIDGE UNIVERSITY
AND DEUTSCH PROFESSOR OF PHILOSOPHY AT THE
UNIVERSITY OF CALIFORNIA, BERKELEY

It is worth noting that Voltaire was spectacularly odious toward Rousseau, particularly with regard to *La nouvelle Héloïse*, which he described as "stupid, bourgeois, impudent, boring," and he did his best to get it suppressed.

Williams, *Truth and Truthfulness* (2002), 303n28.

Diderot's my Enlightenment hero, much more than Voltaire, who I think was a mildly despotic and unpleasing individual, vastly overestimated in his influence.

Interview at Williams's home in Oxford, summer 2002, from Baggini and Stangroom, *What More Philosophers Think* (2007), 145.

Garry Wills (1934–)

PULITZER PRIZE–WINNING AMERICAN AUTHOR,
CRITIC, AND PROFESSOR OF HISTORY AT
NORTHWESTERN UNIVERSITY

He is often thought to be the American Voltaire, an enemy of religion in a sense that none of the others was. But Paine insisted on his own Deism, which is obviously not atheism. Deism, like theism, is simply "God-ism" (from *Deus* in Latin, *Theos* in Greek). In fact, Paine wrote his most reviled book, *The Age of Reason*, in France, where he opposed the extremism of some French Revolutionaries.

Wills commenting on Thomas Paine in *Head and Heart* (2007), 154.

Tom Wolfe (1931–2018)

AMERICAN NOVELIST, CRITIC, AND ONETIME
NEW JOURNALIST

Chomsky's politics enhanced his reputation as a great linguist, and his reputation as a great linguist enhanced his reputation as a political solon, and his reputation as a political solon inflated his reputation from great linguist to all-around genius, and the genius inflated the solon into a veritable Voltaire, and the veritable Voltaire inflated the genius of all geniuses into a philosophical giant . . . Noam Chomsky.

Wolfe, "The Origins of Speech" (2016), 29. Excerpted from "Noam Charisma," chap. 4 in Wolfe's book *The Kingdom of Speech* (2016), 4.

William Wordsworth (1770–1850)

ENGLISH POET

". . . this dull product of a Scoffer's pen."

The Wanderer, commenting on a copy of *Candide* owned by The Solitary in Wordsworth's *The Excursion* (1814), book 2, 74.

Frank Lloyd Wright (1867–1959)

AMERICAN ARCHITECT

Your wonderful portrait makes me the American Voltaire.

Wright to the renowned Canadian photographer Yousuf Karsh, who took his photo in 1952. Quoted in Francis, "How Karsh Pictures Celebrities" (1952), 224. Ironically, a year later the English architect Lionel Brett called Wright the Rousseau of modern architecture and Le Corbusier its Voltaire.

Damon Young (1975–)

AUSTRALIAN WRITER AND PHILOSOPHER

For Voltaire, the garden did not symbolize monkish quietism—quite the contrary. . . . It was a bold metaphor for compassion, responsibility and pragmatism—a call to improve his immediate surroundings.

Young, *Voltaire's Vine and Other Philosophies* (2014), 169.

Ferney required practical expertise, continual labour, and devotion. And likewise for civil institutions: the estate stood for France as a whole, which deserved to be governed wisely, benevolently, tolerantly. This is the point of Voltaire's conclusion: Candide's garden required careful, attentive custodianship—one that nurtured the community as well as the soil.

Young, *Voltaire's Vine and Other Philosophies* (2014), 170.

Émile Zola (1840–1902)

FRENCH JOURNALIST, PLAYWRIGHT, SHORT STORY WRITER, AND NOVELIST

Je ne considère point Voltaire comme un poète, un philosophe, un historien ou un romancier; je le considère comme une force dont s'est servie la vérité, ou plutôt encore comme l'individualité la plus complète et la plus en lumière du glorieux dix–huitième siècle.

I do not regard Voltaire as a poet, a philosopher, a historian or a novelist; I regard him as a force used by Truth, or rather the most complete individuality, and the brightest light of the glorious eighteenth century.

In Zola's book review column "Livres d'aujourdhui et de demain," in the April 3, 1866, issue of *L'Événement,* a short-lived Parisian daily; reprinted in Zola's *Œuvres complètes* (1968), 10:427.

1694   Born François-Marie Arouet in late November, in or near Paris, the son of François Arouet, a notary with court and aristocratic connections. His mother, née Marie-Marguerite Daumard, dies in 1701, when François is seven years old. As a boy, his family calls him "Zozo."

1704   Enters the Jesuit *collège* Louis-le-Grand, where he receives a classical education and makes lifelong friendships with the future duc de Richelieu and the brothers René-Louis and Marc-Pierre d'Argenson, government ministers under Louis XV.

1711   Finishes his schooling at Louis-le-Grand and, despite his announced intention to become a writer, is obliged by his father to study law.

1713   Spends four months at The Hague as secretary to the French ambassador in the Netherlands, the marquis de Châteauneuf, brother of Voltaire's godfather.

1714   In Paris, during his brief apprenticeship in the law, he meets a fellow clerk, Nicolas-Claude Thieriot, who becomes a lifelong friend and correspondent.

1716   One year after the death of Louis XIV, he is exiled from Paris to Sully-sur-Loire and accused of writing satirical verse about the regent.

1717   Imprisoned in the Bastille and charged with writing another satire about the regent.

1718   Adopts the pseudonym Voltaire, believed to be an acronym of Arouet l. j. (*le jeune*). His first play, the tragedy *Œdipe*, is applauded at the Comédie-Française in Paris.

1722   Death of his father. Travels to Brussels, The Hague, and Amsterdam. Frequents the exiled Tory politician Lord Bolingbroke at Bolingbroke's country estate, La Source, near Orléans.

1723   Royal censors refuse to permit publication of *La Ligue*, Voltaire's epic poem about one of his greatest heroes, Henri IV. The poem is later revised and renamed *La Henriade*.

1726　After a row with the chevalier de Rohan (whose men give Voltaire a thrashing in the street), he is again imprisoned in the Bastille and released provided that he leave Paris. He departs for London, where he soon masters spoken and written English. He reconnects with Bolingbroke and meets Jonathan Swift, John Gay, Alexander Pope, Lord Chesterfield, and Prime Minister Robert Walpole.

1728　*La Henriade* is published in London in French and dedicated to Queen Caroline of England. After almost two years in England, Voltaire returns to France in 1729.

1730　Begins writing *La Pucelle*, a sacreligious mock epic poem about Joan of Arc. His tragedy *Brutus*, inspired by Shakespeare, premieres in Paris.

1731　His first history, *Histoire de Charles XII*, is published.

1732　His third major tragedy, *Zaïre*, is successfully staged.

1733　*Letters Concerning the English Nation* is published in London. His liaison with Mme du Châtelet begins. *Le Temple du Goût* is published.

1734　The French edition of the *Letters Concerning the English Nation*, the *Lettres philosophiques*, is published in Rouen and immediately censored. After a scandal at court, he and Émilie, the marquise du Châtelet, move into the château de Cirey in eastern France owned by her absent husband, a career military man.

1736　Voltaire begins a correspondence with Frederick of Prussia that will last until his death. He publishes *Le Mondain*, a breezy but scandalous poem about luxury and the good life that compels him to leave France and go to Holland.

1738　*Élémens de la philosophie de Neuton* is published in Amsterdam, followed by the *Discours en vers sur l'homme*, inspired by Pope's *Essay on Man* (1734–1735).

1740　Voltaire and Émilie spend two months in Brussels.

1741　Premiere of *Le Fanatisme, ou Mahomet*.

1743　Elected a fellow of the British Royal Society.

1745　In favor (briefly) at Versailles, with the support of Mme de Pompadour. Voltaire is appointed historiographer to the king, writes librettos for two operas by Rameau (*Le Princesse de Navarre* and *Le Temple de la gloire*), and dedicates his play *Mahomet* to the pope. Begins a secret sexual relationship with his niece, Mme Marie-Louise Denis.

1746   Elected to the Académie française. Appointed *Gentilhomme ordinaire de la chambre du Roi.*

1747   *Memnon*, later titled *Zadig*, is the first of his short pieces of fiction to be published. Voltaire and Mme du Châtelet leave Paris for Cirey.

1749   Émilie dies giving birth to a child fathered by the poet Saint-Lambert. Voltaire returns to Paris, where he and Mme Denis briefly share the same house.

1750   Accepts Frederick the Great's invitation to join his court in Prussia.

1751   *Le Siècle de Louis XIV* is published in Berlin.

1753   After a messy falling out with Frederick, Voltaire leaves Prussia. The king has him placed under house arrest in Frankfurt. Voltaire and Mme Denis reside in Colmar for a little over a year.

1754   In December, Voltaire and Mme Denis spend three months at the château de Prangins in the Pays de Vaud, not far from Geneva.

1755   Voltaire and Mme Denis move into Les Délices, a mansion on an estate inside the Republic of Geneva. Voltaire resides there on and off until he is fully settled at Ferney in 1760. In late November he learns of the earthquake and massive loss of life in Lisbon. *La Pucelle* is published in a pirated edition.

1756   Publishes the *Poème sur le désastre de Lisbonne* and his first avowed edition of the *Essai sur les mœurs.*

1758   Acquires the *seigneurie* and château de Tournay near the west shore of Lake Geneva, on French territory, one mile north of the city of Geneva.

1759   Acquires and begins refurbishing the *seigneurie* and château de Ferney, also in France, a mile northwest of Tournay, where he becomes renowned as the "Patriarch of Ferney." *Candide* is published anonymously in editions all over Europe.

1760   First use of the words *Écrasez l'infâme* ("Crush the despicable"), Voltaire's catchphrase in the struggle for enlightened religious toleration and justice in human affairs.

1761   The first volumes of a thirty-six-volume set of his writings, edited and translated into English by Tobias Smollett and Thomas Francklin, are published in London.

1763   The *Traité sur la tolérance à l'occasion de la mort de Jean Calas* is published. Voltaire champions the cause of the French Huguenot Calas, unjustly condemned to death in Toulouse in 1762.

1764   Publishes the *Dictionnaire philosophique portatif* in editions reprinted
        and often enlarged several times over the next few years. Dr. John
        Morgan, cofounder of the Medical College at the University of
        Pennsylvania, is received by Voltaire at Ferney.

1765   Thanks to Voltaire's campaign on his behalf and Voltaire's high-
        placed connections, Calas is posthumously rehabilitated.

1770   Publication of the multivolume *Questions sur l'Encyclopédie* begins.

1776   Takes in twenty-year-old Reine-Philiberte Rouph de Varicourt, the
        daughter of an impoverished neighbor, who is otherwise destined for
        a convent. Nicknamed by Voltaire "Belle et Bonne," she is regarded
        as his adoptive daughter and in November 1777 is married off to the
        marquis de Villette, who, in September 1778, purchases the estate at
        Ferney after Voltaire's death.

1778   Returns to Paris after an absence of twenty-eight years and is hailed
        at the Académie française and at the Théâtre-Français. He and Benja-
        min Franklin meet and embrace at the Académie des Sciences. After
        his death on May 30 in the hôtel de Villette on the quai des Théatins,
        his corpse is smuggled out of Paris and secretly buried in Champagne.
        Catherine the Great buys Voltaire's library from his niece, Mme
        Denis.

1781   Jean-Antoine Houdon's seated marble statue of Voltaire, commis-
        sioned by Mme Denis, one of the greatest masterpieces of
        eighteenth-century art, is exhibited at the Salon of Painting and
        Sculpture sponsored by the royal Académie de peinture et de
        sculpture.

1783   Publication of the seventy-volume Kehl edition of the *Œuvres
        complètes de Voltaire* begins, financed and edited by the playwright
        Beaumarchais (*Le Barbier de Séville*, *Le Mariage de Figaro*), who also
        helped finance French assistance to the American army during the
        American Revolution.

1791   The quai des Théatins is renamed quai Voltaire. Voltaire's remains are
        transported in a solemn procession through the heart of Paris, past the
        house in which he died, and placed in the crypt of the Panthéon, to be
        joined in 1794 by the remains of Jean-Jacques Rousseau.

1828   James Fenimore Cooper tours Voltaire's house and estate at
        Ferney.

1831   Publication of a seventy-two-volume set of the *Œuvres de Voltaire*,
        edited by Adrien Beuchot, begins.

1865   *Candide*, a twice-weekly newspaper, is founded by Gustave Tridon and Auguste Blanqui.

1867   Publication of volume 1 of Gustave Desnoiresterres's eight-volume biography, *Voltaire et la société au XVIIIe siècle* (1867–1876).

1870   The boulevard du Prince-Eugène in Paris's eleventh arrondissement is renamed boulevard Voltaire.

1871   Communards burn a guillotine on the boulevard Voltaire opposite a bronze cast of Houdon's seated statue of Voltaire.

1872   Lord Morley, the English journalist and prolific author of lives of great men, publishes the first full-fledged biography of Voltaire in English.

1877   Publication of the fifty-two-volume Moland edition of the *Œuvres complètes de Voltaire* begins.

1878   The Paris daily *Le Voltaire* is founded. Victor Hugo delivers a speech in Voltaire's honor during the centennial commemoration of his death.

1881   The first American biography of Voltaire, James Parton's 1,300-page, two-volume work published by Houghton, Mifflin, is later described as the "most complete, and the best" life of Voltaire "ever written."

1885   On July 14, a statue of Voltaire by Joseph-Michel Caillé is inaugurated on the quai Malaquais in Paris, near the Institut de France.

1903   In England, Evelyn Beatrice Hall [S. G. Tallentyre] publishes her influential biography *The Friends of Voltaire*. Among its American readers are Clarence Darrow and Will Durant.

1911   The French Danton-class battleship *Voltaire* is launched at Toulon.

1916   Founders of the Dada movement meet at the Cabaret Voltaire in Zurich.

1923   The HMS *Voltaire*, an auxiliary cruiser in the British Royal Navy, is launched.

1924   The defunct newspaper *Candide* is revived as a political and literary weekly.

1928   Random House publishes a deluxe limited edition of *Candide*, illustrated by the graphic artist Rockwell Kent.

1929   The City of Geneva purchases Voltaire's former home, Les Délices. The U.S. Treasury department declares a French edition of *Candide* obscene and seizes a shipment of books imported by a Boston bookseller.

1933   George Arliss, Academy Award winner for Best Actor in 1929–1930, stars in the Warner Brothers "bio-pic" *Voltaire*. Doris Kenyon plays Madame de Pompadour, and Reginald Owen plays Louis XV.

1939   In June, just before World War II begins in Europe, E. M. Forster peeks at Voltaire's château through the front gate.

1944   In December, four months after the Liberation of Paris, Paul Valéry evokes the memory and cultural significance of Voltaire for France in a moving address delivered at the Sorbonne.

1952   Les Délices at Geneva becomes the Institut et Musée Voltaire, with Theodore Besterman as director.

1955   Besterman launches the *Studies on Voltaire and the Eighteenth Century* series, commenced at Les Délices, to be continued, fifteen years later, at the University of Oxford.

1956   Leonard Bernstein's comic operetta *Candide* opens on Broadway, with a libretto by Lillian Hellman and lyrics by the poet Richard Wilbur; it closes after just two months.

1957   Nancy Mitford's best seller *Voltaire in Love* is published.

1959   Yale University history professor Peter Gay's study *Voltaire's Politics* is published.

1960   During a Council of Ministers meeting in December 1960, Charles de Gaulle is urged to order the arrest of Jean-Paul Sartre for his well-publicized opposition to the government's policies in Algeria. De Gaulle's reported response: "You don't put Voltaire in jail."

1961   *Le Nouveau Candide*, a weekly newspaper, is launched; its contributors include the novelist and essayist Jean Dutourd, *Le Figaro* political cartoonist Jacques Faizant, and Jean-Jacques Sempé, whose drawings later appear on the cover of the *New Yorker*.

1965   Simon & Schuster publishes *The Age of Voltaire*, volume 9 in Will and Ariel Durant's popular series *The Story of Civilization*.

1968   Publication by the Voltaire Foundation, headed by Theodore Besterman, of the *Œuvres complètes de Voltaire* begins, and within the *OCV*, the second, "definitive" edition of Voltaire's correspondence.

1971   After a bitter dispute with the City of Geneva, Besterman moves his Voltaire Foundation operation to the University of Oxford.

1973   The English industrial/techno pop band Cabaret Voltaire is formed. A poster for the group is seen on the bedroom wall of the teen slacker played by Matthew Broderick in the 1986 film *Ferris Bueller's Day Off*.

1974　A revised and condensed, one-act version of Leonard Bernstein's *Candide*, directed by Hal Prince, begins a successful two-year run on Broadway.

1979　In Paris, an exhibition at the Bibliothèque Nationale, *Voltaire: Un homme, un siècle*—a tardy bicentennial tribute, 201 years after Voltaire's death—runs from January 23 through April 22.

1980　The graduating class at the elite state school, the École Nationale d'Administration Française—the *promotion Voltaire*—boasts three up-and-coming French politicians: President François Hollande, Prime Minister Dominique de Villepin, and government minister Ségolène Royal.

1982　A third, "opera house" production of *Candide*, also directed by Hal Prince (libretto by Hugh Wheeler), opens at the New York City Opera and becomes the standard version staged around the world.

1985　Publication of volume 1 of René Pomeau's five-volume biography *Voltaire en son temps*.

1988　In the planning stages of the combined live-action and animated comedy *Who Framed Roger Rabbit*, the film's villain, Judge Doom (played by Christopher Lloyd), has a pet vulture named Voltaire.

1994　Commemoration of the 300th anniversary of Voltaire's birth features a comprehensive exhibition at the Hôtel de la Monnaie in Paris and a joint international congress in Paris and Oxford. Thierry Meyssan founds the nonprofit, center-left organization Réseau Voltaire, with a website at www.voltairenet.org.

1996　The Voltaire Society of America is formed in New York City.

1997　Zadig & Voltaire, the Paris-based ready-to-wear luxury clothing line, is founded.

1998　La Tour Voltaire goes up in the La Défense business district outside Paris. In 2019 BlackRock, the New York–based global investment manager ("the world's biggest shadow bank"), purchases the skyscraper.

1999　The French government acquires the château de Ferney.

2000　Andrew Brown, former assistant and successor to Besterman as director of the Voltaire Foundation, establishes the Société Voltaire, based in Ferney-Voltaire. *La Faute à Voltaire*, directed by Abdellatif Kechiche, is screened at the Venice International Film Festival.

2001　The Société Voltaire publishes the first volume in its series of scholarly journals, *Cahiers Voltaire*. In the United States, *Voltaire & Jefferson: The*

Sage of Ferney and the Man from Monticello, an award-winning, twenty-three-minute documentary narrated by Cliff Robertson and produced for the Voltaire Society of America, airs on the local PBS station in New York City.

2009　In Melbourne, the Victorian Council for Civil Liberties, Australia's oldest human rights association, merges with the activist group Free Speech Victoria. Together they present the first annual Liberty Victoria Voltaire Award to an individual or organization that has made an outstanding contribution to free speech. In 2011 the joint recipients were Wikileaks and Julian Assange.

2010　Voltaire Gazmin begins six years of service as Secretary of National Defense in the Philippines.

2011　The French writer Frédéric Lenormand publishes the first in a series of historical whodunits called *Voltaire mène l'enquête.* Later titles include *Le Diable s'habille en Voltaire* (2013) and *Élémentaire, mon cher Voltaire!* (2015).

2012　In France, Robert Ménard, Dominique Jamet, Denis Cheyrouze, and Emmanuelle Duverger launch the far-right news aggregator website Boulevard Voltaire.

2015　Voltaire's name is invoked after the horrific Islamic terrorist attack in Paris on the offices of the French satirical weekly *Charlie Hebdo.*

2016　In Geneva, the International Publishers Association (IPA) awards its first annual IPA Prix Voltaire to Raif Badawi of Saudi Arabia. Major publishers such as HarperCollins, Oxford University Press, Penguin Random House, and Simon & Schuster provide most of the roughly $10,000 prize money. The IPA Prix Voltaire, formerly the Freedom to Publish Prize, was established to recognize a significant contribution to the defense and promotion of the freedom to publish.

2018　On May 31, one day after the 240th anniversary of Voltaire's death, French president Emmanuel Macron officiates at the reopening of the château de Ferney, which for several years had been closed for extensive repairs and renovations.

2019　Les Arènes publishes volume 2 of *Voltaire Amoureux,* a multitome "biopic" *en bande dessinée* (distributed by Hachette), written and illustrated by Clément Oubrerie, who, in an interview, describes Voltaire as a "super personnage de comédie, un peu à la Woody Allen." Hypothesis Brewing Company (Chicago) begins marketing an India pale ale called Voltaire.

2020   On June 22, as part of a nationwide protest against France's colonial past and its role in the slave trade—prompted by civil unrest in the United States following the death of Black Lives Matter martyr George Floyd—vandals splash red paint on a statue of Voltaire in the *square* Honoré-Champion in Paris, next to the Institut de France.

2021   The Voltaire Foundation publishes the last volume of text in its 203-volume series of Voltaire's complete works.

FURTHER READING (AND VIEWING) IN ENGLISH

If a college or public library does not have any of the material listed here, it might be available through interlibrary loan. Peter Gay's monograph, the volumes edited by Nicholas Cronk, Donald M. Frame, and G. K. Noyer, and the biographies by Ian Davidson, Nancy Mitford, and Roger Pearson are still in print. Used copies of the other texts generally can be purchased via Amazon.com or eBay; the DVD may be ordered from Films Media Group (www.films.com/id/1584).

BIOGRAPHY

Aldington, Richard. *Voltaire*. London: G. Routledge, 1925.

Besterman, Theodore S. B. *Voltaire*. New York: Harcourt, Brace & World, 1969.

Davidson, Ian. *Voltaire: A Life*. London: Profile Books, 2010.

Davidson, Ian. *Voltaire in Exile*. London: Atlantic Books, 2004.

Maurois, André. *Voltaire*. Translated by Hamish Miles. London: Thomas Nelson and Sons, 1938.

Mitford, Nancy. *Voltaire in Love*. New York: Harper & Row, 1957. Reprint, with an introduction by Adam Gopnik, New York: New York Review Books, 2012.

Morley, John. *Voltaire*. London: Chapman and Hall, 1872.

Orieux, Jean. *Voltaire*. Translated by Barbara Bray and Helen R. Lane. New York: Doubleday, 1981.

Parton, James. *Life of Voltaire*. 2 vols. Boston: Houghton, Mifflin and Company, 1881.

Pearson, Roger. *Voltaire Almighty: A Life in Pursuit of Freedom*. New York: Bloomsbury, 2005.

CANDIDE AND OTHER TALES

Candide, Zadig, and Other Stories. Translated by Donald M. Frame, with an introduction by John R. Iverson. New York: Signet Classic (New American Library), 2001. (Frame's translation was first published in 1961.)

CORRESPONDENCE

Brooks, Richard A., ed. and trans. *The Selected Letters of Voltaire*. New York: New York University Press, 1973.

Hall, Evelyn Beatrice [S. G. Tallentyre], ed. and trans. *Voltaire in His Letters: Being a Selection from His Correspondence*. London: John Murray, 1919.

SPECIALIZED STUDIES

Cronk, Nicholas, ed. *The Cambridge Companion to Voltaire*. Cambridge: Cambridge University Press, 2009.

Cronk, Nicholas. *Voltaire: A Very Short Introduction*. Oxford: Oxford University Press, 2017.

De Beer, Gavin, and André-Michel Rousseau, eds. *Voltaire's British Visitors*. In *Studies on Voltaire and the Eighteenth Century*, vol. 49. Geneva: Institut et Musée Voltaire, 1967.

Gay, Peter. *Voltaire's Politics: The Poet as Realist*. Princeton, NJ: Princeton University Press, 1959. Reprint, New Haven, CT: Yale University Press, 1988.

Noyer, G. K., ed. and trans. *Voltaire's Revolution: Writings from His Campaign to Free Laws from Religion*. Amherst, NY: Prometheus Books, 2015.

VIDEO

Apgar, Garry, cowritten and edited by George W. Gowen and Patrick H. Ryan. *Voltaire & Jefferson: The Sage of Ferney and the Man from Monticello*. DVD. 23 min. Produced and directed by Dennis Powers, Patrick H. Ryan, and Rawn Fulton. Narrated by Cliff Robertson. Princeton, NJ: Films for the Humanities, 2001.

ACKNOWLEDGMENTS

The Quotable Voltaire marks the second major accomplishment of the nonprofit Voltaire Society of America Inc., founded in 1997 with George W. Gowen as chairman of the board and James W. Reid as president. In 2001, our award-winning, twenty-three-minute documentary *Voltaire & Jefferson: The Sage of Ferney and the Master of Monticello*, produced by Dennis A. Powers, was completed, thanks primarily to the devotion and persistence of George Gowen, who also arranged for the film to be broadcast on WNET, the public television station in New York City. George brought the same dynamic qualities to bear in helping this project come to fruition.

We owe a debt of gratitude to the following individuals who have provided vital material or moral support for this project: Mathew K. Apgar; Stephen Michael Apgar; Stephen Ashworth; W. Nat Baker; Theodore E. D. Braun; Andrew Brown; Gerald Leonard Cohen; Nicholas Cronk; Simon Davies; Lu-Vada Dunford, Julia Goddard; Shaun O'L. Higgins; Laurence A. Jarvik; Kathleen Jones; Sergueï Karp; John O'Neill; Lynette Papadogianis, development coordinator with Golub and Company; Richard Pershan; Gillian Pink; François Roussiau, treasurer of the association "Les amis de Jean Guéhenno"; Yale Law librarian Fred Shapiro; Thelma Snyder; W. R. Sphar III; Don Surber; Peter M. Urbach; Steven Wander; Mark Weiner; Servanne Woodward; and Robert Zaretsky. We also wish to acknowledge the generous financial support of Joseph D. Allen III, Susan J. Alpine, Nat Baker, Ted Braun, Edward J. Foley III, the Fred and Gertrude Perlberg Foundation Inc., Norman F. Hapke Jr., Shaun Higgins, Larry Jarvik, Bill Lanni, Rog Sphar, and Sue Ann Raring, who made a donation in memory of her husband Andrew M. Raring, a college roommate and fraternity brother, like Rog Sphar, of Garry Apgar.

Finally, we are immensely grateful to Greg Clingham, former director of the Bucknell University Press, for his keen interest in *The Quotable Voltaire*, and to production editor John Donohue and copy editor Sue Sakai of Westchester Publishing Services for their superb professionalism. During the final stages of the production process, John was a delight to work with on the editing, proofing, and design of the interior of the book.

BIBLIOGRAPHY

VOLTAIRE'S COMPLETE WORKS

Beaumarchais, Pierre-Augustin Caron de, ed. *Œuvres complètes de Voltaire.* 70 vols. Kehl: Imprimerie de la Société Littéraire-Typographique, 1783–1790.

Besterman, Theodore S. B., et al., eds. *Œuvres complètes de Voltaire: The Complete Works of Voltaire.* 216 vols. to date of a projected 220 vols. Geneva: The Voltaire Foundation, 1968–2018. (This total does not include the 50 volumes of Voltaire's correspondence that are counted among the *Complete Works.*)

Beuchot, Adrien-Jean-Quentin, ed. *Œuvres de Voltaire avec Préfaces, Avertissements, Notes, etc.* 70 vols. Paris: Chez Lefèvre, Libraire, Firmin Didot Frères, and Lequien Fils, 1828–1834.

Cramer, Gabriel, and Philibert Cramer, eds. *Collection complette des Œuvres de Mr. de Voltaire, première édition.* 27 vols. Geneva, 1756–1775.

Moland, Louis, ed. *Œuvres complètes de Voltaire. Nouvelle édition avec notices, préfaces, variantes, table analytique, les notes de tous les commentateurs et des notes nouvelles, conforme pour le texte à l'édition de Beuchot.* 52 vols. Paris: Garnier Frères, 1877–1885.

Oeuvres de M. *de Voltaire. Nouvelle Edition. Revue, corrigée & considérablement augmentée, avec des figures en taille-douce.* Vol. 4. Amsterdam: Chez Etienne Ledet & Compagnie, 1739. Of a five-volume series, published 1738–1744.

Oeuvres de M. de Voltaire. Nouvelle Edition, Revuë, corrigée, augmentée par l'Auteur; & enrichie de Figures en Taille-douce. 2 vols. Amsterdam: Jacques Desbordes/Estienne Ledet & Compagnie, 1732.

Oeuvres de M. *de Voltaire. Nouvelle Edition: Revue, corrigée et considerablement augmentee par l'auteur enrichie de Figures en Taille-douce.* 9 vols. Dresden: Chez George Conrad Walther, 1748–1750.

Oeuvres de M. *de Voltaire. Nouvelle Edition: Revue, corrigée et considerablement augmentée par l'auteur enrichie de Figures en Taille-douce.* 8 vols. Dresden: Chez George Conrad Walther, 1752–1756.

Oeuvres diverses de Monsieur de Voltaire. Nouvelle édition. Recueillie avec soin, enrichie de Piéces Curieuses, & la seule qui contienne ses véritables Ouvrages. Avec Figures en Taille-Douce. Tome sixiéme. London: Chez Jean Nourse, 1746.

Smollett, Tobias, Thomas Francklin, M.A., and Others, eds. and trans. *The Works of Mr. de Voltaire. Translated from the French. With Notes, Historical and Critical.* 36 vols. London: J. Newbery, R. Baldwin, W. Johnston, S. Crowder, T. Davies, J. Coote, G. Kearsley, 1761–1770.

Voltairiana. 4 vols. Edited and translated by Mary Julia Young. London: J. P. Hughes, 1805.

The Works of Voltaire: A Contemporary Version. Translated by William F. Fleming. 42 vols. New York: E. R. DuMont, 1901.

COMPILATIONS OF VOLTAIRE'S WRITINGS

The Dramatic Works of Mr. de Voltaire. Edited by Tobias Smollett, Thomas Francklin, M.A., and Others. 7 vols. London: J. Newbery, R. Baldwin, S. Crowder, and Co., J. Coote, T. Davies, W. Johnston, R. Francklin, G. Kearsley, 1761–1763. These volumes were published as part of the thirty-six-volume Smollett et al. edition of *The Works of Mr. de Voltaire* (1761–1770).

Mélanges de littérature, d'histoire et de philosophie. 1757. In *Collection complète des Œuvres de Mr. De Voltaire*, vol. 4. https://books.google.com/books.

Mélanges de Poésies, de littérature, d'histoire et de philosophie. Vol. 2. Geneva, 1757. https://books.google.com/books.

Mélanges philosophiques, littéraires, historiques, &c. Vol. 1. Geneva, 1771. https://books.google.com/books.

Mélanges philosophiques, littéraires, historiques, &c. Vol. 2. Geneva, 1771. https://books.google.com/books.

Mélanges philosophiques, littéraires, historiques, &c. Vol. 4. Geneva, 1771. https://books.google.com/books.

Mélanges philosophiques, littéraires, historiques, &c. Vol. 6. Geneva, 1777. https://books.google.com/books.

Miscellaneous Poems. By Mr. De Voltaire. Translated from the French, By T. Smollett, M.D., T. Francklin, M.A. and others. London: J. Newbery, R. Baldwin, S. Crowder, and Co., 1764. Vol. 33 in the Smollett et al. edition of *The Works of Mr. de Voltaire* (1761–1770). https://books.google.com/books.

Nouveaux Mélanges philosophiques, historiques, critiques, &c. &c. &c. 19 vols. Geneva: Cramer, 1765–1775.

Œuvres complètes de Voltaire. Mélanges littéraires. 2 vols. Paris: Chez Antoine-Augustin Renouard, 1821.

Œuvres de M. de Voltaire. Nouvelle édition, Considérablement augmentée, Enrichie de Figures en Taille-douce. Tome III. 1751.

Œuvres de Monsieur de V***. Romans; Contes allégoriques, philosophiques, &c. Nouvelle Édition. Vol. 1. Neuchâtel, 1771.

Piéces détachées, attribuées à divers hommes célèbres, &c. Vol. 2. 1775.

Pièces nouvelles de Monsieur de Voltaire. "Amsterdam," 1769. https://books.google.com/books.

Poèmes et discours en vers, Œuvres complètes de Voltaire. Vol. 12. Edited by Pierre-Augustin Caron de Beaumarchais. Kehl: Imprimerie de la Société Littéraire-Typographique, 1784.

Poësies mêlées, &c. Vol. 3. 1774. Vol. 20 in *Collection Complette des Œuvres de Mʳ. de ****.

Questions sur l'Encyclopédie, par des Amateurs. Première partie. 9 vols. [Geneva: Cramer,] 1770–1772.

Recueil de nouvelles pièces fugitives en prose et en vers. Nouvelle Edition, revûë & corrigée. Par M. de Voltaire. "A Londres," "Aux Dépens de la Société," 1741.

Recueil de nouvelles pièces fugitives en prose et en vers, par M. de Voltaire. London, 1741.

Recueil de pieces fugitives en prose et en vers. Par M. de V***. 1740. https://books.google.com/books.

Seconde Suite des mélanges de littérature, d'histoire, et de philosophie &c. 1761. In *Collection complette des Œuvres de Mr. de. . . . . . . , Seconde partie.*

Suite des mélanges de littérature, d'histoire et de philosophie. 1757. Vol. 5 in the 27-volume series *Collection complette des Œuvres de Mr. de Voltaire, première édition,* edited by Gabriel Cramer and Philibert Cramer. Geneva, 1756–1775. https://books.google.com /books.

Suite des mélanges de littérature, par Mr. de Voltaire. Avec un supplément aux Mélanges de poésie. Tome quatorzieme. "Londres," 1773. https://books.google.com/books.

Théatre complet de M'. de Voltaire. 5 vols. Geneva, 1768. In *Collection Complette des Œuvres de M'. de Voltaire.*

Troisieme suite des mélanges de poesie, de littérature, d'histoire et de philosophie. 1765.

Voltaire: Political Writings. Edited and translated by David Williams. Cambridge: Cambridge University Press, 1994.

CORRESPONDENCE OF VOLTAIRE

Aldington, Richard, ed. *Letters of Voltaire and Frederick the Great.* New York: Brentano's, 1927.

Besterman, Theodore, and Frédéric Deloffre, eds. *Voltaire. Correspondance.* 13 vols. Paris: Gallimard (La Pléiade), 1978–1993. (Unlike the Besterman series, the Pléiade edition contains no letters addressed to Voltaire.)

Besterman, Theodore S. B., ed. *The Complete Works of Voltaire. Correspondence and Related Documents. Definitive Edition.* Vols. 85–135. Geneva: Institut et Musée Voltaire, 1968–1977.

Beuchot, Adrien-Jean-Quentin, ed. *Œuvres de Voltaire avec préfaces, avertissements, notes, etc. Correspondance—Tome XI.* Vol. 54. Paris: Chez Lefèvre, libraire, 1832.

Francklin, Thomas, trans. *Letters, from M. de Voltaire. To Several of His Friends.* Dublin: H. Saunders, 1770.

Hall, Evelyn Beatrice [S. G. Tallentyre], ed. and trans. *Voltaire in His Letters: Being a Selection from His Correspondence.* London: John Murray, 1919.

"IIme homélie. Sur la superstition." In *Homelies prononcées à Londres en 1765. Dans une assemblée particuliere,* 30–49. 1767. https://books.google.com/books.

INDIVIDUAL WORKS BY VOLTAIRE

L'A, B, C, Dialogue curieux. "A Londres": "Chez Robert Freeman," 1762. https://books .google.com/books.

L'A, B, C, ou Dialogues entre A. B. C. In *La Raison Par Alphabet. Sixiéme édition, revuë, corrigée & augmentée par l'Auteur. Second Partie,* 2:199–339. 1769. (Modern edition: Theodore S. B. Besterman et al., eds., *Œuvres complètes de Voltaire,* vol. 65a, edited by Roland Mortier and Christophe Paillard [2011].)

"Abus des mots." In *Questions sur l'Encyclopédie, par des Amateurs,* 1:52–57. 1770. https:// books.google.com/books.

"Académie." In *Questions sur l'Encyclopédie, par des Amateurs,* 1:57–61. 1770. https://books .google.com/books.

Additions à l'Essay sur l'Histoire générale, Et sur l'Esprit & les Mœurs des Nations, depuis Charlemagne jusqu'à nos jours. 1763. https://books.google.com/books.

Adélaïde du Guesclin, Tragédie. In *Théatre Complet de Mr de Voltaire.* Vol. 3. Geneva: [Gabriel Cramer], 1768. https://books.google.com/books.

"Adultère." In *Questions sur l'Encyclopédie, par des Amateurs*, 1:76–90. 1770. https://books.google.com/books.

The Age of Louis XIV. To Which Is Added, an Abstract of the Age of Louis XV. 2 vols. Translated by Richard Griffith. London: Fielding and Walker, 1779.

Alzire, ou les Américains. Tragédie de M. de Voltaire. Représentée à Paris pour la première fois le 27 Janvier, 1736. Paris: Chez Jean-Baptiste-Claude Bauche, 1736. https://gallica.bnf.fr/ark:/12148/bpt6k57464038.texteImage. (Modern edition: Theodore S. B. Besterman et al., eds., *Œuvres complètes de Voltaire*, vol. 14, ed. Theodore E. D. Braun [1989].)

"Amitié." In *Questions sur l'Encyclopédie, par des Amateurs*, 1:205–207. 1770. https://books.google.com/books.

"Amour-propre." In *Questions sur l'Encyclopédie, par des Amateurs*, 1:213–215. 1770. https://books.google.com/books.

"Amour socratique." In *Questions sur l'Encyclopédie, par des Amateurs*, 1:136–140. 1774. https://books.google.com/books.

Annales de l'Empire depuis Charlemagne. Par l'Auteur du Siècle de Louis XIV. Tome premier. Nouvelle édition, Où l'on a inséré les corrections de l'Auteur. Basel: Chez Jean-Henri Decker, 1754.

"Anthropophages." In *Questions sur L'Encyclopédie, par des Amateurs*, 1:356–367. 1770. https://books.google.com/books.

"Antiquité." In *Questions sur l'Encyclopédie, par des Amateurs*, 1:339–355. 1770. https://books.google.com/books.

"Argent." In *Questions sur l'Encyclopédie, par des Amateurs*, 2:118–129. 1770. https://books.google.com/books.

"Arianisme." In *Questions sur l'Encyclopédie, par des Amateurs*, 2:129–143. 1770. https://books.google.com/books.

"Aristote." In *Questions sur l'Encyclopédie, par des Amateurs*, 2:147–162. 1770. https://books.google.com/books.

"Art dramatique." In *Questions sur l'Encyclopédie, par des Amateurs*, 2:189–250. 1770. https://books.google.com/books.

"A Son Altesse Sérénissme Madame la Duchesse du Maine." In *Oreste, tragédie, par M. Arouet de Voltaire*, iii–xxi. 1750. https://books.google.com/books.

"Athéisme." In *Questions sur l'Encyclopédie, par des Amateurs*, 2:283–327. 1770. https://books.google.com/books.

"Augustin." In *Questions sur L'Encyclopédie, par des Amateurs.* Seconde partie, 353–356. 1770.

"Avis à un journaliste." *Mercure de France*, November 1744, 2–41.

Avis au Public sur les Parricides imputés aux Calas et aux Sirven. 1766.

"Bacchus." In *Questions sur l'Encyclopédie, par des Amateurs*, 3:10–16. 1770. https://books.google.com/books.

La Bégueule. Conte moral. 1772.

Besterman, Theodore S. B. et al., eds. *Œuvres complètes de Voltaire*, vol. 49B. Edited by Raymond Trousson. Geneva: The Voltaire Foundation, 2009.

Le Brutus de Monsieur de Voltaire, avec un Discours sur la Tragedie. Paris: Chez Je. Fr. Josse, 1731. (Modern edition: Theodore S. B. Besterman et al., eds., *Œuvres complètes de Voltaire*, vol. 5, ed. John Renwick [1998].)

Brutus, Tragédie de M. de Voltaire. Nouvelle edition. Revûë & corrigée par l'Auteur. Paris: Chez Prault fils, 1736. https://books.google.com/books.

Les Cabales, Œuvre pacifique. Par M. de Voltaire. "A Londres," 1772. (Modern edition: Theodore S. B. Besterman et al., eds., *Œuvres complètes de Voltaire,* vol. 74B, ed. Nicholas Cronk [2006].)

Candide or Optimism. Edited by Norman L. Torrey. New York: Appleton-Century-Crofts, 1946.

Candide, ou L'Optimisme, Par Mr. de Voltaire. Premiere Partie. Edition revue, corrigée & augmentée par L'Auteur. Aux Delices, 1763.

Candide, ou L'Optimisme, Traduit de l'allemand de Mr. le Docteur Ralph. [Geneva: Gabriel Cramer], 1759. (Modern edition: *Candide ou l'optimisme,* edited by René Pomeau [Paris: Éditions A.-G. Nizet, 1979]; reprinted in Theodore S. B. Besterman et al., eds., *Œuvres complètes de Voltaire,* vol. 48, ed. René Pomeau [1980].)

Candide, Zadig, and Other Stories. Translated by Donald M. Frame, with an introduction by John Iverson. New York: Signet Classic (New American Library), 2001. (Frame's translation was first published in 1961.)

"Caractère." In *Dictionnaire philosophique portatif par Mr. De Voltaire,* 59–61. 1764.

"Caractère." In *Questions sur l'Encyclopédie, par des Amateurs,* 2:87–89. 1770.

"Catéchisme de l'Honnête-homme, ou Dialogue Entre un Caloyer & un Homme de bien." In *L'Evangile de la raison. Ouvrage postume. De M. D. V. & D. F.* "A Londres": "Aux depens de la Compagnie de Jesus," 1764.

Ce qui plait aux Dames. "Partout": Chez de Libraires François, 1764.

"Chaine, ou Génération des événemens." In *Questions sur l'Encyclopédie, par des Amateurs,* 3:288–292. 1770. https://books.google.com/books.

Charlot, ou La comtesse de Givri, comédie, Représentée sur le Théâtre de F***. Au mois de Septembre 1767. Geneva: Chez Merlin, 1767. (Modern edition: Theodore S. B. Besterman et al., eds., *Œuvres complètes de Voltaire,* vol. 61B, ed. Thomas Wynn [2012].)

Les Choses utiles et agréables. 3 vols. "Berlin" [Geneva], 1769–1770.

"Climat." In *Questions sur l'Encyclopédie, par des Amateurs,* 4:13–22. 1771. https://books.google.com/books.

Les Colimaçons du Reverend Pere L'Escarbotier. 1768. In *Pièces nouvelles de Monsieur de Voltaire.* 1769.

Collection complete des Œuvres de Monsieur de Voltaire, Nouvelle Édition, Augmentée de ses dernieres Pieces de Théâtre, & enrichie de 61 Figures en taille-douce. Vol. 6. "A Amsterdam": "Aux Dépens de la Compagnie," 1764.

Collection Complette des Œuvres de M. de Voltaire. Vols. 8–10. Geneva, 1769.

Collection Complette des Œuvres de Mr. de Voltaire. Vols. 21–24. Geneva, 1774.

Collection complette des Oeuvres de Mr. de Voltaire, Seconde edition. Vol. 17. Geneva, 1757.

Commentaire historique sur les Oeuvres de l'auteur de La Henriade. &c. avec les Piéces originales & les preuves. Basel: Chez les Héritiers de Paul Duker, 1776.

Commentaires sur Corneille. In *Œuvres complètes de Voltaire. Commentaires sur Corneille II: Appendice,* vol. 32. In *Œuvres complètes de Voltaire. Nouvelle edition.* Paris: Garnier frères, 1880.

Commentaire sur l'Esprit des Loix De Montesquieu Par Mr. de Voltaire. 1778.

"The Complete History of England, etc." A review of a French edition of David Hume's *History of England.* In *Supplément à la Gazette littéraire de l'Europe,* May 2, 1764, 193–200.

"Conseils à un journaliste, Sur la Philosophie, l'Histoire, le Théâtre, les Pièces de Poësie, les Mélanges de littérature, les Anecdotes Littéraires, les Langues, & le Stile." In *Collection complete des Œuvres de Monsieur de Voltaire, Nouvelle Édition* 6:13–61. 1764. https://gallica.bnf.fr/ark:/12148/bpt6k72000w.r=Collection%20 complete%20des%20%C5%92uvres%20de%20Monsieur%20de%20Voltaire%2C%20 Nouvelle%20%C3%89dition%2C%20Augment%C3%A9e%20de%20ses%20dernieres %20Pieces%20de%20Th%C3%A9%C3%A2tre%2C%20&%20enrichie%20de%20 61%20Figures%20en%20otaille-douce?rk=21459;2.

Contes de Guillaume Vadé. [Geneva]: [Cramer], 1764. https://books.google.com /books.

Copie d'une Lettre à un premier Commis. June 20, 1733. In *Oeuvres diverses de Monsieur de Voltaire,* 4:245–250. 1746. (Modern edition: Theodore S. B. Besterman et al., eds., *Œuvres complètes de Voltaire,* vol. 9, ed. Pierre Rétat [1999].)

"De la vertu & du vice." In *Traité de Métaphysique.* 1734–1735. First published in *Philosophie générale: Métaphysique, morale, et théologie, Œuvres complètes de Voltaire,* 32:67–76. Edited by Pierre-Augustin Caron de Beaumarchais. Kehl: Imprimerie de la Société Littéraire-Typographique, 1784.

"De l'histoire." In *Questions sur l'Encyclopédie, par des Amateurs,* 7:17–91. 1771. https:// books.google.com/books.

"De l'histoire des Quakers." In *Oeuvres de Mʳ. de Voltaire. Nouvelle edition, Revue, corri-gée et considerablement augmentée par l'auteur,* 4:159–189. 1739. https://books.google .com/books.

"De l'horrible danger de la lecture." In *Nouveaux Mélanges philosophiques, historiques, critiques, &c. &c. &c. Troisième partie,* 159–161. 1765.

Le Dépositaire (1769). In *Théâtre complet de Mr. de Voltaire,* 7:241–356. 1772. https://books .google.com/books.

"Deuxième Discours, de la Liberté." In *Discours en vers sur l'homme,* in *Recueil de pieces fugitives en prose et en vers par M. de V***,* 58–62. 1740.

Dialogue de Pégase et du vieillard. "A Londres": Chez la Société Typographique, 1774. (Modern edition: *Dialogue de Pégase et du vieillard, otes de M. de Morza,* in Theo-dore S. B. Besterman et al., eds., *Œuvres complètes de Voltaire,* vol. 76, ed. Nicholas Cronk [2013].)

"Dialogue III. Entre un philosophe et un contrôleur-général des finances." In *Oeuvres de Mʳ. de Voltaire: Nouvelle édition revue, corrigée et considerablement augmentée par l'auteur enrichie de figures en taille-douce,* 3:262–270. 1752.

Dialogues d'Évhémère. "Londres" [Amsterdam]: [Marc-Michel Rey], 1777; 2nd ed., 1779.

Diatribe du docteur Akakia, Médecin du Pape: Decret de l'inquisition; et Rapport des Profes-seurs de Rome, Au sujet d'un Prétendu Président. "Rome," 1753.

Dictionnaire philosophique. In *Œuvres complètes de Voltaire,* vol. 37, edited by Pierre-Augustin Caron de Beaumarchais. Kehl: Imprimerie de la Société Littéraire-Typographique, 1784.

Dictionnaire philosophique, portatif. "Londres," 1764. (Modern edition: Theodore S. B. Besterman et al., eds., *Œuvres complètes de Voltaire,* vols. 35–36, ed. Christiane Mer-vaud [1994].) https://books.google.com/books.

Dictionnaire philosophique, portatif. Nouvelle Édition. "A Londres," 1765. https://books .google.com/books.

Dictionnaire philosophique, portatif. Sixieme Edition revue, corrigée & augmentée de XXXIV. Articles par l'Auteur. Vol. 2. "Londres," 1767. https://books.google.com /books.

Dictionnaire philosophique portatif, ou Supplément à l'Édition de 1765. Revue, corrigé & augmenté de XXXVII Articles par l'Auteur. "A Londres," circa 1765. https://books .google.com/books.

Dictionnaire philosophique, portatif par Mr. De Voltaire. "A Londres," 1764. https://books .google.com/books.

Le Dimanche, ou les Filles de Minée, Poëme Adressé par M. De Voltaire, sous le nom de M. de la Visclede, à Madame Harnarche. "À Londres": "Aux Dépens de la Société," 1775. https://gallica.bnf.fr/ark:/12148/bpt6k8417684.image.

Le Dîner du comte de Boulainvilliers par Mr. St. Hiacinthe. 1728.

Discours en vers sur l'homme. 1737–1738. In *Recueil de pieces fugitives en prose et en vers par M. de V***,* 51–94 (1740), and *Mélanges de Poésies, de littérature, d'histoire et de philoso- phie,* 2:7–53 (1757). (Modern edition: *Épîtres ou Discours en vers sur l'homme,* in Theodore S. B. Besterman et al., eds., *Œuvres complètes de Voltaire,* vol. 17, ed. Haydn T. Mason [1991].)

Discours prononcez dans l'Académie Françoise, Le Lundi 9 Mai MDCCXLVI. A la Réception de M. de Voltaire. Paris: L'Imprimerie de Jean-Baptiste Coignard, 1746.

Discours sur la tragédie à Mylord Bolingbrooke. See preface to the 1736 edition of *Brutus.* (Modern edition: Theodore S. B. Besterman et al., eds., *Œuvres complètes de Voltaire,* vol. 5, ed. John Renwick [1998].)

Dissertation sur la tragédie ancienne et moderne, a son Eminence Monseigneur le Cardinal Querini, noble vénitien, Éveque de Brescia, bibliothécaire du Vatican (1748). In *La tragé- die de Sémiramis, Et quelques autres Piéces de Littérature.* 1750.

"Dissertation the IId. Upon Liberty." In *Miscellaneous Poems. By Mr. De Voltaire. Trans- lated from the French, By T. Smollet, M.D., T. Francklin, M.A. and others,* 251–258. London: J. Newbery, R. Baldwin, S. Crowder, and Co., 1764. Vol. 32 in *The Works of Voltaire: A Contemporary Version.* Translated by William F. Fleming. 42 vols. New York: E. R. DuMont, 1901.

"Divorce." In *Questions sur l'Encylopédie,* 3:339–341. 1770.

"Du mot *Quisquis* de Ramus, ou La Ramée." In *Questions sur l'Encyclopédie, par des Ama- teurs,* 6:262–279. 1771.

Élémens de la philosophie de Neuton, Mis à la portée de tout le monde. Amsterdam: Etienne Ledet & Compagnie, 1738. https://books.google.com/books.

"Éloge historique de la Raison, prononcé dans une académie de province, par M. . . . . ." (1774). In *Nouveaux Mélanges philosophiques, historiques, critiques, &c. &c. Dix-septième partie,* 189–203. 1775. (Modern edition: Theodore S. B. Besterman et al., eds., *Œuvres complètes de Voltaire,* vol. 76, ed. Jean Dagen [2013].)

L'Enfant prodigue, comédie en vers dissillabes, Représentée sur le Théatre de la Comédie Fran- çaise le 10 Octobre 1736. Paris: Chez Prault, 1738. (Modern edition: Theodore S. B. Besterman et al., eds., *Œuvres complètes de Voltaire,* vol. 16, ed. John Dunkley and Russell Goulbourne [2003]; English translation in Tobias Smollett, Thomas Francklin, M.A., and Others, eds. and trans., *The Works of Mr. de Voltaire,* vol. 14 [1762].)

"Enthousiasme." In *Dictionnaire philosophique portatif. Nouvelle Édition, Revue, corrigée & augmentée de divers Articles par l'Auteur,* 163–165. 1765.

Épître à Horace, par M. de Voltaire. 1772 [fourteen-page pamphlet]. Also published as "Fragmens d'une Épître à Horace, par M. de Voltaire." In *Mercure de France,* Decembre 1772, 55–60. https://books.google.com/books. (Modern edition: Theodore S. B. Besterman et al., eds., *Œuvres complètes de Voltaire,* vol. 74B, ed. Nicholas Cronk [2006].)

Épître à l'auteur du nouveau livre des trois imposteurs. In *Trois Épîtres de Mr. de Voltaire,* 9–12. 1769. https://books.google.com/books.

Épître à Madame Denis, sur l'agriculture, inscribed "A Ferney, ce 14 Mars 1761." In *Troisieme suite des mélanges de poesie, de littérature, d'histoire et de philosophie.* 1765. (Modern edition: Theodore S. B. Besterman et al., eds., *Œuvres complètes de Voltaire,* vol. 51B, ed. David Williams [2013].)

Épître de l'auteur, en arrivant dans sa terre près du lac de Genève, en mars 1755. In *Mélanges de Poésies, de littérature, d'histoire et de philosophie.* 1756. (Modern edition: Theodore S. B. Besterman et al., eds., *Œuvres complètes de Voltaire,* vol. 45A, ed. Nicholas Cronk [2009].)

Epitre sur l'amour de l'étude, à Madame la Marquise Du Chastelet, Par un Elève de Voltaire, avec des notes du maitre. Paris: Chez J. B. Sajou, Imprimeur, 1815.

L'Esprit de Monsieur de Voltaire. Edited by Claude Villaret. 1759.

L'Esprit de Monsieur de Voltaire. Auquel on a joint L'Oracle des Nouveaux philosophes. Edited by Claude Villaret. "Amsterdam": Aux depens de la Compagnie, 1760.

Essai sur les mœurs et l'esprit des nations. Vols. 1–3. Geneva, 1769. In *Collection complette des Œuvres de Mr. de Voltaire, première édition,* edited by Gabriel Cramer and Philibert Cramer, vols. 8–10. (Modern editions: René Pomeau, ed., *Essai sur les mœurs et l'esprit des nations . . . Nouvelle et dernière édition* (1770), 4:138–139; Bruno Bernard, John Renwick, Nicholas Cronk, and Janet Godden, eds., *Œuvres complètes de Voltaire. Essais sur les moeurs et l'esprit des nations (VIII),* vols. 22–25, 26A–26C [Oxford: The Voltaire Foundation, 2009–2015].)

Essai sur les mœurs et l'esprit des nations, et sur les principaux faits de l'histoire, depuis Charlemagne jusqu'à Louis XIII. Vol. 2. Geneva, 1761.

Essai sur les mœurs et l'esprit des nations, et sur les principaux faits de l'histoire, depuis Charlamagne, jusqu'à Louis XIII. Nouvelle et dernière édition, Revue, corrigée & considérablement augumentée. Vol. 4. 1770.

Essai Sur l'Histoire universelle. 3 vols. Leipzig: George Conrad Walther, 1754.

Essai sur l'histoire universelle depuis Charlemagne; Par Mr. de Voltaire, gentilhomme ordinaire de la chambre du roi de France; des académies de Paris, de Londres, de Petersbourg, de Boulogne, de Rome, de la Crusca &c. Vol. 4. Bâle: George Conrad Walther, 1757.

Essay on Epick Poetry. Dublin: J. Hyde, 1728.

Essay sur le siècle de Louis XIV. Par Mr. de Voltaire. [1740].

Essay sur l'histoire générale, et sur les moeurs et l'esprit des nations, depuis Charlemagne jusqu'à nos jours. Vol. 4. 1756. https://books.google.com/books.

Essay sur l'histoire générale, et sur les moeurs et l'esprit des nations, depuis Charlemagne jusqu'à nos jours. Vol. 6. 1757. https://books.google.com/books.

Essay sur l'histoire générale, et sur les moeurs et l'esprit des nations, depuis Charlemagne jusqu'à nos jours. Vol. 7. 1757. https://books.google.com/books.

Essay sur l'histoire générale, et sur les moeurs et l'esprit des nations, depuis Charlemagne jusqu'à nos jours. Nouvelle Edition, revuë, corrigée, & augmentée. Vol. 2. 1756.

Essay sur l'histoire générale, et sur les moeurs et l'esprit des nations, depuis Charlemagne jusqu'à nos jours. Nouvelle Edition, revuë, corrigée, & augmentée. Vol. 5. 1761.

"Étrennes à Uranie." 1748. In Pierre Clément, *Les Cinq Années Littéraires, ou Nouvelles littéraires, &c. Des Années 1748, 1749, 1750, 1751 et 1752*, 1:13. 1754.

"Examen d'une pensée de Pascal sur l'homme." In *Questions sur l'Encyclopédie, par des Amateurs. Premiere partie*, 434–435. 1774. https://books.google.com/books.

L'Examen Important de Milord Bolingbroke, Ecrit sur la fin de 1736. In *Recueil nécessaire*, 153–289. 1765 [1766]. (Modern edition: Theodore S. B. Besterman et al., eds., *Œuvres complètes de Voltaire*, vol. 62, ed. Roland Mortier [1987].)

"Exhortation à l'agonie d'un curé de C.D." In *Nouveaux Melanges philosophiques, historiques, critiques, &c. &c. &c. Dixiéme partie*, 382–384. 1770.

"Fanatisme." In *Dictionnaire philosophique, portatif*, 190–193. 1765.

Le Fanatisme, ou Mahomet le Prophete, Tragédie. Amsterdam: Chez Etienne Ledet & Compagnie, 1743. (Modern edition: Theodore S. B. Besterman et al., eds., *Œuvres complètes de Voltaire*, vol. 20B, ed. Christopher Todd [2002].)

"Femme." In *Questions sur l'Encyclopédie, par des Amateurs*, 6:29–46. 1771. https://books .google.com/books.

"La Fête de Bellébat. À son Altesse sérénissime Mademoiselle de Clermont." 1725. In *Nouveaux Melanges philosophiques, historiques, critiques, &c. &c. &c. Dixiéme partie*, as "Exhortation à l'agonie d'un curé de C.D." (1770), 382–384, and as "Exhortation faite au curé de Courdimanche en son agonie," in *Œuvres complètes de Voltaire*, vol. 12, edited by Pierre-Augustin Caron de Beaumarchais, 360–362. Kehl: Imprimerie de la Société Littéraire-Typographique, 1784.

"Folie." In *Questions sur l'Encyclopédie, par des Amateurs*, 6:127–131. 1771. https://books .google.com/books.

"Génie." In *Questions sur l'Encyclopédie, par des Amateurs*, 6:252–258. 1771. https://books .google.com/books.

"Goût." In Denis Diderot, Jean le Rond d'Alembert, et al., *Encyclopédie, ou Dictionnaire raisonné des Sciences, des Arts et des Métiers, par une Société de Gens de Lettres*, vol. 7. Paris: Chez Briasson, David, et al., 1757.

"Gouvernement." In *Questions sur l'Encyclopédie, par des Amateurs*, 6:298–320. 1771. https://books.google.com/books.

La Henriade. In *Oeuvres de M. de Voltaire. Nouvelle Edition. Revuë, corrigée, augmentée par l'Auteur; & enrichie de Figures en Taille-douce*. Vol. 1. Amsterdam: Chez Jacques Desbordes, 1732.

La Henriade de Mr. de Voltaire. London, 1728. https://books.google.com/books. (Modern edition: Theodore S. B. Besterman et al., eds., *Œuvres complètes de Voltaire*, vol. 2, ed. O. R. Taylor [1970].)

Hérode et Mariamne, Tragédie de M. de Voltaire. Paris: Chez Noel Pissot at François Flahaut, 1725. https://books.google.com/books. (Modern edition: *Hérode et Mariamne*, in Theodore S. B. Besterman et al., eds., *Œuvres complètes de Voltaire*, vol. 57A, ed. Michael Freyne [2014].)

Histoire de l'Empire de Russie, in *Histoire de Charles XII, Roi de Suède, divisée en huit livres, Avec l'Histoire de l'Empire de Russie sous Pierre le Grand, en deux Parties divisées par Chapitres*, in *Collection complette des Œuvres de Mr. de Voltaire, première édition*, edited by Gabriel Cramer and Philibert Cramer, 2: 297–590. Geneva, 1768. https:// books.google.com/books.

Historical and Critical Memoirs of the Life and Writings of M. De Voltaire. Dublin: Printed for L. White, P. Wogan, P. Byrne, J. Cash, W. McKenzie, J. Moore and J. Jones, 1786.

"Homme" (under the subheading "De l'homme dans l'état de pure nature"). In *Questions sur l'Encyclopédie, par des Amateurs*, 3:422–435. 1774.

"Homme" (under the subheading "De l'homme dans l'état de pure nature"). In *Questions sur l'Encyclopédie, par des Amateurs*, 7:91–113. 1771. https://books.google.com/books.

Les Honnêtetés litteraires &c. &c. &c. 1767. https://books.google.com/books.

"Idée." In *Dictionnaire philosophique, portatif. Sizieme Edition revue, corrigée & augmentée de XXXIV. Articles par l'Auteur*, 2:284–285. London, 1767.

The Important Examination of the Holy Scriptures, Attributed to Lord Bolingbroke, but Written by M. Voltaire, and First Published in 1736. London: R. Carlile, 1819.

L'Ingénu, Histoire véritable, Tirée des Manuscrits du Père Quesnel. Geneva ["Utrecht"]: Cramer, 1767. (Modern edition: Theodore S. B. Besterman et al., eds., *Œuvres complètes de Voltaire*, vol. 63C, ed. Richard A. Francis [2006].)

Jeannot et Colin. In *Contes de Monsieur de Voltaire ou de Guillaume Vadé*, 59–70. 1764. (Modern edition: Theodore S. B. Besterman et al., eds., *Œuvres complètes de Voltaire*, vol. 57B, ed. Christiane Mervaud [2014].)

"Langues." In *Questions sur l'Encyclopédie, par des Amateurs*, 7:299–320. 1771. https://books.google.com/books.

"Larmes." In *Questions sur l'Encyclopédie, par des Amateurs*, 4:44–45. 1774. https://books.google.com/books.

A Letter from Mr. Voltaire to M. Jean Jacques Rousseau. London: Printed for J. Payne, 1766.

Letters Concerning the English Nation. By Mr. de Voltaire. Translated by John Lockman. London: C. Davis and A. Lyon, 1733. https://books.google.com/books.

"Lettre Civile et Honnête à l'Auteur Malhonnête de la Critique de l'Histoire Universelle de M. de V***. Qui n'a jamais fait d'Histoire Universelle." *Journal Encyclopédique*, March 1, 1760, 83–99.

Lettre de Gérofle à Cogé (1767). In *Les Choses utiles et agréables*. Vol. 2. "Berlin" [Geneva], 1769.

*Lettre de M. de V*** avec Plusieurs pièces galantes et nouvelles de differens auteurs*. "A La Haye" [Rouen]: Chez Pierre Poppy, 1744.

Lettre d'un Quakre, A Jean-George Le Franc de Pompignan. [1763]. https://books.google.com/books. (Modern edition: *Lettres d'un Quaker à Jean-George* and *Seconde Lettre du Quaker*, in Theodore S. B. Besterman et al., eds., *Œuvres complètes de Voltaire*, vol. 57A, ed. Simon Davies [2014].)

Les Lettres d'Amabed, &c., traduits par l'abbé Tamponet. In *Nouveaux Mélanges philosophiques, historiques, critiques, &c. &c. Huitiéme Partie*, 188–260. 1769.

*Lettres de M. de V*** avec plusieurs pieces de differens auteurs*. "A La Haye" [Rouen]: Chez Pierre Poppy, 1738.

*Lettres Ecrites de Londres sur les Anglois et autres sujets par M. D. V***.* "A Basle" [London], 1734. https://books.google.com/books.

Lettres philosophiques. Basel, 1734. (Modern edition: Gerhardt Stenger, ed. [Paris: Flammarion, 2006].)

Lettres philosophiques. 2 vols. Edited by Gustave Lanson. Paris: Marcel Didier, 1964.

Lettres philosophiques par M. de V. . . . . Rouen: [Jore], 1734. https://books.google.com/books.

"Liberté de penser." In *Dictionnaire philosophique, portatif. Sizieme Edition revue, corrigée & augmentée de XXXIV. Articles par l'Auteur. Tome second*, 332–337. "Londres," 1767.

"Livres." In *Questions sur l'Encyclopédie, par des Amateurs*, 7:338–348. 1771. https://books.google.com/books.

"Loix." In *Questions sur l'Encyclopédie, par des Amateurs*, 7:352–358. 1771. https://books
.google.com/books.

"Luxe." In *Questions sur l'Encyclopédie, par des Amateurs*, 8:22–24. 1771. https://books
.google.com/books.

Mélanges de philosophie avec des figures. 1756. In *Collection Complette des Œuvres de Mr. de
Voltaire*, vol. 3. https://books.google.com/books.

Mémoires pour servir à la vie de Mr. de Voltaire. Ecrits par lui-même. 1784.

"Mémoire sur la Satire par Mr. Voltaire, De l'Accadémie Françoise, Gentilhomme ordinaire du Roi & Historiographe de France." In *Le Papillon, ou Lettres parisiennes*,
152–160. 1746.

Memoirs of the Life of Voltaire. Written by Himself. Translated from the French. London:
Printed for G. Robinson, 1784.

La Mérope Françoise, avec quelques petites pièces de littérature. Paris: Chez Prault, 1744.
(Modern edition: Theodore S. B. Besterman et al., eds., *Œuvres complètes de Voltaire*,
vol. 17, ed. Jack R. Vrooman and Janet Godden [1991].)

*La Merope tragedia Con Annotazioni dell'Autore, e con la sua Risposta alla Lettera del Sig. di
Voltaire. Aggiungesi per altra mano la version Francese del Sig. Freret, e la Inglese del Sig.
Ayre, con una Confutazione della Critica ultimamente stampata.* Translated by Scipione
Maffei. Verona: Stamperia di Dionigi Ramanzini, 1745.

*Micromégas de Mr. de Voltaire, Avec une Histoire des Croisades & Un Nouveau plan de l'his-
toire de l'esprit humain. Par le meme*, 1–40. "A Londres": J. Robinson, 1752. (Modern
editions: *Micromégas, Zadig, Candide*. Edited and presented by René Pomeau [Paris:
Flammarion, 2006]; Theodore S. B. Besterman et al., eds., *Œuvres complètes de Voltaire*, vol. 20c, ed. Nicholas Cronk and J. B. Shank [2017].)

Le Mondain. 1736. Paris: Inventaire Ye35,013. https://gallica.bnf.fr/ark:/12148/bpt6k85957
4s/f1.image.

[*Le Mondain, ou l'Apologie du Luxe*]. As *L'Homme du Monde, ou Défense du Mondain*, in
*Oeuvres de Mʳ. de Voltaire. Nouvelle Edition, Revue, corrigée & considérablement augmen-
tée*, 113–119. 1739. https://books.google.com/books. (Modern edition: Theodore S. B.
Besterman et al., eds., *Œuvres complètes de Voltaire*, vol. 15, ed. Haydn T. Mason
[2003].)

La Mort de César, Tragédie par M. de Voltaire. Paris: Chez Je. Fr. Josse, 1736. https://
books.google.com/books. (Modern edition: Theodore S. B. Besterman et al., eds.,
Œuvres complètes de Voltaire, vol. 8, ed. D. J. Fletcher [1998].)

Notebooks (undated). (Modern edition: Theodore S. B. Besterman, ed., *Voltaire's Notebooks*. 2 vols. Geneva: Voltaire Institut et Musée Voltaire, 1952.)

Notebooks (undated). (Modern edition: Theodore S. B. Besterman, ed., *Voltaire's Notebooks I and II*. 2 vols. In *Œuvres complètes de Voltaire*, vols. 81–82. Geneva: Voltaire
Institut et Musée Voltaire, 1968.)

Nouveaux Melanges philosophiques, historiques, critiques, &c. &c. &c. Dixiéme partie. 1770.

Œdipe, Tragédie. Rev. ed. In *Oeuvres de Mʳ. de Voltaire: Nouvelle édition revue, corrigée et
considerablement augmentée par l'auteur*, 4:23–106. 1748.

Œdipe, tragédie. Par Monsieur de Voltaire. Paris: Chez Pierre Ribou et Jacques Ribou,
1719. (Modern edition: Theodore S. B. Besterman et al., eds., *Œuvres complètes de
Voltaire*, vol. 1A, ed. John Renwick [2001].)

"Onan et Onanisme." In *Questions sur l'Encyclopédie, par des Amateurs*, 4:186–188. 1774.

"Oracle." In *Questions sur l'Encyclopédie, par des Amateurs*, 4:190–195. 1774.

Oreste, Tragédie, Par M. Arouet de Voltaire. Paris: Chez P. G. Le Mercier and M. Lambert, 1750.

The Orphan of China. A Tragedy. Edinburgh: A. Donaldson, 1759.

L'Orphelin de la Chine, Tragédie, Par M. de Voltaire, Représentée pour la premiére fois à Paris, le 20 Août 1755. Paris: Chez Michel Lambert, 1755. (Modern edition: Theodore S. B. Besterman et al., eds., *Œuvres complètes de Voltaire*, vol. 45A, ed. Basil Guy [2009].)

"Ortographe." In *Questions sur l'Encyclopédie, par des Amateurs*, 8:161–162. 1771. https:// books.google.com/books.

Le Papillon, ou Lettres parisiennes; Ouvrage, qui contiendra tout ce qui se passera d'interés- sant, de plus agréable & de plus nouveau dans tous les Genres. Vol. 1. The Hague: Chez Antoine van Dole, Libraire, 1746.

Le Pauvre Diable: Ouvrage en Vers aisés, de feu Mr. Vadé. Paris, 1758. https://books.google .com/books.

Les Pensées de Monsieur de Voltaire. Vol. 1 ("Première partie"). 1768.

Pensées philosophiques de M. de Voltaire, ou Tableau encyclopédique des Connaissances hu- maines, contenant, L'esprit, Principes, Maximes, Caractéres, Portraits, &c. tirés des Ou- vrages de ce célebre Auteur, & rangés suivant l'ordre des matiéres. Vol. 1. 1766.

Pensées, remarques et observations de Voltaire. Paris: Barbar, Pougens, Fuchs, 1802.

"Pensées sur l'administration publique." In *Collection complete des Œuvres de Monsieur de Voltaire. Nouvelle Édition*, 17:62–71. 1764.

"Pensées sur le gouvernement." In *Oeuvres de M. de Voltaire. Nouvelle édition, revue, cor- rigée et considérablement augmentée par l'auteur*, 6:iii–xii. 1752. https://books.google .com/books. (Modern edition: *Pensées sur l'administration*, in Theodore S. B. Bester- man et al., eds., *Œuvres complètes de Voltaire*, vol. 32A, ed. Ahmad Gunny and David Williams [2006].)

Le Philosophe ignorant. 1766. https://books.google.com/books. (Modern edition: Theodore S. B. Besterman et al., eds., *Œuvres complètes de Voltaire*, vol. 62, ed. Roland Mortier [1987].)

A Philosophical Dictionary. From the French of M. de Voltaire. 6 vols. Translated by John G. Gurton. London: J. and H. L. Hunt, 1824.

A Philosophical Dictionary. From the French of M. de Voltaire. A New and Correct Edition. Dublin: Bernard Dornin, 1793.

La Philosophie de l'Histoire, Par feu l'Abbé Bazin. "A Amsterdam": Chez Changuion, 1765. From the edition in the Bibliothèque de l'Arsenal, Paris. https://gallica.bnf.fr/ark: /12148/btv1b8618430t.image. (Modern edition: Theodore S. B. Besterman et al., eds., *Œuvres complètes de Voltaire*, vol. 59, ed. J. H. Brumfitt [1969].)

The Philosophy of History by M. de Voltaire. Glasgow: Printed for Robert Urie, 1766. https://books.google.com/books.

"Plagiat." In *Questions sur l'Encyclopédie, par des Amateurs*, 4:251–253. 1774. https://books .google.com/books.

Poëmes sur le désastre de Lisbonne et sur la loi naturelle avec des préfaces des notes, &c. Gene- va [1756]. https://gallica.bnf.fr/ark:/12148/bpt6k5727289v.texteImage. (Modern edi- tion: Theodore S. B. Besterman et al., eds., *Œuvres complètes de Voltaire*, vol. 45A, ed. David Adams and Haydn T. Mason [2009].)

Poësies mêlées, &c. Vol. 3. Geneva, 1774. (Vol. 20 in *Collection Complette des Œuvres de M^r. de ****.)

"Des Poëtes." In *Mélanges philosophiques, littéraires, historiques, &c.*, 2:417–420. Geneva, 1771.

Précis de l'Ecclésiaste, en vers, par Mr. de Voltaire. Paris, 1759. (Modern edition: Theodore S. B. Besterman et al., eds., *Œuvres complètes de Voltaire*, vol. 49A, ed. Marie-Hélène Cotoni [2010].)

"Préface. D'une Edition d'Oedipe de 1729." In *Oeuvres de M. de Voltaire. Nouvelle Edition. Revue, corrigée & considérablement augmentée, avec des Figures en Taille-douce. Tome second*, 1:5–23. 1738.

Preface to "Fragment d'une lettre écrite par M. de Voltaire à un membre de l'Académie de Berlin." In *Oeuvres de M^r. de Voltaire: Nouvelle édition revue, corrigée et considerablement augmentée par l'auteur enrichie de figures en taille-douce Tome premier.* Dresden: Chez George Conrad Walther, 1752.

"Prières." In *Questions sur l'Encyclopédie, par des Amateurs*, 9:179–181. 1772. https://books .google.com/books.

La Pucelle d'Orléans, ou Jeanne d'Arc, Poeme en Seize Chants Par M. De V——. "Imprimé a Tebsterahn, par Pyr Mardechanburg," 1756.

La Pucelle d'Orléans, Poème, divisé en vingt chants, Avec des notes. Nouvelle Edition, corrigée, augmentée & collationnée sur le Manuscrit de l'Auteur. 1762. (Modern edition: Theodore S. B. Besterman et al., eds., *Œuvres complètes de Voltaire*, vol. 7, ed. Jeroom Vercruysse [1970].)

La Pucelle d'Orléans, Poëme Héroï-comique en Dix-huit chants. "A Londres," 1780.

"Puissance, Toute-Puissance." In *Questions sur l'Encyclopédie, par des Amateurs*, 8:254–261. 1771. https://books.google.com/books.

"Quaker ou Qouacre, ou Primitif, ou Membre de la primitive Église Chrétienne, ou Pensilvanien, ou Philadelphien." In *Questions sur l'Encyclopédie, par des Amateurs*, 9:199–202. 1773. https://books.google.com/books.

"Qu'est-ce que la loi naturelle?" In "Loi naturelle. Dialogue," in *Questions sur l'Encyclopédie, par des Amateurs*, 7:348–352. 1771.

Questions sur l'Encyclopédie, par des Amateurs. Première partie. Vol. 1. 1770. One of nine vols., published 1770–1772. https://books.google.com/books. (Modern edition: Theodore S. B. Besterman et al., eds., *Œuvres complètes de Voltaire*, vols. 38–43, ed. Nicholas Cronk and Christiane Mervaud [2007–2013].)

Questions sur l'Encyclopédie, par des Amateurs. Vol. 6. 1775. In *Collection Complette des Œuvres de Mr. de Voltaire*, vols. 21–24.

La Raison par Alphabet. Septieme Édition, revuë, corrigée & augmentée par l'Auteur. Première Partie. A–I. 1773 [title page incorrectly reads 1763].

La Raison par Alphabet. Sixiéme édition, revuë, corrigée & augmentée par l'Auteur. Seconde Partie. L–V. 1769.

Recueil de pièces fugitives en prose et en vers. 1740. https://books.google.com/books.

Receuil des facéties parisiennes, Pour les six premiers mois de l'an 1760. [1760]. https://books .google.com/books.

Recueil nécessaire. "A Leipsik," 1765 [1766]. (Anthology containing some texts not written by Voltaire.)

"Réfutation directe" ("contre les Critiques de M. La Beaum"). In *Le Siècle politique de Louis XIV. ou lettres du Vicomte Bolingbroke sur ce sujet.* "A Sieclopolie": "Aux depens de la Compagnie," 1753. https://books.google.com/books.

Relation de la mort du Chevalier de La Barre par Mr. CASS ** Avocat au Conseil du Roi, à Mr. le Marquis de Beccaria. "A Amsterdam" [Geneva], 1766 [1767].

Remarques, pour servir de supplément à l'Essay sur l'Histoire générale et sur les mœurs et l'esprit des Nations, depuis Charlemagne jusqu'à nos jours. 1763.

Romans, contes philosophiques, &c. Geneva, 1771. (Vol. 13 in *Collection Complette des Œuvres de Mr. de Voltaire.*)

Rome sauvée, Tragédie de M. de Voltaire. Berlin: Chez Étienne de Bourdeaux, 1752.

Rome sauvée, Tragédie. Par M. De Voltaire. Amsterdam: Chez Charles Warletthius, 1755.

"Sens commun." In *Dictionnaire philosophique portatif. Nouvelle Édition, Revue, corrigée & augmentée de divers Articles par l'Auteur,* 317–319. "A Londres," 1765.

Septième discours sur la vraie vertu, in *Discours en vers sur l'homme* (1738). In *Mélanges de Poésies, de littérature, d'histoire et de philosophie.* Vol. 2. 1757.

Le Sermon des Cinquante. 1749. (Modern edition: Theodore S. B. Besterman et al., eds., *Œuvres complètes de Voltaire,* vol. 49A, ed. J. Patrick Lee [2010].)

Le Siècle de Louis XIV. Edited by René Pomeau, with a preface by Nicholas Cronk. Paris: Gallimard (Folio Classique), 2015.

Le Siècle de Louis XIV. Vol. 1. In *Œuvres complètes de Voltaire,* vol. 22, edited by Pierre-Augustin Caron de Beaumarchais. Kehl: Imprimerie de la Société Littéraire-Typographique, 1785.

Siécle de Louis XIV, Auquel on a joint Un Précis du Siécle de Louis XV. Geneva, 1769. Vol. 11 in *Collection Complette des Œuvres de Mr. de Voltaire.* https://books.google.com/books.

Siécle de Louis XIV, Auquel on a joint Un Précis du Siécle de Louis XV. Geneva, 1772.

Siécle de Louis XIV. Nouvelle Edition, Revuë & augmentée; à laquelle on a ajouté un précis du siécle de Louis XV. Tome troisieme. 1768. https://books.google.com/books.

Le Siecle de Louis XIV. Nouvelle edition revue par l'auteur et considerablement augmentée. Tome second. Dresden: Chez George Conrad Walther, 1753.

Le Siècle de Louis XIV. Publié par M. de Francheville conseiller aulique de sa Majesté, & membre de l'académie roiale des sciences & belles lettres de prusse. 2 vols. Berlin: Chez C. F. Henning, 1751. https://books.google.com/books. (Modern edition: Theodore S. B. Besterman et al., eds., *Œuvres complètes de Voltaire,* vols. 38–43, ed. Nicholas Cronk and Christiane Mervaud [2007–2013].)

"Sixième Discours, De la Nature de l'homme." In *Discours en vers sur l'homme,* in *Recueil de pieces fugitives en prose et en vers par M. de V***,* 86–94. 1740.

Socrate, ouvrage dramatique, traduit de l'anglais de feu M. Tompson. "Amsterdam," 1759.

"Sophiste." In *Questions sur l'Encyclopédie, par des Amateurs,* 8:337–339. 1771. https://books.google.com/books.

"Sottise des deux parts." 1728. In *Oeuvres de Mr. de Voltaire: Nouvelle édition revue, corrigée et considerablement augmentée par l'auteur,* 167–174. 1750. (Modern edition: Theodore S. B. Besterman et al., eds., *Œuvres complètes de Voltaire,* vol. 3A, ed. Jean Dagen [2004].)

Le Sottisier de Voltaire: Publié pour la première fois d'après une copie authentique faite sur le manuscrit autographe conservé au musée de l'Hermitage à Saint-Pétersbourg. Preface by Louis-Antoine Léozoun Le Duc. Paris: Librairie de Bibliophiles, 1880.

"Sur Mr. Locke." In *Réflexions sur les Anglais,* in *Oeuvres de Mr. de Voltaire. Nouvelle Edition, Revue, corrigée & considérablement augmentée,* 233–242. 1739. https://books.google.com/books.

Tancrède, Tragédie; Par Mr. De Voltaire. Geneva: Chez les Frères Cramer, 1761.

Le Temple du Goust. [Amsterdam]: A l'enseigne de La Vérité, chez Hierosme [Jore], 1733. https://books.google.com/books. (Modern edition: *Le Temple du goût.* In Theodore S. B. Besterman et al., eds., *Œuvres complètes de Voltaire*, vol. 9, ed. O. R. Taylor [1999].)

"Testicules." In *Questions sur l'Encyclopédie, par des Amateurs*, 4:437–440. 1774. https://books.google.com/books.

"Tolérance." In *Dictionnaire philosophique portatif. Nouvelle Édition, Revue, corrigée & augmentée de divers Articles par l'Auteur*, 329–333. "A Londres," 1765.

La tragédie de Sémiramis, Et quelques autres Piéces de Littérature. Paris: Chez P. G. Le Mercier, Imprimeur-Libraire, 1750. https://books.google.com/books.

Traité de Métaphysique. 1734–1735. First published in *Philosophie générale: Métaphysique, morale, et théologie.* In *Œuvres complètes de Voltaire*, vol. 40, edited by Pierre-Augustin Caron de Beaumarchais. Kehl: Imprimerie de la Société Littéraire-Typographique, 1784.

Traité sur la Tolérance. [Geneva]: [Cramer], 1763. https://books.google.com/books.

"Les Trois Manières" (1763). In *Contes de Guillaume Vadé*, 23–35. [Geneva]: [Cramer], 1764.

La Voix du sage et du Peuple. "Amsterdam": Chez le Sincère, 1750.

Voltaire's Philosophical Dictionary. Edited and translated by H. I. Woolf. New York: Alfred A. Knopf, 1924.

Zadig; Or, The Book of Fate. An Oriental History, Translated from the French Original of Mr Voltaire. London: John Brindley, 1749.

Zadig ou La Destinée. Histoire orientale. 1748. https://books.google.com/books. (Modern edition: Theodore S. B. Besterman et al., eds., *Œuvres complètes de Voltaire*, vol. 30B, ed. Haydn T. Mason [2004].)

La Zayre, de M. de Voltaire, Representée à Paris aux mois d'Aoust, Novembre & Décembre 1732. Augmentée de l'Epitre Dédicatoire. Paris: Chez Jean-Baptiste Bauche, 1733. https://gallica.bnf.fr/ark:/12148/bpt6k71854s.image. (Modern edition: Eva Jacobs, ed., *Zaïre, tragédie*, in Theodore S. B. Besterman et al., eds., *Œuvres complètes de Voltaire*, vol. 8, ed. D. J. Fletcher [1998]; English translation: Albany Wallace, *Zaire A Dramatic Poem (Translated from the French Tragedy of Voltaire, and Turned into English Rhyme Verse)* [Worthing, 1854].)

"Zoroastre." In *Questions sur l'Encyclopédie, par des Amateurs*, 9:81–88. 1772. https://books.google.com/books.

OTHER AUTHORS AND SOURCES

Abitbol, William. *Les Écrivains et de Gaulle.* Paris: Albin Michel, 1999.

Adams, Abigail, and John Adams. *The Book of Abigail and John: Selected Letters of the Adams Family, 1762–1784.* Edited by L. H. Butterfield, Marc Friedlaender, and Mary-Jo Kline. Cambridge, MA: Harvard University Press, 1975.

Adams, Henry. *The Education of Henry Adams.* Washington, DC: privately printed, 1907.

Adams, John. *A Defence of the Constitutions of Government of the United States, Against the Attacks of M. Turgot in his Letter to Dr. Price, Dated the Twenty-second of March, 1778.* Vol. 3. London: C. Dilly and John Stockdale, 1788.

Adams, John. *The Works of John Adams, Second President of the United States.* 10 vols. Edited by Charles Francis Adams. Boston: Charles C. Little and James Brown, 1851–1856.

Aldington, Richard. *Voltaire*. London: G. Routledge, 1925.

Aldrich, Robert, and Garry Wotherspoon, eds. *Who's Who in Gay and Lesbian History*. Vol. 1, *From Antiquity to the Mid-Twentieth Century*. London: Routledge, 2001.

Aldridge, Alfred Owen. *Voltaire and the Century of Light*. Princeton, NJ: Princeton University Press, 1975.

Allen, Bruce. "Washington's Poisonous Games: Gore Vidal Concludes His Cycle." *Washington Times*, October 8, 2000, B8.

Amicus. "Anecdotes of the Late Dr. Smith." *The Bee, or Literary Weekly Intelligencer* (Edinburgh), May 11, 1791, 2–8.

Andrews, Wayne. *Voltaire*. New York: New Directions, 1981.

"Anecdotes of Mons. de Voltaire in his present situation at Fernex in Burgundy, near Geneva." In *The Annual Register, or a View of the History, Politicks, and Literature, For the Year 1767*, section "Characters," 59–73. London: J. Dodsley, 1768.

"Anecdotes of Voltaire: Collected from the Conversation of several inhabitants of Geneva, and from various learned Characters." *The Edinburgh Magazine, or Literary Miscellany*, June 1786, 409–412.

Angremy, Annie, Madeleine Barbin, Michel Brunet, and Marie-Laure Chastang. *Voltaire: Un Homme, un siècle*. Paris: Bibliothèque Nationale, 1979. Exhibition catalogue.

L'Année littéraire. Vol. 1. Amsterdam: Chez Ch. J. Panckoucke, Libraire, 1763.

The Annual Register, or a View of the History, Politicks, and Literature, For the Year 1765. London: J. Dodsley, 1766.

The Annual Register, or a View of the History, Politicks, and Literature, For the Year 1767. London: J. Dodsley, 1768.

Apgar, Garry. *L'Art singulier de Jean Huber: Voir Voltaire*. Paris: Adam Biro, 1995.

Apgar, Garry. *Mickey Mouse: Emblem of the American Spirit*. San Francisco: Walt Disney Family Foundation Press, 2015.

Apgar, Garry. "'Sage comme une image': Trois siècles d'iconographie voltairienne." *Nouvelles de l'estampe*, July 1994, 4–44.

Apgar, Garry. "Une Célébration bien discrète." *Le Monde*, September 8, 1978, 2.

Apgar, Garry. "Voltaire, Superstar." *Paris Metro*, June 21, 1978, 15.

Apgar, Garry, cowritten and edited by George W. Gowen and Patrick H. Ryan. *Voltaire & Jefferson: The Sage of Ferney and the Man from Monticello*. DVD. 23 min. Produced and directed by Dennis Powers, Patrick H. Ryan, and Rawn Fulton. Narrated by Cliff Robertson. Princeton, NJ: Films for the Humanities, 2001.

Aptheker, Herbert. *The American Revolution, 1763–1783*. New York: International Publishers, 1960.

ArkDem14. "Gore Vidal: An American Voltaire." *Daily Kos*, August 2, 2012. https://www.dailykos.com/stories/2012/8/2/1115901/-Gore-Vidal-An-American-Voltaire.

Arnold, Matthew. "The Bishop and the Philosopher." *Macmillan's Magazine*, January 1863, 241–256.

Auden, W. H. *Collected Poetry of W. H. Auden*. New York: Random House, 1945.

Auden, W. H. "A Great Democrat." *The Nation*, March 25, 1939, 352.

Ayer, J. J. "A Sanctified Voltaire." *The Spectator*, December 11, 1936, 1051–1052.

Baggini, Julian. *The Pig That Wants to Be Eaten: 100 Experiments for the Armchair Philosopher*. New York: Plume, 2006.

Baggini, Julian, and Jeremy Stangroom, eds. *What More Philosophers Think*. London: Continuum, 2007.

Bailyn, Bernard. *To Begin the World Anew: The Genius and Ambiguities of the American Founders*. New York: Alfred A. Knopf, 2003.

Bakunin, Mikhail. *God and the State*. Edited and translated by Carolo Cafiero and Élisée Reclus. Boston: Benjamin Tucker, 1883. Reprint, New York: Dover, 1970.

Bakunin, Mikhail. *L'Empire Knouto-Germanique et la Révolution sociale*. Paris: P.-V. Stock, Editeur, 1908. In Bakunin, *Œuvres*, vol. 3 (1908).

Bakunin, Mikhail. *Œuvres*. 6 vols. Paris: P. V. Stock, 1895–1913.

Ballou, Maturin M. *Notable Thoughts about Women: A Literary Mosaic*. Boston: Houghton, Mifflin and Company, 1882.

Ballou, Maturin M. *Treasury of Thought: Forming an Encyclopedia of Quotations from Ancient and Modern Authors*. Boston: James R. Osgood and Company, 1872.

Barnes, Julian. "A Candid View of *Candide*." *The Guardian*, July 1, 2011. https:// www .theguardian.com/books/2011/jul/01/candide-voltaire-rereading-julian-barnes.

Barthes, Roland. "Le Dernier des écrivains heureux." Preface to *Romans et contes* by Voltaire, 9–17. Paris: Gallimard, 1972.

Barthes, Roland. "Voltaire, le dernier des écrivains heureux." *Actualité littéraire* (Bulletin des Clubs des Libraires de France), March 1958, 13–15. Reprinted as the preface to *Romans et contes de Voltaire*. Paris: Club des Libraires de France, 1958.

Barthes, Roland. "Voltaire, le dernier des écrivains heureux." In Barthes, *Essais critiques*, 1:94–100. Paris: Le Seuil, 1964.

Barzun, Jacques. *From Dawn to Decadence: 500 Years of Western Cultural Life; 1500 to the Present*. New York: HarperCollins, 2000.

Barzun, Jacques. *A Jacques Barzun Reader: Selections from His Works*. Edited by Michael Murray. New York: HarperCollins, 2002.

Barzun, Jacques. "Why Diderot?" In *Varieties of Literary Experience*, edited by Stanley Burnshaw, 31–44. London: Peter Owen, 1962.

Barzun, Jacques, and Wendell Hertig Taylor. *A Catalogue of Crime*. New York: Harper & Row. 1971. Revised and enlarged edition, 1989.

Baudelaire, Charles. *Baudelaire, His Prose and Poetry*. Edited by T. R. Smith. New York: Boni and Liveright, 1919.

Baudelaire, Charles. *The Essence of Laughter and Other Essays, Journals, and Letters*. Edited by Peter Quennell. New York: Meridian Press, 1956.

Baudelaire, Charles. *Mon cœur mis à nu*. Edited by Claude Pichois. Geneva: Droz, 2001.

Baudelaire, Charles. *Œuvres posthumes et correspondance inédites*. Edited by Eugène Crépet. Paris: Maison Quantin, 1887.

Beauvoir, Simone de. *Le Deuxième sexe: Les faits et les mythes*. Paris: Gallimard, 1953.

Beauvoir, Simone de. *The Second Sex*. Translated by Constance Borde and Sheila Malovany-Chevallier. New York: Alfred A. Knopf, 2009.

Benítez, Miguel. "Voltaire Libertin: l'*Épître à Uranie*." *Revue Voltaire*, no. 8 (2008): 99–135.

Benrekassa, Georges. "Civilisation and Civility." In *Encyclopedia of the Enlightenment*, 2 vols., edited by Michel Delon, 1:266–271. London: Routledge, 2001.

Bentley, E. C. *Baseless Biography*. London: Constable & Co., 1939.

Berlin, Isaiah. "The Divorce between the Sciences and the Humanities." The Second Tykociner Memorial Lecture, University of Illinois, Urbana, March 14, 1974.

Berlin, Isaiah. *Freedom and Its Betrayal: Six Enemies of Human Liberty*. Princeton, NJ: Princteon University Press, 2002.

Berlin, Isaiah. *The Proper Study of Mankind: An Anthology of Essays*. Edited by Henry Hardy. London: Chatto & Windus, 1997.

Bernardin de Saint-Pierre, Jacques-Henri. *Harmonies de la nature*. Vol. 1. Edited by Louis Aimé-Martin. Paris: Chez Méquignon-Marvis, 1815.

Bernardin de Saint-Pierre, Jacques-Henri. *Harmonies of Nature*. 3 vols. Translated by W. Meeston. London: Baldwin, Cradock, and Joy, 1815.

Besterman, Theodore S. B. *Voltaire*. New York: Harcourt, Brace & World, 1969.

Black, Conrad. *Richard M. Nixon: A Life in Full*. New York: PublicAffairs, 2007.

Blake, William. *The Selected Poems of William Blake*. Edited by Bruce Woodcock. Ware, UK: The Wordsworth Poetry Library, 1994.

Blankfort, Michael. "George S. Kaufman: Anarcho-Cynicist." *The New Masses*, October 16, 1934, 29.

Bloom, Harold. *The Western Canon: The Books and School of the Ages*. New York: Houghton Mifflin Harcourt, 1994.

Borges, Jorge Luis. Preface (*Prólogo*) to Voltaire, *Cuentos*. Edited and translated by Carlos Pujol. Madrid: Hyspamerica, 1986.

Boswell, James. *Boswell on the Grand Tour: Germany and Switzerland, 1764*. Edited by Frederick Pottle. New York: McGraw-Hill, 1953.

Boswell, James. *James Boswell: The Journal of His German and Swiss Travels, 1764*. Edited by Marlies K. Danziger. New Haven, CT: Yale University Press, 2008.

Boswell, James. *The Life of Samuel Johnson, LL.D. Comprehending an Account of His Studies and Numerous Works in Chronological Order*. 2 vols. London: Printed by Henry Baldwin, for Charles Dilly, in the Poultry, 1791.

Bottiglia, William F., ed. *Voltaire: A Collection of Critical Essays*. Englewood Cliffs, NJ: Prentice-Hall, 1968.

Boufflers, Stanislas-Jean de. *Lettres de Monsieur le chevalier de Boufflers pendant, son voyage en Suisse, à Madame sa mère en 1764*. 1771.

Bourgeois, Émile. *France Under Louis XIV (Le Grand Siècle): Its Arts—Its Ideas*. Translated by Cashel Hoey. New York: Charles Scribner's Sons 1897.

Brackman, Harold. "The New York Times Whitewashes Voltaire and 'The Dark Enlightenment.'" *The Algemeiner*, January 8, 2019. http://www.algemeiner.com /2019/01/08/the-new-york-times-whitewashes-voltaire-and-the-dark-enlighten ment.

Bradbury, Ray. "Walt Disney, the Man Who Invented a Better Mouse." *Los Angeles Times*, November 14, 1976, U3.

Brett, Lionel. "Wright in New York." *New Republic*, November 16, 1953, 19–20.

"Brisbane Rites to Be Monday." *El Paso Herald-Post*, December 26, 1936, 11.

Brogan, Denis W. "The English Voltaire. Tom Paine: Citizen of the World." *Times Literary Supplement*, January 30, 1937.

Brogan, Denis W. "Tom Paine: Citizen of the World." In *American Themes*, 65–76. New York: Harper & Brothers, 1949.

Brooks, Richard A., ed. and trans. *The Selected Letters of Voltaire*. New York: New York University Press, 1973.

Brooks, Van Wyck. *The Ordeal of Mark Twain*. New York: E. P. Dutton & Company, 1920.

Brougham, Henry, Lord. *Lives of Men of Letters and Science, Who Flourished in the Time of George III*. London: Charles Knight and Co., 1845.

Bruun, Geoffrey. *The Enlightened Despots*. 2nd ed. New York: Holt, Rinehart and Winston, 1967.

Buffier, Claude. "Comment le sens commun ne se trouve pas également dans tous les hommes." In *Traité des premières véritez, et de la source de nos jugemens*, chap. 9. Paris: Chez Jean-Luc Nyon, 1724.

Buffier, Claude. *Traité des premières véritez, et de la source de nos jugemens*. Paris: Chez Jean-Luc Nyon, 1724.

Burke, Edmund. *Reflections on the Revolution in France*. London: James Dodsley, November 1790.

Burke, Edmund. *Selected letters of Edmund Burke*. Edited by Harvey C. Mansfield Jr. Chicago: University of Chicago Press, 1984.

Burney, Charles. *The Present State of Music in France and Italy: or, The Journal of a Tour through those Countries, undertaken to collect Materials for a General History of Music*. London: T. Becket and Co., 1771.

Burnshaw, Stanley, ed. *Varieties of Literary Experience*. New York: New York University Press, 1962.

Burton, Richard Francis, Sir, ed. and trans. *The Book of the Thousand Nights and a Night: A Plain and Literal Translation of the Arabian Nights Entertainment*. 10 vols. Stoke Newington, UK: The Kama Shastra Society, 1885.

Buruma, Ian. *Voltaire's Coconuts or Anglomania in Europe*. London: Weidenfeld & Nicolson, 1999.

Campan, Jeanne-Louise-Henriette. *Journal anecdotique de Mme Campan, ou Souvenirs recueillis dans ses entretiens*. Edited by Pierre Maigne. Paris: Baudouin Frères, 1824.

Campbell, Jeremy. "A Lunch as Good as a Matinee." *The Gleaner* (Kingston, Jamaica), September 21, 1974, 8.

Camus, Albert. *Carnets: Mai 1935–Février 1951*. Paris: Gallimard, 1962.

Camus, Albert. *Carnets: 1942–1951*. Translated by Philip Thody. London: Hamish Hamilton, 1963.

Camus, Albert. *Carnets II: Janvier 1942–Mars 1951*. Paris: Gallimard, 1964.

Carlyle, Thomas, ed. *German Romance: Specimens of Its Chief Authors*. Vol. 4. Edinburgh: William Tait, 1827.

Carlyle, Thomas. *On Heroes, Hero-Worship, and the Heroic in History*. London: James Fraser, 1841.

Casanova, Giacomo. *Histoire de ma vie*. 12 vols. Paris: Librairie Plon, 1960–1962.

Casanova, Giacomo. *History of My Life*. Vol. 6. Translated by Willard R. Trask. New York: Harcourt, Brade & World, 1968.

Chambertrand, Gilbert de. *Femme, qu'y a-t-il entre moi et toi?* Basse-Terre, Guadeloupe: Jeunes Antilles, 1976.

Chateaubriand, François-René, Vicomte de. *The Beauties of Christianity*. Vol 2. Edited by Henry Kett. Translated by Frederic Shoberl. London: Henry Colburn, 1813.

Chateaubriand, François-René, Vicomte de. *Le Génie du Christianisme, ou Beautés de la Religion Chrétienne*. Vol. 2. Paris: Chez Migneret, 1802.

Châtelet, Émilie Le Tonnelier de Breteuil, Marquise du. *Selected Philosophical and Scientific Writings*. Edited by Judith P. Zinsser. Translated by Judith P. Zinsser and Isabelle Bour. Chicago: University of Chicago Press, 2009.

Chesterfield, Philip Dormer Stanhope, Fourth Earl of. *Letters Written by the Late Right Honourable Philip Dormer Stanhope, Earl of Chesterfield, to His Son, Philip Stanhope, Esq; Late Envoy Extraordinary at the Court of Dresden*. Vol. 4. 3rd ed. London: J. Dodsley, 1774.

Chesterton, G. K. *"All I Survey": A Book of Essays*. New York: Dodd, Mead, 1933.

Chesterton, G. K. *All Things Considered*. London: Methuen & Co., 1908.

Chesterton, G. K. "Miracles and Agnosticism," *The Illustrated London News*, July 7, 1923, 2.

Chesterton, G. K. "The Spirit of the Eighteenth Century," *Illustrated London News*, January 31, 1925, 6.

Christian, James L. *Philosophy: An Introduction to the Art of Wondering*. 10th ed. Belmont, CA: Wadsworth, Cengage Learning, 2009.

Clark, Kenneth. *Civilisation: A Personal View*. New York: Harper & Row, 1969.

Clayden, P. W. *The Early Life of Samuel Rogers*. London: Smith, Elder & Co., 1887.

Clément, Pierre. *Les Cinq Années Littéraires, ou Nouvelles littéraires, &c. Des Années 1748, 1749, 1750, 1751 et 1752*. Vol. 1. The Hague: Ant. De Groot et fils and Pierre Gosse Junior, 1754. https://books.google.com/books.

Clémentin, Jean. "J'suis pas enceinte, j'suis obèse." *Le Canard Enchaîné*, August 8, 1979, 4.

Cochran, Peter. *Byron at the Theatre*. Newcastle: Cambridge Scholars Publishing, 2009.

Coleridge, Samuel Taylor. "Essay V." *The Friend: A Literary, Moral, and Political Weekly Paper*, no. 8 (October 5, 1809): 114–126.

Coleridge, Samuel Taylor. *The Friend: A Series of Essays in Three Volumes . . . with Literary Amusements Interspersed*. Vol. 1. New ed. London: Rest Fener, 1818.

Coleridge, Samuel Taylor. *Notes and Lectures upon Shakespeare and Some of the Old Poets and Dramatists with Other Literary Remains of S. T. Coleridge*. Edited by Sara Fricker Coleridge. Vol. 1. London: William Pickering, 1849.

Collection des lettres sur les miracles. Écrites à Geneve. Et à Neufchatel. Par Mr. le Proposant Théro, Monsieur Covelle, Monsieur Néedham, Mr. Beaudinet, & Mr. de Montmolin, &c. Neufchâtel, 1765.

Condorocet, Marie-Jean-Antoine-Nicolas Caritat, Marquis de. *Vie de Voltaire, par M. le marquis de Condorcet; suivie des Mémoires de Voltaire Ecrits par lui-même*. In *Oeuvres complètes de Voltaire*. Vol. 70. Kehl: Imprimerie de la Société Littéraire-Typographique, 1789.

Cooke, Alistair. "An Introduction to H. L. Mencken." In *The Vintage Mencken*, v–xii. New York: Vintage Books, 1955.

Cooper, James Fenimore. *Sketches of Switzerland, by an American*. 2 vols. Philadelphia: Carey, Lea, & Blanchard, 1836.

Cousin, Victor. "Leçons de philosophie, ou Essai sur les facultés de l'âme, par M. Laromiguière . . . Premier extrait." *Journal des Savans*, April 1819, 195–202.

Cronk, Nicholas, ed. *The Cambridge Companion to Voltaire*. Cambridge: Cambridge University Press, 2009.

Cronk, Nicholas. "Préface." In *Le Siècle de Louis XIV*, edited by René Pomeau, 7–26. Paris: Gallimard (Folio Classique), 2015.

Cronk, Nicholas. *Voltaire: A Very Short Introduction*. Oxford: Oxford University Press, 2017.

Cronk, Nicholas. "Voltaire and the One-Liner." *OUPblog*, March 10, 2017. https://blog.oup.com/2017/03/voltaire-works-one-liner.

d'Argenson, René-Louis de Voyer de Paulmy, marquis. *Mémoires et journal inédit du marquis d'Argenson*. Vol. 4. Edited by Charles-Marc-René de Voyer d'Argenson. Paris: Chez P. Jannet, Libraire, 1858.

Dark, Sidney. "The English Voltaire: Jonathan Swift—Satirist." *John O'London's Weekly* 12, no. 295 (November 29, 1924): 322.

Darnton, Robert. *The Literary Underground of the Old Regime*. Cambridge, MA: Harvard University Press, 1982.

Darrow, Clarence. Introduction to *The Best of All Possible Worlds: Voltaire's Romances and Tales*. New York: Vanguard Press, 1929.

Darrow, Clarence. *Voltaire*. Chicago: The Workers' University Society, 1918.

Darrow, Clarence, and Wallace Rice. *Infidels and Heretics*. Boston: Stratford Company, 1929.

Davidoff, Henry. *A World Treasury of Proverbs from Twenty-Five Languages*. New York: Random House, 1946.

Davidson, Ian. *Voltaire: A Life*. London: Profile Books, 2010.

Davidson, Ian. *Voltaire in Exile*. London: Atlantic Books, 2004.

De Beer, Gavin, and André-Michel Rousseau, eds. *Voltaire's British Visitors*. In *Studies on Voltaire and the Eighteenth Century*, vol. 49. Geneva: Institut et Musée Voltaire, 1967.

Debs, Eugene V. *Letters of Eugene V. Debs: 1919–1926*. Edited by J. Robert Constantine. Champaign: University of Illinois Press, 1990.

de Cleyre, Voltairine. "Thomas Paine." In *Selected Works of Voltairine de Cleyre*, edited by Alexander Berkman, 276–283. New York: Mother Earth Publishing Association, 1914.

de Feller, Abbé François-Xavier. *Dictionnaire historique, ou Histoire abrégée des hommes qui se sont fait un nom par leur génie, leurs talens, leurs vertus, leurs erreurs ou leurs crimes, depuis le commencement du monde jusqu'à nos jours. Nouvelle edition*. Vol. 7. Paris: Chez Méguignon Fils Aîné, 1818.

Derogy, Jacques. "Le Défi des 343." *L'Express*, April 12–18, 1971, 15.

Desnoiresterres, Gustave. *Voltaire et la société au XVIIIe siècle*. 8 vols. Paris: Didier et Cie, Libraires-Éditeurs, 1867–1876.

Dickieson, Brenton. "Mark Twain's Letters from Earth: A Pre-/Post-Screwtapian Discovery." *A Pilgrim in Narnia* (blog), September 14, 2016. https://apilgriminnarnia.com/2016/09/14/letters-from-earth/.

Dickieson, Brenton. "William Morris' Nonsense from Nowhere." *A Pilgrim in Narnia* (blog), May 29, 2017. https://apilgriminnarnia.com/2017/05/29/william-morris-nonsense-from-nowhere/.

Diderot, Denis. *Correspondance*. Vol. 6. Edited by Georges Roth. Paris: Éditions de Minuit, 1961.

Diderot, Denis. *Le Neveu de Rameau*. Edited by Jean Fabre. Geneva: Librairie Droz, 1977.

Diderot, Denis. *Œuvres complètes*. Vol. 13. Edited by Roger Lewinter. Paris: Le Club Français du Livre, 1972.

Diderot, Denis. *Œuvres complètes de Diderot*. 20 vols. Edited by Jules Assézat and Maurice Tourneux. Paris: Garnier Frères, 1875–1877.

Diderot, Denis. *Œuvres complètes de Diderot: Correspondance II: Lettres à Mlle Volland—Lettres à l'abbé Le Monnier—Lettres à Mlle Jodin / Correspondance générale*. Vol. 19. Edited by Jules Assézat and Maurice Tourneux. Paris: Garnier Frères, 1876.

Diderot, Denis. *Œuvres complètes de Diderot: Oeuvres diverses II / Correspondance I: Lettres à Falconet—Lettres à Mlle Volland*. Vol. 18. Edited by Jules Assézat and Maurice Tourneux. Paris: Garnier Frères, 1876.

Diderot, Denis. *Œuvres inédites de Diderot: Le Neveu de Rameau. Voyage de Hollande.* Paris: Chez J.-L.-J. Brière, 1821.

Diderot, Denis. *Salons 1765.* Vol. 2. 2nd ed. Edited by Jean Seznec. Oxford: Clarendon Press, 1979.

Diderot, Denis, Jean le Rond d'Alembert, et al. *Encyclopédie, ou Dictionnaire raisonné des Sciences, des Arts et des Métiers, par une Société de Gens de Lettres.* Vol. 6. Paris: Chez Briasson, David, et al., 1756.

Diderot, Denis, Jean le Rond d'Alembert, et al. *Encyclopédie, ou Dictionnaire raisonné des Sciences, des Arts et des Métiers, par une Société de Gens de Lettres.* Vol. 7. Paris: Chez Briasson, David, et al., 1757.

Diderot, Denis, Jean le Rond d'Alembert, et al. *Encyclopédie, ou Dictionnaire raisonné des Sciences, des Arts et des Métiers, par une Société de Gens de Lettres.* Vol. 8. Neuchâtel: Chez Samuel Faulche & Compagnie, 1765.

Dieckmann, Herbert. *Inventaire du fonds Vandeul et inédits de Diderot.* Geneva: Librairie Droz, 1951.

Dilthey, Wilhelm. "Das achtzehnte Jahrhundert und die geschichtliche Welt." In *Wilhelm Diltheys Gesammelte Schriften*, vol. 3, edited by Paul Ritter, 209–268. Leipzig: B. G. Teubner, 1927.

Dirda, Michael. "When the World Spoke French." *Salon*, September 6, 2011.

Disraeli, Isaac. *Curiosities of Literature. First Series.* New York: William Pearson & Co., 1835.

Disraeli, Isaac. *The Literary Character; or the History of Men of Genius, Drawn from Their Own Feelings and Confessions.* Vol. 2. 4th ed., rev. London: Henry Colburn, 1828.

Dorris, George E. "Scipione Maffei amid the Dunces." *Review of English Studies* 16, no. 63 (August 1965): 288–290.

Dostoyevsky, Fyodor. *The Brothers Karamazov.* Translated by Richard Pevear and Larissa Volokhonsky. New York: Farrar, Straus and Giroux, 1992.

Doyle, Arthur Conan. *Through the Magic Door.* London: Smith, Elder & Co., 1907.

Dumas père, Alexandre. "Impressions de voyage" ("VI. Le Tour du lac"). *Revue des Deux Mondes*, July 15, 1833, 171–190.

Dumas père, Alexandre. *Travels in Switzerland.* Translated by R.W. Plummer and A. Craig Bell. London: A. Owen, 1958.

Dumersan, Théophile-Marion. *Chants et Chansons populaires de la France. Troisième série.* Paris: H.-L. Delloye, Éditeur, 1843, *notice* "Le Café."

Durant, Will. *Philosophy and the Social Problem.* New York: Macmillan Company, 1917.

Durant, Will. *The Story of Philosophy.* New York: Simon and Schuster, 1926.

Durant, Will, and Ariel Durant. *The Age of Voltaire.* New York: Simon and Schuster, 1965.

Dutourd, Jean. *Le Spectre de la rose.* Paris: Flammarion, 1986.

Dutourd, Jean. *Pluche ou l'amour de l'art.* Paris: Flammarion, 1967.

Duvernet, Jean. *Vie de Voltaire.* Paris: Flammarion, 1967.

Duvernet, Théophile Imageon. *La Reconnaissance de Le Kain, envers M. de Voltaire, son bienfaiteur.* Paris, 1778.

Duvernet, Théophile Imageon. *La Vie de Voltaire, par M***.* Geneva, 1786.

Dwight, Timothy. *The Duty of Americans, at the Present Crisis, Illustrated in a Discourse, Preached on the Fourth of July, 1798.* New Haven, CT: Thomas and Samuel Green, 1798.

Dwight, Timothy. *The Triumph of Infidelity: A Poem.* [Hartford, CT?], 1788.

Eagleton, Terry. *Culture.* New Haven, CT: Yale University Press, 2016.

Eckermann, Johann Peter. *Gespräche mit Goethe in den lezten Jahren seines Lebens, 1823–1832.* Vol. 3. Leipzig: F. A. Brockhaus, 1836.

Edelman, Julia. *Love Voltaire Us Apart: A Philosopher's Guide to Relationships.* London: Icon Books, 2016.

Eliot, T. S. *Die Einheit der Europäischen Kultur.* Berlin: Carl Habel Verlagsbuchhandlung, 1946.

Eliot, T. S. *Notes towards the Definition of Culture.* London: Faber & Faber, 1948.

Emerson, Ralph Waldo. *The Conduct of Life.* Boston: Ticknor and Fields, 1860.

L'Esprit des journaux français et étrangers. Vol. 1. Brussels, 1805.

Fadiman, Clifton, and André Bernard, eds. *Bartlett's Book of Anecdotes.* Rev. ed. Boston: Little, Brown & Co., 2000.

Faguet, Émile. *Dix-huitième siècle: Études littéraires.* Paris: H. Lecene et H. Oudin, 1890.

Faguet, Émile. *Voltaire.* Paris: Lecène, Oudin et Cie., 1895.

Fast, Howard. "Free Speech for Fascists?" *The New Masses,* January 11, 1944, 18.

Fazy, Henri, Émile Yung, Jules Cougnard, et al. *Genève Suisse: le livre du centenaire, 1814–1914.* Geneva: A. Jullien, 1914.

Fellows, Otis. *From Voltaire to La Nouvelle Critique: Problems and Personalities.* Geneva: Librairie Droz, 1970.

Fife, Graeme. *The Terror: The Shadow of the Guillotine: France, 1792–1794.* New York: St. Martin's Press, 2006.

Fisher, Henry W. *Abroad with Mark Twain and Eugene Field: Tales They Told to a Fellow Correspondent.* New York: Nicholas L. Brown, 1922.

Flaubert, Gustave. *Bouvard et Pécuchet: Œuvre posthume.* Vol. 6 in *Œuvres complètes de Flaubert.* Paris: Louis Conard, Libraire-éditeur, 1910.

Flaubert, Gustave. *Correspondance, 1850–1859.* Vol. 2. Paris: Club de l'Honnête Homme, 1974.

Flaubert, Gustave. *Correspondance, 1859–1871.* Vol. 3. Paris: Club de l'Honnête Homme, 1975.

Flaubert, Gustave. *Correspondance, 1871–1877.* Vol. 4. Paris: Club de l'Honnête Homme, 1975.

Flaubert, Gustave. *Correspondance, 1877–1880.* Vol. 5. Paris: Club de l'Honnête Homme, 1975.

Foges, Peter. "Hitchens's Atheism, Intact." Letter to the editor, *New York Times,* May 19, 2016, A26.

Fontenelle, Bernard le Bovier de. "De l'origine des Fables." In *Entretiens sur la pluralité des mondes Par Monsieur de Fontenelle, de l'Académie Françoise. Nouvelle Edition, augmentée de Pieces diverses,* 353–385. Paris: Michel Brunet, 1724.

Forster, E. M. "Ferney." In *Two Cheers for Democracy,* 340–344. London: Edward Arnold, 1951.

Forster, E. M. "Happy Ending." *New Statesman,* November 2, 1940, 442.

Forsythe, Robert [a.k.a., Kyle Crichton]. "Strictly from Anger." *The New Masses,* August 2, 1937, 21.

Foster, John Bellamy, Brett Clark, and Richard York. *Critique of Intelligent Design: Materialism versus Creationism from Antiquity to the Present.* New York: Monthly Review Press, 2008.

France, Anatole. *La Vie littéraire*. Vol. 1. Paris: Calmann-Lévy, 1888.

France, Anatole. *Les Matinées de la Villa Saïd: Propos d'Anatole France, recueillis par Paul Gsell*. Edited by Paul Gsell. Paris: Bernard Grasset, 1921.

Francis, Dvon. "How Karsh Pictures Celebrities." *Popular Science*, October 1952, 220–225, 256, 258, 260.

Franklin, Benjamin. *The Papers of Benjamin Franklin*. Vol. 11. Edited by Leonard W. Labaree. New Haven, CT: Yale University Press, 1967.

Frederick II. *Éloge de Voltaire lu à l'académie royale des Sciences et belles-lettres de Berlin, dans une assemblée publique extraordinairement convoquée, pour cet objet, le 16 novembre 1778 (par sa Majesté le Roi de P . . .)*. Berlin: Chez J. J. Decker, 1788.

Frederick II. *Oeuvres posthumes de Frédéric II, Roi de Prusse*. Vol. 8. 2nd ed. Berlin: Chez Voss et Fils et Decker et Fils, 1788.

"A Frenchman on Mark Twain and His Criticisms of Bourget." *Literary Digest*, March 2, 1895, 11.

Fréron, Élie-Catherine, ed. *L'Année littéraire*. Vol. 6. Paris: Chez Delalain, 1770.

Freud, Sigmund. *Civilisation and Its Discontents*. Translated by Joan Riviere. London: Hogarth Press, 1930.

Freud, Sigmund. *Ungbehagen in der Kultur*. Vienna: Internationaler Psychoanalytischer Verlag, 1930.

Fuller, Margaret. *Conversations with Goethe in the Last Years of His Life*. Boston: Hilliard, Gray, and Company, 1839.

Gabriel Márquez, García. *Del amor y otros demonios*. Mexico City: Editorial Diana, 1994.

Gabriel Márquez, García. *Of Love and Other Demons*. Translated by Edith Grossman. New York: Vintage Books, 1995.

Galantière, Lewis. "Voltaire." In *Atlantic Brief Lives*, edited by Louis Kronenberger, 848–850. Boston: Little, Brown and Company, 1965.

The Galaxy of Wit: Or, Laughing Philosopher, Being a Collection of Choice Anecdotes, Many of Which Originated in or about "The Literary Emporium." 2 vols. Boston: J. Reed, 1880.

Gay, Peter. "The Enlightenment." *Horizon*, Spring 1970, 40–45.

Gay, Peter. *The Party of Humanity: Essays in the French Enlightenment*. New York: Alfred A. Knopf, 1964.

Gay, Peter. *Voltaire's Politics: The Poet as Realist*. Princeton, NJ: Princeton University Press, 1959. Reprint, New Haven, CT: Yale University Press, 1988.

Gay, Peter, and Gerald J. Cavanaugh, eds. *Historians at Work*. 4 vols. New York: Harper & Row, 1972–1975.

Geary, James. *Wit's End: What Wit Is, How It Works, and Why We Need It*. New York: W. W. Norton, 2018.

Gerard, Alexander. *An Essay on Taste with Three Dissertations on the same Subject by Mr. De Voltaire. Mr. D'Alembert, F.R.S. Mr. De Montesquieu*. London: A. Millar, 1759.

Getlen, Larry. "Ben Franklin Was the Country's First Fame Whore." *New York Post*, June 17, 2017. https://nypost.com/2017/06/17/ben-franklin-was-the-countrys-first -fame-whore/.

Gibbon, Edward. *The Letters of Edward Gibbon*. 3 vols. Edited by J. E. Norton. London: Cassell & Co., 1956.

Gibbon, Edward. *The Miscellaneous Works of Edward Gibbon, Esquire. With Memoirs of His Life and Writings, Composed by Himself*. 3 vols. Edited by John Lord Sheffield. Dublin: Printed for P. Wogan et al., 1796.

Gide, André. "Notes sur Voltaire." *Nouvelle Revue Française*, April 1937, 524–537.

Glucksmann, André. "André Glucksmann: L'Europe sera voltairienne ou ne sera pas." Interview with André Glucksmann by Julien Bisson. *L'Express*, February 5, 2015. https://www.lexpress.fr/culture/livre/andre-glucksmann-l-europe-sera-voltairienne -ou-ne-sera-pas_1675118.html.

Goethe, Johann Wolfgang von. *Rameaus Neffe: Ein Dialog*. Leipzig: G. J. Göschen, 1805.

Goldberger, Howard. Letter to the editor, *New York*, April 18, 1998, 8.

Goodman, Robert Walter. "The Uses of Satire." Letter to the editor, *The New Masses*, August 24, 1937, 22.

Gopnik, Adam. *Angels and Ages: A Short Book about Darwin, Lincoln, and Modern Life*. New York: Knopf, 2009.

Gopnik, Adam. "Are Liberals on the Wrong Side of History?" *New Yorker*, March 20, 2017, 88–93.

Gopnik, Adam. Introduction to *Voltaire in Love* by Nancy Mitford, vii–xxi. New York: New York Review Books, 2012.

Gopnik, Adam. "Voltaire's Garden: The Philosopher as a Campaigner for Human Rights." *New Yorker*, March 7, 2005, 74–81.

Goulemot, Jean, André Magnan, and Didier Masseau, eds. *Inventaire Voltaire*. Paris: Quarto, 1995.

Gray, John. *Seven Types of Atheism*. New York: Farrar, Straus & Giroux, 2018.

Grimm, Friedrich Melchior, and Denis Diderot, et al. *Correspondance littéraire, philosophique, critique, par Grimm, etc.* Vol. 1. Edited by Maurice Tourneux. Paris: Garnier Frères, 1877.

Grimm, Friedrich Melchior, and Denis Diderot, et al. *Correspondance littéraire, philosophique et critique, adressée à un Souverain d'Allemagne, depuis 1753–jusqu'en 1769*. Vol. 6. Première Partie. Paris: F. Buisson, 1813.

Grimm, Friedrich Melchior, and Denis Diderot, et al. *Correspondance littéraire, philosophique et critique, adressée à un Souverain d'Allemagne, depuis 1770–jusqu'en 1782*. Vol. 1. Paris: F. Buisson, 1812.

Grimm, Friedrich Melchior, and Denis Diderot, et al. *Correspondance littéraire, philosophique et critique, adressée à un Souverain d'Allemagne, depuis 1770–jusqu'en 1782*. Vol. 4. Seconde Édition, revue et corrigé. Paris: F. Buisson, 1812.

Grimm, Friedrich Melchior, and Denis Diderot, et al. *Correspondance littéraire, philosophique et critique, adressée à un Souverain d'Allemagne, pendant une partie des années 1775–1776, et pendant les années 1782 à 1790, inclusivement*. Vol. 2. Troisième et dernière Partie. Paris: F. Buisson, 1813.

Grimm, Herman Friedrich. *Fünfzehn Essays: Voltaire und Frankreich; Friedrich der Grosse und Macaulay*. Berlin: Ferd. Dümmler's Berlagsbuchhandlung, 1874.

Grimm, Herman Friedrich. *Literature*. Translated by Sarah H. Adams. Boston: Cupples, Upham, & Co., 1886.

Guéhenno, Jean. "Glorieuses fautes." *Le Monde*, July 4, 1978, 1, 13.

Hall, Evelyn Beatrice [S. G. Tallentyre]. *The Friends of Voltaire*. London: Smith, Elder, & Co., 1906.

Hall, Evelyn Beatrice [S. G. Tallentyre]. *The Life of Voltaire*. 2 vols. London: Smith, Elder, & Co., 1903.

Hall, Evelyn Beatrice [S. G. Tallentyre], ed. and trans. *Voltaire in His Letters: Being a Selection from His Correspondence*. London: John Murray, 1919.

Hall, Henry Noble. "From Voltaire's Scribbling Books." *Encore: A Continuing Anthology*, July 1945, 83–85.

Hamill, Pete. *Piecework: Writings on Men and Women, Fools and Heroes, Lost Cities, Vanished Calamities and How the Weather Was*. Boston: Little, Brown and Company, 1996.

Hamilton, Alexander. *The Papers of Alexander Hamilton*. Vol. 26. Edited by Harold C. Syrett. New York: Columbia University Press, 1979.

Hamilton, William. "The Essential Character by Which Our Primary Beliefs, or the Principles of Common Sense, Are Discriminated." In *Philosophy of Sir William Hamilton*, edited by O. W. Wight. New York: D. Appleton, 1855.

Hammer, Carl, Jr. *Goethe and Rousseau: Resonances of the Mind*. Lexington: University Press of Kentucky, 2015.

Harbottle, Thomas Benfield, and Philip Hugh Dalbiac, eds. *Dictionary of Quotations (French and Italian)*. London: Swann Sonnenschein & Co., 1901.

Harris, Kenneth. "Kenneth Harris Talks to Bertrand Russell." *Western Mail* (Cardiff), February 14, 1970, Weekend Magazine section, 7.

Harris, Mark. *The Heart of Boswell: Six Journals in One Volume*. New York: McGraw-Hill, 1981.

Harvey, Paul. "Ozark Folks Dispel Trouble with Homilies." *Del Rio News Herald*, June 20, 1982, 26.

Haslett, Tobi. "The Private Intellectual." *NewYorker*, October 19, 2015. https://www.newyorker.com/books/page-turner/the-private-intellectual.

Hayat, Jeannine. "Marcher boulevard Voltaire ou monter à bord du Thalys." *Le Huffington Post* (French edition), September 3, 2015.

Hayes, Kevin J. *George Washington: A Life in Books*. Oxford: Oxford University Press, 2017.

Hayward, John. "The Cliffhanger, Jan. 29." *Human Events*, January 29, 2013. https://humanevents.com/2013/01/29/the-cliffhanger-jan-29.

Hecht, Ben. *A Child of the Century*. New York: Simon and Schuster, 1954.

Henry, Patrick. "Contre Barthes." In *Studies on Voltaire and the Eighteenth Century*, vol. 249, 19–36. Oxford: The Voltaire Foundation, 1987

Hertzberg, Arthur. *The French Enlightenment and the Jews: The Origins of Modern Anti-Semitism*. New York: Columbia University Press, 1968.

Hertzberg, Arthur. Letter to the editor. *New York Times Book Review*, September 30, 1990, 50.

Hill, Aaron. *The Tragedy of Zara. As it is Acted at the Theatre-Royal, in Drury-Lane, By His Majesty's Servants. The Second Edition*. London: John Watts, 1736.

Hill, Aaron. *The Works of the Late Aaron Hill, Esq*. 4 vols. London: Printed for the Benefit of the Family, 1753.

Himmelfarb, Milton. "Paganism, Religion and Modernity." *Commentary*, November 1968, 89–96.

"Historical and Critical Memoirs of the Life and Writings of M. De Voltaire [. . .]." *The Political Herald, and Review: Or, a Survey of Domestic and Foreign Politics; and a Critical Account of Political and Historical Publications* (London), no. 12 (December 1786): 444–449.

Hitchens, Christopher. *God Is Not Great: How Religion Poisons Everything*. Toronto: McLelland & Stewart, 2008.

Hitchens, Christopher. "Thinking Thrice about the Jewish Question." In *Hitch-22: A Memoir*. New York: Twelve, 351–381.

Hofstadter, Richard. *Anti-Intellectualism in American Life*. New York: Vintage Books, 1963.

Holmes, Richard. "Voltaire's Grin." *New York Review of Books*, November 30, 1995, 49–55.

Horace. *Les poësies d'Horace, Traduites en françois*. Vol. 3. Translated by Noël-Etienne Sanadon. Paris: Chez Moreau, 1756.

Houssaye, Arsène. *Le Roi Voltaire*. Paris: Lévy Frères, 1858.

Howells, William Dean. *My Mark Twain: Reminiscences and Criticisms*. New York: Harper & Brothers, 1910.

Hugo, Victor. *Choses vues* (1846). In *Œuvres complètes: Histoire*, vol. 11. Paris: Robert Laffont, 1987.

Hugo, Victor. *Depuis l'exil: 1870–1885*. Paris: Librairie de l'édition nationale, 1895.

Hugo, Victor. "Le Centenaire de Voltaire." Speech at the Théâtre de la Gaité in Paris, May 30, 1878. Published in *Le Rappel*, June 1, 1878.

Hugo, Victor. *Littérature et philosophie mêlées*. Vol. 1. Paris: Eugène Renduel, 1834.

Hugo, Victor. *Océan prose* (1866–1869). In *Œuvres complètes: Politique*, vol. 10. Paris: Robert Laffont, 1989.

Hugo, Victor. *William Shakespeare*. Paris: A. Lacroix, Verboeckhoven et Compagnie, Éditeurs, 1864.

Hume, David. *The Letters of David Hume*. Vol. 1. Edited by J. Y. T. Greig. Oxford: Clarendon Press, 1932. Reprint, Oxford: Oxford University Press, 2011.

Humes, James C. *The Wit & Wisdom of Benjamin Franklin*. New York: HarperCollins, 1995.

Hunt, Leigh. *The Town: Its Memorable Characters and Events*. London: Smith, Elder and Co., 1848.

Huxley, Aldous. "The Author of 'Eminent Victorians.'" *Vanity Fair*, September 1922, 41.

Huxley, Aldous. "On Re-Reading Candide." In *On the Margin*, 12–17. London: Chatto & Windus, 1923.

Huxley, Aldous. *On the Margin*. London: Chatto & Windus, 1923.

Huxley, Aldous. *Time Must Have a Stop*. Garden City, NY: Sun Dial Press, 1944.

Huxley, T. H. "On the Method of Zadig: Retrospective Prophecy as a Function of Science." *Nineteenth Century: A Monthly Review*, June 1880, 929–940.

James, Clive. *Cultural Amnesia: Necessary Memories from History and the Arts*. New York: W. W. Norton, 2007.

Jeanson, Henri. "Lettres ou pas lettres: Lettre à Jean Giono." *Le Canard Enchaîné*, December 20, 1944, 4.

Jefferson, Thomas. *The Papers of Thomas Jefferson*. Vol. 8. Edited by Julian P. Boyd. Princeton, NJ: Princeton University Press, 1953.

Jefferson, Thomas. *The Papers of Thomas Jefferson, Retirement Series*. Vol. 3. Edited by J. Jefferson Looney. Princeton, NJ: Princeton University Press, 2006.

Joubert, Joseph. *Pensées, essais et maximes*. Vol. 2. Paris: Librairie de Charles Gosselin, 1842.

Joubert, Joseph. *Recueil des Pensées de M. Joubert*. Paris: Imprimerie Le Normant, 1838.

Journet, René, and Guy Robert. *Contribution aux études sur Victor Hugo*. 2 vols. Paris: Annales littéraires de l'Université de Besançon, 1979.

Kaplan, Justin. *Mr. Clemens and Mark Twain: A Biography*. New York: Simon & Schuster, 2003.

Kates, Gary. *Monsieur d'Eon Is a Woman: A Tale of Political Intrigue and Sexual Masquerade*. New York: Basic Books, 1995.

Keate, George. *The Alps*. London: R. and J. Dodsley, 1763.

Keate, George. *Ferney: An Epistle to Monsieur de Voltaire*. London: R. and J. Dodsley, 1763.

Kelly, Christopher, and Roger D. Masters, eds. *The Collected Writings of Rousseau: Confessions and Correspondence, Including the Letters to Malesherbes*. Lebanon, NH: University Press of New England, 1995.

Kerr, Walter. "Candide." *New York Herald Tribune*, December 3, 1956, 10.

Kerr, Walter. "Is This the Best of All Possible 'Candides'?" *New York Times*, December 30, 1973, "Arts and Leisure" section, 1.

Kielmansegge, Friedrich. *Diary of a Journey to England in the Years 1761–1762*. Translated by Philippa Kielmansegg. London: Longmans, Green, and Co., 1902.

Kirk, Russell. *The Conservative Mind: From Burke to Santayana*. Chicago: Henry Regnery Company, 1953.

Kirn, Walter. Post on Kirn's Twitter account, @walterkirn, July 5, 2017. https://twitter .com/walterkirn/status/882793385123131393.

Kronenberger, Louis. "Candide." In *The Polished Surface: Essays in the Literature of Worldliness*. New York: Alfred A. Knopf, 1969.

Labadie-Lagrave, Gaston. "Les appréciations des Américains sur l'oeuvre de Paul Bourget." *Le Figaro: Supplément littéraire*, February 2, 1895, 19.

La Barre de Beaumarchais, Antoine de. *Amusemens littéraires: Ou Correspondance Politique, Historique, Philosophique, Critique & Galante*. Vol. 2. The Hague: Jean Van Duren, 1741.

La Beaumelle, Laurent Angliviel de. *Observations sur L'Esprit des Loix, ou L'Art de lire ce livre, de l'entendre et d'en juger*. Amsterdam: Chez Pierre Mortier, 1751.

Lacombe, Jacques. *Voltaire portatif: Pensées philosophiques de M. de Voltaire, ou Tableau encyclopédique des connaissances humaines*. Vol. 1. [Paris], 1766. https://books.google .com/books.

Lacombe de Prézel, Honoré. *Dictionnaire des portraits historiques, anecdotes, et traits remarquables des hommes illustres*. Paris: Chez Lacombe, Libraire, 1758.

Lacroix, Alexis. "Nous avons besoin d'un Voltaire dans l'âge de Trump." L'Express .com, November 15, 2018. https://www.lexpress.fr/culture/nous-avons-besoin-d-un -voltaire-dans-l-age-de-trump_2048088.html.

Lamport, Felicia. "Dictionaries: Our Language Right or Wrong." *Harper's*, September 1959, 49–54.

Lanson, Gustave. *Histoire de la littérature française*. 4th ed. Paris: Libraire Hachette, 1896.

Lanson, Gustave. "Voltaire." In *La Grande Encyclopédie: Inventaire raisonné des sciences, des lettres et des arts par une société de gens de lettres*, 31 vols., edited by Marcellin Bertholet et al., 31:1117–1129. Paris: Société Anonyme de la Grande Encyclopédie, 1902.

Lanson, Gustave. *Voltaire*. Paris: Société Anonyme de la Grande Encyclopédie, 1906.

Lapham, Lewis H. *Waiting for the Barbarians*. New York: Verso, 1997.

Laski, Harold J. "Is Laughter a Weapon? A Symposium." *The New Masses*, September 14, 1937, 16.

Leith, James A. "Les Trois Apothéoses de Voltaire." *Annales historiques de la Révolution française* (April–June 1979): 161–209.

Lekain, Henri-Louis. *Mémoires de Henri Louis Lekain, publiés par son fils aîné: suivis d'une correspondance (inédite) de Voltaire, Garrick, Colardeau, Lebrun, etc.* Paris: Chez Colnet, Chez Debray, Chez Mongie, 1801.

Lessing, Gottfried Ephraim. *Laokoon oder über die Grensen der Mahlerei und Poesie.* Vol. 1. Berlin: Christian Friedrich Voss, 1766.

Leupin, Alexandre. *La passion des idoles: Religion et politique, la Bible, la Chanson de Roland.* Paris: Harmattan, 2000.

Lévis, Pierre-Marc-Gaston, duc de. *Maximes, préceptes et réflexions sur différens sujets de morale et de politique.* 5th ed. Paris: Charles Gosselin, Libraire, 1825.

Leysenne, Pierre. *Le Bréviaire des Éducateurs et des Pères de Famille.* Paris: Hachette, 1903.

"The Life of the Late Celebrated Dr. Edward Young." In *Annual Register, or a View of the History, Politicks, and Literature, For the Year 1765,* section "Characters," 31–36. London: J. Dodsley, 1766.

Ligne, Charles-Joseph Lamoral, prince de. *Mémoires et mélanges historiques et littéraires.* Vol. 2. Paris: Ambroise Dupont et Cie, 1827.

Linguet, Simon-Nicolas-Henri. *Examen des ouvrages de M. de Voltaire, Considéré comme Poëte, comme Prosateur comme Philosophe.* Brussels: Chez Lemaire, 1788. https://books.google.com/books.

Lintilhac, Eugène. "Le vrai 'système' de Jean-Jacques Rousseau." *La Nouvelle Revue* 75 (March 1892): 109–120.

Lippmann, Walter. "The Near Machiavelli." *New Republic,* May 31, 1922, 12–14.

Lithwick, Dahlia. "Last Count for the Recount." Slate.com, December 12, 2000. https://www.slate.com/articles/news_and_politics/supreme_court_dispatches/2000/12/last_count_for_the_recount.html.

Lockhart, J. G. *Memoirs of the Life of Sir Walter Scott, Bart.* Vol. 7. Philadelphia: Carey, Lea, & Blanchard, 1838.

Longchamp, Sébastian. *Anecdotes sur la vie privée de Monsieur de Voltaire.* Edited by Frédéric Eigeldinger and Raymond Trousson. Paris: Champion, 2009.

Longchamp, Sébastian, and Jean-Louis Wagnière. *Mémoires sur Voltaire et sur ses ouvrages.* 2 vols. Edited by Jacques-Joseph-Marie Decroix. Paris: Aimé André, 1826.

Lowell, James Russell. *Among My Books: Six Essays.* London: Macmillan & Co., 1870.

Lynd, Robert. "The Decline and Fall of Hell." In *The Book of This and That,* 48–49. London: Mills and Boon, 1915.

Macauley, Thomas Babington. "Life and Writings of Addison." *The Edinburgh Review or Critical Journal,* July 1843, 193–260.

"Mae West: Philosophy." *The Straits Times* (Singapore), October 28, 1934. http://maewest.blogspot.com/2012/10.

Maistre, Joseph de. *Les Soirées de Saint-Pétersbourg: ou, Entretiens sur le gouvernement temporel de la Providence, suivis d'un Traité sur les sacrifices.* Paris: Librairie grecque, latine et française, 1821.

Manji, Irshad. *Liberty and Love: The Courage to Reconcile Faith and Freedom.* New York: Atria Books, 2011.

Manzano, María, Ildikó Sain, and Enrique Alonso, eds. *The Life and Work of Leon Henkin: Essays on His Contributions.* Cham, Switzerland: Birkhäuser, 2014.

Marty, Joseph. *Les Principaux monuments funéraires du Père-Lachaise, de Montmartre, du Mont-Parnasse et autres cimetières de Paris.* Paris: Amédée Bédelet, 1839.

Mason, Haydn. *Voltaire: A Biography.* Baltimore: Johns Hopkins University Press, 1981.

Maugham, Somerset. *The Summing Up.* London: William Heinemann, 1938.

Mauriac, François. *Mémoires intérieurs.* Paris: Flammarion, 1959.

Mauriac, François. *Mémoires intérieurs.* Translated by Gerard Hopkins. New York: Farrar, Straus & Cudahy, 1961.

Maurois, André. "An Appreciation of Voltaire." Translated by Lowell Bair. In Voltaire, *Candide.* New York: Bantam Books, 1959.

Maurois, André. *Voltaire.* Paris: Gallimard, 1935.

Maurois, André. *Voltaire.* Translated by Hamish Miles. London: Thomas Nelson and Sons, 1938.

Meacham, Jon. *American Gospel: God, the Founding Fathers, and the Making of a Nation.* New York: Random House, 2006.

Mencken, H. L. *A Book of Burlesques.* New York: Alfred A. Knopf, 1920.

Mencken, H. L. *The Philosophy of Friedrich Nietzsche.* Boston: Luce and Company, 1908.

Mercier, Vivian. Review of *The Portable Jonathan Swift* by Carl Van Doren and Jonathan Swift. *Commonweal,* July 23, 1948, 361–362.

Michelet, Jules. *Histoire de la révolution française.* Vol. 1. Paris: Chamerot, 1847.

Michelet, Jules. *The History of the French Revolution.* Translated by Charles Cocks. 2 vols. London: H. G. Bohn, 1847.

Miller, Merle. *On Being Different: What It Means to Be a Homosexual.* New York: Random House, 1971.

Mitford, Nancy. *Madame de Pompadour.* New York: Random House, 1954.

Mitford, Nancy. *Voltaire in Love.* New York: Harper & Row, 1957. Reprint, with an introduction by Adam Gopnik, New York: New York Review Books, 2012.

Montagu, Elizabeth. *The Letters of Mrs. Elizabeth Montagu, with Some of the Letters of Her Correspondents.* 3 vols. London: T. Cadell and W. Davies, 1813.

Montesquieu, Charles de Secondat, Baron de. *Œuvres posthumes, pour servir de supplément aux différentes éditions in-12 qui ont paru jusqu'a present.* Paris: Chez Plassan, Chez Bernard, and Chez Grégoire, 1798.

Montfort, François Salvat de. *Gasconiana, ou Recueil des bons mots, des pensées les plus plaisantes, et des rencontres les plus vives des Gascons.* Amsterdam: Chez François L'Honoré, 1708.

Moore, Hugh. *A Dictionary of Quotations from Various Authors in Ancient and Modern Languages with English Translations.* London: Whittaker, Treacher, & Co., 1831.

Moore, John. *A View of Society and Manners in France, Switzerland, and Germany: With Anecdotes relating to some Eminent Characters.* Vol. 1. London: W. Strahan and T. Cadell, 1779.

Moos, Malcolm. Introduction to H. L. Mencken, *On Politics: A Carnival of Buncombe,* ed. Malcolm Moos, xi–xxii. Baltimore: Johns Hopkins University Press, 1956.

Morand, Paul. *Journal inutile 1968–1972.* Vol. 1. Paris: Gallimard, 2001.

Morand, Paul. "Mise au vert" ("Chroniques"). *La Parisienne,* August 1953, 1072–1073.

Morgan, John. *The Journal of Dr. John Morgan of Philadelphia: From the City of Rome to the City of London 1764.* Philadelphia: J. B. Lippincott, 1907.

Morley, Christopher. *Swiss Family Manhattan.* Garden City, NY: Doubleday, Doran and Co., 1932.

Morley, John. *Voltaire*. London: Chapman and Hall, 1872.

Mott, Frank Luther, and Chester E. Jorgenson. *Benjamin Franklin: Representative Selections*. New York: American Book Co., 1936.

Mozart, Wolfgang Amadeus. *Briefe*. Edited by Willi Reich. Zurich: Manesse Verlag, 1948.

Mozart, Wolfgang Amadeus. *The Letters of Wolfgang Amadeus Mozart, 1769–1791*. Vol. 1. Translated by Lady Grace Wallace. Oxford: Oxford University Press, 1865.

Murphy, Arthur [Charles Ranger]. "*To Monsieur* Voltaire." *The Gray's Inn Journal*, no. 12 (December 15, 1753): 68–71.

Musset, Alfred de. "Rolla." *Revue des deux mondes*, August 15, 1833, 369–393.

Naipaul, V. S. "Cannery Row Revisited." *Daily Telegraph Magazine*, April 3, 1970, 24–27, 29–30.

Naipaul, V. S. "Steinbeck in Monterey." In *The Writer and the World: Essays*. New York: Alfred A. Knopf, 2002.

Nash, Ogden. *Good Intentions*. New York: Little, Brown & Co., 1942.

Nathan, George Jean. *The Intimate Notebooks of George Jean Nathan*. New York: A. A. Knopf, 1932.

Nicolardot, Louis. *Ménage et finances de Voltaire: Avec une introduction sur les moeurs des cours et des salons au XVIIIᵉ siècle*. Paris: E. Dentu, Libraire-Éditeur, 1854.

Nietzsche, Friedrich. *Ecce Homo. Wie man wird, was man ist*. Leipzig: Isel-Verlag, 1908.

Nietzsche, Friedrich. *Human, All Too Human: A Book for Free Spirits*. In *Political Writings of Friedrich Nietzsche: An Edited Anthology*, edited and translated by Frank Cameron and Don Dombowsky, 75–100. Basingstoke, UK: Macmillan, 2008.

Nietzsche, Friedrich. *Menschliches, Allzumenschliches. Ein Buch für freie Geister*. Chemnitz, Germany: Verlag von Ernst Schmeitzner, 1878.

Noble, William T. "'Unstuck in Time' . . . a Real Kurt Vonnegut: The Reluctant Guru of Searching Youth." *Detroit Sunday Magazine*, June 18, 1972. Reprinted in *Conversations with Kurt Vonnegut*, edited by William Rodney Allen, 57–65. Jackson: University Press of Mississippi, 1988.

Nock, Albert Jay. *Memoirs of a Superfluous Man*. New York: Harper & Brothers, 1943. Facsimile reprint edition, Auburn, AL: Ludwig von Mises Institute, 2007.

Noël, François-Joseph-Michel, and L.-J.-M. Carpentier. *Philologie française ou Dictionnaire étymologique, critique, historique, anecdotique, littéraire*. Vol. 2. Paris: Libraire Le Normant Père, 1831.

Nolte, William. *H. L. Mencken: Literary Critic*. Middletown, CT: Wesleyan University Press, 1964.

Nouvelle anthologie françoise, ou Choix des épigrammes & madrigaux de tous les Poëtes François depuis Marot jusqu'à ce jour. Vol. 1. Paris: Delalain, Libraire, 1769.

Novak, Michael. "It's Not All Relative." *New York Times*, October 16, 1998, A27.

Noyer, G. K., ed. and trans. *Voltaire's Revolution: Writings from His Campaign to Free Laws from Religion*. Amherst, NY: Prometheus Books, 2015.

Noyes, Alfred. *Voltaire*. New York: Sheed and Ward, 1936.

"Obama's Speech in Lansing, Michigan." *New York Times*, August 4, 2008. http://www.nytimes.com/2008/08/04/us/politics/04text-obama.html.

O'Hagan, Andrew. "Norman Mailer: The Art of Fiction." *Paris Review*, Summer 2007. Reprinted in *The Paris Review Interviews*, vol. 3, 399–435. New York: Picador, 2008.

Orieux, Jean. *Voltaire*. Translated by Barbara Bray and Helen R. Lane. New York: Doubleday, 1981.

Orieux, Jean. *Voltaire ou la royauté de l'esprit*. Paris: Flammarion, 1966. Paperback ed. 2 vols. Paris: Flammarion Champs, 1977.

Ormesson, Jean d'. *Une Autre histoire de la littérature française: Les Lumières*. Paris: J'ai lu, 2000.

Orwell, George. *The Collected Essays of George Orwell*. Vol. 4, *In Front of Your Nose, 1945–1950*. Edited by Sonia Orwell and Ian Angus. London: Secker & Warburg, 1968.

Orwell, George. "Mark Twain—The Licensed Jester." *Tribune*, November 26, 1943, 14–15.

Ostertag, Bob. "Gulf Disaster: The Fatal Flaw in Obama's 'Don't Make the Perfect the Enemy of the Good' Politics." *Huffington Post*, July 6, 2010. http://www.huffington post.com/bob-ostertag/gulf-disaster-the-fatal-f_b_566428.html.

Parini, Jay, ed. *Gore Vidal: Writer against the Grain*. New York: Columbia University Press, 1992.

Parker, Theodore. *Ten Sermons of Religion*. London: John Chapman, 1853.

Parton, James. *The Life and Times of Aaron Burr*. New York: Mason Brothers, 1858.

Parton, James. *Life of Voltaire*. 2 vols. Boston: Houghton, Mifflin and Company, 1881.

Pater, Walter. "Winckelmann." *Westminster Review*, October 1867, 80–110.

Pearson, Roger. Introduction to *Candide and Other Stories*, vii–xliii. Oxford: Oxford University Press, 1990.

Pearson, Roger. *Voltaire Almighty: A Life in Pursuit of Freedom*. New York: Bloomsbury, 2005.

Pearson, Roger. "Voltaire's Luck: The French Philosopher Outsmarts the Lottery." *Lapham's Quarterly*, Summer 2016. http://www.laphamsquarterly.org/luck/voltaires -luck.

Peregrine, Anthony. "Nine Things That Might Surprise You about Christmas in France." *The Telegraph*, December 24, 2019. https://www.telegraph.co.uk/travel/desti nations/europe/france/articles/Christmas-in-France-nine-things-that-might-sur prise-you/.

Perelman, S. J. *S. J. Perelman: Critical Essays*. Edited by Steven H. Gale. Oxon: Rout-ledge, 2016.

Perey, Lucien [Luce Herpin], and Gaston Maugras. *La vie intime de Voltaire aux Délices et à Ferney, 1754–1778, d'après des lettres et des documents inédits*. 2nd ed. Paris: Cal-mann-Levy, 1885.

Peyre, Henri. *Writers and Their Critics: A Study of Misunderstanding*. Ithaca, NY: Cornell University Press, 1944.

Peyrefitte, Roger. *L'Enfant de cœur*. Paris: Albin Michel, 1978.

Peyrefitte, Roger. *L'Illustre écrivain*. Paris: Albin Michel, 1978.

Peyrefitte, Roger. Preface to *Romans de Voltaire*, 5–7. Paris: Gallimard (Le Livre de Poche), 1961.

Pidgin, Charles Felton. *Theodosia, The First Gentlewoman of Her Time: The Story of Her Life, and a History of Persons and Events Connected Therewith*. Boston: C. M. Clark Publishing Co., 1907.

Pinto, Isaac. *Apologie pour la nation juive ou Réflexions critiques sur le premier chapitre du VII. Tome des Oeuvres de Monsieur de Voltaire, au Sujet des Juifs*. Amsterdam: Chez J. Joubert, 1762.

Pomeau, René. *D'Arouet à Voltaire: 1694–1734*. Vol. 1 in Pomeau's five-volume biography, *Voltaire en son temps* (1988–1994). 2nd ed. Oxford: Voltaire Foundation, 1998.

Pomeau, René. *De la cour au jardin, 1750–1759.* Vol. 3 in *Voltaire en son temps.* Oxford: Voltaire Foundation, 1991.

Pomeau, René. *La Religion de Voltaire.* Paris: Nizet, 1956; 2nd ed., Paris: Nizet, 1969.

Pomeau, René. *On a voulu l'enterrer: 1770–1791.* Vol. 5 in *Voltaire en son temps.* Oxford: Voltaire Foundation, 1994.

Pomeau, René. "Voltaire's Religion." In *Voltaire: A Collection of Critical Essays,* edited by William F. Bottiglia, 140–148. Englewood Cliffs, NJ: Prentice Hall, 1968.

Poniatowski Stanislas-Auguste, and Marie-Thérèse Geoffrin. *Correspondance inédite du roi Stanislas-Auguste Poniatowski et de Madame Geoffrin.* Edited by Charles de Moüy. Paris: E. Plon, 1875.

Le Porte-feuille d'un Homme de Gout, ou L'Esprit de nos meilleurs poëtes. Nouvelle Édition, Considérablement augmentée. Vol. 3. Amsterdam: Chez Delalain, 1770.

Porter, Laurence M. *A Gustave Flaubert Encyclopedia.* Westport, CT: Greenwood Press, 2001.

Potts, Rolf. "The Henry Ford of Literature." *The Believer,* September 2008. http://www.believermag.com/issues/200809/?read=article_potts.

Powys, John Cowper. *Suspended Judgments: Essays on Books and Sensations.* New York: G. Arnold Shaw, 1916.

Rae, John. *Life of Adam Smith.* London: Macmillan & Co., 1895.

Ratcliffe, Susan, ed. *Concise Oxford Dictionary of Quotations.* Oxford: Oxford University Press, 2006.

Recueil de planches sur les sciences, les arts libéraux et les arts méchaniques, avec leur explication. Paris: Chez Briasson, David, Le Breton, Durand, 1763.

Redman, Ben Ray. *The Portable Voltaire.* New York: Viking Press, 1949.

Rickels, Laurence A., ed. *Looking after Nietzsche: Interdisciplinary Encounters with Merleau-Ponty.* Albany: State University of New York Press, 1990.

Rocques de Montgaillard, Abbé Gabriel-Maurice. *Histoire de France: depuis la fin du règne de Louis XVI jusqu'à l'année 1825.* Vol. 3. Paris: Moutardier, Libraire-éditeur, 1827.

Rollins, Alfred B., Jr. *Roosevelt and Howe.* New Brunswick, NJ: Transaction Publishers, 1962.

Rousseau, Jean-Jacques. *Correspondance complète de Jean-Jacques Rousseau.* Vol. 4. Edited by R. A. Leigh. Geneva: Institut et Musée Voltaire, 1967.

Rousseau, Jean-Jacques. *Lettres de J. J. Rousseau.* [Paris], 1765.

Rousseau, Jean-Jacques. *Œuvres complètes.* Vol. 1. Edited by Michel Launay. Paris: Éditions du Seuil, 1967.

Rousseau, Jean-Jacques. *Seconde Partie des Confessions de J. J. Rousseau, Citoyen de Geneve. Édition enrichie d'un nouveau recueil de ses Lettres.* Vol. 3. Neuchâtel: De l'Imprimerie de L. Fauche-Borel, 1790.

Roy, Claude. "Un Fauteuil nommé Voltaire." *L'Express,* June 12, 1958. https://www.lexpress.fr/culture/livre/1958-un-fauteuil-nomme-voltaire_2025774.html.

Rushdie, Salman. "How Politics Took a Leaf from Voltaire's Garden." *The Guardian,* April 27, 2002. http://www.theguardian.com/books/2002/apr/27/francoismmariearouet devoltaire.salmanrushdie.

Sand, George. "Lettres de George Sand à Gustave Flaubert." *La Nouvelle Revue,* March 15, 1883, 30–61.

Scalia, Antonin. *Scalia Speaks: Reflections on Law, Faith, and Life Well Lived.* Edited by Christopher J. Scalia and Edward Whelan. New York: Crown Forum, 2017.

Scheff, David. "Playboy Interview: Camille Paglia." *Playboy*, May 1995, 51–64.

Schlegel, Friedrich. *Geschichte der alten und neuen Litteratur: Vorlesungen gehalten zu Wien im Jahre 1812*. Wien: K. Schaumburg und Compagnie, 1815.

Schlosser, Friedrich Christoph. *Geschichte des achtzehnten Jahrhunderts und des neunzehnten bis zum Sturz des französischen Kaiserreichs*. Vol. 3. Heidelberg: J. C. B. Mohr, 1842.

Schlosser, Friedrich Christoph. *History of the Eighteenth Century and of the Nineteenth till the Overthrow of the French Empire*. Vol. 2. Translated by D. Davison. London: Chapman and Hall, 1844.

Scott, James C. *Seeing Like a State: How Certain Schemes to Improve the Human Condition Have Failed*. New Haven, CT: Yale University Press, 1998.

Sedgwick, Catharine Maria. *Letters from Abroad to Kindred at Home*. 2 vols. London: Edward Moxon, 1841.

Seldes, Gilbert. "Motion Pictures." *Scribner's*, March 1938, 65–66, 68.

Seldes, Gilbert. *The 7 Lively Arts*. New York: Harper & Row, 1924.

Shabad, Rebecca. "Ryan Says He Doesn't Want to Negotiate with Democrats on Health Care." CBS.com, March 30, 2017. http://www.cbsnews.com/news/paul-ryan-says-he-doesnt-want-to-negotiate-with-democrats-on-health-care.

Shaftesbury, Anthony Ashley-Cooper, 3rd Earl of. *Characteristicks of Men, Manners, Opinions, Times*. 3 vols. 1711.

Shapiro, Ben. *The Right Side of History: How Reason and Moral Purpose Made the West*. New York: Broadside Books, 2019.

Sharp, William. "Literary Geography. The Thames from Oxford to the Nore." *The Pall Mall Magazine* 32, no. 131 (March 1904): 378–390.

Shattuck, Roger. *Forbidden Knowledge: From Prometheus to Pornography*. New York: Harcourt Brace & Company, 1996.

Shaw, George Bernard. *Saint Joan: A Chronicle Play in Six Scenes and an Epilogue*. New York: Brentano's, 1924.

Sheen, Bishop Fulton J. *Old Errors and New Labels*. New York: The Century Company, 1931.

Sherlock, Martin. *Letters from an English Traveller. Translated from the Original French Printed at Geneva and Paris. With Notes. A New Edition, Revised and Corrected*. London: J. Nichols, T. Cadell, P. Elmsly, H. Payne, and N. Conant, 1780.

Sherlock, Martin. *Lettres d'un voyageur anglois*. London: 1779.

Simon, Julian L., ed. *The State of Humanity*. Oxford: Blackwell Publishers, 1995.

Simond, Louis. *Switzerland; Or, A Journal of a Tour and Residence in That Country, in the Years 1817, 1818, and 1819*. 2 vols. London: John Murray, 1822–1823.

Smith, Paul J. "Montaigne in the World." In *The Oxford Handbook of Montaigne*, edited by Philippe Desan, 287–305. Oxford: Oxford University Press, 2016.

Smith, Sydney. Review of *Discourses on Various Subjects* by Dr. Thomas Rennel. *The Edinburgh Review, or Critical Journal*, October 1802, 83–91.

Snow, Philippa. "Paris Hilton Is the Greatest Performance Artist of Our Time." *i-D* (i-d.vice.com), May 16, 2019. https://i-d.vice.com/en_uk/article/j5wgad/paris-hilton-is-the-greatest-performance-artist-of-our-time.

Sollers, Philippe. "Il manque, Voltaire, là!" Interview with Frédéric Joignot. *Le Monde*, April 9, 2015. https://www.lemonde.fr/culture/article/2015/04/09/philippe-sollers-il-manque-voltaire-la_4612249_3246.html.

Spence, Joseph. *Observations, Anecdotes, and Characters of Books and Men: Collected from Conversation*. Vol. 1. Edited by James M. Osborn. Oxford: Clarendon Press, 1966.

Staël, Germaine de. *De l'Allemagne*. 3 vols. Paris: H. Nicolle, 1810.

Starobinski, Jean. "Est-il tolérant? Est-il odieux?" *Journal de Genève et Gazette de Lausanne/Samedi littéraire*, April 30–May 1, 1994, 1–2.

Starobinski, Jean. "Le fusil à deux coups de Voltaire." *Revue de métaphysique et de morale*, July–September 1966, 277–291.

Starobinski, Jean. *Le Remède dans le mal: Critique et légitimation de l'artifice à l'âge des Lumières*. Paris: Gallimard, 1989.

Stendhal [Henri Beyle]. *Vie de Henri Brulard*. 2 vols. Paris: Henry Debraye, 1913.

Stephen, James Fitzjames. *Liberty, Fraternity, Equality*. London: Smith & Elder, 1873.

Stevens, Jessi Jezewska. "The Hidden Power of the Passive Protagonist." Lithub.com, March 5, 2020. https://lithub.com/the-hidden-power-of-the-passive-protagonist.

Stone, Robert. *A Flag for Sunrise*. New York: Alfred A. Knopf, 1981.

Stout, Rex. *Gambit*. New York: Viking Press, 1962.

Strachey, Lytton. "Voltaire." *Athenæum*, August 1, 1919, 677–679.

Strachey, Lytton. "Voltaire." *New Republic*, August 6, 1919, 14–16.

Strachey, Lytton. "Voltaire and England." *The Edinburgh Review or Critical Journal*, October 1914, 392–411.

Surber, Don. "Bill Keller Wasn't Defending Robert Novak." July 2006. http://donsurber.blogspot.com/2006/07.

Swift, Jonathan ["J.S.D.D.D.S.P.D."]. "A short Account of the Author." In Voltaire, *Essay on Epick Poetry*. Dublin: J. Hyde, 1728.

Taylor, Peter Shawn. "Voltaire Wasn't Prepared to Die Defending the Right to Free Speech, But We Can Still Learn from Him." *National Post*, June 7, 2017. https://nationalpost.com/opinion/peter-shawn-taylor-voltaire-wasnt-prepared-to-die-defending-the-right-to-free-speech-but-we-can-still-learn-from-him.

Taylor, Philip M. *Munitions of the Mind: A History of Propaganda from the Ancient World to the Present Day*. 3rd ed. Manchester: Manchester University Press, 2003.

Tendron, Édith. *Anatole France inconnu*. Liège, Belgium: Editions du CEFAL, 1995.

Thacker, Christopher. *The Wildness Pleases: The Origins of Romanticism*. New York: St. Martin's Press, 1983.

Thatcher, Margaret. *Statecraft: Strategies for a Changing World*. New York: HarperCollins, 2003.

Thompson, Mark. *Enough Said: What's Gone Wrong with the Language of Politics?* New York: St. Martin's Press, 2016.

Thurber, James. "Something to Say." *New Yorker*, July 30, 1932, 17–19.

Torrey, Norman L. Introduction to *Candide or Optimism*, ix–x. Translated by Richard Aldington. Revised and edited by Norman L. Torrey. New York: Appleton-Century-Crofts, 1946.

Torrey, Norman L. *Les Philosophes: The Philosophers of the Enlightenment and Modern Democracy*. New York: Capricorn Books, 1961.

Traub, James. *John Quincy Adams: Militant Spirit*. New York: Basic Books, 2016.

Trimble, Esther. J. *A Hand-book of English and American Literature*. Philadelphia: Eldredge & Brother, 1883.

Tronchin, Henry. *Le Conseiller François Tronchin et ses amis: Voltaire, Diderot, Grimm etc. d'après des documents inédits*. Paris: Librairie Plon, 1895.

Trublet, Nicolas-Charles-Joseph. *Essais sur divers sujets de Littérature et de Morale.* Vol. 4. Paris: Chez Briasson, 1760.

Trublet, Nicolas-Charles-Joseph. "Suite sur M. de Fontenelle, par M. l'Abbé Trublet." *Mercure de France,* August 1757, 48–79.

Turnbull, Paul. "'Une Marionette Infidèle': The Fashioning of Edward Gibbon's Reputation as the English Voltaire." In *Edward Gibbon: Bicentenary Essays,* edited by David Womersley, 279–307. Oxford: The Voltaire Foundation, 1997.

Turner, Frank M. *European Intellectual History from Rousseau to Nietzsche.* Edited by Richard A. Lofthouse. New Haven, CT: Yale University Press, 2014.

Updike, John. "The Ten Greatest Works of Literature, 1001–2000: *A Eurocentric List Totted Up for the 1998 World Almanac.*" In *More Matter: Essays and Criticism,* 846–847. New York: Random House, 1999.

Valéry, Paul. *Voltaire: Discours prononcé le 10 décembre 1944 en Sorbonne.* Paris: Domat-Montchrestien, 1945.

Van Buren, Abby. "Dear Abby." *Eagle Gazette* (Lancaster, Ohio), March 17, 1974, 19.

Vercruysse, Jeroom, ed. *Les Éditions encadrées des Œuvres de Voltaire de 1775.* In *Studies on Voltaire and the Eighteenth Century,* vol. 168. Oxford: The Voltaire Foundation, 1977.

Versaille, André. "De l'héritage de Voltaire et de ce que nous n'en avons pas fait." Blog no. 21, LeMonde.fr, April 2017. http://andreversaille.blog.lemonde.fr.

Vidal, Gore. *Lincoln: A Novel.* New York: Random House, 1984.

Viereck. Peter. *Conservative Thinkers: From John Adams to Winston Churchill.* New York: D. Van Nostrand, 1956.

Villette, Charles-Michel de. *Œuvres du Marquis de Villette.* London, 1784.

Vinet, Alexandre. *Histoire de la Littérature française au dix-huitième siècle.* Paris: Chez les Éditeurs, 1853.

"Voltaire on the Fleet." *The Spectator,* June 10, 1916, 713.

"Voltaire's 'Candide' Is Adjudged Obscene by Treasury of U.S." *Chicago Tribune,* May 23, 1929, 2.

Voltariana ou Eloges amphigouriques de Fr. Marie Arrouet. Paris, 1748.

Vonnegut, Kurt, Jr. *Conversations with Kurt Vonnegut.* Edited by William Rodney Allen. Jackson: University Press of Mississippi, 1988.

Vonnegut, Kurt, Jr. "Hypocrites You Always Have with You." *The Nation,* April 19, 1980, 469.

Wade, Ira O. *The Intellectual Development of Voltaire.* Princeton, NJ: Princeton University Press, 1969.

Wade, Ira O. *The Search for a New Voltaire: Studies in Voltaire Based upon Material Deposited at the American Philosophical Society.* Philadelphia: American Philosophical Society, 1958.

Wade, Ira O. *Studies on Voltaire with Some Unpublished Papers of Mme du Châtelet.* Princeton, NJ: Princeton University Press, 1947. Reprint, New York: Russell & Russell, 1967.

Wade, Ira O. "Towards a New Voltaire." In *The Search for a New Voltaire: Studies in Voltaire Based upon Material Deposited at the American Philosophical Society,* 105–114. Philadelphia: American Philosophical Society, 1958.

Walker, Ian. "Leveson Wins on Long-windedness." Letter to the editor, *Financial Times,* November 30, 2012. https://www.ft.com/content/94cc5db2-3a2a-11e2-a00d-00144feabdco.

Wallemacq, Thomas. "Clément Oubrerie: 'Voltaire est un super personnage de comédie, un peu à la Woody Allen.'" *Metro*, October 5, 2019. http://fr.metrotime.be/2019/10/05 /must-read/clement-oubrerie-voltaire-est-un-super-personnage-de-comedie-un-peu -a-la-woody-allen.

Warman, Caroline et al., ed. and trans. *Tolerance: The Beacon of the Enlightenment.* Cambridge: Open Book Publishers, 2016.

Watson, Charles [Lord Moran]. *Churchill: Taken from the Diaries of Lord Moran; The Struggle for Survival, 1940–1965.* Boston: Houghton Mifflin, 1966.

Weightman, John. "Cultivating Voltaire." *New York Review of Books*, June 18, 1970, 35–37.

Wendell, Barrett. *A Literary History of America.* New York: Charles Scribner's Sons, 1900.

White, Edmund. *Fanny: A Fiction.* New York: Ecco/HarperCollins, 2003.

Whitman, Walt. *Specimen Days & Collect.* Philadelphia: David McKay, 1887.

Wight, O. W., ed. *Philosophy of Sir William Hamilton.* New York: D. Appleton, 1855.

Wilde, Oscar. "To Read or Not to Read" (unsigned). *Pall Mall Gazette* 43, no. 6521 (February 8, 1886): 11.

Williams, Bernard. *Truth and Truthfulness: An Essay in Genealogy.* Princeton, NJ: Princeton University Press, 2002.

Wills, Garry. *Head and Heart: American Christianities.* New York: Penguin Press, 2007.

Wolfe, Tom. *The Kingdom of Speech.* New York: Little, Brown and Company, 2016.

Wolfe, Tom. "The Origins of Speech: In the Beginning Was Chomsky." *Harper's*, August 2016, 25–40.

Wood, Rev. James. *Dictionary of Quotations from Ancient and Modern, English and Foreign Sources.* New York: Frederick Warne and Co., 1893.

Wootton, David. *Candide and Related Texts.* Indianapolis: Hackett Publishing, 2000.

Wordsworth, William. *The Excursion, Being a Portion of The Recluse, A Poem.* London: Longman, Hurst, Rees, Orme, and Brown, 1814.

Young, Damon. *Voltaire's Vine and Other Philosophies: How Gardens Inspired Great Writers.* London: Rider Books, 2014.

Young, Edward. *The Complete Works, Poetry and Prose, of the Rev. Edward Young, LL.D., Formerly Rector of Welwyn, Hertfordshire, &c. Revised and Collated with the Earliest Editions.* Vol. 2. London: William Tegg and Co., 1854.

Ziegler, Jean. *Une Suisse au-dessus de tout soupçon.* Paris: Seuil, 1976.

Zola, Émile. "Livres d'aujourdhui et de demain." *L'Evénement*, April 3, 1866.

Zola, Émile. *Œuvres complètes.* 15 vols. Edited by Henri Mitterand. Paris: Cercle du livre précieux, 1966–1969.

INDEX

Note: Page numbers in *italics* indicate figures.

ABOUT THE EDITORS

GARRY APGAR is president of the Voltaire Society of America. His most recent books are *Mickey Mouse: Emblem of the American Spirit* and *Quotes for Conservatives*. A cartoonist and a former freelance writer, he has a BA in French from Washington and Lee University, a PhD in the history of art from Yale University, and a *maître-ès-lettres* in *Lettres Modernes* from the Université de Paris IV/Sorbonne.

EDWARD M. LANGILLE, a graduate of Université de la Sorbonne-Nouvelle and a member of the board of directors of the Voltaire Society of America, is professor of French language and literature at St. Francis Xavier University, Antigonish, Nova Scotia. Professor Langille's scholarship has been honored by the French government, which in 2004 awarded him the rank of Chevalier in the Order of Arts and Letters.